Presented to

The Official Guide to American Historic Inns

Rated "Outstanding" by Morgan Rand.

Winner of Benjamin Franklin Award -- Best Travel Guide

"Readers will find this book easy to use and handy to have. The Sakaches have conveyed their love of historic inns and have shared that feeling and information in an attractive and inviting guide. An excellent, well-organized and comprehensive reference for inngoers and innkeepers alike." Inn Review, Kankakee, Illinois.

" ... thoughtfully organized and look-ups are hassle free ... well-researched and accurate ... put together by people who know the field. There is no other publication available that covers this particular segment of the bed & breakfast industry — a segment that has been gaining popularity among travellers by leaps and bounds. The information included is valuable and well thought out." Morgan Directory Reviews

"This is the best bed and breakfast book out. It outshines them all!" Maggie Balitas, Rodale Book Clubs

*"Most of us military families have lived all over the world, so it takes an unusual book, service or trip to excite us! As I began to look through **The Official Guide to American Historic Bed & Breakfast Inns and Guesthouses** by Tim and Deborah Sakach, my heart beat faster as I envisioned what a good time our readers could have visiting some the very special historic bed and breakfast properties."* Ann Crawford, Military Living

"Many of those listed have served as travel stops for more than 200 years, and include several chosen as National Landmarks. The vignettes and sketches capture the charm of these often unusual settings. The book presents the opportunity to relax in settings visited by George Washington, Andrew Jackson, Daniel Webster and other notables." Don James, Los Angeles Times.

*"Thank you for **The Official Guide to American Historic Inns**. It is such a beautiful, fascinating and educational treasure. We love it. We are anxious to share the guide with several friends who will also be travelling."* B. N. Sheldon

*"A staff member discovered listings for two of his all-time favorite B&Bs and wholeheartedly agrees with **The Official Guide's** comments on the same."* Kacey Jordan, Daily Sun Post.

" ... helps you find the very best hideways (many of the book's listings appear in the National Register of Historic Places.)" Country Living

"A great book! An excellent reference. I keep it by my desk and refer to it often." Jim Burns, Travel Editor, Los Angeles Herald Examiner.

Also recommended by:

Changing Times
Women's Day
USA Today
Library Journal
Publishers Weekly
Book-of-the-Month Club News

The Official Guide to
American Historic Inns
Second Edition
Includes 4900 Bed & Breakfast and Country Inns

Formerly called:
The Official Guide to
**American Historic
Bed & Breakfast**
Inns and Guesthouses

The Official Guide to

American Historic Inns
Second Edition
Includes 4900 Bed & Breakfast and Country Inns

Formerly called:
The Official Guide to
**American Historic
Bed & Breakfast**
Inns and Guesthouses

Deborah Edwards Sakach
Timothy J. Sakach

Association of American Historic Inns
Dana Point, California

Published by:

> The Association of American Historic Inns
> P. O. Box 336
> Dana Point, California 92629

Front cover:

> Sword Gate Inn, Charleston, South Carolina.

Photos by Timothy Sakach Photos.

Publisher's Cataloging in Publication Data
> Sakach, Timothy J & Deborah Edwards
> The Official Guide to American Historic Inns

1. Bed & Breakfast Accommodations -- United States, Directories, Guide Books.
2. Travel -- Historic Inns, Directories, Guide Books.
3. Bed & Breakfast Accommodations -- Historic Inns , Directories, Guide Books.
4. Hotel Accommodations -- Bed & Breakfast Inns, Directories, Guide Books.
5. Hotel Accommodations -- United States, Inns, Directories, Guide Books.
I Title . II Author. III American Historic Inns, The Official Guide
ISBN 0-9615481-2-6 Softcover
Library of Congress: ISSN 1043-1195   87-71501

647'.947

Printed in the United States of America

Contents

Acknowledgments   viii

How to use this book   ix

The Association of American Historic Inns
  Listings by State   1

Directory of American Historic Inns   225

Reservation Services   279

State Tourism Information   287

Inn Associations   289

Awards   292

Inns of Interest   293

Inns by Name   295

Discount Certificates   302

Inn Evaluation Form   305

To Elmer and Marge, my parents
In celebration of their 50th year of marriage

Our appreciation and thanks goes to each of the inn-keepers who provided reams of historical information, brochures, drawings, copies of newspaper articles, photographs, and local folklore about their inns. Most of all we are grateful for their constant enthusiasm and support for the project all along the way.

We give special credit to our artist Claire Read, whose skill and dedication helped produce some of the finest pen and ink inn drawings we have seen. We also appreciate the assistance of artist Raul Bustamonte.

To our sons Tim and David for their ideas, advice, inspections, encouragement, and assistance we express our deep appreciation and to our son Stephen, for his journalistic experience and sharp eye, and to our daughter Suzanne who keeps us on our toes.

A heartfelt thanks to Catherine Bowers, our editor, for her many insightful suggestions and skill, and to Sandy Imre whose assistance and skill with a computer was crucial to making this edition possible.

Tim & Deborah Sakach

How to use this book

In this expanded second edition we hope to provide the inn traveller with as much information as is economically feasible to include in a single volume. The resources included here are rarely found in traditional guide books. We concentrate on only historic inns — those in buildings dating prior to 1940. These include B&Bs, country inns, guesthouses, and city inns. Some have recently opened. Others have been operating for hundreds of years and have a long rich history. All of the places have stories to tell. It is these places and stories we hope to preserve.

Nearly all listed here are commercially run inns of the types mentioned above. We have not included private homes (homestays), except in rare instances. All currently active homestays can be reached through the reservation services included in this book.

Book structure

After many years of experience, making reservations for thousands of prospective inn-goers and using the available guides, it seemed that the most logical structure for a guide be alphabetical — by state, by city, and by the inn's name. Our experience with regionally organized references at times proved very frustrating, particularly when we knew in advance the name of the city but not the arbitrary region. Considering the fact that most of us already know the fifty states and the regions they define, what better structure could there be?

We also found that by using a road map in conjunction with this guide, it is very easy to locate the city using the map's index and coordinates. Nearby cities can also be checked very quickly.

Some of the inns desired to also be included under the listing for a nearby city or town. This is helpful to travelers who may not be familiar with the proximity of a lesser known town to a major city. This cross reference should be checked if you are considering a stay at the major city.

Codes

The listings use codes where possible to help condense the information. We have kept the use of codes to a minimum and have used them only to refer to those things with which we are all very familiar.

Credit Cards:

Visa	(no change)
MC	Master Charge
AE	American Express

CB	Carte Blanche
DC	Diner's Club
DS	Discover Card

Beds:

K	King size bed
Q	Queen-size bed
D	Double size bed
T	Twin beds
W	Waterbed
C	Crib available.

Meals:

Continental breakfast: coffee, juice, toast, or pastry.

Continental-plus breakfast: A continental breakfast plus a variety of breads, cheeses, fruit.

Deluxe continental: more elaborate version of the continental plus. Eggs Flambeau?

Full breakfast: Coffee, juice, breads and an egg or meat entree.

B&B: Breakfast (full or continental) included in the price of the room.

AP: American Plan. All three meals are included in the price of the room. Check to see if quoted for two people or per person.

.MAP: Modified American Plan. Breakfast and dinner are included in the price of the room.

EP: European Plan. No meals are included.

"Seen in:"

We have added a new feature to the listings. If the inns provided us with excerpts from verifiable articles appearing in magazines or newspaper, or perhaps radio and TV shows, we have indicated the source in the listing. These articles may be available either from the source as reprints or through libraries.

Rates

Unless indicated with a "pp" (per person) all rates are double occupancy. Those marked with "**" can be booked either directly or through a reservation service or travel agent.

All rates are listed as ranges. The range covers both off-season low rates and busy season high rates. When making reservations you should check the rates which are always subject to change. The information is current at press time.

Comments

We have requested that innkeepers provide us with actual guest comments and with the names and address of the guests making the comment. If the names were not provided we did not use the comment.

INNspections

This book contains 1001+ major listings of historic inns plus a comprehensive directory of more than 5000 historic inns. Each year the authors travel across the country visiting hundreds of inns. However, to undertake an inspection of all historic inns prior to publication of information about them is an impossible task. Last year we travelled more than 20,000 miles. In the years since 1981 we have visited inns in almost every part of the country. But there is no way that anyone can visit them all. Surprisingly, more than once we have been told that we were the only authors to have visited the inns in some popular areas.

However, "inspecting" inns is not the major focus of our travels. We want to visit as many as possible, photograph them, get to know the innkeepers and the inns. There are inns that are models of fineness. And there are others that are rustic — some travellers may consider these intolerable — which we have enjoyed and hated to leave — old buildings with lots of charm and character managed by some of the finest people you would ever have the pleasure of meeting. We cherish the memories inns have offered from the pristine to the rustic, and only rarely have we come across a "bad" inn — poorly kept and poorly managed. These do not survive. Travel is an adventure into the unknown, full of surprises and rewards. The uniqueness, a reflection of our individuality, is the magic that makes travelling from inn to inn the delightful experience it is.

If you wish to participate in evaluating your inn experiences, use the **Inn Evaluation Form** in the back of the book. You might want to make copies of this form prior to departing on your journey.

Minimum stay requirements

When travelling in peak seasons, expect two night minimums. In some areas two night minimums are required at all times on weekends.

Advance Reservations Required

For weekend travel and travel to resort areas during peak season, advance reservations are always required. Some inns fill up six to twelve weeks in advance.

What to do if all the inns you call are full:

Ask the inn for recommendations, perhaps a new inn has opened or there might be one a little off the beaten path.

Call a reservation service for that area. See **Reservation Services** in this book.

Call the local Chamber of Commerce in the town you hope to visit. They may know of inns that have recently opened.

Call or write to the state tourism bureau. See the **State Tourism Information** section.

Contact an Inn Association serving the local area. They may be able to refer you to new inns. See the **Inn Associations** section in this book.

Andrew Jackson's birthplace, Mecklenburg County, N.C.

Alabama

Mentone

Mentone Inn
Highway 117, PO Box 284
Mentone AL 35984
(205) 634-4836

Circa 1927. Mentone is a refreshing stop for those looking for the cool breezes and natural air-conditioning of the mountains. Here antique treasures mingle with modern-day conveniences and a sun deck and spa complete the experience. Sequoyah Caverns, Little River Canyon and DeSoto Falls are moments away. There is also a cabin on the grounds and the inn has its own hiking trails.
Location: On Lookout Mountain in northeast Alabama.
**Rates: $35-$70. May 1-Oct 31.
Innkeeper(s): Amelia & Bob Brooks.
12 Rooms. 12 Private Baths. Guest phone available. Beds: QT. Meals: Full breakfast. Jacuzzi. Conference room.

Mobile

Vincent-Doan Home
1664 Springhill Ave
Mobile AL 36604
(205) 433-7121

Circa 1827. This is not only the oldest house in Mobile but also the last remaining example of French Creole architecture. The house has been restored and retains its original roof line, galleries and facade. Each bedroom has a fireplace and provides direct access to the gallery overlooking the garden.
Rates: $50.
3 Rooms. 3 Private Baths. Guest phone in room. TV in room. Beds: DT. Meals: Full breakfast. Fireplaces. CCs: Visa, MC.

Alaska

Anchorage

Alaska Private Lodgings
PO Box 110135 South Station
Anchorage AK 99511
(907) 345-2222
Susan Hansen operates this bed and breakfast reservation service. She lists several historic properties including an original log house built by a pioneer.
Rates: $30-$55.

McCarthy Wilderness B&B
Box 111241
Anchorage AK 99511
(907) 277-6867
Circa 1917. This cabin, once occupied by the territorial commissioner, is in the National Register. It was the mother lode powerhouse for mines up McCarthy Creek, and copper mines can still be viewed.
Location: South Central Alaska.
Innkeeper(s): Bob & Bobbie Jacobs.
6 Rooms. Beds: QT. Meals: B&B. Jacuzzi. Sauna. Conference room. Rafting, glacier trekking, horseback riding, ghost towns.
"Loved every minute. Just wish we could have stayed longer."

Homer

Driftwood Inn
135-T W Bunnell Ave
Homer AK 99603
(907) 235-8019
Circa 1920. Clean, comfortable and unpretentious, the Driftwood Inn is in a historic building on the shores of Kachemak Bay. The inn caters to families and sportsmen and all-you-can-eat breakfasts are a special feature. There are spectacular mountain and water views.
Location: On the beach with views of mountains, glaciers and the bay.
Rates: $35-$70.
Innkeeper(s): Jeff & Gail Murphy.
8 Rooms. 7 Private Baths. Guest phone available. TV available. Meals: Full breakfast. Sauna. Moose watching, wildflower photography.

Arizona

Phoenix

Prescott Pines Inn
See: Prescott, AZ

Squaw Peak Inn
4425 E Horseshoe Rd
Phoenix AZ 85028
(602) 990-0682

Circa 1929. A classic example of regional architecture, this house was a favorite of Frank Lloyd Wright. He

often brought his students here to admire its use of adobe and other natural Arizona materials. Clark Gable used it as a hideaway. The guest house is separate from the main house, and both kitchen and living room have native stone fireplaces. It is built of California redwood and features log beamed ceilings.
Location: Northeast slope of Squaw Peak Mountain Preserve.
**Rates: $45-$125.
Innkeeper(s): Bill & Ann Epley.
5 Rooms. 5 Private Baths. Guest phone in room. TV in room. Beds: KQT. Meals: Continental breakfast. Fireplaces. Pool. Volleyball court. Member Mi Casa, Su Casa.
"Please! Don't change a thing!! Great atmosphere."

Westways Resort
PO 41624
Phoenix AZ 85080
(602) 582-3868

Circa 1939. This Spanish Mediterranean house originally constructed in the Thirties, has been completely renovated and now reflects a contemporary southwestern tone. The inn is on an acre landscaped with plants from the various regions of Arizona. There are desert cactus, palm trees, grapefruit and orange trees, as well as semi-tropical plantings and mountain pines. A Mexican fountain is the centerpiece of the courtyard.
Location: Northwest Phoenix, adjacent to Arrowhead Country Club.
**Rates: $78-$105.
Innkeeper(s): Darrell Trapp & Brian Curran.
6 Rooms. 5 Private Baths. Guest phone in room. TV in room. Beds: QD. Meals: B&B. Jacuzzi. Handicap access provided. Conference room. Fireplaces. Pool. CCs: Visa, MC, AE, DS.
"Personalized service that made our stay memorable."

Prescott

Marks House Inn
203 E Union
Prescott AZ 86303
(602) 778-4632 (800)822-8885

Circa 1894. In the 1890s four prominent residences dominated Nob Hill, including the Marks house. It was built by Jake Marks, cattle rancher and mine owner. Now in the National Historic Register, this Victorian mansion provides a special setting in which to enjoy rare

antiques, gracious breakfasts, and majestic sunsets.
Location: Ninety miles north of Phoenix. One block from Courthouse Square.
**Rates: $65-$110.
Innkeeper(s): Gregory & Bonnie Miller.
5 Rooms. 5 Private Baths. Guest phone available. Beds: KQ Meals: B&B Conference room. Fireplaces. Fishing, hiking, art fairs. May Territorial Days. World's oldest rodeo, July.
Seen in: *Member of B&B in Arizona.*
"Exceptional!"

Prescott Pines Inn
901 White Spar Rd
Prescott AZ 86303
(602) 445-7270

Circa 1902. A white picket fence and ten stately pines flank this one-

time dairy farm, and four renovated cottages were shelter for the farm hands. Rose, cream, and blue colors reflect the inn's country Victorian elegance and the veranda looks out over an acre of lawn and gardens.

Near the flagstone patio a tree swing beckons to the young at heart.
Location: One-and-a-third miles south of Courthouse Plaza.
Rates: $40-$125.
Innkeeper(s): Jean Will and Michael Acton.
13 Rooms. 13 Private Baths. Guest phone in room. TV in room. Beds: KQC. Meals: B&B. Handicap access provided. Conference room. Fireplaces. CCs: Visa, MC, DS.
Seen in: *Sunset Magazine*
"Great place, great food, great people...thanks!"

Scottsdale

Squaw Peak Inn
See: Phoenix, AZ

Sedona

Garland's Oak Creek Lodge
PO Box 152, Hwy 89A
Sedona AZ 86336
(602) 282-3343
Circa 1930. Two mountain orchards surround the original log homestead providing peaches, ap-

ples, pears, apricots, plums and cherries in season. Rustic log cabins, set around the lodge, overlook Oak Creek (a stocked fishing stream) or the gardens. Some are tucked into the apple orchard while others have views of red cliff walls. Gourmet country cooking includes organically grown vegetables. A massive stone fireplace dominates the dining room. Day trips from the inn include the Painted Desert, Petrified Forest, Indian reservations and ghost towns.
Location: Eight miles north of Sedona.
Rates: $120-$150 April-Nov 1.
Innkeeper(s): Gary & Mary Garland.
15 Rooms. 15 Private Baths. Guest phone available. Beds: KDC. Meals: MAP. Fireplaces. CCs: Visa, MC. Nearby horseback riding, golf, hiking. Clay tennis court.

Seen in: *Scottsdale Scene, Tempe Daily News, Food & Wine.*

Saddle Rock Ranch
255 Rock Ridge Dr
Sedona AZ 86336
(602) 282-7640
Circa 1939. This historic ranch house is constructed of native red rock with beamed ceilings and wood and flagstone floors. The guest suites have fieldstone fireplaces and panoramic vistas of the surrounding red rocks, and Nipper, the RCA Victor dog, greets visitors at the front door. The house has often been featured in motion pictures depicting the Old West.
Location: On two acres of hillside.
**Rates: $88-$98.
Innkeeper(s): Fran & Dan Bruno.
3 Rooms. 3 Private Baths. Guest phone available. TV available. Beds: KQ Meals: Continental plus. Jacuzzi. Conference room. Fireplaces. Pool. Archeological and back-country jeep expeditions. Horseback riding nearby.
"Thank you for sharing your ranch with us...it has been the highlight of our trip."

Tempe

Mi Casa-Su Casa Bed & Breakfast
PO Box 950
Tempe AZ 85281
(602) 990-0682 (800) 456-0682
Circa 1882. This reservation service represents homes throughout the state, and coordinator Ruth Young knows Arizona like her own backyard. A few of her listings are historic homes and depict the full southwest experience. An American territorial adobe in Tucson is a favorite and has been meticulously restored. Blooming garden courtyards add to its elegance. A directory describes a wide selection of private homestays and historic dude ranches represented by Mi Casa-Su Casa.
Location: Covers Arizona as well as New Mexico, Utah, and Nevada.

Tucson

La Posada Del Valle
1640 N Campbell Ave
Tucson AZ 85719
(602) 795-3840
Circa 1920. This southwest adobe has 18-inch-thick walls and the house wraps around a courtyard with a fountain. Ornamental orange trees surround the property, across the street from the University Medical Center. All the rooms have outside entrances and open to the patio or overlook the courtyard. A Twenties decor includes a fainting couch. Afternoon tea is served and there is turn down service.
Location: Walking distance to the University of Arizona.
**Rates: $80-$100.
Innkeeper(s): Charles & Debbi Bryant.
5 Rooms. 5 Private Baths. Guest phone in room. TV available. Beds: KQT. Meals: Continental plus breakfast. Fireplaces. CCs: Visa, MC. Full breakfast served on weekends. Individual heating and cooling in each room.
Seen in: *Gourmet.*

Mi Casa-Su Casa
See: Tempe, CA

Arkansas

Brinkley

The Great Southern Hotel
127 West Cedar
Brinkley AR 72021
(501) 734-4955
Circa 1913. Built on the site of a hotel that burned to the ground, the Great Southern Hotel is a Victorian

building with frontage on the Rock Island tracks and adjacent to the Union passenger depot. Both the hotel and depot are owned by the Prince family, and this is now a national historic district. The hotel was recently restored and an elegant and serene atmosphere prevails. There are two balconies and a wraparound veranda.
Location: Midway between Memphis and Little Rock.
Rates: $36-$40.
Innkeeper(s): Stanley & Dorcas Prince.
4 Rooms. 4 Private Baths. Guest phone available. TV in room. Meals: Full breakfast. Sauna. Conference room. Fireplaces. CCs: Visa, MC, AE. Fishing and duck and quail hunting.
"Absolutely terrific! Beautiful."

Eureka Springs

Dairy Hollow House
Rt 4 Box 1
Eureka Springs AR 72632
(501) 253-7444
Circa 1888. This restored Ozark farmhouse was the first of Eureka

Springs' bed and breakfast inns. Outstanding *"Nouveau'zarks"* cuisine is available by reservation. The innkeeper is the author of several books including the award-winning *Dairy Hollow House Cookbook.*
Location: At the junction of Spring & Dairy Hollow Road.
Rates: $69-$149.
Innkeeper(s): Ned Shank & Crescent Dragonwagon.
5 Rooms. 5 Private Baths. Guest phone available. Beds: QDT. Meals: Full breakfast. Jacuzzi. Conference room. CCs: All.
Seen in: *Christian Science Monitor, Los Angeles Times.*
"The height of unpretentious luxury."

The Heartstone Inn and Cottages
35 King's Highway
Eureka Springs AR 72632
(501) 253-8916
Circa 1903. Described as a "pink and white confection", this handsome restored Victorian with its wraparound verandas is located in

the historic district. The inn is filled with antiques. Pink roses line the

picket fence surrounding the inviting garden.
Location: Northwest Arkansas.
Rates: $51-$75.
Innkeeper(s): Iris & Bill Simantel.
12 Rooms. 12 Private Baths. Guest phone available. TV in room. Beds: KQC. Meals: Full breakfast. Conference room. Fireplaces. CCs: Visa, MC. Small weddings. Private cottages available.
"Extraordinary! Best breakfasts anywhere!"
"Our fourth stay and it gets better each time."

The Piedmont House
165 Spring St
Eureka Springs AR 72632
(501) 253-9258
Circa 1880. An original guest book from the inn's days as a tourist home is a cherished item here. The Piedmont offers the best views in town and is in the National Register.
Rates: $55-$65.
Innkeeper(s): Rose & Larry Olivet.
8 Rooms. 8 Private Baths. Guest phone available. TV available. Beds: DT. Meals: Full breakfast. Handicap access provided. CCs: Visa, MC. Walking distance to downtown shops and restaurants.

"Wonderful atmosphere and your per-sonalities are exactly in sync with the surroundings."

Mountain View

The Commercial Hotel
A Vintage Guesthouse
PO Box 72
Mountain View AR 72560
(501) 269-4383

Circa 1920. The inn's wraparound porches are a focal point for local

musicians who often play old-time music. If you rock long enough you're likely to see an impromptu hootenanny in the Courthouse Square across the street. Since there are no priceless antiques children are welcome but you may have to watch them (and yourself) because there's a tempting first-floor bakery that's always "fixin up" divinity cookies, macaroons and hot breads.
Location: In the Ozarks.
Rates: $34-$49. All year.
Innkeeper(s): Todd and Andrea Budy.
8 Rooms. 3 Private Baths. Guest phone available. Beds: QDC. Meals: B&B. CCs: MC. White water rafting, horseback riding, caverns. Gourmet bakery on site.
Seen in: *Midwest Living, New York Times, Dan Rather & CBS.*

California

Albion

Fensalden Bed & Breakfast
PO Box 99
Albion CA 95410
(707) 937-4042

Circa 1860. Originally a stagecoach station, Fensalden looks out over the

Pacific Ocean as it has for more than one-hundred years. The Tavern Room has witnessed many a rowdy scene and bullet holes are evident in the original redwood ceilings. The inn provides twenty acres for walks, whale-watching, viewing deer and bicycling.
Location: Seven miles south of Mendocino on Hwy 1.
Rates: $75-$125.
Innkeeper(s): Scott & Frances Brazil.
7 Rooms. 7 Private Baths. Guest phone available. Beds: KQ. Meals: Full breakfast. Handicap access provided. CCs: Visa, MC.

Anaheim

Anaheim Country Inn
856 South Walnut St
Anaheim CA 92802
(714) 778-0150

Circa 1910. An elegant Craftsman farmhouse built by Mayor John Cook, the inn is surrounded by

nearly an acre of lawns, gardens and avocado trees. Detailed woodwork

graces the entry and staircase, and beveled and leaded windows cast rainbows in the parlor and dining room. There are balconies and a circular porch, and just outside the honeymoon suite is a gazebo and spa.
Location: One mile from Disneyland.
**Rates: $50-$70.
Innkeeper(s): Lois Ramont & Marilyn Watson.
9 Rooms. 6 Private Baths. Guest phone available. Beds: QT. Meals: Full breakfast. Jacuzzi. Conference room. CCs: All.
"My husband is still telling anyone who'll listen how good the breakfasts were."

Angels Camp

Cooper House
1184 Church St
Angels Camp CA 95222
(209) 736-2145

Circa 1911. This Craftsman bungalow was built by Dr. George Cooper. A magnificent greenstone fireplace is the focal point of the living room, while a spacious veranda overlooks the garden path as it winds down to a gazebo. Many of the inn's furnishings were once

owned by the well-known Archie Stevenot, "Mr. Mother Lode" and guests can visit the nearby Stevenot Winery. Angels Camp is the home of Mark Twain's celebrated Jumping Frog of Calaveras County.
Rates: $56-$70.
Innkeeper(s): Mark & Jeannette Chandler.
3 Rooms. 3 Private Baths. Guest phone available. Beds: QDT. Meals: Full breakfast. CCs: Visa, MC. Bicycling, backpacking on foot or horseback, gold panning, skiing.
"The house is lovely, your breakfast was great and your hospitality unsurpassed!"

Aptos

Apple Lane Inn
6265 Soquel Dr
Aptos CA 95003
(408) 475-6868

Circa 1870. Ancient apple trees border the lane that leads to this Victorian farmhouse set on two acres of

gardens and fields. Built by the Porter brothers, founding fathers of Aptos, the inn is decorated with Victorian wallpapers and hardwood floors. The original wine cellar still exists, as well as the old barn and apple drying shed used for storage after harvesting the orchard. Miles of beaches are within walking distance.

Rates: $65-$110.

Innkeeper(s): Ann Farley

5 Rooms. 4 Private Baths. Guest phone available. TV available. Beds: KQD. Meals: Full Conference room. Fireplaces. CCs: Visa, MC. Darts and horseshoes. close to beaches, golfing, fishing, hiking.

Seen in: *1001 Decorating Ideas, New York Times.*

"Our room was spotless and beautifully decorated. Mrs. Farley is a delightful innkeeper."

Mangels House
570 Aptos Creek Rd, PO Box 302
Aptos CA 95001
(408) 688-7982

Circa 1886. Claus Mangels built this country house when he started

the California sugar beet industry with the famous Spreckels family. The inn, on four acres, is reminiscent of a southern mansion with its encircling veranda, lawns and orchards. It is bounded by the Forest of Nisene Marks with 10,000 acres of redwoods creeks and trails. Just three-quarters of a mile away is Monterey Bay.

Location: Central Coast.

Rates: $68-$90.

Innkeeper(s): Jacqueline Fisher.

5 Rooms. 2 Private Baths. Guest phone available. Beds: KQT. Meals: Full breakfast. Conference room. CCs: Visa, MC.

"Compliments on the lovely atmosphere. We look forward to sharing our discovery with friends and returning with them."

Arroyo Grande

Guest House
120 Hart Lane
Arroyo Grande CA 93420
(805) 481-9304

Circa 1850. This New England Colonial is set among old-fashioned gardens and was built by an eastern sea captain. The flavor of that period is kept alive with many family heirlooms and a colorful garden terrace. It is seventeen miles south of San Luis Obispo.

Location: In the village.

Rates: $50.

Innkeeper(s): Mark V. Migger.

3 Rooms. Guest phone available. Beds: QD. Meals: Hearty breakfast. Wineries, beaches, and antique shops nearby. Hearst Castle.

"The charm of the home is only exceeded by that of the hosts."

"This home is a treasure, beautiful!"

Rose Victorian Inn
789 Valley Rd
Arroyo Grande CA 93420
(805) 481-5566

Circa 1885. Once the homestead for a large walnut farm, this picturesque Victorian features a tower that rises four stories providing views of meadows, sand dunes and the ocean. Surrounded by a white picket fence, it is decorated with authentic Victorian furnishings. A 30-foot rose arbor leads to a gazebo in the garden, a favorite setting for weddings. Rates include dinner from the inn's restaurant.

Location: Halfway between Los Angeles and San Francisco.

Rates: $125 MAP.

Innkeeper(s): Ross & Diana Cox.

8 Rooms. 3 Private Baths. Guest phone available. Beds: KQ. Meals: Full breakfast, 5-course dinner. Handicap access provided. Conference room. CCs: Visa, MC.

Seen in: *Los Angeles Times, Daughters of Painted Ladies.*

Auburn

Red Castle Inn
See: Nevada City, CA

Avalon

The Inn On Mt. Ada
Box 2560, 207 Wrigley Rd
Avalon CA 90704
(213) 510-2030

Circa 1921. This Georgian mansion was built on a hillside by the famous Wrigley family. Mr. Wrigley brought the Chicago Cubs to Avalon for spring training and would watch them from the house. Once the summer White House for Presidents Coolidge and Harding, its breathtaking ocean and bay views are framed by a multitude of wide windows and terraces. Weekends are booked six months ahead.

Rates: $170-$390.

Innkeeper(s): Marlene McAdam, Wayne & Susie Griffin.

6 Rooms. 6 Private Baths. Guest phone available. Beds: Q. Meals: Full breakfast. Conference room. Fireplaces.

Seen in: *Los Angeles Times, Chicago Tribune.*

Benicia

Union Hotel
401 First St
Benicia CA 94510
(707) 746-0100

Circa 1882. Once a famed bordello, this old clapboard hotel has been renovated and purified with whitewash, polished brass, and stained glass. The inn is set in a picturesque town that served as the capital of California for one year. Guest rooms are filled with antiques and each has a whirlpool tub. Some rooms feature water views of Carquinez Strait.

Location: Forty-five minutes from San Francisco.

**Rates: $70-$120.

Innkeeper(s): Andrea Barrett.

12 Rooms. 12 Private Baths. Guest phone in room. TV in room. Beds: KQ. Meals: Full breakfast. Jacuzzi. Handicap access provided. CCs: Visa, MC, AE, DC.

Seen in: *Travel & Leisure, Bon Appetit.*

Berkeley

Gramma's Inn

2740 Telegraph
Berkeley CA 94705
(415) 549-2145

Circa 1905. Three buildings comprise Gramma's, one a Tudor house. All are decorated with Victorian antiques and there are 12 rooms with fireplaces. Handmade quilts and cookies and milk served in the evening are favorite Gramma amenities.
Location: Two miles from Oakland.
**Rates: $71-$130.
Innkeeper(s): Craig Runyon.
30 Rooms. 28 Private Baths. Guest phone in room. TV in room. Beds: KQDT. Meals: Continental. Handicap access provided. Conference room. Fireplaces. CCs: Visa, MC. Wine and cheese.
Seen in: *Sunset.*

Big Bear City

Gold Mountain Manor

1117 Anita, PO Box 2027
Big Bear City CA 92314
(714) 585-6997

Circa 1926. This spectacular log mansion was once a hideaway for

the rich and famous. Eight fireplaces provide a roaring fire in each room in fall and winter. The Lucky Baldwin Room features a hearth made from stones of gold gathered in the famous Lucky Baldwin mine nearby. In the Clark Gable room is the fireplace Gable and Carole Lombard enjoyed on their honeymoon.
Location: Two hours northeast of Los Angeles and Orange Counties.
Rates: $70-$135.
Innkeeper(s): Lynn Montgomery & Richard Kriegler.
7 Rooms. 6 Private Baths. Guest phone available. Beds: Q. Meals: Full breakfast. Jacuzzi. Conference room. Fireplaces. Skiing, hiking, lake activities.
"A majestic experience! In this magnificent house, history comes alive!"

Big Bear Lake

Knickerbocker Mansion

869 S Knickerbocker Rd
Big Bear Lake CA 92315
(714) 866-8221

Circa 1917. The inn is one of the few vertically designed log structures in the area. It was built of local lumber by Bill Knickerbocker, first

damkeeper of Big Bear, and is set against a backdrop of trees. Spacious front lawns provide seating for the annual summer "Astronomy Weekends" led by Griffith Park Observatory astronomers.
Location: One-quarter mile south of Big Bear Village.
**Rates: $85-$150.
Innkeeper(s): Phyllis Knight.
10 Rooms. 6 Private Baths. Guest phone available. TV in room. Beds: KQ. Meals: Full breakfast. Jacuzzi. Handicap access provided. Conference room. Horseback riding, skiing, parasailing, water slide. Astronomy weekends, weddings.
Seen in: *Los Angeles Magazine, Yellow Brick Road.*
"Best breakfast I ever had. We especially enjoyed the hot tub with its terrific view."

Big Sur

Deetjen's Big Sur Inn

Hwy One
Big Sur CA 93920
(408) 667-2377

Circa 1938. Norwegians Helmut and Helen Deetjen, built these casual, rustic cabins on several acres in a canyon two miles from the ocean. Today they are managed by a

non-profit corporation and provide employment for local residents. Two cottages overlook a bubbling stream and some have fireplaces and down comforters. The restaurant serves candlelight dinners Thursday through Sunday. The adventurous will appreciate the setting and the whimsy but due to the rustic nature of the accommodations this is not for the faint of heart.
Location: Twenty-eight miles south of Carmel.
Rates: $45-$80.
Innkeeper(s): Bettie Walters & Doris Jolicoeur.
20 Rooms. 13 Private Baths. Guest phone available. Beds: TW. Meals: EP, breakfast and dinner available. Handicap access provided. Fireplaces. Hiking trails and beaches nearby.
Seen in: *New York Times, California Magazine.*

Calistoga

Brannan Cottage Inn

109 Wapoo Ave
Calistoga CA 94515
(707) 942-4200

Circa 1860. This Greek Revival cottage was built as a guest house for the old Calistoga Hot Springs

Resort. Behind a white picket fence towers the original palm tree

planted by Sam Brannan and noted by Robert Louis Stevenson in his "Silverado Squatters." Five graceful arches, an intricate gingerbread gableboard, and unusual scalloped ridge-cresting make for a charming holiday house. Hand-painted flower stencils of sweet peas, wild iris, violets, morning glories and wild roses are part of the fresh country Victorian decor.
Location: Napa Valley.
**Rates: $90-$100.
Innkeeper(s): Jan & Scott Sofie.
6 Rooms. 6 Private Baths. Guest phone available. Beds: Q. Meals: Full breakfast. Handicap access provided. Conference room. Fireplaces. CCs: Visa, MC. Ballooning, petrified forest, hot springs, gliding, wine tasting.
Seen in: *Travel Age West, Los Angeles Herald Examiner, Chicago Tribune.*
"I think of you as the caretakers of romance in our busy world."

Scarlett's Country Inn
3918 Silverado Trail N
Calistoga CA 94515
(707) 942-6669
Circa 1900. This restored farmhouse occupies property that was a Wappo Indian campground in the days when they migrated from

the mountains in winter. There are green lawns and refreshing country vistas in a woodland setting at the edge of vineyards. Fruit trees abound and guests are free to sample their wares. Breakfast is often taken beneath the apple trees or poolside.
Location: Napa Valley wine country.
**Rates: $75-$95.
Innkeeper(s): Scarlett & Derek Dwyer.
3 Rooms. 3 Private Baths. Guest phone in room. TV available. Beds: QC. Meals: Continental-plus breakfast. Pool. CCs: Visa, MC.
"Wonderful, peaceful, serene."

Wine Way Inn
1009 Foothill Blvd
Calistoga CA 94515
(707) 942-0680
Circa 1915. In the garden of this white Craftsman house is a gazebo set on a lushly planted hillside,

providing spectacular views across Calistoga to the mountains beyond. Inside the inn are beamed ceilings, leaded glass cabinets and 19-century English and American antiques. Allen's grandfather was humorist Chic Sale, and each guest room features books such as *The Specialist* (about a gentleman who specializes in building outhouses).
**Rates: $65-$100.
Innkeeper(s): Allen & Dede Good.
6 Rooms. 6 Private Baths. Guest phone available. Beds: QD. Meals: Full breakfast. Fireplaces. CCs: Visa, MC. Mudbaths in town, golf, tennis, horseback riding nearby. Air conditioning.
Seen in: *Los Angeles Times.*
"We loved being here and loved meeting Dede & Allen. Such personal service!"

Carmel

Cypress Inn
7th & Lincoln Streets, PO Box 7
Carmel CA 93921
(408) 624-3871
Circa 1929. The Cypress Inn is a small Mediterranean-style hotel in the heart of Carmel. Period details include oak floors, imported Italian tiles, and beamed cathedral ceilings, all carefully restored. There is a large living room with fireplace, an intimate library overlooking a private garden courtyard, and ocean views.
Location: In the center of the village.
**Rates: $89-$159.
Innkeeper(s): David Wolf.

33 Rooms. 33 Private Baths. Guest phone in room. TV in room. Beds: KQT. Meals: Continental. CCs: Visa, MC, AE.
Seen in: *Travel & Leisure, Country Inns.*

Happy Landing Inn
Monte Verde between 5th & 6th
Carmel CA 93921
(408) 624-7917
Circa 1925. Built as a family retreat, this early Comstock-design inn has evolved into one of Carmel's most romantic places to stay. The Hansel-and-Gretel look is

accentuated with a central garden and gazebo, pond and flagstone paths. There are cathedral ceilings and the rooms are filled with antiques.
Location: Four blocks to the beach and 1 1/2 blocks to the village.
Rates: $75-$120.
Innkeeper(s): Bob Anderson & Dick Stewart.
7 Rooms. 7 Private Baths. Guest phone available. Beds: KQ. Meals: Continental breakfast. Handicap access provided. CCs: Visa, MC.

Chico

Bullard House
256 E First Avenue
Chico CA 95926
(916) 342-5912
Circa 1902. City fathers bestowed the Golden Rose Award for restoration excellence upon Bullard House,

a country Victorian home. It was also selected as "Decorator Dream

House". The inn is centrally located for guests who want to be close to Chico State College or historic Bidwell Mansion.
Rates: $50-$60.
Innkeeper(s): Bob Anderson & Dick Stewart.
4 Rooms. Guest phone available. Meals: Continental breakfast. Hunting, fishing and boating.

Chula Vista

Dickinson Boal Mansion
See: National City, CA

Cloverdale

Abrams House Inn
314 N Main St
Cloverdale CA 95425
(707) 894-2412
  Circa 1870. This restored Victorian is one of the oldest buildings in Cloverdale. It was built by the Abrams family and there is a brick

building on the property believed to have been the town's first jail. Ask for the suite with four-poster bed and private porch.
Location: Sonoma County wine country.
**Rates: $45-$90.
Innkeeper(s): Mary & David Hood.
4 Rooms. 1 Private Baths. Guest phone available. Beds: KQT. Meals: Full breakfast. Conference room. Fireplaces. CCs: Visa, MC. Bicycling, wine tasting, fishing, canoeing, boating.

Vintage Towers Inn
302 N Main St
Cloverdale CA 95425
(707) 894-4535
  Circa 1900. This gracious Victorian has three towers - square, round and an octagon. Guests can try a different room each time they visit or

enjoy the luxurious master suite downstairs. Bicycles are provided for riding to several nearby vineyards.
Location: Six blocks from Russian River.
**Rates: $65-$110. Feb. to Dec.
Innkeeper(s): James Mees & Garrett Hall.
7 Rooms. 5 Private Baths. Guest phone available. TV available. Beds: KQDT. Meals: Full breakfast. Conference room. Fireplaces. CCs: Visa, MC, AE. Wineries, white water rafting, horseback riding, fishing. Special meals by prior arrangement.

Coloma

Coloma Country Inn
PO Box 502, #2 High St
Coloma CA 95613
(916) 622-6919
  Circa 1852. The inn is set in the middle of 300-acre Gold Discovery State Park, so guests can walk to the

blacksmith, tinsmith and one-room schoolhouse, as well as Sutter's Mill, site of California's first gold discovery. The inn was built by Hugh Miller, owner of Coloma's Fashion Billard Saloon. Antique beds, primitives, stenciling and country decor complement an idyllic five-acre setting, with duck pond and gazebo in the garden.
Location: Heart of the Gold Country, Coloma, where the Gold Rush began.
**Rates: $68.
Innkeeper(s): Alan & Cindi Ehrgott.

5 Rooms. 1 Private Baths. Guest phone available. Beds: D. Meals: Full breakfast. Fireplaces. Hot air ballooning with host, white water rafting. Wine seminars.
Seen in: Country Living, Los Angeles Times.

Vineyard House
Cold Spring Rd, PO Box 176
Coloma CA 95613
(916) 622-2217
  Circa 1878. Ulysses Grant is said to have made a speech from the balcony of this 19-room house built by Robert Chalmers, winery owner. The parlor is decorated in a Victorian

fashion with velvet-covered furniture and antiques. In the basement a saloon occupies the house's former wine cellar. It is said that when Mr. Chalmers became insane as a result of syphilis, his wife had him chained in the basement. The house is rumored to be haunted but it doesn't seem to disturb the conviviality found in the dining room almost any evening.
Location: Off Highway 49.
**Rates: $54-$64.
Innkeeper(s): Gary, Frank, Darlene Herrera. David van Buskirk.
7 Rooms. Guest phone available. Beds: KQDT. Meals: Continental or full. Conference room. CCs: Visa, MC. Hiking, white-water rafting, ballooning. Old melodramas next door.
Seen in: United, Sierra Heritage, Sacramento Union.

Crowley Lake

Rainbow Tarns
PO Box 1097
Crowley Lake CA 93546
(619) 935-4556
  Circa 1920. Just south of Mammoth Lakes, at an altitude of 7,000 feet, is this secluded retreat on three acres of ponds, open meadows and hills. Country-style here includes luxury

touches such as a double jacuzzi tub and a skylight for star-gazing. In the Thirties, ponds on the property served as a "U-Catch-Em": folks rented fishing poles and paid ten cents an inch for the fish they caught. Nearby Crowley Lake is still one of the best trout-fishing areas in California. Corrals are povided should you bring your horse.
Location: Eight-tenths of a mile north of Tom's Place.
Rates: $85-$125.
Innkeeper(s): Lois Miles.
2 Rooms. 2 Private Baths. Guest phone available. TV available. Beds: QDT. Meals: Full breakfast. Jacuzzi. Handicap access provided. Fireplaces. Skiing, horseback riding, back packing, fishing, hunting.

Davenport

New Davenport Bed & Breakfast
31 Davenport Ave
Davenport CA 95017
(408) 425-1818

Circa 1902. Captain John Davenport came here to harvest the gray whales that pass close to shore

during migration. The oldest remaining original building is modest in appearance and began as a public bath. It also became a bar, restaurant and dance hall before being converted to a private home. Completely renovated, it now houses four of the inn's rooms.
Location: Halfway between Carmel and San Francisco on the coast.
**Rates: $55-$105.
Innkeeper(s): Bruce & Marcia McDougal.
12 Rooms. 12 Private Baths. Guest phone in room. Beds: KQ. Meals: Full breakfast. Handicap access provided. CCs: Visa, MC, AE.
"We have been in California for over 25 years and never knew there was a Davenport! I cannot express the

wonderful thrill at the first glimpse of our room with its lovely country appeal and garden."

Dulzura

Brookside Farm
1373 Marron Valley Rd
Dulzura CA 92017
(619) 468-3043

Circa 1928. From the farmhouse, ancient oaks shade terraces that lead to a murmuring brook. Behind a nearby stone barn there is a grape arbor and beneath it, a spa. Each room in the inn and its two cottages is furnished with vintage pieces and handmade quilts. Adventurous hikers can explore mines dating from the gold rush of 1908. Edd and Judy, former award-winning restaurant owners, give gourmet cooking classes.
Location: Thirty-five minutes southeast of San Diego.
**Rates: $45-$65.
Innkeeper(s): Edd & Judy Guishard.
9 Rooms. 6 Private Baths. Guest phone available. Beds: QD. Meals: Full breakfast. Jacuzzi. Handicap access provided. Conference room. Fireplaces.
Seen in: *California Magazine, San Diego Home & Garden.*
"Our stay at the farm was the most relaxing weekend we've had in a year."

Elk

Elk Cove Inn
PO Box 367
Elk CA 95432
(707) 877-3321

Circa 1883. This mansard-style Victorian was built as a guest house for lumber baron L. E. White. Operated as a full-service country inn for over 21 years, Elk Cove Inn commands

majestic views from atop a scenic bluff. Two cabins and an addition

feature large bay windows, skylights, and Victorian fireplaces. Antiques, hand-embroidered linens, and sun-dried sheets add to the amenities. Below the inn is an expansive driftwood-strewn beach. French and German specialities are served in the ocean-view dining rooms.
Location: 6300 S Hwy 1, 15 miles south of Mendocino.
Rates: $88-$168.
Innkeeper(s): Hildrun-Uta Triebess.
6 Rooms. 6 Private Baths. Guest phone available. Beds: Q. Meals: Full breakfast and MAP Saturdays. Handicap access provided. Fireplaces. Ocean kayaking, beachcombing, tennis, golf, wine tasting.
Seen in: *AAA & Mobil guidebooks.*

Harbor House
5600 S Hwy 1
Elk CA 95432
(707) 877-3203

Circa 1916. Built by a lumber company for executives visiting from the East, the inn is constructed en-

tirely of redwood. The parlor's vaulted, carved ceiling and redwood paneling were sealed by hot beeswax and hand rubbed. Edwardian decor adds elegance to the guest rooms. Views of the ocean and arches carved in the massive rocks that jut from the sea may be seen from the blufftop cottages. Benches nestle along a path edged with wildflowers as it winds down the bluff to the sea.
Rates: $110-$165.
Innkeeper(s): Dean & Helen Turner.
9 Rooms. 9 Private Baths. Guest phone available. Meals: Full breakfast and dinner included.

Eureka

Carter House
1033 Third St
Eureka CA 95501
(707) 445-1390

Circa 1982. The Carters found a pattern book in an antique shop and built this inn according to a plan

featuring an 1890 San Francisco Victorian. (The architect, Joseph Newsom, also designed the Carson House across the street.) There are three open parlors with bay windows and marble fireplaces, and guests are free to visit the kitchen in quest of coffee and views of the bay. The inn is famous for its Apple Almond Tart featured in *Gourmet* magazine.
Location: Corner of Third & L streets in Old Town.
Rates: $55-$165.
Innkeeper(s): Mark & Christi Carter.
7 Rooms. 4 Private Baths. Guest phone available. TV available. Beds: QD. Meals: Full breakfast. Conference room. CCs: Visa, MC, AE.

"We've traveled extensively throughout the U.S. and stayed in the finest hotels. You've got them all beat!! The accommodations, the food, the atmosphere and the friendly hosts are the very best of the best."

Ferndale

Shaw House Inn
PO Box 250, 703 Main St
Ferndale CA 95536
(707) 786-9958

Circa 1854. The Shaw House is thought to be the second oldest inn in California. It is an attractive Gothic house with gables, bays and

balconies set back on an acre of garden. An old buckeye tree frames the front gate, and in the back a secluded deck overlooks a creek. Nestled under the wallpapered gables are several guest rooms filled with antiques and fresh flowers. New owners have brought new zest to this lovely old inn.
**Rates: $55-$95.
Innkeeper(s): Norma & Ken Bessingpas.
6 Rooms. 2 Private Baths. Guest phone available. Beds: KQT. Meals: Continental-plus breakfast. Conference room. Fireplaces. CCs: Visa, MC. Bikes available, hiking, sleeping, reading.

Fort Bragg

Country Inn
632 N Main St
Fort Bragg CA 95437
(707) 964-3737

Circa 1890. The Union Lumber Company once owned this two-story townhouse built of native redwood. It features rooms with slanted

and peaked ceilings. Several of the rooms have fireplaces. Camellia trees, flower boxes, and a white picket fence accent the landscaping, while just two blocks away a railroad carries visitors on excursions through the redwoods.
Rates: $58-$95.
Innkeeper(s): Don & Helen Miller.
8 Rooms. 8 Private Baths. Guest phone available. Beds: KQ. Meals: Continental-plus breakfast. Handicap access provided. Fireplaces. CCs: Visa, MC, AE.

"Each room is so charming, how do you choose one?"

Grey Whale Inn
615 N Main St
Fort Bragg CA 95437
(707) 964-0640

Circa 1915. Built in the classic style, with weathered, old growth redwood, this stately historic building served as the Redwood Coast Hospital until 1971. A skillfully ex-

ecuted renovation has created airy and spacious rooms, most with fireplaces and some with ocean views.
Location: Two blocks from center of town in historic North Fort Bragg.
Rates: $60-$125.
Innkeeper(s): Colette Bailey.
16 Rooms. 16 Private Baths. Guest phone available. TV in room. Beds: KQT. Meals: Full breakfast. Handicap access provided. Conference room. Fireplaces. CCs: Visa, MC, AE.
Seen in: *San Francisco Examiner.*

"Just spent the loveliest week in our traveling history...the inn surpassed any Hyatt Regency in service and attitude. The accommodations were superb."

Noyo River Lodge
500 Casa Del Noyo Dr.
Fort Bragg CA 95437
(707) 964-8045

Circa 1868. Located on a two-and-one-half acre pinnacle of wooded land overlooking the Noyo River, the harbor and fishing village, the lodge is a mansion once owned by the local lumber baron. Paths on the grounds lead to romantic picnic spots under the redwoods. Each guest room is furnished with antiques and is lined with a fine cedar no longer available to builders. The lodge's restaurant provides picturesque views overlooking the river and fireside dining.
Rates: $65-$100.
Innkeeper(s): Joe Patton & Ellie Singel.
7 Rooms. 7 Private Baths. Guest phone available. Beds: KQ. Meals: Full breakfast. Fireplaces. CCs: Visa, MC. Horseback riding on beach, whale watching trips, steam train ride. State and national parks.

"Such beauty and serenity, words cannot describe. We left the city in search of peace and tranquility and discovered it here."

Pudding Creek Inn
700 N Main St
Fort Bragg CA 95437
(707) 964-9529

Circa 1889. Originally constructed by a Russian count, the inn's two

picturesque Victorian buildings are adjoined by an enclosed garden with begonias, fuchsias and ferns. Rumor has it that there could be jewels buried on the grounds because the count is said to have fled his homeland with riches that were not his own.
Location: Corner of Bush and North Main.
**Rates: $49-$78. Feb-Dec.
Innkeeper(s): Marilyn & Gene Gundersen.
10 Rooms. 10 Private Baths. Guest phone available. Beds: KQDT. Meals: Full breakfast. CCs: Visa, MC.

"Best stop on our trip!"

Freestone

Green Apple Inn
520 Bohemian Hwy
Freestone CA 95472
(707) 874-2526

Circa 1862. On five acres of redwoods, apple trees and blackberry bushes, this farmhouse was built by Trowbridge Wells, squire, pundit, grocer and postman. Freestone was once the site of a Pomo Indian holy ground and a Russian experimental wheat farm.
Location: Sonoma county.
**Rates: $65 to 85. a
Innkeeper(s): Roger & Rosemary Hoffman.
4 Rooms. 2 Private Baths. Guest phone available. Beds: QD. Meals: Full breakfast. Handicap access provided. Fireplaces. CCs: Visa, MC. Horseback riding nearby, deep sea fishing, river boats, biking.
Seen in: *Auto Club, Sonoma Monthly, San Francisco Chronicle.*

"The Green Apple is a cosy inn. Not rushed but you can take your time." Emma, age 6.

Garberville

Benbow Inn
445 Lake Benbow Dr
Garberville CA 95440
(707) 923-2124

Circa 1926. The Benbow family commissioned famous architect Albert Far to design this Tudor-style inn, an imposing sight set among Japanese maples and an English

rose garden. Each summer the park service builds a dam to form a lake, creating a sandy beach and backdrop for Shakespeare plays performed in July and August. The lobby and main rooms of the inn are filled with fine paintings, antiques, old clocks and books. The dining room overlooks green lawns leading down to the banks of the Eel River.
Location: On the Eel River, two miles south of Garberville.
**Rates: $78-$220.
Innkeeper(s): Patsy & Chuck Watts.
55 Rooms. 55 Private Baths. Guest phone available. TV in room. Beds: KQDT. Meals: EP Jacuzzi. Fireplaces. CCs: Visa, MC. Lake swimming, hiking, biking. Afternoon tea & scones, wine.

"An astonishing place with charm by the ton!! This is our fifth visit."
"Both of us commented on how wonderful the service was everywhere in the hotel."

Georgetown

American River Inn
Orleans Street, PO Box 43
Georgetown CA 95634

(916) 333-4499
Circa 1853. Just a few miles from where gold was discovered in Coloma stands this completely re-

stored boarding house. Mining cars dating to the original Woodside Mine Camp are visible and the lode still runs under the inn, although no one knows exactly where. A famous nugget from the mine weighed in at 126 ounces! There is a spring-fed pool on the property.
Rates: $61-$71.
Innkeeper(s): Neal & Carol.
20 Rooms. 5 Private Baths. Guest phone available. Beds: KQ. Meals: Full breakfast. Handicap access provided. Pool. CCs: Visa, MC. White water rafting on the American River.

"Our home away from home. We fell in love here in all its beauty and will be back for our 4th visit in April, another honeymoon for six days."

Grass Valley

Annie Horan's
415 W Main St
Grass Valley CA 95945
(916) 272-2418

Circa 1874. Mine-owner James Horan built this splendid Victorian house for his wife Mary. Today the exterior, parlor and guest quarters are as they were at the height of

Gold Country opulence. Just beyond the inn are shops, pubs, restaurants and other spots frequented by Mark Twain, Bret Harte and Presidents Grant, Harrison and Cleveland.
Location: Downtown Grass Valley.
**Rates: $55-$85.
Innkeeper(s): Tom & Pat Kiddy.
4 Rooms. 4 Private Baths. Guest phone available. TV available. Beds: Q. Meals: Continental plus. Conference room. CCs: Visa, MC. Rafting, fishing, boating, gold panning, skiing.

Swan-Levine House
328 S Church St
Grass Valley CA 95945
(916) 272-1873
Circa 1880. Originally built by a local merchant, this Queen Anne Victorian was sold to Dr. John Jones who converted it into a hospital. It served the area as a medical center until 1968. Innkeepers and artists Howard and Margaret Levine renovated the home for their three children, and as a printmaking studio and guesthouse. The old surgery is a guest room with rose-painted walls, octagonal white floor tiles, and grand views from the wicker-furnished turret.
Rates: $50-$70.
Innkeeper(s): Howard Levine
4 Rooms. 1 Private Baths. Guest phone available. TV available. Beds: KQT. Meals: Full breakfast. Fireplaces. Pool. CCs: Visa, MC Swimming, badminton and nearby skiing, hiking, fishing. Etching instruction at the inn.

Guerneville

Santa Nella House
12130 Hwy 116
Guerneville CA 95466
(707) 869-9488
Circa 1870. This Victorian farmhouse was the residence of the builder of the Santa Nella Winery. It was also the site of one of the first

sawmills in the redwood lumber area and served as a stage coach stop. An enchanting trail winds down to the Russian River, and there is a sun deck and old pool table on the property. High ceilings, red carpets and antiques set the stage for a relaxing stay.
Rates: $70-$80. Feb 20-Jan 5.
Innkeeper(s): Alan "Ed" & Joyce Ferrington.
4 Rooms. 4 Private Baths. Guest phone available. TV available. Beds: DXL. Meals: Full breakfast. Jacuzzi. Conference room. CCs: Visa, MC, AE. Canoeing, horseback riding, berry picking, wine tasting. Trail to Russian River, deck.
"It is rare to find a home as warm and gracious as its owners."
"Thank you so much for making our honeymoon special. We plan to come back every year for our anniversary."

Half Moon Bay

Mill Rose Inn
615 Mill St
Half Moon Bay CA 94019
(415) 726-9794
Circa 1903. This Victorian country inn is situated on the original Miramontes land grant and played an important part in local coastal

history. English country gardens bloom year round under the magical hand of innkeeper and landscape designer Terry Baldwin. Canopy beds, claw-foot tubs, hand-painted fireplaces, and an inside garden spa create an opulent setting in which to relax.
**Rates: $125-$195.
Innkeeper(s): Eve & Terry Baldwin.
6 Rooms. 6 Private Baths. Guest phone in room. TV available. Beds: KQ. Meals: Full breakfast. Jacuzzi. Conference room. Fireplaces. CCs: Visa, MC, AE. Horseback riding, beach, wineries, whale watching. Musicians and masseuses on call.
Seen in: *New York Times, LA Times, Dallas Morning News.*

"One of the loveliest retreats this side of the Cotswolds." San Diego Union.

Healdsburg

Abrams House Inn
See: Cloverdale, CA

Camellia Inn
211 North St
Healdsburg CA 95448
(707) 433-8182
Circa 1869. An elegant Italianate Victorian townhouse, the Camellia Inn has twin marble parlor fireplaces and an ornate mahogany dining-room fireplace. Antiques fill the guest rooms, complementing Palladian windows and classic interior moldings. The award-winning grounds feature 30 varieties of camellias and are accentuated with a pool.
Location: Heart of the Sonoma Wine Country.
**Rates: $55-$95.
Innkeeper(s): Ray & Del Lewana.
8 Rooms. 7 Private Baths. Guest phone available. Beds: QT. Meals: Full breakfast. Handicap access provided. Pool. CCs: Visa, MC.

Grape Leaf Inn
539 Johnson St
Healdsburg CA 95448
(707) 433-8140
Circa 1900. This magnificently restored Queen Anne home was built in what was considered the "Nob Hill" of Healdsburg and was typical of a turn-of-the-century middle-class dream house. It is situated near the Russian River and the town center. Seventeen skylights provide an abundance of sunlight, fresh air, and stained glass. Guest rooms feature antiques and several have whirlpool tubs.
**Rates: $60-$95.
Innkeeper(s): Kathy Cookson.
7 Rooms. 7 Private Baths. Beds: KQ. Meals: Full breakfast. Jacuzzi. Fireplaces. CCs: Visa, MC. Bicycles, canoeing. Lake Sonoma water sports. Wine and cheese in the a
"Reminds me of my grandma's house."

Haydon House

321 Haydon St
Healdsburg CA 95448
(707) 433-5228

Circa 1912. This unique home shows the influence of several architectural styles. It has the curving

porch and general shape of a Queen Anne Victorian, the expansive areas of siding and unadorned columns of the Bungalow style, and the exposed roof rafters of the Craftsman style.
Location: Western Sonoma County, heart of the wine country.
Rates: $65-$110.
Innkeeper(s): Richard & Joanne Claus.
8 Rooms. 4 Private Baths. Guest phone available. Beds: QT. Meals: Full breakfast. Conference room. CCs: Visa, MC.

"Adjectives like class, warmth, beauty, thoughtfulness with the right amount of privacy, attention to details relating to comfort, all come to mind. Thank you for the care and elegance."

Madrona Manor

PO Box 818 1001 Westside
Healdsburg CA 95448
(707) 433-4231

Circa 1881. Surrounded by eight acres of manicured lawns and woodlands, this majestic three-story mansion was built as a vacation home for John Paxton, a San Francisco businessman. Embellished with turrets, bay windows, porches and a mansard roof, the inn provides views of surrounding vineyards. Massive antique furnishings such as a four-poster canopied bed and a rosewood piano provide guests with an elegant country atmosphere. More casual guest rooms are in the Gothic-style carriage house.
Location: In the heart of the wine country, Sonoma County.
Rates: $82.50-$125.
Innkeeper(s): John & Carol Muir.
20 Rooms. 20 Private Baths. Guest phone in room. Beds: KQDT. Meals: Full breakfast. Handicap access provided.

Conference room. Fireplaces. CCs: Visa, MC, AE, DS. Canoeing, wine tasting, picnics. golf and tennis nearby.
Seen in: *Northern California Home & Garden, Gourmet, Country Inns.*

"Our fourth visit and better every time."

Homewood

Rockwood Lodge

5295 W Lake Blvd, PO Box 544
Homewood CA 95718
(916) 525-4663 (800)722-4849

Circa 1930. On the west shore of Lake Tahoe, the Rockwood Lodge is situated among towering pines near the Kaiser estate where *The Godfather, Part II* was filmed. There is a

small historic marina nearby. The inn features a huge indigenous rock fireplace, hand-hewn beams and pine paneling. European and American antiques, together with tall bedsteads and puffy down comforters, give a luxurious touch. Ask for the room with the seven-foot Roman tub.
Location: Lake Tahoe.
Rates: $100-$150.
Innkeeper(s): Louis Reinkens, Constance Stevens.
4 Rooms. 4 Private Baths. Beds: QD. Meals: Full breakfast. Fireplaces. Skiing, hiking.
Seen in: *Sunset, New York Times Magazine, Ski.*

Idyllwild

Wilkum Inn

26770 Hwy 243, PO Box 1115
Idyllwild CA 92349
(714) 659-4087

Circa 1939. Idyllwild's history includes lumbering and sawmills, and much of the knotty pine in the original part of the inn was repor-

tedly milled in the area. There are pine-crafted stair rails unique to the area's construction in the Thirties. The inn is noted for its Old World charm.
Location: South of village center, 3/4 mile.
**Rates: $55-$75.
Innkeeper(s): Annamae Chambers & Barbara Jones.
5 Rooms. 2 Private Baths. Guest phone available. Beds: QDT. Meals: Full breakfast. Handicap access provided. Fireplaces. Horseback riding. hiking.

Inverness

Ten Inverness Way

10 Inverness Way
Inverness CA 94937
(415) 669-1648

Circa 1904. Shingled in redwood, this bed and breakfast features a stone fireplace, good books, player piano and access to a great hiking area. Views from the breakfast room invite you to include a nature walk in your day's plans. According to local folklore a ghost used to call Ten Inverness Way his home, but since the innkeepers had each room blessed, he seems to have disappeared, and the inn has become known for its peace and refreshment.
Location: Near Point Reyes National Seashore.
Rates: $90-$100.
Innkeeper(s): Mary Davies.
4 Rooms. Guest phone available. Meals: Full breakfast. Jacuzzi. Fireplaces. Birdwatching, horsebacking, hiking nearby.
Seen in: *LA Times, New York Times, Travel & Leisure, Sunset.*

Ione

The Heirloom
214 Shakeley Lane, PO Box 322
Ione CA 95640
(209) 274-4468
Circa 1863. A two-story Colonial with columns and balconies, the an-

tebellum Heirloom has a spacious, private English garden. Inside, there are many family heirlooms and a square grand piano once owned by Lola Montez. The building was dedicated by the Native Sons of the Golden West as a historic site.
Location: California Gold Country.
Rates: $50-$85.
Innkeeper(s): Melisande Hubbs & Patricia Cross.
6 Rooms. 4 Private Baths. Guest phone available. Beds: KQ. Meals: Full breakfast.
"As usual our stay was unforgettable."

Jamestown

National Hotel
Main Street, PO Box 502
Jamestown CA 95327
(209) 984-3446
Circa 1859. One of the oldest continuously operating hotels in California, the inn maintains its

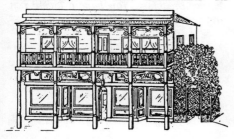

original redwood bar at which thousands of dollars in gold dust were spent. The restaurant is considered to be one of the finest in the Mother Lode.

Location: Center of town.
Rates: $45-$75.
Innkeeper(s): Stephen Willey.
8 Rooms. 8 Private Baths. Guest phone available. TV available. Beds: QT. Meals: Continental-plus breakfast. Conference room. CCs: Visa, MC. Gold panning.
Seen in: *Bon Appetit.*
"Excellent, wonderful place!"

Julian

Pine Hills Lodge
2960 La Posada Way, PO Box 2260
Julian CA 92036
(619) 765-1100
Circa 1912. Nestled among tall, whispering pine trees, stately oaks, and wildflowers, the lodge is situated on eight rolling acres at

4,500 feet. There are quaint rooms with shared baths in the rustic main building. Cabins dot the landscape surrounding the lodge, some with patios and fireplaces.
Rates: $50-$125.
Innkeeper(s): Donna Goodman.
18 Rooms. 12 Private Baths. Guest phone available. Beds: KQDT. Meals: Full breakfast. Conference room. Fireplaces. Pool. CCs: Visa, MC, AE, DC. Barbeque dinner theater.

Kyburz

Strawberry Lodge
Hwy 50
Kyburz CA 95720
(916) 659-7030
Circa 1935. Nestled in the Sierra Nevada Mountains high above Lake Tahoe, Strawberry Lodge was named for Ira Fuller Berry. (It was said that he was so tight-fisted that he passed off straw for hay to teamsters driving their wagons up to the lodge. When they arrived, they would yell, "Got any more of

that straw, Berry?") The lodge features brass beds and hand-painted furniture. Nearby, golden eagles nest on the high cliffs of Lover's Leap.
Location: 15 miles west of Lake Tahoe.
**Rates: $33-$100.
Innkeeper(s): Richard Mitchell.
39 Rooms. 34 Private Baths. Guest phone available. TV available. Beds: KQT. Meals: EP. Conference room. Fireplaces. Pool. CCs: Visa, MC, AE. German brown and rainbow trout fishing, swimming, tennis. Dancing in the dance room.
Seen in: *San Francisco Examiner.*

La Jolla

The Bed & Breakfast Inn at La Jolla
7753 Draper Ave
La Jolla CA 92037
(619) 456-2066
Circa 1913. The architect Irving Gill, father of tilt slab construction, built this home once occupied by John Phillip Souza and his family. All the guest rooms are beautifully designed but honeymooners often choose the room with the white canopy bed, fireplace and white sofa. Each room has one of Betty's fresh floral arrangements, and there are garden and ocean views.
Location: One block to the ocean.
**Rates: $70-$185.
Innkeeper(s): Betty P. Albee.
16 Rooms. 15 Private Baths. Guest phone available. TV available. Beds: QT. Meals: Full breakfast. Handicap access provided. Fireplaces. CCs: Visa, MC. Tennis across the street. swimming, surfing, sunning.
Seen in: *Innsider, Country Inns.*
"Perfection, elegance, style! May I buy this room?"

Laguna Beach

Carriage House
1322 Catalina St
Laguna Beach CA 92651
(714) 494-8945
Circa 1920. A Laguna Beach historical landmark, this inn has a Cape clapboard exterior. It once housed

an art gallery and a bakery, and then was converted into apartments with large rooms and kitchens. Now as a cozy inn, each room has a private parlor. Outside is a courtyard fountain shaded by a large carrotwood tree with hanging moss.
Location: Two & one-half blocks from the ocean.
**Rates: $90-$110.
Innkeeper(s): Dee & Vernon Taylor.
6 Rooms. 6 Private Baths. Guest phone available. TV available. Beds: KQDT. Meals: Continental-plus breakfast. Swimming, shopping.
"A true home away from home with all the extra touches added in."

Casa Laguna
2510 S Coast Hwy
Laguna Beach CA 92651
(714) 494-2996
Circa 1930. A romantic combination of California Mission and Spanish Revival architecture, the

inn's Mission House and cottages were built in the early Thirties. The casitas were added in the Forties. The hillside setting of secluded gardens, winding paths, and flower-splashed patios invites guests to linger and enjoy ocean views or watch the sunset from the Bell Tower high above the inn.
Location: On an ocean view hillside.
**Rates: $95-$150.
Innkeeper(s): Jerry & Luanne Siegel.
20 Rooms. 20 Private Baths. Guest phone in room. TV in room. Beds: KQTC. Meals: Continental-plus breakfast. Conference room. Fireplaces. Pool. CCs: Visa, MC, AE, DC.
Seen in: *Los Angeles Magazine.*
"We had such a wonderful time at your delightful inn that we have regretted leaving every day we have been home."

Eiler's Inn
741 S Coast Hwy
Laguna Beach CA 92651
(714) 494-3004

Circa 1940. This New Orleans-style inn surrounds a lush courtyard and fountain. The rooms are decorated with antiques and wallpapers. Wine and cheese is served in the evening in front of the fireplace. Named after Eiler Larsen, famous town greeter of Laguna, the inn is just a stone's throw from the beach on the ocean-side of Pacific Coast Highway.
Location: In the heart of the village.
Rates: $95-$150.
Innkeeper(s): Jonna Iverson.
12 Rooms. 12 Private Baths. Guest phone available. TV available. Beds: KQT. Meals: Continental-plus breakfast. Fireplaces.
"Who could find a paradise more relaxing than an old-fashioned bed and breakfast with Mozart and Vivaldi, a charming fountain, wonderful fresh-baked bread, ocean air, and Henk's conversational wit?"

Lake Arrowhead

Storybook Inn
See: Sky Forest, CA

Little River

Glendeven
8221 N Hwy 1
Little River CA 95456
(707) 937-0083
Circa 1867. Lumber merchant Isaiah Stevens built this farmhouse set on a two-acre headland meadow

with the bay of Little River in the distance. White clapboard siding and high pitched roof lines reflect the architecture of Stevens' native Maine. The sound of waves rolling onto the beach can often be heard. Ask for the Eastlin Suite with its inlaid Louis XVI rosewood bed, fireplace, and view of the bay.
Location: One-half mile to Mendocino.
Rates: $85-$125.

Innkeeper(s): Jan & Janet deVries.
10 Rooms. 10 Private Baths. Beds: QDT. Meals: Continental plus. Jacuzzi. Fireplaces. CCs: Visa, MC. Tennis, golf, horseback riding nearby. wonderful hiking.
Seen in: *Arizona Republic, Contra Costa Times.*

The Victorian Farmhouse
7001 N Hwy 1, PO Box 357
Little River CA 95456
(707) 937-0697
Circa 1877. Built as a private residence this Victorian farmhouse is located on two-and-a-half acres in

Little River, two miles south of the historic village of Mendocino. The inn offers a relaxed country setting with deer, quail, flower gardens, an apple orchard and a running creek (School House Creek). There are ocean views from the front porch but a short walk will take you to the shoreline.
Rates: $75-$90.
Innkeeper(s): George & Carole Molnar.
10 Rooms. 10 Private Baths. Guest phone available. Beds: KQ. Meals: Continental-plus breakfast. Handicap access provided. Conference room. Fireplaces. CCs: Visa, MC. Horseback riding, canoeing, fishing, golf and hiking nearby. Garden weddings are popular.
"This morning when we woke up at home we really missed having George deliver breakfast. You have a lovely inn and you do a super job."

Los Angeles

Eastlake Victorian Inn
1442 Kellam Ave
Los Angeles CA 90026
(213) 250-1620

Circa 1887. Faithfully restored, decorated and furnished, the

Eastlake Victorian Inn is situated in Los Angeles' first historic preservation zone. Private tours of two National Register Victorian homes are available, as well as old-fashioned hot-air ballooning, murder mysteries, and other nearby attractions.
Location: Near downtown and the Music Center.
Rates: $45-$125. All year.
Innkeeper(s): Murray Burns & Planaria Price.
7 Rooms. 2 Private Baths. Guest phone available. TV available. Beds: Q. Meals: B&B. Conference room. CCs: Visa, MC, AE.
Seen in: *USA Today, Travel & Leisure, Travel Holiday, Sunset.*
"Incomparably romantic!" Los Angeles Times.

Salisbury House
2273 W 20th St
Los Angeles CA 90018
(213) 737-7817

Circa 1909. Located in Arlington Heights, the inn is part of the old West Adams area of Los Angeles. It

features original stained and leaded glass windows, wood-beamed ceilings, and an abundance of wood paneling and has been used as a

location for movies and commercials. Salisbury House is known for its gourmet breakfasts and old-fashioned graciousness.
**Rates: $60-$75.
Innkeeper(s): Alice & Si Torvend.
5 Rooms. 3 Private Baths. Guest phone available. TV available. Beds: KQT. Meals: Full breakfast. CCs: Visa, MC, AE.
"The finest bed and breakfast we've seen. Not only is the house exquisite but the hospitality is unmatched!"

Terrace Manor
1353 Alvarado Terrace
Los Angeles CA 90006
(213) 381-1478

Circa 1902. This three-story Tudor is a National Register Landmark house. The inn is tastefully decorated and displays extraordinary stained-glass windows installed by the builder who owned a stained glass factory at the turn of the century.
**Rates: $55-$85.
Innkeeper(s): Sandy & Shirley Spillman.
5 Rooms. 5 Private Baths. Guest phone available. Beds: KQ. Meals: Full breakfast. Conference room. Fireplaces. CCs: Visa, MC, AE.
"Lovely! Sandy does magic in the parlor; Shirley in the kitchen!

Mariposa

Meadow Creek Ranch
Bed & Breakfast Inn
2669 Triangle Rd
Mariposa CA 95338
(209) 966-3843

Circa 1858. This Wells Fargo stagecoach stop is now a rambling farmhouse framed by a black walnut tree and old-fashioned climbing roses. A cozy country cottage in back is called the "Chicken Coop" but is decorated with a white carpet, canopy bed and antiques. There are three guestrooms in the main house.
Location: Halfway between two southern entrances into Yosemite.
**Rates: $55-$75.
Innkeeper(s): Bob & Carol Shockley.
4 Rooms. 1 Private Baths. Guest phone available. Beds: QT. Meals: Full breakfast. Fireplaces. CCs: Visa, MC, AE. Yosemite skiing, horseback riding, river rafting.
Seen in: *Gazette, Signature, Los Angeles Times.*

"A wonderful spot to begin a trip through the Gold Country or into Yosemite."

Mendocino

Elk Cove Inn
See: Elk, CA

Glendeven
See: Little River, CA

Headlands Inn
PO Box 132
Mendocino CA 95460
(707) 937-4431

Circa 1868. Originally built as a small barbershop on Main Street, the building became the elegant "Oyster and Coffee Saloon" in 1884. Later, horses pulled the house over log

rollers to its present location. The new setting provides spectacular views of the ocean, rugged coastline, and sunsets. Antiques, paintings, and fireplaces warm each guest room and there is a romantic honeymoon cottage in the back garden.
Location: Two blocks from the center of the village.
Rates: $85-$110.
Innkeeper(s): Pat & Rod Stofle.
5 Rooms. 5 Private Baths. Guest phone available. Beds: KQT. Meals: Full breakfast. Handicap access provided. Fireplaces. Hiking in state parks, redwood groves, wineries, little theater.
"If a Nobel Prize were given for breakfasts, you would win hands down. A singularly joyous experience!!"

Howard Creek Ranch
See: Westport, CA

Joshua Grindle Inn
44800 Little Lake Rd, PO Box 647
Mendocino CA 95460
(707) 937-4143

Circa 1879. The town banker Joshua Grindle built this New England-style home on two acres. The decor is light and airy, with Early American antiques, clocks and

quilts. In addition to the house, there are rooms in the water tower and in a cottage. Six of the guest rooms have fireplaces and some have views over the town to the ocean.
Location: On the Pacific Ocean.
Rates: $65-$95.
Innkeeper(s): Bill & Gwen Jacobson.
10 Rooms. 10 Private Baths. Guest phone available. Beds: QT. Meals: Full breakfast. Handicap access provided. Fireplaces. CCs: Visa,, MC, AE.
Seen in: *Peninsula, Copley News Service.*
"We are basking in the memories of our stay. We loved every moment."

MacCallum House Inn
45020 Albion St
Mendocino CA 95460
(707) 937-0289
Circa 1882. Built by William H. Kelley for his newly wed daughter Daisy MacCallum, the MacCallum House Inn is a splendid example of New England architecture in the Victorian village of Mendocino. Besides the main house, accommodations include the barn, carriage house, greenhouse, gazebo and water tower rooms.
Location: North Coast.
**Rates: $45-$125. All year.
Innkeeper(s): Melanie & Joe Reding.
20 Rooms. 7 Private Baths. Guest phone available. Beds: KQTC. Meals: Full breakfast. Dinner available. Handicap access provided. CCs: Visa, MC, AE.
Seen in: *California Visitors Review.*

Mendocino Village Inn
44860 Main St, PO Box 626
Mendocino CA 95460
(707) 937-0246
Circa 1882. Originally the home of physician Dr. William McCornack, this graceful Victorian has been beautifully restored and is one of the architectural gems of Mendocino. A variety of rooms offer

both Victorian and country decor and seven have fireplaces with

wood laid neatly each night. Just beyond a white picket fence is the ocean and the pleasures of the North Coast.
Location: Walking distance to everything in the village.
Rates: $55-$110. All year.
Innkeeper(s): Sue & Tom Allen.
12 Rooms. 10 Private Baths. Guest phone available. Beds: Q. Meals: Full breakfast. CCs: Visa, MC.
"Thanks for making our visit very special! We enjoyed the ambience you provided - Vivaldi, Diamond Lil, homemade breakfast and of course, Mendocino charm!"

Noyo River Lodge
See: Fort Bragg, CA

The Victorian Farmhouse
See: Little River, CA

Whitegate Inn
PO Box 150, 499 Howard St
Mendocino CA 95460
(707) 937-4892
Circa 1883. When it was first built, the local newspaper called it "one of the most elegant and best appointed residences in town." There are bay windows, a steep gabled roof, redwood siding and fishscale shingles.

Original wallpaper adorns one of the double parlors where an antique Hamilton pump organ and inlaid

pocket doors add to the atmosphere. Other elegant touches are the silver, Baccarat crystal and Rosenthal china used at breakfast.
Rates: $65-100. All year.
Innkeeper(s): Patricia Patton.
5 Rooms. 5 Private Baths. Beds: QD.
Meals: Full breakfast. Fireplaces.
"Made our honeymoon a dream come true."

Mill Valley

Mountain Home Inn
810 Panoramic Hwy
Mill Valley CA 94941
(415) 381-9000
Circa 1912. At one time the only way to get to Mountain Home Inn was by taking the train up Mount Tamalpais. With 22 trestles and 281 curves it was called "the crookedest railroad in the world" but the round-trip cost only $1.40 from San Francisco. Then as now, it was always worth the trip to marvel at the spectacular view of San Francisco Bay. Each guest room has a view of the mountain, valley or bay.
Location: Mt. Tamalpais.
**Rates: $108-$178.
Innkeeper(s): Ed & Susan Cunningham.
10 Rooms. 10 Private Baths. Guest phone available. TV available. Beds: KQ.
Meals: B&B. Jacuzzi. Handicap access provided. Conference room. Fireplaces. CCs: Visa, MC. Ocean beach 10 minutes away. Above giant redwoods of Muir Woods.
Seen in: *San Francisco Examiner, California Magazine.*
"A luxurious retreat. Echoes the grand style and rustic feeling of national park lodges." Ben Davidson, *Travel and Leisure.*

Monterey

Old Monterey Inn
500 Martin St
Monterey CA 93940
(408) 375-8284
Circa 1929. Built in the Tudor style with half-timbers, the ivy-covered Old Monterey Inn looks and feels like an English country house. Sheltering an acre of pansies, roses, peonies and rhododendrons are redwood, pine and old oak trees. Brick pathways and a hammock beckon

guests to the garden. Most of the guest rooms have wood-burning fireplaces, skylights and stained-glass windows.
Rates: $130-$195. All year.
Innkeeper(s): Ann & Gene Swett.
10 Rooms. 10 Private Baths. Guest phone available. Beds: KQT. Meals: Continental-plus breakfast. Fireplaces.
Seen in: *Los Angeles Times, PSA magazine, San Francisco Focus.*
　"Bed and Breakfast Inn of the Year." Hideaway Report.

The Jabberwock
598 Laine St
Monterey CA 93940
(408) 372-4777
　Circa 1911. Set in a half-acre of gardens, this Victorian inn provides

views of Monterey Bay and its famous barking seals. There are huge Victorian beds complete with lace-edged sheets and goose-down comforters. Early evening hor d'oeuvres and aperitifs are served in an enclosed veranda.
Location: Four blocks above Cannery Row, the beach and Monterey Aquarium.
Rates: $85-$160. All year.

Innkeeper(s): Jim & Barbara Allen.
7 Rooms. 3 Private Baths. Guest phone available. Beds: KQ. Meals: Full breakfast. Conference room. Fireplaces. Cookies & milk to tuck you in. Fisherman's Wharf, Seventeen-Mile Drive.
Seen in: *Sacramento Bee, San Francisco Examiner, Los Angeles Times.*
　"Not only were the accommodations delightful but the people were equally so."

Murphys

Dunbar House, 1880
PO Box 1375
Murphys CA 95247
(209) 728-2897
　Circa 1880. A picket fence frames this Italianate home built by Willis

Dunbar for his bride. Later, distinguished sons served in the State Assembly and ran the Dunbar Lumber Company. On the porch, rocking chairs overlook century-old gardens while inside are antiques, lace, quilts and claw-foot tubs. Breakfast is delivered to your room in a picnic basket, or you may join others by the fireplace in the dining room.
**Rates: $60-$70. All year.
Innkeeper(s): Bob & Barbara Costa.
5 Rooms. 5 Private Baths. Guest phone available. TV available. Beds: KD. Meals: Full breakfast. Conference room. Fireplaces. CCs: Visa, MC. Tennis, swimming and fishing nearby. skiing 39 miles. Winery and gold panning tours.
　"Your beautiful gardens and gracious hospitality combine for a super bed and breakfast."

Murphy's Hotel
457 Main St
Murphys CA 95247
(209) 728-3444
　Circa 1856. Built as a stopover for visitors to the Calaveras Big Trees, a grove of giant sequoias, the hotel's many guests have included such

notables as President Grant, Mark Twain and Horatio Alger. The hotel still is a center for social activity in town, and there is a 20-room modern motel adjacent to the main building.
Location: In the historic Gold Rush town of Murphys.
**Rates: $48-$55. All year.
Innkeeper(s): Robert Walker.
9 Rooms. Guest phone available. TV available. Meals: Continental breakfast. Conference room. CCs: Visa, MC, AE. Caverns, fishing, gold panning, golf, art galleries.

Napa

Brannan Cottage Inn
See: Calistoga, CA

Coombs Residence "Inn on the Park"
720 Seminary St
Napa CA 94559
(707) 257-0789
　Circa 1852. This two-story Victorian was built as the home of Frank Coombs, son of Nathan

Coombs who laid out the city of Napa and was ambassador to Japan during President Harrison's term. The inn is decorated with European

and American antiques. Across the street is historic Fuller Park.
Location: One hour from San Francisco.
Rates: $75-$95. All year.
Innkeeper(s): Dave & Pearl Campbell.
4 Rooms. 1 Private Baths. Guest phone available. TV available. Beds: KQDT.
Meals: Full breakfast. CCs: Visa, MC.

"We feel like we are back in Europe! Your hospitality is unmatched! Simple elegance with warm friendly atmosphere. Our favorite B&B, a house with its own personality."

Napa Inn
1137 Warren St
Napa CA 94559
(707) 257-1444
Circa 1885. This Victorian mansion is nestled in the heart of the wine

country in a quiet neighborhood. Some rooms have kitchens. A short stroll takes you to shaded parks, gourmet and family restaurants or you can pack a picnic lunch and start off for an afternoon of wine-touring.
Location: In the historic district.
Rates: $80-$90. All year.
Innkeeper(s): Doug & Carol Morales.
4 Rooms. 2 Private Baths. Beds: KQ.
Meals: Continental-plus breakfast.

Shady Oaks Country Inn
See: St. Helena, CA

National City

Dickinson Boal Mansion
1433 East 24th St
National City CA 92050
(619) 477-5363
Circa 1887. This large Queen Anne Victorian built by Col. William Dickinson, the founder of Chula Vista, is situated on two acres. There are seven fireplaces, stained glass win-

dows, and an ornate bannister. Although only in the beginning stages

of renovation, those interested in historic preservation may be interested in the process and the owner anticipates needing 15 years to complete the restoration.
Rates: $75-$85.
Innkeeper(s): Jim Ladd and Connie Marquez.
3 Rooms. 1 Private Baths. Beds: K.
Meals: B&B.
Seen in: *San Diego Union*.

Nevada City

Downey House
517 West Broad St
Nevada City CA 95959
(916) 265-2815
Circa 1869. This Eastlake Victorian is situated amid Nevada City's noted Victorians atop Nabob Hill.

There are six sound-proofed guest rooms, a curved veranda, and in the garden a pond and restored red barn. One can stroll downtown when the evening streets are lit by the warm glow of gas lights.
Location: On Nabob Hill close to the Historic District.
Rates: $60-$80. All year.
Innkeeper(s): Miriam Wright.
6 Rooms. 6 Private Baths. Guest phone available. TV available. Beds: QD.
Meals: Full breakfast. CCs: Visa, MC.

Tennis, fishing, gold panning, boating, water-skiing, wineries. Horse-drawn carriages, trolley.
"The best in Northern California."
"Wonderful food, lovely room and yard."

Red Castle Inn
109 Prospect St
Nevada City CA 95959
(916) 265-5135
Circa 1857. The Smithsonian has lauded the restoration of this four-

story Gothic Revival known as "The Castle" by townsfolk. The roof is laced with wooden icicles and the balconies are festooned with gingerbread. Within, there are intricate moldings, antiques, Victorian wallpapers, canopy beds and fireplaces. Verandas provide views of dogwood, apple and pine trees, as well as a pond and fountain.
Location: One hour north of Sacramento and 2 1/2 hours from San Francisco.
**Rates: $65-$95. All year.
Innkeeper(s): Conley & Mary Louise Weaver.
8 Rooms. Guest phone available. Beds: QD. Meals: Full breakfast. Handicap access provided. Fireplaces. CCs: Visa, MC. Cross-country skiing, swimming, tennis, golf, white-water rafting.
Seen in: *Signature, Sacramento, B&B Innviews*.
"A place of warmth and comfort. You have the true knowledge of what it takes to run a five-star, first-class bed and breakfast inn."

Newport Beach

Doryman's Inn
2102 W Ocean Front
Newport Beach CA 92663
(714) 675-7300
Circa 1880. Romantic Victorian rooms overlook the ocean and Newport pier at the Doryman's. French

and American antiques enhance luxury appointments such as Italian marble sunken bathtubs, gilt-edged beveled mirrors, and etched French glass fixtures. Ferns and skylights are everywhere, and candlelit dinners are catered by one of Newport's finest gourmet seafood restaurants.
Location: Oceanfront.
**Rates: $135-$275. All year.
Innkeeper(s): Michael Palitz.
10 Rooms. 10 Private Baths. TV available. Beds: KQ. Meals: Continental-plus breakfast. Jacuzzi. Handicap access provided. Conference room. Fireplaces. CCs: Visa, MC, AE, DC,CB. All water sports are nearby.
"Terrific service." Neil & Marsha Diamond.
"Had a wonderful stay." Jerry Lewis.

Nipomo

The Kaleidoscope Inn
Box 1297, 130 E Dana St
Nipomo CA 93444
(805) 929-5444
Circa 1887. Joseph Dana, a sea captain from New England, fell in love with this area and married a

Spanish senorita. Afterwards, he petitioned the Mexican government and was given all the land from the foothills to the sea. Inside this gingerbread Victorian are antique sofas, an old wooden trunk of Patty's great, great grandmother and vintage photographs. Sunlight filtering through the stained glass windows creates a kaleidoscope effect.
Location: Twenty miles south of San Luis Obispo, near Pismo Beach.
**Rates: $65-$70. All year.
Innkeeper(s): Patty & Bill Linane, Dorothy Memeo.
3 Rooms. Guest phone available. Beds: QT. Meals: Continental-plus breakfast.

Jacuzzi. Fireplaces. CCs: Visa, MC. Golfing, horseback riding, mineral springs, wind surfing. Dinner & theater reservations.
Seen in: *Santa Maria Times.*
"A fantasy stay - the best B&B we've stayed in."

Ojai

Ojai Manor Hotel
210 E Matilija
Ojai CA 93023
(805) 646-0961
Circa 1874. Once a schoolhouse, this is Ojai's oldest building. Turn-of-the-century furnishings are combined with modern prints and sculpture for an original decor. In the parlor are blue velvet couches and a big willow chair next to an old pot-bellied stove where sherry is served in the evening. Several good restaurants are nearby.
Location: One block from Main Street.
Rates: $70-$80. All year.
6 Rooms. Meals: Continental-plus breakfast. CCs: Visa, MC. Walk to shops & restaurants. drive to hot springs.
Seen in: *Country Inns.*
"Best hotel we've ever stayed in and best breakfast we've ever had."
"A feast for all the senses, an esthetic delight."

Pacific Grove

Gosby House Inn
643 Lighthouse Ave.
Pacific Grove CA 93950
(408) 375-1287
Circa 1887. Built as an upscale Victorian inn for visitors to the old

Methodist retreat, this yellow mansion features an abundance of

gables, turrets and bays. During renovation the innkeeper slept in all the rooms to determine just what antiques were needed and how the beds should be situated. Gosby House is in the National Register.
Location: Six blocks from the ocean.
**Rates: $90-$145. All year.
Innkeeper(s): Kelly Short.
22 Rooms. 20 Private Baths. Guest phone available. Beds: QC. Meals: Full breakfast. Conference room. Fireplaces. CCs: Visa, MC, AE, DS. Afternoon tea & hors d'oeuvres.
Seen in: *Los Angeles Times.*

Green Gables Inn
104 5th St
Pacific Grove CA 93950
(408) 375-2095
Circa 1888. This half-timbered Queen Anne Victorian appears as a fantasy of gables overlooking spec-

tacular Monterey Bay. The parlor has stained-glass panels framing the fireplace and bay windows looking out to sea. A favorite focal point is an antique carousel horse. Most of the guest rooms have panoramic views of the ocean, fireplaces, gleaming woodwork, soft quilts, and flowers.
Location: On Monterey Bay four blocks from Monterey Bay Aquarium.
**Rates: $95-$150. All year.
Innkeeper(s): Roger & Sally Post with Claudia Long.
11 Rooms. 7 Private Baths. Guest phone available. TV available. Beds: QD. Meals: Full breakfast, afternoon tea. Conference room. Fireplaces. CCs: Visa, MC, AE, DS. Picnicking, scuba diving, swimming, golfing. Honeymoon packages.

House of Seven Gables
555 Ocean View
Pacific Grove CA 93950
(408) 372-4341
Circa 1886. At the turn of the century, Lucie Chase, a wealthy widow and civic leader from the East Coast,

embellished this Victorian with gables and verandas taking full ad-

vantage of its spectacular setting on Monterey Bay. All guest rooms feature ocean views and there are elegant antiques, intricate Persian carpets, and beveled-glass armoires. Sea otters, harbor seals, and whales may often be seen from the inn.
Location: Oceanfront.
**Rates: $85-$165. All year.
Innkeeper(s): The Flatley family - John, Nora, Susan, Fred, Ed.
14 Rooms. 14 Private Baths. Guest phone available. TV available. Beds: KQD. Meals: Continental-plus breakfast. Handicap access provided. Nightly turn-down service. Cannery Row, 17-Mile Drive, Fisherman's Wharf.
Seen in: *Woman's Day, Innsider, Los Angeles Times.*
"Charlene and I enjoyed our recent stay enormously. We have been to the Monterey area several times but this will always remain our most memorable trip."

Old St Angela Inn
321 Central Ave
Pacific Grove CA 93950
(408) 372-3246
Circa 1890. Formerly a convent, this Cape-style inn has been restored and includes a glass solarium where a champagne breakfast is served. Under the gazebo in the back garden is a jacuzzi. The ocean is a block away.
**Rates: $75-$135.
Innkeeper(s): Donna & Carmen.
8 Rooms. 5 Private Baths. Guest phone available. Beds: QDT. Meals: Full champagne breakfast. Jacuzzi. Fireplaces. CCs: Visa, MC. Special rates for mid-week off season.
"Outstanding inn and outstanding hospitality."

Roserox Country Inn By-The-Sea
557 Ocean View Blvd
Pacific Grove CA 93950
(408) 373-7673

Circa 1904. Roserox was designed and built by Dr. Julia Platt, first woman mayor of Pacific Grove, as well as Doctor of Zoology and world-renowned scientist. This is a

warm and intimate four-story inn, enhanced by original patterned oak floors and ten-foot-high redwood beamed ceilings.
Location: Oceanfront.
Rates: $85-$185. All year.
Innkeeper(s): Dawn Browncroft.
8 Rooms. 4 Private Baths. Guest phone available. Beds: QT. Meals: Full country breakfast. Conference room.
Seen in: *This Month's Magazine.*
"I could never return to Monterey without staying at Roserox."

Pismo Beach

The Kaleidoscope Inn
See: Nipomo, CA

Placerville

Chichester House Bed & Breakfast
800 Spring St
Placerville CA 95667
(916) 626-1882
Circa 1892. D.W. Chichester, a partner in the local sawmill, built

this house for his wife and it is said to be the first home in Placerville with built-in plumbing. Guests enjoy the pump organ in the parlor,

the fireplaces, a library and conservatory. The guest rooms are decorated with family treasures and antiques.
Rates: $65-$70.
3 Rooms. 3 Private Baths. Meals: Full gourmet breakfast.
"The most relaxing and enjoyable trip I've ever taken."

James Blair House
2985 Clay St
Placerville CA 95667
(916) 626-6136
Circa 1901. James Blair, a Placerville lumberman, built this Queen Anne Victorian with a three-story turret and conservatory. There are stained glass windows, an elegant parlor, and fine interior woodwork. Guests can relax on wide porches or walk to Old Hangtown. Ask to stay in the romantic turret room.
Rates: $45-$70. All year.
Innkeeper(s): Patsy & Richard Thompson.
4 Rooms. 2 Private Baths. Guest phone available. Beds: QD. Meals: Full breakfast and restaurant. Fireplaces. CCs: Visa, MC. Downhill & cross country skiing, river rafting, gold panning.
"Your house is beautiful and your hospitality was wonderful."

Point Richmond

East Brother Light Station
117 Park Pt
Point Richmond CA 94801
(415) 233-2385
Circa 1873. Managed by a non-profit organization, this lighthouse inn is located on an acre of island. Guest quarters, furnished simply, are situated in the outbuildings and on the second story of the innkeeper's Victorian house. The light has been automated since 1969.
Location: Ten minutes from dock.
Rates: $250 MAP.
Innkeeper(s): Linda & Leigh Hurley.
4 Rooms. 2 Private Baths. Meals: Continental plus, dinner included.
Seen in: *Uncommon Lodgings.*

Quincy

The Feather Bed
542 Jackson St, PO Box 3200
Quincy CA 95971

(916) 283-0102

Circa 1893. Englishman Edward Huskinson built this charming Queen Anne house shortly after he

began his mining and real estate ventures. The inn has a secluded cottage with its own deck and claw-foot tub. Other rooms in the main house overlook downtown Quincy or the mountains. Check out a bicycle to explore the countryside.
Location: In the heart of Plumas National Forest.
**Rates: $50-$75. All year.
Innkeeper(s): Chuck & Dianna Goubert.
6 Rooms. 6 Private Baths. Guest phone available. TV available. Beds: Q. Meals: Full breakfast. Conference room. CCs: Visa, MC, AE. Horseback riding, water sports, cross country skiing, hiking. Bicycles available.

"After living and traveling in Europe where innkeepers are famous, we have found The Feather Bed to be one of the most charming in the U.S. and Europe!"

Rancho Cucamonga

Christmas House Bed & Breakfast Inn
9240 Archibald Ave
Rancho Cucamonga CA 91730
(714) 980-6450

Circa 1904. This Queen Anne Victorian has been renovated in period elegance, emphasizing its intricate

wood carvings and red and green stained-glass windows. Once surrounded by 80 acres of citrus groves and vineyards, the wide, sweeping veranda is still a favorite place for looking out over lawns and palm trees. The elegant atmosphere attracts the business traveler, romance-seeker and vacationer.
Location: East of downtown Los Angeles, 3 miles from Ontario Airport.
Rates: $55-$105. All year.
Innkeeper(s): Jay & Janice Ilsley.
5 Rooms. 3 Private Baths. Guest phone available. TV available. Beds: D. Meals: Full breakfast on weekends. Conference room.
Seen in: *Los Angeles Times*.

Red Bluff

Faulkner House
1029 Jefferson St
Red Bluff CA 96080
(916) 529-0520

Circa 1890. Built by jeweler Herman Wiendieck, this Queen Anne Victorian was bought by Dr. and

Mrs. James L. Faulkner in 1933. The house has original stained-glass windows, ornate molding, and eight-foot pocket doors separating the front and back parlors. Church bells nearby chime the hour as you relax on the porch.
**Rates: $43-$60. All year.
Innkeeper(s): Harvey & Mary Klingler.
4 Rooms. 1 Private Baths. Guest phone available. Beds: QD. Meals: Full breakfast. Conference room. Fishing, hiking, skiing.
"A delightful B&B, tastefully decorated with beautiful antiques."

Sacramento

Amber House
1315 22nd St

Sacramento CA 95816
(916) 444-8085

Circa 1905. This Craftsman-style bungalow on the city's Historic Preservation Register is in a neighborhood of fine old homes eight blocks from the capitol. Each room is named for a famous poet and features stained glass, English antiques, selected volumes of poetry and fresh flowers. Ask for Lord Byron where you can soak by candlelight in the jacuzzi.
Location: Seven blocks to the capitol.
**Rates: $70-$125. All year.
Innkeeper(s): Michael & Jane Richardson.
5 Rooms. 5 Private Baths. Guest phone in room. TV available. Beds: QD. Meals: Full gourmet breakfast. Jacuzzi. Conference room. Fireplaces. CCs: Visa, MC, AE. Near old town, convention center, river rafting. Bicycles available.

Briggs House B&B
2209 Capitol Ave
Sacramento CA 95816
(916) 441-3214

Circa 1901. Surrounded by stately trees, this elegantly restored Cube colonial is filled with European and American antiques, creating a set-

ting of peaceful splendor. The spacious rooms have rich wood paneling, inlaid hardwood floors, and oriental rugs. Guests are welcome to raid the refrigerator where wine, sparkling water, and cider are kept.

Location: Midtown, seven blocks from the capitol.
Rates: $60-$95. All year.
Innkeeper(s): Sue, Barbara, Kathy, Paula, & Leslie.
7 Rooms. 5 Private Baths. Guest phone in room. Beds: KQT. Meals: Full breakfast. Jacuzzi. Sauna. Conference room. CCs: Visa, MC, AE.
Seen in: *Motorland, San Francisco Bay Views, California Lodging Update*.
"I have experienced a real change in what is accomplished at business meet-

ings held at inns as opposed to hotel rooms. People become friendlier, more relaxed and more productive. The sense of caring...nurtures the harried traveler."

"We have enjoyed country inns around the world, and this ranks as one of the top small inns."

Hartley House Inn
700 22nd St
Sacramento CA 95816
(916) 447-7829

Circa 1906. Original hitching posts grace the front of this stunning

Colonial Revival inn. What was formerly known as Mrs. Murphy's boarding house has been restored with elegant antiques and silk wallpapers. There is a large collection of antique wall clocks and chiming grandfather clocks.
Location: Downtown.
**Rates: $55-$85. All year.
Innkeeper(s): Randall Hartley.
5 Rooms. 5 Private Baths. Guest phone in room. TV in room. Beds: Q. Meals: Full gourmet breakfast. Conference room. Fireplaces. CCs: All. Water skiing, horseback riding, bicycling.
Seen in: *Yellow Brick Road, Sacramento Bee.*

"Breakfasts are as lavish as the inn."

Saint Helena

Cornerstone B&B Inn
1308 Main St
Saint Helena CA 94574
(707) 963-1891

Circa 1891. This old stone building has been renovated and is a European-style hostelry with twelve spacious rooms furnished in the Victorian period. Nearby attractions are the famous hot springs and mud baths, and concerts in the vineyards.

**Rates: $55-$85. All year.
Innkeeper(s): Margie Hinton.

12 Rooms. TV available. Beds: KQDT. Meals: Continental-plus breakfast. Conference room. CCs: California checks. Ballooning, gliders, geysers, bicycling.

Ink House
1575 St Helena Hwy
Saint Helena CA 94574
(707) 963-3890

Circa 1884. Theron H. Ink owned thousands of acres in Marin, Napa

and Sonoma counties and invested in livestock, wineries and mining. He built this Italianate Victorian with a glass-walled observatory on top of the house. From this room and the guest rooms, visitors can enjoy 360-degree views of the Napa Valley and surrounding vineyards.
Location: In the heart of Napa Valley wine country.
**Rates: $80-$95. All year.
Innkeeper(s): Lois & George Clark.
4 Rooms. 4 Private Baths. Guest phone available. TV available. Beds: QD. Meals: Continental breakfast. Nearby wine tours, spas & mud baths, soaring, ballooning.

"Your hospitality of home and heart have made us feel so much at home. This is a place and a time we will long remember."

Shady Oaks Country Inn
399 Zinfandel
Saint Helena CA 94574
(707) 963-1190

Circa 1880. This country home sits on two acres of oak and walnut trees. Adjacent to the house is a winery built in 1883, possessing the original stone walls. It now serves as a luxurious guest suite. Rooms in the main house feature such items as original wallpaper, a claw-foot

tub, private deck or views of the gardens and vineyards. Guests often choose to play croquet or sometimes ask the innkeeper to pack one of her perfect picnic baskets.
Location: Two miles south of town among the finest wineries in the valley.
**Rates: $50-$120. All year.
Innkeeper(s): Lisa Wild-Runnells & Jon Runnells.
4 Rooms. 4 Private Baths. Guest phone available. Beds: KQ. Meals: Full gourmet breakfast. Handicap access provided. Fireplaces. CCs: Visa, MC, AE. Hammock, croquet, bicycles.

"This spot is a little piece of heaven! We are really spoiled now."

San Diego

Britt House
406 Maple St
San Diego CA 92103
(619) 234-2926

Circa 1887. This lavish Queen Anne Victorian house was once the home of the Scripps family. Mr.

Scripps created a chain of 35 newspapers and one of them, the San Diego Sun, was begun simply to irritate the Spreckels, owners of the Union-Tribune. The house is noted for an unusual two-story rose and blue stained glass window depicting morning, noon, and night. Other features include carved oak fretwork, a golden oak staircase and

turrets. There are formal English gardens.
Location: City, parkside.
**Rates: $85-$105. All year.
Innkeeper(s): Dawn Martin.
10 Rooms. 1 Private Baths. Guest phone available. TV available. Beds: Q. Meals: Full breakfast & afternoon tea. Handicap access provided. Picnics and special dinners by arrangement.
Seen in: *LA Magazine, California Magazine, Toronto Sun.*
"The 'Gold Standard' for California B&B's."

Brookside Farm
See: Dulzura, CA

Heritage Park
Bed & Breakfast Inn
2470 Heritage Park Row
San Diego CA 92110
(619) 295-7088
Circa 1889. Situated on a seven-acre Victorian park in the heart of Old Town, this is one of seven

preserved classic structures. Built for Hartfield and Myrtle Christian it was featured in *The Golden Era* as an "outstandingly beautiful home of Southern California." It has a variety of chimneys, shingles, a two-story corner tower, and a wraparound porch.
Location: In the heart of historic Old Town where San Diego began.
**Rates: $75-$115. All year.
Innkeeper(s): Lori Chandler.
9 Rooms. 3 Private Baths. Guest phone available. Beds: QT. Meals: Full breakfast. Handicap access provided. CCs: Visa, MC. Walking distance to golf and tennis. sportsfishing 5 miles. Candlelight dinners in room.
Seen in: *Los Angeles Herald Examiner, Yellow Brick Road.*
"A beautiful step back in time. Peaceful and gracious."

Surf Manor & Cottages
PO Box 7695
San Diego CA 92107
(619) 225-9765
Circa 1930. Four of the original beach cottages remaining in the popular area of South Mission Beach, Surf Manor provides quiet

accommodations with a living room, bedroom, kitchen and bath in each cottage. Guests enter through a picket fence and onto a small front porch. An English garden surrounds each one, and only steps away are both the Pacific Ocean beach and the bay.
Location: South Mission Beach.
**Rates: $60-$90. All year.
Innkeeper(s): Jerri Grady.
4 Rooms. 4 Private Baths. Beds: D. Meals: B&B. Water sports.

The Bed & Breakfast Inn at La Jolla
See: La Jolla, CA

San Francisco

Art Center Wamsley
Bed & Breakfast
1902 Filbert St
San Francisco CA 94123
(415) 567-1526
Circa 1857. The Art Center Bed & Breakfast was built during the Louisiana movement to San Francisco during the Gold Rush. The building was next to what is reputed to have been Washer Woman's Cove, a freshwater lagoon at the foot of Laguna Street that served as the village laundry. It was the only permanent structure on the path between the Presidio and Yerba Buena village. There are four guest apartments here, convenient to

much of San Francisco. Ask for the penthouse apartment.
Location: Two blocks south of Lombard (Rt 101) on the corner of Laguna.
**Rates: $65-$115. All year.
Innkeeper(s): George & Helvi Wamsley.
4 Rooms. 4 Private Baths. Guest phone available. TV in room. Beds: QT. Meals: Stocked kitchen. Jacuzzi. Fireplaces. CCs: All.

Green Apple Inn
See: Freestone, CA

Mill Rose Inn
See: Half Moon Bay, CA

Moffatt House
431 Hugo St
San Francisco CA 94122
(415) 661-6210
Circa 1910. A simple two-story Edwardian home, the Moffatt House has a vivid stained glass window that contrasts with its light, neutral interior. Guest rooms are artfully decorated. Some guests linger to enjoy garden views while others take in the neighborhood shops, bakeries and cafes. The Haight-Ashbury district and Golden Gate Park are nearby.
Location: One block from Golden Gate Park.
Rates: $34-$49. All year.
Innkeeper(s): Ruth Moffatt.
4 Rooms. Guest phone available. TV in room. Beds: QTC. Meals: Continental-plus breakfast. CCs: Visa, MC.
"It was neat and clean...excellent breakfast. I would return."

Petite Auberge

863 Bush St
San Francisco CA 94108
(415) 928-6000

Circa 1919. This five-story hotel features an ornate baroque design with curved bay windows. Now transformed to a French country inn there are antiques, fresh flowers, and country accessories. Most rooms also have working fireplaces. It's a short walk to the Powell Street cable car.
Location: Two-and-a-half blocks from Union Square.
**Rates: $105-$195.
Innkeeper(s): Carolyn Vaughan.
26 Rooms. 26 Private Baths. Meals: Full breakfast. CCs: Visa, MC, AE.

Spencer House

1080 Haight St
San Francisco CA 94117
(415) 626-9205

Circa 1890. This opulent mansion, which sits on three city lots, is one of San Francisco's finest examples of Queen Anne Victorian architecture. Ornate parquet floors, original wallpapers, gaslights, and antique linens are featured. Breakfast is served with crystal and silver in the elegantly paneled dining room.
Location: Ten minutes from the wharf.
**Rates: $75-$130. All year.
Innkeeper(s): Barbara & Jack Chambers.
6 Rooms. 3 Private Baths. Guest phone available. TV available. Beds: KQD. Meals: Full breakfast. Conference room. Fireplaces.

Spreckels Mansion

737 Buena Vista West
San Francisco CA 94117
(415) 861-3008

Circa 1887. The Spreckels family built this rare Colonial Revival

across from Buena Vista Park, on a hill with spectacular views of the

city. The stained-glass windows and gaslight fixtures are all original. Request the Sugar Baron Suite and enjoy a canopied bed and free-standing tub in view of the fireplace. The next morning if you ask, your breakfast will be brought up on a silver tray.
Location: On a wooded hilltop near the Panhandle of Golden Gate Park.
**Rates: $88-$190. All year.
Innkeeper(s): Jonathan Sharron & Kathleen Austin.
10 Rooms. 8 Private Baths. Guest phone in room. TV available. Beds: Q. Meals: Continental-plus breakfast. Fireplaces. CCs: Visa, MC, AE. Afternoon social hour before the fireplace.
Seen in: *Travel & Leisure, Bay View Magazine.*
"Well, it's the closest thing to heaven that we've found."

Union Street Inn

2229 Union St
San Francisco CA 94123
(415) 345-0424

Circa 1902. This graceful Edwardian withstood the 1906 earthquake, and provides a tranquil garden setting complete with blooming lilacs, camellias and violets. The Carriage House, with its own jacuzzi, is the most romantic room of all, nestled just beyond the garden.
Location: In the heart of San Francisco's fine dining and shopping area.
Rates: $75-$125. All year.
Innkeeper(s): Helen Stewart & Charlene Browne.
6 Rooms. 6 Private Baths. Guest phone in room. TV available. Beds: KQTC. Meals: Continental-plus breakfast. Jacuzzi. Wine Country, Muir Woods tours pick up at the inn.
Seen in: *Los Angeles Times, Travel & Leisure.*

White Swan Inn

845 Bush St
San Francisco CA 94108
(415) 775-1755

Circa 1908. This four-story Nob Hill hotel has a marble facade and was originally called Hotel Louise. Heavy beveled glass doors open to a large reception area with granite floors, an antique carousel horse, and English artworks. Bay windows and a rear deck contribute to the feeling of an English garden inn. The guest rooms are decorated with softly colored English wallpapers

and prints. All rooms have fireplaces and turn down service is provided.
Location: In the heart of downtown.
**Rates: $145-$250. All year.
Innkeeper(s): Carolyn Vaughan.
27 Rooms. 27 Private Baths. Guest phone in room. TV in room. Beds: KQC. Meals: Continental-plus breakfast. Conference room. Fireplaces. CCs: Visa, MC, AE, DS. Afternoon tea and hors d'oeuvres.

San Juan Capistrano

Hospitality Plus

PO Box 388
San Juan Capistrano CA 92693
(714) 496-6953

Circa 1910. This reservation service features over 50 houses and arranges stays in historic homes up the coast of California. The house in San Juan Capistrano is a Mission Revival mansion built for the John Forster family who once owned Mission San Juan Capistrano. Built around courtyards with fountains, rose gardens, and tiled porticos, a Capistrano legend has been assigned to each room. In its heyday the mansion served as a social hub, and today it is one of Southern California's most elegantly appointed homes.
Location: Three blocks from the Mission, four blocks from the train station.
**Rates: $55-$155. All year.
9 Rooms. 3 Private Baths. Guest phone available. TV available. Beds: KQ. Meals: Full breakfast. Conference room. Fireplaces. CCs: Visa, MC, AE. Two miles to whale watching, parasailing, rocky cliffs, sandy beach. Bike path to ocean.
Seen in: *New York Times, Changing Times, Country Living.*

San Luis Obispo

Country House Inn
See: Templeton, CA

San Rafael

Casa Soldavini
531 "C" St
San Rafael CA 94901
(415) 454-3140
Circa 1932. Linda Soldavini's grandparents built this home and on the walls she proudly hangs pictures of her family, the first Italian settlers in San Rafael. Grandfather Joseph, a winemaker, originally planned and planted what are now the lush gardens that surround the home. There are many antiques original to the house.
Location: Fifteen minutes north of Golden Gate Bridge.
**Rates: $55-$65. All year.
Innkeeper(s): Linda Soldavini-Cassidy & Dan Cassidy.
3 Rooms. 1 Private Baths. Guest phone available. TV available. Beds: QT. Meals: Continental-plus breakfast. Fireplaces. Within 30-45 minutes to woods, beaches, horses, wineries.
"Wonderful, quaint, convenient. Love it."

Santa Ana

The Craftsman
2900 N Flower St
Santa Ana CA 92706
(714) 543-1168
Circa 1910. This two-story Colonial Revival with multiple gables was built by the Smiley family. They were orange growers in Orange County and an original orange grove remains across the street. The house is one of the few stately homes still in the area and has been restored to its original beauty, furnished in American and Danish antiques.
Location: Disneyland area in Orange County.
Rates: $50. All year.
Innkeeper(s): Philip & Irene Chinn.
2 Rooms. Guest phone in room. TV available. Beds: Q. Meals: Full breakfast. Fireplaces. Pool. Tennis and swimming.

Santa Barbara

Blue Quail Inn
1908 Bath St
Santa Barbara CA 93101
(805) 687-2300
Circa 1915. The inn and cottages are decorated in a charming country style. The Hummingbird is a cottage guest room featuring a chaise longue, queen-size, white iron bed, and a private brick patio. Hot apple cider is served each evening and picnic lunches are available.
Location: Quiet residential area near town and the beach.
**Rates: $65-$90. All year.
Innkeeper(s): Jeanise Suding Eaton, Sue Occhiuto.
9 Rooms. 5 Private Baths. Guest phone available. Beds: KQT. Meals: Continental-plus breakfast. Fireplaces. CCs: Visa, MC. Bicycles available at no charge. nearby gliding, wine tasting.
Seen in: *Los Angeles Times.*
"Mahvolous, simply maaahvolous! Loved everything. And just think, I'm here on a business trip - boy, love this job! I'll be back for sure - business of course."

Cheshire Cat Inn
36 W Valerio
Santa Barbara CA 93101
(805) 569-1610
Circa 1892. The Eberle family built two graceful homes side by side, one a Queen Anne, the other a Colonial Revival. President McKinley was entertained here on his visit to Santa Barbara. There is a pagoda-like porch, and a square and a curved bay. There are rose gardens, grassy lawns and a gazebo. Laura Ashley wallpapers are featured here and in the owner's other inn, an 1199 manor in Scotland.
Location: Downtown.
**Rates: $109-$159. All year.
Innkeeper(s): Christine Dunstan & George Mari.
11 Rooms. 11 Private Baths. Guest phone in room. TV available. Beds: KQT. Meals: Continental-plus breakfast. Jacuzzi. Conference room.
Seen in: *Two on the Town, KABC, Los Angeles Times, Santa Barbara Magazine.*

Glenborough Inn
1327 Bath St
Santa Barbara CA 93101

(805) 966-0589
Circa 1880. This Craftsman-style inn recreates the turn-of-the-century atmosphere in the main house, and

there is also an 1880's cottage reminiscent of the Victorian era. Inside are antiques, rich wood trim, and elegant fireplace suites with canopy beds. There's always plenty of firewood and an invitation to the secluded garden hot tub. Breakfasts are homemade and have been written up in *Bon Appetit* and *Chocolatier*.
**Rates: $65-$150. All year.
Innkeeper(s): Pat Morgan, Pat Hardy, JoAnn Bel.
9 Rooms. 5 Private Baths. Guest phone available. Beds: Q. Meals: Full gourmet breakfast. Jacuzzi. Fireplaces. CCs: Visa, MC, AE. Nearby sailing, scuba diving, tennis, horseback riding, wineries.
Seen in: *Houston Post, Los Angeles Times.*
"Both Tom & I are terminal romantics and as it is obvious that you must be also, suffice it to say that for grace & style you are hereby awarded the Blue Ribbon."
"The Glenborough is a favorite spot of mine. These innkeepers are real pros." Chocolatier.

Harbour Carriage House
420 West Montecito Street
Santa Barbara CA 93101
(805) 962-8447
Circa 1900. The Harbour Carriage House, set behind a white picket fence, consists of two historic homes adorned with fish-scale shingles and gabled roofs. Guest rooms are named for wildflowers and decorated with a combination of French and English country antiques. Try Forget-Me-Not and enjoy a private spa, a fireplace and a view of the mountains from the canopied, king-size bed.
Location: Two blocks to the beach, close to downtown.
**Rates: $85-$155. All year.

Innkeeper(s): Jeanise Suding Eaton.
9 Rooms. 9 Private Baths. Guest phone in room. TV available. Beds: KQ. Meals: Full breakfast. Jacuzzi. Handicap access provided. Fireplaces. CCs: Visa, MC. Biking, horseback riding, sailing, wine tasting, gliding.
Seen in: *Los Angeles Times.*

"Thank you for a lovely weekend. If it wouldn't be any trouble could we have your recipes for the delicious breakfast?"

Old Yacht Club Inn
431 Corona Del Mar
Santa Barbara CA 93103
(805) 962-1277

Circa 1912. This California Craftsman house was the home of

the Santa Barbara Yacht Club during the Roaring Twenties. It was opened as Santa Barbara's first B&B and has become renowned for its gourmet food and superb hospitality. Nancy is the author of *The Old Yacht Club Inn Cookbook.*
Location: East Beach.
**Rates: $60-$90. All year.
Innkeeper(s): Nancy Donaldson, Sandy Hunt & Lu Carouso.
9 Rooms. 7 Private Baths. Guest phone available. TV available. Beds: KQT. Meals: Full gourmet breakfast. Jacuzzi. Conference room. CCs: Visa, MC, AE.
Seen in: *Los Angeles Magazine, Valley Magazine.*

"Donaldson is one of Santa Barbara's better-kept culinary secrets."

Olive House
1604 Olive St
Santa Barbara CA 93101
(805) 962-4902

Circa 1904. This California Craftsman house was saved from demolition in 1980, and moved to its present location atop a slight rise. Features include bay windows and window seats, stained and leaded glass, a parlor with redwood-

paneled wainscots, coffered ceilings, and a studio grand piano. Tea or wine and hors d'oeuvres are served in front of the fireplace in the afternoon.
**Rates: $80-$100. All year.
Innkeeper(s): Lois & Bob Poire.
5 Rooms. 5 Private Baths. Guest phone available. TV available. Beds: QD. Meals: Continental-plus breakfast. Conference room. Fireplaces. CCs: Visa, MC.
"Thank you for providing not only a lovely place to stay but a very warm and inviting atmosphere."

Red Rose Inn
1416 Castillo St
Santa Barbara CA 93101
(805) 966-1470

Circa 1886. This inn is pictured in the Santa Barbara Historical Society's publication *Survivors* as

one of the city's outstanding examples of Victorian architecture. Fully restored with polished hardwood floors, stained glass windows, and an elegant walnut fireplace, the inn features antique furnishings throughout. There is a rose garden, and a large avocado tree shades the patio. A bed believed to have been owned by Abraham Lincoln highlights one of the guest rooms.
Location: Four blocks from downtown, fourteen blocks from the ocean.
**Rates: $55-$100. All year.
Innkeeper(s): Dana & Chrysa Olson.
5 Rooms. 3 Private Baths. Guest phone available. Beds: Q. Meals: Continental-

plus Breakfast. CCs: Visa, MC. Bicycles available from the inn.
Seen in: *Santa Barbara Magazine, LA Times.*

"One of the most exquisite B&Bs in Southern California. The Red Rose Inn is our favorite place!"

Simpson House Inn
121 East Arrellaga St
Santa Barbara CA 93101
(805) 963-7067

Circa 1874. If you were one of the Simpson family's first visitors, you

would have arrived in Santa Barbara by stagecoach or sea because the railroad was not completed for another 14 years. A stately Italianate house, the inn is graciously decorated. It is situated on an acre of lawns and gardens secluded behind a ten-foot-tall eugenia hedge. Mint juleps are often served in the early evening and are particularly enjoyable under the shade of the magnolia trees.
Location: Five minute walk to downtown Santa Barbara and Historic District.
**Rates: $85-$130.
Innkeeper(s): Gillean Wilson, Linda & Glyn Davies.
6 Rooms. 5 Private Baths. Guest phone available. Beds: KQD. Meals: Full breakfast. Handicap access provided. Conference room. Fireplaces. CCs: Visa, MC. Hiking, biking, surfing, windsurfing nearby. Complementary bicycles.
Seen in: *Country Inns Magazine, Santa Barbara Magazine.*

"Perfectly restored and impeccably furnished. Your hospitality is warm and heartfelt and the food is delectable."

The Parsonage
1600 Olive St
Santa Barbara CA 93101
(805) 962-9336

Circa 1892. Built for the Trinity Episcopal Church, The Parsonage is one of Santa Barbara's most notable Queen Anne Victorians. It is nestled between downtown Santa Barbara

and the foothills, in a quiet residential, upper eastside neighborhood. The inn has ocean and mountain views and is within walking distance of the mission, shops, theater, and restaurants.
****Rates: $70-$130.
Innkeeper(s): Hilde Michemore.
6 Rooms. 6 Private Baths. Meals: Full breakfast.

Villa d' Italia
**780 Mission Canyon Rd
Santa Barbara CA 93105
(805) 687-6933**
Circa 1919. This Mediterranean villa home was built by Secondino Ferragamo. The Music Academy of the West originated here and Maestro Padarewski once filled the villa with his music. The ceilings are 20-feet high and there are flowers, plush towels and aromatic delights emanating from the kitchen.
**Rates: $95-$125. All year.
Innkeeper(s): Captain & Mrs. A. J. Van Tuyl.
2 Rooms. 2 Private Baths. Guest phone available. Beds: KQ. Meals: Three-course gourmet breakfast. Handicap access provided. Fireplaces. Sailing, biking tennis.

Santa Clara

Madison Street Inn
**1390 Madison St
Santa Clara CA 95050
(408) 249-5521**
Circa 1890. This Queen Anne Victorian still has the original doors

and locks. "No Peddlers or Agents" is engraved in the cement of the original carriageway, but guests always receive a warm and gracious welcome. High-ceilinged rooms are furnished in antiques, oriental rugs, and Victorian wallpapers.
Location: Ten minutes from San Jose.
**Rates: $60-$80.

Innkeeper(s): Ralph & Teresa Wigginton.
5 Rooms. 3 Private Baths. Guest phone available. TV available. Beds: QT. Meals: B&B. Jacuzzi. Sauna. Pool. CCs: Visa, MC, AE.

Santa Cruz

Apple Lane Inn
See: Aptos, CA

Babbling Brook
Bed & Breakfast Inn
**1025 Laurel St
Santa Cruz CA 95060
(408) 427-2437**
Circa 1909. This inn was built on the foundations of an 1870 tannery and a 1790 grist mill. Secluded, yet

within the city, the inn features a cascading waterfall and meandering creek on its acre of gardens and redwoods. Country French decor, cozy fireplaces, and deep soaking whirlpool tubs are luxurious amenities of the Babbling Brook.
Location: North end of Monterey Bay.
**Rates: $95-$125. All year.
Innkeeper(s): Tom & Helen King.
12 Rooms. 12 Private Baths. Guest phone available. TV available. Beds: KQ. Meals: Full breakfast. Jacuzzi. Handicap access provided. Fireplaces. CCs: Visa, MC, AE, DS. Tennis, and ocean are walking distance. Inn-to-inn tour package.
"We were impressed with the genuine warmth of not only the inn but the two of you. The best breakfast we've had outside our own home!"

Chateau Victorian
**118 First St
Santa Cruz CA 95060
(408) 458-9458**
Circa 1890. Chateau Victorian was built by a prosperous young sea captain from the east coast who made Santa Cruz his home port. On one of his journeys he met and fell in love with a native girl from the

Solomon Islands. He sent his ship on without him after instructing the crew to tell the story that he had died at sea. Years later, nearing death, he tried to return home to Santa Cruz but died aboard ship. Now his Victorian house is an elegant inn with a fireplace in each room.
Location: One block from the beach near the boardwalk and wharf.
Rates: $80-$110.
Innkeeper(s): Franz & Alice-June Benjamin.
7 Rooms. 7 Private Baths. Guest phone available. Beds: Q. Meals: Continental-plus breakfast. Conference room. Fireplaces. CCs: Visa, MC, AE. Golfing, fishing, sailing, ballooning, whale watching.
Seen in: *Times Tribune, Santa Cruz Sentinel, Good Times.*
"Certainly enjoyed our most recent stay and have appreciated all of our visits."
"I had a delightful time this past weekend. Chateau Victorian is charming."

Cliff Crest
**407 Cliff St
Santa Cruz CA 95060
(408) 427-2609**
Circa 1887. Warmth, friendliness and comfort characterize this elegantly restored Queen Anne Victorian. An octagonal solarium, tall stained-glass windows, and a belvedere overlook Monterey Bay and the Santa Cruz mountains. The mood is airy and romantic. The spacious gardens were designed by John McLaren, landscape architect for Golden Gate Park. Antiques and fresh flowers fill the rooms, once home to William Jeter, Lieutenant Governor of California.
Location: One-and-a-half blocks from the beach and boardwalk.
**Rates: $75-$115. All year.
Innkeeper(s): Sharon & Bruce Taylor.
5 Rooms. 5 Private Baths. Guest phone available. Beds: KQ. Meals: Full hearty breakfast. CCs: Visa, MC, AE. Hammock.

Santa Monica

Channel Road Inn
**219 West Channel Road
Santa Monica CA 90402
(213) 454-7577**

Circa 1912. This shingle-clad building is a rare example of a variation

of the Colonial Revival Period, one of the few remaining in Los Angeles. The abandoned home was saved from the city's wrecking crew by Susan Zolla with the encouragement of the local historical society. Many amenities for business guests and beach visitors are available, and there is a spectacular cliffside spa.
Location: One block from the ocean.
**Rates: $85-$140. All year.
Innkeeper(s): Susan Zolla & Jean Root.
14 Rooms. 14 Private Baths. Guest phone in room. TV available. Beds: KQD. Meals: Full breakfast. Jacuzzi. Handicap access provided. Conference room. Fireplaces. CCs: Visa, MC, AE. Horseback riding nearby, bicycles provided for beach bike path. Picnic lunches on request.

Sausalito

Casa Madrona Hotel
801 Bridgeway
Sausalito CA 94965
(415) 332-0502 (800)288-0502
Circa 1885. This Victorian mansion started as a lumber baron's mansion but as time went on additional

buildings were added giving it a European look. A registered Sausalito Historical Landmark, it is the oldest building in town. Each room has a unique name such as "Lord Ashley's Lookout" or "Kathmandu", and the appointments are as varied as the names. The inn faces San Francisco Bay enabling guests to frequently enjoy the barking seals, the evening fog and the arousing sunsets.
Location: Downtown Sausalito.
Rates: $60-$195.
Innkeeper(s): John W. Mays.
37 Rooms. 37 Private Baths. Guest phone in room. TV in room. Jacuzzi. Conference room. CCs: All. Checks not accepted.
"Had to pinch myself several times to be sure it was real! Is this heaven? With this view it sure feels like it."

Sausalito Hotel
16 El Portal
Sausalito CA 94965
(415) 332-4155
Circa 1900. The inn was built in the Mission Revival style as a hotel for sailors, ferry and train travelers in the bootlegging heyday of Sausalito's history. Now refurbished, all rooms are decorated with Victorian antiques.
Location: Adjacent to the ferry landing in the heart of Sausalito.
Rates: $65-$140. All year.
Innkeeper(s): Manager Liz MacDonald, owner Gene Hiller.
15 Rooms. 9 Private Baths. Guest phone in room. TV in room. Beds: KQDTC. Meals: Continental-plus breakfast. Fireplaces. CCs: Visa, MC, AE, DC. Windsurfing, sailing, golf. all water sports nearby.

Seal Beach

Seal Beach Inn & Gardens
212 5th St
Seal Beach CA 90740
(213) 493-2416
Circa 1924. This is an exquisitely restored inn with fine antiques and historical pieces. Outside, the gardens blaze with color and there are Napoleonic *jardinieres* filled with flowers. A 300-year-old French fountain sits in the pool area and an antique Parisian fence surrounds the property. Nearby, in the historic

area, is a Red Car on Electric Street, a reminder of the time the Holly-

wood crowd came to Seal Beach on the trolley to gamble and drink rum.
Location: 300 yards from the ocean, five minutes from Long Beach.
**Rates: $88-$155. All year.
Innkeeper(s): Marjorie Bettenhausen.
23 Rooms. 23 Private Baths. Guest phone available. TV in room. Beds: KQTC. Meals: Full breakfast. Conference room. Pool. CCs: Visa, MC, AE, DB. Gondola packages and honeymoon packages.
Seen in: *Brides Magazine, Country Inn Magazine.*
"The closest thing to Europe since I left there."

Sky Forest

Storybook Inn
PO Box 362
Sky Forest CA 92385
(714) 336-1483
Circa 1939. Formerly known as the Foutch Estate, this 9,000-square-foot home illustrates Mr. Foutch's romantic flair with its abundant mahogany paneling bleached to match the color of his bride's hair! Two massive brick fireplaces dominate the main lobby. The three-story inn has enclosed solariums and porches. A hot tub nestled under ancient oaks provides views of snow-capped mountains, forests and on clear days, the Pacific Ocean.
Location: 28717 Highway 18.
**Rates: $79-$150.
Innkeeper(s): Kathleen & John Wooley.
9 Rooms. 9 Private Baths. Guest phone available. TV available. Beds: KQD. Meals: Full breakfast. Jacuzzi. Handicap access provided. Conference room. Fireplaces. CCs: Visa, MC. Horseback riding, skiing, hiking, water skiing.
Seen in: *Los Angles Times.*

Sonoma

Overview Farm
15650 Arnold Dr
Sonoma CA 95476
(707) 938-8574

Circa 1880. This Victorian farmhouse was once a part of the famed Spreckels estate. It has been

revitalized to capture the gracious living styles of turn-of-the-century Sonoma. Large guest rooms with ten-foot ceilings house a fine collection of early American treasures. Manicured gardens, espaliered fruit trees, and captivating views complement the beauty of the interior.
Rates: $92.50. All year.
Innkeeper(s): Judy & Robert Weiss.
3 Rooms. 3 Private Baths. Guest phone available. Beds: QD. Meals: Full breakfast.
Seen in: *Los Angeles Times.*

Victorian Garden Inn
316 E Napa St
Sonoma CA 95476
(707) 996-5339

Circa 1870. Authentic Victorian gardens cover more than an acre of grounds surrounding this Greek Revival farmhouse. Pathways wind around to secret gardens and guests can walk to world-famous wineries and historical sites. All rooms are decorated with the romantic flair of the innkeeper, an interior designer. Ask to stay in the renovated water tower.
**Rates: $69-$125.
Innkeeper(s): Donna Lewis.
4 Rooms. 3 Private Baths. Guest phone available. Beds: QT. Meals: Full breakfast. Conference room. Fireplaces. Pool. CCs: Visa, MC, AE. Winery tours, swimming, nearby golf, tennis, bicycles. Full consierge services.
Seen in: *Denver Post.*

Sonora

The Ryan House Bed & Breakfast
153 S Shepherd St
Sonora CA 95370
(209) 533-3445

Circa 1855. This homestead-style house is set well back from the street in a quiet residential area.

Green lawns and gardens with 35 varieties of roses surround the house. Each room is individually decorated with handsome antiques.
Location: Two blocks from the heart of historic Sonora.
Rates: $50-$65. All year.
Innkeeper(s): Nancy & Gary Hoffman.
4 Rooms. 2 Private Baths. Guest phone available. Beds: QD. Meals: Full breakfast. CCs: Visa, MC, DC.
"Everything our friends said it would be: warm, comfortable and great breakfasts. You made us feel like long-lost friends the moment we arrived."

Sutter Creek

Nancy & Bob's 9 Eureka Street Inn
55 Eureka Street, PO Box 386
Sutter Creek CA 95685
(209) 267-0342

Circa 1916. A California bungalow, this inn mirrors the graciousness and charm of a bygone era. It is filled with rich woods, antiques, and stained-glass windows, and all the guest rooms are decorated in the manner of the past.
Location: Highway 49 in the Gold Country.
Rates: $65-$75. Feb.-Dec.
Innkeeper(s): Nancy & Bob Brahmst.
5 Rooms. 5 Private Baths. Guest phone available. Beds: QT. Meals: Full breakfast. Conference room. CCs: Visa, MC.

Tahoe City

Mayfield House
256 Grove St, PO Box 5999
Tahoe City CA 95730
(916) 583-1001

Circa 1930. Norman Mayfield, Lake Tahoe's pioneer contractor, built this home of wood and stone. Julia Morgan, the architect responsible for the Hearst Castle, was a frequent guest. Dark-stained pine-paneling, beamed ceiling, and a large stone fireplace make an inviting living room. Many of the rooms have either mountain, woods, or golf course views.
Location: Downtown on Highway 28.
Rates: $65-$100.
Innkeeper(s): Janie Kaye.
6 Rooms. 3 Private Baths. Guest phone available. Beds: KQT. Meals: Full breakfast. Jacuzzi. Handicap access provided. Fireplaces. CCs: Visa, MC. Horseback riding skiing, water sports, bicycles.

Templeton

Country House Inn
91 Main St
Templeton CA 93465
(805) 434-1598

Circa 1886. This Victorian home, built by the founder of Templeton, is

set off with gardens bordered by roses. It was designated as a historic site in San Luis Obispo County and all the rooms are decorated with antiques and fresh flowers. Hearst Castle and six wineries are nearby.
Location: Twenty miles north of San Luis Obispo on Hwy 101.
**Rates: $65-$80. All year.
Innkeeper(s): Dianne Garth.
5 Rooms. 2 Private Baths. Guest phone available. Beds: KQ. Meals: Full break-

fast. Fireplaces. CCs: Visa, MC. Horseback riding, tennis, waterskiing, wine tasting.

"A feast for all the senses, an esthetic delight."

Ventura

La Mer
411 Poli St
Ventura CA 93001
(805) 643-3600

Circa 1890. The second floor of this three-story Cape Cod Victorian overlooks the heart of historic San Buenaventura and the spectacular

California coastline. Each room is decorated to capture the feeling of a specific European country. French, German, Austrian, Norwegian and

English-style accommodations are available. Gisela, your hostess, is a native of Siegerland, Germany.
Location: Second house north of city hall.
**Rates: $70-$125. All year.
Innkeeper(s): Gisela & Michael Baida.
5 Rooms. 5 Private Baths. Guest phone available. TV available. Beds: Q. Meals: Full Bavarian breakfast. CCs: Visa, MC. Biking or walking to the beach a few blocks away. Goose down feather beds.
Seen in: *Los Angeles Times, Ventura Star Press.*

"Where to begin? The exquisite surroundings, the scrumptious meals, the warm feeling from your generous hospitality?!? What an unforgettable weekend in your heavenly home."

Westport

Howard Creek Ranch
40501 North Hwy, PO Box 121
Westport CA 95488
(707) 964-6725

Circa 1871. First settled as a land grant of thousands of acres, Howard Creek Ranch is now a 20-acre farm with sweeping views of the Pacific Ocean, sandy beaches, and rolling

mountains. A 75-foot bridge spans a creek that flows past barns and outbuildings to the beach 200 yards away. The farmhouse is surrounded

by green lawns, an award-winning flower garden, and grazing cows and horses. This rustic rural location is highlighted with antiques and collectibles.
Location: Mendocino Coast on the ocean.
Rates: $50-$85.
Innkeeper(s): Charles & Sally Grigg.
7 Rooms. 3 Private Baths. Guest phone available. Beds: KQD. Meals: Hearty ranch breakfast. Jacuzzi. Sauna. Pool.

"Of the dozen or so inns on the West Coast we have visited, this is easily the most enchanting one."

Colorado

Aspen

Sardy House
128 E Main St
Aspen CO 81611
(303) 920-2525

Circa 1892. This Queen Anne Victorian was built by J. William Atkinson, an owner of the Little Annie

Mine and Aspen's first freight company. The mansion is built with thick brick walls, sandstone detailing, and wood ornamental trim. A Colorado blue spruce on the grounds is more than 90 feet tall, the tallest in Aspen. There are deluxe guest rooms in both the main house and the carriage house. At the Sardy House guests enjoy the ultimate in pampered luxury.
**Rates: $100-$395. Closed May.
Innkeeper(s): Jayne Poss.
21 Rooms. 21 Private Baths. Guest phone in room. TV in room. Beds: KQT. Meals: Full breakfast. Jacuzzi. Sauna. Conference room. Fireplaces. Pool. CCs: All. Tennis, rafting, horses, gliding, ballooning, water skiing.
Seen in: *Country Inns.*

"I was overwhelmed by your attention to details. A job well done!"

Boulder

Briar Rose B&B
2151 Arapahoe
Boulder CO 80302
(303) 442-3007

Circa 1897. Known locally as the McConnell House, this English-style

brick house is situated in a neighborhood originally composed of bankers, attorneys, miners and carpenters. The inn recently received the Award of Excellence from the City of Boulder. Fresh flowers, handmade feather comforters and turn down service with chocolates add to the atmosphere.
Rates: $49-$98.
Innkeeper(s): Kit Riley & Emily Hunter.
11 Rooms. 6 Private Baths. Guest phone in room. TV available. Beds: QDTC. Meals: Continental plus. Conference room. Fireplaces. CCs: All.

"It's like being at Grandma's; the cookies, the tea, the welcoming smile."

Colorado Springs

Hearthstone Inn
506 N Cascade Ave
Colorado Springs CO 80903
(719) 473-4413

Circa 1885. This elegant Queen Anne is actually two houses joined by an old carriage house. It has been

restored as a period showplace with six working fireplaces, carved oak staircases, and magnificent antiques throughout. A lush, green lawn, suitable for croquet, surrounds the house, and flower beds match the Victorian colors of the exterior.
Location: A resort town at the base of Pikes Peak.
**Rates: $51-$99.
Innkeeper(s): Dot Williams & Ruth Williams.
25 Rooms. 23 Private Baths. Guest phone available. Beds: KQDC. Meals: Full breakfast. Conference room. Fireplaces. CCs: Visa, MC, AE. Working fireplaces.
Seen in: *Rocky Mountain News.*

"We try to get away and come to the Hearthstone at least twice a year because people really care about you!"

Holden House-1902
1102 W Pikes Peak Ave
Colorado Springs CO 80904
(719) 471-3980

Circa 1902. This Victorian home was built by the Holden family who had mining interests in Cripple Creek, Silverton and Leadville. An old iron fence frames the wide

verandas and three-story turret. The inn is filled with Victorian antiques and family heirlooms.
Location: Near the historic district of Old Colorado City.
**Rates: $46-$60.
Innkeeper(s): Sallie & Welling Clark.
3 Rooms. 3 Private Baths. Guest phone available. TV available. Beds: QD. Meals: Full breakfast. Fireplaces. CCs: Visa, MC. Horseback riding, skiing, tennis nearby. Honeymoon package.
Seen in: *Rocky Mountain News, Pikes Peak Journal.*
"Your love of this house and nostalgia makes a very delightful experience."

Cripple Creek

Imperial Hotel
123 N Third St
Cripple Creek CO 80813
(719) 689-2922 (719)689-2713
Circa 1896. Although not a bed and breakfast, this is the only original Cripple Creek hotel still standing. There is a collection of Gay Nineties memorabilia and the inn is known for its excellent cuisine. A cabaret-style melodrama is performed twice daily.
**Rates: $40.
Innkeeper(s): Stephen & Bonnie Mackin.
26 Rooms. 12 Private Baths. Guest phone available. Beds: QDT. Meals: No meals included. Conference room. CCs: All.
Seen in: *Rocky Mountain News.*
"This was truly an experience of days gone by - we loved our stay!"

Denver

Queen Anne Inn
2147 Tremont Place
Denver CO 80205
(303) 296-6666
Circa 1879. This Queen Anne was designed by Colorado's most famous architect Frank Edbrooke. There are many elegant furnishings,

including pillared canopy beds and a wraparound mural of an aspen grove in the turret peak. Music, art, and a grand oak stairway add to the Victorian experience. In an area of meticulously restored homes and flower gardens, the inn is four blocks from the central business district.
Location: In the Clement Historic District.
Rates: $54-$99.
Innkeeper(s): Ann & Chuck Hillestad.
10 Rooms. 10 Private Baths. Guest phone available. Beds: KQ. Meals: Continental-plus breakfast. Conference room. CCs: All.
Seen in: *Elle, New York Times.*
Selected by *Bridal Guide Magazine* as one of "America's Top Ten" wedding night locations.

The Oxford Alexis
1600 17th St
Denver CO 80202
(800) 228-5838 (303)628-5400
Circa 1891. This five-story Richardsonian brick hotel was renovated in 1983 and placed in the

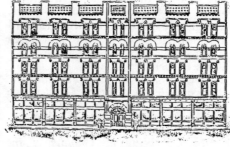

National Register of Historic Places. During restoration some of the painted chandeliers were discovered to be made of sterling silver. Each room is individually decorated with English and French antiques.
**Rates: $85-$115.
Innkeeper(s): Peter White.
81 Rooms. 81 Private Baths. Guest phone in room. Beds: KQTC. Meals: EP. Jacuzzi. Handicap access provided. Con-

ference room. Fireplaces. CCs: All. Health club use.
Seen in: *Pacific Northwest Magazine, Dallas Morning News.*

Empire

The Peck House
PO Box 423
Empire CO 80438
(303) 569-9870
Circa 1860. Built as a residence for gold mine owner James Peck, this is the oldest hotel still in operation in Colorado. Many pieces of original

furniture brought here by ox cart remain in the inn, including a red antique fainting couch and walnut headboards. Rooms such as Mountain View provide magnificent views of the eastern slope of the Rockies, and a panoramic view of Empire Valley can be seen from the old front porch.
**Rates: $35-$65.
Innkeeper(s): Gary & Sally St. Clair.
11 Rooms. 9 Private Baths. Guest phone available. Beds: DT. Meals: EP. Jacuzzi. CCs: All.
Seen in: *American West, Rocky Mountain News, Denver Post, Colorado Homes.*

Golden

The Dove Inn
711 14th St
Golden CO 80401
(303) 278-2209
Circa 1889. An airy bay window of this charming Victorian overlooks giant blue spruce and the foothills of the Rockies. Breakfast is served before the 100-year-old fireplace or outdoors on the porch or deck. In

the same neighborhood are the beautiful old homes that housed the

leaders of the former territorial capital of Colorado and the Colorado School of Mines is two blocks away. The innkeepers prefer married couples.
**Rates: $36-$54.
Innkeeper(s): Ken & Jean Sims.
6 Rooms. 6 Private Baths. Guest phone available. TV in room. Beds: Q. Meals: Full breakfast. Cross-country skiing at 8,000 feet.
"Our first experience at a bed and breakfast was delightful, thanks to your hospitality at The Dove Inn."

Green Mountain Falls

Outlook Lodge
Box 5
Green Mountain Falls CO 80819
(719) 684-2303
Circa 1889. Outlook Lodge was originally the parsonage for the historic Church in the Wildwood. Hand-carved balustrades surround a verandah that frames the alpine village view, and inside are many original antique furnishings. Marshmallows are roasted by the

fire in the evening. This secluded mountain village is nestled at the foot of Pikes Peak, 15 minutes from Colorado Springs.
Rates: $32-$40.
11 Rooms. 2 Private Baths. TV available. Beds: QTC. Meals: Continental-plus breakfast. Handicap access provided. Conference room. Fireplaces. Pool. CCs: Visa, MC. Swimming, fishing, volleyball, tennis, riding stables. Melodramas, concerts.

Hesperus

Blue Lake Ranch
16919 Hwy 140
Hesperus CO 81326
(303) 385-4537
Circa 1900. Built by Swedish immigrants, this renovated Victorian farmhouse is surrounded by spectacular flower gardens and a white picket fence. The inn is filled with comforts such as down quilts, vases of fresh flowers and family antiques. The property is designated as a wildlife refuge and there are two cabins overlooking trout-filled Blue Lake. In the evening guests enjoy soaking in the jacuzzi under clear, star-studded skies, and in the morning dining on Tia's gourmet breakfasts.
Location: Twenty minutes from Durango.
**Rates: $70-$125. May to October.
Innkeeper(s): David & Tia Alford.
6 Rooms. 5 Private Baths. Guest phone available. TV in room. Beds: Q. Meals: Restaurant. Jacuzzi. Sauna. Handicap access provided. Conference room. Fireplaces. Fishing, swimming, hiking.
"What a paradise you have created - we would love to return!!"

Silver Plume

Brewery Inn
246 Main St, PO Box 473
Silver Plume CO 80476
(303) 571-1151 (303)674-5565
Circa 1890. The Brewery Inn is a restored Victorian with fireplaces, antiques, wallpapers and down comforters. Located within the Sil-

ver Plume National Historic District, a walk through the town recaptures the feeling of an 1880's silver mining town. Nearby is the Silver Plume Museum and the Georgetown Loop Narrow Gauge train ride.
Location: Fifty miles west of Denver, I-70 exit 226.
Rates: $40-$60.
Innkeeper(s): Mary P. Joss & Jeanette Rizzardi.
4 Rooms. 1 Private Baths. Guest phone available. Beds: QT. Meals: B&B. Restaurant. Conference room. CCs: Visa, MC.
"Charming, cozy, comfortable! It makes one ponder the real need for the 'necessities' of life, (TV, telephone). It was wonderful to go back and be free of everyday stresses."

Connecticut

Bolton

Jared Cone House
25 Hebron Rd
Bolton CT 06043
(203) 643-8538

Circa 1775. Once the town post office and library, this is a lavishly

embellished Georgian post-and-beam house. There are seven fireplaces and a dramatic Palladian window on the second floor. A pond at the rear of the property provides ice skating for both townsfolk and guests, and in spring, sugar maples surrounding the house are tapped for the inn's breakfasts.
Location: Ten miles east of Hartford via I-384 & Exit #5.
Rates: $45-$70. All year.
Innkeeper(s): Jeff & Cinde Smith.
3 Rooms. 1 Private Baths. Guest phone available. TV available. Beds: Q. Meals: Full Breakfast. Conference room. Fireplaces. Sleigh rides, hay rides, cross-country skiing. Canoe to lend.
Seen in: *Manchester Herald, Weekend Plus.*
"*Beautiful colonial home, delightful breakfasts.*"

Bristol

Chimney Crest Manor
5 Founders Dr
Bristol CT 06010
(203) 582-4219

Circa 1930. This 32-room Tudor mansion possesses an unusual castle-like arcade and a 45-foot

living room with a stone fireplace at each end. Many of the rooms are embellished with oak paneling and ornate plaster ceilings. The inn is located in the Federal Hill District, an area of large colonial homes.
**Rates: $65-$95. All year.
Innkeeper(s): Dan & Cynthia Cimadamore.
4 Rooms. 4 Private Baths. Guest phone available. TV in room. Beds: Q. Meals: Full breakfast. Conference room. Fireplaces. Pool. CCs: Visa, MC. Ballooning, cross-country skiing, sleigh rides, tubing. Honeymoon and anniversary weekends.
Seen in: *Record-Journal.*

Clinton

Captain Dibbell House
21 Commerce St
Clinton CT 06413
(203) 669-1646

Circa 1865. Built by a sea captain, this graceful Victorian house is only two blocks from the harbor where

innkeeper Ellis Adams sails his own vessel. A ledger of household accounts dating from the mid-1800s is on display, and there are fresh flowers and fruit baskets in each guest room.
Location: Exit 63 & I-95, south on Rt 1, east for 1 block, left on Commerce.
Rates: $45-$60. May to Oct. 30.
Innkeeper(s): Ellis & Helen Adams.
3 Rooms. 2 Private Baths. Guest phone available. TV available. Beds: QTD. Meals: Full Breakfast. Fireplaces. CCs: Visa, MC. Boating, swimming, fishing, hiking, bicycling.
Seen in: *Clinton Recorder.*
"*This was our first experience with B&B and frankly, we didn't know what to expect. It was GREAT! The Adams were relaxed and charming and little personal touches added to our delight.*"

Coventry

Maple Hill Farm Bed & Breakfast
365 Goose Lane
Coventry CT 06423
(203) 742-0635

Circa 1731. This historic farmhouse still possesses its original kitchen cupboards and a flour bin used for generations. Family heirlooms and the history of the former homeowners are shared with guests.

There is a three-seat outhouse behind the inn. Visitors, of course, are

provided with modern plumbing, as well as a screened porch and greenhouse in which to relax.
**Rates: $50-$60. All year.
Innkeeper(s): Tony & Mary Beth Felice.
3 Rooms. Guest phone available. TV available. Beds: TDC. Meals: Continental plus. Fireplaces. Pool. CCs: Travelers checks. Swimming, golf, biking, horseback riding, volleyball.
"Comfortable rooms and delightful country ambience."

Deep River

Riverwind
209 Main St
Deep River CT 06417
(203) 526-2014
Circa 1850. Renovated almost single-handedly by the innkeeper

herself, this inn has a wraparound gingerbread porch filled with gleaming white wicker furniture. Antiques from Barbara's Virginia home are used throughout and there are fireplaces everywhere including a

twelve-foot cooking fireplace in the keeping room.
Rates: $75-$135. All year.
Innkeeper(s): Barbara Barlow.
4 Rooms. 4 Private Baths. Beds: D. Meals: Full breakfast. CCs: Visa, MC. Badminton, croquet.
Seen in: *The Hartford Courant, New Haven Register.*
"If we felt any more welcome we'd have our Time subscription sent here."
"As innkeepers in Newport, Rhode Island, we rate your inn a 10."

East Windsor

Stephen Potwine House
84 Scantic Rd
East Windsor CT 06088
(203) 623-8722
Circa 1831. Acres of farmland surround this old homestead. In keeping with its rural setting a country decor has been chosen, and rooms look out over a pond shaded by graceful willow trees. Two goats and a barn complete the picture. The hosts' special interests are highlighted in seminars on stress management, music imagery and other renewal experiences. Sturbridge Village is 30 miles away.
Rates: $25-$55. May to Nov.
Innkeeper(s): Bob & Vangy Cathcart.
4 Rooms. 1 Private Baths. Guest phone available. TV available. Beds: QTD. Meals: Full breakfast. Jacuzzi. Fireplaces. Swimming, tennis.

Glastonbury

Butternut Farm
1654 Main St
Glastonbury CT 06033
(203) 633-7197
Circa 1720. This Colonial house sits on two acres of woodlands. Prize-

winning goats, pigeons, and chickens are housed in the old barn on

the property. Eighteenth-century Connecticut antiques including a cherry highboy and cherry pencil-post canopy bed, are placed throughout the inn, enhancing the natural beauty of the pumpkin-pine floors and brick fireplaces.
Location: South of Glastonbury Center, 1 1/2 miles, 15 minutes to Hartford.
Rates: $64-$78. All year.
Innkeeper(s): Don Reid.
4 Rooms. 2 Private Baths. Guest phone in room. TV in room. Beds: QD. Meals: Full breakfast. Fireplaces.

Greenwich

Homestead Inn
420 Field Point Rd
Greenwich CT 06830
(203) 869-7500
Circa 1799. The Homestead began as a typical farmhouse built by a judge and gentleman farmer, Augus-

tus Mead. Later it was remodeled in a fanciful Carpenter Gothic style. The full veranda is filled with wicker furnishings and offers views of rolling lawns and trees. Renovated by well-known designers John and Virginia Saladino, the inn now has a fine collection of antiques, an intimate library with fireplace, and a classic French restaurant.
Rates: $82-$165. All year.
Innkeeper(s): Nancy & Lessie Davison.
23 Rooms. 23 Private Baths. Guest phone available. TV available. Meals: Continental breakfast, full extra. CCs: All.

Hartford

Chimney Crest Manor
See: Bristol, CT

Maple Hill Farm B&B
See: Coventry, CT

Lakeville

Wake Robin Inn
Rt 41
Lakeville CT 06039
(203) 435-2515

Circa 1898. Once the Taconic School for Girls, this inn is located on 15 acres of landscaped grounds in the Connecticut Berkshires. A library has been added as well as antique furnishings. The recently renovated property also includes a few private cottages.
Rates: $85-$150. All year.
Innkeeper(s): H.J.P. Manassero.
40 Rooms. 40 Private Baths. Guest phone in room. TV in room. Beds: KQT. Meals: Restaurant. Jacuzzi. Sauna. Conference room. Fireplaces. CCs: Visa, MC, AE. Swimming, cycling, horseback riding.

Litchfield

Tollgate Hill Inn
Route 202 and Tollgate Rd
Litchfield CT 06759
(203) 567-4545

Circa 1745. Formerly known as the Captain Bull Tavern, the inn underwent extensive renovations in 1983. Listed in the National Register, features include Indian shutters, wide pine-paneled walls, a Dutch door fireplace, and an upstairs ballroom. Next door is a historic schoolhouse that contains four of the inn's guestrooms.
Rates: $90-$130.
10 Rooms. 10 Private Baths. Guest phone available. Beds: QD. Meals: Continental. Restaurant. CCs: All. Tennis.
Seen in: *Food & Wine, Travel & Leisure.*

Mystic - Noank

Palmer Inn
25 Church St
Mystic - Noank CT 06340
(203) 572-9000

Circa 1907. This gracious seaside mansion was built for shipbuilder Robert Palmer, Jr. by shipyard craftsmen. It features a two-story grand columned entrance, mahogany beams, a mahogany staircase, quarter-sawn oak floors, and

14-foot ceilings. The Lincrusta wallcovering, original light fixtures, and nine stained-glass windows remain.
Location: Two miles from Mystic.
Rates: $90-$150. All year.
Innkeeper(s): Patricia W. Cornish.
6 Rooms. 4 Private Baths. Guest phone available. Beds: KQT. Meals: Continental plus. Conference room. Fireplaces. CCs: Visa, MC. Sailing, tennis, museums.
Seen in: *Yankee Magazine, The Norwalk Hour.*
"Tops for luxury." Water Escapes, by Whittemann & Webster.

Mystic

Harbour Inne and Cottage
Edgemont Street
Mystic CT 06355
(203) 572-9253

Circa 1898. This recently remodeled home has a three bedroom cottage with cedar interiors and its own kitchen. There are views of the Mystic River and Fishers Island Sound and picnic tables are situated along the waterfront. Nearby canoe and row boats rentals are available.
**Rates: $35-$85. All year.
Innkeeper(s): Charley Lecouras, Jr.
4 Rooms. 4 Private Baths. Guest phone available. TV in room. Beds: F. Meals: EP. Canoeing, fishing, row boats.

Red Brook Inn
PO Box 237
Mystic CT 06372
(203) 572-0349

Circa 1740. Situated on a bluff surrounded by seven acres of woodland, the inn and stagecoach stop have been recently restored and each has a traditional center chimney. There are 13 fireplaces in the inn. All rooms are furnished with period antiques such as canopy beds and many rooms have working

fireplaces. Breakfast is served in the large keeping room of the Haley Tavern in front of a great hearth.
Rates: $65-$150.
Innkeeper(s): Ruth Keyes.
11 Rooms. 11 Private Baths. Guest phone available. TV available. Beds: QD. Meals: B&B. Jacuzzi. Fireplaces. CCs: Visa, MC.
Seen in: *Travel & Leisure, Yankee Magazine.*

New Hartford

Cobble Hill Farm
Steel Rd
New Hartford CT 06057
(203) 379-0057 (203) 379-3828

Circa 1796. This rambling Colonial inn was selected by *Country Living Magazine* as one of their favorite ten

inns in the country. It is located in Litchfield Hills on 40 acres of gardens, meadows, woodlands, and wildlife. Deer and wild turkeys can be seen strolling along the dirt road. A spring-fed pond is filled with tadpoles and trout, and the barn houses horses, chickens, and pigs.
Location: Foothills of the Berkshires.
**Rates: $95. April 1 - Jan 1
Innkeeper(s): Jo & Don McCurdy.
4 Rooms. 3 Private Baths. Guest phone available. TV available. Beds: KQDC. Meals: Full breakfast. Fireplaces. Hay & sleigh rides, horseback riding, tubing on river, swimming.
"Do you know what it's like to relive one's happy childhood except in technicolor? We loved it. The accommodations and food were excellent, too."

New Haven

The Inn at Chapel West
1201 Chapel St
New Haven CT 06511
(203) 777-1201

Circa 1847. This green-and-white Victorian has recently undergone a two-million-dollar renovation. Its lavish appointments include items such as a Bavarian canopy bed,

mahogany and French country furnishings, and a musical doll collection. Maple woodwork, parquet floors and seven fireplaces adorn the inn. There are crystal glasses in the bathrooms and Laura Ashley prints on the walls.
Location: Downtown, one block from the Yale campus.
**Rates: $100-$175. All year.
Innkeeper(s): Steven Schneider.
10 Rooms. 10 Private Baths. Guest phone in room. TV in room. Beds: KQC. Meals: Continental. Handicap access provided. Conference room. Fireplaces. CCs: Visa, MC, AE, DC. Tours, theater.
Seen in: *New York Times, Business Digest of Greater New Haven.*

New Milford

Homestead Inn
5 Elm St
New Milford CT 06776
(203) 354-4080
Circa 1853. Built by the first of three generations of John Prime

Treadwells, the inn was established 80 years later. Victorian architecture includes high ceilings, spacious rooms and large verandas. There is a small motel adjacent to the inn. Marilyn Monroe and Arthur Miller were among the Homestead's famous guests.

Location: North of Danbury, 15 miles.
Rates: $47-$66. All year.
Innkeeper(s): Rolf & Peggy Hammer.
14 Rooms. 14 Private Baths. Guest phone available. TV in room. Beds: QTDC. Meals: Continental plus. CCs: Visa, MC, AE, DS. Golf, hiking, downhill and cross-country skiing.
"One of the homiest inns in the U.S.A. with most hospitable hosts. A rare bargain to boot."

New Preston

Inn on Lake Waramaug
North Shore Rd
New Preston CT 06777
(203) 868-0563
Circa 1795. Set on a hill overlooking Lake Waramaug, with acres of spacious lawns and towering sugar

maples, this Colonial inn is well known for its guest rooms and cuisine. An indoor pool and sauna provide respite in winter while a private beach awaits in summer. Host John Koiter has been a whitewater rafting guide and a member of the ski patrol.
Location: Northwest Connecticut.
**Rates: $128-$168. All year.
Innkeeper(s): John & Karen Koiter.
23 Rooms. 23 Private Baths. Guest phone available. TV in room. Beds: QTD. Meals: MAP, restaurant. Sauna. Handicap access provided. Conference room. Fireplaces. Pool. CCs: Visa, MC, AE. Swimming, tennis, sailing, canoes, golf, skiing.
Seen in: *Washington Journal, Business Weekly, Record Journal.*
"Guests, innkeepers and a pony all give the Inn on Lake Waramaug the kind of country inn character that most inns can only hope for." New England Get Aways."

Norfolk

Manor House
Maple Ave, Box 447
Norfolk CT 06058
(203) 542-5690
Circa 1898. Charles Spofford, designer of London's underground

system, built this home with many gables, exquisite cherry paneling,

and grand staircase. There are Moorish arches and Tiffany windows. Guests can enjoy hot mulled cider after a sleigh ride, hay ride, or horse-and-carriage drive along the country lanes nearby.
Rates: $50-$130. All year.
Innkeeper(s): Hank & Diane Tremblay.
9 Rooms. 6 Private Baths. Guest phone available. TV available. Beds: KQT. Meals: Full breakfast. Conference room. Fireplaces. CCs: Visa, MC, AE. Cross-country skiing, hiking, biking, riding stables.
Seen in: *Boston Globe, The Journal, Philadelphia Inquirer.*
"Queen Victoria, eat your heart out."

Mountain View Inn
Rt 272
Norfolk CT 06058
(203) 542-5595
Circa 1875. Imagine yourself bundled in blankets in a horse-drawn sleigh, as it slides silently through virgin snow, back to the warmth and comfort of Victorian Mountain View. There are fine antiques and collectables in all the rooms and gourmet dining on site at Mayfield's restaurant.
**Rates: $60-$100. May - November.
Innkeeper(s): Alan & Michele Sloane.
11 Rooms. 8 Private Baths. Guest phone available. TV available. Beds: TD. Meals: Continental Plus, Restaurant. Conference room. Fireplaces. CCs: Visa, MC. Swimming, hiking, horseback riding, rafting, cross-country skiing.
"Newly decorated with delightful results." B&B Travelers Review.

Norwalk

Silvermine Tavern
Silvermine & Perry Aves
Norwalk CT 06850
(203) 847-4558
Circa 1786. The Silvermine consists of the Old Mill, the Country Store, the Coach House, and the Tavern it-

self. Primitive paintings and furnishings, as well as family heirlooms, decorate the inn. Guest rooms and dining rooms overlook the Old Mill, the waterfall, and swans gliding across the millpond.
Rates: $60.
Innkeeper(s): Frank Whitman, Jr.
10 Rooms. 10 Private Baths. Meals: B&B. CCs: All.

Old Lyme

Old Lyme Inn
85 Lyme St
Old Lyme CT 06371
(203) 434-2600
Circa 1850. This elegantly restored mansion features original wall

paintings in its front hall, portraying historic Old Lyme buildings and the scenic countryside. Elegance is reflected throughout the inn with marble fireplaces, antique mirrors, and Victorian and Empire furnishings.
Rates: $75-$115. Closed Mondays.
Innkeeper(s): Diana Field Atwood.
13 Rooms. 13 Private Baths. Guest phone available. TV available. Beds: QT. Meals: Continental breakfast, restaurant. Handicap access provided. CCs: All.
"Gracious and romantic rooms with exquisite dining, our favorite inn!"

Salisbury

Under Mountain Inn
Rt 41
Salisbury CT 06068
(203) 435-0242
Circa 1710. Situated on three acres, this was originally the home of iron

magnate Jonathan Scoville. A thorned locust tree, rumored to be the oldest in Connecticut, shades the inn. Paneling that now adorns the pub was discovered hidden between the ceiling and attic floorboards. The boards were probably placed there in violation of a colonial law requiring all wide lumber to be given to the King of England. British-born Peter was happy to reclaim it in the name of the Crown.
**Rates: $75. All year.
Innkeeper(s): Peter & Marged Higginson.
7 Rooms. 7 Private Baths. Guest phone available. Beds: QTD. Meals: MAP. CCs: Visa, MC, AE. Golf, tennis, horseback riding, boating, hiking, swimming, bikes.
Seen in: *Travel & Leisure, Country Inns Magazine.*
"You're terrific!"

Somersville

The Old Mill Inn
63 Maple St
Somersville CT 06072
(203) 763-1473
Circa 1850. Owners of the old woolen mill bought this home at the turn-of-the-century, and it was oc-

cupied by the storekeeper of the Somersville general store. The dining room walls are painted with flowering shrubs and trees in keeping with the inn's landscaping. In the old mill there are two furniture factories and a shop producing Shaker reproductions.
Location: Five miles east of Exit 47 on I-91, 1 block south of Rt. 190.
Rates: $45-$50. All year.
Innkeeper(s): Ralph & Phyllis Lumb.
4 Rooms. 2 Private Baths. Guest phone available. TV available. Beds: TF. Meals: Full breakfast. Golf, horseback riding.
"We loved staying here! You are both delightful. P.S. We slept like a log."

Thompson

Samuel Watson House
Rt 193
Thompson CT 06277
(203) 923-2491
Circa 1767. Samuel Watson built this pillared Georgian mansion for

his bride, and it gave her, as well as present-day visitors, views of what is called the prettiest common in New England. All guest rooms feature working fireplaces. The innkeepers also operate the Sea Wings Gallery and Workshop where they display their hand-carved shore birds.
Location: Thompson Hill Historic District on the common.
Rates: $50-$60. All year.
Innkeeper(s): Bob & JoAnn Godfrey.
4 Rooms. Guest phone available. TV available. Beds: QTC. Meals: Full breakfast. Conference room. Fireplaces. Boating, swimming, golf, cross-country skiing.
Seen in: *Observer Extra, Putnam Patriot Observer.*
"A home of great charm and warmth and it belongs to just the right people. Thank you for letting us share it and your deliciously groaning board."

Tolland

Tolland Inn
63 Tolland Green, Box 717
Tolland CT 06084
(203) 872-0800
Circa 1800. This white clapboard house on the village green originally provided lodging for travelers on the old Post Road between New York and Boston. After extensive renovation, the Tolland Inn has been opened once again and has been refurbished with antiques and many

furnishings made by the innkeeper. Nearby is the town hall and the Old Jail Museum.
Location: On the village green, 1/2 mile to exit 68 & I-84.
Rates: $30-$50.
Innkeeper(s): Susan & Stephen Beeching.
5 Rooms. 3 Private Baths. Guest phone available. Beds: DT. Meals: B&B. Fireplaces. CCs: Visa, MC.

Westbrook

Captain Stannard House
138 S Main St
Westbrook CT 06498
(203) 399-7565
Circa 1850. Captain Elbert Stannard became a seaman at 14, and later commanded many famous

ships. At 21, he built this gracious Georgian home complete with a widow's walk. It eventually became the Menunketesuck Inn, and has now been restored to its former beauty. Antiques, a wood-burning

stove, and hot mulled cider are available for today's guests.
Rates: $60-$150. All year.
Innkeeper(s): Ray & Elaine Grandmaison.
9 Rooms. 9 Private Baths. Guest phone available. TV available. Beds: TD. Meals: Full breakfast. Conference room. Fireplaces. CCs: Visa, MC, AE, DC. Biking, tennis, fishing, evening cruises.

Woodbury

Curtis House
Main St
Woodbury CT 06798
(203) 263-2101
Circa 1754. Perhaps the oldest continuously operating inn in the state, the Curtis House began as the Orenaug Inn run by Anthony Stoddard. In 1900, the roof was raised and a third floor of eight rooms laid out in anticipation of a boom from a scheduled trolley service. All the guest rooms in the main house have canopied beds. Regional Yankee fare such as chowders, bisques and crusted pot pies are served at the inn.
Rates: $30-$70. All year.
Innkeeper(s): The Hardisty family.
18 Rooms. 12 Private Baths. Guest phone in room. TV in room. Meals: EP, Continental, Restaurant. Handicap access provided. Conference room. Fireplaces.

CCs: Visa, MC. Swimming, boating, hiking, bicycling, golf.

Woodstock

Inn at Woodstock Hill
Plaine Hill Rd
Woodstock CT 06267
(203) 928-0528
Circa 1816. This classic Georgian house with its black shutters and white clapboard exterior reigns over 14 acres of rolling farmland. Inside are several parlors, pegged-wood floors, English country wallpapers,

floral chintzes and a fireplace for each room. The inn was recently renovated at a cost of $1.5 million, but the barn with its cupola remains untouched and stalls still display names such as Topsy and Primrose.
**Rates: $55-$140. All year.
Innkeeper(s): Ruth Jensen.
19 Rooms. 19 Private Baths. Guest phone in room. TV available. Beds: QT. Meals: Continental-plus breakfast. Conference room. Fireplaces. CCs: Visa, MC. Horseback riding, skiing.
Seen in: *The Hartford Courant.*

Delaware

Laurel

Spring Garden
Rt 1 Box 283-A
Laurel DE 19956
(302) 875-7015

Circa 1780. This gracious white brick and clapboard, country plantation was built in a Federal architec-

ture with Georgian overtones. It features outstandingly preserved 18th-century heart pine paneling, four fireplaces, and wide-planked floors. Lawns and meadows bloom with lilies and lilacs and a stream meanders through the inn's forest.
Location: Fourteen miles north of Salisbury, MD.
**Rates: $50-$70. All year.
Innkeeper(s): Gwen North.
6 Rooms. 2 Private Baths. Guest phone available. TV available. Beds: DT. Meals: Full breakfast, gourmet. Handicap access provided. Conference room. Fireplaces. Bicycling, horseback riding, badminton, tennis, swimming, fishing.
Seen in: The Sun, Newsday.

"The warmest, most gracious hostess on the Eastern Shore. We rated all the inns we stayed in on a scale of one to ten. You got the ten."

New Castle

David Finney Inn
216 Delaware St
New Castle DE 19720
(302) 322-6367

Circa 1683. There has been a tavern here since 1683 although the oldest parts of the inn only date to 1713. George Washington was a frequent guest and two of the signers of the Declaration of Independence stayed here. In 1794 two buildings were put together to form the present inn, a Dutch Colonial. A courtyard garden shaded by an old walnut tree is in the back of inn. The guest rooms are decorated with pine antiques and have views of the Delaware River or of the village green. A highly acclaimed restaurant, a member of the Master Chef's Institute, is on the premises.
Location: In the center of New Castle.
Rates: $60-$100. All year.
Innkeeper(s): Judy Piser.
17 Rooms. 17 Private Baths. Meals: Restaurant. CCs: All.

The Jefferson House
Bed & Breakfast
The Strand at the Wharf
New Castle DE 19720
(302) 323-0999 (302)322-8944

Circa 1800. Overlooking the Strand and the Delaware River, the Jefferson House served as a hotel, a rooming house, and a shipping company office during colonial times. On the side lawn is a "William Penn landed here" sign. The inn features heavy paneled doors, black marble mantels over the fireplaces and a fanlight on the third floor. Cobblestone streets add to the

quaintness of this old river town, the first capital city of the colonies.
Location: Mid-Atlantic region.
**Rates: $65. All year.
Innkeeper(s): Dr. & Mrs. Mel Rosenthal.
3 Rooms. 3 Private Baths. Guest phone available. TV in room. Beds: D. Meals: Full breakfast, restaurant. Fireplaces.

William Penn Guest House
206 Delaware St
New Castle DE 19720
(302) 328-7736

Circa 1682. William Penn slept here. In fact, his host Arnoldus de LaGrange witnessed the ceremony in which Penn gained possession of the Three Lower Colonies. Mrs. Burwell who lived next door to the historic house 'gained possession' of it one day about twenty years ago while her husband was away. After recovering from his wife's surprise purchase, Mr. Burwell rolled up his sleeves and set to work restoring the house. Guests may stay in the very room slept in by Penn.
Rates: $35. All year.
Innkeeper(s): Irma & Richard Burwell.
4 Rooms. TV available. Beds: DT. Meals: Continental plus.

Rehoboth Beach

Pleasant Inn Lodge
31 Olive Ave
Rehoboth Beach DE 19971
(302) 227-7311

Circa 1928. Originally on the ocean front, this Victorian four-square house was moved a block away after Rehoboth's Great Storm of 1918. The inn is comfortably fur-

nished with antiques. Broad verandas and several common rooms invite guests to lounge whether they choose a bedroom or apartment. No meals are served but there is coffee and many restaurants are within walking distance.
Rates: $45-$65. All year.
Innkeeper(s): Peck Pleasanton.
10 Rooms. 10 Private Baths. Guest phone available. TV available. Beds: KQTW. Meals: Continental plus. CCs: Visa, MC. Water skiing, fishing, charter boats, ocean.

Florida

Amelia Island

1735 House
584 S Fletcher Ave
Amelia Island FL 32034
(904) 261-5878

Circa 1928. Perched right at the edge of the Atlantic, the inn is just about fifteen steps across the sand to the ocean (any closer and it

would be below the tide line). All the rooms in this New England clapboard-style inn are actually suites. Antiques, wicker and rattan add to the decor and comfort of the rooms. A lighthouse-type building is popular with families. Breakfast is delivered to your door in a picnic hamper.
Location: Oceanfront.
**Rates: $55-$85. All year.
Innkeeper(s): Gary & Emily Grable.
5 Rooms. 5 Private Baths. Guest phone available. TV in room. Beds: KQT. Meals: Full breakfast, continental plus. CCs: Visa, MC, AE. Tennis, golf, horseback riding.

"It was a delightful surprise to find a typical old New England inn in Florida. The charm of Cape Cod with warm ocean breezes and waves lapping at the door."

Apalachicola

Gibson Inn
PO Box 221
Apalachicola FL 32320
(904) 653-2191

Circa 1907. James Buck of South Carolina built this Victorian hotel of cypress and heart pine lumber that he handpicked. Purchased by the Gibson sisters in the Twenties the

inn was known for its elegant parties. Recently renovated, two stories of verandas and a roof-top cupola adorn the inn. Rich woodwork, a flaired staircase and globe lamps prepare guests for antique-filled rooms and a pleasing dining room.
Location: Highway U.S. 98.
**Rates: $50-$100. All year.
Innkeeper(s): Michael J. Koun & JoAnn Dearing.
31 Rooms. 31 Private Baths. Guest phone in room. TV in room. Beds: KQTC. Meals: Full breakfast, restaurant. Handicap access provided. Conference room. CCs: Visa, MC, AE. Tennis, golf, fishing.
Seen in: The Stuart News, South Florida.

Cedar Key

Historic Island Hotel
Box 460
Cedar Key FL 32625
(904) 543-5111

Circa 1849. This old hotel was never elegant but it has tremendous character and a rich history. At one time it housed both Union and Confederate armies, although not at the same time. A leisurely veranda, a pot-bellied stove, paddle-fans, and canopies of mosquito netting are reminiscent of days gone by when Pearl Buck used the hotel as a writing retreat. Two red-headed parrots maintain a vigil in the lobby.
Location: Gulf of Mexico Islands - 55 miles west of Gainesville.
Rates: $60-$73. All year.
Innkeeper(s): Marcia Rogers.
10 Rooms. 6 Private Baths. Guest phone available. TV available. Beds: KD. Meals: Full breakfast, restaurant, gourmet Handicap access provided. Conference room. Swimming, boating.
Seen in: Chicago Tribune.

"When you step through the double screen doors, you enter a different world, a world of the Caribbean Islands, or even the South Pacific."

Coral Gables

Hotel Place St. Michel
162 Alcazar Ave
Coral Gables FL 33134
(305) 444-1666

Circa 1926. Although the architecture is Spanish in character, the inn's carefully selected paintings and antiques help to establish a French country inn feeling in many

of the rooms. Fresh flowers, and turn down service with Italian chocolates add to the ambience. The hotel's restaurant is locally favored for its French deli takeout and French-Continental cuisine.

**Rates: $70 - $110.

Innkeeper(s): Stuart N. Bornstein & Alan H. Potamkin.

28 Rooms. 28 Private Baths. Guest phone in room. TV in room. Beds: KQ. Meals: Continental breakfast. Handicap access provided. Conference room. CCs: Visa, MC, AE, DC. Golf, water skiing, tennis.

Seen in: *Esquire, Miami Herald, South Florida.*

"It was positively divine, all of it. I look forward to retuning."

Fernandina Beach

Bailey House
PO Box 805
Fernandina Beach FL 32034
(904) 261-5390

Circa 1895. This elegant Queen Anne Victorian was a wedding present Effingham W. Bailey gave to

his bride. He was a steamship agent and shocked the locals by spending the enormous sum of $10,000 to build the house with all its towers, turrets, gables, and verandahs. The parlor and dining room open to a fireplace in a reception hall with the inscription "Hearth Hall - Welcome All". A spirit of hospitality reigned in this home from the beginning.

Location: On Amelia Island.
**Rates: $55-$85. All year.
Innkeeper(s): Ken Nolan with owners Tom & Diane Hay.

4 Rooms. 4 Private Baths. Guest phone available. TV in room. Beds: QDT. Meals: Continental-plus breakfast. Fireplaces. CCs: MC. Beach, horseback riding, tennis golf in the vicinity. Bicycles for guests.

Seen in: *Victorian Homes, St. Petersburg Times.*

"Well, here we are back at Mickey Mouse land. I think we prefer the lovely Bailey House!"

Holmes Beach

Harrington House B&B
5626 Gulf Dr
Holmes Beach FL 34217
(813) 798-9933

Circa 1925. A mere 40 feet from the water and set among oak trees and palms is this gracious home constructed of 14-inch-thick coquina blocks. A 20-foot-high beamed ceil-

ing, fireplace, Twenties wallpaper, and French doors are features of the living room. All the guest rooms have four-poster beds and antique wicker furnishings with French doors opening onto a deck overlooking the swimming pool and water.

Rates: $65-$85.

Innkeeper(s): Walt & Betty Spangler.

5 Rooms. 5 Private Baths. Guest phone available. TV in room. Beds: DT. Handicap access provided. Pool. CCs: Visa, MC. Moonlight beach walks, theater.

Jacksonville

House on Cherry St
1844 Cherry St
Jacksonville FL 32205
(904) 384-1999

Circa 1912. Blooming flowers fill the pots that line the circular entry stairs to this Federal-style house on tree-lined Cherry Street. It was moved in two pieces to its present site on St. Johns River in the historic Riverside area. Traditionally decorated rooms include collections of decoy ducks and old clocks that chime and tick. Most rooms overlook the river. Your hosts are a social worker and family doctor.

**Rates: $55-$65.

Innkeeper(s): Carol Anderson

4 Rooms. 2 Private Baths. Guest phone available. TV in room. Beds: QDT. Meals: B&B.

Seen in: *Florida Wayfarer.*

Key West

Colours Key West
410 Fleming St
Key West FL 33040
(305) 294-6977

Circa 1889. This Victorian mansion has been completely renovated and has maintained all the original architectural detail including 14-foot ceilings, chandeliers, polished wood floors and graceful verandahs. The house is said to be haunted by Hetty, a ghost who has been seen by many folks over the years. The innkeeper states that the inn is for the liberal-minded adult only.

Location: Historic Old Town District.
**Rates: $69-$149. All year.
Innkeeper(s): James Remes.

12 Rooms. 10 Private Baths. Guest phone in room. TV available. Beds: KD. Meals: Continental-plus breakfast. Pool. CCs: Visa, MC, AE. Water skiing, snorkling, scuba diving, boating. Turn down service, cocktails.

Seen in: *Sunshine News/Sun Sentineal.*

"I have stayed at several guest houses in Key West - none compare. Constant clean towels and the freshness of everything is impressive."

Heron House
512 Simonton St
Key West FL 33040
(305) 294-9227

Circa 1856. One of the oldest homes remaining in Key West, this house is an early pre-1860 example of Conch architecture. Bougainvillea, jasmine and orchids bloom in the tropical gardens. Light and airy

rooms have a tropical feeling with wicker furnishings.
Location: One block from Duval St. in center of Historic District.
**Rates: $45-$95. All year.
Innkeeper(s): Fred Gribelt.
18 Rooms. 18 Private Baths. Guest phone available. Beds: D. Meals: Continental-plus breakfast. Pool. CCs: Visa, MC, AE. Complete free-weight gym.

Island City House

411 William St
Key West FL 33040
(305) 294-5702
Circa 1880. This house was built for a wealthy Charleston merchant who later converted it to a small

hotel, anticipating the arrival of the railroad in 1912. Restored by two active preservationists, Island City House and Arch House provide apartments in beautifully restored environs with turn-of-the-century decor. Private porches and ceiling fans are historical amenities that remain.
**Rates: $115-$175.
Innkeeper(s): Valerie Kieffer & Gary Ross.
30 Rooms. 24 Private Baths. Guest phone available. TV available. Beds: KD. Meals: Continental-plus breakfast. Jacuzzi. Pool. CCs: Visa, MC, AE. Deep sea fishing, sailing, shelling, diving two blocks away.
Seen in: *Palm Beach Daily News*.

"We really enjoyed our stay and have decided we're going to visit the Keys every year and stay at our new-found 'home', apartment #4."

Key West B&B Popular House

415 William St
Key West FL 33040
(305) 296-7274
Circa 1890. This pink and white Victorian rests behind a white picket fence. It was constructed by ship-builders with sturdy heart-pine walls and 13-foot ceilings. There are two stories of porches and the inn is located in the center of the Historic District.
Location: Two blocks to the Gulf.
**Rates: $45-$100. May to Dec.
Innkeeper(s): Jody Carlson.
7 Rooms. 2 Private Baths. Guest phone available. Beds: KQT. Meals: Continental-plus breakfast. Jacuzzi. Sauna. Conference room. CCs: Visa, MC, AE. Fishing, shopping, hemmingway house tours, all water sports.
"The essence of charming."

Watson House

525 Simonton
Key West FL 33040
(305) 294-6712
Circa 1860. This home was purchased by an Ohio couple during the Civil War and remodeled to be-

come a Bahama-style home, ideal for its sub-tropical climate. In 1986 after two years of restoration, the house became the recipient of the Excellence in Rehabilitation award granted by the Historic Florida Keys Preservation Board.
**Rates: $95-$215. April to Dec.
Innkeeper(s): Joe Beres, Ed Czaplicki.
3 Rooms. 3 Private Baths. Guest phone in room. TV in room. Beds: Q. Meals: AP. Jacuzzi. Pool. CCs: Visa, MC. All suites with kitchens.

Lake Wales

Chalet Suzanne

319 W Starr Ave, Drawer AC
Lake Wales FL 33859-9003
(813) 676-6011
Circa 1928. Carl & Vita Hinshaw are carrying on the traditions begun by Carl's mother, Bertha, who was

known as a world traveler, gourmet cook and antique collector. Following the stock market crash and the double disaster of her husband's death, she turned her home into an inn and dining room. The whimsical architecture includes gabled roofs, balconies, spires and steeples. The restaurant has received the Craig Claiborne award as one of the 121 best restaurants in the world.
Location: Four miles north of Lake Wales.
**Rates: $75-$145. All year.
Innkeeper(s): Carl & Vita Hinshaw.
32 Rooms. 32 Private Baths. Guest phone in room. TV in room. Beds: KQDTC. Meals: EP. Handicap access provided. Conference room. Pool. CCs: Visa, MC, AE, DC. Lawn games, golf and tennis nearby. private airstrip and lake. Murder mystery weekends.
Seen in: *USA Today, Dallas Morning News, Woman's Day*.
"I now know why everyone always says 'Wow!' when they come up from dinner. Please don't change a thing."

Miami

B&B Company

PO Box 262
Miami FL 33243
(305) 661-3270
Circa 1900. Marcella Schaible operates this reservation service for private homestays that includes a historic stone house in the Coconut Grove area of Miami. Formerly a restaurant frequented by area socialites, the home is constructed of

stone and situated on a street lined with banyan trees. There is a huge fireplace in the living room and two gardens outside. A 20-mile-long bikepath is nearby.
Location: Several homes in Greater Miami.
Rates: $55. Meals: Full breakfast.

Hotel Place St. Michel
See: Coral Gables, FL

Orlando

Chalet Suzanne
See: Lake Wales, FL

St. Augustine

Casa de Solana
21 Aviles St
St. Augustine FL 32084
(904) 824-3555
Circa 1763. A Spanish military leader, Don Manuel Solana built this home in the early European settle-

ment. The thick coquina-shell walls, high ceilings with dark, hand-hewn beams and polished hand-pegged floors are part of the distinctive flavor of this period. Two working Majorcan fireplaces are in the carriage house. An elegant ten-foot-long mahogany table is the site of a southern breakfast.
Location: In the Historic District.
**Rates: $100-$125.
Innkeeper(s): Faye L. McMurray.
4 Rooms. 4 Private Baths. Guest phone available. TV in room. Beds: KQT. Meals: Full breakfast. Handicap access provided. Conference room. CCs: Visa, MC, AE, DC.
Seen in: *House Beautiful.*

Kenwood Inn
38 Marine St
St. Augustine FL 32084
(904) 824-2116
Circa 1865. The Kenwood was originally built as a summer home but has taken in guests for over a hundred years. Early records show

that it was advertised as a private boarding house as early as 1886. Rooms are decorated in periods ranging from the simple Shaker decor to more formal colonial and Victorian styles.
Location: One block from the bayfront.
Rates: $55-$75. All year.
Innkeeper(s): Mark, Kerrianne & Caitlin Constant.
13 Rooms. 13 Private Baths. Guest phone available. TV available. Beds: KQ. Meals: Continental breakfast. Fireplaces. Pool. CCs: Visa, MC.

St. Francis Inn
279 St George St
St. Augustine FL 32084
(904) 824-6068
Circa 1791. Long noted for its hospitality, the St. Francis Inn is near the oldest house in town. A classic example of Old World ar-

chitecture, it was built by Senor Garcia who received a Spanish grant to the plot of land. Coquina, a limestone formed of broken shells and corals cemented together and found on Anastasia Island was the main building material. St. Augustine was founded in 1565.

Location: In the St. Augustine Historic District, the nation's oldest city.
**Rates: $38-$85. All year.
Innkeeper(s): Marie Register.
16 Rooms. 16 Private Baths. TV in room. Beds: KQTC. Meals: Hearty continental breakfast. Pool. CCs: Visa, MC.
"We have stayed at many nice hotels but nothing like this. We are really enjoying it."

St. Petersburg

Bayboro House on Old Tampa Bay
1719 Beach Dr, SE
St. Petersburg FL 33701
(813) 823-4955
Circa 1904. The Bayboro has a Victorian flavor and was built by one of

the founding fathers of the city, C. A. Harvey. He was the first real estate developer and the first to have the vision to construct the port. The house is across from Lassing Park and faces Old Tampa Bay. It has an unobstructed view.
Location: Off exit 9 (I-275), downtown St. Petersburg.
Rates: $45-$55. All year.
Innkeeper(s): Gordon & Antonia Powers.
3 Rooms. 3 Private Baths. Guest phone available. TV in room. Beds: QDT. Meals: Continental-plus breakfast. CCs: Visa, MC.
"A lovely room and the house itself a handsome structure. Special touches from the fine linen, pretty quilts, plants, shells and lovely antique furniture made my brief stay enjoyable."

Tampa

Harrington House B&B
See: Holmes Beach, FL

Georgia

Atlanta

Beverly Hills Inn
65 Sheridan Dr. NE
Atlanta GA 30305
(404) 233-8520

Circa 1929. Period furniture and polished wood floors decorate this

inn located in the Buckhead neighborhood. There are private balconies, kitchens, and a library with a collection of newspapers and books. The Governor's Mansion, Neiman-Marcus, Saks, and Lord & Taylor are five minutes away.
Location: North on Peachtree 15 minutes then 1/2 block off Peachtree.
**Rates: $64-$74.
Innkeeper(s): Lyle & Bonnie Kleinhaus.
18 Rooms. 18 Private Baths. Guest phone in room. TV in room. Beds: Q. Meals: Continental plus. Conference room. CCs: Visa, MC, AE.
"A three-star left bank hotel in a prime residential area."

Augusta

Telfair Inn
326 Greene St
Augusta GA 30901

(404) 724-3315

Circa 1888. Telfair is a collection of 17 Victorian houses in the heart of historic Olde Town. Each one has been renovated and decorated with four-poster beds, fireplaces, whirlpool baths, antiques, and gleaming hardwood floors. The inn's private 40-foot cabin cruiser *Lady Telfair*, often often takes guests for a cocktail cruise along the Savannah River. There is also a large conference center.
**Rates: $41-$85. All year.
Innkeeper(s): Lee Edwards.
89 Rooms. 89 Private Baths. Guest phone in room. TV in room. Beds: KQTC. Meals: Full breakfast, restaurant. Jacuzzi. Handicap access provided. Conference room. Fireplaces. Pool. CCs: Visa, MC, AE, DC. Tennis, swimming. Private cabin cruiser.
"A great experience! Thanks for everything. The service here is excellent!"

Macon

1842 Inn
353 College St
Macon GA 31201
(912) 741-1842

Circa 1842. Judge John J. Gresham, cotton merchant and founder of the

Bibb Manufacturing Company, built this antebellum Greek Revival house. It features graceful columns, elaborate mantels, crystal chandeliers and oak parquet floors inlaid

with mahogany. Guest rooms boast cable TV discreetly tucked into antique armoires, and there are whirlpool baths available in the main house and in an adjoining Victorian cottage.
**Rates: $60-$90. All year.
Innkeeper(s): Aileen P. Hatcher
22 Rooms. 22 Private Baths. Guest phone in room. TV in room. Beds: KQTC. Meals: Full breakfast. Jacuzzi. Handicap access provided. Conference room. Fireplaces. CCs: Visa, MC, AE.
Seen in: *The Christian Science Monitor, Southern Living.*
"The best B&B we've seen! Deserves all four stars!."

Mountain City

York House
Box 126
Mountain City GA 30562
(404) 746-2068

Circa 1896. Bill and Mollie York opened the York House as an inn in 1896 and it has operated continuously ever since. Two stories of

shaded verandas overlook tall hemlocks, Norwegian spruce, lawns and mountains. Adjacent to the Old Spring House is a stand of pines that provide a romantic setting for weddings. Breakfast is carried to the room each morning on a silver tray

and each room is plumbed with natural spring water.
**Rates: $45-$70. All year.
Innkeeper(s): Phyllis & Jimmy Smith.
13 Rooms. 13 Private Baths. Guest phone available. TV in room. Beds: DC. Meals: Full breakfast. Handicap access provided. Conference room. Fireplaces. CCs: Visa, MC. Skiing, horseback riding, hiking, swimming.

Saint Mary's

Riverview Hotel
105 Osborne St
Saint Mary's GA 31558
(912) 882-3242
Circa 1916. This hotel is located on the banks of the St. Mary's River near the ferry to Cumberland Island

National Seashore. It was renovated in 1976, and there is a veranda filled with rocking chairs. Guests can tour pre-Civil-War Oak Grove Cemetery, and the Okefenokee Swamp is an hour away.
Location: St. Mary's river, 30 miles north of Jacksonville, Florida.
**Rates: $32-$49. All year.
Innkeeper(s): Jerry Brandon.
18 Rooms. 18 Private Baths. Guest phone available. TV in room. Beds: KD. Meals: Restaurant. CCs: Visa, MC, AE, DC.

Saint Simon's Island

Little St. Simons Island
PO Box 1078 G
Saint Simon's Island GA 31522
(912) 638-7472
Circa 1917. Once a part of Butler Plantation, Little St. Simons Island was purchased at the turn of the century by the Berolzheimer family. Deer roam freely and eagles soar over 10,000 acres of pristine forests, fresh water ponds, isolated beaches, and marshland. There are more than 200 species of birds, and guests can

enjoy horseback riding on miles of private trails. The Hunting Lodge,

filled with books and memorabilia, is the gathering spot for the island.
Location: A privately owned island 20 minutes offshore from St. Simons.
**Rates: $250 double. Feb-Nov 15.
Innkeeper(s): Ben Gibbens.
12 Rooms. 12 Private Baths. Guest phone available. Beds: KQT. Meals: All meals provided. Jacuzzi. Conference room. Fireplaces. Pool. CCs: Visa, MC. Canoeing, horseback riding, birdwatching, fishing. Naturalist-led explorations.
Seen in: *Meeting Destinations.*
"The staff is unequaled anywhere."

RSVP Savannah B&B Reservations
See: Savannah, GA

Savannah

"417" The Haslam-Fort House
417 East Charlton St
Savannah GA 31401
(912) 233-6380
Circa 1872. This is a free-standing three-story brick townhouse built in

an Italianate style with a colorful full side garden. Located on a quiet square, the two-bedroom suite has a living room, full bath and country kitchen. The inn's attractive decor has been featured in several magazines and newspapers.
Location: In the heart of Savannah's Historic District.
Rates: $65-$150. All year.

Innkeeper(s): Alan Fort & Richard McClellan.
2 Rooms. 1 Private Baths. Guest phone in room. TV in room. Beds: KTC. Meals: Continental plus. Handicap access provided.
"Alan is by far the most qualified host I've met. He gives 'home away from home' a brand new meaning."

Ballastone Inn
14 E Oglethorpe Ave
Savannah GA 31401
(912) 236-1484
Circa 1835. The inn is located in the heart of the largest historic district in the nation (2 1/2 square miles). Four stories of luxurious furnishings are accentuated with authentic Savannah colors and Scalamandre fabrics. Theme rooms include Greek Revival, English, and Egyptian. Turndown service features pralines and brandy, a southern touch.
**Rates: $90-$125.
Innkeeper(s): Richard Carlson & Tim Hargus.
19 Rooms. 19 Private Baths. Guest phone in room. TV in room. Beds: KQ. Meals: continental plus. Jacuzzi. Handicap access provided. Fireplaces. CCs: Visa, MC, AE. Carriage rides, ocean is 17 miles for boating, swimming. Elevator, jacuzzis, breakfast in bed.
"To a fabulous inn - magnificent!" Patricial Neal.

Foley House Inn
14 W Hull St
Savannah GA 31401
(912) 232-6622
Circa 1896. Fine craftsmen have faithfully restored the inn, and there is a fireplace in each room. An-

tiques, silver, china, oriental rugs and hand-colored engravings come from around the world. Churches, museums, galleries and the waterfront are within walking distance.

**Rates: $85-$180. All year.
Innkeeper(s): Susan Steinhauser.
20 Rooms. 20 Private Baths. Guest phone available. TV available. Beds: KQDTC. Meals: Continental plus. Jacuzzi. Fireplaces. CCs: Visa, MC, AE.

"I'll send all my romantic friends here."

Forsyth Park Inn

102 W Hall St
Savannah GA 31401
(912) 233-6800

Circa 1893. This graceful yellow and white three-story Victorian features bay windows and a large veranda overlooking Forsyth Park.

Sixteen-foot ceilings, polished parquet floors of oak and maple, and a handsome oak stairway provide an elegant background for the guestrooms. There are twelve fireplaces, four whirlpool tubs, marble baths and four-poster beds.
Location: Savannah's historic district, opposite Forsyth Park.
Rates: $60-$90. All year.
Innkeeper(s): Hal & Virginia Sullivan.
10 Rooms. 10 Private Baths. Guest phone available. Beds: KQT. Meals: Continental. Jacuzzi. Fireplaces. CCs: Visa, MC, AE. Tennis, jogging.
Seen in: *Savannah Morning News.*

"Breathtaking, exceeded my wildest dreams."

Jesse Mount House

209 W Jones St
Savannah GA 31401
(912) 236-1774

Circa 1854. A Greek Revival townhouse, Jesse Mount has two spacious, luxurious three-bedroom suites complete with gas-burning fireplaces. There is a Savannah-style

walled garden. Exceptional antiques include a coach used by Tom Thumb to meet Queen Victoria, gilded harps and a grand piano. The hostess is an internationally-known concert harpist. A pre-Revolutionary London clock chimes gently to urge you to step from your historic lodgings into the compelling charm of Old Savannah.
Location: In historic district of Savannah.
Rates: $70-$130. All year.
Innkeeper(s): Howard Crawford & Lois Bannerman.
2 Rooms. 2 Private Baths. Guest phone in room. TV in room. Beds: QC. Meals: Full breakfast.
Seen in: *Savannah Morning News.*

"Marvelous. We enjoyed your gracious hospitality, delicious breakfast, and elegant surroundings."

Liberty Inn 1834

128 W Liberty St
Savannah GA 31401
(912) 233-1007 (800)637-1007

Circa 1834. In 1949, the innkeepers met for their first date at the Liberty Cafe. Many years later they purchased it and converted it to an inn.

A National Register Landmark, it was constructed of clapboard over brick and has survived many Savannah fires. The builder, Colonel Williams, was a publisher, bookseller, and six-time mayor of the city. Period pieces, original fireplaces, and exposed interior brick walls are featured.
Location: Northeast corner of Liberty & Barnard Streets.
Rates: $93-$150. All year.
Innkeeper(s): Frank & Janie Harris, Iris Rogers, Manager.
5 Rooms. 7 Private Baths. Guest phone in room. TV in room. Beds: Q. Meals: Full breakfast. Jacuzzi. Fireplaces. CCs: Visa, MC, AE. River harbor cruises.
Seen in: *The Orlando Sentinel, Savannah Morning News.*

"Incredibly beautiful. Perfectly charming."

Olde Harbour Inn

508 E Factors Walk
Savannah GA 31401
(912) 234-4100

Circa 1892. This building once housed Tidewater Oil Company and in 1930 the Alexander Blue Jean Manufactory. Now converted to condos, the units are decorated in a traditional style and each suite overlooks the Savannah River.
**Rates: $89-$109. Mar - Aug.
24 Rooms. 24 Private Baths. Guest phone in room. TV in room. Beds: QTC. Meals: Continental plus. CCs: Visa, MC, AE. Riverfront Vacation package.

Remshart-Brooks House

106 W Jones St
Savannah GA 31401
(912) 234-6928

Circa 1853. Remshart-Brooks House is in the center of the historic district. Guests enjoy a terrace-garden suite with bedroom, living room, bath and kitchen. Home-baked delicacies enhance the continental breakfast.
Location: Center of historic district.
Rates: $60-$80. All year.
Innkeeper(s): Anne Barnett.
1 Rooms. 1 Private Baths. Guest phone in room. TV in room. Beds: Q. Meals: Full breakfast.

RSVP Savannah B&B Reservation Service

417 E Charlton St
Savannah GA 31401
(912) 232-7787

Circa 1848. This service specializes in the traveler seeking history and beauty, from South Carolina's Low

Country to Georgia's Sea Islands. Accommodations are available in an elegantly restored inn, guest house,

private home or villa on the water. Areas include Savannah, Tybee and St. Simons Islands, in Georgia, and Beaufort and Charleston in South Carolina.
Rates: $60-$175. All year.
Innkeeper(s): Alan Fort.
140 Rooms. 140 Private Baths. Guest phone in room. TV in room. Beds: KQTC. Meals: Full breakfast, continental, rest. Jacuzzi. Handicap access provided. Fireplaces. Pool. CCs: Visa, MC, AE. Golf, tennis, sailing, deep sea fishing, water sports.

Senoia

Culpepper House
Corner Of Broad At Morgan, PO Box 4
Senoia GA 30276
(404) 599-8182
  Circa 1871. This Queen Anne Victorian was built by a Confederate veteran and later occupied for fifty years by Dr. Culpepper. It has its original moldings, stained glass windows and mantelpieces and is decorated in cozy Victorian clutter and comfortable whimsy. The inn offers guests Southern hospitality at its finest.
Rates: $45-$55.
Innkeeper(s): Mary Brown.
3 Rooms. 1 Private Baths. Guest phone available. TV available. Beds: QDT. Meals: B&B.

The Veranda - (Hollberg Hotel)
252 Seavy St
Senoia GA 30276-0177
(404) 599-3905
  Circa 1907. This 9,000 square foot hotel housed notables such as William Jennings Bryan before it was turned into a private estate in the Thirties. Doric columns adorn the verandas and the inn is surrounded by tall trees. Inside are walnut bookcases previously owned by President William McKinley. Collections of kaleidoscopes, Victorian hair combs, paperweights and walking canes add to the decor.
Location: Thirty miles south of Altanta airport.
**Rates: $65-$85. All year.
Innkeeper(s): Jan & Bobby Boal.
9 Rooms. 9 Private Baths. Guest phone available. Beds: QTC. Meals: Full breakfast. Jacuzzi. Handicap access provided. Conference room. Fireplaces. CCs: Visa, MC, DS. Golf, tennis, fishing.
Seen in: *The Newnan Times Herald, Good Times, After Hours.*
  "*The mystique and reality of The Veranda are that you're being elaborately entertained by friends in their private home.*"
  "*The Veranda is a time machine that allows you to step back into the Victorian age.*"

Tybee Island

RSVP Savannah B&B Reservations
See: Savannah, GA

Hawaii

Haiku, Maui

Haikuleana Bed & Breakfast Inn

69 Haiku Rd
Haiku, Maui HI 96708
(808) 575-2890

Circa 1850. This plantation house sits among pineapple fields and Norfolk pine trees. There are high ceilings and a tropical decor with the flavor of Hawaiian country life. The porch looks out over exotic gardens, and beaches and waterfalls are nearby.
Location: Twelve miles east of Kahului.
**Rates: $60. All year.
Innkeeper(s): Denise & Clark Champion.
2 Rooms. Guest phone available. TV available. Beds: QT. Meals: Full breakfast.

"Great, great, extra great! Maui is paradise thanks to your daily guidance, directions and helpful hints."

Honolulu

Manoa Valley Inn

2001 Vancouver Dr
Honolulu HI 96822
(808) 947-6019 (800)634-5115

Circa 1919. An Iowa lumber executive built this mansion situated on a half-acre of lush greenery. Gables supported by fanciful buttresses add a unique detail to the inn, now in the National Register. Lanais furnished with white wicker overlook Diamond Head. The guest rooms are filled with carefully chosen antiques, reproduction wallpapers and cozy comforters.
Location: On the island of Oahu.
Rates: $80-$145. All year.
Innkeeper(s): Marianne Schultz.
8 Rooms. 5 Private Baths. Guest phone in room. TV available. Beds: KQD. Meals: Continental. Conference room. Fireplaces. CCs: Visa, MC. Pool table, croquet.
Seen in: *Discover Hawaii.*

Koloa, Kauai

Poipu Bed & Breakfast Inn

2720 Hoonani Rd
Koloa, Kauai HI 96756
(808) 742-1146 (800) 552-0095

Circa 1933. This restored plantation house is one block from the beach.

Handcrafted wood interiors, traditional lanais, carousel horses, and pine antiques decorate the inn. Each room has a private bath and some have whirlpool tubs. One can hear the sound of the ocean and a nearby stream.
Location: Poipu Beach.
**Rates: $50-$150. All year.
Innkeeper(s): Dotti Cichon.
6 Rooms. 6 Private Baths. Guest phone available. TV in room. Beds: KQTC. Meals: Full breakfast, continental plus. Jacuzzi. Handicap access provided. Conference room. Pool. CCs: Visa, MC. Swimming, surfing, boating, horseback riding, golf, tennis. Afternoon tea, popcorn with movies.

"Thank you for sharing your home as well as yourself with us. I'll never forget this place, it's the best B&B we've stayed at."

Lahaina, Maui

The Lahaina Hotel

127 Lahainaluna Road
Lahaina, Maui HI 96761
(808) 661-0577

Circa 1963. Originally built in the 1860s as a hotel for whalers, the bar became famous for brawls. A 16-foot killer whale stuffed and hanging overhead was the target for harpoons, a version of barroom darts. After a fire in 1963, the hotel was rebuilt in a frontier storefront style. All rooms have balconies and some have ocean views.
Rates: $85-$135.
12 Rooms. 12 Private Baths. Beds: D. Meals: Restaurant on premises. CCs: Visa, MC.

Idaho

Coeur d'Alene

Greenbriar Bed & Breakfast
315 Wallace
Coeur d'Alene ID 83814
(208) 667-9660

Circa 1908. Winding mahogany staircases, woodwork and window seats are features of Greenbriar, now

in the National Register. Antiques, imported Irish down comforters with linen covers, sheer curtains, and gabled ceilings decorate the guest rooms. It is four blocks from Lake Coeur d'Alene, one of the most beautiful lakes in the country.
Rates: $35-$65. All year.
Innkeeper(s): Kris McIluenna.
7 Rooms. 4 Private Baths. Guest phone available. Beds: KQTC. Meals: Full breakfast, restaurant. CCs: Visa, MC. Canoeing, bicycling, skiing, snowmobiling.

Illinois

Chicago

Burton House
Bed & Breakfast Inn
1454 N Dearborn Pkwy
Chicago IL 60610
(312) 787-9015

Circa 1877. The Bullock-Folsom Mansion, as it is known locally, was the Chicago White House during Grover Cleveland's term. It has been owned by the same family since it was built, and much of early California was built by members of the Bullock and Folsom families. A grand lobby on the first floor displays the magnificent Eastlake interiors seen throughout the inn. Each bedroom has a marble fireplace and gilded ceiling.
**Rates: $90-$120. All year.
Innkeeper(s): Ralph d'Neville-Raby.
3 Rooms. 3 Private Baths. Guest phone available. TV in room. Beds: QTD. Meals: EP, full breakfast. Fireplaces. CCs: MC, AE. Shopping.

Collinsville

Maggie's Bed & Breakfast
2102 N Keebler Rd
Collinsville IL 62234
(618) 344-8283

Circa 1890. A rustic, two-acre wooded area surrounds this friendly Victorian, once a boarding house. Rooms feature 14-foot ceilings and are furnished with exquisite antiques and art objects collected on world-wide travels. Just ten minutes

away is downtown St. Louis, the Gateway Arch and the Mississippi riverfront.
Location: Ten minutes from St. Louis.
Rates: $25-$45.
Innkeeper(s): Maggie Leyda.
5 Rooms. 1 Private Baths. Guest phone available. Beds: QDTC. Meals: Full breakfast. Jacuzzi. Conference room.
"We enjoyed a delightful stay. You've thought of everything. What fun!"

Galena

Avery Guest House
606 S Prospect St
Galena IL 61036
(815) 777-3883

Circa 1859. Avery Guest House is named for Major George Avery who served in the Civil War and later led parades through Galena each year. The house was originally owned by a steamboat captain and later by a

wagon-maker. There is a porch swing for leisurely evenings. Breakfast is served in the sunny dining room with bay windows overlooking the Galena River Valley.
Rates: $40-$50. All year.
Innkeeper(s): Flo & Roger Jensen.
4 Rooms. Guest phone available. TV available. Beds: QTC. Meals: Continental plus. Handicap access provided. CCs: Visa, MC. Horseback riding, swimming, skiing, hiking, bicycling.
Seen in: *The Galena Gazette*.
"We've stayed in several B&Bs and this one is the most pleasant and friendly."

Belle Aire Mansion
11410 Rt 20 W
Galena IL 61036
(815) 777-0893

Circa 1834. Situated on 16 acres including a barn and windmill, the

Belle Aire Mansion originally began as a log cabin. Remodeled in 1879, the charming white Federal-style

house features a two-story columned porch looking out over lawns and a circular drive. Original logs and flooring as well as a fieldstone basement remain. Decor is early American and country. The hosts have two small children and welcome children of all ages.
Location: Thirteen miles east of Dubuque, Iowa.
Rates: $60-$65. All year.
Innkeeper(s): Lorraine Svec & Linda Cook.
4 Rooms. 1 Private Baths. Guest phone available. TV available. Beds: TDC. Meals: Full breakfast. Downhill and cross-country skiing, golf, horseback riding, hiking.
"Loved the house and the hospitality!"

Mars Avenue Guest House

515 Mars Ave
Galena IL 61036
(815) 777-3880

Circa 1854. President Grant kept his horses in the barn here when he

came to town. Later, the house featured a commercial tea room. It's decorated in a country style with hand-cut stencils. Rooms are named for the owners' grandmothers and a portrait hangs in each guest room. Handmade quilts have been collected for cozy evenings.
Location: Five blocks from town.
Rates: $50. All year.
Innkeeper(s): Nan Wick.
4 Rooms. Guest phone available. TV available. Beds: KTD. Meals: Full breakfast. CCs: Visa, MC. Shopping.

Stillman's Country Inn

513 Bouthillier
Galena IL 61036
(815) 777-0557

Circa 1858. This grand Victorian mansion, built by merchant Nelson

Stillman, is just up the hill from Ulysses S. Grant's house, and Grant

and his wife dined here often. The tower of the house was a hideout for slaves escaping through the Underground Railroad. Original working fireplaces and handsome antiques grace the guest rooms.
Location: Across from General Grant's house.
Rates: $55-$85. All year.
Innkeeper(s): Pam & Bill Lozeau.
5 Rooms. 5 Private Baths. Guest phone available. TV in room. Beds: QD. Meals: Continental breakfast. Conference room. Fireplaces. CCs: Visa, MC, AE, DS.
Seen in: *National Geographic Traveler, Telegraph Herald.*

Geneva

The Oscar Swan Country Inn

1800 W State St
Geneva IL 60134
(312) 232-0173

Circa 1902. This turn-of-the-century estate, built by local landowners, has been opened for bed and breakfast by Hans and Nina Heymann, both educators. The inn is 6,000 square feet on seven acres of trees and lawns.
Rates: $60-$125.
7 Rooms. 2 Private Baths. Guest phone available. Beds: KQD. Meals: Full breakfast.

Lanark

Standish House

540 W Carroll St
Lanark IL 61046
(815) 493-2307

Circa 1882. Four generations of Standishes were associated with this Queen Anne Victorian house, and the current owner is Norman Standish, a descendant of Captain Myles Standish. Furnishings include English antiques from the 17th and 18th centuries. During Thanksgiving

the innkeepers sponsor a series of lectures on pilgrim history.
Location: One-hundred-twenty miles west of Chicago on route 64.
Rates: $50-$65. All year.
Innkeeper(s): Maggie Aschenbrenner.
5 Rooms. 1 Private Baths. Guest phone available. TV available. Beds: QT. Meals: Full breakfast. CCs: Visa, MC. Skiing, fishing, hunting, hiking. Pilgrim history lectures.
Seen in: *Prairie Advocate, Northwestern Illinois Dispatch.*

Winnetka

Chateau des Fleurs

552 Ridge Rd
Winnetka IL 60093
(312) 256-7272

Circa 1936. This is an authentic French-style country home near Lake Michigan. The lawn and terraced English gardens are shaded by cottonwoods, willows and apple trees. A Steinway baby grand piano is in the living room and there is a library available to guests. The Northwestern Train to the Chicago Loop is four blocks away.
Location: Thirty minutes to the Chicago Loop.
Rates: $80.
Innkeeper(s): Sally Ward.
3 Rooms. Guest phone in room. TV available. Beds: KDT. Meals: Continental plus. Jacuzzi. Fireplaces. Pool. Jogging, golf.

Indiana

Batesville

Sherman House Restaurant & Inn
35 S Main Street
Batesville IN 47006
(812) 934-2407

Circa 1852. This hotel has been in business for more than 100 years,

and during this century it acquired a Tudor facade. The restaurant is the focal point of town with business meetings and frequent banquets in the Chalet Room. There are several covered bridges nearby.
**Rates: $32-$45.
25 Rooms. 25 Private Baths. Guest phone available. TV in room. Beds: QTC. Meals: EP. Conference room. CCs: Visa, MC, AE. Weekend and tour packages.

Crawfordsville

Davis House
1010 W Wabash Ave
Crawfordsville IN 47933
(317) 364-0461

Circa 1870. Sampson Houston built this colonial house from brick manufactured on site. He was a colonel in the homeguards, a farmer, minister, and land speculator developing the town. Stately

bedrooms have private baths and comfortable beds.
Location: South on I-74.
**Rates: $35-$50. All year.
Innkeeper(s): Jan Stearns.
4 Rooms. 4 Private Baths. Guest phone in room. TV available. Beds: QTDC. Meals: Full breakfast. Conference room. Fireplaces. CCs: Visa, MC, AE. Canoeing, fishing, hiking.
"This is just wonderful. I've never stayed in a cleaner B&B."

Evansville

Brigadoon Bed & Breakfast Inn
1201 SE Second St
Evansville IN 47713
(812) 422-9635

Circa 1892. This Victorian inn is approached through a white picket fence. Built for a railroad executive, it is in the historic area near downtown and the river. The Forbes family completely restored the house adding extra baths and insulation to the interior bedroom walls. The parlor and library are open to guests.
Location: Old Ohio River city.
Rates: $35-$45. All year.
Innkeeper(s): Kathee Forbes.
4 Rooms. 2 Private Baths. Guest phone in room. TV available. Beds: QC. Meals:

Full breakfast. Handicap access provided. Conference room. CCs: Visa, MC. Horse racing, zoo.
"These 14 hours of pure enjoyment have been a delight. Throughout the 26 countries I've traveled not one B&B has matched your hospitality."

Fort Wayne

The Candlewyck B & B
331 W Washington Blvd
Fort Wayne IN 46802
(219) 424-2643

Circa 1914. This California Craftsman-style bungalow features beveled glass and stained-glass windows throughout. There are oak-

beamed ceilings in the parlor and dining room as well as oak floors and woodwork. The hostess is an interior designer and her talents are displayed in the carefully chosen antiques, accessories, and wallcoverings that fill the inn.
Location: Two blocks from Convention Center, across from the library.
**Rates: $40-$55.
Innkeeper(s): Jan & Bob Goehringer.
5 Rooms. Guest phone available. TV available. Beds: QDT. Meals: Full breakfast on weekends. Fireplaces.
"Very enjoyable! You certainly know how to make guests feel like friends."

Indianapolis

Country Roads Guesthouse
See: Westfield, IN

Hollingsworth House Inn
6054 Hollingsworth Road
Indianapolis IN 46254
(317) 299-6700

Circa 1854. This Greek Revival farmhouse is in the National Register. The four acres of the inn add to the restful and elegant atmosphere. Haviland china makes breakfast a special treat. The inn is next to a 120-acre park.
Rates: $75.
Innkeeper(s): Ann Irvine & Susan Muller.
5 Rooms. 5 Private Baths. Guest phone available. Meals: Continental breakfast.
CCs: Visa, MC.

Stewart Manor
612 E 13th St
Indianapolis IN 46202
(317) 634-1711

Circa 1870. Old North Side Historic District is noted for its many Victorian mansions. Stuart Manor is a

three-story Italianate with handsome woodwork, pocket doors and the original gas chandeliers. There is a ballroom on the second floor and a large landing with pink and green stained glass windows highlighted by polished woodwork and a pink chaise.
**Rates: $50-$100.
Innkeeper(s): Eileen Stewart.
4 Rooms. 4 Private Baths. Guest phone available. TV available. Beds: D. Meals: Continental plus. Conference room. Fireplaces. CCs: Visa, MC.
Fabulous! A great place to spend our wedding night. If we had known it was so beautiful, we'd have planned to have the wedding here!"

Knightstown

Old Hoosier House
Rt 2 Box 299-I
Knightstown IN 46148
(317) 345-2969

Circa 1836. The Old Hoosier House was owned by the Elisha Scovell family, friends of President Martin Van Buren. They named their child after him. Features of this early Victorian house include tall, arched windows and a gabled entrance. Rooms are air-conditioned and decorated with antiques and lace curtains. Only Hoosier breakfasts are served here.
Location: Greensboro Pike and Rd. 750 S.
Rates: $55.
Innkeeper(s): Jean & Tom Lewis.
4 Rooms. 1 Private Baths. Guest phone available. Meals: Full breakfast.
"We had such a wonderful time at your house. Very many thanks."

Mishawaka

The Beiger Mansion Inn
317 Lincoln Way E
Mishawaka IN 46544
(219) 256-0365

Circa 1903. This neo-classical limestone mansion was built to satisfy Susie Beiger's wish for a Newport-style estate resembling that of a Rhode Island friend. Palatial rooms that were once a gathering place for local society now welcome guests who seek gracious accommodations. Notre Dame, St. Mary's and Indiana University in South Bend are nearby.
Location: Northern Indian.
Rates: $65-$125.
10 Rooms. 5 Private Baths. Meals: Continental-plus breakfast. Conference room. CCs: Visa, MC. Afternoon hors d'oeuvres.

Morgantown

The Rock House
380 W Washington St
Morgantown IN 46160
(812) 597-5100

Circa 1894. James Smith Knight built this stone house with tower rooms, a three-room basement, and

an attic and delivery room. Knight made concrete blocks years before they were popular, and embedded stones and rocks in them before they were dry. He also used seashells, jewelry, china dolls and even an animal skull to decorate the blocks. There is still a dumbwaiter used to lower food to the basement for cooling during the summer.
Location: Ten miles north of Brown County/Nashville.
Rates: $35-$55. All year.
Innkeeper(s): Doug & Marcia Norton.
5 Rooms. 3 Private Baths. Guest phone available. TV available. Beds: TD. Meals: Full breakfast. Lake, skiing.

Nashville

The Rock House
See: Morgantown, IN

Paoli

Braxtan House Inn
Bed & Breakfast
210 N Gospel St
Paoli IN 47454
(812) 723-4677

Circa 1893. Thomas Braxtan, son of original Quaker settlers, was a business owner and stock trader and built this Victorian house. It has 21 rooms and became a hotel when nearby mineral springs lured guests to Paoli. Oak, cherry, chestnut, and maple woodwork are featured. The inn is furnished in antiques and highlighted with stained and leaded glass.
Location: Downtown Paoli on state road 37N.
Rates: $30-$65.
Innkeeper(s): Terry & Brenda Cornwell.
8 Rooms. 3 Private Baths. Guest phone available. TV available. Beds: DT. Meals: Full breakfast. Conference room. CCs:

Visa, MC. Skiing, swimming, fishing, golf, tennis.

Westfield

Country Roads Guesthouse
2731 W 146th St
Westfield IN 46074
(317) 846-2376

Circa 1890. Just north of Indianapolis this 100-year-old farmhouse and barn sits on four acres. There are high ceilings, a kitchen fireplace and antique furniture. A swimming pool, basketball court, and air-conditioning are among the modern amenities.
Location: Near Indianapolis.
Rates: $36. All year.
Innkeeper(s): Phil Pegram.
2 Rooms. Guest phone in room. Beds: T. Meals: Continental. Fireplaces. Swimming, basketball.

Iowa

Amana Colonies

Die Heimat Country Inn
Main St
Amana Colonies IA 52236
(319) 622-3937

Circa 1854. The Amana Colonies is a German settlement listed in the National Register. This two-story clapboard inn houses a collection of

handcrafted Amana furnishings of walnut and cherry. Country-style quilts and curtains add personality to each guest room. Nearby are museums, a winery, and a woolen mill that imports wool from around the world.
Location: South of Cedar Rapids, west of Iowa City.
Rates: $27-$45. All year.
Innkeeper(s): Don & Sheila Janda.
19 Rooms. 19 Private Baths. Guest phone available. TV in room. Beds: QD. Meals: Continental-plus breakfast. CCs: Visa, MC, DS. Nature trail, golf course. Hayrack tour package.

"Staying at Die Heimat has been one of our life's highlights. We loved the clean rooms, comfortable beds and history connected with your establishment."

Avoca

Victorian Bed and Breakfast Inn
425 Walnut St
Avoca IA 51521
(712) 343-6336

Circa 1904. This Victorian was built by Fred Thielsen, a local contractor and builder. The house is outstanding for its fishscale shingling and golden pine woodwork. Detailed columns enhance the parlor and dining rooms. Midwestern antiques and locally made quilts decorate the guest rooms.
Rates: $32-$46.
Innkeeper(s): Rodney & Andrea Murray.
4 Rooms. Meals: Full breakfast. CCs: Visa, MC.

Bellvue

Mont Rest
300 Spring St
Bellvue IA 52031
(319) 872-4220

Circa 1893. Mont Rest was built by Seth Lewellyn Baker, developer of the Chicago suburb of Glen Ellyn. A

compulsive gambler, he played high-stakes poker from the turret

and within three years lost his home. Since the architecture is an unusual mix of styles the owners and the Iowa Historical Society labeled it Gothic Steamboat Revival. A clearly Victorian atmosphere prevails inside.
Location: On a nine-acre wooded bluff overlooking the Mississippi River.
Rates: $50-$75.
Innkeeper(s): Fred & Nancy Davison.
5 Rooms. Guest phone available. TV available. Beds: Q. Meals: Full breakfast. Jacuzzi. Conference room. Fireplaces. CCs: Visa, MC. Potter's mill, fishing, nature center, doll museum. Lunch and dinner on request.
Seen in: *Quad City Times, The Register.*

Decorah

Old World Inn
See: Spillville, IA

Dubuque

Redstone Inn
504 Bluff St
Dubuque IA 52001
(319) 582-1894

Circa 1894. The Redstone Inn, a twenty-three room duplex, was built by pioneer industrialist A. A. Cooper as a wedding gift for his daughter Nell. The side occupied by Nell's family is a grand Victorian generously embellished with turrets and porches. Maple and oak woodwork, beveled, leaded and stained-glass windows and marble and tile fireplaces are elegant features. Dubuque conservationists and business people converted the mansion into a luxurious antique-filled inn.

**Rates: $65-$140. All year.
Innkeeper(s): Debbie Gnesinger, manager.
15 Rooms. 15 Private Baths. Guest phone in room. TV in room. Beds: QTDC. Meals: Continental-plus breakfast. Jacuzzi. Conference room. Fireplaces. CCs: Visa, MC, AE. Dickens Christmas and ski packages.
Seen in: *Country Inns Magazine, Journal Star.*

"The staff and accommodations made me feel like a queen!"

Stout House

**1105 Locust
Dubuque IA 52001
(319) 582-1890**

  Circa 1890. This Richardsonian-Romanesque mansion was built by Frank D. Stout for $300,000. The intricate wood carvings were a showcase for the finest skilled craftsmen of the day, working in rosewood, maple, oak and sycamore. One of the ten wealthiest men in Chicago, Stout entertained Dubuque's upper crust elegantly in his rough-hewn sandstone house.
**Rates: $65-$85.
Innkeeper(s): Tom & Mary Morobray.
6 Rooms. 2 Private Baths. Guest phone available. TV in room. Beds: Q. Meals: Full breakfast. Conference room. CCs: Visa, MC, AE, DC.
Seen in: *Telegraph Herald, Country Inns Magazine.*

Spencer

The Hannah Marie Country Inn

**Rt 1, Hwy 71 S
Spencer IA 51301
(712) 262-1286 (712) 332-7719**

  Circa 1910. This beautifully restored farmhouse is Northwest Iowa's first country inn. Guestrooms

are decorated with Iowa-made quilts, antiques and lace curtains and the Sweetheart room has an in-room claw-foot tub with pillows. Amenities include dessert, evening wine, fruit baskets and flowers. Afternoon teas include Queen Victoria's Chocolate Tea, or Tea with the Mad Hatter, all served in costume. Green lawns and golden fields of corn surround the inn and the scent of freshly mowed hay accompanies guests who are given walking sticks and parasols for strolling to the old creek for a country picnic.
Location: Six miles south of Spencer.
Rates: $50-$60. May to Nov 15.
Innkeeper(s): Mary Nichols & Dave Nichols.
3 Rooms. 3 Private Baths. Guest phone in room. Beds: QDT. Meals: Full couuntry breakfast. Jacuzzi. CCs: Visa,

MC. Museums, antiquing. Afternoon tea included in room price.
Seen in: *Innsider.*

Spillville

Old World Inn

**331 S Main St
Spillville IA 52168
(319) 562-3739 (319)562-3186.**

  Circa 1871. This brick general store has been a brewery, livery stable, hardware store and residence. Most recently it was a Czech restaurant. It is located in the Czech village that

inspired Antonin Dvorak to compose the "American Quartet." He worked on the New World Symphony here in 1893. Lodging is upstairs.
Location: Walking distance to Dvorak exhibit.
Rates: $35.
Innkeeper(s): Juanita Loven.
4 Rooms. 4 Private Baths. Guest phone available. Beds: DT. Meals: EP. Restaurant on premises. Conference room. CCs: Visa, MC. Skiing, canoeing, roller skating.
Seen in: *Des Moines Register, Cedar Rapids Gazette.*

  "Rooms are delightful! Very charming atmosphere."

Kansas

Council Grove

The Cottage House
25 N Neosho
Council Grove KS 66846
(316) 767-6828

Circa 1876. Council Grove is the birthplace of the Santa Fe Trail and The Cottage House is located on it.

The building grew from a boarding house to an elegant home and then hotel of a local banker. Listed in the National Register of Historic Places, the inn is a beautiful example of Victorian architecture in a prairie town.
Location: Northeast Kansas, intersection of 56 & 177.
**Rates: $24-$48. All year.
Innkeeper(s): Connie Essington
26 Rooms. 26 Private Baths. Guest phone in room. TV in room. Beds: KQTC. Meals: EP. Jacuzzi. Sauna. Handicap access provided. Conference room. CCs: Visa, MC, AE, DS. Historic sites, golf in town, lake nearby. Dinner package, group tours.
Seen in: *Manhattan Mercury, The Gazette.*
"A walk back into Kansas history; preserved charm and friendliness."

Lawrence

Halcyon House
1000 Ohio
Lawrence KS 66044

(913) 841-0314

Circa 1886. This charming Victorian has been renovated and features a large parlor. Outside is a patio and pleasant yard. The University of Kansas is three blocks from the house.
Location: Twenty-five miles west of Kansas City.
Rates: $40-$69.
Innkeeper(s): Esther Wolfe & Gail Towle.
8 Rooms. 3 Private Baths. TV available. Meals: Full breakfast. CCs: Visa, MC, AE.

Melvern

Schoolhouse Inn
106 E Beck, PO Box 175
Melvern KS 66510
(913) 549-3473

Circa 1870. This charming, three-story building was once a country schoolhouse. Stone from local quar-

ries and large timbers were used during construction. A bar counter in the reception room was purchased from the old Wigger Grocery, and upstairs is a cabinet from St. Mary's College and an old church pew, part of the country decor.
Location: Eighty miles southwest of Kansas City.

Rates: $35-$40.
Innkeeper(s): Mary & Bill Fisher.
4 Rooms. 2 Private Baths. Guest phone available. TV available. Beds: Q. Meals: Full breakfast. CCs: Visa, MC, AE. Swimming and boating at Melvern Lake.
Seen in: *Journal-Free Press.*
"We just love the way you have fixed up the building with all of its history but the most charming aspect of the inn are its hosts and their overflowing hospitality."

Saint Mary's

Morning Star Inn
110 W Bertrand
Saint Mary's KS 66536
(913) 437-6851

Circa 1902. The Morning Star was originally a convent built for the Sisters of Charity. They occupied it until 1975, when they returned to their Motherhouse in Leavenworth. Afterwards, the convent was the site of an annual haunted house, free health department checkups, and bridge parties. In keeping with convent tradition, the new owners named each room for a saint or priest and decorated it accordingly.
Location: West of Kansas City, thirty minutes.
Rates: $36.50-$84.50.
Innkeeper(s): Ann Smith & Adele Frederick.
8 Rooms. 1 Private Baths. Guest phone in room. TV in room. Beds: KD. Meals: Full breakfast. Jacuzzi. Conference room. CCs: Visa, MC, AE. Horseback riding, museums nearby. Limo service from airport.
"Delicious, delightful and delectable Sunday brunch. A perfect replica of the best in New York and Connecticut."

Kentucky

Bardstown

Jailer's Inn
111 W Stephen Foster Ave
Bardstown KY 40004
(502) 348-5551
   Circa 1819. The old jail was constructed of native limestone with

two cells and an upstairs dungeon to house prisoners. The back building, sometimes referred to as the new jail, is completely surrounded by a stone wall. Jailer's Inn was a residence for many years.
Location: South of Louisville 35 miles.
Rates: $55-$75. March to Dec.
Innkeeper(s): Challen & Fran McCoy.
4 Rooms. Guest phone available. TV available. Meals: Continental breakfast. CCs: Visa, AE. Dinner train and drama package.
   "One of the oldest and most picturesque houses in Bardstown, a city noted for its fine homes." Joe Creason of the Courier Journal.

Old Talbott Tavern
Court Square, 107 W Stephen Foster
Bardstown KY 40004
(502) 348-3494
   Circa 1779. Old Talbott Tavern claims to be the oldest continuously operating "western" stagecoach inn in America. The stone building is filled with antiques, and there are several murals painted by the family of Prince Philippe of France. There are fireplaces in the six original guest rooms, and in addition to the pub, three dining rooms on the property.
Rates: $50-$62.
Innkeeper(s): Bill & Jim Kelley.
6 Rooms. 6 Private Baths. Meals: EP. CCs: Visa, AE, DC.

Berea

Boone Tavern Hotel
Main St, CPO 2345
Berea KY 40403
(606) 986-9358
   Circa 1909. This white, three-story Georgian hotel is run by a non-profit organization for the benefit of Berea College. The school is famous for a work-study program that makes a college education available to motivated students from the Kentucky mountains. To enjoy an example of Kentucky's finest dining, make reservations and be sure to arrive on time, since there is only one seating.
Location: Center of Berea College campus.
Rates: $49-67.
Innkeeper(s): J.B. Morgan.
59 Rooms. 59 Private Baths. Guest phone in room. TV in room. Beds: QD. Meals: Full breakfast. Handicap access provided. Conference room. CCs: Visa, MC, AE, DS. Tennis, gym. Alumni packages. Berea College nearby.

Covington

Amos Shinkle Townhouse
215 Garrard St
Covington KY 41011
(606) 431-2118
   Circa 1854. The facade of this restored mansion is Greco-Italianate. The cast iron fence and gate in front

are echoed in the cast iron filigree on the porch. Inside there are impressive crown moldings highlighted by stenciling in a surrounding border. Massive carved bedsteads, 16-foot ceilings, and rococo Revival chandeliers add to the formal elegance. Southern hospitality is practiced here.
Location: Fifteen minute walk to downtown Cincinnati.
**Rates: $55-$90. All year.
Innkeeper(s): Bernie Moorman.
7 Rooms. 7 Private Baths. Guest phone available. TV available. Beds: QD. Meals: Full breakfast. Jacuzzi. Conference room. Fireplaces. CCs: Visa, MC, DC. Stroll to an authentic paddlewheel boat, or carriage ride.
Seen in: *Bluegrass Magazine, Cincinnati Magazine, Cincinnati Post.*
   "It's like coming home to family and friends."

Georgetown

Log Cabin B&B
350 N Broadway
Georgetown KY 40324
(502) 863-3514

Circa 1809. This rustic Kentucky log cabin was restored by the McKnight family and has a shake-shingle roof and chinked logs. The huge fieldstone fireplace often holds a roaring fire and there is a kitchen and upstairs loft bedroom. Country decor and collections fill the house. Art Linkletter and Alex Haley enjoyed visits here.
Location: Two miles off I-75, ten miles from Lexington.
Rates: $60. All year.
Innkeeper(s): Clay & Sanis McKnight.
Fireplaces.
Seen in: *Lexington Herald Leader.*

Harrodsburg

Shakertown At Pleasant Hill
Rt 4
Harrodsburg KY 40330
(606) 734-5411

Circa 1805. A non-profit organization preserves and manages this nineteenth-century Shaker village set in a pleasant hill-top meadow. The inn's rooms are spread out in fifteen restored Shaker buildings. The old road running through the village is a National Landmark and is restricted to foot traffic. Parking is available near the guest quarters. The rooms are appointed with reproductions of authentic Shaker furnishings — each piece copied from originals in the Center Family House Museum. Air conditioning is hidden and all rooms have privated baths, but there are no closets. Instead, clothes (and sometimes chairs, and lighting fixtures) are hung on Shaker Pegs spaced about one foot apart on all four walls of the room. Costumed interpreters in the craft buildings describe Shaker culture and craft.
Location: Twenty five miles southwest of Lexington off Harrodsburg Road.
Rates: $40 - $70. All year.
Innkeeper(s): Anne Voris.
78 Rooms. 78 Private Baths. Guest phone in room. TV in room. Beds: TD. Meals: EP. Hearty Shaker Breakfast, $5.50. CCs: None.
"We can't wait to return! We treasure our memories here of peaceful, pleasant days."

Lexington

Log Cabin B&B
See: Georgetown, KY

Louisville

Braxtan House Inn B&B
See: Paoli, IN

Murray

Diuguid House
603 Main St
Murray KY 42071
(502) 753-5470

Circa 1895. When this Victorian house was built there was a tax on the number of rooms and each

closet was counted as a room so the family did without closets, using freestanding wardrobes. Thick brick walls make it soundproof, and there are stained glass windows and intricate oak woodwork.
Location: Downtown Murray.
**Rates: $30-$35. All year.
Innkeeper(s): Helena & Lorene Celano.
3 Rooms. Guest phone available. TV available. Beds: QTC. Meals: Full breakfast. Conference room. Fireplaces. CCs: Visa, MC. Horseback riding, tennis, boating within 15 miles.
Seen in: *The Murray State News.*
"We enjoyed our visit in your beautiful home and your hospitality was outstanding."

Louisiana

Jackson

Asphodel Plantation
Rt 2 Box 89
Jackson LA 70748
(504) 654-6868

Circa 1820. The main house is in the National Register. The Levy House belonged to a merchant in Jackson and was moved here in 1968 for a restaurant. There is an overseer's cottage and a train depot.
Location: North of Baton Rouge.
**Rates: $40-$70.
18 Rooms. 18 Private Baths. Guest phone available. TV available. Beds: KQC. Meals: Full breakfast, restaurant. Jacuzzi. Conference room. Fireplaces. Pool. CCs: Visa, MC, AE. Hiking, swimming, bird watching.

Napoleonville

Madewood Plantation
Rt 2 Box 478
Napoleonville LA 70390
(504) 369-7151

Circa 1848. Six massive Ionic columns support the central portico

of this striking Greek Revival mansion framed by live oaks and ancient magnolias. Overlooking Bayou Lafourche, it was designed by Henry Howard, a noted architect from Cork, Ireland. Elegant double parlors, a ballroom, library, music

room and dining room are open to guests.
Location: Seventy-five miles from New Orleans.
Rates: $85-$150. All year.
Innkeeper(s): Keith & Millie Marshall.
9 Rooms. 9 Private Baths. Guest phone available. TV available. Beds: QTD. Meals: MAP, full breakfast. Conference room. Fireplaces. CCs: DC.
Seen in: *Travel & Leisure.*

"We have stayed in many hotels, other plantations and English manor houses and Madewood has surpassed them all in charm, hospitality and food."

New Orleans

A Hotel, The Frenchman
417 Frenchman St
New Orleans LA 70116
(504) 948-2166

Circa 1860. Two townhouses built by Creole craftsmen have been total-

ly renovated, including the slave quarters. The original site was

chosen to provide easy access to shops and Jackson Square and the location today is still prime. Historic homes, quaint shops, and fine restaurants are immediately, at hand and the Old Mint and French Market are across the way. All rooms are furnished with period antiques.
Location: The French Quarter.
**Rates: $64-$99.
Innkeeper(s): Mark Soubie, Jr.
25 Rooms. 25 Private Baths. Guest phone in room. TV in room. Beds: QC. Meals: Full breakfast, restaurant. Jacuzzi. Handicap access provided. Conference room. Fireplaces. Pool. CCs: Visa, MC, AE. Swimming.

"Still enjoying wonderful memories of my stay at your charming hotel...such a delightful respite from the frantic pace of the Quarter."

Cornstalk Hotel
915 Royal St
New Orleans LA 70116
(504) 523-1515

Circa 1805. This home belonged to Judge Francois Xavier-Martin, the

author of the first history of Louisiana and the first Chief Justice of Louisiana's Supreme court. Andrew Jackson stayed here and another guest, Harriet Beecher Stowe wrote *Uncle Tom's Cabin* after viewing the nearby slave markets. The Civil War followed the widely-read publication. Surrounding the inn is a 150-year-old wrought-iron cornstalk fence. Stained-glass windows, oriental rugs, fireplaces and antiques grace the inn.
Location: In the heart of the French Quarter.
Rates: $65-$105. All year.
Innkeeper(s): Debbie & David Spencer.
14 Rooms. 14 Private Baths. Guest phone in room. TV available. Beds: KQDT.
Meals: Continental. CCs: Visa, MC, DC.

Dauzat House
337 Burgandy St
New Orleans LA 70130
(504) 524-2075
  Circa 1788. Located three blocks from Canal Street and two blocks from Bourbon Street, Dauzat House contains a lobby that was once the cottage of Marie Lareau, voodoo queen. There are two slave quarters converted to full suites with living rooms and kitchens and a 200-year-old courtyard with a swimming pool. Because of its location in the heart of the French Quarter the inn-keepers require adherence to a list of policies and regulations. Write to the inn for information.
Rates: $75-$500. All year.
Innkeeper(s): Richard Nicolais & Donald Dauzat.
8 Rooms. 5 Private Baths. Guest phone in room. TV in room. Beds: T. Meals: Full breakfast. Conference room. Fireplaces. Pool. Swimming.
Seen in: *Esquire Magazine, Playboy Magazine.*

Dusty Mansion
2231 General Pershing
New Orleans LA 70115
(504) 891-6061
  Circa 1913. Located in one of New Orleans historic districts near the St. Charles street car line, this home features hardwood floors and is furnished with antiques and reproductions. On Sunday a champagne brunch is served.
**Rates: $35-$50.
Innkeeper(s): Bob & Cynthia Riggs.

4 Rooms. 2 Private Baths. Guest phone available. TV available. Beds: QDC.
Meals: Continental-plus breakfast.

Grenoble House
329 Dauphine
New Orleans LA 70112
(504) 522-1331
  Circa 1854. Grenoble House consists of several renovated historic buildings in the French Quarter. There are several suites and a spa and pool are available.
Location: In the heart of the French Quarter.
**Rates: $125-$300.
Innkeeper(s): Carlos Flores.
  Guest phone in room. TV in room.
Meals: EP. Jacuzzi. Pool. CCs: Visa, MC, AE.

Lafitte Guest House
1003 Bourbon St
New Orleans LA 70116
(504) 581-2678 800/331-7971
  Circa 1849. This elegant French manor house has been meticulously restored. In the heart of the French

Quarter, there is easy access to world-famous restaurants, museums, antique shops and rows of Creole and Spanish cottages. The house is filled with fine antiques and paintings collected from around the world.
Location: Heart of the French Quarter.
**Rates: $65-$115. All year.
Innkeeper(s): Steve Guyton.
14 Rooms. 14 Private Baths. Guest phone in room. TV available. Beds: KQ. Meals: Continental. Fireplaces. CCs: Visa, MC, AE, DC.
Seen in: *Glamour Magazine, Antique Monthly.*

"This old building offers the finest lodgings we have found in the city." McCall's Magazine.

Lamothe House
621 Esplanade Ave
New Orleans LA 70116
(504) 947-1161 (800)367-5858
  Circa 1840. A carriageway that formerly cut through the center of many French Quarter buildings was

enclosed at the Lamothe House in 1866, and is now the foyer. Splendid Victorian furnishings enhance moldings, high ceilings, and hand-turned mahogany railings along the stairways. Gilded opulence goes unchecked in the Mallard and Layfayette suites. Registration takes place in the second-story salon.
Innkeeper(s): William Prentiss.
20 Rooms. 20 Private Baths. Guest phone in room. TV in room. Beds: TD. Meals: Continental. Conference room. Fireplaces. CCs: Visa, MC, AE.
Seen in: *Houston Post, Travel & Leisure.*

Nine-O-Five Royal Hotel
905 Rue Royal St
New Orleans LA 70116
(504) 523-0219
  Circa 1890. A quaint European style hotel, the Nine-O-Five is a

colonial with balconies overlooking the southern charm of Royal Street. There are eighteen-foot ceilings, antique furnishings and kitchenettes.
Location: French quarter.
Rates: $455-$95. All year.
Innkeeper(s): J.J. Morell.
10 Rooms. 10 Private Baths. Guest phone available. TV in room. Beds: KQD. Meals: EP. CCs: Travelers checks.

St. Charles Guest House
1748 Prytania St
New Orleans LA 70130
(504) 523-6556
Circa 1850. Reminiscent of a European *pensione*, the St. Charles Guest House has served visitors for

more than 30 years. Located in the residential lower Garden district the St. Charles Streetcar is nearby. This is a good choice for seasoned travelers who want an economical, clean and basic accommodation with friendly and helpful hosts.
Rates: $38-$58.
Innkeeper(s): Joanne & Dennis Hilton.
36 Rooms. 23 Private Baths. Guest phone available. Beds: TD. Meals: Continental. Pool. CCs: Visa, MC, AE.
Seen in: *Chicago-Sun Times*.
"You had an intuitive understanding of how a group like ours should experience New Orleans."

Stone Manor Hotel
3800 St. Charles Ave
New Orleans LA 70115
(504) 899-9600 504/522-5558
Circa 1908. This house was built in the Richardson Romanesque style by famed New Orleans architect Emile Weil. A neighboring property, the Unity Temple, is in the Frank Lloyd Wright manner and the contrast between these two buildings is of great interest to architects. The

house served as the French Consulate in the 1920s and '30s and is one of few remaining stone mansions on the avenue.
**Rates: $60-$150. All year.
Innkeeper(s): David & Debi Spencer.
9 Rooms. 5 Private Baths. Guest phone in room. TV in room. Beds: KQTC. Meals: Continental breakfast. Handicap access provided. Pool. CCs: Visa, MC, AE.

The Prytania Park Hotel
1525 Prytania St
New Orleans LA 70130
(800) 862-1984 (504)524-0427
Circa 1834. This hotel consists of a Victorian building and a new building. Request the older rooms to

enjoy the English Victorian reproduction furnishings, garden chintz fabrics and 14-foot ceilings. Some of these rooms have fireplaces. Rooms in the new section feature refrigerators, microwaves and contemporary furnishings. It is one-half block from the historic St. Charles Avenue streetcar.
Location: Lower Garden District.
Rates: $49-$79. All year.
Innkeeper(s): Judy Faget.
62 Rooms. 62 Private Baths. Guest phone in room. TV in room. Beds: KQT. Meals: Continental-plus. CCs: Visa, MC, AE, DC. Jogging.
Seen in: *New York Times*.
*"A little jewel."*Baton Rouge Advocate.

New Roads

Pointe Coupee Bed & Breakfast
605 E Main St
New Roads LA 70760
(504) 638-6254
Circa 1850. The inn is actually four houses, two embellished with gingerbread. One of the houses was constructed at Waterloo, but because of frequent floods was moved here around 1900. Another is a lakefront cottage. Saint Mary's Catholic Church is next door and the False River is four blocks away.
**Rates: $40. All year.
Innkeeper(s): Rev. and Mrs. Miller Armstrong.
10 Rooms. 2 Private Baths. Guest phone available. TV available. Beds: DT. Meals: Full breakfast. Handicap access provided. Conference room. Fireplaces. Water sports.

Saint Francisville

Barrow House
524 Royal St
Saint Francisville LA 70775
(504) 635-4791
Circa 1809. This saltbox with a Greek Revival addition was built during Spanish Colonial times. Antiques in the house date from 1840-1860, and include a Mississippi plantation bed with full canopy and a massive rosewood armoire crafted by the famous New Orleans cabinetmaker Mallard. One room has a Spanish moss mattress, traditional Louisiana bedding material used for more than 200 years. Six nearby plantations are open for tours.
Rates: $55-$80.
Innkeeper(s): Shirley Dittloff
4 Rooms. 4 Private Baths. Beds: Q. Meals: Continental breakfast.
Seen in: *Louisiana Life*.

St. Francisville Inn
118 N Commerce St
PO Drawer 1369
Saint Francisville LA 70775
(504) 635-6502
Circa 1880. A general merchant, Morris Wolf, built this Victorian Gothic often referred to as the Wolf-Schlesinger House. It is located in

the center of the business district. There are 14-foot ceilings and all the rooms open onto a New Orleans-style courtyard.
Location: Between Natchez and New Orleans.
Rates: $35-$55. All year.
Innkeeper(s): Florence & Dick Fillet.
9 Rooms. 9 Private Baths. Guest phone in room. TV in room. Beds: KTD. Meals: Full breakfast, restaurant. Conference room. CCs: Visa, MC, AE, DC.

Shreveport

Fairfield Place
2221 Fairfield Ave
Shreveport LA 71104
(318) 222-0048
   Circa 1890. This blue Victorian is in the Highland Restoration District, a neighborhood of gracious mansions framed by stately oaks. French hand-printed Victorian reproduction wallpaper adorns the foyer. Brad-

bury papers provide the background for the French, English, German and Scandinavian antiques in the guest rooms. Two rooms feature upholstered walls of English floral chintz. Guests enjoy the secluded New Orleans courtyard, porches and gardens that bloom year round.
Rates: $60-$85.
Innkeeper(s): Janie Lipscomb.
6 Rooms. 6 Private Baths. Guest phone in room. TV in room. Beds: KQT. Meals: B&B. CCs: Visa, MC, AE. Smoking in courtyard and gardens only.
Seen in: *Dallas Herald, Veranda Magazine.*

The Columns on Jordan
615 Jordan
Shreveport LA 71101
(318) 222-5912
   Circa 1898. This Classical Revival house in the historic district features four Gothic columns, and is surrounded by stately magnolia trees whose white blooms reach to the upstairs porch in the spring. Guest rooms are decorated in period furnishings. The pool was constructed in the shape of a bone by order of the owner, an orthopedic surgeon.
Rates: $58-$68.
Innkeeper(s): Judith Simonton.
5 Rooms. 4 Private Baths. Guest phone available. TV available. Beds: KDT. Meals: B&B. Jacuzzi. Conference room. Pool. CCs: Visa, MC, AE. Bicycles available.
Seen in: *The Shreveport Times, Travel Times CBS.*

White Castle

Nottoway
PO Box 160, Mississippi River Rd
White Castle LA 70788
(504) 545-2409
   Circa 1859. Virginian John Hampden Randolph built the

South's largest plantation home. Twenty-two columns support the exterior structure, a combination of Greek Revival and Italianate architecture. Listed in the National Register, the mansion is over 53,000 square feet. The White Ballroom is the most famous of Nottoway's 64 rooms.
**Rates: $90-$250.
13 Rooms. 13 Private Baths. Guest phone available. TV in room. Beds: QT. Meals: Full breakfast. Pool. CCs: Visa, MC. Tennis nearby.
   "Southern hospitality at its finest. Your restaurant has got to be Louisiana's best kept secret."

Maine

Bar Harbor

Graycote Inn
40 Holland Ave
Bar Harbor ME 04609
(207) 288-3044

Circa 1881. On an acre of land in town, this summer house was built

for Christopher Leffingwell, the Episcopal Bishop of Maine. It has served as a guest house since 1929 and was recently restored. King-size canopy beds, antiques, and fireplaces provide luxury. The ocean, harbor and shops are a four-block stroll from the inn.
Rates: $55-$90. May to Nov.
Innkeeper(s): William & Darlene DeMao.
10 Rooms. 4 Private Baths. Guest phone available. Beds: KQ. Meals: Full breakfast, continental plus. Fireplaces. CCs: Visa, MC. Hiking, bicycling, horseback riding, canoe and kayak rentals.
"We appreciated your hospitality. Your inn is by far our favorite."

Hearthside Inn
7 High St
Bar Harbor ME 04609
(207) 288-4533

Circa 1907. Originally built for a doctor, this three-story shingled

house sits on a quiet street in town. Guests enjoy four working fireplaces and a porch. The parlor includes a library and fireplace, and the music room holds a studio grand piano. Five minutes away is Acadia National Park.
Rates: $45-$90.
Innkeeper(s): Susan & Barry Schwartz.
9 Rooms. 7 Private Baths. Guest phone available. Beds: DQ. Meals: B&B. Fireplaces. CCs: Visa, MC. Near skiing, hiking, whale watching, boating, swimming.
"I have only one word to describe this place, Wow! My wife and I are astonished at the splendor of the place, the warmth of your care and the beauty of the surroundings."

Holbrook House
74 Mount Desert
Bar Harbor ME 04609
(207) 288-4970

Circa 1880. A local merchant built this Victorian inn in the Bar Harbor double-bracket style, for vacationers

who came to enjoy the beauty of Mt. Desert Island. The inn is located in the town's historic corridor. There is a library, sunroom, and parlor.
Location: Mt. Desert Island.
Rates: $75-$90. Jn 15-Oct 15.
Innkeeper(s): Dorothy & Mike Chester.
10 Rooms. 10 Private Baths. Guest phone available. TV available. Beds: QT.

Meals: Full breakfast. CCs: Visa, MC, AE. Acadia National Park entrance one mile.
"When I selected Holbrook House all my dreams of finding the perfect little country inn came true."

Ledgelawn Inn
66 Mount Desert
Bar Harbor ME 04609
(207) 288-4596

Circa 1904. Gables, bays, columns and verandas are features of this

rambling three-story summer house located on an acre of wooded land within walking distance to the waterfront. The red clapboard structure sports black shutters and a mansard roof. The inn is filled with antiques and fireplaces and there is a sitting room and library.
Rates: $85-$160. April 1-Nov 30.
Innkeeper(s): Nancy & Michael Miles.
38 Rooms. 38 Private Baths. Guest phone available. TV in room. Beds: KQDWC. Meals: B&B. Jacuzzi. Sauna. Conference room. Fireplaces. Pool. CCs: Visa, MC, AE. Bike riding, canoeing, water sports.

Manor House Inn
W St, Historic District
Bar Harbor ME 04609
(207) 288-3759

Circa 1887. Colonel James Foster built this 22-room Victorian mansion

now in the National Register. It is an example of the tradition of gracious summer living for which Bar Harbor was and is famous. In addition to the main house there are several charming cottages situated in the extensive gardens on the property. The innkeeper has written a history of the inn and Bar Harbor.
Location: 106 West Street.
Rates: $74-$140. April to Nov.
Innkeeper(s): Jan Matter.
14 Rooms. 14 Private Baths. Guest phone available. TV available. Beds: KQT. Meals: Continental plus. Fireplaces. Pool. CCs: Visa, MC, AE. Horseback riding, bicycling, hiking, canoeing.
"Wonderful honeymoon spot!"

Mira Monte Inn
69 Mount Desert St
Bar Harbor ME 04609
(207) 288-4263 (207) 846-4784
(winter)

Circa 1864. A gracious 18-room Victorian mansion, the Mira Monte

has been newly renovatd in the style of early Bar Harbor. It features period furnishings, pleasant common rooms, a library and wraparound porches. Situated on estate grounds, there are sweeping lawns, paved terraces, and many gardens. The inn was one of the ear-

liest of Bar Harbor's famous summer cottages.
Location: Five minute walk from the waterfront, shops and restaurants.
**Rates: $75-$105. May to October.
Innkeeper(s): Marian Burns.
11 Rooms. 11 Private Baths. TV in room. Beds: KQT. Meals: Full breakfast. Fireplaces. CCs: Visa, MC, AE. Swimming, outdoor games, tennis.
On our third year at your wonderful inn in beautiful Bar Harbor. I think I enjoy it more each year. A perfect place to stay in a perfect environment."

Stratford House Inn
45 Mount Desert St
Bar Harbor ME 04609
(207) 288-5189

Circa 1900. Lewis Roberts, Boston publisher of Louisa Mae Alcott's *Little Women* constructed a 10-bedroom

cottage for his guests. It was modeled on Shakespeare's birthplace in an English Tudor style with Jacobean period furnishings and motifs throughout. The rooms are all furnished with antiques such as four-poster mahogany and brass bow-bottom beds. The entrance and dining room are paneled in ornate black oak.
Rates: $55-$100. May to October
Innkeeper(s): Barbara & Norman Moulton.
10 Rooms. 8 Private Baths. Guest phone available. TV in room. Beds: KQ. Meals: Continental. Handicap access provided. Fireplaces. CCs: Visa, MC, AE. Swimming, boating, fishing, hiking, mountain climbing.
"Marvelous visit. Love this house. Great hospitality."

The Maples
16 Roberts Ave
Bar Harbor ME 04609
(207) 288-3443

Circa 1903. This summer cottage is a 15-room Victorian, tastefully re-

stored and filled with colonial and Victorian furnishings. The cottage annex next door, also a part of the inn, was built by Frank Whitmore, stationmaster for the Maine Central Railroad Ferry which operated from the town pier. The inn is within walking distance of shops, boutiques, crafts, and restaurants.
Rates: $60-$85. All year,
Innkeeper(s): Michele & Rick Suydam.
10 Rooms. 8 Private Baths. Guest phone available. Beds: DT. Meals: Continental plus. Fireplaces. CCs: Visa, MC. Horseback riding, hiking, bicycling, swimming, fishing, tennis.

Bar Mills

Royal Brewster
Bed & Breakfast
Box 307, Corner Rt 202 & 112
Bar Mills ME 04004
(207) 929-3012

Circa 1805. Master builder Joseph Woodman constructed this impres-

sive Federal house for Dr. Royal Brewster. There is an Adams-style carved mantle over the library fireplace, and a semi-flying staircase. Original sliding Indian shutters remain in many window casings. The hostess is from Manchester, England and the atmosphere is reminiscent of an English bed and breakfast where guests are treated as one of the family.
**Rates: $65. All year.
Innkeeper(s): Marian & Bill Parker.
4 Rooms. Guest phone available. TV available. Beds: DT. Meals: Full breakfast. Conference room. Fireplaces. CCs: Visa. Golf, beaches, amusement parks, mountains.
Seen in: *Portland, Maine, Evening Express.*

Bath

Fairhaven Inn
RR 2 Box 85, N Bath Rd
Bath ME 04530
(207) 443-4391

Circa 1790. With its views of the Kennebec River, this site was so attractive that Pimbleton Edgecomb

built his colonial house where a log cabin had previously stood. His descendants occupied it for the next 125 years. Antiques and country furniture fill the inn. Meadows and lawns, and woods of hemlock, birch and pine cover the inn's 27 acres.
Rates: $45-$70. All year.
Innkeeper(s): George & Sallie Pollard.
9 Rooms. 1 Private Baths. Guest phone available. TV available. Beds: QT. Meals: Full breakfast. Conference room. Fireplaces. Cross-country skiing, snowshoeing, beaches nearby.
"The Fairhaven is now marked in our book with a red star, definitely a place to remember and visit again."

Belfast

The Jeweled Turret Inn
16 Pearl St
Belfast ME 04915
(207) 338-2304

Circa 1898. This grand Victorian is named for the staircase that winds

up the turret, lighted by stained and leaded glass panels and jewel-like embellishments. It was built for attorney James Harriman. Dark pine beams adorn the ceiling of the den,

and the fireplace is constructed of bark and rocks from every state in the Union. Elegant antiques furnish the guest rooms of this National Register home.
Rates: $45-$65. All year.
Innkeeper(s): Carl & Cathy Heffentrager.
7 Rooms. 7 Private Baths. Guest phone available. Beds: QDT. Meals: Full breakfast. Fireplaces. Swimming, horseback riding, golf, tennis, deep sea fishing. Afternoon tea.
"This was the most fun we had in all of the places we've seen all week."

Bethel

Hammons House
Broad St
Bethel ME 04217
(207) 824-3170

Circa 1859. Built by Congressman David Hammons, this is an elegant

Greek Revival with a side-hall plan. William Upson converted the adjacent barn to a small summer theater in the early 1920s. Every day a full country breakfast is served. The inn is surrounded by porches, a patio, and beautiful perennial gardens.
Location: Centrally located on the village common.
Rates: $65-$75. All year.
4 Rooms. Guest phone available. TV available. Beds: DT. Meals: Full breakfast. Conference room. Fireplaces. CCs: Visa, MC.
"The charm of your home was a highlight of our New England tour."

Blue Hill

Blue Hill Farm Country Inn
Rt 15
Blue Hill ME 04614
(207) 374-5126

Circa 1832. This farm, situated at the foot of Blue Hill Mountain, spans 48 acres of woods and fields. There is a trout pond and brook on the property, and the restored barn holds a comfortable living room and dining area. Dinner may be arranged while making room reservations. The farm has been in continuous operation since 1840.
Rates: $53+. All year.
Innkeeper(s): Jim & Marcia Schatz.
14 Rooms. 7 Private Baths. Guest phone available. TV available. Beds: QD. Meals: Full breakfast.
"One of the most relaxing experiences ever - perfect beds, ultimate quiet."

Boothbay Harbor

Admiral's Quarters
105 Commercial St
Boothbay Harbor ME 04538
(207) 633-2474

Circa 1820. Set on a knoll looking out to the sea, the inn is composed of two sea captain's houses. Captain

Sawyer built his house with a prominent widow's watch, and it features rounded windows and views of Boothbay Harbor and the town. The inn is decorated in a Twenties style.
Location: On the point of Commercial, facing up the harbor.
Rates: $50-$70. All year.
Innkeeper(s): Jean E. & George Duffy.
8 Rooms. 8 Private Baths. TV in room. Beds: DT. Meals: Restaurant. CCs: Visa, MC. Boating, cruises, shopping.
"Unbelievable views. Jean, please book us for next year."

Boothbay

Kenniston Hill Inn
Rt 27
Boothbay ME 04537
(207) 633-2159

Circa 1786. Six fireplaces warm this white clapboard, center-chimney

colonial set amidst four acres of gardens and woodlands. It was built by David Kenniston, a prominent shipbuilder and landowner, and was occupied by the Kennistons for more than one hundred years. The parlor has a huge, open hearth fireplace. For several years the inn was used as a country club and later as a restaurant.
**Rates: $60-$80. April to Nov.
Innkeeper(s): Paul & Ellen Morissette.
8 Rooms. 8 Private Baths. Guest phone available. Beds: KQD. Meals: EP, restaurant. Fireplaces. CCs: Visa, MC. Golf, deep sea fishing, horseback riding, bicycling.

"England may be the home of the original bed and breakfast, but Kenniston Hill Inn is where it has been perfected!"

Bridgton

Noble House
PO Box 180
Bridgton ME 04009
(207) 647-3733

Circa 1903. This inn is tucked among three acres of old oaks and a

grove of pine trees, providing an estate-like view from all guest rooms. The elegant parlor contains a library, grand piano and hearth. Bed chambers are furnished with antiques, wicker and quilts. A hammock placed at the water's edge provides a view of the lake and Mt. Washington. The inn's lake frontage also allows for canoeing at sunset and swimming.
Location: Forty miles northwest of Portland.
Rates: $55-$75. All year.
Innkeeper(s): Jane & Dick Starets & family.
7 Rooms. 4 Private Baths. Guest phone available. TV available. Beds: QDT. Meals: Full breakfast. Jacuzzi. Fireplaces. Swimming, fishing, hiking, boating, canoe & paddle boats for guest.

Brunswick

Harraseeket Inn
See: Freeport, ME

The Bagley House
See: Freeport, ME

Camden

Blue Harbor House
67 Elm St, Rt 1
Camden ME 04843
(207) 236-3196

Circa 1835. James Richards, Camden's firt settler, built this Cape

house on a 1768 homesite. (The King granted him the land as the first person to fulfill all the conditions of a settler.) An 1806 carriage house has been refurbished to offer private suites. The bustling harbor is a five-minute walk.
Location: Camden Village.
Rates: $60-$100. All year.
Innkeeper(s): Bob & Connie Hood.
6 Rooms. 4 Private Baths. Beds: QD. Meals: Full breakfast. CCs: MC, AE. Sailing, fishing, swimming, hiking, horse-

back riding, golf, bikes. Member of Maine Innkeepers Association.

"Breakfast is as good a B&B experience as you can find. Bob entertains you and guides you thru Maine while you sample Connie's incredible recipes."

Broad Bay Inn & Gallery
See: Waldoboro, ME

Edgecombe-Coles House
64 High St, HCR 60 Box 3010
Camden ME 04843
(207) 236-2336

Circa 1830. Admiring the view of Pebnobscot Bay, Chicago lawyer

Chauncey Keep built this house on the foundation of a sea captain's house. By 1900, his 22-room cottage was too small and he built a 50-room mansion up the hill, retaining this as a guest house. Country antiques set the tone and many rooms command a spectacular ocean view.
Location: North of Camden Harbor on Highway 1.
Rates: $60-$120. All year.
Innkeeper(s): Terry & Louise Price.
6 Rooms. 6 Private Baths. Guest phone available. TV in room. Beds: KQDT. Meals: Full breakfast. Fireplaces. CCs: Visa, MC, AE, DC. Skiing, mountain climbing, fishing, sailing, hiking, tennis, golf.

"A beautiful view, beautiful decor and a lovely hostess make this a very special place." Shelby Hodge, *Houston Post.*

Hawthorne Inn
9 High St
Camden ME 04843
(207) 236-8842

Circa 1890. This yellow and white, towered Victorian sits on a green lawn set against a backdrop of woods near the harbor. The spacious grounds offer many water views. A carriage house boasts private decks, jacuzzis and apartments, and there are additional rooms in the main house. The English hostess serves afternoon tea and biscuits in the drawing room.
Rates: $55-$125. All year.
Innkeeper(s): Pauline & Brad Staub.

11 Rooms. 8 Private Baths. Guest phone available. TV in room. Beds: QTC. Meals: Full breakfast. Jacuzzi. Fireplaces. CCs: Visa, MC. Sailing, hiking, boating, outdoor theater.

Maine Stay Bed & Breakfast
22 High St
Camden ME 04843
(207) 236-9636

Circa 1813. One of Camden's treasured colonials, the Maine Stay is depicted in a painting *1840, Camden* at the Farnsworth Museum in Rockland, Maine. Decorated with period furnishings the inn has a large country dining room with adjoining deck. Guest rooms and parlors are spacious, and it is a five-minute walk to the center of the village and the Camden Harbor. The innkeeper is president of the Bed & Breakfast Society of Camden.
Rates: $68-$104. April - Nov.
Innkeeper(s): Jacques & Carol Gagnon.
8 Rooms. Guest phone available. TV in room. Beds: QDT. Meals: Full breakfast. Conference room. Fireplaces. Sailing, windsurfing, skiing, tennis, golf, hiking, swimming.

Castine

The Manor
Battle Ave, PO Box 276
Castine ME 04421
(207) 326-4861

Circa 1895. Built for Commodore Fuller of the New York Yacht Club

this is a shingle-style cottage of grand proportions. Traditionally the Club begins its annual summer cruise in Castine. On five acres of lawns and gardens, the inn is reminiscent of magnificent summer holidays at the turn of the century. Public rooms include the Hunting Room, the Billiard Room, and the Library.

Rates: $55-$95.
Innkeeper(s): Paul & Sara Brouillard.
Meals: Continental. Cross-country skiing, golf, tennis, charter sailing, hiking.
"Beautiful and elegant - a very special place. We will return!! With friends!"

Center Lovell

Center Lovell Inn
Rt 5
Center Lovell ME 04016
(207) 925-1575

Circa 1805. A wraparound porch connects the original farmhouse

with a Cape-style annex added in 1830. Governor of Florida, Eckley Stearns, transformed this house into its present Mississippi steamboat style with the addition of a mansard roof and third floor. Acclaimed by *Architectural Digest*, the inn overlooks Kezar Lake Valley with a panoramic view of the White Mountains.
Location: Western Maine mountains along the New Hampshire border.
Rates: $42-$145. May to October.
Innkeeper(s): Bil & Susie Mosca.
11 Rooms. 7 Private Baths. Guest phone available. TV available. Beds: DT. Meals: Full breakfast, EP, gourmet. Jacuzzi. Sauna. Conference room. Fireplaces. Pool. CCs: Visa, MC, AE. Horseback riding, golf, swimming, hiking, canoeing, kayaking.
Seen in: *New York Magazine, Architectural Digest.*
"Finest food I have ever eaten in 40 states and 30 countries, located in one of the most beautiful areas anywhere."

Clark Island

Craignair Inn
Clark Island Rd
Clark Island ME 04859
(207) 594-7644

Circa 1930. Craignair originally was built to house stonecutters working in nearby granite quarries.

Overlooking the docks of the Clark Island Quarry, where granite schooners once were loaded, this roomy, three-story inn is tastefully decorated with local antiques.
Rates: $60-$72. July to Sept.
Innkeeper(s): Norman & Terry Smith.
20 Rooms. 5 Private Baths. Guest phone available. Beds: DTC. Meals: Full breakfast, gourmet. CCs: Visa, MC. Tennis, horseback riding, sailing.
"We thoroughly enjoyed our stay with you. Your location is lovely and private. Your dining room and service and food were all 5 star!"

Damariscotta

The Brannon Bunker
PO Box 045, HCR 64
Damariscotta ME 04543
(207) 563-5941

Circa 1820. This Cape-style house has been a home to many generations of Maine residents, one of whom was captain of a ship that sailed to the Arctic. During the Twenties, the barn served as a dance hall. Later, it was converted into comfortable guest rooms.
Rates: $40-$55. All year.
Innkeeper(s): Joe & Jeanne Hovance.
8 Rooms. 4 Private Baths. Guest phone available. TV available. Beds: QTC. Meals: Continental plus. Fireplaces. CCs: Visa, MC.
"Wonderful beds, your gracious hospitality and the very best muffins anywhere made our stay a memorable one."

Dennysville

Lincoln House Country Inn
Rts 1 & 86
Dennysville ME 04628
(207) 726-3953

Circa 1787. Theodore Lincoln, ancestor of Abraham Lincoln and son of Benjamin Lincoln, who accepted

the sword of surrender from Cornwallis after the American

Revolution, built this house. The four-square colonial looks out to the Dennys River and its salmon pools. John James Audubon stayed here on his way to Labrador, and loved the house and family so much that he named the Lincoln Sparrow in their honor.
Rates: $58. May to October.
Innkeeper(s): Mary & Jerry Haggerty.
6 Rooms. Guest phone available. Beds: DT. Meals: MAP, restaurant. Conference room. Fireplaces. CCs: Visa, MC, AE. Bird watching, hiking, fishing, boating, cross-country skiing.

East Boothbay

Linekin Village Bed & Breakfast
Ocean Point Rd, Rt 96
East Boothbay ME 04544
(207) 633-3681

Circa 1882. Located on Linekin Bay, this center-chimney Cape was expanded with a second floor in 1900. A porch wraps around the house and old rocking chairs provide a restful site overlooking the garden. The inn has its own pier for fishing and boating.
Location: On Linekin Bay.
**Rates: $35-$45. May to October.
Innkeeper(s): Larry T. Cooley.
3 Rooms. Guest phone available. Beds: DT. Meals: Full breakfast. Swimming, fishing, boating, hiking.

"Very relaxing, just what I needed. Charming and cheap."

Eastport

Artists Retreat
29 Washington St
Eastport ME 04631
(207) 853-4239

Circa 1846. A stately Victorian house with gracious, elegant interiors, the inn is furnished with the original ornately carved, marble-topped furniture and knicknacks. Victoriana buffs will enjoy the 19-century atmosphere of this island city.
Rates: $35-$45. All year.
Innkeeper(s): Joyce Weber.
5 Rooms. Guest phone available. TV available. Beds: QT. Meals: Full breakfast Conference room. CCs: Visa, MC.

Weston House
26 Boynton Street
Eastport ME 04631
(207) 853-2907

Circa 1810. Jonathan Weston, an 1802 graduate of Harvard, built this

Federal-style house on a hill overlooking Passamaquoddy Bay. John Audubon stayed here as a guest of the Westons while awaiting passage to Labrador in 1833.
Rates: $35-$50. All year.
Innkeeper(s): John & Jett Peterson.
5 Rooms. Guest phone in room. TV in room. Beds: KQT. Meals: Full breakfast. Conference room. Fishing, golf, hiking, bicycling, boating.

Eliot

High Meadows Bed & Breakfast
Rt 101
Eliot ME 03903
(207) 439-0590

Circa 1736. A ship's captain built this house now filled with remembrances of colonial days. At

one point, it was raised and a floor added underneath, so the upstairs is older than the downstairs. It is convenient to factory outlets, great dining, and historic Portsmouth's beaches and theater.
Rates: $50-$60. Jan. to April.
Innkeeper(s): Elaine Raymond.
5 Rooms. 3 Private Baths. Guest phone available. TV available. Beds: TW. Meals: Continental plus. Conference room. Fireplaces. Golf, tennis, whale watching.

"High Meadows was the highlight of our trip."

Freeport

Harraseeket Inn
162 Main St
Freeport ME 04032
(207) 865-9377

Circa 1850. The tavern and drawing room of this inn are decorated in

the Federal style. Guest rooms are furnished with antiques and half-canopied beds, and some have whirlpools and fireplaces. The L.L. Bean store is two blocks away, and other outlet stores nearby are Ralph Lauren, Laura Ashley and Anne Klein.
**Rates: $60-$190. All year.
Innkeeper(s): Paul & Nancy Gray.
54 Rooms. 54 Private Baths. Guest phone in room. TV in room. Beds: KQCD. Meals: EP, Restaurant, Gourmet. Jacuzzi. Handicap access provided. Conference room. Fireplaces. CCs: All. Golf, sailing, fishing.
Seen in: *Village Bed & Breakfast.*

Isaac Randall House
Independence Drive
Freeport ME 04032
(207) 865-9295

Circa 1823. Isaac Randall's Federal-style farmhouse was once a dairy farm and a stop on the Under-

ground Railway for slaves escaping into Canada. Randall was a descendant of John Alden and Priscilla Mullins of the *Mayflower*. Longfellow immortalized their romance in *The Courtship of Miles Standish.*
Rates: $50-$85. May to Oct. 31.
Innkeeper(s): Jim & Glynrose Friedlander.

8 Rooms. 6 Private Baths. Guest phone available. TV in room. Beds: KQC. Meals: Full breakfast. Jacuzzi. Handicap access provided. Conference room. Fireplaces. Cross country skiing, hiking.

"Enchanted to find ourselves surrounded by all your charming antiques and beautiful furnishings."

The Bagley House
RR 3 Box 269C
Freeport ME 04032
(207) 865-6566

Circa 1772. Six acres of fields and woods surround the Bagley House

that was once an inn, a store, and a schoolhouse. Guest rooms are decorated with colonial furnishings and hand-sewn Maine quilts, and many boast working fireplaces. For breakfast, guests gather in the country kitchen in front of a huge brick fireplace and beehive oven.
Location: Route 136, Durham.
Rates: $70-$80. All year.
Innkeeper(s): Sigurd A. Knudsen, Jr.
5 Rooms. 2 Private Baths. Guest phone available. Beds: QTF. Meals: Full breakfast. Conference room. Fireplaces. CCs: Visa, MC, AE. Cross country skiing, hiking, croquet.

"I had the good fortune to stumble on the Bagley House. The rooms are well appointed and the new innkeeper is as charming a host as you'll find."

Greenville

Greenville Inn
PO Box 1194
Greenville ME 04441
(207) 695-2206

Circa 1895. The Greenville Inn sits on a hill a block from town and the shoreline of Moosehead Lake, the largest lake completely contained in any one state. A wealthy lumbering family built the house and ten years were needed to complete the cherry and mahogany paneling. There are six fireplaces with carved mantels

and mosaics. From the dining room guests have an excellent water view.
Location: Moosehead Lake.
Rates: $38-$65. All year.
Innkeeper(s): The Schnetzer's.
14 Rooms. 7 Private Baths. Guest phone available. TV available. Beds: KQTC. Meals: EP, Full, Restaurant, Gourmet. Handicap access provided. Conference room. Fireplaces. CCs: Visa, MC. Cross country & downhill skiing, boating, hunting, fishing.
Seen in: *Maine Times.*

Hulls Cove

Inn at Canoe Point
Rt 3 Box 216A
Hulls Cove ME 04644
(207) 288-9511

Circa 1889. This oceanfront inn has served as a summer residence for

several generations of families escaping city heat. Guests are treated to the gracious hospitality of the past, surrounded by the ocean and pine forests. They can relax on the deck overlooking Frenchman's Bay, or pursue outdoor activities in the National Park.
Rates: $90-$165. All year.
Innkeeper(s): Don Johnson.
6 Rooms. 4 Private Baths. Guest phone available. TV available. Beds: KQTF. Meals: Full breakfast. Conference room. Fireplaces.
Seen in: *Portland Monthly Magazine.*

Kennebunkport

1802 House
Box 646A Locke St
Kennebunkport ME 04046
(207) 967-5632

Circa 1802. Many of the guest rooms in 1802 House possess fireplaces and all are decorated with colonial wallpapers and antiques such as four-poster beds. The ringing of a ship's bell announces breakfast and guests dine overlooking a golf course next to the inn. Water sports, fall foliage, cross-country skiing and the Seashore Trolley Museum are all popular attractions.
**Rates: $74-$94. All year.
Innkeeper(s): Sal & Pat Ledda.
8 Rooms. 8 Private Baths. TV available. Beds: QTD. Meals: Full breakfast. Fireplaces. CCs: Visa, MC, AE. Golf, tennis, cross country skiing, hiking, boating.

Captain Lord Mansion
Pleasant & Green, PO Box 800
Kennebunkport ME 04046
(207) 967-3141

Circa 1812. In the National Register, the Captain Lord Mansion was built during the War of 1812,

and is one of the finest examples of Federal architecture on the coast of Maine. A four-story spiral staircase winds up to the cupola where one can view the town and the Kennebunk River and Yacht Club. At one time, there was a street entrance so villagers could climb the stairs to view inbound ships without bothering the family. There are 13 rooms with fireplaces and a romantic cottage with a fireplace in the bathroom.
Rates: $59-$79. All year.
Innkeeper(s): Bev Davis & Rick Litchfield.
18 Rooms. 18 Private Baths. Guest phone available. Beds: K Meals: Full breakfast. Jacuzzi. Conference room.

Fireplaces. CCs: Visa, MC, DS. Cross country skiing, cruises, sailing, beaches Seen in: *AAA, Colonial Homes, Yankee, New England Get Aways.*

"A showcase of elegant architecture, with lovely remembrances of the past. Meticulously clean and splendidly appointed. It's a shame to have to leave."

Harbor Inn
PO Box 538A
Kennebunkport ME 04046
(207) 967-2074

Circa 1903. Tucked behind a white iron Victorian fence is the Harbor

Inn. A yellow canopy covers the stairs leading to the veranda, from which you can hear the quiet purring of fishing boats or smell the fresh, sea air. Guest rooms are furnished with canopied or four-poster beds, period lighting, oriental rugs, and antique coverlets. The inn's kitchen has blue iris stained-glass windows and an old wood stove set on a brick hearth. Just past the inn, where the Kennebunk River runs to the sea, are Spouting Rock and Blowing Cave.
Rates: $65-$135. May 15-Dec. 15.
Innkeeper(s): Charlotte & Bill Massmann.
8 Rooms. 8 Private Baths. Beds: D. Meals: Full breakfast. Fireplaces. Golf, tennis, biking, boating, fishing.
"Everything is beautifully done. It's the best we've ever been to."

Inn at Harbor Head
RR 2 Box 1180
Kennebunkport ME 04046
(207) 967-5564

Circa 1898. This rambling, shingled saltwater farmhouse is on the water in historic Cape Porpoise - the quiet side of Kennebunkport. The inn has been elegantly restored, and offers outstanding views of the harbor, ocean and islands. Ancient apple

trees shield it from the road and a back terrace leads down to the seashore.
Rates: $85-$140. All year.
Innkeeper(s): Joan & David Sutter.
4 Rooms. 4 Private Baths. Guest phone available. Beds: KQT. Meals: Gourmet. CCs: Visa, MC. Swimming.
Seen in: *The Boston Globe.*
"Your lovely home is our image of what a New England B&B should be. Unbelievably perfect! So glad we found you."

Inn on South Street
PO Box 478A, South St
Kennebunkport ME 04046
(207) 967-5151

Circa 1807. Built in the Greek Revival style, the inn now stands on a quiet side street. It was towed here

by oxen from its original location on the village green, because a wealthy citizen complained that it was cutting off her river view. The inn boasts a handsome 'good-morning' staircase, original pine-plank floors, hand-planed wainscoting and an old-fashioned herb garden.
Innkeeper(s): Jacques & Eva Downs.
3 Rooms. 3 Private Baths. Guest phone in room. Beds: QT. Meals: Full breakfast. Fireplaces. CCs: AE. Water sports, hiking, bicycling, walking.
Seen in: *Summertime.*
"Superb hospitality. We were delighted by the atmosphere and your thoughtfulness."

Kylemere House 1818
South Street, PO Box 1333
Kennebunkport ME 04046
(207) 967-2780

Circa 1818. Located in Maine's largest historic district, Kylemere House was built by Daniel Walker, descendant of an original Kennebunkport family. In 1895, Maine artist and architect Abbot Graves purchased the property and used the barn as his studio. He named the house Crosstrees for the husband and wife maple trees planted on either side of the front door. Today only one maple remains at the entrance to this center-chimney colonial.
Rates: $60-$85. May to Dec.
Innkeeper(s): Mary & Bill Kyle.
5 Rooms. 3 Private Baths. Guest phone available. Beds: KQT. Meals: Full breakfast. CCs: AE.
Seen in: *Boston Globe.*
"Beautiful inn. Outstanding hospitality. Thanks for drying our sneakers, fixing our bikes. You are all a lot of fun!"

Maine Stay Inn and Cottages
Maine St, PO Box 500A
Kennebunkport ME 04046
(207) 967-2117

Circa 1860. In the National Register, this is a square-block

Italianate contoured in a low hip-roof design. Later additions of the Queen Anne period include a suspended spiral staircase, crystal windows, ornately carved mantels and moldings, bay windows and porches. A sea captain built the handsome cupola that became a favorite spot for making taffy and in the Twenties, a place from which to spot offshore rumrunners. Guests enjoy afternoon tea with stories of the Maine Stay's heritage.
Location: In the Kennebunkport National Historic District.
Rates: $68-$104. April to Nov.
Innkeeper(s): Jacques & Carol Gagnon.
17 Rooms. 17 Private Baths. Guest phone available. TV available. Beds: QC. Meals: EP or B&B. Handicap access provided. Conference room. CCs: Visa, MC, AE.
"Beautifully decorated home. Clean, clean accommodations, cute cottages."

Old Fort Inn

Old Fort Ave, PO Box M 24
Kennebunkport ME 04046
(207) 967-5353

Circa 1880. The Old Fort Inn is a luxurious mini-resort nestled in a secluded setting with an English

garden. It has a tennis court, fresh water swimming pool and shuffleboard. Bikes are also available. Country furniture, primitives, and china are featured in an antique shop on the property. The ocean is just a block away.
Rates: $86-$185. April-Oct.
Innkeeper(s): Sheila & David Aldrich.
16 Rooms. 16 Private Baths. Guest phone available. Beds: KQT. Meals: Full breakfast. Jacuzzi. CCs: Visa, MC, AE, DS. Bicycling, swimming, golf.
Seen in: *Country Inns.*

"My husband and I have been spending the last two weeks in August at the Old Fort Inn for years. It combines for us a rich variety of what we feel a relaxing vacation should be."

Port Gallery Inn

PO Box 1367
Kennebunkport ME 04046
(207) 967-3728

Circa 1891. This Victorian mansion was given to Captain Titcomb,

builder of the largest ships on the Kennebunk River. Kennebunkport, summer home of the rich and famous, is in the National Register of Historical Places with 26 different architectural styles. The inn features

a Marine Art Gallery specializing in paintings of old seafaring days.
Location: Corner of Spring & Main Streets.
**Rates: $98-$149. All year.
Innkeeper(s): Francis & Lucy Morphy.
7 Rooms. 7 Private Baths. Guest phone in room. TV in room. Beds: QD. Meals: Continental. CCs: Visa, MC, DC. Golf, tennis, hiking, canoeing, bicycling.
Seen in: *The Globe Pequot Press.*

Sundial Inn

PO Box 1147
Kennebunkport ME 04043
(207) 967-3850

Circa 1891. This yellow and white clapboard house faces the ocean and

Kennebunk Beach. The inn is decorated with country Victorian antiques, and some rooms have a whirlpool. An elevator makes for easy access. Beachcombing for sand dollars, sea shells and sea urchins is a popular pastime, along with enjoying splendid views from the porch rockers and guest rooms.
Location: Beach Avenue #49.
Rates: $45-$160. All year.
Innkeeper(s): Pat & Larry Kenny.
34 Rooms. 34 Private Baths. Guest phone in room. TV in room. Beds: QT. Meals: Full breakfast. Jacuzzi. Handicap access provided. Conference room. Fireplaces. CCs: Visa, MC, AE, DC. Member Maine Innkeeper Association.,

" My time on your porch watching the sea was the best part of my vacation. Whenever I am stressed I wander back in my mind to a day at the Sundial where I found such inner peace."

The White Barn Inn

Beach Street, RR 3 Box 387
Kennebunkport ME 04046
(207) 967-2321

Circa 1840. Over the past 150 years, various owners have added onto this farmhouse and its signature white barn. Each addition to the rambling grey structure has been distinctive. Stately Queen Anne furnishings, soft down sofas, bright floral prints, and country tweeds decorate the suites. There are four-posters and whirlpool tubs

in some rooms. Candlelight dining is popular in the three-story barn.
Location: South of Portland 1/2 hour, I-95 1-1/2 hour North of Boston.
**Rates: $90-$170. All year.
Innkeeper(s): Laurie Bongiorno & Carol Hackett.
24 Rooms. 24 Private Baths. Guest phone available. TV available. Beds: KQTC. Meals: MAP, Continental Plus, Full, Rest. Jacuzzi. Conference room. Fireplaces. CCs: Visa, MC, AE. Golf, tennis, downhill skiing, beach.

"It is clear you are in the business of very fine hospitality and we appreciated the warm welcome we received from you and your staff."

Welby Inn

Ocean Avenue, PO Box 774
Kennebunkport ME 04046
(207) 967-4655

Circa 1900. The Welby Inn possesses a gambrel-style roof and a large

common room with a Victorian motif. The innkeeper's watercolors of flowers and her floral arrangements decorate the interiors. Breakfast is served in the dining room or on the breakfast roof overlooking the garden. It is a five-minute walk to the ocean, galleries and fine restaurants.
Rates: $55-$75. All year.
Innkeeper(s): David Knox & Betsy Rogers-Knox.
7 Rooms. 5 Private Baths. Guest phone available. Beds: QTF. Meals: Full breakfast. Conference room. CCs: AE. Golf, tennis, bicycling, fishing, whale watching.

"I'm glad we found this place before Gourmet Magazine discovers it and the rates increase!"

Naples

The Inn at Long Lake
Lake House Road, PO 806
Naples ME 04055
(207) 693-6226

Circa 1906. This recently reopened inn housed the overflow guests from the Lake House Resort 80 years ago,

when guests traveled on the Oxford-Cumberland Canal. Each room is named for a historic canal boat and is decorated to match. Stephen and Leslie once owned a bath shop so they've been creative with the 16 brand new ones they've installed.
Rates: $59-$69. All year.
Innkeeper(s): Stephen & Leslie Vlachos.
16 Rooms. 16 Private Baths. Guest phone available. TV in room. Beds: QT. Meals: Continental plus. Fireplaces. CCs: Visa, MC, AE. Golf, waterskiing, boating, bicycling, cross country skiing.
"Convenient location, tastefully done and the prettiest inn I've ever stayed in."

New Harbor

Gosnold Arms
Northside Road, Rt 32
New Harbor ME 04554
(207) 677-3727

Circa 1870. This is a remodeled, sparkling-white saltwater farmhouse with a steamboat wharf and a glassed-in dining porch overlooking the water. A Smith College dorm mother assembled several cottages in addition to the rooms in the house, creating a congenial family atmosphere. One cottage is a rustic pilot house picked up, helm and all, off a steamboat and nestled bayside.

Rates: $42-$89. June 13-Sept.2.
Innkeeper(s): The Phinney family.

26 Rooms. 19 Private Baths. Guest phone available. Beds: QTCD. Meals: Full breakfast. Conference room. Fireplaces. CCs: Visa, MC.
Seen in: *New York*.

Newcastle

The Newcastle Inn
River Road
Newcastle ME 04553
(207) 563-5685

Circa 1860. The Newcastle Inn is a Federal-style colonial that has been

an inn since the early 1920s. Located on the Damariscotta River, the neighbors just behind the inn are 97 sailboats. Honeymooners like the room with the old-fashioned canopy bed, and many rooms look out over the water and the town. Breakfast consists of four courses and there is a five-course dinner.
Location: Tidal Damariscotta River.
Rates: $60-$80. All year.
Innkeeper(s): Ted & Chris Sprague.
15 Rooms. 15 Private Baths. Guest phone available. Beds: KQT. Meals: Full breakfast. Fireplaces. CCs: Visa, MC. Cross country skiing, golf, bicycling, swimming, fishing.
Seen in: *Yankee Magazine, Coastal Journal, The Weekly Courier.*
"Standing ovation for the food, atmosphere and innkeepers!"

Portland

Harraseeket Inn
See: Freeport, ME

Isaac Randall House
See: Freeport, ME

Noble House
See: Bridgton, ME

Royal Brewster B&B
See: Bar Mills, ME

The Bagley House
See: Freeport, ME

The Inn at Long Lake
See: Naples, ME

Searsport

Homeport Inn
Rt 1, East Main St
Searsport ME 04974
(207) 548-2259

Circa 1862. Captain Joshua Nickels built this home on Penobscot Bay. On top of the two-story house is a

widow's walk. A scalloped picket fence frames the property. Fine antiques, black marble fireplaces, a collection of grandfather clocks and elaborate ceiling medallions add to the atmosphere.
**Rates: $50-$65.
Innkeeper(s): Dr. & Mrs. F. George Johnson.
10 Rooms. 6 Private Baths. Guest phone available. TV available. Beds: QT. Meals: Full breakfast. English Pub. Handicap access provided. Fireplaces. CCs: Visa, MC, AE, DC. Golf, sailing, cruises, bicycle rentals.

McGilvery House
PO Box 588
Searsport ME 04974
(207) 548-6289

Circa 1860. A prominent sea captain, William McGilvery, built this

handsome estate in the mansard domestic style with a soaring center-gambrel gable. Guest rooms provide excellent views of Penobscot Bay, and some feature ornate marble fireplaces.

**Rates: $45. All year.
Innkeeper(s): Sue Omness & Stephen Stier.
3 Rooms. 3 Private Baths. Guest phone available. Beds: Q. Meals: Full breakfast. Fireplaces. Boating, museums.
Seen in: *The Courier-Gazette.*

"It was a thrill being in your lovely home. Your personal touches are evident everywhere. The breakfasts are tops. We'll be back."

Southwest Harbor

Lindenwood Inn
PO Box 1328
Southwest Harbor ME 04679
(207) 244-5335

Circa 1906. Sea Captain Mills named his home The Lindens after stately linden trees that line the front lawn. The cypress paneling retains its original finish and adorns the entrance and dining room. Gull's Nest and Casablanca are among the rooms overlooking the harbor.
Location: Mt. Desert Island.
Rates: $35-$75. All year.
Innkeeper(s): T. Gardiner, Marilyn & Matthew Brower.
7 Rooms. 3 Private Baths. Guest phone available. TV available. Beds: QTD. Meals: Full breakfast. Fireplaces. Boating, hiking, biking, golf, swimming, horse back riding.
"We had a lovely stay at your inn. Breakfast, room and hospitality were all first rate. You made us feel like a special friend instead of a paying guest."

The Island House
Box 1006
Southwest Harbor ME 04679
(207) 244-5180

Circa 1830. The first guests arrived at Deacon Clark's door as early as 1832. Steamboat service from Boston began in the 1850s and The Island House became a popular summer hotel. Among guests was Ralph Waldo Emerson. In 1902 the hotel was taken down and rebuilt as two separate homes with much of the

woodwork from the original building.
Location: Mount Desert Island (Acadia National Park).
Rates: $50-$60. May to Oct. 31.
Innkeeper(s): Ann R. Gill.
4 Rooms. 1 Private Baths. Guest phone available. TV available. Beds: QW. Meals: Continental plus. Fireplaces. Horse back riding, swimming, canoeing, sailing, bicycling. Piano.
"Island House is a delight from the moment one enters the door! We loved the thoughtful extras. You've made our vacation very special!"

The Kingsleigh Inn
PO Box 1426
Southwest Harbor ME 04679
(207) 244-5302

Circa 1904. This seaside village has been home to fishermen and boat-builders for generations. After stop-

ping by the inn's country kitchen for lemonade, guests gravitate to the flower-filled veranda to watch the harbor waters. Waverly wall coverings and fabrics decorate the rooms. Book the turret suite with its spectacular harbor views and four-poster bed.
Rates: $35-$95. May to Nov. 1.
Innkeeper(s): Jim & Kathy King.
7 Rooms. 5 Private Baths. Guest phone available. Beds: Q. Meals: Full breakfast. Fireplaces. Horseback riding, canoeing, hiking, swimming, sailing.
"Very romantic and wonderfully decorated. We'll always treasure our stay with you."

Surry

Surry Inn
PO Box 25
Surry ME 04684
(207) 667-5091

Circa 1834. Surry inn was originally built for passengers traveling by steamship. The driveway is called Stagecoach Lane because the steamboat met the stage at the inn's private beach in Contention Cove. The inn features stenciled walls and New England decor and is noted for excellent dinners.
Rates: $42-$58. All year.
Innkeeper(s): Peter Krinsky.
13 Rooms. 11 Private Baths. Guest phone available. TV available. Beds: QT. Handicap access provided. Conference room. Fireplaces. CCs: Visa, MC. Boating, swimming, croquet.
"Wonderful food! Peaceful, quiet and comfortable."

Waldoboro

Broad Bay Inn & Gallery
Main Street, PO Box 607
Waldoboro ME 04572
(207) 832-6668

Circa 1905. This colonial inn lies in the heart of an unspoiled coastal vil-

lage. There are Victorian furnishings throughout and some guest rooms have canopy beds. Afternoon tea is served on the deck. A barn on the property is a gallery and often the site of art workshops.
**Rates: $35-$65. All year.
Innkeeper(s): Jim & Libby Hopkins.
4 Rooms. 1 Private Baths. Guest phone available. TV available. Beds: FT. Meals: Full breakfast, Restaurant. Fireplaces. CCs: Visa, MC. Swimming, fishing, cross country skiing, sleigh rides.
"Breakfast was so special - I ran to get my camera. Why, there were even flowers on my plate."

Tide Watch Inn

PO Box 94, Pine St
Waldoboro ME 04572
(207) 832-4987

Circa 1850. Located on the waterfront, the Tide Watch is a twin or mirror colonial erected by

brothers who wished to live side by side. The first five-masted schooners were built in front of the house, and for a time the inn was a boarding house for the shipbuilders.
Rates: $30-$40. All year.
Innkeeper(s): Mel & Cathy Hanson.
4 Rooms. 1 Private Baths. Guest phone available. TV available. Beds: QTF. Meals: Full breakfast. CCs: Visa, MC, AE, DC. Boating, cross country & downhill skiing,

"*Sumptuous breakfasts. We can't wait to come back.*"

Weld

Kawanhee Inn Lakeside Lodge

Lake Webb
Weld ME 04285
(207) 585-2243 778-4306, winter.

Circa 1930. This country inn sits on a hill in the midst of woods, overlooking Lake Webb and the mountains beyond. Guest rooms are located in the lodge or in several lakefront cottages. The lodge fireplace is so large it can accommodate four-foot-long logs. A white sandy beach is popular for sunning and swimming.
Rates: $47 & up.
Innkeeper(s): Jeff & Marti Strunk & Sturges Butler.
25 Rooms. 11 Private Baths. CCs: Visa, MC.
Seen in: *New England Monthly*.

Wiscasset

The Squire Tarbox Inn

RR 2 Box 620
Wiscasset ME 04578
(207) 882-7693

Circa 1765. North of Bath, deep into the country and woods, Squire

Tarbox built his rambling farmhouse around a building originally constructed in 1763. Today, the rooms are warm and comfortable in the inn and in the remodeled hayloft. The innkeepers raise Nubian goats, all photogenic, that have become part of the entertainment (milking and goat cheese). A house-party atmosphere pervades the inn.
Location: Route 144, 8-1/2 miles on Westport Island.
**Rates: $40-$150. May to Oct.
Innkeeper(s): Bill & Karen Mitman.
11 Rooms. 11 Private Baths. Guest phone available. Beds: KQTD. Meals: MAP. Continental breakfast. Fireplaces. CCs: Visa, MC, AE. Sailing, fishing, sand dunes, ocean.
Seen in: *Washington Post, Hartford Courant.*

"*Your hospitality was warm, friendly, well-managed and quite genuine. That's a rarity, and it's just the kind we feel best with.*"

York Harbor

York Harbor Inn

Rt 1A Box 573
York Harbor ME 03911
(207) 363-5119

Circa 1637. The core building of the York Harbor Inn is a small log cabin constructed on the Isles of Shoals. It was moved and reassembled at this dramatic location overlooking the entrance to York Harbor, and is now a gathering room with a handsome stone fireplace. There is an English-style

pub in the cellar of the inn with booths made from horse stalls.
**Rates: $35-$55. All year.
Innkeeper(s): Joe & Garry Dominguez.
32 Rooms. 27 Private Baths. Guest phone available. TV available. Beds: Q. Meals: Full breakfast, Gourmet,Restaurant. Jacuzzi. Handicap access provided. Conference room. Fireplaces. CCs: Visa, MC, AE. Golf, tennis, boating, fishing, theater.
Seen in: *New York Times, Down East.*

"*It's hard to decide where to stay when you're paging through a book of country inns. This time we chose well.*"

York

Dockside Guest Quarters

PO Box 205, Harris Island
York ME 03909
(207) 363-2868 (207) 363-4800 (Dining)

Circa 1885. Harris Island, the site of Dockside and its companion marina, was the smallpox quaran-

tine area for York in 1632. This Maine house is typical of the large, cottage-style New England summer home. It is on a peninsula overlooking York Harbor and the ocean. There are antiques of museum quality. Guest accommodations are in the main house and several newer cottages.
Location: Harris Island, Maine Rt. 103
**Rates: $44-$105. May to October.
Innkeeper(s): The Lusty Family.
22 Rooms. 20 Private Baths. Guest phone available. TV available. Beds: KQTC. Meals: AP, EP, continental plus. Handicap access provided. Conference room. Fireplaces. CCs: Visa, MC. Deep sea fishing, tennis, golf.
Seen in: *Boston Globe.*

"*We've been back many years. All in all, it's a paradise for us, the scenery, location, maintenance, living quarters, etc.*"

Maryland

Annapolis

Gibson's Lodging
110-114 Prince George St
Annapolis MD 21401
(301) 268-5555
Circa 1786. This Georgian house in the heart of the Annapolis Historic

District was built on the site of the Old Courthouse, circa 1680. Two historic houses make up the inn and there is an annex built in 1988. All the rooms, old and new are furnished with antiques. Only a few yards away is the City Dock Harbor and within two blocks is the Naval Academy visitor's gate.
Rates: $55-$120. All year.
Innkeeper(s): Eileen Fitzgerald.
20 Rooms. 7 Private Baths. Guest phone in room. TV in room. Beds: QT. Meals: Continental. Conference room. Fireplaces. CCs: Visa, MC, AE.

Prince George Inn
232 Prince George St
Annapolis MD 21401
(301) 263-6418
Circa 1884. The Prince George Inn is a three-story brick townhouse comfortably furnished with an emphasis on Victorian decor. The guest parlor, breakfast room, porch and courtyard offer areas for relaxing. In the heart of the colonial city, the inn is near restaurants, museums, shops,

and the City Dock. The Naval Academy is two blocks away. Your hostess operates a walking-tour service.
Location: Historic District of Annapolis.
**Rates: $65. All year.
Innkeeper(s): Bill & Norma Grovermann.
4 Rooms. Guest phone available. TV available. Beds: QDT. Meals: Continental plus. Fireplaces. CCs: MC. Sailing, walking tours.

Baltimore

Admiral Fell Inn
888 S Broadway
Baltimore MD 21231
(301) 522-7377
Circa 1850. This inn is three buildings, the oldest of which is a red brick, three-story columned structure with a Victorian facade. At one time the complex served as a boarding house for sailors and a vinegar bottling plant. Each room is tastefully furnished with period pieces.
**Rates: $90-$135. All year.
Innkeeper(s): Jim Widman.
40 Rooms. 40 Private Baths. Guest phone in room. TV in room. Beds: K. Meals: Full breakfast. Jacuzzi. Handicap access provided. Conference room. CCs: Visa, MC, AE. Boating, shopping.

Betsy's Bed & Breakfast
1428 Park Ave
Baltimore MD 21217
(301) 383-1274
Circa 1895. This four-story townhouse with 13-foot ceilings features many elegant architectural touches. The hallway floor is laid in alternating strips of oak and walnut and there are six carved marble fireplaces. The most elaborate,

carved in fruit designs, is in the dining room. The inn is decorated with handsome brass rubbings made by the owner during a stay in England.
Location: Downtown, about 1.5 miles north of Inner Harbor.
Rates: $60-$65. All year.
Innkeeper(s): Betsy Grater.
3 Rooms. 1 Private Baths. Guest phone available. TV in room. Beds: KQT. Meals: Full breakfast. Jacuzzi. CCs: Visa, MC, AE. Swimming, tennis.
Seen in: *The Peabody Reflector.*
"What hotel room could ever compare to a large room in a 115-year old house with 10-foot ceilings and a marble fireplace with hosts that could become dear long-time friends?"

Mensana Inn
See: Stevenson, MD

Society Hill Government House
1125 N Calvert St
Baltimore MD 21202
(301) 752-7722
Circa 1827. This is the official guest house for Baltimore's visiting dignitaries as well as the general public. Three townhouses comprise the inn, located in the Mt. Vernon historic district. Features include chandeliers, ornate wallpapers, and Victorian decor. Each bedchamber has its own view.
Rates: $90-$110.
Innkeeper(s): Deborah Fisher & Laura Hernandez.
18 Rooms. 18 Private Baths. Guest phone in room. TV in room. Beds: KQDC. Meals: Full breakfast. Handicap access provided. Conference room. Fireplaces. CCs: Visa, MC, AE, DC.

Society Hill Hotel
58 W Biddle St
Baltimore MD 21201
(301) 837-3630

Circa 1890. This townhouse has been converted for lodging and includes a distinctive bar and restaurant with romantic dining rooms. The country-inn decor includes brass beds, fresh flowers and elaborate Victorian furnishings. Breakfast is brought to the room. Within walking distance is Meyerhoff Symphony Hall, and the Lyric Opera House.
Rates: $70-$110.
Innkeeper(s): Kate Hopkins.
15 Rooms. 15 Private Baths. Guest phone in room. TV in room. Beds: KQT. Meals: Full breakfast, restaurant.

Society Hill Hopkins
3404 St Paul St
Baltimore MD 21218
(301) 235-8600

Circa 1920. The embassy-like atmosphere of this inn make it popular for small meetings as well as romantic getaways. Antiques and original art fill the rooms, decorated in a variety of period styles. Breakfast may be taken in the guest room or dining room.
Rates: $90-$130.
Innkeeper(s): Joanne Fritz & Paul Fogarty.
26 Rooms. 26 Private Baths. Guest phone in room. TV in room. Meals: Full breakfast. CCs: Visa, MC, AE, DC.

The Shirley-Madison Inn
205 W Madison St
Baltimore MD 21201
(301) 728-6550

Circa 1880. An elegant Victorian mansion located in a downtown historic neighborhood, the Shirley-Madison Inn has an English stairway of polished ash that winds up four stories. The original 100-year-old lift still carries no more than three guests. The inn is decorated with Victorian and Edwardian antiques and turn-of-the-century artwork. The Inner Harbor, business district, and cultural centers are a short walk away.
Location: Ten blocks from the Inner Harbor.
**Rates: $55-$95. All year.
Innkeeper(s): Ellen Roberts, Minica Gescue, Daniel Houck.

27 Rooms. 27 Private Baths. Guest phone in room. TV in room. Beds: QT. Meals: Continental plus. Conference room. CCs: Visa, MC, AE.
"Charming, comfortable rooms, reasonable rates and friendly staff."

Twin Gates
308 Morris Ave
Baltimore MD 21093
(301) 252-3131 (800) 635-0370

Circa 1857. While renovating Twin Gates, the innkeepers discovered

two secret rooms used to hide runaway slaves heading north by means of the Underground Railroad. One of them is a small, half-height room that, prior to renovation, was accessed through a trap-door in the room above. All the public rooms have 12-foot ceilings and are decorated with antiques.
Location: Lutherville, a Victorian village north of Baltimore.
**Rates: $70. All year.
Innkeeper(s): Gwen & Bob Vaughan.
6 Rooms. 2 Private Baths. Guest phone available. TV available. Beds: Q. Meals: Full breakfast. Fireplaces. Winery tours. National Aquarium.
Seen in: *The Towson Flier.*

Chestertown

White Swan Tavern
231 High St
Chestertown MD 21620
(301) 778-2300

Circa 1730. During the 1978 restoration of the inn, an archeological dig discovered that before 1733 the site was a tannery operated by the Shoemaker of Chestertown. His one-room dwelling is now converted to a guest room. After additions to the building, it became a tavern in 1793, and was described as "situated in the center of business...with every attention given to render comfort

and pleasure to such as favor it with their patronage."
Location: Eastern shore of Maryland. Downtown historic district.
Rates: $75-$100. All year.
Innkeeper(s): Mary Susan Maisel.
6 Rooms. 6 Private Baths. Guest phone available. TV available. Beds: QDTC. Meals: Full breakfast. Conference room.

Denton

Sophie Kerr House
Rt 3 Box 7-B, Kerr & 5th Aves
Denton MD 21629
(301) 479-3421

Circa 1861. This two-story white colonial sits on a spacious lawn away from the road. It was the birthplace of Sophie Kerr, an Eastern Shore writer. A four-star French country restaurant is within walking distance and two state parks are nearby.
Location: Downtown Denton, Route 404 to Fifth Avenue.
Rates: $35. All year.
Innkeeper(s): John & Thelma Lyons.
5 Rooms. TV available. Beds: KQTC. Meals: Full breakfast. Pool. Antique and craft shops.
Seen in: *Pittsburg Press.*
"John and Thelma make a stay there fun. We met them in the garden with two guests from Manhattan. We joined the party and had a terrific time."

Frederick

National Pike Inn
See: New Market, MD

Spring Bank Inn
7945 Worman's Mill Rd
Frederick MD 21701
(301) 694-0440

Circa 1881. Both Gothic Revival and Italianate architectural details

are featured in this brick Victorian. High ceilings accommodate 10-foot arched windows and the original interior shutters remain. The parlor has a marbleized slate fireplace and there is original hand-stenciling in the billiards room. Victorian and Chippendale furnishings have been collected from the family's antique shop. Black birch, pine, maple, and poplar trees dot the inn's ten acres.
Location: Two and a half miles north of Frederick Historic District.
Rates: $70-$85. All year.
Innkeeper(s): Beverly & Ray Compton.
6 Rooms. 1 Private Baths. Guest phone available. Beds: D. Meals: Full breakfast, continental plus. CCs: AE. Fishing, bicycling, canoeing, cross-country skiing.
Seen in: *The Washington Post, Los Angeles Times.*

Tran Crossing
121 E Patrick St
Frederick MD 21701
(301) 663-8449
Circa 1877. This elegant three-story townhouse in the heart of the Frederick Historic District is noted for its attractive mansard roof and

stately entrance. A spiral staircase leads to rooms where guests enjoy gaslights and period furnishings.

Historical sites within walking distance include the location of the first official rebellion against the Stamp Act.
**Rates: $80-$100. All year.
Innkeeper(s): Mr. & Mrs. Frederick Tran.
2 Rooms. 1 Private Baths. Guest phone in room. Beds: Q. Meals: Full breakfast. Conference room. Fireplaces. Hiking, tennis, swimming, bicycling.
"The room was perfect, as fine a B&B as we have stayed at anywhere. You'll see us again."

Harwood

Oakwood
4566 Solomons Island Rd
Harwood MD 20776
(301) 261-5338
Circa 1840. A private lane winds through towering poplar, hickory and maple trees to Oakwood, a gracious two-and-a-half story Federal-style manor. Extensive terraced gardens include old-fashioned flowers and there are deep woods surrounding the inn. Interiors feature 11-foot ceilings and six fireplaces. An imposing dining room is appointed with a large dining table, a period sideboard, and chandeliers. Guest rooms are filled with antiques. Outbuildings include a spring house, butler's house and pond.
Location: Thirty miles southeast of Washington, D.C.
**Rates: $60. March - Nov 15.
Innkeeper(s): Dr. Joan and Dennis Brezina.
2 Rooms. Guest phone available. TV available. Beds: DT. Meals: Continental plus. Fireplaces. Water sports.
Seen in: *The Washington Post.*
"A special glimpse at nature's beauty. Such a tranquil spot. Delightful! Beautiful!"

New Market

National Pike Inn
9 W Main St
New Market MD 21774
(301) 865-5055
Circa 1796. This brick Federal house with red shutters has a unique widow's watch which was added in 1900. The National Pike was the East-West connection be-

tween Baltimore and points west, and towns along the road were located eight miles apart which was as far as herds could be driven in one day. Of the eight inns in New Market only two remain. The inn's colonial decor includes wingback chairs, oriental rugs and four-poster beds.
Rates: $60-$85. All year.
Innkeeper(s): Tom & Terry Rimel.
5 Rooms. 2 Private Baths. Guest phone available. TV available. Beds: QDT. Meals: Full breakfast. Fireplaces. CCs: Visa, MC. Tennis, golf, cross-country skiing, hiking.
"You really make us feel at home. We appreciate your making this getaway so special."

Strawberry Inn
17 Main St, PO Box 237
New Market MD 21774
(301) 865-3318
Circa 1860. Strawberry Inn is a restored Maryland farmhouse located in the center of a 200-year-old Na-

tional Historic Register town. The white Victorian clapboard house is furnished with antiques, of course, since New Market is the antique capital of Maryland.
Rates: $55-$85.
Innkeeper(s): Jane & Ed Rossig.
5 Rooms. 5 Private Baths. Beds: QT. Meals: B&B. Conference room.
"A tiny jewel in a Victorian setting." New York Times.

Owings Mills

Mensana Inn
See: Stevenson, MD

Pikesville

Mensana Inn
See: Stevenson, MD

Saint Michaels

Kemp House Inn
412 S Talbot St
Saint Michaels MD 21663
(301) 745-2243
  Circa 1805. This two-story Georgian house was built by Col. Joseph Kemp, a shipwright and one of the town forefathers. The inn is appointed in period furnishings accentuated by candlelight. Guest rooms include patchwork quilts, a collection of four-poster rope beds, and old-fashioned nightshirts. There are several working fireplaces. Robert E. Lee is said to have been a guest.
Rates: $60-$95. All year.
Innkeeper(s): Stephen & Diane Cooper.
7 Rooms. 3 Private Baths. Beds: Q. Meals: Full breakfast. Fireplaces. CCs: Visa, MC. Waterskiing, hunting, boating, fishing, bicycling, crabbing.

Sharpsburg

Inn At Antietam
PO Box 119
Sharpsburg MD 21782
(301) 432-6601

  Circa 1908. Eight acres of meadows surround this gracious white Victorian framed by English walnut trees. A columned veranda provides views of the countryside, the town with its old stone churches, and the Blue Mountains. Gleaming floors accentuate romantically designed Victorian guest rooms. An inviting smokehouse features beamed ceilings, a wide brick fireplace, and handsome upholstered chairs.
Rates: $55-$85. All year.
Innkeeper(s): Betty N. Fairbourn.
5 Rooms. 5 Private Baths. Guest phone available. Beds: QDT. Meals: EP, full breakfast. Conference room. Fireplaces. CCs: MC. Hiking, bicycling, cross-country skiing, golf, tennis. Civil War battlefield tours.
"A romantic setting and a most enjoyable experience."

Stevenson

Mensana Inn
1718 Greenspring Valley Rd
Stevenson MD 21153
(301) 653-2403
  Circa 1900. Edmund Burke, one of Teddy Roosevelt's Rough Riders,

built this colonial on 18 acres, high on a hill overlooking the Green Spring Valley. Trophies from African hunting expeditions hang on the living room wall, including a rhino, Cape buffalo and wart hog. The inn is furnished with antiques and oriental rugs.
Location: Ten minutes to Pikesville, 15 minutes to Baltimore.
**Rates: $140. Jan.3-Dec.18
Innkeeper(s): Lee Hendler.
8 Rooms. 8 Private Baths. Guest phone in room. TV in room. Beds: T. Meals: Family style. Sauna. Conference room. CCs: Visa, MC, AE, DC. Racquet club, tennis.
"I feel like Scarlet O'Hara, living at Tara. Where's Rhett?"

Towson

Mensana Inn
See: Stevenson, MD

Vienna

Tavern House
111 Water St, PO Box 98
Vienna MD 21869
(301) 376-3347
  Circa 1760. River views are available from the guest rooms of this tavern, popular during colonial days. The inn has been renovated and the polished wood floors and white plaster walls provide the backdrop for simple antique furnishings and reproductions. Five fireplaces at the inn include a cooking hearth in the cellar.
Location: On Nanticoke River at the Maryland Eastern Shore.
Rates: $55-$60.
Innkeeper(s): Harvey & Elise Altergott.
4 Rooms. Meals: Continental plus. Fireplaces. CCs: Visa, MC. Bicycles available.
Seen in: *Baltimore Magazine.*

Massachusetts

Amherst

Deerfield Inn
See: Deerfield, MA

Andover

Sherman-Berry House
See: Lowell, MA

Ashfield

Ashfield Inn
Main St
Ashfield MA 01330
(413) 628-4571
Circa 1919. This handsome Georgian mansion was built as a summer

home for Milo Belding. Enormous porches overlook spectacular perennials and herb gardens, and there are views of the lake, hills and countryside. Nestled in the gardens are several tree swings. The romantic interior includes a reception hall and a grand stairway.
Rates: $70-$80. All year.
Innkeeper(s): Scott & Stacy Alessi.
8 Rooms. Guest phone available. TV available. Beds: QDTC. Meals: Full breakfast. Fireplaces. CCs: Visa, MC, AE. Golf, skiing, hiking, swimming.
"Privacy, elegance, fabulous food, amenities (like terry robes, flowers and fruit) that made me feel pampered.

Wonderful hospitality in a spectacular romantic setting."

Auburn

Captain Samuel Eddy House Inn
609 Oxford St
Auburn MA 01501
(508) 832-5282
Circa 1765. This beautiful 18th-century farmhouse has been painstak-

ingly restored by the innkeepers. The south parlor is decorated with colonial furniture while the north parlor has modern furnishings and a TV. Carilyn often cooks over the hearth and sometimes dresses in a colonial frock to present breakfast. An herb garden and flock of geese are behind the inn.
**Rates: $48-$58. All year.
Innkeeper(s): Jack & Carilyn O'Toole.
5 Rooms. 5 Private Baths. Guest phone available. TV available. Beds: QT. Meals: Full breakfast, MAP. Conference room. Fireplaces. Pool. CCs: Visa, MC. Hiking, skating, swimming.
Seen in: *The Boston Herald.*
"Like stepping back in time."

Barnstable

Ashley Manor
3660 Olde Kings Hwy, PO Box 856
Barnstable MA 02630
(508) 362-8044
Circa 1699. The first addition to this house was built in 1750 and a succession of expansions occurred over the years. Besides the wide-

board flooring (usually reserved for the king) and huge, open-hearth fireplaces with beehive ovens, there is a secret passageway connecting the upstairs and downstairs suites. It was thought to be a hiding place for Tories during the Revolutionary War. The inn now rests gracefully on two acres of manicured lawns sprinkled with cherry and apple trees.
**Rates: $85-$125. All year.
Innkeeper(s): Donald & Fay Bain.
6 Rooms. 6 Private Baths. Guest phone available. Beds: Q. Meals: Full breakfast. Sportfishing, boating, tennis.
Seen in: *Boston Globe.*
"This is absolutely perfect! So many very special, lovely touches."

Thomas Huckins House
2701 Main St, Rt 6A
Barnstable MA 02630
(508) 362-6379
Circa 1705. Merchants and shippers, the Huckins family settled in Barnstable in 1639. Thomas built

this Cape half-house across from Calves Pasture Lane, common grazing land used by the colonists. There is a ten-foot fireplace and original paneling, windows, hinges and latches. American antique furnishings with canopy beds add to the gracious feeling of the inn. Just down the road is a graveyard where slate headstones bear the names of early residents.
Location: Cape Cod
Rates: $55-$85. All year.
Innkeeper(s): Burt & Eleanor Eddy.
3 Rooms. 3 Private Baths. Guest phone available. TV available. Beds: QD. Meals: Full breakfast. Fireplaces. CCs: Visa, MC.

"Your home is even warmer and more charming in person than the lovely pictures in Early American Life."

Barnstable Village

Beechwood
2839 Main St
Barnstable Village MA 02630
(508) 362-6618
Circa 1853. Beechwood is a carefully restored Queen Anne house offer-

ing period furnishings, fireplaces and ocean views. Its warmth and elegance make it a favorite hideaway for couples looking for a peaceful return to the Victorian nineteenth century. The inn is named for rare old beech trees that shade the veranda.

Location: Cape Cod's historic North Shore.
Rates: $85-$125. All year.
Innkeeper(s): Anne & Bob Livermore.
6 Rooms. 6 Private Baths. Guest phone available. Beds: KQF. Meals: Full breakfast. CCs: Visa, MC, AE. Golf, beaches, whale watching.

"Your inn is pristine in every detail. We concluded that the innkeepers, who are most hospitable, are the best part of Beechwood."

Charles Hinckley House
Olde Kings Highway, PO Box 723
Barnstable Village MA 02630
(508) 362-9924
Circa 1809. Built by shipwright Charles Hinckley, direct descendant

of the last governor of Plymouth Colony, the inn is a fine example of Federal colonial architecture. A twin chimney, hip-roofed, post-and-beam structure, the house is an award-winning restoration. Standing watch over one of Cape Cod's most photographed wildflower gardens, the inn is a short walk down a quiet lane to the bay.
**Rates: $94-$135. All year.
Innkeeper(s): Les & Miya Patrick.
4 Rooms. 4 Private Baths. Guest phone available. Beds: Q. Meals: Full breakfast. Fireplaces.
Seen in: *Country Living Magazine, Historic Preservation.*

"A wonderful, sophisticated and intimate hideaway. This inn experience was truly fantastic, punctuated by Miya's incredible gourmet breakfasts."

Bernardston

Bernardston Inn
Church St
Bernardston MA 01337
(413) 648-9282
Circa 1905. The present building was erected on the site of an old coach inn. Recently renovated, the

Bernardston Inn has ceiling fans, claw-foot bathtubs, and guest rooms with antique furnishings.
Location: Junction Routes 5 & 10.
Rates: $38-$68. All year.
Innkeeper(s): Tory A.O. Holmes & Steven Pardoe.
7 Rooms. 7 Private Baths. Guest phone available. TV available. Beds: QT. Meals: Full breakfast. Restaurant. CCs: Visa, MC.

"Delighted with the charming atmosphere, excellent accommodations and outstanding service."

Boston

A Cambridge House, B&B
See: Cambridge, MA

Coach House Inn
See: Salem, MA

Host Homes of Boston
PO Box 117, Waban Branch
Boston MA 02168
(617) 244-1308
Circa 1864. This stately townhouse sits on Commonwealth Avenue with its tall elms and grassy mall. Less than one block away is the Ritz Carlton and Boston Common. The house was built for the Robbins family, prominent clockmakers of the period. Later it served as a private social club providing cultural and intellectual programs as well as overnight lodging for members. A grand staircase, moldings and high ceilings add to the atmosphere.
Location: Homes in Beacon Hill, Back Bay, Cambridge, Greater Boston.
Rates: $90.
7 Rooms. 5 Private Baths. Beds: DT. Meals: Continental breakfast. Handicap access provided. CCs: Visa, MC, AE.

The Federal House

48 Fayette
Boston MA 02116
(617) 350-6657

Circa 1836. This is a beautifully restored Federal townhouse with flower-filled window boxes. Most

guest rooms have fireplaces and period furniture including four-posters and wing chairs. It is within walking distance to Quincy Market, Copley Square, Public Garden and Downtown Crossing. For easy transportation to the Kennedy Library, Logan Airport and Harvard Square the green, red and orange lines of the public transit system are close by.
**Rates: $85-$110.
Innkeeper(s): Joan Lautenschleger.
3 Rooms. 1 Private Baths. Guest phone in room. TV in room. Beds: QD. Meals: Continental breakfast. Fireplaces.
Seen in: *The Providence Journal.*

"A lovely home away from home. Our room is beautiful, the breakfast was right on, and your restaurant and touring advice was super."

The Summer House

See: Sandwich, MA

The Terrace Townhouse

60 Chandler St.
Boston MA 02116
(617) 350-6520

Circa 1870. Located on a South End cobblestone street, this old brownstone has been restored and features handsome antiques, fresh flowers, and crystal chandeliers. Copley Place, the Back Bay Amtrak station and rapid transit, are nearby. Parking lots are a few blocks away.
Rates: $105-$125.
Innkeeper(s): Gloria Belknap
5 Rooms. 3 Private Baths. TV in room. Beds: KQD. Meals: Continental breakfast.

Seen in: *Country Inns Magazine.*

Brewster

Bramble Inn

Rt 6a 2019 Main St
Brewster MA 02631
(508) 896-7644

Circa 1861. The venerable Bramble Inn is composed of three buildings. The main house containing a restaurant and lodging, and the house next door with five guest rooms, are of Greek Revival architecture. The Captain Bangs Pepper House on the other side is a Federal-style built in 1793. Williamsburg and Laura Ashley fabrics and wall coverings decorate the inn.
Location: Walking distance to the ocean.
**Rates: $65-$85. April to Dec.
Innkeeper(s): Ruth & Cliff Manchester.
11 Rooms. 11 Private Baths. Guest phone available. Beds: QD. Meals: Full breakfast, gourmet restaurant. CCs: Visa, MC, AE, DC. Tennis, swimming, bicycling.
Seen in: *The Boston Globe, The Boston Herald, Bon Appetit.*

"Adventurous cuisine in a romantic setting." Providence Journal.

Old Manse Inn

1861 Main St, PO 839
Brewster MA 02631
(508) 896-3149

Circa 1800. This old sea captain's house is tucked behind tall trees and has a gracious mansard roof. It was built by Captain Knowles, and served as a link in the Underground Railroad during the Civil War. The rooms are decorated with old-fashioned print wallpapers, original paintings and antiques.
Location: Cape Cod.
Rates: $60-$80. April to Nov.
Innkeeper(s): Sugar & Doug Manchester.
9 Rooms. 9 Private Baths. Guest phone available. Beds: KQTD. Meals: Full breakfast. Restaurant. Handicap access provided. CCs: Visa, MC, AE. Tennis, golf swimming, bicycling, fishing.

"Our stays at the Old Manse Inn have always been delightful. The innkeepers are gracious, the decor charming and the dining room has a character all its own."

Old Sea Pines Inn

2553 Main St
Brewster MA 02631
(508) 896-6114

Circa 1900. This turn-of-the-century mansion on three-and-one-half

acres of lawns and trees was formerly the Sea Pines School of Charm and Personality for Young Women, established in 1907. Recently renovated, the inn displays elegant wallpapers and a grand sweeping stairway. It is located near beaches and bike paths, as well as village shops and restaurants.
Location: Cape Cod.
**Rates: $36-$95. All year.
Innkeeper(s): Stephen & Michele Rowan.
14 Rooms. 9 Private Baths. Guest phone available. Beds: TD. Meals: Full breakfast, restaurant. Conference room. Fireplaces. CCs: Visa, MC, AE, DC,DS. Beaches, tennis, golf.

"The loving care applied by Steve, Michele and staff is deeply appreciated."

Brookline

Beacon Street Guest House

1047 Beacon St
Brookline MA 02146
(800) 872-7211 (617)232-0292

Circa 1900. This four-story brick and sandstone building was originally a private home built by Silas and Luther Merril and designed by G. Wilton Lewis. The house is an example of Queen Anne and Romanesque Revival and is five minutes from Harvard and five blocks from Fenway. Restaurants, theaters, and shops are nearby.
Location: West of Boston.
**Rates: $35-$65. April to Nov.
Innkeeper(s): Jessica McGovern & Morris Fuller.
14 Rooms. 9 Private Baths. Guest phone available. TV available. Beds: TDC. Meals: Continental. Fireplaces. CCs: Visa, MC, AE, DC.

"Quiet, charming. Real Boston flavor."

Cambridge

A Cambridge House
Bed & Breakfast Inn
2218 Massachusetts Ave
Cambridge MA 02140
(617) 491-6300

Circa 1892. Listed in the National Register, A Cambridge House has

been restored to its turn-of-the-century elegance. A remarkable carved cherry fireplace dominates the den, and some rooms have four-poster canopy beds and fireplaces. The library is often the setting for mulled cider, wine or tea served fireside on brisk afternoons. Parking is available and the subway is four blocks away.
Location: Minutes from downtown Boston.
**Rates: $59-$139. All year.
Innkeeper(s): Ellen Riley & Tony Femmino.
12 Rooms. 1 Private Baths. Guest phone in room. TV in room. Beds: QT. Meals: Full breakfast. Fireplaces. CCs: Visa, MC, AE.
Seen in: *Evening Magazine.*

"I'm afraid you spoiled us quite badly! Your home is elegant, charming and comfortable. Breakfasts were delicious and beautifully served."

Centerville

Copper Beech Inn
497 Main St
Centerville MA 02632
(508) 771-5488

Circa 1820. At the site of the largest copper beech tree on Cape Cod you'll find this white clapboard house, built by Captain Hillman Crosby. The Crosby name has long been associated with boat builders and fast sailing ships. Preserved and restored, this Cape-style inn is shaded by elms and surrounded by

hedges. Summer theater, fine restaurants, and the beach are nearby.
Rates: $65-$75. All year.
3 Rooms. 3 Private Baths. Guest phone available. TV available. Beds: KD. Meals: Full breakfast. CCs: Visa, MC, AE. Bicycling, ocean beach.

"Everything we were looking for, clean and private, but best of all were our wonderful hosts. They made us feel very much at home and made delicious breakfast."

Chatham, Cape Cod

Chatham Town House Inn
11 Library Lane
Chatham, Cape Cod MA 02633
(508) 945-2180

Circa 1881. This three-story sea captain's house was built by Daniel

Webster Nickerson, a descendant of William Nickerson who came over on the *Mayflower*. Resting on two acres in the village, the inn is surrounded with charming gardens. Victorian wallpapers, hand stenciling and canopy beds are features of most guest rooms and there are two cottages with fireplaces. Hospitality is provided by an international staff and Scandanavian hosts.
Rates: $98-$155.
Innkeeper(s): Russell & Svea Marita Peterson.
Meals: Full breakfast.
Seen in: *Cape Cod Times, New York Times, Yankee Magazine.*

Concord

Anderson-Wheeler
Homestead
154 Fitchburg Turnpike
Concord MA 01742
(617) 369-3756

Circa 1890. When Route 117 was the main road between Boston and

Fitchburg the Lee family operated a stagecoach stop here. They provided room and board, a change of horses, and a leather and blacksmith shop. The building burned in 1890 and a Victorian house was built by Frank Wheeler, developer of rust-free asparagus. The property has remained in the family, and the veranda overlooks an extensive lawn and Sudbury River.
**Rates: $55-$75. All year.
Innkeeper(s): David & Charlotte Anderson.
5 Rooms. 1 Private Baths. Guest phone available. TV in room. Beds: KTCD. Meals: Continental plus. Conference room. CCs: Visa, MC. Bird-watching, horseback riding, cross-country skiing.

"The five nights spent with you were the most comfortable and most congenial of the whole cross-country trip."

Colonel Roger Brown House
1694 Main St
Concord MA 01742
(508) 369-9119

Circa 1775. The oldest house in West Concord was the home of Minuteman Roger Brown who fought at the Old North Bridge. The frame for this center-chimney colonial was raised April 19th, the day the battle took place. Other parts of the house were built in 1708. Next door is the Damon Mill now developed as an office complex with a fitness club available to guests.
Rates: $70-$80.
5 Rooms. 5 Private Baths. Guest phone in room. TV in room. Beds: QDT. Meals: Continental-plus breakfast. Jacuzzi. Sauna. Fireplaces. Pool. CCs: Visa, MC, AE, DC. Golf, canoeing, skiing, tennis.

Seen in: *Middlesex News.*
"He won't stay anywhere else!" Secretary.

Hawthorne Inn
462 Lexington Rd
Concord MA 01742
(508) 369-5610

Circa 1870. The Hawthorne Inn is situated on land that once belonged to Ralph Waldo Emerson, the Alcotts and Nathaniel Hawthorne. It was here Bronson Alcott planted his fruit trees, made pathways to the Mill Brook, and erected his Bath House. Hawthorne purchased the land and repaired a path leading to his home with trees planted on either side. Two of these trees still stand. Across the road is Hawthorne's House, The Wayside. Next to it is the Alcott's Orchard House, and Grapevine Cottage where the Concord grape was developed. Nearby is Sleepy Hollow Cemetery where Emerson, the Alcotts, the Thoreaus, and Hawthorne were laid to rest.
**Rates: $85-$150. All year.
Innkeeper(s): G. Burch & M. Mudry.
7 Rooms. 7 Private Baths. Guest phone available. Beds: TCD. Meals: Continental plus. Fireplaces. Cross country skiing, swimming.
"Surely there couldn't be a better or more valuable location for a comfortable, old-fashioned country inn."

Sherman-Berry House
See: Lowell, MA

Deerfield

Deerfield Inn
The Street
Deerfield MA 01342
(413) 774-5587

Circa 1885. Deerfield was settled in 1670 and a few years later survived an Indian massacre. Farmers still

unearth bones and axeheads when they plow. Now, 50 beautifully re-

stored colonial and Federal homes line mile-long The Street, considered by many to be the loveliest street in New England. The inn is situated at the center of this peaceful village and is filled with antiques from historic Deerfield's remarkable collection. The village has been designated a national historic site.
Location: Middle of historic village.
Rates: $58-$125. All year.
Innkeeper(s): Karl & Jane Sabo.
23 Rooms. 23 Private Baths. Guest phone in room. TV available. Beds: KQT. Meals: Full breakfast. Restaurant. Handicap access provided. Conference room. Fireplaces. CCs: Visa, MC, AE, DC. Golf, downhill & cross country skiing, buggy rides.
Seen in: *The Recorder-Greenfield, Travel Today, Daily Hampshire Gazette.*
"We've stayed at many New England inns, but the Deerfield Inn ranks among the best."

Dennis

Four Chimneys Inn
946 Main St, Rt 6A
Dennis MA 02638
(508) 385-6317

Circa 1881. This spacious Victorian stands across from Lake Scargo, which legend says was created at the command of an Indian chief whose daughter needed a larger fishbowl for her goldfish. The village maidens dug the lake with clam shells and all the fish happily multiplied. The inn has eight-foot windows, high ceilings, a cozy library and parlor, and a gracious summer porch from which to view the "fishbowl."
Location: Cape Cod.
Rates: $45-$80. All year.
Innkeeper(s): Christina Jervant & Diane Robinson.
9 Rooms. 7 Private Baths. Guest phone available. Beds: QDT. Meals: Continental. Conference room. CCs: Visa, MC. Bicycling, tennis, golf, fishing, swimming, theatre.
Seen in: *The Littleton Independent.*

Isaiah Hall
Bed & Breakfast Inn
152 Whig St
Dennis MA 02638
(508) 385-9928

Circa 1857. Adjacent to the Cape's oldest cranberry bog is this Greek Revival farmhouse built by Isaiah Hall, a cooper. He designed and patented the original barrel for shipping cranberries, and his brother Henry Hall cultivated the first bogs in North America. In 1948, Dorothy Ripp, an artist, established the inn. Many examples of her art work remain.
Location: Cape Cod.
**Rates: $40-$75. April to Oct.
Innkeeper(s): Marie & Dick Brophy.
11 Rooms. 10 Private Baths. Guest phone available. TV available. Beds: QD. Conference room. Fireplaces. CCs: Visa, MC, AE. Swimming, golf, tennis.

Duxbury

Black Friar Brook Farm
636 Union Street
Duxbury MA 02332
(617) 834-8528

Circa 1708. Josiah Soule, grandson of pilgrim George Soule, built this saltbox house on 11 acres of farmland, part of an original land grant of 150 acres. Gun-stock beams and colonial antiques are featured, and the private guest suite includes a bedroom, sitting room and dining area. The hostess runs a reservation service for other New England homestays.
Rates: $45-$50. March to Nov.
Innkeeper(s): Ann & Walter Kopke.
2 Rooms. Guest phone available. TV in room. Beds: KT. Meals: EP. Fireplaces. Beach.

East Orleans

Parsonage
202 Main St, PO Box 1016
East Orleans MA 02643
(508) 255-8217

Circa 1770. This 18-century parsonage is a Cape house, complete with ancient wavy glass in the win-

dows and antique furnishings throughout. There are dormer windows and a sitting area in the spacious loft room. Breakfast is served in the courtyard or in guest rooms. Main Street, the road to Nauset Beach, is lined with the old homes of sea captains and other early settlers.
Rates: $45-$50. May to Oct.
Innkeeper(s): Chris & Lloyd Shand.
2 Rooms. Meals: Continental breakfast. Beaches, tennis, bicycling.
Seen in: *Miami Herald.*

"Your hospitality was as wonderful as your home. Your home was as beautiful as Cape Cod. Thank you!!"

Ships Knees Inn
Beach Rd
East Orleans MA 02643
(508) 255-1312

Circa 1817. This is a 190-year-old restored sea captain's house located

just a short walk to the ocean and Nauset Beach. Guest rooms feature beamed ceilings, four-poster beds piled with quilts, and a special colonial color scheme. A few overlook Orleans Cove.
Location: One-and-a-half hours from Boston.
Rates: $38-$78. All year.
Innkeeper(s): Carol & Dick Hurlburt.
22 Rooms. 9 Private Baths. Guest phone available. TV in room. Beds: KQDTC. Meals: Continental. Pool. Golf, swimming, tennis.

"Warm, homey and very friendly atmosphere. Very impressed with the beamed ceilings."

East Sandwich

Wingscorton Farm Inn
11 Wing Blvd
East Sandwich MA 02537
(617) 888-0534

Circa 1757. Wingscorton is a working farm on seven acres of lawns, gardens and orchards, and adjoining

a short walk to a private ocean beach. This Cape Cod manse, built by a Quaker family, is a historical landmark on what was once known as the King's Highway, the oldest historical district in the United States. All the rooms are furnished with working fireplaces (one with a secret compartment where runaway slaves hid) as well as fully restored antiques. Breakfast features fresh produce with eggs, meats and vegetables from the farm's livestock and gardens.
Location: North Side of Cape Cod, off Route 6A.
Rates: $90-$125. All year.
Innkeeper(s): Dick Loring & Sheila Weyers.
Guest phone available. TV in room. Fireplaces. CCs: Visa, MC. Boating, fishing, whale watching.

Edgartown

Chadwick Inn
67 Winter St
Edgartown MA 02539
(508) 627-4435

Circa 1840. The winding staircase in this Greek Revival house was

crafted by the carpenter who built the Edgartown Old Whaling Church tower. You may wish to stay in the original house with its high ceilings, fireplaces, antiques, and canopy beds, or in the newer Garden Wing. Guests enjoy the veranda with views of the spacious lawn and blooming flower beds. Just down the block are numerous shops and galleries.
Location: Center of Edgartown.
Rates: $50-$225. All year.
Innkeeper(s): Peter & Jurate Antioco.

15 Rooms. 15 Private Baths. Guest phone available. TV available. Beds: KQT. Meals: Full breakfast. Handicap access provided. Fireplaces. CCs: Visa, MC, AE. Swimming, horseback riding, bicycling.
Seen in: *Cape Cod Life.*

"Wonderful hospitality. I hated to leave, it's such a comfortable, caring inn."

Charlotte Inn
S Summer St
Edgartown MA 02539
(508) 627-4751

Circa 1860. A widow's walk tops this white clapboard sea captain's house. Traditional early American antiques, down comforters and four-poster beds add romance and elegance. Inside the inn are a restaurant, gift shop, and the Edgartown Art Gallery.
Rates: $32-$195.
24 Rooms. Meals: Full breakfast.

Edgartown Inn
56 N Water
Edgartown MA 02539
(508) 627-4794

Circa 1798. The Edgartown Inn was originally built as a home for whaling Captain Worth. (Fort Worth, Texas, was later named for his son.) The house was converted to an inn around 1820 when Daniel Webster was a guest. The innkeeper admonished his children not to "sop the platter" in Webster's presence, that is, not to dip their bread into the gravy. To the delight of the children, Webster himself "sopped the platter." Later, Nathaniel Hawthorne stayed here and proposed to the innkeeper's daughter Eliza Gibbs (who turned him down).
Location: Martha's Vineyard.
Rates: $50-$135. All year.
Innkeeper(s): Liliane & Earle Radford.
22 Rooms. 12 Private Baths. TV available. Meals: Full breakfast. Tennis, golf, sailing.

Point Way Inn
104 Main St, Box 128
Edgartown MA 02539
(508) 627-8633

Circa 1840. The reception area of Point Way Inn is papered with navigational charts from a 4,000-mile cruise the innkeepers made with their two daughters. After the voyage, they discovered this old sea captain's house and completely renovated it, filling it with New England antiques, period wallpapers, and canopied beds. There are working fireplaces and French doors opening onto private balconies. Croquet can be played on the lawn in view of Linda's flower gardens.

Location: Martha's Vineyard.
Rates: $115-$185. All year.
Innkeeper(s): Ben & Linda Smith.
15 Rooms. 15 Private Baths. Guest phone available. TV available. Beds: QTC. Meals: Full breakfast. Conference room. Fireplaces. CCs: Visa, MC, AE. Croquet, golf, horseback riding, bicycling.

"One of the most pleasant old New England inns around." The Boston Monthly.

The Arbor
222 Upper Main St
Edgartown MA 02539
(508) 627-8137

Circa 1890. This house was originally built on the adjoining is-

land of Chappaquidick and was moved over to Edgartown on a barge at the turn of the century. Located on the bicycle path, it is walking distance from downtown and the harbor. Guests may relax in the hammock, have tea on the porch, or walk the unspoiled island beaches of Martha's Vineyard.

**Rates: $70-$90. May to Oct.
Innkeeper(s): Peggy Hall.
10 Rooms. 8 Private Baths. Guest phone available. Beds: QDWT. Meals: Continental. Fireplaces. CCs: MC, AE. Beaches, bike trails, sailing, fishing, nature.

"Thank you so much for your wonderful hospitality! You are a superb hostess. If I ever decide to do my own B&B your example would be my guide."

Falmouth

Captain Tom Lawrence House
75 Locust St
Falmouth MA 02540
(508) 540-1445

Circa 1861. After completing five

whaling trips around the world, each four years in length, Captain Lawrence retired at 40 and built this house. There is a Steinway piano here now, and elegantly furnished guest rooms, some with canopied beds. The house is near the beach, bikeway, ferries and train station. Freshly ground grain is used much as it was in the 1800s, with blueberry pancakes a frequent specialty.

Location: Cape Cod.
Rates: $48-$75. All year.
Innkeeper(s): Barbara Sabo-Feller.
6 Rooms. 4 Private Baths. Guest phone available. Beds: KQT. Meals: Full breakfast. Fireplaces. CCs: Visa, MC. Golf, tennis, swimming, bicycling.

"This is our first B&B experience. Better than some of the so-called 4-star hotels!! We loved it here."

Mostly Hall
27 Main St
Falmouth MA 02540
(508) 548-3786

Circa 1849. Albert Nye built this southern plantation house with

wide verandas and a cupola to observe shipping in Vineyard Sound. It was a wedding gift for his New Orleans bride. Because of the seemingly endless halls on every floor, some 30 feet long, it was whimsically called Mostly Hall.

Location: In the historic district across from the village green.
Rates: $70-$95. All year.
Innkeeper(s): Caroline & Jim Lloyd.
6 Rooms. 6 Private Baths. Guest phone available. TV available. Beds: Q. Meals: Full breakfast, gourmet. Fireplaces. Bicycling, tennis, golf, swimming, boating, theater.
Seen in: *Sunday Cape Cod Times.*

"Of all the inns we stayed at during our trip, we enjoyed Mostly Hall the most. Imagine, southern hospitality on Cape Cod!!"

Palmer House Inn
81 Palmer Ave
Falmouth MA 02540
(508) 548-1230

Circa 1901. It's just a short walk to the village common from this turn-of-the-century Victorian. The

original stained glass windows and rich woodwork are typical of the gracious homes in the historic district of Falmouth.

Location: Historic district of Falmouth.
Rates: $65-$87. All year.
Innkeeper(s): Phyllis & Bud Peacock.
8 Rooms. 8 Private Baths. Guest phone available. TV available. Beds: DWT. Meals: Full breakfast, gourmet. Fireplaces. CCs: Visa, MC. Beach, tennis, golf, bicycling.

"Exactly what a New England inn should be!"
"The meals were fantastic."

The Inn At One Main Street
One Main St
Falmouth MA 02540
(508) 540-7469

Circa 1892. The Inn was originally the residence of an early Cape Cod

family. In the Fifties it became The Victorian House offering lodging to guests visiting Falmouth. It is just off the village green in the historic district.
**Rates: $75-$95.
Innkeeper(s): Alan Cassidy.
8 Rooms. 8 Private Baths. Guest phone available. Beds: QT. Meals: Full breakfast. Conference room. Fireplaces. CCs: Visa, MC. Beaches, fine restaurants, summer theaters, bike paths.

"The art of hospitality in a delightful atmosphere, well worth traveling 3,000 miles for."

Village Green Inn
40 W Main St
Falmouth MA 02540
(508) 548-5621
   Circa 1804. The inn was originally built in the Federal style for Brad-

dock Dimmick, son of Revolutionary War General Joseph Dimmick. Later Cranberry King John Crocker, moved the house onto a granite slab foundation remodeling it in the Victorian style. There are inlaid floors, large porches and gingerbread trim.
Location: Falmouth's historic village green.
Rates: $80-$95. All year.
Innkeeper(s): Linda & Don Long.
5 Rooms. 5 Private Baths. Guest phone available. TV in room. Beds: QD. Meals: Full breakfast. Fireplaces. Boating, sailing, fishing, water skiing, tennis, horses.
"Like we've always said, it's the innkeepers that make the inn!"

Wyndemere House at Sippewissett
718 Palmer Ave
Falmouth MA 02193
(508) 540-7069
   Circa 1797. Lord Wyndemere left Sussex, England under mysterious

circumstances relating to his wife's disappearance. He built this Paul Revere-style colonial home and became known for his reclusive lifestyle and his many political and civil liberties writings. After additions and renovations the house has become a country inn.
Location: Take 28 South Sippenwissett exit. One mile from town.
**Rates: $75-$95. May to October.
Innkeeper(s): Carole F. Railsback.
6 Rooms. 4 Private Baths. Guest phone available. Beds: KDT. Meals: Full breakfast. Fireplaces.

Great Barrington

Seekonk Pines Inn
142 Seekonk Cross Rd
Great Barrington MA 01230
(413) 528-4192
   Circa 1832. Known as the Crippen Farm from 1835-1879, Seekonk Pines

Inn now includes both the original farmhouse and a Dutch Colonial wing. Throughout the years, major alterations were made to this New England frame house. Green lawns, gardens and meadows surround the inn. The name *Seekonk* was the local Indian name for the Canadian geese

which migrate through this part of the Berkshires.
Rates: $60-$84. All year.
Innkeeper(s): Linda & Chris Best.
7 Rooms. 3 Private Baths. Guest phone available. TV available. Beds: QTDC. Meals: Full breakfast. Pool. Cross-country & downhill skiing, theater.
"Of all the B&B's we trekked through, yours was our first and most memorable!

Harwich Port

Captain's Quarters
85 Bank St
Harwich Port MA 02646
(508) 432-0337
   Circa 1850. This Victorian house features a classic wraparound porch,

gingerbread trim, an authentic turret room and a graceful, curving front stairway. It is situated on an acre of sunny lawns, broad shade trees and colorful gardens. The inn is a five-minute walk to sandy Bank Street Beach and is close to town.
Location: One-and-a-half hours from Boston.
**Rates: $50-$85. April to Oct.
Innkeeper(s): David & Kathleen Van Gelder.
6 Rooms. 6 Private Baths. Guest phone available. TV available. Beds: Q. Meals: Continental plus. Pool. CCs: Visa, MC, AE. Fishing, boating, tennis.
"Accommodations are very comfortable and attractive. This is our favorite inn!"

Dunscroft By the Sea
24 Pilgrim Rd
Harwich Port MA 02646
(508) 432-0810
   Circa 1922. This gambrel-roofed house sits behind a split-rail fence at

the end of a winding brick driveway. Inside the handsome columned entrance is an extensive library and a living room with a piano. Best of all is the candlelit bed chamber with turned down bed and the music of ocean waves rolling onto the private beach on Nantucket Sound, 300 feet from the inn.

Location: One-and-a-half hours from Boston on Cape Cod.

**Rates: $72-$125. All year.

Innkeeper(s): Wally & Alyce Cunningham.

9 Rooms. 9 Private Baths. Guest phone available. Beds: KQTC. Meals: Full breakfast. Fireplaces. Horseback riding, cross-country skiing, fishing, golf, tennis.

"A quaint and delightful slice of New England. Your generous hospitality is greatly appreciated. Your place is beautiful."

Holyoke

Yankee Pedler Inn
1866 Northampton St.
Holyoke MA 01040
(413) 532-9494

Circa 1875. Five buildings comprise this Connecticut River Valley

inn. There is a tavern and dining room decorated with brass lamps, Blue Onion china, copper pieces and Currier & Ives prints. The kitchen has no doors, an invitation to guests to visit and watch their dinner being prepared. All the rooms are decorated in an Early American style and some include canopy beds.

**Rates: $58-$80.

Innkeeper(s): The Banks family.

47 Rooms. 47 Private Baths. Guest phone in room. TV in room. Beds: KQDTC. Meals: EP. Conference room. Fireplaces. CCs: Visa, MC, AE, DC. Ten minutes to skiing Mt. Tom.

Hyannis

Captain Sylvester Baxter House
Park Square Village, 156 Main St
Hyannis MA 02601

(508) 775-5611

Circa 1855. Captain Baxter, shipmaster, became a state senator and built this house for his family. (His

father helped to build the old mill in town.) In 1855, Baxter's wife gathered a group of ladies in her parlor and started the local literary association. Guest rooms have television, air-conditioning and private baths.

Rates: $55-$85. All year.

Innkeeper(s): N. Krajewski & R.D. Arenstrup.

9 Rooms. 9 Private Baths. Guest phone available. TV in room. Beds: QD. Meals: Continental plus. Fireplaces. Pool. CCs: Visa, MC. Golf, tennis, concerts.

Hyannisport

Copper Beech Inn
See: Centerville, MA

Lenox

Birchwood Inn
7 Hubbard St, Box 2020
Lenox MA 01240
(413) 637-2600

Circa 1764. This house was enlarged to become Hubbard Tavern in 1798. It was next purchased by

state senator and Judge Azariah Egleston. The Dana family lived here from 1885 to 1953. Lenox was considered the nation's literary cen-

ter in the 1800s with Edith Wharton, Henry Ward Beecher, Hawthorne, Longfellow and Melville living in the area. The gracious parlor, dining room with its elegant fireplace and showcase gardens make Birchwood a special place.

Location: Near Berkshire.

**Rates: $75-$175. All year.

Innkeeper(s): Arnold, Sandra & Laura Hittleman.

11 Rooms. 9 Private Baths. Guest phone available. TV available. Beds: QT. Meals: Full breakfast. Handicap access provided. Conference room. Fireplaces. CCs: Visa, MC. Cross country & downhill skiing, hiking, biking, golf, tennis.

"Inn-credible! Inn-viting! Inn-spiring! Inn-comparable! The Birchwood is our ultimate getaway. Wonderful ambiance, great food and the finest hosts ever met."

Brook Farm Inn
15 Hawthorne St
Lenox MA 01240
(413) 637-3013

Circa 1890. Brook Farm Inn is named after the original Brook Farm, a literary commune that sought to combine thinker and

worker through a society of intelligent, cultivated members. In keeping with that theme, this gracious Victorian inn offers poetry and writing seminars and has a 650-volume poetry library. Canopy beds, Mozart, and a swimming pool tend to the spirit.

Rates: $55-$125. All year.

Innkeeper(s): Bob & Betty Jacob.

12 Rooms. 12 Private Baths. Guest phone available. Beds: QTF. Meals: Full breakfast. Fireplaces. Pool. CCs: Visa, MC. Hiking, swimming.

Seen in: *Berkshire Eagle*.

"We loved everything about your inn, especially the friendliness and warmth

of both of you. The only bad thing about your inn is leaving it!"

Cliffwood Inn
25 Cliffwood St
Lenox MA 01240
(413) 637-3330

Circa 1904. This stately manor was built in the Stanford White style for a former ambassador to France. Its

gracious columned entrance leads to interiors with polished hardwood floors, high ceilings and fine furnishings. Six of the guest rooms have fireplaces. Nearby historical sites in the area include the home of Herman Melville and the Edith Wharton estate.
Rates: $80-$125. All year.
Innkeeper(s): Joy & Scottie Farrelly.
8 Rooms. 6 Private Baths. Guest phone available. TV available. Beds: KQT. Meals: Continental plus. Conference room. Fireplaces. Swimming.
"Our weekends at your fantastic retreat have been some of our sweetest memories over the past two years."

Colonel Ashley Inn
See: Sheffield, MA

East Country Berry Farm
830 East St
Lenox MA 01240
(413) 442-2057

Circa 1798. At the time of the French and Indian War, a land grant was given to the widow and children of Captain Stevens. Later, the farm was owned by the Sears family for approximately 150 years. Now, two historic, restored farmhouses combine to create the inn which is located on 23 acres of lawn, fields, trees and flowers.
Location: Two-and-a-half hours from Boston.
**Rates: $45-$125. All year.
Innkeeper(s): Rita F. Miller.
7 Rooms. 3 Private Baths. Guest phone available. Beds: KQTC. Meals: Full breakfast. Fireplaces. Downhill & cross country skiing, hiking, horseback riding.
Seen in: *Boston Globe.*

Garden Gables Inn
141 Main St
Lenox MA 01240
(413) 637-0193

Circa 1770. Several distinctive gables adorn this home set on five

wooded acres, and deer occasionally wander into the garden to help themselves to fallen apples. Breakfast is served in the dining room which overlooks tall maples, flower gardens and fruit trees. The swimming pool was the first built in the county and is still the longest.
**Rates: $55-$125. All year.
Innkeeper(s): Mario & Lynn Mekinda.
10 Rooms. 10 Private Baths. Guest phone available. Beds: KQT. Meals: Full breakfast. Jacuzzi. Fireplaces. Skiing, swimming, hiking, tennis, golf, horseback riding.
"Charming and thoughtful hospitality. You restored a portion of my sanity and I'm very grateful."

The Gables Inn
103 Walker St, Rt 183
Lenox MA 01240
(413) 637-3416

Circa 1885. At one time this was the home of Pulitzer Prize-winning novelist Edith Wharton. The Queen Anne-style Berkshire cottage features a handsome eight-sided library and Mrs. Wharton's own four-poster bed. The inn has an unusual indoor swimming pool with jacuzzi and tennis courts and a popular gourmet restaurant.
Rates: $60-$135. All year.
Innkeeper(s): Mary & Frank Newton.
14 Rooms. 14 Private Baths. Guest phone available. TV available. Beds: QTW. Meals: Continental plus. Jacuzzi. Fireplaces. Pool. CCs: Visa, MC, AE. Tennis, swimming.
"You made us feel like old friends and that good feeling enhanced our pleasure. In essence it was the best part of our trip."

Underledge Inn
76 Cliffwood St
Lenox MA 01240
(413) 637-0236

Circa 1876. Drive along Cliffwood Street under an archway of greenery, then up Underledge's winding drive

to a peaceful setting overlooking the Berkshire Hills. The inn sits resplendently atop four acres providing rooms with sunset views. In the foyer is an exquisite oak staircase and floor-to-ceiling oak fireplace. A solarium is the setting for breakfast. Just down the street are quaint shops and fine restaurants.
Rates: $60-$130. All year.
Innkeeper(s): Marcie & Cheryl Lanoue.
9 Rooms. 9 Private Baths. Guest phone available. TV available. Beds: KQ. Meals: Full breakfast. Fireplaces. CCs: Visa, AE. Golf, tennis, swimming.
"We were received like a guest in a luxurious private house. We now think of Underledge as our summer home."

Village Inn
16 Church St
Lenox MA 01240
(413) 637-0020

Circa 1771. Four years after the Whitlocks built this Federal-style

house they converted it and two adjoining barns for lodging. Since 1775 it has operated as an inn, and a six-year renovation has just been completed. Stenciled wallpapers, maple floors, and four-poster canopied beds decorate the rooms. Best of all, traditional afternoon tea includes scones and clotted cream.
Location: In the heart of the Berkshires.
**Rates: $70-$130.

Innkeeper(s): Clifford Rudisill & Ray Wilson.
29 Rooms. 27 Private Baths. Guest phone available. TV available. Beds: KQT. Meals: EP, Restaurant, MAP. Jacuzzi. Conference room. Fireplaces. CCs: Visa, MC. Hiking, cross country & downhill skiing, tennis, golf, horses.
Seen in: *Country Inns of America.*

"Kathy and I stayed at your beautiful inn in early October. It was the highlight of our trip to New England."

Walker House
74 Walker St
Lenox MA 01240
(413) 637-1271
Circa 1804. This beautiful Federal-style house sits in the center of the village on three acres of graceful

woods and restored gardens. Guest rooms have fireplaces and private baths and each is named for a favorite composer such as Beethoven, Mozart, or Handel. The innkeepers' musical backgrounds include associations with the San Francisco Opera, the New York City Opera, and the Los Angeles Philharmonic. The Houdeks occasionally sponsor Walker House concerts.
Location: Route 183 & 7A.
Rates: $45-$125. All year.
Innkeeper(s): Richard & Peggy Houdek.
8 Rooms. 8 Private Baths. Guest phone available. TV available. Beds: KQT. Meals: Full breakfast. Handicap access provided. Conference room. Fireplaces. Bicycles, croquet, badminton, tennis, swimming, skiing, hiking.

"We had a grand time staying with fellow music and opera lovers! Breakfasts were lovely."

Lexington

Sherman-Berry House
See: Lowell, MA

Lowell

Sherman-Berry House
163 Dartmouth St
Lowell MA 01851
(617) 459-4760
Circa 1893. This Queen Anne Victorian is shaded by a spreading

sugar maple that drops leaves on the wraparound porch when fall begins. The front and back parlors have fireplaces and are filled with antiques. Beside the staircase is a dramatic stained-glass window. Well-behaved children of all ages are invited to pump the player piano, turn the kaleidoscope, and peer through the stereoscope.
**Rates: $45-$55. All year.
Innkeeper(s): Susan Scott & David Strohmeyer.
2 Rooms. Guest phone in room. TV available. Meals: Full breakfast. Fireplaces.
Seen in: *The Sun.*

"A fantastic two night stay! Loved all the lovely things surrounding us, the table settings and food fantastic."

Marblehead

Spray Cliff on the Ocean
25 Spray Avenue
Marblehead MA 01945
(617) 631-6789
Circa 1910. Panoramic views stretch out in grand proportions from this English Tudor mansion set high above the Atlantic. The inn provides a spacious and elegant atmosphere inside and the grounds of the inn include a brick terrace is surrounded by lush flower gardens where eider ducks, black cormorants and seagulls abound.
Location: Fifteen miles north of Boston.
Rates: $85-$110. All year.

Innkeeper(s): Richard & Diane Pabich.
5 Rooms. 5 Private Baths. Guest phone available. Beds: KQD. Meals: Full breakfast. CCs: Visa, MC, AE, DC.

Nantucket

Century House
10 Cliff Rd, Box 603
Nantucket MA 02554
(508) 228-0530
Circa 1833. Captain Calder built this Federal-style house and supplemented his income by taking in

guests when the whaling industry slowed down. This is the oldest continually operating inn on the island. It is surrounded by other large homes on a knoll in the historic district. A short walk away are museums, beaches and restaurants. The inn's motto for the last 100 years has been, "An inn of distinction on an island of charm." Ask about the inn's secluded rose covered cottage.
**Rates: $50-$105.
10 Rooms. 8 Private Baths. Guest phone available. Beds: KQDTW. Meals: Continental-plus breakfast. Handicap access provided. Fireplaces. Surfing, wind surfing, sandcastle building, biking.

"We loved the inn and the staff. Our stay here really was enjoyed."

Corner House
49 Centre St, PO Box 1828
Nantucket MA 02554
(508) 228-1530
Circa 1723. The Corner House is a charming 18th-century inn. Architectural details such as the original pine floors, paneling and fireplaces have been preserved. A screened porch overlooks the English perennial garden where guests often take afternoon tea. There are more than 400 buildings in the historic district of town. The

main street was laid out in 1697, and paved in 1837 with cobblestones from Gloucester.
Rates: $80-$120. All year.
Innkeeper(s): Sandy & John Knox-Johnston.
14 Rooms. 14 Private Baths. Guest phone available. TV in room. Beds: KQTD. Meals: Full breakfast, Continental plus. Conference room. CCs: Visa, MC.
Seen in: *Detroit Free Press, The Atlanta Journal, Newsday.*
"The most beautiful place we've ever been to and the most comfortable!!"

Four Chimneys
38 Orange St
Nantucket MA 02554
(508) 228-1912
Circa 1839. The Four Chimneys is located on famous Orange Street

where 126 sea captains built mansions. Captain Frederick Gardner built this Greek Revival, one of the largest houses on Nantucket Island. The Publick Room is a double parlor with twin fireplaces. Outdoors are porches across three levels of the house with views of the harbor and beyond.
Rates: $90-$145. April to Dec.
Innkeeper(s): Elizabeth York.
10 Rooms. 10 Private Baths. Guest phone available. TV available. Beds: QD. Meals: Continental breakfast. Conference room. Fireplaces. CCs: Visa, MC, AE. Golf, boating, fishing, swimming, tennis.
Seen in: *Country Home.*

Jared Coffin House
29 Broad St
Nantucket MA 02554
(508) 228-2400
Circa 1845. Jared Coffin was one of the island's wealthiest shipowners and the first to build a three-story mansion. Its brick walls and slate roof resisted the Great Fire of 1846 and, in 1847 it was purchased by the Nantucket Steamship Company for use as a hotel. Additions were made and a century later the Nantucket Historical Trust purchased and restored the house. Today the inn consists of five historic houses and a 1964 building. The oldest is the Swain House.
Rates: $90-$135.
Innkeeper(s): Phil and Margaret Read.
58 Rooms. 58 Private Baths. Guest phone in room. TV available. Beds: QDT.
Meals: EP. CCs: All.

Quaker House
5 Chestnut St
Nantucket MA 02554
(508) 228-0400
Circa 1847. The recently renovated Quaker House is situated on a quiet side street in the Nantucket Historic District. Guest rooms are furnished with oriental rugs and period antiques that include brass, iron and carved wood. Its restaurant has been recommended for reasonable rates and outstanding breakfasts.
9 Rooms. 9 Private Baths. Beds: QD.
Meals: Full breakfast. Restaurant. CCs: Visa, MC.

Ships Inn
13 Fair St
Nantucket MA 02554
(508) 228-0040
Circa 1812. Located near the waterfront, this four-story house

was built by Captain Obed Starbuck and is the birthplace of abolitionist

Lucretia Mott. Many of the guest rooms are named for ships that the Captain commanded and authentic furnishings have been selected. The Captain's Table is the inn's restaurant.
Location: Nantucket Island.
Rates: $55-$90. All year.
Innkeeper(s): Joyce Berruet & John Krebs.
12 Rooms. 10 Private Baths. Beds: DT.
Meals: Full restaurant, Continental. Fireplaces. CCs: Visa, MC, AE. Fishing, swimming, boating.

The Woodbox
29 Fair St
Nantucket MA 02554
(508) 228-0587
Circa 1709. Captain Bunker built this house and then an adjoining

house two years later. Eventually they were made into one by cutting into the sides of both. As Nantucket's oldest inn, the Woodbox posseses a gourmet dining room with low beamed ceilings, pine-paneled walls and Early American atmosphere.
Rates: $95-$150. June to Oct.
Innkeeper(s): Dexter Tutein.
9 Rooms. 9 Private Baths. Guest phone available. Beds: KQTD. Meals: EP, Restaurant. Handicap access provided. Conference room. Fireplaces. Swimming, tennis, bicycling.
Seen in: *Wharton Alumni Magazine.*
"Best breakfast on the island."
Yesterday's Island.

West Moor Inn
Off Cliff Rd
Nantucket MA 02554
(508) 228-0877
Circa 1917. Only 300 yards from the beach, this house was built as a wedding gift for a member of the Vanderbilt family. It is situated on two acres at the crest of a hill providing splendid views of meadows, moors and the village.

The yellow shingled house has a library furnished with antique wick-

er and the guest rooms have wallpapers, fine percale sheets and antique pillow covers.
Location: One mile from Nantucket center.
Rates: $90-$165. May to Oct.
Innkeeper(s): Mary Schoen.
9 Rooms. 7 Private Baths. Guest phone available. TV available. Beds: KQ. Meals: Full breakfast, Gourmet. Jacuzzi. Fireplaces. CCs: Visa, MC, AE. Beach.
Seen in: *Inquirer, Mirror.*
"Thank you for a wonderful week. Super place, super innkeeper."

North Eastham

The Penny House
Rt 6 Box 238
North Eastham MA 02651
(508) 255-6632
Circa 1751. Captain Isaiah Horton built this house with a shipbuilder's bow room. Traditional wide-planked floors and 200-year-old beams buttress the ceiling of the public room. The Captain's Quarters is the largest guest room with its own fireplace and motto: *Coil up your ropes and anchor here, Til better weather doth appear.*
Location: Route 6, Cape Cod.
**Rates: $65-$75. All year.
Innkeeper(s): Bill & Margaret Keith.
12 Rooms. 2 Private Baths. Guest phone available. Beds: KQT. Meals: Full breakfast. Fireplaces. CCs: Visa, MC. Bicycling, fishing.
"Enjoyed my stay tremendously. My mouth waters thinking of your delicious breakfast."

Northampton

Deerfield Inn
See: Deerfield, MA

Northfield

Centennial House
94 Main St
Northfield MA 01360
(413) 498-5921
Circa 1811. John Nevers paid $600 for the Stearns brothers, the finest

builders in the area, to construct this colonial house. (Nevers was a Revolutionary War colonel and became a lawyer and legislator.) For years this was the home of the president of Northfield-Mount Hermon School. The parlor is paneled in pine and has exposed beams and a fireplace. The Connecticut River is nearby.
Rates: $45-$65. All year.
Innkeeper(s): Marguerite L. Lentz.
5 Rooms. 2 Private Baths. Guest phone available. TV available. Beds: QTF. Meals: Full breakfast. Conference room. Fireplaces. CCs: Visa, MC. Cross country skiing, hiking, bicycling.
"An enchanting haven in New England!"

Oak Bluffs

Nashua House
30 Kennebec Ave
Oak Bluffs MA 02557
(508) 693-0043
Circa 1873. Methodist campgrounds first occupied Oak Bluffs as a religious retreat. Later, the area was designed by William Copeland, a landscape architect. His idea was to provide "curving ways around open spaces that lent themselves to a meandering stroll, casual encounters between neighbors, a sense of grace, ease, leisure and appreciation of natural beauty." The Victorian guest house is part of Copeland's design.
Location: Martha's Vineyard.
Rates: $29-$60. April to Nov.
Innkeeper(s): Harvy & Son.

15 Rooms. TV available. Beds: WF. Meals: Full breakfast. CCs: Visa, MC. AE. Bicycling, beach activities, water sports.
Seen in: *The Boston Sunday Globe.*

Petersham

Winterwood at Petersham
North Main St
Petersham MA 01366
(508) 724-8885
Circa 1842. The town of Petersham is often referred to as a museum of Greek Revival architecture, and one

of the grand houses facing the common is Winterwood. Originally a summer home, it boasts fireplaces in almost every room and the two-room suite has twin fireplaces. Private dining is available for small groups.
Rates: $80-$100. All year.
Innkeeper(s): Jean & Robert Day.
5 Rooms. 5 Private Baths. Guest phone available. Beds: TF. Meals: Continental plus. Conference room. Fireplaces. CCs: Visa, MC, AE. Hiking, cross country skiing.
Seen in: *Boston Globe.*
"Between your physical facilities and Jean's cooking, our return to normal has been made even more difficult. Your hospitality was just a fantastic extra to our total experience."

Provincetown

Land's End Inn
22 Commercial St
Provincetown MA 02657
(508) 487-0706
Circa 1908. Built as a shingle-style summer cottage for Charles Higgins, a Boston merchant, Land's End stands high on a hill overlooking Provincetown and all of Cape Cod Bay. Part of the Higgins' collection of oriental wood carvings and

stained glass is housed at the inn. Furnished lavishly in a Victorian style, the inn offers a comforting atmosphere for relaxation and beauty.
Rates: $62-$100. All year.
Innkeeper(s): David Schoolman.
14 Rooms. 10 Private Baths. Guest phone available. Beds: F. Meals: Full breakfast. Swimming, bicycling.

Somerset House
378 Commercial St
Provincetown MA 02657
(508) 487-0383
   Circa 1850. Somerset House is 100 feet from the beach and is easily

identified by its profusely planted front garden. It became a guest house in 1928, and rooms are filled with Victorian and modern furnishings. Provincetown Playhouse and restaurants are nearby.
Rates: $40-$75. All year.
Innkeeper(s): Jon Gerrity.
13 Rooms. 10 Private Baths. Guest phone available. Beds: KTD. Meals: EP. Fireplaces. CCs: Visa, MC, AE. Fishing, bicycling, horses.
Seen in: *New York Times*.
   "Meticulously clean and comfortable. Your garden is the talk of the town."

Rehoboth

Perryville Inn
157 Perryville Rd
Rehoboth MA 02769
(508) 252-9239
   Circa 1824. The Perryville Inn was a dairy farm for more than 140 years. Then, the original two-story colonial was remodeled into a handsome three-story Victorian in 1897. (The house was raised and an additional floor added underneath.) The pasture is now a public golf course but the icehouse remains. There are

old stone walls, a mill pond, trout stream and wooded paths. Inside the inn, cozy rooms are decorated with comfortable antiques.
**Rates: $40-$75. All year.
Innkeeper(s): Tom & Betsy Charnecki.
5 Rooms. 3 Private Baths. Guest phone available. Beds: QTD. Meals: Full breakfast, Continental plus. CCs: Visa, MC, AE. Hay & sleigh rides, cross country skiing, golf, tennis, bicycles.
Seen in: *The Providence Journal-Bulletin*.

Rockport

Inn on Cove Hill
37 Mt Pleasant St
Rockport MA 01966
(508) 546-2701
   Circa 1791. Pirate gold found at Gully Point paid for this Federal-style house. An exquisitely-crafted

spiral staircase, random-width, pumpkin-pine floors, and hand-forged hinges display the artisan's handiwork. A picket fence and granite walkway invite guests to stay at a truly historic inn.
Rates: $44-$80. April to Oct.
Innkeeper(s): John & Margorie Pratt.
   Guest phone available. TV in room. Beds: QTD.
   "Everything was superb. Love your restorations, your muffins and your china."

Old Farm Inn
291 Granite St
Rockport MA 01966
(508) 546-3237
   Circa 1799. This old red farmhouse remains a charming example of period country style. Rustic beams, paneling, wide-pine flooring and six fireplaces are original. The initials of James, grandson of the earliest owner are chiseled on the old granite gatepost along with the date,

1799. *The Yankee Bodleys*, a novel by Naomi Babson, is based on the lives of people who lived on the farm in the 1830s.
Location: At Halibut Point on Cape Ann.
Rates: $60-$80. April to Dec.
Innkeeper(s): The Balzarini Family.
7 Rooms. 4 Private Baths. Guest phone available. TV in room. Beds: KQTDC. Meals: Full breakfast, Continental plus. Fireplaces. CCs: Visa, MC. Tennis, fishing, golf, bicycling, horse back riding.
   "We had a wonderful time, the room was so cozy. A fantastic stay with wonderful hosts!"

Rocky Shores Inn
Eden Rd
Rockport MA 01966
(508) 546-2823
   Circa 1905. This grand country mansion was built on wooded land

selected to provide maximum views of Thacher Island and the open sea. There are seven unique fireplaces, handsome woodwork, and a graceful stairway. Guest rooms are in the main house or in several cottages nestled against the trees. Lawns flow from the mansion down to the picturesque shoreline.
Location: On a knoll overlooking the ocean.
**Rates: $82.
Innkeeper(s): Gunter & Renate Kostka.
10 Rooms. 10 Private Baths. Guest phone available. TV in room. Beds: QT. Meals: Continental-plus. Conference room. Fireplaces. CCs: Visa, MC. Nearby whale watching, sailing, fishing, diving, tennis, golf.
   "Fabulous! You and your inn are a five-star rating as far as we are concerned."

Rutland

The General Rufus Putnam House
344 Main St
Rutland MA 01543
(508) 886-4256
   Circa 1750. This restored Federal house, listed in the National

Register, was the home of General Rufus Putnam, founder of Marietta, Ohio. A memorial tablet on the

house states that "to him it is owing...that the United States is not now a great slaveholding empire." Surrounded by tall maples and a rambling stone fence, the inn rests on seven acres of woodlands and meadows. There are eight fireplaces, blue Delft tiles, and a beehive oven. Afternoon tea and breakfast is served fireside in the keeping room where the hostess may often be found in period dress.
Location: Rural/Central Massachusetts.
Rates: $75-$90. All year.
Innkeeper(s): Gordon & Marcia Hickory.
3 Rooms. 1 Private Baths. Guest phone available. TV available. Beds: DTC.
Meals: Full breakfast. Fireplaces. Pool. Swimming, golf, fishing, concerts.
Seen in: *Sunday Telegram.*
   "*We were thrilled not only with the beauty of the place but the luxury and the best hospitality.*"
   "*How pleased we were to have business in Boston that would offer us the opportunity to visit Rufus again.*"

Salem

Amelia Payson Guest House
16 Winter St
Salem MA 01970
(508) 744-8304
   Circa 1845. This elegantly restored two-story wooden house is a prime example of Greek Revival architecture. Located in the heart of the Salem Historic District, it is a short walk to shops, museums and the wharf. Ask for the room with the canopy bed.
Location: Thirteen miles north of Boston.
Rates: $50-$85. All year.
Innkeeper(s): Ada & Donald Roberts.
4 Rooms. 2 Private Baths. Guest phone available. TV in room. Beds: TD. Meals:

Full breakfast, EP. Fireplaces. CCs: Visa, MC, AE, DS. Whale watching.
   "*Your hospitality has been a part of my wonderful experience.*"

Coach House Inn
284 Lafayette St
Salem MA 01970
(508) 744-4092
   Circa 1879. Captain Augustus Emmerton was one of the last Salem

natives to earn his living from maritime commerce. He was master of the barkentine *Sophronia* and the ship *Neptune's Daughter* that sailed to Zanzibar and the Orient. Emmerton's house is an imposing example of Second Empire architecture situated two blocks from the harbor. The House of Seven Gables and the Salem Witch Museum are nearby.
Rates: $69-$76.
11 Rooms. 9 Private Baths. Guest phone available. TV in room. Beds: DT. Meals: B&B. Fireplaces. CCs: Visa, MC, AE.
Seen in: *The North Shore.*

Salem Inn
7 Summer St
Salem MA 01970
(508) 741-0680
   Circa 1834. Captain Nathaniel West, first owner of this historical building, believed that his home should be maintained in readiness for him after returning to shore at his journey's end. Today that same philosophy is practiced for guests of the Salem Inn. The guest rooms are uniquely decorated with homey touches and there are two-room suites with kitchens for families.
Location: Historic downtown.
Rates: $65-$90. All year.
Innkeeper(s): Richard & Diane Pabich.
23 Rooms. 23 Private Baths. Guest phone in room. TV in room. Beds: KQT. Meals: Full breakfast.
   "*Delightful, charming. Our cup of tea.*"

Stephen Daniels House
1 Daniels St
Salem MA 01970
(508) 744-5709
   Circa 1667. This lovely 300-year-old captain's house is one of the few three-story homes of this vintage still intact. A large walk-in fireplace graces the common room and each guest room includes antique furnishings, a canopy bed, and a fireplace. A pleasant English garden filled with colorful blooms surrounds the house.
**Rates: $60-$77. All year.
Innkeeper(s): Catherine Gill.
4 Rooms. 1 Private Baths. TV available. Beds: DT. Meals: Continental. Full by arrangement. Conference room. Fireplaces. CCs: AE. Bicycles available.
   "*Like going back to earlier times.*"

Sandwich

Captain Ezra Nye House
152 Main St
Sandwich MA 02563
(508) 888-6142
   Circa 1829. Captain Ezra Nye built this house after a record-shattering Halifax to Boston run, and the state-

ly Federal-style house reflects the opulence and romance of the clipper ship era. Hand-stenciled walls and museum-quality antiques decorate the interior. Within walking distance are the Doll Museum, the Glass Museum, restaurants, shops, the famous Heritage Plantation, and the beach and marina.
**Rates: $40-$65. All year.
Innkeeper(s): Elaine & Harry Dickson.
6 Rooms. 4 Private Baths. Guest phone available. TV available. Beds: KQT. Meals: Continental plus. Conference room. Fireplaces. CCs: Visa, MC. Piano.
   "*The prettiest room and most beautiful home we have been to. Thank you for everything. We had a wonderful time.*"

The Summer House
158 Main St
Sandwich MA 02563
(508) 888-4991

Circa 1835. The Summer House is a handsome Greek Revival in a setting

of historic homes and public buildings. (Hiram Dillaway, one of the owners, was a famous moldmaker for the Boston & Sandwich Glass Company.) The house is fully restored and decorated with antiques and hand-stitched quilts. Four of the guest rooms have black marble fireplaces. The porch overlooks old-fashioned perennial gardens, antique rose bushes, and a 70-year-old rhododendron hedge.
Location: Center of village, Cape Cod.
Rates: $35-$70. March to Dec.
Innkeeper(s): David & Kay Merrell.
5 Rooms. 1 Private Baths. Guest phone available. Beds: KQT. Meals: Full breakfast. Fireplaces. CCs: Visa, MC. Beach.
Seen in: Country Living Magazine.

"This is just full of charm. As beautiful as a fairy world."

Sheffield

Centuryhurst
Bed & Breakfast
Box 486 Main St
Sheffield MA 01257
(413) 229-8131

Circa 1800. Dr. William Buell built this house to contain both his home and an office for country doctors in the area. There are unique archways and an unusually large fireplace with a beehive bake oven. The inn serves as an antique shop specializing in Wedgwood and antique clocks.
Rates: $52-$58. All year.
Innkeeper(s): Ronald & Judith Timm.
4 Rooms. Guest phone available. TV available. Beds: TF. Meals: Full breakfast, continental. Conference room.

Fireplaces. Pool. CCs: Visa, MC, AE. Bicycling, hiking, fishing, tennis, golf, canoeing, horses.
Seen in: Travel and Leisure.

Colonel Ashley Inn
Bow Wow Road, RR 1, PO Box 142
Sheffield MA 01257
(413) 229-2929

Circa 1814. Although this isn't actually Colonel Ashley's house, the innkeeper is Colonel Ashley's direct

descendant. The Colonel founded Sheffield, and in 1774 wrote a declaration of independence. His slave Mum Beth overheard the declaration and sued for her own independence. She was the first slave in America to win freedom through the courts. The Colonel Ashley inn is a center-chimney farmhouse in a picturesque setting at the intersection of two country roads. It is flanked by a historic schoolhouse and a hired man's cottage.
Location: Twenty-five minutes from Tanglewood.
**Rates: $50-$95. May to March.
Innkeeper(s): Nancy & Gery Torborg.
4 Rooms. 4 Private Baths. Guest phone in room. TV in room. Beds: QTC. Meals: Full breakfast, Restaurant. Conference room. Fireplaces. CCs: Visa, MC. Swimming, golf, tennis, lawn games.
Seen in: Getaways for Gourmets, The Zenith Traveler.

"Thanks so much for another peaceful, serene, carefree, thought provoking, educational and thoroughly enjoyable weekend. You make us feel like family."

Staveleigh House
PO 608, South Main St
Sheffield MA 01257
(413) 229-2129

Circa 1821. The Reverand Bradford, minister of Old Parish Congregational Church, the oldest church in the Berkshires, built this home for his family. Mysteriously, the name Staveleigh is carved into

the mantel of the living room fireplace. Afternoon tea is served here. The house is located next to the town green, in the shade of century-old trees.
Rates: $70-$85. All year.
Innkeeper(s): Dorothy Marosy & Marion Whitman.
5 Rooms. 2 Private Baths. Guest phone available. Beds: QTD. Meals: Full breakfast. Fireplaces. Skiing, horseback riding, hiking, bicycling, canoeing.
Seen in: Los Angeles Times, Country Inns of America.

"Exceptionally good."

South Egremont

Egremont Inn
Old Sheffield Rd
South Egremont MA 01258
(413) 528-2111

Circa 1780. This three-story inn is adjacent to a quiet, tree-lined stream where guests have spent many a

summer day. There are private tennis courts on the premises. A wraparound porch is decorated with white wicker and guest rooms are furnished with antiques. There is a tavern and a dining room.
Rates: $70-$150. All year.
Innkeeper(s): John Black.
23 Rooms. 23 Private Baths. Guest phone available. TV available. Beds: QD. Meals: MAP, EP, Restaurant. Fireplaces. Pool. CCs: Visa, MC, AE. Swimming, tennis, golf, hiking, riding.

Weathervane Inn
PO Box 388
South Egremont MA 01258
(413) 528-9580

Circa 1785. Nine years were spent restoring this rambling old house that was formerly a kennel, store, and dance studio. Long ago, it was also an inn. Today high ceilings,

handsome moldings, and a beehive oven are featured attractions.

Location: Main Street, Route 23.
Innkeeper(s): Vincent & Anne Murphy.
12 Rooms. 12 Private Baths. Guest phone available. TV available. Beds: KQT. Meals: Full breakfast, Restaurant. Handicap access provided. Conference room. CCs: Visa, MC, AE. Downhill & cross country skiing, fishing, tennis, golf.
Seen in: *New York Times, Berkshire Eagle, Berkshire Business Journal.*

"...the Murphy family exemplifies the best tradition of New England hospitality." Berkshire Business Journal.

South Lee

Historic Merrell Tavern Inn
Rt 102 Main St
South Lee MA 01260
(413) 243-1794

Circa 1794. This elegant stagecoach inn was carefully preserved under supervision of the Society for the Preservation of New England Antiquities. Architectural drawings of Merrill Tavern have been preserved by the Library of Congress. Eight fireplaces in the inn include two that were used for cooking with original beehive and warming ovens. An original circular birdcage bar now serves as a check-in desk. Comfortable rooms feature canopy and four-poster beds and Hepplewhite and Sheraton-style antiques.

Rates: $65-$120. All year.
Innkeeper(s): Charles & Faith Reynolds.
8 Rooms. 8 Private Baths. Guest phone available. Beds: TD. Meals: Full breakfast. Fireplaces. CCs: Visa, MC, AE. Downhill & cross-country skiing.

"One of the most authentic period inns on the East Coast." The Discerning Traveler.

South Sudbury

Longfellow's Wayside Inn
Wayside Inn Rd
South Sudbury MA 01776
(617) 443-8846

Circa 1702. Henry Ford endowed the non-profit corporation that manages the Wayside Inn in 1944, to preserve it as a historic and literary shrine. The inn's second owner is known to have led the colonists of Sudbury on the march to Concord on April 19, 1775, toward the Old North Bridge. Originally opened as How's Tavern in 1702, it later became Red Horse Tavern. Finally, in 1897, a new owner, acknowledging the popular association with Longfellow's poem, *Tales of a Wayside Inn*, changed the name. The Old Barroom, Longfellow's Parlor, the pianoforte and grandfather clock are all here. A reproduction Grist Mill, and the Redstone Schoolhouse are open for touring. Allow six to twelve months ahead for reservations.

Rates: $52.50 & up.
10 Rooms. 10 Private Baths. Beds: TD. Conference room. CCs: All major.

Stockbridge

Colonel Ashley Inn
See: Sheffield, MA

Sturbridge

Captain Samuel Eddy House Inn
See: Auburn, MA

Commonwealth Inn
11 Summit Ave
Sturbridge MA 01566
(617) 347-7603

Circa 1890. This 16-room Victorian house overlooks the Quinebaug River just a few minutes from Old Sturbridge Village. Two parlors, each with a marble fireplace, is

available to guests. The inn is decorated in a country style. The

veranda has two gazebos, one on each end.

Rates: $40-$55.
Innkeeper(s): Kevin MacConnell.
8 Rooms. 5 Private Baths. Guest phone available. TV in room. Meals: Full breakfast. Jacuzzi. Fireplaces.

Vineyard Haven

Captain Dexter House
100 Main St, PO Box 2457
Vineyard Haven MA 02568
(508) 693-6564

Circa 1843. Captain Dexter House was the home of sea captain Rodolphus Dexter. Authentic 18th-century

antiques, early American oil paintings and oriental rugs are among the inn's appointments. There are Count Rumford fireplaces and hand-stenciled walls in several rooms. Located on a street of fine historic homes, the inn is a short stroll to the beach.

Location: Martha's Vineyard.
**Rates: $55-$130. All year.
Innkeeper(s): Julia Ross & Roberta Pieczenik.
8 Rooms. 8 Private Baths. Guest phone available. Beds: KQT. Meals: Continental. Conference room. Fireplaces. CCs: Visa, MC, AE. Horseback riding, wind surfing, bicycling, tennis, boating.

"The house is sensational. Your hospitality was all one could expect.

You've made us permanent bed and breakfast fans."

Lothrop Merry House

Owen Park Box 1939
Vineyard Haven MA 02568
(508) 693-1646

Circa 1790. Eight yoke of oxen moved this house to its present

beach-front location. A wedding gift from father to daughter, the house has a classic center chimney and six fireplaces. Breakfast is served in season on the flower bedecked patio overlooking stunning harbor views. A private beach beckons at the end of a sloping lawn.
Location: Martha's Vineyard.
Rates: $68-$113. All year.
Innkeeper(s): John & Mary Clarke.
7 Rooms. 4 Private Baths. Guest phone available. Beds: QTC. Meals: Continental. CCs: Visa, MC. Golf, tennis, bicycling, sailing, canoeing.
"It is the nicest place we've ever stayed."

Ware

The Wildwood Inn

121 Church St
Ware MA 01082
(413) 967-7798

Circa 1880. This yellow Victorian has a wraparound porch and a beveled glass front door. American primitive antiques include a collection of New England cradles, and there is a cobbler's bench, a sled, and a spinning wheel. The inn's two acres are dotted with maple, chestnut and apple trees, and through the woods is a river.
Rates: $34-$62. All year.
Innkeeper(s): Margaret Lobenstine.
5 Rooms. Guest phone available. Beds: QTD. Meals: Full breakfast. Fireplaces.

CCs: Visa, MC, AE. Tennis, canoeing, swimming, hiking, cross country skiing.
Seen in: *The Boston Globe.*

West Barnstable

Honeysuckle Hill

591 Main St
West Barnstable MA 02668
(508) 362-8418

Circa 1825. This Queen Anne Victorian built by Josiah Goodspeed is

in the National Register. Guest rooms are decorated with Victorian sofas, Peter Rabbit memorabilia, and St. Louis antiques. Feather beds, Laura Ashley linens and fluffy pillows are among the other amenities.
Location: Cape Cod.
**Rates: $85-$95. All year.
Innkeeper(s): Barbard & Bob Rosenthal.
3 Rooms. 3 Private Baths. Guest phone available. TV available. Beds: KQ. Meals: Full breakfast. Conference room. Fireplaces. CCs: Visa, MC, AE. Bicycling, beach.
"The charm, beauty, service and warmth shown to guests are impressive, but the food overwhelms. Breakfasts were divine!" Judy Kaplan, *St. Louis Journal.*

West Harwich

Cape Cod Sunny Pines B&B

77 Main Street
West Harwich MA 02671
(508) 432-9628

Circa 1900. Caleb Chase of Chase and Sanbourne coffee fame built this house as a parsonage for the local Baptist Church. It later became the town library and then, in the Forties, a guest house. An Irish candlelight breakfast is served. The innkeeper was an oceanographer for 20 years.
**Rates: $30-$75. All year.
Innkeeper(s): Jack & Eileen Connell.
6 Rooms. 6 Private Baths. Guest phone in room. TV in room. Beds: KQT. Meals:

Full breakfast, Gourmet extra. Fireplaces. Pool. CCs: Visa, MC, AE. Hiking, bicycling, swimming, fishing, water sports. Irish candlelight breakfast.

Lion's Head Inn

186 Belmont Rd PO 444
West Harwich MA 02671
(508) 432-7766

Circa 1804. This Cape half-house was built by sea captain Thomas Snow. Original pine floors and a ship's ladder staircase are features of the inn. It is decorated in antiques and traditional furnishings and several old maps hang in the Map Room, once used as a study for Captain Snow.
**Rates: $72-$85. All year.
Innkeeper(s): Kathleen & William Lockyer.
4 Rooms. 2 Private Baths. Guest phone available. Beds: KT. Meals: Full breakfast. Fireplaces. CCs: Visa, MC. Badminton, beach, fishing, boating, golf.
"The best innkeepers we have met on the Cape!"

Worcester

Captain Samuel Eddy House Inn

See: Auburn, MA

Samuel Watson House

See: Thompson, CT

Yarmouth Port

Liberty Hill Inn

77 Main St
Yarmouth Port MA 02675
(508) 362-3976

Circa 1825. This Greek Revival mansion is located on the site of the original Liberty Pole dating from

Revolutionary times. To benefit the Cape Cod Conservatory of Music several local decorators restored the rooms. There are outstanding English gardens and the inn's setting on the hill affords views of Cape Cod Bay. On historic Old King's Highway, it's a brief walk to antique shops, auctions, and restaurants.
Rates: $50-$80. All year.
Innkeeper(s): Beth & Jack Flanagan.
5 Rooms. 5 Private Baths. Guest phone available. TV available. Beds: KQT. Meals: Continental.

"I loved the large airy room and the bay view."

Old Yarmouth Inn
223 Main St
Yarmouth Port MA 02675
(508) 362-3191
Circa 1696. The Old Yarmouth was originally built as an inn and is one of America's oldest. There is a guest register from the 1860s when it was called the Sears Hotel. Traveling salesmen often stayed here and according to the register they sold such items as Henry's Vermont Linament, lightning rods, sewing machines and drilled-eye needles. Today this venerable inn has rooms with antiques, but also cable television and air-conditioning.
Location: King's Highway, Route 6A.
Rates: $55-$80. All year.
Innkeeper(s): Shane Peros.
5 Rooms. 5 Private Baths. Guest phone available. TV in room. Beds: QT. Meals: Continental plus. Restaurant. CCs: Visa, MC, AE, DC. Beaches.
Seen in: *The Register, Travel News.*

Michigan

Allegan

Winchester Inn
524 Marshall St
Allegan MI 49010
(616) 673-3621

Circa 1863. This neo-Italian Renaissance mansion was built of double-layer brick and has been restored to

its original beauty. Surrounded by a unique hand-poured iron fence, the inn is decorated with period antiques and romantically furnished bed chambers. Choices include amenities such as a canopy bed or fireplace and whether to have breakfast in the elegant dining room or in bed.
**Rates: $45-$95.
Innkeeper(s): Marge & Shawn Gavan, Gail & Keith Miller.
5 Rooms. 5 Private Baths. Guest phone available. TV available. Beds: QT. Meals: Full breakfast. Handicap access provided. Conference room. CCs: Visa, MC. Skiing, boating, horseback riding, fishing. Murder mystery weekends.
Seen in: *Architectural Digest*.
"This is one of Michigan's loveliest country inns."

Ann Arbor

The Homestead
See: Saline, MI

Big Bay

Big Bay Lighthouse Bed & Breakfast
3 Lighthouse Rd
Big Bay MI 49808
(906) 345-9957

Circa 1896. With 4,500 feet of frontage on Lake Superior this landmark lighthouse commands 534 acres of forests and five acres of lawn. The interior of the lighthouse features a brick fireplace and several guest rooms look out to the water. The tower room on the top floor boasts truly unforgettable views.
Location: Four miles northeast of Big Bay.
Rates: $75-$100. All year.
Innkeeper(s): Buck & Marilyn Gotschall.
6 Rooms. 7 Private Baths. Guest phone available. Beds: DT. Meals: Full breakfast. Sauna. Conference room. Fireplaces. Hiking, bicycling, skiing.
Seen in: *Los Angeles Times, USA Today*.
"The fact that anyone who has ever met Buck Gottschall or stayed at the Lighthouse will tell everyone they know that they have to go there, in my opinion, makes Buck Gottschall the Ambassador of the year." Vic Krause, State Representative.

Detroit

Bed & Breakfast in Michigan
Detroit MI
(313) 561-6041

Circa 1905. The Marvin Stanton family built this Victorian, known locally as the Little White House because of its two-story pillared portico. Henry Ford II attended school here when it was a private boys school. The entrance features 10-foot-high doors with etched glass and the interiors boast oak woodwork and floors. All the rooms are furnished with antiques. It is represented by B&B in Michigan, a reservation agency at PO Box 1731, Dearborn MI 48121. Call Diane Shields for arrangements.
Location: One mile from Belle Isle.
Rates: $70-$75.
7 Rooms. 7 Private Baths. Meals: Continental. Fireplaces.

Grand Rapids

Kemah Guest House
See: Saugatuck, MI

Holland

Old Wing Inn
5298 E 147th Ave
Holland MI 49423
(616) 392-7362

Circa 1844. This home was built for Rev. George Smith, a missionary for an Ottawa Indian colony. In the National Register, it is the oldest house in town. In May, Holland's tulip festival draws many gardeners into the area. A Dutch village and wooden shoe factories are nearby.
Location: One-ane-a-half miles east of US 31.
Innkeeper(s): Chuck & Chris Lorenz.
5 Rooms. 2 Private Baths. Meals: Continental plus. CCs: Visa, MC.

The Parsonage

6 E 24th St
Holland MI 49423
(616) 396-1316

Circa 1908. Members of Prospect Park Christian Reformed Church

built this Queen Anne as their parsonage and over the years it housed nine different pastors and their families. Rich oak woodwork, antique furnishings, and leaded glass are found throughout the inn. There are two sitting rooms, a formal dining room, garden patio and summer porch. The inn flies a B&B flag designed by the hosts and available at The Parsonage.
Location: Close to Hope College.
Rates: $50-$70. All year.
Innkeeper(s): Bonnie Verwys.
4 Rooms. Guest phone available. TV available. Beds: DT. Meals: Full breakfast, continental plus. Conference room. CCs: MC. Cross-country skiing, golf, tennis, boating.
"Charming, we slept so well!"

Lakeside

The Pebble House

15093 Lakeshore Rd
Lakeside MI 49116
(616) 469-1416

Circa 1912. Built during the Arts and Crafts Movement, Pebble House is named for the small beach

stones selected to construct portions of the exterior, fence and fireplace. An enclosed porch, tennis courts and decks are popular spots along

with the lake view. The inn is furnished with Empire pieces.
Rates: $80-$90. All year.
Innkeeper(s): Jean & Ed Lawrence.
7 Rooms. 7 Private Baths. Guest phone available. Beds: KD. Meals: Full breakfast. Handicap access provided. Fireplaces. CCs: Visa, MC. Tennis, cross-country skiing, beach, nature centers.
Seen in: *Chicago Sun-Times.*
"Beautiful place, wonderful hospitality, cute cats."

Marquette

Big Bay Lighthouse

See: Big Bay, MI

Mendon

The Mendon Country Inn

440 W Main St
Mendon MI 49072
(616) 496-8132

Circa 1873. This two-story inn was constructed with St. Joseph River clay bricks fired on the property. There are eight-foot windows, high ceilings and a walnut staircase. Country antiques are accentuated with rag rugs, collectibles, and bright quilts and the Indian Room has a fireplace. A creek runs by the property and a romantic courting canoe is available to guests. Depending on the season guests may also borrow a tandem bike or arrange for an Amish sleigh ride.
Location: Halfway between Chicago and Detroit.
**Rates: $40-$72. All year.
Innkeeper(s): Dick & Dolly Buerkle.
11 Rooms. 11 Private Baths. Guest phone available. TV available. Beds: QD. Meals: Full breakfast. Jacuzzi. Handicap access provided. Conference room. Fireplaces. CCs: Visa, MC, AE. Fishing, tennis, golf, bicycles, swimming, cross-country skiing.
Seen in: *Innsider.*
"A great experience. Good food and great hosts. Thank you."

Niles

Yesterdays Inn

518 N 4th
Niles MI 49120
(616) 683-6079

Circa 1875. Nearly every style of architecture can be found on Fourth Street in the historical district. This distinctive Italianate house has a graceful porch and tall shuttered windows. The walls are 12 inches thick with the interior plaster applied directly onto the brick. The innkeepers maintain a collection of antique oriental chests.
Location: Eight miles north of South Bend.
Rates: $50-$55.
Innkeeper(s): Dawn & Phil Semler.
5 Rooms. 5 Private Baths. Jacuzzi.

Northport

Old Mill Pond Inn

202 W Third St
Northport MI 49670
(616) 386-7341

Circa 1895. This three-story summer cottage nestles among tall trees

and is surrounded by extensive gardens including a Roman garden with fountain and statues. Inside the house is an unusual collection of pieces from around the world. Breakfast is served by the fireside or on the screened porch with its white wicker furnishings. Shops and restaurants are within two blocks and the beach is a quarter of a mile.
Rates: $65. June to Nov.
Innkeeper(s): David Chrobak.
6 Rooms. Guest phone available. TV available. Beds: QT. Meals: Full breakfast. Fireplaces. CCs: Visa, MC. Sailing, fishing, swimming, hiking.

Port Sanilac

Raymond House Inn
M-25, 111 S Ridge St
Port Sanilac MI 48469
(313) 622-8800

Circa 1871. Uri Raymond, owner of Michigan's first hardware store,

built this Gothic house with its gingerbread facade and white icicle trim dripping from the eaves. The inn is filled with antiques and features classic moldings, high ceilings and a winding staircase. The innkeeper is a sculptor and works as a restoration artist at the U. S. Capitol. Be sure to visit the historic lighthouse nearby.
Location: I-94 to Port Huron, then 30 miles on M-25.
**Rates: $50. May to Nov.
Innkeeper(s): Shirley Denison.
7 Rooms. 7 Private Baths. Guest phone available. TV available. Beds: Q. Meals: Continental plus. Fireplaces. Sport fishing, swimming, sailing, golf, bicycling, scuba diving.
"A warm, friendly, relaxed, homey atmosphere like visiting friends and family."

Saline

The Homestead
9279 Macon Rd
Saline MI 48176
(313) 429-9625

Circa 1851. The Homestead is a two-story brick farmhouse situated on 50 acres of fields, woods and river. The house has 15-inch-thick walls and is furnished with Victorian antiques and family heirlooms. This was a favorite camping spot for Indians while they salted their fish, and many arrowheads have been found on the farm. Ac-

tivities include long walks through meadows of wildflowers and cross-

country skiing in season. It is 40 minutes from Detroit and Toledo and five minutes from Ann Arbor.
Location: Southeastern Michigan, within six miles of I-94 & US23.
**Rates: $26-$55. All year.
Innkeeper(s): Shirley Grossman.
5 Rooms. Guest phone in room. TV available. Beds: DT. Meals: Full breakfast. Conference room. CCs: Visa, MC, DC, CB. Golf, tennis.
"One of the nicest B&Bs we've ever stayed in."

Saugatuck

Kemah Guest House
633 Pleasant St
Saugatuck MI 49453
(616) 857-2919

Circa 1906. Stained-glass windows, beamed ceilings, and stone and tile fireplaces are features of this house.

There is a billiard room, and a Bavarian rathskeller with German inscriptions on the wall and original wine kegs. Deco Dormer, a guest room with a mahogany bedroom suite, was featured in a 1926 *Architectural Digest*. That same year, a Frank Lloyd Wright-style solarium with its own waterfall was added to the house. Kemah is situated on two hilltop acres with views of the water. There is also a cave on the property.
Rates: $75-$95. All year.
Innkeeper(s): Cindi & Terry Tatsch.
7 Rooms. Guest phone available. TV available. Beds: DT. Meals: Continental

plus. Conference room. Fireplaces. CCs: Visa, MC. Golf, sailing, cross-country skiing.
"What a wonderful time we had at Kemah. Thank you for a delightful stay. Your home is very special."

Maplewood Hotel
428 Butler St Box 1059
Saugatuck MI 49453
(616) 857-2788

Circa 1860. On the quiet village green in the center of Saugatuck

stands the Maplewood Hotel. Built during Michigan's lumber era, the elegant three-story Greek Revival boasts four massive wooden pillars, each 25-feet high. The interiors include crystal chandeliers, period furniture, and well-appointed lounge areas.
Rates: $400-$134. All year.
Innkeeper(s): Donald & Harriet Mitchell.
13 Rooms. 13 Private Baths. Guest phone available. TV in room. Beds: KQC. Meals: Continental, gourmet dining room. Conference room. Pool. CCs: Visa, MC, AE. Swimming.
"Staying at the Maplewood provided the pleasure of listening to classical music on the player grand piano. It was so easy vacationing...steps from boutiques, art galleries and antique shops."

The Kirby House
294 W Center St, PO Box 1174
Saugatuck MI 49453
(616) 857-2904

Circa 1890. This impressive Victorian sits behind a picket fence and is framed by tall trees. The inn has four fireplaces and a grand staircase.

A veranda wraps around three sides.
Location: Near Lake Michigan.
Rates: $55-$75. All year.
Innkeeper(s): Marsha & Loren Kontio.
10 Rooms. 4 Private Baths. Guest phone available. Beds: QDT. Meals: Full breakfast. Jacuzzi. Fireplaces. Pool. CCs: Visa, MC, AE. Beachcombing, hiking, swimming.
Seen in: *Michigan Today Magazine*.

The Park House
888 Holland St
Saugatuck MI 49453
(616) 857-4535
Circa 1857. This Greek Revival is the oldest residence in Saugatuck

and was constructed for the first mayor. Susan B. Anthony was a guest here for two weeks in the 1870s, and the local Women's Christian Temperance League was established in the parlor. A country theme pervades the inn with antiques, old woodwork, and pine floors.
**Rates: $49-$75. All year.
Innkeeper(s): Lynda & Joe Petty.
8 Rooms. 8 Private Baths. Guest phone available. TV available. Beds: Q. Meals: Continental plus. Handicap access provided. Conference room. Fireplaces. CCs: Visa, MC. Cross-country skiing, swimming, hiking.
Seen in: *Innsider, Gazette*.

The Parsonage
See: Holland, MI

Tecumseh

Boulevard Inn
904 W Chicago Blvd
Tecumseh MI 49286
(517) 423-5169
Circa 1854. Chosen as a designer showcase home for the local historical society, this sparkling Italianate Victorian displays friendly white

gingerbread, lavender clapboard, and curlicued brackets. Inside are 10-foot ceilings, ornate borders, bay windows, an elegant parlor, antiques and chandeliers. A romantic gazebo looks out over flower gardens and landscaped grounds.
Innkeeper(s): Gary & Judy Hicks
8 Rooms. Guest phone available.
Seen in: *Better Homes & Gardens, Small Towns in Michigan*.

Traverse City

Warwickshire Inn
5037 Barney Rd
Traverse City MI 49684
(616) 946-7176
Circa 1902. The Warwickshire is a farm home located in a country setting, yet with a panoramic view of Traverse City. Spacious rooms feature turn-of-the century Victorian furnishings. Afternoon tea and breakfast are served elegantly on fine china.
Location: Two miles west of City Center.
Rates: $68.
Innkeeper(s): Dan & Pat Warwick.
3 Rooms. 3 Private Baths. Meals: Full breakfast.

Minnesota

Cannon Falls

Quill & Quilt
615 W Hoffman St
Cannon Falls MN 55009
(507) 263-5507

Circa 1897. This colonial Revival, a three-story gabled house, has six bay windows and several porches

and decks. The inn features a well-stocked library, a front parlor with a fireplace, and handsomely decorated guest rooms. A favorite is the room with a double whirlpool tub, two bay windows, king-size, oak canopy bed and Victorian chairs.
Location: Forty-five miles from Minneapolis/St. Paul, and Rochester.
**Rates: $55-$95. All year.
Innkeeper(s): Denise Anderson & David Karpinski.
4 Rooms. 4 Private Baths. Guest phone in room. TV available. Beds: KQD. Meals: AP, full breakfast. Jacuzzi. Fireplaces. CCs: Visa, MC. Bicycling, hiking, canoeing, cross-country skiing, tubing.
"What a pleasure to find the charm and hospitality of an English country home while on holiday in the United States."

Chaska

Bluff Creek Inn
1161 Bluff Creek Dr
Chaska MN 55318
(612) 445-2735

Circa 1864. This two-story brick Victorian folk home was built on land granted by Abe Lincoln to one of the earliest settlers in the area. It boasts a wide veranda and three summer porches. Family antiques are accentuated by Laura Ashley and Merrimekko quilts and linens. A three-course breakfast is served in the country dining room with Bavarian Crystal and old English China.
Rates: $65-$85. All year.
Innkeeper(s): Anne Karels.
4 Rooms. 1 Private Baths. Guest phone available. Beds: QD. Meals: Full breakfast. Fireplaces. CCs: Visa, MC. Bike trails, cross-country skiing, walking paths.

Grand Marais

Naniboujou Lodge
HC 1 Box 505
Grand Marais MN 55604
(218) 387-2688

Circa 1928. Built originally as an exclusive private club, this cedar and cypress lodge was constructed on land that includes a mile of Lake Superior shoreline. Babe Ruth and Jack Dempsey were charter members, but after the stock market crash of 1929 the club fell into financial straits. Now rejuvenated, the lodge possesses Minnesota's largest native rock fireplace, and a dining room painted in brilliant colors with

Cree Indian designs on the vaulted ceilings and walls.
Location: On the shores of Lake Superior, 15 miles east of Grand Marais.
Rates: $35-$60. May 15-Oct. 15
Innkeeper(s): Tim & Nancy Ramey.
29 Rooms. 15 Private Baths. Guest phone available. TV available. Beds: QDT. Meals: EP. Fireplaces. CCs: Visa, MC, AE, DC. Hiking, cross-country skiing.
Seen in: *Twin Cities Reader.*

Harmony

Michel Farm Vacations
Rt 1 Box 914
Harmony MN 55939
(507) 886-5392

Circa 1889. This is an association of working farm families located in southeastern Minnesota and northeastern Iowa. There are dairy farms, an Amish colony, country lanes, and winding trout streams in the area. One family shares its secret bass-fishing spots while another gives buggy rides and jeep excursions through the woods. Many of the quaint farmhouses and old barns are historic.
40 Rooms. Beds: QT. Meals: Full breakfast.

Lanesboro

Scanlan House
708 Park Ave S
Lanesboro MN 55949
(507) 467-2158

Circa 1890. This gracious Victorian, a National Register house, was built

by the Scanlans, successful merchants and bankers. Window boxes and garden areas have been added. There are stained-glass windows throughout, and carved oak woodwork adorns the dining room and staircase.
**Rates: $45-$55. All year.
Innkeeper(s): Mary, Gene & Kirsten Mensing.
5 Rooms. 1 Private Baths. Guest phone available. TV in room. Beds: QC. Meals: Full breakfast. Conference room. Fireplaces. CCs: Visa, MC, AE. Skiing, bicycles, golf, tennis, tubing, canoeing.
Seen in: *Post-Bulletin*.

"A fantastic weekend. Your decorating is so homey and fun."

Minneapolis/St. Paul

Chatsworth Bed & Breakfast
See: Saint Paul, MN

Quill & Quilt
See: Cannon Falls, MN

Scanlan House
See: Lanesboro, MN

The Northrop House
See: Owatonna, MN

University Club of St. Paul
See: Saint Paul, MN

Morris

The American House
410 E Third St

Morris MN 56267
(612) 589-4054

Circa 1900. One block from the Morris Campus of the University of Minnesota, this is a two-story house with a wide veranda. It is decorated in a country style with original stencil designs, stained glass, and family heirlooms. The Elizabeth Room holds a Jenny Lind bed with a hand-crocheted bedcover.
Location: One block from University of Morris campus.
Rates: $30-$44. All year.
Innkeeper(s): Karen Berget.
3 Rooms. Guest phone available. TV available. Beds: D. Meals: Full breakfast. Conference room. Bicycling, cross-country skiing, tennis, hunting, golf.

"We certainly enjoyed ourselves last week. It was one of the best B&Bs we've visited!"

Owatonna

The Northrop House
358 E Main St
Owatonna MN 55060
(507) 451-4040

Circa 1890. This inviting, three-story Victorian house was built as a wedding present from a father to his daughter. The Northrop family, noted scholars and statesmen, purchased it later. The library features a fireplace and Victorian furnishings, and in the west parlor there is a grand piano. One of the guest rooms has a marble fireplace.
Rates: $44-$49. All year.
Innkeeper(s): Nancy Rowe & Greg Northrop.
3 Rooms. Guest phone available. TV available. Beds: T. Meals: Full breakfast. Conference room. Fireplaces. CCs: Visa, MC. Bicycling, parks.

"Excellent coffee, great breakfast."

Red Wing

Pratt-Taber Inn
706 W Fourth
Red Wing MN 55066
(612) 388-5945

Circa 1876. City treasurer A. W. Pratt built this Italianate house during the town centennial, adding star-studded porch detailing to the gingerbread trim to celebrate the event. Feather-painted slate

fireplaces and gleaming butternut woodwork provide a backdrop for early Renaissance Revival and country Victorian furnishings. There is a Murphy bed hidden in the library buffet. Other library items include 1,000 stereoptican slides and a Victrola. Secret bureau drawers, authentic Victorian wallpapers, dress-up clothes and hand-stenciling add to the atmosphere.
Location: Fifty-five miles south of the Twin Cities.
**Rates: $69-$89. All year.
Innkeeper(s): Jane Walker, Jan Mc-Dermott, Darrell Molander.
6 Rooms. 2 Private Baths. Guest phone available. TV available. Beds: KQDT. Meals: Full breakfast. Handicap access provided. Conference room. Fireplaces. CCs: Visa, MC. Golf, hiking, bicycling.
Seen in: *Better Homes & Gardens, Midwest Living*.

"When I need a peaceful moment I dream of the Pratt-Taber and the big screened-in porch and the church bells chiming a favorite tune."

Rochester

Canterbury Inn
Bed & Breakfast
723 2nd St SW
Rochester MN 55902
(507) 289-5553

Circa 1890. Ornate scrollwork adorns the four gables of this three-story, red gingerbread Victorian. The house dates from the time of a tor-

nado instrumental in opening the Mayo Clinic, three blocks away.

Carved oak spindles grace the stairway and fireplaces enhance the Victorian decor. A proper afternoon tea is served.
**Rates: $55-$65.
Innkeeper(s): Mary Martin & Jeffrey Van Sant.
4 Rooms. 4 Private Baths. Guest phone in room. TV available. Beds: KQT. Meals: Full breakfast, gourmet extra. Jacuzzi. Conference room. Fireplaces. CCs: Visa, MC. Canoeing, golf, tennis, cross-country skiing. Pick up service from airport.
Seen in: *Dispatch.*

"Rochester's B&B treasure." Bill Farmer, *St. Paul Pioneer Press.*

Saint Paul

Chatsworth Bed & Breakfast
984 Ashland
Saint Paul MN 55104
(612) 227-4288

Circa 1902. This three-story red Victorian is framed by maple and basswood trees. Guest rooms are decorated in an international theme

except for the Four Poster Room, which features a canopy bed, whirlpool bath, mirrored armoire, and a wallpaper of roses that covers both the ceiling and the walls. Vegetarian breakfasts are available and the innkeeper is known for her cranberry bread.
Rates: $42-$85. All year.
Innkeeper(s): Donna & Earl Gustafson.
5 Rooms. 2 Private Baths. Guest phone available. Beds: KQT. Meals: Full breakfast. Conference room. Fireplaces.
Seen in: *St. Paul Pioneer Press and Dispatch.*

"Wonderful and romantic surroundings everywhere. So beautifully kept, fresh and clean. Tremendous service."

University Club of St. Paul
420 Summit Ave

Saint Paul MN 55102
(612) 222-1751

Circa 1912. This Tudor Revival mansion is modeled after the Cambridge and Oxford Clubs in London, established to enhance literary, cultural and social activities

for the well-educated. Fine English antiques and oil paintings of English landscapes decorate the interiors. In the Grill Bar, F. Scott Fitzgerald's initials can be found carved beside those of other club members. There is a library, dining room, the Fireside Room and a fitness center.
Rates: $35-$75. All year.
5 Rooms. 3 Private Baths. TV available. Beds: QT. Meals: Restaurant. Sauna. Conference room. Fireplaces. Pool. CCs: Visa, MC, AE, DC. Tennis, exercise room, playground.
Seen in: *Minnesota USA Magazine.*

Spring Valley

Chase's
508 N Huron Ave
Spring Valley MN 55975
(507) 346-2850

Circa 1879. This brick, Second Empire house is in the National Register and features a mansard roof, arched windows, and a long porch. Several parlors and the guest

rooms display antiques for sale. Beds include a walnut Renaissance Revival hooded bed, a pine canopy bed, and a golden oak, six-foot-tall double bed.
**Rates: $50-$60. Closed January.
Innkeeper(s): Bob & Jeannine Chase.
5 Rooms. 2 Private Baths. Guest phone available. TV available. Beds: KQD. Meals: Full breakfast. Fireplaces. CCs: Visa, MC. Trout fishing, cross-country skiing, hiking, canoeing.
"It's so beautiful!"

Stillwater

Lowell Inn
102 N Second St
Stillwater MN 55082
(612) 439-1100

Circa 1930. The Palmer family has operated this Williamsburg-style hotel since Christmas Day 1930, collecting antiques and fine tableware all this time. The George

Washington Room is a parlor containing collections of Dresden china, a Charles III Sheffield silver service, Williamsburg ladder-back chairs, and colonial draperies. A natural spring bubbles in the Garden Room. Guest rooms include four suites with jacuzzi baths.
Rates: $89-$239. All year.
Innkeeper(s): Arthur & Maureen Palmer.
21 Rooms. 21 Private Baths. Guest phone in room. Beds: KQC. Meals: AP, EP, Restaurant. Jacuzzi. Conference room. CCs: Visa, MC, AE, DC. Downhill & cross-country skiing, hiking, canoeing, biking, swimming. European or American plans available.
Seen in: *New York Times.*

Mississippi

Chatham

Mount Holly
Box 140
Chatham MS 38731
(601) 827-2652
   Circa 1855. This 20-room mansion, on six acres fronting Lake

Washington, is in the Italianate style. It has 24-inch-thick walls of brick. Most of the rooms are 25 by 25 feet. All bedrooms open off a large second-floor ballroom, including a room with a 12-foot-high canopy bed. Antique furnishings, bordered ceilings, and chandeliers decorate the interior.
Location: On beautiful Lake Washington.
Rates: $75. Feb. to Dec.
Innkeeper(s): Ann & T.C. Woods, Jr.
5 Rooms. 4 Private Baths. Guest phone in room. TV available. Beds: KQT. Meals: Full breakfast. Conference room. Fireplaces. CCs: Visa, MC. Fishing, skiing, sailing.
Seen in: *Southern Living.*

Jackson

Millsaps-Buie House
628 N State St
Jackson MS 39202
(601) 352-0221
   Circa 1888. Major Millsaps, founder of Millsaps College, built

this stately mansion 100 years ago and it has remained in the family. A

handsome, columned entrance, bays and gables are features of the house, decorated by Berle Smith designer for Mississippi's governor's mansion. The parlor features a French dating bench and a grand piano and the guestrooms are appointed in antiques and canopied beds.
Rates: $65-$120. All year.
11 Rooms. 11 Private Baths. Guest phone in room. TV in room. Beds: KQT. Meals: Continental plus. Conference room. CCs: Visa, MC, AE, DC.
Seen in: *New York Times.*

Lorman

Rosswood Plantation
Hwy 552
Lorman MS 39096
(601) 437-4215
   Circa 1857. Rosswood is a stately, columned mansion in an original plantation setting. Here guests may find antiques, buried treasure, ghosts, a slave revolt, a Civil War battleground, the first owner's diary and genuine southern hospitality. Voted the "prettiest place in the

country" by *Farm & Ranch Living,* the manor is a Mississippi Landmark and is in the National Register.
Rates: $65-$75. All year.
Innkeeper(s): Jean & Walt Hylander.
4 Rooms. 4 Private Baths. Guest phone in room. TV in room. Beds: Q. Meals: Full breakfast. Conference room. CCs: Visa, MC.
Seen in: *Farm and Ranch Living.*
   "The plantation to see if you can only see one."

Natchez

Dunleith
84 Homochitto
Natchez MS 39120
(601) 446-8500 (800)443-2445
   Circa 1856. This is a Greek Revival plantation house. During the Civil War the Davis family raised thoroughbred horses here, and the story goes that when they heard Union officers were coming to take their horses, they hid their favorites in the cellar under the dining room. The officers ate dinner and heard nothing so the horses were saved. Rare French Zubar mural wallpaper decorates the dining room.
**Rates: $75-$130. All year.
Innkeeper(s): Nancy Gibbs.

11 Rooms. 11 Private Baths. Guest phone in room. TV in room. Beds: QDT. Meals: Full breakfast. Conference room. Fireplaces. CCs: Visa, MC, AE, DC.

"The accommodations at the mansion were wonderful. Southern hospitality is indeed charming and memorable!"

Monmouth Plantation
36 Melrose
Natchez MS 39120
(800) 828-4531

Circa 1818. Monmouth was the home of General Quitman who be-

came acting Governor of Mexico, Governor of Mississippi, and a U. S. Congressman. In the National Register, the inn features antique four-poster and canopy beds, turn-down service, and an evening cocktail hour. Guests Jefferson Davis and Henry Clay enjoyed the same acres of gardens, pond and walking paths available today.
**Rates: $75-$135.
14 Rooms. 14 Private Baths. Guest phone in room. TV in room. Beds: KQT. Meals: Full breakfast. Handicap access provided. Conference room. CCs: Visa, MC, AE.

"The best historical inn we have stayed at anywhere."

Rosswood Plantation
See: Lorman, MS

Port Gibson

Oak Square
1207 Church St
Port Gibson MS 39150
(601) 437-4350

Circa 1850. Six, 22-foot fluted Corinthian columns support the front gallery of this 30-room Greek Revival plantation. The owners furnished the mansion with heirloom antiques collected from family members who lived in Mississippi for

more than 200 years. The parlor holds a carved rosewood Victorian suite, original family documents, and a collection of Civil War memorabilia. Enormous oaks and magnolia trees grace the grounds.
Location: US 61 between Natchez & Vicksburg.
**Rates: $65-$75. All year.
Innkeeper(s): Mr. & Mrs. William D. Lum.
10 Rooms. 10 Private Baths. Guest phone in room. TV in room. Beds: QT. Meals: Full breakfast. CCs: Visa, MC, AE.
Seen in: *Quad-City Times, The Dallas Morning News.*

"We just cannot say enough about the wonderful ambiance of Oak Square...except it is even better than four stars."

Vicksburg

Cedar Grove Mansion Inn
2200 Oak St
Vicksburg MS 39180
(601) 636-1605

Circa 1840. It's easy to relive *Gone With the Wind* at this grand antebellum estate built by John Klein as a wedding present for his bride. Visitors sip mint juleps and watch gas chandeliers flicker in the finely appointed parlors. The children's rooms and master bedroom contain their original furnishings. Although Cedar Grove survived the Civil War, a Union cannonball is still lodged in the parlor wall. Four acres of gardens include fountains and gazebos.
**Rates: $65-$115. All year.
Innkeeper(s): Glen Williams.
17 Rooms. 17 Private Baths. Guest phone available. TV in room. Beds: KQ. Meals: EP. Jacuzzi. Handicap access provided. Conference room. Fireplaces. Pool. CCs: Visa, MC. Swimming.
Seen in: *Vicksburg Post.*

Mount Holly
See: Chatham, MS

Rosswood Plantation
See: Lorman, MS

The Corners
601 Klein St
Vicksburg MS 39180
(601) 636-7421 (800) 444-7421

Circa 1872. Listed in the National Register, the Corners was built as a wedding present. It is an interesting combination of architectural styles including Steamboat Gothic,

Louisiana Raised Cottage, Italianate, Greek Revival, and Vicksburg Pierced Columns. Lovely antiques and canopy beds fill the mansion and it's the only inn in Vicksburg with original parterre gardens and view of the Mississippi River from the front gallery.
Rates: $65-$85. All year.
Innkeeper(s): Cliff & Bettye Whitney.
7 Rooms. 6 Private Baths. Guest phone in room. TV in room. Beds: QT. Meals: Full breakfast. Handicap access provided. Conference room. Fireplaces. CCs: Visa, MC.
Seen in: *Vicksburg Post.*

"The highlight of our trip was the night we spent in Vicksburg with you. It was just great!"

The Duff Green Mansion
1114 First East St
Vicksburg MS 39180
(601) 636-6968

Circa 1856. The 12,000 square-foot Duff Green Mansion is considered one of the finest examples of Palladian architecture in Mississippi. It was a wedding gift to Mary Lake Green from her parents, Judge and Mrs. William Lake, who built the adjacent house, Lakemont. During the siege of Vicksburg, Mary Green gave birth in one of the caves next to the mansion and named her son Siege Green. Handsome furnishings

highlight the spacious and elegantly renovated rooms.

Location: Vicksburg Historic District.

**Rates: $75-$140. March to Dec.

Innkeeper(s): Sally Bullard & Tom De-Rossette.

7 Rooms. 7 Private Baths. Guest phone available. TV in room. Beds: KQC. Meals: Full breakfast. Jacuzzi. Sauna. Fireplaces. CCs: Visa, MC, AE. Swimming.

"The service could not have been better. We've stayed in a number of B&B inns in different parts of the country over the years and we rate you #1."

Missouri

Branson

Branson House
120 4th St
Branson MO 65616
(417) 334-0959

Circa 1920. A landscape architect for the Missouri State Park system, A. L. Drumeller built this bungalow house surrounding it with rock

walls, gardens and orchards. Exposed beam ceilings, built-in glass cabinets, and pine woodwork are features. From its hillside location, the veranda overlooks the town and Lake Taneycomo. Sherry is served in the late afternoon and in the evening, cookies and milk are dispensed.
Location: Downtown.
Rates: $50-$70. April to Nov.
Innkeeper(s): Mrs. Opal Kelly.
7 Rooms. 7 Private Baths. Guest phone available. TV available. Beds: DT. Meals: Gourmet plus. Fireplaces. Fishing, boating, water sports.
"Thank you so much for your warm hospitality. It really made our trip special."

Hannibal

Garth Woodside Mansion
RR 1
Hannibal MO 63401
(314) 221-2789

Circa 1871. This Italian Renaissance mansion is set on 39 acres of

meadow and woodland. Authentic Victorian antiques fill the house, and an unusual flying staircase with no visible means of support vaults three stories. Best of all is the Samuel Clemens room where Mark Twain slept in a "button bed". It is said that once Buffalo Bill Cody and Mr. Clemens met here.
Location: Just off highway 61.
**Rates: $51-$63. All year.
Innkeeper(s): Irv & Diane Feinberg.
8 Rooms. 4 Private Baths. Guest phone available. TV available. Beds: D. Meals: Full breakfast. Conference room. Fireplaces. CCs: Visa, MC. Riverboat rides.
Seen in: *Country Inns, Chicago-Sun Times.*
"So beautiful and romantic and relaxing, we forgot we were here to work." Jeannie and Bob Ransom, *Innsider.*

The Fifth Street Mansion
Bed & Breakfast
213 S Fifth St
Hannibal MO 63401
(314) 221-0445

Circa 1865. This 20-room Italianate house displays the typical extended eaves and heavy brackets, tall windows, and decorated lintels. There is a cupola affording views of the town. Mark Twain was invited to dinner here by the Garth family and joined Laura Frazer (his Becky Thatcher) for the evening. An enormous stained-glass window lights the stairwell, and the library stained-glass window holds the family crest. The library also features hand-grained walnut paneling.
Location: North of St. Louis 100 miles.
Rates: $40-$60. All year.
Innkeeper(s): Donalene & Mike Andreotti.
8 Rooms. 4 Private Baths. Guest phone available. TV available. Beds: QTC. Meals: Full breakfast. Fireplaces. Mississippi river cruises.
"We thoroughly enjoyed our visit. Terrific food and hospitality!"

Jamesport

Richardson House B & B
PO 227
Jamesport MO 64648
(816) 684-6664 (816) 684-6234

Circa 1900. This intimate, five-room house is situated on a farm at the edge of Jamesport, and was built

by the Richardson family who delivered rural mail by horse and buggy. Careful restoration makes an attractive background for the country antiques that furnish the house, now owned by the Richardson's grandaughter. The entire house is rented to one party at a time, and home-cooked meals fresh from the farm are available.

**Rates: $45-$55. All year.
Innkeeper(s): Jayla Smith, Rebecca Richardson, owner.
5 Rooms. Guest phone available. TV available. Beds: QDT. Meals: Full breakfast. Conference room. CCs: Visa, MC. Fishing, hunting, hiking, bicycling, canoeing, horseback riding. Farm tours for children.

Kansas City

Doanleigh Wallagh
**217 E 37th St
Kansas City MO 64111
(816) 753-2667**

Circa 1900. This Georgian-style inn is located in the Hyde Park area. Overlooking the park, the inn is decorated in English and American antiques. A pump organ and grand piano dominate the living room. One guest room has a woodburning fireplace, another has twin canopy beds.
Location: Five minutes from Crown Center and Country Club Plaza.
Rates: $60-$90.
Innkeeper(s): Ed & Carolyn Litchfield.
5 Rooms. 5 Private Baths. Guest phone available. Beds: KQT. Meals: Full breakfast. Conference room. Fireplaces. CCs: Visa, MC. Tennis across the street. Airport pickup, business meetings and weddings.

Richardson House B&B
See: Jamesport, MO

Saint Charles

Boone's Lick Trail Inn
**1000 South Main St
Saint Charles MO 63301
(314) 947-7000**

Circa 1840. This Greek Revival brick and limestone house overlooks the Missouri River State Trail and the Lewis and Clark Trail. From the front gallery guests may watch the horse-drawn carriage go by Frontier

Park. The inn is furnished with antiques, lace curtains and old quilts.
Location: 10 minutes from St. Louis airport.
Rates: $65.
Innkeeper(s): V'Anne Mydler
6 Rooms. 4 Private Baths. Guest phone available. TV available. Beds: QDT. Meals: Continental plus. CCs: Visa, MC. Art museums, the ferry, historic district. Missouri River, Louis & Clark launching site.
Seen in: *St. Louis Post Dispatch, Midwest Motorist.*
"Makes your trip back in time complete."

Saint Louis

Lafayette House
**2156 Lafayette Ave
Saint Louis MO 63104
(314) 772-4429**

Circa 1876. Captain James Eads, designer and builder of the first trussed bridge across the Mississippi

River, built this Queen Anne mansion as a wedding present for his daughter Margaret. The rooms are furnished in antiques and there is a suite with a kitchen on the third floor. The house overlooks Lafayette Park.
Location: In the center of St. Louis.
Rates: $35-$60. All year.
Innkeeper(s): Sarah & Jack Milligan.
6 Rooms. 2 Private Baths. Guest phone available. TV available. Beds: QDC. Meals: Full breakfast.
"We had a wonderful stay at your house and enjoyed the furnishings, delicious breakfasts, and friendly pets."

Maggie's Bed & Breakfast
See: Collinsville, IL

The Coachlight B&B
**1 Grandview Heights
Saint Louis MO 63131
(314) 965-4328**

Circa 1904. This three-story, brick house is in an exclusive district of elegant homes once considered "private places" where homeowners even owned the streets. The neighborhood has been beautifully maintained and is near St. Louis and Washington Universities. The parlor features Queen Anne furnishings with Laura Ashley prints. Please request Coachlight when you call the reservation center.
Location: Central West End.
Rates: $60-$75. All year.
Innkeeper(s): Reservations are made by River Country B&B.
3 Rooms. 3 Private Baths. Guest phone in room. TV in room. Beds: QDT. Meals: Continental plus. Conference room. Fireplaces. CCs: Visa, MC. Zoo, art museums.

Springfield

Walnut Street B&B
**900 E Walnut St
Springfield MO 65806
(417) 864-6346**

Circa 1894. This three-story Queen

Anne gabled house has cast iron Corinthian columns and a veranda. Polished wood floors and antiques are featured throughout, and upstairs is the gathering room with a fireplace. The McCann Room is a guest room with two bay windows. A full breakfast is served including items such as Peach Stuffed French Toast.
Rates: $60-$85. All year.
Innkeeper(s): Nancy & Karol Brown.
6 Rooms. 6 Private Baths. Guest phone available. TV available. Beds: QT. Meals: Full breakfast. Handicap access provided. Conference room. Fireplaces. CCs: Visa, MC. Boating, fishing, sports center.

Washington

Zachariah Foss Guest House
4 Lafayette
Washington MO 63090
(314) 239-6599 (800)332-5223

Circa 1846. Zachariah and Amelia Foss arrived from Maine with their

five children and selected this spot on the Missouri River, across from the steamboat landing, for their new home. Amelia was a schoolteacher and opened the first private English-speaking schoolhouse in this German settlement. Constructed in a Federal style the house is three stories of clapboard and stone. This private historic retreat is rented to one party at a time and can accommodate from one to six guests. Antique-filled rooms, a his-and-hers claw-foot bathtub, a tandem bike and Missouri wine are among the luxuries provided.
Location: West of St. Louis, 45 minutes.
Rates: $110-$130. All year.
Innkeeper(s): Sunny & Joy Drewel, Janet Berlener.
7 Rooms. 1 Private Baths. Beds: DT. Meals: B&B. CCs: Visa, MC. Linen & Lace shop on the premises.
Seen in: *Country Home.*

Montana

Big Sky

Lone Mountain Ranch
PO Box 145
Big Sky MT 59716
(406) 995-4644

Circa 1920. A cross-country ski center and guest ranch, this was one of the first ranches in Gallatin

Canyon. Situated in a meadow, posh log cabins with fireplaces border a tumbling trout stream. An extensive Indian artifact collection is housed in several ranch buildings. There are 45 miles of groomed trails for skiers and in summer, guests fish world-famous trout streams or take part in dozens of other activities.
Location: Forty miles south of Bozeman Mountain.
**Rates: From $590pp/wk. April to Dec.
Innkeeper(s): Mike Aukeny, Bob & Viv Schaap.
20 Rooms. 20 Private Baths. Guest phone available. Beds: QT. Meals: AP. Jacuzzi. Handicap access provided. Conference room. Fireplaces. CCs: Visa, MC. Horseback riding, cross-country skiing, fly fishing. Horse-drawn sleigh ride dinners.
Seen in: *The New York Times, Town & Country Magazine.*
"Meals couldn't be better! From the sack lunches to the gourmet dinner, it was all delicious. We'll be back with friends."

Billings

Pitcher Guest House
See: Red Lodge, MT

Bozeman

Lone Mountain Ranch
See: Big Sky, MT

Voss Inn
319 S Willson
Bozeman MT 59715
(406) 587-0982

Circa 1883. The Voss Inn is a restored two-story house with a large front porch and a Victorian parlor. Old-fashioned furnishings include an upright piano and chandelier. In the morning a full breakfast is served with fresh baked rolls kept in a unique warmer built into an ornate 1880's radiator.
Location: Four blocks south of downtown.
**Rates: $50-$70. All year.
Innkeeper(s): Ken & Ruthmary Tonn.
6 Rooms. 6 Private Baths. Meals: Full breakfast. CCs: Visa, MC, DC.

Great Falls

Three Pheasant Inn
626 5th Ave N
Great Falls MT 59401
(406) 453-0519

Circa 1910. This Victorian house, newly opened as an inn, features glassed-in sun porches and common rooms that include a parlor and library. Outside there are gardens, a 100-year-old fountain, and a gazebo.

On occasion the innkeepers allow guests to bring pets.
Rates: $35-$45.
Innkeeper(s): Doug & Amy Sloan
4 Rooms. 1 Private Baths. Guest phone available. Meals: Full brunch style breakfast.

Red Lodge

Pitcher Guest House
2 S Platt PO 1148
Red Lodge MT 59068
(406) 446-2859

Circa 1910. This completely refurbished house is built in the Finnish

fashion of quiet, clean and sound construction. It is an unhosted house with a kitchen available to one family or couple at a time. Antiques, and stenciled cabinets and wallpapers decorate the interior.
Rates: $55 & up. All year.
Innkeeper(s): Ruth & Robert Pitcher.
11 Rooms. 2 Private Baths. Guest phone in room. TV in room. Beds: QT. Meals: Kitchenette. Fireplaces. Horseback riding, cross-country skiing, golf, fishing, hiking.
Seen in: *Family Circle Magazine, The Billings Gazette.*
"Such charm! A doll house in adult proportions. We're definitely coming back."

Nebraska Nevada

Omaha

Offutt House
140 N 39th St
Omaha NE 68131
(402) 553-0951

Circa 1894. This two-and-a-half story, 14-room house is built like a chateau with a steep roof and tall

windows. During the 1913 tornado, although almost every house in the neighborhood was leveled, the Offutt house stood firm. It is said that a decanter of sherry was blown from the dining room to the living room without anything spilling. The large parlor features a handsome fireplace, a wall of books and an inviting white sofa.
Location: One block from downtown.
**Rates: $40-$60. All year.
Innkeeper(s): Jeannie K. Swoboda.
7 Rooms. 2 Private Baths. Guest phone in room. TV in room. Beds: KDT. Meals: Full breakfast, gourmet. Conference room. Fireplaces. CCs: Visa, MC, AE. Sightseeing, walking.
"Hospitable, comfortable, lovely."

Carson City

Winters Creek Ranch
1201 US 395 North
Carson City NV 89701
(702) 849-1020

Circa 1865. This ranch features 50 acres of meadows and ponderosa pines as well as spectacular views of the Sierra Nevada Mountains. Cycling, fishing, and hiking can be enjoyed without leaving the ranch. During winter, the outdoor hot tub is a favorite with the gazebo overhead and snow on the ground.
Location: Fifteen minutes south of Reno, 11 miles north of Carson City.
Rates: $75-$85.
Innkeeper(s): Myronn Sayan & Susan Hannah.
3 Rooms. 3 Private Baths. Guest phone available. Beds: QD. Meals: Full breakfast. Jacuzzi. Fireplaces.
Seen in: *Reno Gazette, Sacramento Bee.*

Virginia City

Edith Palmer's Country Inn
South B Street, PO Box 756
Virginia City NV 89440
(702) 847-0707

Circa 1862. This white clapboard two-story country house has a wine cellar with walls two feet thick. The addition of a skylight makes this a romantic setting for dining and for weddings. Furnishings are country antiques, and the inn is within easy walking distance of the historic district of Virginia City.
Rates: $65-$75.
Innkeeper(s): Earlene Brown.
5 Rooms. 3 Private Baths. Meals: Full gourmet breakfast. Conference room.

New Hampshire

Bedford

Bedford Village Inn
2 Old Bedford Road
Bedford NH 03102
(603) 472-2001

Circa 1810. Built by Josiah Gordon, the Bedford Inn stands as a

landmark restoration of a farm estate. There are Indian shutters, exposed chestnut beams, and working fireplaces. Situated in the converted barn, the inn's guest rooms feature king-size beds and canopied four-posters. Public spaces include the Milk Room Lounge and viewing porches perched in the original barn silos. A herd of French *Charolais* cows graze with their calves in adjacent pastures.
**Rates: $125-$375 MAP.
Innkeeper(s): Maureen Woolford.
14 Rooms. 14 Private Baths. Guest phone in room. TV in room. Beds: K. Meals: Continental breakfast, restaurant. Jacuzzi. Handicap access provided. Conference room. CCs: All. Cross-country skiing on property. Corporate packages. Seen in: *Travelhost Magazine.*

"Thank you for the gracious hospitality. I was extremely happy with the accommodations and the food and wine were exquisite."

Bethlehem

The Bells
Strawberry Hill, PO Box 276
Bethlehem NH 03574
(603) 869-2647

Circa 1892. This unique Queen Anne house is a wonderful example

of Victorian ingenuity. Basically square with wraparound porches, the roofline has been orientalized which makes the house look like a pagoda. Eighty hand-carved wooden bells hang under the second floor eaves and eight large tin bells hang from the upper corners of the roofs. According to local folklore the builder constructed the house for his son, a missionary to the Far East.
Location: In the heart of the White mountains, USR & 302.
**Rates: $40-$60. All year.
Innkeeper(s): Bill & Louise Sims.
4 Rooms. 4 Private Baths. Guest phone available. TV available. Beds: TD. Meals: Full breakfast. Golf, fishing, tennis, swimming, hiking, cross-country skiing.

"It was so nice to be fussed over, not to mention being treated like old friends. Everything was superb and we went bananas over the decor!"

The Mulburn Inn
Main St
Bethlehem NH 03574
(603) 869-3389

Circa 1913. This summer cottage was known as The Ivie Estate. Mrs. Ivie and Mrs. Frank Woolworth of 'Five and Dime' fame were sisters. Many of the Ivie and Woolworth family members vacationed here in summer. Cary Grant and Barbara Hutton spent their honeymoon at the mansion. Polished oak staircases and stained glass windows add to the atmosphere.
**Rates: $50-$65. All year.
Innkeeper(s): Linda & Moe Mulkigian, Bob & Cheryl Burns.
7 Rooms. 7 Private Baths. Guest phone available. TV available. Beds: KQTD. Meals: Full breakfast. Fireplaces. CCs: Visa, MC, AE. Hiking, bicycling, swimming, fishing, tennis, skiing.

"You have put a lot of thought, charm, beauty and warmth into the inn. Your breakfasts were oh! so delicious!!"

Bradford

Bradford Inn
Main St
Bradford NH 03221
(603) 938-5309

Circa 1898. The Bradford Hotel was the most elaborate lodging in

town when it first boasted of electricity, a coal furnace and a large

dining room. Now restored and polished to its original turn-of-the-century charm, guests can once again enjoy the grand staircase, the wide halls, parlors, high ceilings and sunny rooms.
Location: Rural country village.
Rates: $59-$79. All year.
Innkeeper(s): Connie & Tom Mazol.
14 Rooms. 14 Private Baths. Guest phone available. TV in room. Beds: DTC. Meals: Continental or full breakfast, MAP Handicap access provided. CCs: Visa, MC, DS.

"We enjoyed excellent breakfasts and dinners while at the Bradford Inn as well as a clean and spacious suite and a most pleasant host and hostess."

Mountain Lake Inn
Rt 114
Bradford NH 03221
(603) 938-2136 (800)662-6005
Circa 1760. This white colonial house is situated on 167 acres, 17 of which are lakefront. A sandy beach

on Lake Massasecum is inviting for sunning but guests often prefer to take out the canoe and the rowboat. The Pine Room has floor-to-ceiling windows that look out to the garden. A 75-year-old Brunswick pool table is in the lounge, along with a wood-burning fireplace.
**Rates: $70-$80. All year.
Innkeeper(s): Carol & Phil Fullerton.
9 Rooms. 9 Private Baths. Guest phone available. TV available. Beds: KQTC. Meals: Full breakfast, MAP. Conference room. Fireplaces. CCs: Visa, MC. Swimming, skiing, snowshoeing packages, country cooking weekend.
Seen in: *Country Inns.*

"We loved your place! From the moment I entered the door that afternoon and caught the aroma of a country dinner I was hooked. You give the inn such personal warmth."

Bridgewater

Pasquaney Inn
On Newfound Lake
Star Rt 1 Box 1066
Bridgewater NH 03222
(603) 744-2712
Circa 1840. The Pasquaney Inn was a stopover point on the Old Star Route from Boston to Montreal. It

was built originally for lodging and is in the classic style of a New England resort with white clapboard siding, tall windows and a broad veranda stretching the length of the inn. It faces the sandy beaches of what is purported to be one of the cleanest, clearest lakes in the world. The mountains are just beyond.
Rates: $35-$50. All year.
Innkeeper(s): Barbara & Bud Edrick - Pamela & Sean Smith.
26 Rooms. 18 Private Baths. Beds: QT. Meals: Full breakfast, MAP. Fireplaces. CCs: Visa, MC, AE. Swimming, fishing, boating, cross-country & downhill skiing.

Campton

Mountain Fare Inn
Mad River Rd
Campton NH 03223
(603) 726-4283
Circa 1850. This white farmhouse is surrounded by flower gardens in

the summer and unparalleled foliage in the fall. Often, ski teams, family reunions and other groups are found enjoying the outdoors here with Mountain Fare as a base.

In the winter everyone seems to be a skier and in the summer there are boaters and hikers. The inn is decorated in a casual New Hampshire-style country decor.
Location: Two hours from Boston in the White Mountains.
Rates: $24-$35. All year.
Innkeeper(s): Susan & Nick Preston.
9 Rooms. 6 Private Baths. Guest phone available. TV available. Beds: DTC. Meals: Full breakfast, MAP, EP. Fireplaces. Golf, hiking, biking, cross-country skiing, tennis, fishing.
"Charming and casual. Truly country."

Centre Harbor

Red Hill Inn
RD 1 Box 99M
Centre Harbor NH 03226
(603) 279-7001
Circa 1904. The mansion was once the centerpiece of a 1000-acre estate.

It was called "keewaydin" for the strong north wind that blows across Sunset Hill. When the Depression was over, the inn was sold and new owners included European royalty escaping from Nazi Germany. Now the mansion is a lovely restored country inn with spectacular views of the area's lakes and mountains. From your room you can see the site of the filming of *On Golden Pond.*
Location: Central New Hampshire in the Lakes Region.
Rates: $65-$115.
Innkeeper(s): Don Leavitt & Rick Miller.
23 Rooms. 23 Private Baths. Guest phone in room. TV available. Beds: D. Meals: Restaurant. Jacuzzi. Conference room. Fireplaces. CCs: Visa, MC, AE. Cross-country skiing on groomed trails. rental equipment available.

Concord

Province Inn
See: Strafford, NH

The Meeting House Inn
See: Henniker, NH

Conway

Darby Field Inn
Bald Hill, PO Box D
Conway NH 03818
(603) 447-2181
Circa 1826. This rambling, blue clapboard farmhouse has a huge

fieldstone fireplace, stone patio and outstanding views of the Mt. Washington Valley and the Presidential Mountains. For many years it was called the Bald Hill Grand View lodge but was renamed to honor the first man to climb Mt. Washington, Darby Field.
Location: Half a mile south of Conway.
**Rates: $60-$85pp.
Innkeeper(s): Marc & Maria Donaldson.
16 Rooms. 14 Private Baths. TV available. Beds: DT. Meals: MAP. Pool. CCs: Visa, MC, AE.
"If an inn is a place for a weary traveler to relax, recover and feel the hospitality and warmth of the innkeeper, then the Darby Field Inn is one of the finest."

Merrill Farm Resort
PO Box 2070
Conway NH 03818
(603) 447-3866
Circa 1790. There are six rooms in the main building which is a traditional inn. Other rooms are in the motel or the lodge on the premises. Several 1920's era cabins nestle along the bank of the Saco River. A a maple sugar house stands on the grounds and in the autumn the inn produces its own cider.
Location: Mt. Washington Valley between villages of Conway & N. Conway.
**Rates: $49-$89. All year.
Innkeeper(s): Lee & Chris Gregory.

60 Rooms. 59 Private Baths. Guest phone in room. TV in room. Beds: KQTC. Meals: Full breakfast, continental plus. Jacuzzi. Sauna. Handicap access provided. Conference room. Fireplaces. Pool. CCs: Visa, MC, AE, DC. Swimming, skiing, canoeing, hiking, shuffleboard.
Seen in: *New England Getaways.*

Cornish

Chase House B&B
Rt 12 A, RR 2 Box 909
Cornish NH 03745
(603) 675-5391
Circa 1775. Cornish's first English settler, Dudley Chase, built this Federal house noted for its fine ar-

chitecture. In 1845 it was moved to accommodate the Sullivan County Railroad. Designated a National Landmark, it was the birthplace of Salmon Chase, Governor of Ohio, Secretary of the Treasury for President Lincoln and Chief Justice of the Supreme Court. The Chase Manhattan Bank was named after him.
Location: Two-and-a-half hours from Boston.
Rates: $65-$85. All year.
Innkeeper(s): Hal & Marilyn Wallace.
6 Rooms. 4 Private Baths. Guest phone available. TV available. Beds: QT. Meals: Full breakfast. CCs: Visa, MC. Hiking, canoeing, cross-country skiing, swimming, tennis, golf.
Seen in: *New Hampshire Sunday News.*

Eaton Center

Rockhouse Mountain Farm
Eaton Center NH 03832
(603) 447-2880
Circa 1900. This handsome old house is framed by maple trees on 400 acres of forests, streams, fields and wild flowers. Saddle horses, milking cows, pigs, geese and ducks provide entertainment for city youngsters of all ages. A 200-year

old barn bulges with the fragrance of new-mown hay. There is a private beach on nearby Crystal Lake with rowboats, canoes and sailboats.
Rates: $46-$70. June 15 to Oct.
Innkeeper(s): The Edge family.
15 Rooms. 7 Private Baths. Guest phone available. TV available. Beds: TDC. Meals: MAP. Handicap access provided. Fireplaces. Horseback riding, hiking.
Seen in: *Country Vacations.*

Etna

Moose Mountain Lodge
Moose Mountain
Etna NH 03750
(603) 643-3529
Circa 1938. This old log lodge is perched high on the western side of

Moose Mountain providing views of the Connecticut River Valley and the Green Mountains. The inn's land connects with the Appalachian Trail for extended hikes and ski tours. In the summer the lodge participates in "Canoeing Inn to Inn" on the Connecticut River. Bountiful gardens provide fresh vegetables for lunch and dinner.
Location: Part of town of Hanover.
Rates: $65+. June to March.
Innkeeper(s): Peter & Kay Shuurway.
12 Rooms. Guest phone available. Beds: QTD. Meals: AP, MAP. Conference room. Fireplaces. CCs: Visa, MC. Cross-country skiing, bicycling, hiking, swimming.
"Moose Mountain is just like some of the old European ski lodges, relaxed, warm, friendly, and very comfortable."

Fitzwilliam

Fitzwilliam Inn
Fitzwilliam NH 03447
(603) 585-9000
Circa 1796. For almost 200 years this old New England inn has of-

fered food, lodging and grog. Over the parlor presides a portrait of the

Earl of Fitzwilliam, the 18th century nobleman for whom the town is named. In the rustic pub the innkeeper still provides his own special grog.
Rates: $30-$50. All year.
28 Rooms. 14 Private Baths. Guest phone available. TV available. Beds: KQTC. Meals: Full breakfast, EP, restaurant. Handicap access provided. Conference room. Fireplaces. Pool. CCs: Visa, MC, AE, DC. Cross-country skiing, hiking, fishing.
Seen in: *Boston Globe.*

Franconia

Franconia Inn
Easton Rd
Franconia NH 03580
(603) 823-5542
Circa 1936. This inn was originally built in 1868 when most of the area's

farmers took in summer boarders. Each farmer had a wagon marked with his farm's name and would pick up guests at the train station in Littleton. In the 30s, fire destroyed the old house and it was rebuilt as an inn. A basement rathskeller is well known by the ski-touring circuit. There is also an oak-paneled library upstairs.
Location: Exit 38 off I-93, 2-1/2 miles south on Route 116.
**Rates: $40-$152. May 20-April.
Innkeeper(s): Alec & Richard Morris.
35 Rooms. 35 Private Baths. Guest phone available. TV available. Beds: KQTC. Meals: MAP, EP. Jacuzzi. Conference room. Fireplaces. Pool. CCs: Vica, MC,

AE. Cross-country skiing, tennis, horseback riding, bicycles.
Seen in: *The Philadelphia Inquirer.*
"The piece de resistance of the Franconia Notch is the Franconia Inn." Philadelphia Inquirer.

Lovett's Inn
Rt 18, Profile Rd
Franconia NH 03580
(603) 823-7761
Circa 1784. In the National Register, the main building consists of two connected Cape-style houses.

The lower floor functioned as the kitchen, woodshed and milkroom and the old wash oven remains today next to the original fireplace. Other rooms are in cottages and new additions. Trout streams, Lafayette Brook and a pond dot the inn's 90 acres.
Rates: $85-$130, MAP.
Innkeeper(s): Lan Finlay, General Manager.
30 Rooms. 19 Private Baths. Guest phone available. TV available. Beds: QDTC. Meals: MAP, EP. Handicap access provided. Conference room. Fireplaces. Pool. CCs: All. Gliding, horseback riding, golf nearby. ski trails on premises.
"Room very pleasant, comfortable and clean. Delicious dinner. We appreciated being made to feel welcome and at home."

Gilford

Cartway House Inn
83 Old Lake Shore Rd
Gilford NH 03246
(603) 528-1172
Circa 1771. Overlooking mountains and meadows, this clapboard colonial was built by shipbuilders and is one of ten historic homes in Gilford. This is a popular area for bike tours, cross-country skiing, horseback riding and golf. The innkeepers speak several languages.
**Rates: $52-$58. All year.

Innkeeper(s): Gretchen & Tony Shortway.
9 Rooms. 1 Private Baths. Guest phone available. TV available. Beds: TD. Meals: Full breakfast. Jacuzzi. Fireplaces. CCs: Visa, MC. Skiing, swimming, golf, horseback riding, bicycling.
"Gretchen really knows how to make you feel welcome."

Glen

Bernerhof Inn
Box 381 Rt 302
Glen NH 03838
(603) 383-4414
Circa 1890. This unusual house sports a variety of peaks and gables

and is fronted with a glassed-in greenhouse. There is a common room just inside the entrance called the Zumstein Room and a second floor sitting room. A Finnish sauna is on the property and guests can stroll through the pines to the swimming pool.
Rates: $80-$100. All year.
Innkeeper(s): Ted & Sharon Wroblewski.
9 Rooms. 6 Private Baths. Guest phone available. TV in room. Beds: KQTC. Meals: MAP, Full breakfast, restaurant. Jacuzzi. Sauna. Handicap access provided. Pool. CCs: Visa, MC, AE. Skiing, hiking, rafting, canoeing, kayaking.
Seen in: *The Boston Globe.*
"When people want to treat themselves, this is where they come."

Greenfield

The Greenfield Inn
Box 156
Greenfield NH 03047
(603) 547-6327
Circa 1817. In the 1850s this inn was purchased by Henry Dunklee, innkeeper of the old Mayfield Inn

across the street. When there was an overflow of guests at his tavern, Mr.

Dunklee accommodated them here. Three acres of lawn and a veranda provide views of Crotched, Temple and Monadnock Mountains. Inside are polished wide-board floors and cozy comfortable furnishings.
Location: Southern New Hampshire, 90 minutes from Boston.
Rates: $45-$60.
Innkeeper(s): Vic Mangini.
9 Rooms. 5 Private Baths. Guest phone available. TV in room. Beds: KDQT Meals: Full breakfast. Jacuzzi. Conference room. Fireplaces. CCs: Visa, MC. Mountain climbing, skiing, bicycling, swimming, hunting, golf.

Hanover

Moose Mountain Lodge
See: Etna, NH

Watercourse Way B&B
See: South Strafford, VT

Haverhill

Haverhill Inn
Box 95
Haverhill NH 03765
(603) 989-5961
Circa 1810. This handsome Federal house commands sweeping views of

the Upper Connecticut River Valley and the Vermont hills. Indian shutters, a fireplace in every room, and

an old kitchen hearth and bake oven add to the charm. Cross-country trails start at the back door and in summer, guests often canoe inn-to-inn.
Location: On Route 10.
Rates: $65. All year.
Innkeeper(s): Stephen Campbell & Katharine DeBoer.
4 Rooms. 4 Private Baths. Guest phone available. Beds: QT. Meals: Full breakfast. Fireplaces. Hiking, cross-country skiing, canoeing.

Henniker

The Meeting House Inn & Restaurant
35 Flanders Rd
Henniker NH 03242
(603) 428-3228
Circa 1850. Just up the road from this rural country farmstead is the site of the first meeting house in Henniker. Hearty New England cooking is served in the 200-year-old barn/restaurant. Wide pine floors, brass beds and antique accessories decorate guest rooms in the main house.
Location: Off 114S, 2 miles from Henniker Center.
Rates: $58-$88. All year.
Innkeeper(s): June & Bill Davis, Peter & Cheryl Bakke.
6 Rooms. 6 Private Baths. Guest phone available. TV available. Beds: QTDC. Meals: Full breakfast, gourmet restaurant. Jacuzzi. Sauna. Conference room. CCs: Visa, MC, AE. Downhill & cross-country skiing, golf, swimming, hiking, bicycling
"Thank you for giving us a honeymoon worth waiting eleven years for."

Holderness

Manor On Golden Pond
Rt 3 Box T
Holderness NH 03245
(603) 968-3348
Circa 1903. An Englishman and land developer had a boyhood dream of living in a beautiful mansion high on a hill overlooking lakes and mountains. After he discovered these beautiful 13 acres he brought craftsmen from around the world to build an English-style country man-

sion. Old world charm is accentuated by marble fireplaces and the hand-carved mahogany lobby.
Location: On Squam Lake, 40 minutes north of Concord.
**Rates: $65-$138. May 15 - Oct.
Innkeeper(s): Jan & Pierre Havre.
29 Rooms. 29 Private Baths. Guest phone available. TV available. Beds: KQTC. Meals: EP. Conference room. Fireplaces. Pool. CCs: Visa, MC, AE, DC, DS Boating, canoeing, tennis, swimming, cross-country skiing.
Seen in: *Summer Week.*
"...the setting, the inn itself, the dining, the staff, the fascinating boat tour. Everything was outstanding!"

The Inn on Golden Pond
Rt 3 Box 680
Holderness NH 03245
(603) 968-7269
Circa 1879. Framed by meandering stone walls and split-rail fences more than 100 years old, this inn is

situated on 55 acres of woodlands. Most rooms overlook picturesque countryside and nearby is Squam Lake, setting for the film *On Golden Pond*. An inviting, 60-foot screened porch provides a place to relax during the summer.
Location: Four miles from Exit 24, I-93.
**Rates: $45-$75. All year.
Innkeeper(s): Bill & Bonnie Webb.
9 Rooms. 7 Private Baths. Guest phone available. TV available. Beds: QT. Meals: Full breakfast. Fireplaces. CCs: Visa, MC. Skiing, boating, fishing, swimming.

Jackson

Ellis River House

Rt 16 Box 656
Jackson NH 03846
(603) 383-9339

Circa 1890. Andrew Harriman built this colonial farmhouse, as well as

the village town hall and three-room schoolhouse where the innkeepers' child attends school. Classic antiques fill the guest rooms and each window reveals views of magnificent mountains, the vineyard, or spectacular Ellis River. As a working farm, the Ellis River House includes a population of chickens, geese, ducks, a pony and pigs.
Location: White Mountain area.
Rates: $25-$50pp. All year.
Innkeeper(s): Barry & Barbara Lubao.
6 Rooms. 1 Private Baths. Guest phone available. TV available. Beds: QT. Meals: MAP, full breakfast. Jacuzzi. Fireplaces. CCs: Visa, MC, AE. Cross-country skiing, horseback riding, tennis, golf, biking.
Seen in: *The Mountain Ear*.
"*We have stayed at many B&B's all over the world and are in agreement that the beauty and hospitality of Ellis River House is that of a world class bed & breakfast.*"

Inn At Thorn Hill

PO Box A, Thorn Hill Road
Jackson NH 03846
(603) 383-4242 (603)383-6448

Circa 1895. Follow a romantic drive through the Honeymoon

Covered Bridge to Thorn Hill Road

where this country Victorian stands, built by architect Stanford White. Its 11 acres are adjacent to the Jackson Ski Touring trails. Inside, the decor is Victorian and a collection of antique light fixtures accentuates the guest rooms, pub, drawing room, and parlor.
**Rates: $62-$88. All year.
Innkeeper(s): Peter & Linda LaRose.
20 Rooms. 20 Private Baths. Guest phone available. TV available. Beds: KQT. Meals: MAP, EP, full breakfast. Conference room. Fireplaces. Pool. CCs: Visa, MC, AE. Cross-country skiing, golf, tennis, horseback riding.
Seen in: *Mature Outlook, The Reporter, New England GetAways*.
"*Magnificent, start to finish! The food was excellent but the mountain air must have shrunk my clothes!*"

The Inn at Jackson

PO Box H
Jackson NH 03846
(603) 383-4321

Circa 1900. Architect Stanford White built this inn overlooking the village and White Mountains. The atmosphere is comfortable and inviting, and breakfast is served in a glassed-in porch which provides a panoramic view. In winter, sleigh rides can be arranged and in summer, hay rides and horseback riding.

Rates: $60-$70. All year.
Innkeeper(s): Lori & Steve Tradewell.
6 Rooms. 6 Private Baths. Guest phone available. TV available. Beds: Q. Meals: Full breakfast. Fireplaces. CCs: Visa, MC, AE. Golf, skiing, tennis.
"*We had a terrific time and found the inn warm and cozy and most of all relaxing.*"

Village House

Rt 16A Box 359
Jackson NH 03846
(603) 383-6666

Circa 1860. Village House was built as an annex to the larger Hawthorne

Inn which eventually burned. It is a colonial building, with a porch winding around three sides. The Wildcat River flows by the inn's seven acres, and there is a clay tennis court and shuffleboard set in view of the White Mountains.
Rates: $50-$80. All year.
Innkeeper(s): Robin Crocker, Lori Allen.
10 Rooms. 8 Private Baths. Guest phone available. TV available. Beds: QT. Meals: Full breakfast, restaurant. Pool. CCs: Visa, MC. Tennis, hiking, cross-country skiing, golf, ice skating, horses.
Seen in: *The Foxboro Reporter*.
"*Your hospitality and warmth made us feel right at home. The little extras, such as turn-down service, flowers and baked goods are all greatly appreciated.*"

Jaffrey

Benjamin Prescott Inn

Rt 124 East
Jaffrey NH 03452
(603) 532-6637

Circa 1853. Colonel Prescott arrived on foot in Jaffrey in 1775, with an ax in his hand and a bag of beans

on his back. The family built this classic Greek Revival many years later. Now candles light the windows, seen from the stonewall-lined lane adjacent to the inn. Each room bears the name of a Prescott family member.
Rates: $45-$70. All year.
Innkeeper(s): Richard Kettig.
8 Rooms. 8 Private Baths. TV available. Beds: KQT. Meals: Full breakfast. CCs: Visa, MC. Hiking, climbing, cross-country skiing, sleigh rides.

Jefferson

The Jefferson Inn

Rt 2
Jefferson NH 03583
(603) 586-7998

Circa 1896. This rambling Victorian house features a turret, gables, and verandas. English antiques fill the inn and there are complimentary desserts in the evening.

Innkeeper(s): Greg Brown & Bertie Koelewyn
7 Rooms. 1 Private Baths. Guest phone available. TV available. Beds: TD. Meals: Full breakfast. Conference room. CCs: Visa, MC, AE. Skiing, hiking, swimming, golf, tennis, cycling, horseback riding.

Laconia

Cartway House
See: Gilford, NH

Ferry Point House
Rt 1 Box 335
Laconia NH 03246
(603) 524-0087
Circa 1838. The Pillsbury family of Tilton, New Hampshire built this

16-room waterfront Victorian as their summer residence. Before Winnisquam Bridge was constructed, the Laconia ferry docked at the landing across the road from the inn. A floor-to-ceiling fireplace of New Hampshire rock and crystal dominates the living room. All guest rooms have views of the water.
Location: On picturesque Lake Winnisquam in the Lakes Region.
Rates: $55-$65. May to Sept.
Innkeeper(s): Joe & Diane Damato & Mi-Mere.
5 Rooms. 3 Private Baths. Guest phone available. TV available. Beds: TD. Meals: Full breakfast. Fireplaces. Swimming,

hiking, golf, tennis, water slides, horseback riding. Open weekends after Labor Day.
Seen in: *Regional Update*.
"The house is delightful and the scene across the lake breathtaking. It makes you feel almost in fairyland but the best treasure is the Damato's!"

Manor On golden Pond
See: Holderness, NH

Pasquaney Inn
See: Bridgewater, NH

Littleton

Beal House Inn
247 West Main St
Littleton NH 03561
(603) 444-2661
Circa 1833. This Federal Renaissance farmhouse has been an inn for 54 years. The original barn still

stands, now covered with white clapboard and converted to an antique shop. The inn is furnished with antiques, that are for sale. Beal House is a Main Street landmark as well as the area's first bed and breakfast inn.
**Rates: $5-$90. All year.
Innkeeper(s): Jim & Ann Carver.
14 Rooms. 12 Private Baths. Guest phone available. Beds: KQTC. Meals: Full breakfast, continental plus. CCs: Visa, MC, AE, DC. Downhill & cross-country skiing, hiking, golf, canoeing.
Seen in: *Country Inn*.
"These innkeepers know and understand people, their needs and wants. Attention to cleanliness and amenities, from check-in to check-out is a treasure."

Thayers Inn
136 Main St
Littleton NH 03561
(603) 444-6469
Circa 1843. Ulysses Grant is said to have spoken from the inn's balcony during a federal court hearing. In those days, fresh firewood and candles were delivered to guest

rooms each day as well as a personal thunderjug. The handsome

facade features four 30-foot, hand-carved pillars and a cupola with views of the surrounding mountains.
Rates: $24-$36. All year.
Innkeeper(s): Don & Carolyn Lambert.
40 Rooms. 36 Private Baths. Guest phone in room. TV in room. Beds: DC. Meals: EP, restaurant. CCs: Visa, MC, AE, DC.
Seen in: *Business Life, Vacationer, Upcountry*.
"This Thanksgiving Russ and I spent a lot of time thinking about the things that are most important to us. It seemed appropriate that we should write to thank you for your warm hospitality as innkeepers."

Nashua

Sherman-Berry House
See: Lowell, MA

New London

Follansbee Inn
See: North Sutton, NH

New London Inn
Box 8 Main St
New London NH 03257
(603) 526-2791
Circa 1792. This classic New England inn is situated right on

Main Street and features a two-story

veranda. Inside are bed chambers decorated in colonial furnishings. Guests may dine beside the fire at the inn's restaurant. Colby-Sawyer College is nearby.
**Rates: $70-$85. All year.
Innkeeper(s): Maureen & John Follansbee.
30 Rooms. 30 Private Baths. Guest phone available. TV available. Meals: MAP, full breakfast. Conference room. CCs: Visa, MC.

Newport

The Inn at Coit Mountain
HCR 63, PO 3 Rt 10
Newport NH 03773
(603) 863-3583 (800)367-2364
  Circa 1790. This gracious Georgian was once the home of Rene Cheronette-Champollion a descendant of the famous Egyptologist who deciphered the Rosetta stone. A 35-foot, two-story library adds elegance with its oak paneling and massive granite fireplace. Lake Sunapee is nearby.
Location: Lake Sunapee Region, 8 miles south from Exit 13 on Route 10.
Rates: 45-$135. All year.
Innkeeper(s): Dick & Judi Tatem.
5 Rooms. 1 Private Baths. Beds: KQDTC. Meals: Full breakfast, restaurant, gourmet Handicap access provided. Conference room. Fireplaces. CCs: Visa, MC. Skiing, swimming, boating, fishing, snowmobiling, sleigh rides.

North Conway

Bernerhof Inn
See: Glen, NH

Buttonwood Inn
Mt Surprise Rd, PO Box 3297
North Conway NH 03860
(603) 356-2625
  Circa 1820. This center-chimney, New England-style inn was once a

working farm of more than 100 acres on the mountain. Of the original outbuildings only the

granite barn foundation remains. Through the years the house has been extended to twenty rooms.
Rates: $27-$32. All year.
9 Rooms. 2 Private Baths. Guest phone available. TV available. Beds: DTC. Meals: MAP, full breakfast. Pool. CCs: Visa, MC, AE. Swimming, downhill & cross-country skiing, golfing, hunting.
  "The very moment we spotted your lovely inn nestled midway on the mountainside in the moonlight, we knew we had found a winner."

Cranmore Mt Lodge
Kearsarge Rd, PO Box 1194
North Conway NH 03860
(603) 356-2044
  Circa 1850. Babe Ruth was a frequent guest at this old New England farmhouse when his daughter was owner. One guest room is still decorated with his furnishings. The barn on the property is held together with wooden pegs and contains dorm rooms. There is also an alpine ski rental shop on the premises.
Location: Village of Kearsarge.
Rates: $48-$115. All year.
Innkeeper(s): Dennis & Judy Helfand.
17 Rooms. 5 Private Baths. Guest phone available. TV available. Beds: DT. Meals: MAP, full breakfast. Jacuzzi. Handicap access provided. Fireplaces. Pool. CCs: Visa, MC, AE. Tennis, fishing, hiking, bicycling.
  "Your accommodations are lovely, your breakfasts delicious."

Inn at Thorn Hill
See: Jackson, NH

Peacock Inn
PO Box 1012
North Conway NH 03860
(603) 356-9041
  Circa 1773. The guest book at this inn dates from 1875. Since that time

the inn has been renovated and placed on the federal map as a national landmark. Some of the rooms have skylights as well as brass beds

or canopy beds and antique rockers. Breakfast is served fireside. Across the street flows a babbling brook.
Location: Kearsarge Road, 1 mile from Mt. Cranmore.
**Rates: $78. All year.
Innkeeper(s): Claire & Larry Jackson.
18 Rooms. 16 Private Baths. Guest phone available. TV available. Beds: KQTC. Meals: Full breakfast. Sauna. Conference room. Fireplaces. Pool. CCs: Visa, MC, AE. Swimming, hiking.
  "Although I expected this to be a nice, cozy place, I was not prepared for the royal treatment my family and I received. We cast our vote for Larry and Claire as innkeepers of the year."

Stonehurst Manor
Rt 16
North Conway NH 03860
(603) 356-3271
  Circa 1876. This English-style manor stands on lush, landscaped lawns and 30 acres of pine trees. It

was built as the summer home for the Bigelow family, founder of the Bigelow Carpet Company. Inside the tremendous front door is an elegant display of leaded and stained-glass windows, rich oak woodwork, a winding staircase and a massive, hand-carved oak fireplace.
Rates: $50-$135. All year.
Innkeeper(s): Peter Rattay.
24 Rooms. 22 Private Baths. Guest phone available. TV in room. Beds: QTD. Meals: MAP, EP, Full breakfast, restaurant Jacuzzi. Handicap access provided. Conference room. Fireplaces. Pool. CCs: Visa, MC, AE. Swimming, canoeing, hiking.
Seen in: *The Boston Globe, New York Daily News.*
  "An architecturally preserved replica of an English country house, a perfect retreat for the nostalgic-at-heart." Phil Berthiaume, *Country Almanac.*

The 1785 Inn
Rt 16 at The Scenic Vista
North Conway NH 03860
(603) 356-9025

Circa 1785. The main section of this center-chimney house was built

by Captain Elijah Dinsmore of the New Hampshire Rangers. He was granted the land for service in the American Revolution. Original hand-hewn beams, corner posts, fireplaces, and a brick oven are still visible and operating.
**Rates: $55-$110. All year.
Innkeeper(s): Charlie & Becky Mallar.
13 Rooms. 8 Private Baths. Guest phone available. TV available. Beds: KC. Meals: MAP, full breakfast. Conference room. Fireplaces. Pool. CCs: All. Downhill & cross-country skiing, swimming, fishing, bicycling.
Seen in: *The Valley Visitor.*

"Occasionally in our lifetimes is a moment so unexpectedly perfect that we use it as our measure for our unforgettable moments. We just had such an experience at The 1785 Inn."

North Sutton

Follansbee Inn
PO Box 92, Keyser St
North Sutton NH 03260
(603) 927-4221

Circa 1840. This New England farmhouse was enlarged in 1929, be-

coming an inn, no doubt because of its attractive location on the edge of Kezar Lake. It has a comfortable porch, sitting rooms with fireplaces, and antique-furnished bedrooms. Cross-country skiing starts at the doorstep.
Rates: $65-$85. All year.

Innkeeper(s): Sandy & Dick Reilein.
23 Rooms. 11 Private Baths. Guest phone available. Beds: TD. Meals: Full breakfast. Fireplaces. CCs: Visa, MC. Skiing, golf, tennis, boating, fishing, swimming. Wind surfer, paddleboat.

"Bravo! A great inn experience. Super food."

North Woodstock

Mt. Adams Inn
Rt 3, South Main St
North Woodstock NH 03262
(603) 745-2711

Circa 1875. Situated at a choice spot on the banks of the Moosaiauki River, this is the only hostelry

remaining in the area from the 1800s. Original tin ceilings and cobblestone fireplaces were first enjoyed when visitors came for the summer, taking carriage rides through the mountains. Unique rock formations along the river behind the inn are called the "mummies" and tourists have explored them for more than a century. Authentic Polish cuisine is served in the restaurant.
Rates: $42-$48. All year.
Innkeeper(s): Gloria & Joe Town.
20 Rooms. Guest phone available. TV in room. Beds: DW. Meals: Full breakfast, restaurant. Fireplaces. CCs: Visa, MC. Horseback riding, skiing, golf, tennis, swiming, mountain climbing
Seen in: *Outlook.*

"Last of the grand inns when guests were dropped off by train right across the road."

Northwood

Meadow Farm B&B
Jenness Pond Rd
Northwood NH 03261
(603) 942-8619

Circa 1770. This authentic colonial house is located in a quiet country setting with horses and lake frontage on Jenness Pond. Original features include four fireplaces, paneling, old beams, wide-pine

floors and a keeping room with a bake oven where breakfast is served.
Location: Eighteen miles east of Concord.
Rates: $35-$45. All year.
Innkeeper(s): Douglas & Janet Briggs.
3 Rooms. Guest phone available. TV available. Beds: DT. Meals: Full breakfast. Fireplaces. Swimming, cross-country skiing.

"Thanks so much for sharing your lovely historical home. I feel I now have friends in Northwood."

Plymouth

Crab Apple Inn
RFD 2 Box 200B, Rt 25
Plymouth NH 03264
(603) 536-4476

Circa 1835. Behind an immaculate, white picket fence is a brick Federal house beside a small brook at the foot of Tenney Mountain. There are

fireplaces on the second floor and panoramic vistas from the third floor, and rooms are furnished with canopy beds and claw-foot tubs. The grounds include an English garden and meandering wooded paths.

Location: The Baker River Valley.
Rates: $60-$75. All year.
Innkeeper(s): Bill & Carolyn Crenson
4 Rooms. 2 Private Baths. Guest phone available. Beds: QDT. Meals: Full breakfast. Fireplaces. CCs: Visa, MC. Skiing, hiking, horseback riding, golf.

"We are still excited about our trip. The Crab Apple Inn was the unanimous choice for our favorite place to stay."

Portsmouth

Leighton Inn
69 Richards Ave
Portsmouth NH 03801
(603) 433-2188

Circa 1809. Immediately after cabinetmaker Samuel Wyatt built this fashionable clapboard Federal house, the *Portsmouth Oracle* advertised it for auction in their December 23, 1809 edition. Through an impressive entranceway, Empire antiques accentuate the gracious atmosphere of this handsome home.
Location: North of Boston 55 miles.
Rates: $65-$75. All year.
Innkeeper(s): Catherine Stone.
5 Rooms. 3 Private Baths. Guest phone available. TV available. Beds: QDT. Meals: Full breakfast. CCs: Visa, MC. Tennis, swimming, sailing.
Seen in: *Country Inns.*

"Your hospitality, charm and friendliness was greatly appreciated. You're a terrific cook."

Martin Hill Inn
404 Islington St
Portsmouth NH 03801
(603) 436-2287
Circa 1820. Lieutenant-Governor George Vaughan sold this land in 1710 for 50 British pounds. The Main House, a colonial, contains three guest rooms and the Guest House has four. All bedrooms are decorated in elegant antiques including canopy and four-poster beds, writing tables and sofas or sitting areas. Amenities include air-conditioning.
Rates: $70-$82. All year.
Innkeeper(s): Jane & Paul Harnden.
7 Rooms. 7 Private Baths. Guest phone available. Beds: QDT. Meals: Full breakfast. CCs: Visa, MC.
Seen in: *New Hampshire Profiles, Country Inn Magazine.*

Province Inn
See: Strafford, NH

The Inn at Strawberry Banke
314 Court St
Portsmouth NH 03801
(603) 436-7242
Circa 1790. Around the corner from the waterfront and Strawberry Banke's living museums is the house of Captain Holbrook, who once walked the narrow, winding streets of this beautiful seaport village. Cozy rooms reflect the charm of those bygone days. Strawberry butter is a speciality here and in spring, guests can pick their own

breakfast from the strawberry patch out back.
**Rates: $70-$95. All year.
Innkeeper(s): Tom & Martha Laurie.
7 Rooms. 7 Private Baths. Guest phone available. Beds: QDT. Meals: Full breakfast. Conference room. CCs: Visa, MC, AE.

Snowville

Snowvillage Inn
Box 83, Foss Mt. Rd
Snowville NH 03849
(603) 447-2818
Circa 1850. Frank Simonds, noted World War I historian and government consultant, called his retreat

here "Blighty." The beams in the main house are hand-hewn and were taken from the original 1850 farmhouse. The inn has a spectacular sweeping view of Mt. Washington, and resembles a European mountain home with an Austrian flavor. (The hostess was born in Austria.)
Location: In White Mountains.
Rates: $45-$55. All year.
Innkeeper(s): Peter, Trudy & Frank Cutrone.
19 Rooms. 19 Private Baths. Guest phone available. Beds: KQDT. Meals: MAP, full breakfast, restaurant. Sauna. Conference room. Fireplaces. CCs: Visa, MC, AE. Cross-country skiing, hiking, tennis, volleyball.
Seen in: *New England GetAways, Los Angeles Times.*

"A jewel of a country inn and gourmet food."

Strafford

Province Inn
PO Box 309, Bow Lake
Strafford NH 03884
(603) 664-2457
Circa 1800. This 18th-century colonial estate in an unspoiled

country setting has its own enclosed and heated swimming pool and a lighted tennis court. Nearby is Bow Lake and in the winter snowmobiling, snowshoeing and cross-country skiing start at the inn's back door.
Rates: $50-$55. All year.
Innkeeper(s): Steve & Corky Garboski.
4 Rooms. Guest phone available. TV available. Beds: DT. Meals: Full breakfast. Fireplaces. Pool. Tennis, fishing, golf, swimming, hiking, canoeing.

Sugar Hill

Hilltop Inn
Main Street (Rt 117)
Sugar Hill NH 03585
(603) 823-5695
Circa 1895. This rambling Victorian guest house is located on the quiet main street of town. The rooms are decorated with antiques and there are several cozy common rooms for relaxing after a day of canoeing, horseback riding, or skiing. A spacious deck provides views of the surrounding gardens.
Location: White Mountain National Forest area.
Rates: $50-$85.
Innkeeper(s): Meri & Mike Hern.
6 Rooms. 2 Private Baths. Beds: QDT. Meals: Country breakfast. CCs: Visa, MC, AE. Canoeing, horseback riding. Close to alpine and Nordic skiing.
Seen in: *Boston Globe.*

Ledgeland
Sugar Hill NH 03585
(603) 823-5341

Circa 1926. The main house of this inn is open from June to October

but the private cottages surrounding the inn are available all year. Furnishings are contemporary and there are fireplaces in many of the cottages.
Rates: $55-$90.
23 Rooms. 23 Private Baths. Guest phone available. TV available. Beds: KTC. Meals: Continental plus. Fireplaces. Cross-country skiing, hiking, fishing, tennis, swimming.

"We loved it at Ledgeland. Your place offered the kind of peace and beauty we desperately needed."

The Homestead
Sugar Hill NH 03585
(603) 823-5564

Circa 1802. The current innkeepers are seventh generation descendants

of Sugar Hill's first settler. In 1880, the Teffits began taking in "city boarders". Early settlers carted many of the inn's antiques here with their ox-drawn wagons. In 1917, the Chalet was built with stones from nearby meadows.
Rates: $70-$80. All year.
Innkeeper(s): James & Holly Burris, Essie Serafina.
18 Rooms. 8 Private Baths. Guest phone available. TV available. Beds: KQDT.

Meals: Full breakfast. Fireplaces. CCs: Visa, MC. Cross-country skiing, swimming, tennis, golf, hiking.
Seen in: *Yankee Magazine, Boston Globe, Playboy, Reader's Digest.*

Tamworth

Tamworth Inn
Main St
Tamworth NH 03886
(603) 323-7721

Circa 1833. A sparkling trout stream borders the inn's two acres. Across the street is the Barnstormers

Theater, one of the country's oldest summer stock theaters. It is now in its 57th year under the direction of Francis Cleveland, son of President Grover Cleveland. The Tamworth Pub is on the premises.
Rates: $50-$75. All year.
Innkeeper(s): Ron & Nancy Brembt.
22 Rooms. 10 Private Baths. Guest phone available. TV available. Beds: KQT. Meals: EP, restaurant. Pool. CCs: Visa, MC, AE. Swimming.

"It was great spending the day touring and returning to the quiet village of Tamworth and your wonderful inn."

Wakefield

Wakefield Inn
Mountain Laurel Rd, Rt 1 Box 2185
Wakefield NH 03872
(603) 522-8272

Circa 1803. Early travelers pulled up to the front door of the Wakefield Inn by stagecoach and while they disembarked, their luggage was handed up to the second floor. It was brought in through the door which is still visible over the

porch roof. A spiral staircase, ruffled curtains, wallpapers and a wraparound porch all create the romantic ambience of days gone by. In the dining room an original three-sided fireplace casts a warm glow on dining guests as it did 186 years ago.
Location: Historic district.
Rates: $55-$60. All year.
Innkeeper(s): Harry & Lou Sisson.
6 Rooms. 3 Private Baths. Guest phone available. TV available. Beds: DT. Meals: Full breakfast, restaurant. Fireplaces. CCs: Visa, MC, AE, DC. Cross-country & downhill skiing.
Seen in: *New England GetAways.*

"Comfortable accommodations, excellent food and exquisite decor highlighted by your quilts."

Wolfeboro

Tuc'Me Inn
PO 657
Wolfeboro NH 03894
(603) 569-5702

Circa 1880. Wolfeboro, on the shores of New Hampshire's largest lake, Lake Winnipesaukee, is said to be the oldest summer resort in the United States. This colonial inn is two blocks from the lakefront. A library and two screened porches offer inviting areas for relaxation.
Rates: $67-$73. All year.
Innkeeper(s): Irma Limberger.
7 Rooms. 3 Private Baths. Guest phone available. TV available. Beds: QT. Meals: Full breakfast. Fireplaces. CCs: Visa, MC. Skiing, swimming.
Seen in: *Granite State News.*

"This is the most delightful place I have ever stayed."

New Jersey

Cape May

Abigail Adams Bed & Breakfast
12 Jackson St
Cape May NJ 08204
(609) 884-1371

Circa 1888. The front porch of this Victorian, one of the Seven Sisters, is

only 100 feet from the ocean. There is a free-standing circular staircase, and original fireplaces and woodwork throughout. The decor is highlighted with flowered chintz and antiques, and the dining room is hand-stenciled.
Rates: $55-$95. April to Oct.
Innkeeper(s): Ed & Donna Misner.
5 Rooms. 3 Private Baths. Guest phone available. Beds: QD. Meals: Full breakfast, EP, restaurant. Fireplaces. CCs: Visa, MC. Biking, beaches.

Barnard-Good House
238 Perry St
Cape May NJ 08204
(609) 884-5381

Circa 1865. The Barnard-Good House is a Second Empire Victorian with a mansard roof and original

shingles. A wraparound veranda adds to the charm of this lavender, blue and tan cottage along with the original picket fence and a concrete-formed flower garden. The inn was selected by *New Jersey Magazine* as the number one spot for breakfast in New Jersey.
Rates: $65-$85. April to Nov.
Innkeeper(s): Nan & Tom Hawkins.
5 Rooms. 3 Private Baths. Guest phone available. Beds: KD. Meals: Full breakfast. CCs: Visa, MC.

"Even the cozy bed can't hold you down when the smell of Nan's breakfast makes its way upstairs."

Captain Mey's Inn
202 Ocean St
Cape May NJ 08204
(609) 884-7793

Circa 1881. Named after a Dutch West India captain who named the area, the inn displays its Dutch heritage with table-top Persian rugs, Delft china and imported Dutch lace curtains. The dining room features

chestnut oak Eastlake paneling, and breakfast is served by candlelight.
Rates: $65-$125. All year.
Innkeeper(s): Milly LaCanfora & Carin Feddermann.
9 Rooms. 2 Private Baths. Guest phone available. Beds: QT. Meals: Full breakfast. Conference room. Fireplaces. CCs: Visa, MC. Swimming, tennis, horse & buggy rides.
Seen in: *Americana Magazine, Country Living.*

"The innkeepers pamper you so much you wish you could stay forever."

COLVMNS by the Sea
1513 Beach Dr
Cape May NJ 08204
(609) 884-2228

Circa 1905. Dr. Davis, the Philadelphia physician who created

calamine lotion, built this house in the days when a summer cottage might have 20 rooms, 12-foot ceilings, three-story staircases and hand-carved ceilings. Large, airy

rooms provide magnificent views of the ocean. The innkeepers supply beach tags and towels as well as bikes. Afternoon tea is served.
Rates: $89-$115. All year.
Innkeeper(s): Barry & Cathy Rein.
11 Rooms. 11 Private Baths. Guest phone available. TV available. Beds: Q. Meals: Full breakfast. Conference room. Fireplaces.

Dormer House, International
800 Columbia Ave
Cape May NJ 08204
(609) 884-7446
  Circa 1899. This Colonial Revival estate is three blocks from the ocean and the historic walking mall. It was built by marble-dealer John Jacoby and retains much of the original marble and furniture. Several years ago the inn was converted into guest suites with kitchens.
Location: Corner of Franklin & Columbia in the historic district.
Rates: $45-$90. All year.
Innkeeper(s): Bill & Peg Madden.
8 Rooms. 8 Private Baths. Guest phone available. TV available. Beds: QDT. Meals: EP. CCs: Visa, MC.

Duke of Windsor Inn
817 Washington St
Cape May NJ 08204
(609) 884-1355
  Circa 1896. This Queen Anne Victorian was built by Delaware River boat pilot Harry Hazelhurst and his

wife Florence. They were both six feet tall, so the house was built with large open rooms and doorways, and extra wide stairs. The inn has a carved, natural oak open staircase with stained-glass windows at top and bottom. Five antique chandeliers grace the dining room.
Rates: $50-$85. Feb. to Dec.

Innkeeper(s): Bruce, Fran & Barbara Prichard.
9 Rooms. 7 Private Baths. Guest phone available. Beds: D. Meals: Full breakfast. Fireplaces. CCs: Visa, MC. Tennis, beach.
Seen in: *Philadelphia Inquirer*.
  "Tom and I loved staying in your home! We certainly appreciate all the hard work you put into renovating the house."

Gingerbread House
28 Gurney St
Cape May NJ 08204
(609) 884-0211
  Circa 1869. The Gingerbread is one of eight original Stockton Row Cottages, summer retreats built for families from Philadelphia and Virginia. It is a half-block from the ocean and breezes waft over the wicker-filled porch. The inn is decorated with period antiques and a fine collection of paintings.
Location: One-half block from the beach.
Rates: $68-$110. All year.
Innkeeper(s): Fred & Joan Echevarria.
6 Rooms. 3 Private Baths. Guest phone available. Beds: D. Meals: Continental plus. Fireplaces.

Henry Ludlam Inn
See: Woodbine, NJ

Holly House
20 Jackson St
Cape May NJ 08204
(609) 884-7365
  Circa 1888. Holly House is one of the seven Renaissance Revival cottages famous as Cape May's "Seven Sisters." The inn was designed by Stephen Decatur Button as a Victorian beach house and is in the National  Register. A three-story circular staircase and the original coal-grate fireplaces are highlights. The innkeeper is a former mayor of Cape May.
Rates: $40-$50. All year.
Innkeeper(s): Corinne & Bruce Minnix.
6 Rooms. Guest phone available. Meals: EP. CCs: Visa, MC. Beach.

  "Friendly people. Informal, comfortable mix of old and new."

Humphrey Hughes House
29 Ocean St
Cape May NJ 08204
(609) 884-4428
  Circa 1903. Stained-glass windows mark each landing of the staircase, and intricately carved American chestnut columns add to the atmosphere in this 30-room summer cottage. The land was purchased by the Captain Humphrey Hughes family in the early 1700s and remained in the family till 1980. Dr. Harold Hughes' majestic grandfather clock remains as one of many late Victorian antiques.
Rates: $85-$105. All year.
Innkeeper(s): Lorraine & Terry Schmidt.
11 Rooms. 4 Private Baths. Guest phone available. Beds: KQ. Meals: Full breakfast. Handicap access provided. Fireplaces. Biking, golf, beach.
  "Thoroughly enjoyed our stay. You should be proud of your home and operation."

Mainstay Inn
635 Columbia Ave
Cape May NJ 08204
(609) 884-8690
  Circa 1872. This was once the elegant and exclusive Jackson's

Clubhouse popular with gamblers. Many of the guest rooms and the grand parlor look much as they did in the 1840s. Fourteen-foot ceilings, elaborate chandeliers, a sweeping veranda and a cupola add to the atmosphere. Tom and Sue Carroll received the annual American Historic Inns award in 1988 for their preservation efforts.
Rates: $65-$108. April to Dec 15
Innkeeper(s): Tom & Sue Carroll.
13 Rooms. 9 Private Baths. Guest phone available. Beds: KQ. Meals: Full breakfast. Conference room.

Mason Cottage
625 Columbia Avenue
Cape May NJ 08204
(609) 884-3358

Circa 1871. Since 1940, this house has been open to guests. The curved

mansard wood-shingle roof was built by local shipyard carpenters. Much of the original furniture remains in the house, and it has endured both hurricanes and the 1878 Cape May fire.
**Rates: $65-$105. May to Nov.
Innkeeper(s): Dave & Joan Mason.
5 Rooms. 4 Private Baths. Guest phone available. Beds: D. Meals: Continental plus. CCs: Visa, MC. Trolley tours, carriage rides, walking tours. Honeymoon packages.
"We look forward so much to coming back each summer and enjoying your hospitality and very special inn."

Queen Victoria
102 Ocean St
Cape May NJ 08204
(609) 884-8702

Circa 1881. The Sherwin-Williams Company used this restored seaside villa to illustrate its line of Victorian

paints, and *Victorian Homes* featured 23 color photographs of it. Amenities include afternoon tea and mixers, a fleet of bicycles, and evening turn-down service. Suites feature a jacuzzi, fireplace or private porch.
Location: In the heart of the historic district, one block from the beach.
Rates: $55-$115. All year.

Innkeeper(s): Dane & Joan Wells.
11 Rooms. 9 Private Baths. Guest phone available. TV in room. Beds: KQTDC. Meals: Full breakfast. Jacuzzi. Handicap access provided. Conference room. Fireplaces. CCs: Visa, MC. Bicycling, beach.
"Everything was perfect in a beautiful surrounding."

Sand Castle Guest House
829 Stockton Ave
Cape May NJ 08204
(609) 884-5451

Circa 1873. This Carpenter Gothic was built by John Bullitt, a wealthy Philadelphia lawyer and a key fig-

ure in the development of Cape May in the mid-19th century. The inn is one block from the ocean and the two-mile-long promenade. The decor is a light blend of country and Victorian with lace, oak, quilts and chintz.
Rates: $65-$125. May to Oct. 15.
Innkeeper(s): Eileen, Guy & Kim Brooks.
7 Rooms. 1 Private Baths. Beds: TDC. Meals: Continental plus. Fireplaces. CCs: Visa, MC. Beach.
"Your friendly atmosphere and decor can't be beat. Thanks for making a needed vacation such a pleasant one."

Seventh Sister Guesthouse
10 Jackson St
Cape May NJ 08204
(609) 884-2280

Circa 1888. Most of the Seventh Sister's guest rooms have ocean views. The inn is in the National Register. Extensive wicker and original art collections are featured and three floors are joined by a spectacular central cir-

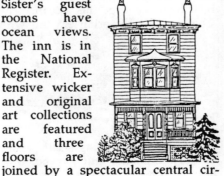

cular staircase. The center of town is one block away.
Rates: $50-$65. March to Dec.
Innkeeper(s): Bob & Jo-Anne Myers.
6 Rooms. Guest phone available. Beds: D. Bicycling, beach.

The Chalfonte
301 Howard St
Cape May NJ 08204
(609) 884-8409

Circa 1878. This 103-room hotel has a rambling veranda, rooms are simple, and the cooking is southern. The cook Helen Dickerson, now in her seventies, has been with the hotel since her mother brought her here at the age of four.
Location: Centrally located in the historic district, 2 blocks from beaches.
**Rates: $42-$87. May to Oct.
Innkeeper(s): Anne LeDuc & Judy Bartella.
103 Rooms. 11 Private Baths. Guest phone available. TV available. Beds: D. Meals: MAP. Conference room. CCs: Visa, MC. Swimming, sailing, tennis, golf, bicycling. Special workshops.
Seen in: *Philadelphia Inquirer, The Washington Times Magazine.*
"Thanks for everything. We had a great time!"

The Wooden Rabbit
609 Hughes St
Cape May NJ 08204
(609) 884-7293

Circa 1838. Robert E. Lee brought his wife to stay at this sea captain's

house to ease her arthritis. The house was also part of the Underground Railroad. Throughout the inn are whimsical touches such as the "rabbit hutch" in the living room which holds a collection of Beatrix Potter figures. The decor is country, with folk art and collec-

tibles that can accommodate hands-on exploration.
Rates: $100-$125. All year.
Innkeeper(s): Greg & Debby Burow.
3 Rooms. 3 Private Baths. Guest phone available. TV in room. Beds: KQT. Meals: Full breakfast, afternoon tea. Fireplaces. CCs: Visa, MC. Swimming, bicycling, tennis, golf.
"The room was perfect, our breakfast delicious. We will be back."

Lyndhurst

The Jeremiah J. Yereance House
410 Riverside
Lyndhurst NJ 07071
(201) 438-9457
Circa 1841. In the National Register, this tiny house was built by a ship joiner who worked at the shipyards on the Passaic River. The inn is adjacent to a one-room schoolhouse built in 1804 which is now a museum of local history. There are cobblestone walks and a wisteria arbor. It is across from a riverside park.
**Rates: $50-$75. All year.
Innkeeper(s): Evelyn & Frank Pezzolla.
4 Rooms. 1 Private Baths. Guest phone in room. TV in room. Meals: Full breakfast, continental plus. Fireplaces. Tennis, bicycling, walking trails.
"A perfect setting to start our honeymoon!"

Ocean Grove

Cordova
26 Webb Ave
Ocean Grove NJ 07756
(201) 774-3084
Circa 1886. Founded as a Methodist retreat, ocean-bathing

and cars were not allowed here until a few years ago, so there are no souvenir shops along the white

sandy beach and wooden boardwalk. The inn has hosted Presidents Wilson, Cleveland and Roosevelt who were also speakers at the Great Auditorium with its 7,000 seats. Guests here feel like family and have the use of kitchen, lounge and barbecue.
**Rates: $30-$66. May to Sept.
Innkeeper(s): Doris & Vlad Chernik.
22 Rooms. 1 Private Baths. Guest phone available. TV available. Beds: TDC. Meals: Full breakfast, continental plus. Swimming, tennis, volleyball, bicycling.
Seen in: *New Jersey Magazine, Asbury Park Press.*
"Warm, helpful and inviting, homey and lived-in atmosphere."

Pine Tree Inn
10 Main Ave.
Ocean Grove NJ 07756
(201) 775-3264
Circa 1880. This small Victorian hotel is operated by longstanding residents of the area and the original innkeeper is Mr. Schneider, now 88 years old. Guestrooms are decorated in antiques and all the rooms are equipped with sinks. Bicycles are available as well as beach towels.
Rates: $42-$85. All year.
Innkeeper(s): Francis & Deborah Goger and Karen Mason.
13 Rooms. 3 Private Baths. Guest phone available. TV in room. Beds: KQT. Meals: Full breakfast. CCs: Visa, MC. Swimming, bicycling, jogging.
Seen in: *Country Living Magazine.*

Spring Lake

Chateau
500 Warren Ave
Spring Lake NJ 07762
(201) 974-2000
Circa 1888. In addition to the lake, this village has a two-mile boardwalk along the ocean. The Chateau is a Victorian era inn with

many rooms providing scenic vistas of the park, lake and gazebo. Borders of flowers surround the white pillared verandas and there are

brick patios, sun-filled balconies and private porches. The Spring Lake Trolley departs every half hour from the front door.
**Rates: $47-$126. April to Oct.
Innkeeper(s): Scott & Karen Smith
35 Rooms. 35 Private Baths. Guest phone in room. TV in room. Beds: KQDC. Meals: Continental plus. Conference room. CCs: Visa, MC, AE. Swimming, surfing, boating, fishing, tennis, golf, bicycling.
Seen in: *Great Water Escapes.*
"One of the top five inns in New Jersey." Mobil Travel Guide.

Kenilworth
1505 Ocean Ave
Spring Lake NJ 07762
(201) 449-5327
Circa 1882. This Victorian inn provides an unobstructed view of

the Atlantic from the front porch, and is located across the street from the boardwalk. The parlor is filled with books, and a Victorian bridal chamber has recently been added. Guests are welcome to barbeque on the side lawn or use the fully equipped kitchen.
**Rates: $60-$90. June 15-Oct.15.
Innkeeper(s): Lesley Mason Mills & Ric Karr.
23 Rooms. 14 Private Baths. Guest phone available. TV available. Beds: QTC. Meals: Full breakfast. Conference room. Swimming, fishing, tennis, golf.
Seen in: *The Christian Science Monitor, Holiday Shore Magazine.*

Sandpiper Hotel
7 Atlantic Ave
Spring Lake NJ 07762
(201) 449-6060
Circa 1888. This historic Victorian inn is just one-quarter of a block from the ocean. It offers romantically appointed rooms, a large wraparound porch, and old-fashioned hospitality. Spring Lake is a lovely Victorian-era community

with an uncluttered two-mile-long oceanfront boardwalk.
Rates: d$65-$125. All year.
15 Rooms. 15 Private Baths. Guest phone in room. TV in room. Beds: KQDT. Meals: Continental, restaurant. CCs: Visa, MC, AE, DC.

Stone Post Inn
115 Washington Ave
Spring Lake NJ 07762
(201) 449-1212

Circa 1882. Originally built as a lodging establishment, the inn was known as the Rest-A-While and then The Washington House. It is located in a quiet residential area surrounded by tree-shaded lawns and gardens, giving it the atmosphere of a private home. European antiques are complemented by a varied collection of family antiques and art.
Location: One block from the ocean and the village.
**Rates: $50-$100. All year.
Innkeeper(s): Julia Paris & daughters Janine & Connie.
20 Rooms. 9 Private Baths. Guest phone available. TV available. Beds: QT. Meals: Full breakfast. Conference room. Fireplaces. CCs: Visa, MC, AE. Tennis, horseback riding, golf, fishing.

The Normandy Inn
21 Tuttle Ave
Spring Lake NJ 07762
(201) 449-7172

Circa 1888. An Italianate villa with Queen Anne influences, the Nor-

mandy Inn features sunburst designs and neoclassical interiors.

Victorian antiques are accentuated by Victorian colors documented and researched by Roger Moss. The house was moved onto the present site around 1910.
Rates: $85-$115. All year.
Innkeeper(s): Michael & Susan Ingino.
20 Rooms. 15 Private Baths. Guest phone available. TV available. Beds: DTC. Meals: Full breakfast. Bicycling.

Stanhope

Whistling Swan Inn
Box 791, 110 Main St
Stanhope NJ 07874
(201) 347-6369

Circa 1900. This Queen Anne Victorian has a limestone wraparound veranda and a tall steep-roofed turret. Family antiques fill the rooms and highlight the polished ornate woodwork, pocket doors and winding staircase. It is a little over a mile from Waterloo Village and the International Trade Zone.
Innkeeper(s): Paula Williams & Joe Mulay.
10 Rooms. 10 Private Baths. Meals: Full breakfast. CCs: Visa, MC, AE.
Seen in: *Sunday Herald.*

Stockton

Woolverton Inn
6 Woolverton Rd
Stockton NJ 08559
(609) 397-0802

Circa 1793. This charming mansard-roofed inn was built by John

Prall, a merchant who owned the Prallsville Mills nearby. The stone

manor house is set among formal gardens. Each room is decorated in a different era and named after one of the previous owners.
Rates: $60-$95. All year.
Innkeeper(s): David Salassi & Louise Warsaw.
11 Rooms. 1 Private Baths. Guest phone available. Beds: KTD. Handicap access provided. Fireplaces. CCs: Visa, MC. Horse back riding, tennis, swimming, cross-country skiing.
Seen in: *New York Magazine, Colonial Homes.*
"Thank you for providing a perfect setting and relaxed atmosphere for our group. You're terrific."

Woodbine

Henry Ludlam Inn
124 S Delsea Dr, RD 3 Box 298
Woodbine NJ 08270
(609) 861-5847

Circa 1760. Each of the guest rooms has a fireplace and view of Ludlam Lake. Canoeing and fishing

are popular activities and the innkeepers make sure you enjoy these at your peak by providing you with a full country breakfast.
Location: Cape May County.
Rates: $45-$75. All year.
Innkeeper(s): Ann & Marty Thurlow.
6 Rooms. 2 Private Baths. Guest phone available. TV available. Fireplaces. CCs: Visa, MC.
"By the time we left we felt like old friends!...I'm afraid that staying with you spoiled us!"

New Mexico

Albuquerque

Casita Chamisa
850 Chamisal Rd NW
Albuquerque NM 87107
(505) 897-4644

Circa 1850. Beneath her old adobe, Kit an archeologist, discovered a deeply stratified Indian village attributed to the Pueblo IV Period, 1300-1650 A.D. After a two-year excavation a viewing site was created. There is an indoor swimming pool and bicycles are available. An aerial tram and hot air ballooning is nearby.
Location: Fifteen minutes from town.
Rates: $60. All year.
Innkeeper(s): Kit & Arnold Sargeant.
3 Rooms. 2 Private Baths. Beds: KQT.
Meals: Continental-plus breakfast. Pool.
CCs: Visa, MC.

W.E. Mauger Estate
701 Roma Ave NW
Albuquerque NM 87102
(505) 242-8755

Circa 1897. This former boarding house is now an elegantly restored Victorian in the National Register. Third floor rooms are done in Art Deco with views of downtown Al-

buquerque and the Sandia Mountains beyond. The second floor is decorated with antiques and lace. The inn is located in an area undergoing renovation, six blocks from the Convention Center.
Location: Central Albuquerque.
Rates: $50-$95 All year.
Innkeeper(s): Richard & Uta Carleno.
6 Rooms. 6 Private Baths. Guest phone available. TV available. Beds: QT. Meals: Continental Plus. Conference room. CCs: Visa, MC, AE. Water skiing, horseback riding, fishing. daily Indian dances. Organized tours of Indian Pueblos & petroglyphs.
Seen in: *Albuquerque Journal*.

"...all because of your hospitality, kindness and warmth...We will always be comparing the quality of our experience to what we experienced during our stay in W.E. Mauger.

Cloudcroft

The Lodge
PO Box 497
Cloudcroft NM 88317
(505) 682-2566

Circa 1899. This 11-room B&B is located in the restored Pavilion, the oldest building at the Lodge at Cloudcroft, an award-winning resort 9,200 feet above Alamogordo and New Mexico's White Sands National Monument. Past guests were Pancho Villa, Judy Garland, and Clark Gable. The new renovation has included a graceful pond and waterfall framed by flowers.
**Rates: $45-$80.
Innkeeper(s): Judy Montoya.
11 Rooms. 9 Private Baths. Guest phone in room. TV in room. Beds: KQDTC. Meals: Continental. Restaurant. Jacuzzi. Sauna. Handicap access provided. Conference room. Fireplaces. Pool. CCs: Visa, MC, AE. Biking, skiing, golf, tennis.

Galisteo

Galisteo Inn
Box 4
Galisteo NM 87540
(505) 982-1506

Circa 1760. This adobe hacienda, framed by ancient cottonwoods, belonged to the same family for 180 years. It is decorated in a New Mexico style with beamed entranceway, plank flooring and whitewashed walls. Regional cuisine features items such as southwestern scones.
Location: Twenty-three miles southeast of Santa Fe.
Rates: $55-$125.
Innkeeper(s): Elizabeth Luster.
10 Rooms. 3 Private Baths. Guest phone available. TV available. Beds: KQT. Meals: Full breakfast. Jacuzzi. Sauna. Handicap access provided. Conference room. Fireplaces. Pool. CCs: Visa, MC. Horseback riding, hiking, massage, exercise center. Art tours.
Seen in: *Innsider*.

Santa Fe

El Paradero
220 W Manhattan
Santa Fe NM 87501
(505) 988-1177

Circa 1912. This was originally a two-bedroom Spanish farmhouse that doubled in size to a Territorial style in 1860, was remodeled as a Victorian in 1912, and became a Pueblo Revival in 1920. All styles are present and provide a walk through many years of history.
Location: Downtown.
**Rates: $40-$95. All year.

Innkeeper(s): Ouida MacGregor & Thom Allen.

12 Rooms. 8 Private Baths. Guest phone in room. TV available. Beds: QT. Meals: EP, gourmet. Handicap access provided. Conference room. Fireplaces. CCs: Visa, MC. Hiking, horseback riding, white water rafting, indian ruins.

Seen in: *Insider Magazine, Country Inns.*

"I'd like to LIVE here."

Grant Corner Inn

122 Grant Ave
Santa Fe NM 87501
(505) 983-6678

Circa 1905. Judge Robinson and his family lived in this colonial manor for 30 years and many couples were married in the parlor. Still a romantic setting, the inn is secluded by a garden with willow trees, and there is a white picket fence. Rooms are appointed with antique furnishings and the personal art collections of the Walter family.

**Rates: $45-$110. All year.
Innkeeper(s): Louise Stewart & Martin Walter.
13 Rooms. 7 Private Baths. Guest phone in room. TV in room. Beds: KQTC. Meals: EP. Handicap access provided. Conference room. Fireplaces. CCs: Visa, MC. Downhill & cross-country skiing, hiking, fishing.

"The very best of everything - comfort, hospitality, food and T.L.C."

Pueblo Bonito

138 W Manhattan
Santa Fe NM 87501
(505) 984-8001

Circa 1883. A large adobe wall surrounds the grounds of this estate,

once the home of a circuit judge. An original Indian oven is attached to the house. Flagstone pathways, old oak trees and a rose garden add to the atmosphere.

Location: Downtown.
**Rates: $50-$150. All year.
Innkeeper(s): Amy & Herb Behm.
18 Rooms. 18 Private Baths. Guest phone available. TV in room. Beds: QC. Meals: Continental plus. Jacuzzi. Sauna. Handicap access provided. Conference room. Pool. CCs: Visa, MC. Hiking, skiing, swimming, tennis, golf, horseback riding, bicycles

"...captured that quaint, authentic Santa Fe atmosphere, yet I didn't feel as if I had to sacrifice any modern conveniences."

Taos

Hacienda del Sol

Box 177
Taos NM 87571
(505) 758-0287

Circa 1800. Mabel Dodge, patron of the arts, purchased this old hacienda as a hideaway for her Indian husband Tony Luhan. The spacious adobe sits among huge cottonwoods, blue spruce, and ponderosa pines, with an uninterrupted view of the mountains that spread across 95,000 acres of Indian lands. Among Dodge's famous guests were Georgia O'Keefe, who painted here, and D. H. Lawrence. The mood is tranquil and on moonlit nights guests can hear Indian drums and the howl of coyotes.

Location: North of Santa Fe at the base of Sangre de Cristo Mountains.
**Rates: $24-$78.
Innkeeper(s): Mari & Jim Ulmer.
3 Rooms. 3 Private Baths. Guest phone available. TV available. Beds: QD. Meals: Continental-plus breakfast. CCs: Visa, MC.

"Your warm friendliness and gracious hospitality have made this week an experience we will never forget!"

La Posada De Taos

309 Juanita Lane, Box 1118
Taos NM 87571
(505) 758-8164

Circa 1900. Located within the historic district in a secluded residential area, La Posada is built in the adobe vernacular of the southwest. Log-beamed ceilings (vigas), polished floors, Mexican headboards, handwoven spreads, and whitewashed walls hung with local serigraphs contribute to the southwestern decor. French doors open onto a garden with views of Taos Mountain. There are four guest rooms and a honeymoon cottage.

Rates: $46-$75.
5 Rooms. 5 Private Baths. TV available. Beds: QT. Meals: B&B. Handicap access provided. Fireplaces.

"Since we left your inn we have talked of our time there often. We look forward to being there again."

The Taos Inn

125 Paseo del Pueblo Norte
Taos NM 87571
(505) 758-2233

Circa 1660. The Taos Inn is a historic landmark with sections dating back to the 1600s. It is a rustic wood and adobe setting with wood-burning fireplaces, vigas, and wrought iron. The exotic tricultural heritage of Spanish, English, and Indian is displayed in hand-loomed Indian bedspreads, antique armoires, Taos furniture, and Pueblo Indian fireplaces.

Location: A quarter block north of historic Taos Plaza.
Rates: $50-$95.
Innkeeper(s): Bruce Ross & Feeny Lipscomb.
40 Rooms. 40 Private Baths. Guest phone in room. TV in room. Handicap access provided. CCs: Visa, MC, AE.
Seen in: *Bon Appetit.*

New York

Albany

The Gregory House
See: Averill Park, NY

Altamont

Appel Inn
Rte 146
Altamont NY 12009
(518) 861-6557

Circa 1765. Originally built as a tavern by Hendrick Appel, this was the site of the first town meeting of

Guilderland. A century later pillars, porches and a Victorian solarium were added. Guests often breakfast in this sunny room with views through trees to winding Black Creek. The innkeeper was a European chef.
Location: 15 miles to Albany & 8 miles to Schenectady.
Rates: $45-$60.
Innkeeper(s): Laurie & Gerd Beckmann.
4 Rooms. Guest phone available. TV available. Beds: QTC. Meals: B&B. Conference room. Fireplaces. Pool. CCs: Visa, MC. Nearby lakes, golf. Fireplaces in bedrooms.
"Accommodations were superb, hosts were gracious and food was delicious. We were delighted."

Amenia

Troutbeck
Box 26, Leedsville Rd
Amenia NY 12501
(914) 373-9681

Circa 1918. This English country estate on 422 wooded acres enjoyed

its heyday in the Twenties. The NAACP was conceived here and the literati and liberals of the period, including Teddy Roosevelt, were overnight guests. Weekend room rates include all meals and spirits as well as luxurious accommodations for a couple. During the week the inn is a corporate retreat and was awarded Executive Retreat of the Year.
Location: Foothills of the Berkshires.
**Rates: $550-$975. All year.
Innkeeper(s): James Flaherty & Kathy Robinson.
31 Rooms. 26 Private Baths. Guest phone available. TV available. Beds: QTDC. Meals: All meals. Jacuzzi. Conference room. Fireplaces. Pool. CCs: AE. Horseback riding, downhill & cross-country skiing, fishing. Tennis courts, swimming pool.
Seen in: *Good Housekeeping, New York Magazine.*
"Connoisseurs of country inns rummage fruitlessly through their memories to summon up an establishment that satisfies their expectations as completely as Troutbeck." Travel & Leisure.

Averill Park

The Gregory House
PO Box 401
Averill Park NY 12018
(518) 674-3774

Circa 1837. This colonial house was built in the center of the village by stockbroker Elias Gregory. It became a restaurant in 1984. The his-

toric section of the building now holds the restaurant while a new portion accommodates overnight guests. It is decorated with Early American braided rugs and four-poster beds.
Location: Minutes from Albany.
**Rates: $50-$70. All year.
Innkeeper(s): Bette & Bob Jewell.
12 Rooms. 12 Private Baths. Guest phone available. TV available. Beds: QT. Meals: Full breakfast, EP, restaurant Fireplaces. Pool. CCs: Visa, MC, AE, DC, CB Swimming.
Seen in: *The Courier, The Sunday Record.*

Buffalo

Rainbow Hospitality
See: Niagara Falls, NY

Burdett

The Red House Country Inn
Picnic Area Rd
Burdett NY 14818
(607) 546-8566

Circa 1844. Nestled within the 13,000-acre Finger Lakes National

Forest, this old farmstead has a large veranda overlooking groomed lawns, flower gardens and picnic areas. Pet Samoyeds, goats, and horses share the seven acres. Next to the property are acres of wild blueberry patches and stocked fishing ponds. The Red House is near Seneca Lake, world-famous Glen Gorge, and Cornell University.
Location: Finger Lakes National Forest, near Watkins Glen.
Rates: $32-$65. All year.
Innkeeper(s): Sandy Schmanke & Joan Martin.
6 Rooms. Guest phone available. TV available. Beds: D. Meals: Full breakfast. CCs: Visa, MC. Cross-country skiing, hiking, swimming.
Seen in: *New York Alive.*
"Delightful. Beautifully located for hiking, cross-country skiing. Guest rooms are charming."

Cazenovia

Brae Loch Inn
5 Albany St
Cazenovia NY 13035
(315) 655-3431

Circa 1805. Here the innkeeper wears a kilt to highlight the Scottish

theme. Four of the oldest rooms have fireplaces. There are Stickley furnishings, and the Princess Diana

Room has a canopy of white eyelet. Guest rooms are on the second floor above the restaurant.
Location: U.S. Route 20.
**Rates: $59-$125. All year.
Innkeeper(s): H. Grey Barr & Doris L. Barr.
12 Rooms. 12 Private Baths. Guest phone available. TV in room. Beds: KQDC. Meals: Continental plus, restaurant. Conference room. Fireplaces. CCs: Visa, MC, AE, DC. Horseback riding, cross-country skiing, golf, hiking.

Cold Spring

Hudson House
2 Main St
Cold Spring NY 10516
(914) 265-9355

Circa 1832. This is a restored Historic Landmark Building located on the banks of a beautiful section of

the Hudson River. The inn is said to be the second oldest inn in continuous operation in New York State. It was built to accommodate the increase in passenger traffic along the river because of a new paddle steamer. The rooms are filled with antiques and many have waterfront views of West Point and the hills.
Location: Hudson River Valley.
Rates: $85-$130. Closed January.
Innkeeper(s): Mary Pat Sawyer.
15 Rooms. 15 Private Baths. Guest phone available. Beds: QTD. Meals: Continental. CCs: Visa, MC, AE. Swimming, sailing.
Seen in: *Vogue, New York Romantic Weekends, Gannett Westchester.*

Cooperstown

Inn at Cooperstown
16 Chestnut St
Cooperstown NY 13326
(607) 547-5756

Circa 1874. In 1986, New York State awarded the Certificate of Achieve-

ment in Historic Preservation for the restoration of this three-story, Second Empire house. A block from Otsego Lake, the inn is within walking distance of most of Cooperstown's attractions.
**Rates: $65-$75. All year.
Innkeeper(s): Michael Jerome.
17 Rooms. 17 Private Baths. Beds: KQTC. Meals: Continental. CCs: Visa, MC, AE, DC, DS Swimming, cross-country skiing, horseback riding, snow tubing.
Seen in: *The Plain Dealer.*

The Inn at Mill Pond
PO Box 167
Cooperstown NY 13326
(315) 858-1654

Circa 1890. This quaint bed and breakfast is located on a mill pond in a historic area. The house has been restored and is furnished with local antiques. Late afternoon tea is served.
Location: Route 80, 10 minutes north of Cooperstown.
Rates: $45. May to October.
Innkeeper(s): Ed & Gail Newton-Condon.
3 Rooms. 1 Private Baths. Guest phone available. Beds: D. Meals: Full breakfast. Golf, fishing, swimming.
"Great stay, we loved it!"

Corning

Rosewood Inn
134 E First St
Corning NY 14830
(607) 962-3253

Circa 1855. Rosewood Inn was originally built as a Greek Revival house. In 1917, the interior and exterior were remodeled in an English Tudor style. The facade includes four, two-story, square columns and arched windows and doors. Original black walnut and oak woodwork grace the interior, decorated with authentic wallpapers, period draperies and fine antiques.
Location: Off U.S. Route 17.
Rates: $45-$75. All year.
Innkeeper(s): Winnie & Dick Peer.
6 Rooms. 4 Private Baths. Guest phone in room. TV available. Beds: QTDC. Meals: Full breakfast. Fireplaces. CCs: Visa, MC, AE, DC.
Seen in: *Syracuse Herald-Journal.*

"Rosewood Inn is food for the soul! You both made us feel like friends instead of guests. We'll be back!"

Cuba

33 South
33 South St
Cuba NY 14727
(716) 968-1387

Circa 1902. This newly opened B&B, a modified Queen Anne Victorian of red brick, was constructed of native cherry and oak from the family farm. An open cherry stair-

case, Palladian glass windows, stained glass and three fireplaces are features. Nearby McKinney Stable housed and bred horses for the Czar of Russia.
Rates: $35-$40. All year.
Innkeeper(s): Jim & Ina Willson.
3 Rooms. 2 Private Baths. Guest phone available. TV available. Beds: QTC. Meals: Full breakfast. Fireplaces. CCs: Visa, MC. Skiing, boating, horses.

Geneseo

American House
39 Main St
Geneseo NY 14454
(716) 243-5483

Circa 1897. The American House was a tavern and stagecoach stop in the early 1800s. When it burned, a private home was built and it is now in the National Register. Centrally located in the village, it's a short walk to the campus of the State University of New York. The second oldest active fox hunt in the country is the Genesee Valley Hunt.
Location: Thirty miles south of Rochester, 60 miles east of Buffalo.
**Rates: $40-$60. All year.
Innkeeper(s): Harry & Helen Wadsworth.

6 Rooms. 2 Private Baths. Guest phone available. TV available. Beds: QTD. Meals: Full breakfast. Fireplaces. Cross-country skiing, horseback riding, swimming, boating.

"You certainly set the tone for Jodi's wedding day. Many thanks from a grandmother who enjoyed every moment of that memorable stay."

Geneva

Inn at Belhurst Castle
PO 609
Geneva NY 14456
(315) 781-0201

Circa 1895. Red Medina stone was chosen to construct this Richardson Romanesque mansion. The inn's sweeping lawns and views of Seneca Lake may be enjoyed anywhere on the property, but the most stunning experience is from the balcony of the Tower suite, a special room with a hot tub and a private staircase that winds up the turret. Exquisitely carved woodwork throughout the inn serves as a backdrop to surprising decorative touches such as a stuffed partridge or a suit of armor.
Rates: $80-$190.
Innkeeper(s): Robert Golden.
12 Rooms. 12 Private Baths. Beds: QT. Meals: EP. Fireplaces. CCs: All. Swimming, sailing, fishing, cross-country skiing.

Glens Falls

The Crislip's Bed & Breakfast
RD 1 Box 57, Ridge Rd
Glens Falls NY 12801
(518) 793-6869

Circa 1820. This Federal-style house was built by Quakers. It was owned by the area's first doctor

who used it as a training center for young interns. There are historic stone walls on the property.
Location: Lake George, Sarasota area.
Rates: $55-$65. All year.

Innkeeper(s): Ned & Joyce Crislip.
3 Rooms. 3 Private Baths. Guest phone available. TV in room. Beds: KD. Fireplaces. CCs: Visa, MC.

Greenville

Greenville Arms
South St
Greenville NY 12083
(518) 966-5219

Circa 1889. William Vanderbilt built this graceful Victorian with Queen Anne gables and cupolas. Seven acres of lush lawns are dotted

with gardens of daffodils, tulips and lilacs. There are floor-to-ceiling fireplaces, chestnut woodwork and wainscoting, and Victorian beadwork over the doorways. Popular painting workshops are often held in summer and fall.
Rates: $35-$50. May to October.
Innkeeper(s): Laura & Barbara Stevens.
20 Rooms. 14 Private Baths. Guest phone available. TV available. Beds: TD. Meals: MAP, full breakfast. Conference room. Fireplaces. Pool. CCs: Visa, MC, AE. Golf, tennis, horseback riding, hiking, bicycling.

"Just a note of appreciation for all your generous hospitality, and wonderful display of attention and affection!"

Groton

Benn Conger Inn
206 W Cortland
Groton NY 13073
(607) 898-5817

Circa 1921. Once home to Benn Conger, founder of Smith-Corona

typewriters, this Greek Revival mansion overlooks the village and presides over 18 acres of rolling fields. The inn is owned and operated by Chef Mark Bloom and wife Patricia who specialize in French and Italian cuisine. Guest rooms are furnished in antiques and feature flannel sheets and warm comforters for frosty evenings.
Location: Finger Lakes area between Ithaca and Cortland.
Rates: $50-$90.
Innkeeper(s): Mark & Patricia Bloom.
4 Rooms. 2 Private Baths. Guest phone available. TV available. Beds: KQD. Meals: Full breakfast. Dinner Tues - Sat. Conference room. Fireplaces. CCs: Visa, MC, AE, DC. Hiking, cross country skiing on premises. nearby wineries. Award-winning wine cellar.
Seen in: *Andrew Harper's Hideaway Report.*

Hyde Park

Village Victorian
See: Rhinebeck, NY

Irvington-on-Hudson

Shadowbrook B&B
821 N Broadway
Irvington-on-Hudson NY 10533
(914) 591-9291
  Circa 1850. This Sleepy Hollow Elizabethan estate was once owned by the Newberry five-and-dime store family and Irving Berlin composed "I'll Be Loving You Always" for the daughter of a previous owner. Its 10 acres include beech, cherry, and apple trees and the original carriage house, stables and gardener's cottage remain. A winding mahogany staircase, nine marble fireplaces, Tiffany windows, and carved mahogany paneling are features. There is a tennis court on the property and guests will enjoy countryside walks to historic sites such as the home of Washington Irving and Lyndhurst.
Location: Thirty minutes from New York City, walking distance to train.
Rates: $65-85.
Innkeeper(s): David & Lenore Person.
7 Rooms. 4 Private Baths. Guest phone available. TV available. Beds: KDT. Handicap access provided. Conference room.

"Fascinating! A wonderful place."

Ithaca

Benn Conger Inn
See: Groton, NY

Peregrine House
140 College Ave
Ithaca NY 14850
(607) 272-0919
  Circa 1874. This eight-bedroom brick Victorian was built by an Englishman who came to town to work on Ezra Cornell's house. It is three blocks from the edge of Cornell campus and a block away from several ethnic restaurants.
Location: Three blocks from Cornell Campus.
**Rates: $75-$89. All year.
Innkeeper(s): Nancy Falconer & Susan Vance.
8 Rooms. 5 Private Baths. Guest phone in room. TV in room. Beds: QTD. Meals: Full breakfast. Fireplaces. CCs: Visa, MC. Boating, swimming, ice skating, cross-country skiing.
Seen in: *Ithaca Daily Journal, Cornell Daily Sun.*
"Elegant, warm, first rate. One is made to feel comfortable and relaxed."

Rose Inn
813 Auburn Rd, Rt 34 N, Box 6576
Ithaca NY 14851-6576
(607) 533-7905
  Circa 1851. This classic Italianate mansion has long been famous for its circular staircase made of Hon-

duran mahogany by a mysterious craftsman. Charles Rosemann is a German hotelier with a degree from the Hotel School in Heidelberg. Sherry is a noted interior designer specializing in pre-Victorian architecture and furniture. The inn is on twenty landscaped acres fifteen minutes from Ithaca and Cornell University.
Rates: $95-$200. All year.

Innkeeper(s): Sherry & Charles Rosemann.
15 Rooms. 15 Private Baths. Guest phone available. TV available. Beds: KQT. Meals: Full breakfast. Handicap access provided. Conference room. CCs: CB. Downhill & cross-country skiing, sailing, windsurfing.
Seen in: *Ithaca Times, New Woman Magazine.*
  "The blending of two outstanding talents, which when combined with your warmth, produce the ultimate experience in being away from home. Like staying with friends in their beautiful home."

Sage Cottage
See: Trumansburg, NY

Keene

The Bark Eater
Alstead Mill Rd
Keene NY 12942
(518) 576-2221
  Circa 1830. Originally a stagecoach stop on the old road to Lake Placid, The Bark Eater (English for the In-

dian word Adirondacks) has been in almost continuous operation since the 1800s. Then it was a full day's journey over rugged, mountainous terrain with two teams of horses. The inn features wide-board floors, fireplaces and rooms filled with antiques.
Location: One mile from town.
**Rates: $75 to 90. All Year.
Innkeeper(s): Joe Pete Wilson and Arley McDevitt
12 Rooms. 4 Private Baths. Guest phone available. TV available. Beds: KQTC. Meals: MAP. Handicap access provided. Conference room. Fireplaces. CCs: AX. All summer & winter sports, horseback riding, cross country skiing. Adironacks high peaks climbing.
  "Staying at a country inn is an old tradition in Europe, and is rapidly catching on in the United States... A stay here is a pleasant surprise for anyone who travels." William Lederer, *Ugly American.*

Kingston

Village Victorian
See: Rhinebeck, NY

Lake George

Lamplight Inn
See: Lake Luzerne, NY

Lake Luzerne

Lamplight Inn
PO Box 70, 2129 Lake Ave (9n)
Lake Luzerne NY 12846
(518) 696-5294

Circa 1890. Howard Conkling, a wealthy lumberman, built this Victorian Gothic estate on land that had been the site of the Warren

County Fair. The home was designed for entertaining since Conkling was a very eligible bachelor. It has 12-foot beamed ceilings, chestnut wainscoting and moldings and a chestnut keyhole staircase all crafted in England.
Rates: $70-$85. May to Oct.
Innkeeper(s): Gene & Linda Merlino.
7 Rooms. 7 Private Baths. Guest phone available. TV available. Beds: QD. Meals: Full breakfast. Fireplaces. CCs: AE. Horseback riding, swimming, cross-country & downhill skiing.
Seen in: *Getaways for Gourmets.*

Lake Placid

Highland House Inn
3 Highland Place
Lake Placid NY 12946
(518) 523-2377

Circa 1910. This inn is situated on the hill in the village, a five-minute walk to Main Street and the Olympic Center. The rooms are decorated in a charming country style. A

separate cottage on the property accommodates groups of up to six people.
Location: Above Main Street in the Lake Placid Village.
**Rates: $37-$50. All year.
Innkeeper(s): Teddy & Cathy Blazer.
9 Rooms. 5 Private Baths. Guest phone available. TV available. Beds: DT. Meals: Full breakfast. Conference room. CCs: Visa, MC. Lakes, beaches, skiing.
Seen in: *Weekender.*

Livingston Manor

Lanza's Country Inn
RD 2 Box 446, Shandelee Rd
Livingston Manor NY 12758
(914) 439-5070

Circa 1901. Located on seven acres, the inn has a country taproom with a fireplace. It is furnished with antiques. There is a separate cottage on the property for groups of four.
Rates: $69-$79. All year.
Innkeeper(s): Dick, Pat & Mickey Lanza.
7 Rooms. 7 Private Baths. Guest phone available. TV available. Beds: QT. Meals: Full breakfast. Fireplaces. CCs: Visa, MC, AE.

Mayville

Plumbush B&B
at Chautauqua
Chautauqua — Stedman RD2
Mayville NY 14757
(716) 789-5309

Circa 1860. Situated on 125 acres of meadows and woodlands, Plumbush is a mauve and pale pink, Italianate Victorian shaded by

towering maples. Eleven foot ceilings accommodate the nine-foot tall arched windows. There is a music room and a staircase winds up to the three-story turret. Hiking and ski trails are currently under development.
**Rates: $55-$75.
Innkeeper(s): George & Sandy Green.
4 Rooms. 4 Private Baths. Beds: DT. One mile to Chautauqua Institute.
Seen in: *Buffalo News, Mayville Centenille.*

Mumford

Genesee Country Inn
948 George St, Box 340
Mumford NY 14511
(716) 538-2500

Circa 1833. This stone house with its two-and-a-half-foot thick limestone walls served as a plaster mill

and later as a hub and wheel factory. Now it is an inn set on six acres with views of streams, woodlands and ponds. There is a deck adjacent to a 16-foot waterfall. Ask for a garden room and enjoy a fireplace and your own balcony overlooking the mill ponds.
Location: Twenty minutes south of Rochester.
**Rates: $75-$115. April to Oct.
Innkeeper(s): Glenda & Gregory Barcklow
9 Rooms. 9 Private Baths. Guest phone in room. TV in room. Beds: QTD. Meals: Full breakfast. Conference room. Fireplaces. CCs: Visa, MC, AE, DC. Tennis, swimming, cross-country skiing, trout fishing.
"You may never want to leave...the stunningly beautiful stenciling (and the authentic 19th-century atmosphere) provide a lovely touch!" Craft & Home Magazine.

New York City

Homestead Inn
See: Greenwich, CT

Incentra Village House
32 8th Ave
New York City NY 10014
(212) 206-0007

Circa 1841. Located in the Greenwich Village area, this guest house is decorated in period furnishings. Most rooms have kitchens and some have fireplaces and air conditioning.
Location: Greenwich Village area.
Rates: $85.
Innkeeper(s): Thomas Brinker & Frank Desmerles.

11 Rooms. 11 Private Baths. Meals: EP. CCs: Visa, MC, AE.

Shadowbrook
See: Irvington-on-Hudson, NY

The Jeremiah J Yereance House
See: Lyndhurst, NJ

Niagara Falls

Rainbow Hospitality
9348 Hennepin Ave
Niagara Falls NY 10011
(716) 283-4794 (716) 874-8797

Circa 1839. This Victorian home is on a tree-lined street in the heart of town. The accommodation consists of a bedroom, bath and private parlor. Guests can walk to the bus and subway and the Convention Center is two miles away. Rainbow Hospitality is a reservation service coordinated by Georgia Brannan. Their listings in Buffalo include a historic home with whirlpool suite.
Location: Historic homes in Niagara Falls and Buffalo.
Rates: $50.
2 Rooms. 1 Private Baths. Meals: Full breakfast.

Oneida

The Pollyanna
302 Main St
Oneida NY 13421
(315) 363-0524

Circa 1860. Roses and iris grace the gardens of this Italian villa. Inside are special collections, antiques and

three Italian-marble fireplaces. Of the two crystal chandeliers, one is still piped for original gas. A hand-crafted white wool and mohair rug runs up the staircase to the rooms

where guests are pampered with bed warmers and down quilts. The innkeeper teaches spinning, felting, bobbin lace and other crafts.
Location: Route 46, 5 miles from Thruway 90, exit off route 5.
**Rates: $35-$65. All year.
Innkeeper(s): Doloria & Ken Chapin.
5 Rooms. Guest phone in room. TV available. Beds: QT. Meals: Full breakfast, gourmet. Conference room. CCs: Visa, MC. Skiing.

"Great hospitality and super breakfast. We really enjoyed all the interesting things."

Penfield

Strawberry Castle B&B
1883 Penfield Rd, Rt 441
Penfield NY 14526
(716) 385-3266

Circa 1875. A rosy brick Italianate villa, Strawberry Castle was once known for the grapes and strawber-

ries grown on the property. Ornate plaster ceilings and original inside shutters are special features. There are six roof levels, carved ornamental brackets, and columned porches topped by a white cupola.
Location: East of Rochester on Route 441.
Rates: $55-$65. All year.
Innkeeper(s): Charles & Cynthia Whited.
3 Rooms. 2 Private Baths. Guest phone available. TV available. Meals: Full breakfast. Conference room. Pool. CCs: Visa, MC, AE. Swimming.
Seen in: *Upstate Magazine.*

"You have a most unusual place. We applaud your restoration efforts and are thankful you've made it available to travelers."

Poughkeepsie

Village Victorian
See: Rhinebeck, NY

Rhinebeck

Beekman Arms
Rt 9
Rhinebeck NY 12572
(914) 876-7077

Circa 1766. Said to be the oldest landmark inn in America, some walls of the Beekman Arms are two and three feet thick. It has seen a variety of guests - among them pioneers, trappers, Indians and Dutch farmers. Among the famous were Aaron Burr, William Jennings Bryan, Horace Greeley and Franklin Roosevelt. Like most old taverns and inns it provided a meeting place for leaders of the day. Victorian furnishings are found throughout. Mr. LaForge is the 28th innkeeper at Beekman Arms.
Location: Center of Village of Rhinebeck.
**Rates: $60-$90. All year.
Innkeeper(s): Charles LaForge.
49 Rooms. 49 Private Baths. Guest phone in room. TV in room. Beds: QT. Meals: Continental, restaurant. Handicap access provided. Conference room. Fireplaces. CCs: Visa, MC, AE, DC. Cross-country skiing, golf, tennis.
Seen in: *New York Times.*

Village Victorian Inn
31 Center St
Rhinebeck NY 12572
(914) 876-8345

Circa 1860. A white picket fence surrounds this appealing yellow-and-white Victorian. It is furnished

in French Victorian fabrics, floral wallpapers, local antiques and canopy or brass beds. Cheese blintzes or eggs Benedict are often the choices for breakfast which is served in the dining room.
**Rates: $85-$120. All year.
Innkeeper(s): Judy & Rich Kohler.
5 Rooms. 5 Private Baths. Guest phone available. TV available. Beds: KQ. Meals: Full breakfast, gourmet. Conference room. Fireplaces. CCs: Visa, MC, AE.

Seen in: *Travel & Leisure Magazine, Weekend Trader.*

"*Thank you for all your hospitality and for making our stay so wonderful. Breakfast was delicious.*"

Rochester

Genesee Country Inn
See: Mumford, NY

Saranac Lake

The Point
Star Route
Saranac Lake NY 12983
(518) 891-5678

Circa 1930. Designed by renowned architect William Distin and built for William Rockefeller, this Adirondack Great Camp has hosted fashionable house parties for the

Vanderbilts, Whitneys and Morgans. No expense was spared to create the elegant, rustic lakefront estate with its walk-in-granite fireplaces, rare Adirondack antiques and massive hand-hewn beams. Each day a cord of wood is needed to fuel all the fireplaces. This lavish camp welcomes those who prefer to rough it with style.
**Rates: $425-$650.
Innkeeper(s): Bill & Claudia McNamee.
11 Rooms. 11 Private Baths. Guest phone available. TV available. Beds: KQT. Meals: All meals and liquor included. Jacuzzi. Conference room. Fireplaces. CCs: MC. Swimming, canoeing, water-skiing. Snow picnics, snow skiing. Old mahogany runabouts.

"*An incredibly beautiful setting. A very special place to return to again and again. Thanks especially to our gracious hosts for their humor and camaraderie.*"

Saratoga Springs

Lamplight Inn
See: Lake Luzerne

The Westchester House
102 Lincoln Ave, PO Box 944
Saratoga Springs NY 12866
(518) 587-7613

Circa 1880. This gracious Queen Anne Victorian has been welcoming

vacationers for more than 100 years. Antiques from four generations of the Melvin's family grace the rooms. Saratoga was a favorite Victorian resort for vacationers who packed their Saratoga trunks and headed off for summers in the Adirondacks. The tradition of high living, culture, romance and health ran strong. Strains of Victor Herbert's music filled the air and Mark Twain, Diamond Jim Brady, and Lil Langtree all participated in the Saratoga summer.
Location: Thirty miles north of Albany in the Adirondack foothills.
Rates: $50-$160. All year.
Innkeeper(s): Bob & Stephanie Melvin.
7 Rooms. 5 Private Baths. Guest phone available. Beds: KD. Meals: Continental plus. Fireplaces. CCs: Visa, MC, AE. Golf, tennis, swimming, cross-country skiing, ice skating. NYC Ballet & Opera at the Arts Center.

"*I adored your B&B and have raved about it to all...One of the most beautiful and welcoming places we've ever been to.*"

Skaneateles

Sherwood Inn
26 W Genesee St
Skaneateles NY 13152
(315) 685-3405

Circa 1807. During the Knickerbocker Tours of the 1820's stagecoaches making the rounds between New York and Niagara Falls chose Isaac Sherwood's tavern as their favorite stopping place. Many of the rooms face scenic Skaneateles Lake. The inn is noted for its continental and American menu.
**Rates: $55-$88. All year.
Innkeeper(s): Ellen Seymour.
16 Rooms. 16 Private Baths. Guest phone in room. TV available. Beds: TDC. Meals: Restaurant. Conference room. Fireplaces. CCs: Visa, MC, AE, DC. Boating, swimming, tennis, skiing, horseback riding.

Syracuse

Brae Loch Inn
See: Cazenovia, NY

The Pollyanna
See: Oneida, NY

Troy

The Gregory House
See: Averill Park, NY

Trumansburg

Sage Cottage
112 E Main St, Box 626
Trumansburg NY 14886
(607) 387-6449

Circa 1855. Andrew Jackson Downing, a prestigious American landscape designer, created this Gothic cottage. To quote Downing, "*Houses should wear an ever smiling expressing of kindly invitation and cordial welcome.*" Sage Cottage boasts a graceful circular staircase and rooms are decorated with antiques and collectibles.
Rates: $34-$40. All year.
Innkeeper(s): Dorry Norris.
4 Rooms. 2 Private Baths. Guest phone available. TV available. Beds: KQTD. Meals: Full breakfast. Handicap access provided. Fireplaces. Swimming, hiking, golf, croquet. Herb classes.
Seen in: *The Ithaca Journal.*

"*I've been singing the praises of the Sage Cottage all week. We loved our stay.*"

Utica

The Pollyanna
See: Oneida, NY

Waterloo

The Historic James R. Webster Mansion
115 E Main St - Rts 5 & 20
Waterloo NY 13165
(315) 539-3032
   Circa 1845. James Russell Webster, relative of Noah and Daniel Webster

and friend of Abraham Lincoln, built this Greek Revival mansion with a classical pillared Greek temple front. In addition to its fine furnishings, there are many collections including rare European clocks of the 17th and 18th centuries. Richly crafted woodwork is found throughout. The inn's fine cuisine was recently acknowledged by membership in the Master Chefs Institute of America.
Location: Routes 5 & 20 between Geneva and Seneca Falls, Exit 41 off I-90.
**Rates: $200. All year.
Innkeeper(s): Leonard & Barbara N. Cohen.
2 Rooms. 2 Private Baths. Guest phone available. Beds: D. Meals: Full breakfast, continental. Conference room. Fireplaces. CCs: Visa, MC. Horseback riding, skiing, fishing, water skiing.
   "Thank you for making our honeymoon a fabulous fairy tale. Wonderful antiques. Absolutely gourmet meals. We think you have reached perfection."

Watkins Glen

The Red House Country Inn
See: Burdett, NY

Westfield

The William Seward Inn
RD 2, S Portage Rd, Rt 394
Westfield NY 14787
(716) 326-4151
   Circa 1821. This two-story Greek Revival estate stands on a knoll overlooking the forest and Lake

Erie. Seward was a Holland Land Company agent before becoming governor of New York. He later served as Lincoln's Secretary of State and is known for the Alaska Purchase. George Patterson bought Seward's home and also became governor of New York. Most of the mansion's furnishings are dated 1790 to 1870 from the Sheraton-Victorian period.
Location: Three hours from Cleveland, Pittsburgh and Toronto.
Rates: $58-$79. All year.
Innkeeper(s): Peter & Joyce Wood.
10 Rooms. 10 Private Baths. Guest phone available. TV available. Beds: KQT. Meals: Full breakfast. Handicap access provided. Conference room. Fireplaces. CCs: Visa, MC. Downhill & cross-country skiing.
Seen in: *The Buffalo News, Pittsburgh Post-Gazette.*
   "The breakfasts are delicious. The solitude and your hospitality are what the doctor ordered."

Westfield House

E Main Rd, PO Box 505
Westfield NY 14787
(716) 326-6262
   Circa 1840. Westfield was part of the Granger Homestead. Benjamin Hopson, a local ice merchant, built a magnificent Gothic Revival addition in 1860. His daughter Lucy used the living room with its large crystal windows as a tea room. The Gothic detailed interiors include a winding

staircase to the six upstairs bed chambers.
Location: Southwestern New York state. Historic Chautauqua County.
Rates: $45 to $65. All year.
Innkeeper(s): Betty & Jud Wilson
6 Rooms. 6 Private Baths. Guest phone available. Beds: KQ. Meals: B&B. Handicap access provided. Conference room. Fireplaces. CCs: Visa, MC. Horseback riding, skiing, Lake Erie And Lake Chautauqua water sports. Complimentary boat rides on Chautauqua Lake.
   "Your accommodations and hospitality are wonderful! Simply outstanding. The living room changes its character by the hour."

Westhampton Beach

1880 Seafield House
2 Seafield Lane
Westhampton Beach NY 11978
(516) 288-1559 (800)346-3290
   Circa 1880. On Westhampton Beach's exclusive Seafield Lane, this country estate includes a pool and tennis court, and it is just a short walk to the ocean beach. The inn is decorated with Victorian antiques, Shaker benches, and Chinese porcelain creating a casual, country inn atmosphere.
Location: Ninety minutes from Manhattan.
**Rates: $75. May to October
Innkeeper(s): Elsie Collins.
2 Rooms. 2 Private Baths. Guest phone available. Beds: D. Meals: EP. Fireplaces. Pool. Tennis, swimming.
   "From the moment we stepped inside your charming home we felt all the warmth you sent our way which made our stay so comfortable and memorable."

North Carolina

Asheville

Cedar Crest Victorian Inn
674 Biltmore Ave
Asheville NC 28803
(704) 252-1389

Circa 1890. This Queen Anne mansion is one of the largest and most

opulent residences surviving Asheville's 1890's boom. A captain's walk, projecting turrets, and expansive verandas welcome guests to lavish interior woodwork and stained glass. All rooms are furnished in antiques with satin and lace trappings.
Rates: $60-$90. All year.
Innkeeper(s): Barbara & Jack McEwan.
13 Rooms. 11 Private Baths. Guest phone available. TV available. Beds: QT. Meals: B&B. Fireplaces. CCs: Visa, MC, DS. Afternoon beverage, evening hot chocolate & tea.
Seen in: *New Woman, Southern Living, Good Housekeeping, House Beautiful.*

Dry Ridge Inn
See: Weaverville, NC

Flint Street Inn
100 & 116 Flint St
Asheville NC 28801
(704) 253-6723

Circa 1915. Side by side, these two lovely old family homes are located in Asheville's oldest neighborhood

and are within comfortable walking distance of downtown. A lovely breakfast room invites guests to linger and 200-year-old oaks, old-fashioned gardens and a fish pond add to the atmosphere.
Location: Montford Historic District.
**Rates: $50-$60.
Innkeeper(s): Rick, Lynne & Marion Vogel.
8 Rooms. 8 Private Baths. Guest phone available. TV available. Beds: D. Meals: Hearty southern breakfast. CCs: Visa, MC, AE.
"Our home away from home."

Heritage Hill
64 Linden Ave
Asheville NC 28801
(704) 254-9336

Circa 1909. Twelve white pillars and a large veranda filled with rocking chairs greet visitors to this colonial house. There are three fireplaces and on cool evenings guests often enjoy wine in front of a cozy fire. The house sits on an acre of park-like grounds with giant maple, oak, pine and dogwood trees. It's a three-block walk to town.
Rates: $40-$60. All year.
Innkeeper(s): Linda & Ross Willard.
9 Rooms. 6 Private Baths. TV in room. Beds: KDT. Meals: Buffet restaurant. Fireplaces. CCs: Visa, MC. Swimming,

skiing, hiking, tennis. Champagne for honeymooners.
"It was the highlight of our trip! Thanks."

Reed House B&B
119 Dodge St
Asheville NC 28803
(704) 274-1604

Circa 1892. This yellow and white Queen Anne Victorian, in the National Register, sports a handsome, three-story tower. During renovation the owners discovered a secret passageway from the top of the tower down between the walls to an exit in the crawl space under the house. Inside the house, rose-colored cherubs decorate the fireplace tile, and there is a grand piano. Rockers and a porch swing occupy the veranda.
Location: South of Asheville.
Rates: $40-$50. May to Nov.
Innkeeper(s): Marge Turcot.
5 Rooms. 1 Private Baths. Guest phone available. TV available. Beds: DTC. Meals: Full breakfast. Fireplaces. CCs: Visa, MC. Golfing, fishing, hiking, rafting.
Seen in: *Old House Journal, CBS Morning Show.*

Richmond Hill Inn
87 Richmond Hill Dr
Asheville NC 28806
(919) 273-9409

Circa 1889. This newly renovated 30-room Victorian mansion was designed for the Pearson family by James Hill, architect of the U. S. Treasury Building. Richmond Pearson was a renowned statesman, Congressman, and friend of Theodore Roosevelt. This elegant estate featured innovations such as

running water, a communication system, and a pulley-operated elevator for moving furniture.
Rates: $80-$160. All year.
12 Rooms. 12 Private Baths. Guest phone in room. TV in room. Beds: KQTC. Meals: Full breakfast. Jacuzzi. Conference room. Fireplaces. CCs: Visa, MC, AE. Fishing, rafting, downhill skiing.

The Old Reynolds Mansion
100 Reynolds Hgts
Asheville NC 28804
(704) 254-0496
Circa 1855. A three-story brick, antebellum mansion listed in the National Register of Historic Places, this handsome inn is furnished with

antiques. There are mountain views from all rooms, wood-burning fireplaces, a two-story veranda, and a swimming pool. It is situated on a four-acre knoll of Reynolds Mountain.
Location: Ten minutes north of downtown Asheville.
Rates: $40-$65. Jan. to April.
Innkeeper(s): Fred & Helen Faber.
10 Rooms. 7 Private Baths. Guest phone available. Beds: QTC. Meals: Continental plus. Fireplaces. Pool. Swimming.
"This was one of the nicest places we have ever stayed, convenient to Asheville but secluded in the mountains. We spent every sundown on the porch waiting for the fox's daily visit."

Beaufort

Captains' Quarters,
Bed & Biscuit
315 Ann St
Beaufort NC 28516

(919) 728-7711
Circa 1902. This two-story, balloon-frame house has a wraparound front porch. Politician and railroad owner

W. S. Chadwick, built the heart-pine home for his daughter Corinne. It is furnished with Victorian antiques and family heirlooms that date to the American Revolution.
Location: Corner of Ann & Turner Streets in the heart of historical district.
**Rates: $50-$90. All year.
Innkeeper(s): Ruby & Captain Dick Collins.
3 Rooms. 3 Private Baths. Guest phone available. TV available. Beds: DT. Meals: Full breakfast, continental plus. Fireplaces. CCs: Visa, MC. Fishing, golf, tennis, beaches.
Seen in: *The News-Times.*
"Your family is simply delightful and your hospitality was more than a pleasure."

Langdon House
135 Craven St
Beaufort NC 28516
(919) 728-5499
Circa 1733. This three-story colonial house witnessed Beaufort pillaged by pirates in 1747, plundered by the British in 1782, occupied by the Union army in 1862, and pounded by the great hurricane of 1879. The atmosphere of the inn is enhanced by a 19th-century pump organ, an Empire secretary, and other antiques. A colonial garden features daisies, cabbage roses and a collection of herbs.
**Rates: $59-$89. All year.
Innkeeper(s): Jimm Prest.
4 Rooms. 4 Private Baths. Guest phone available. Beds: Q. Meals: Full breakfast. Handicap access provided. Conference room. Fireplaces. Sailing, fishing, swimming, boating, tennis, golf, water skiing. Gourmet Belgian waffles.
Seen in: *McCalls, Lookout Magazine.*
"Prest is a historian, a guide, a maitre'd', a confidant. He's your friend."

Brevard

Red House Inn
412 W Probart St
Brevard NC 28712
(704) 884-9349
Circa 1851. Originally built as a trading post, this inn was also the county's first post office and railroad station. It survived the Civil War and years of neglect. Recently renovated, it is furnished with Victorian antiques. The center of town is four blocks away.
**Rates: $32-$47. May to Dec.
Innkeeper(s): Lynne & Peter Ong.
6 Rooms. 1 Private Baths. TV available. Beds: D. Meals: Full breakfast. Handicap access provided. Fireplaces. Hiking.

Bryson City

Folkestone Inn
767 W Deep Creek Rd
Bryson City NC 28713
(704) 488-2730
Circa 1926. This farmhouse is constructed of local stone and rock. Pressed tin ceilings, stained-glass

windows and claw-foot tubs remain. The dining room where breakfast is served features floor-to-ceiling windows on all sides with views of the mountains. There is a stream with a rock bridge on the property, and the Deep Creek entrance to Smoky Mountain National Park with its waterfall views is a ten-minute walk.
Rates: $58. March to Dec.
Innkeeper(s): Norma & Peter Joyce.
6 Rooms. 6 Private Baths. Guest phone available. Beds: D. Meals: Full English breakfast. Fireplaces. Hiking, horseback riding, fishing, tubing, rafting.
"Thanks to you we were able to stop and smell the flowers last weekend! You have a lovely place."

Chapel Hill

Colonial Inn
See: Hillsborough, NC

Fearrington House
See: Pittsboro, NC

Charlotte

The Homeplace B&B
5901 Sardis Rd
Charlotte NC 28226
(704) 365-1936
Circa 1902. This country Victorian house sits on two-and-one-half wooded acres and has a wraparound porch with a gabled entrance. The foyer features a hand-crafted staircase, ten-foot beaded ceilings, and heart-of-pine floors. Guest rooms are decorated with antiques.
Rates: $50-$65. All year.
Innkeeper(s): Frank & Peggy Dearien.
4 Rooms. 2 Private Baths. Guest phone available. TV available. Beds: QT. Meals: Full breakfast. CCs: Visa, MC, AE.
"Everything was perfect. The room was superb, the food excellent!"

Durham

Arrowhead Inn
106 Mason Rd
Durham NC 27712
(919) 477-8430
Circa 1775. The Lipscombe family and later owners made additions to the original white colonial manor house, but none destroyed the handsome fanlight, moldings, wainscoting, mantelpieces, and heart-of-pine floors. Past its doors, Catawba and Waxhaw Indians traveled the Great Path to Virginia. A stone arrowhead and marker at the inn's front door designate the path. Current visitors enjoy a long tradition of hospitality. From time to time, the hosts conduct classes for prospective innkeepers.
**Rates: $50-$85. All year.
Innkeeper(s): Jerry & Barbara Ryan.
8 Rooms. 4 Private Baths. Guest phone available. TV available. Beds: QTDC. Meals: Full breakfast. Conference room. Fireplaces. CCs: Visa, MC, AE. Golf, tennis, fishing nearby.

Seen in: *The Daily Courier*.

Colonial Inn
See: Hillsborough, NC

The Waverly Inn
See: Hendersonville, NC

Edenton

The Lords Proprietors' Inn
300 N Broad St
Edenton NC 27932
(919) 482-3641
Circa 1787. On Albemarle Sound, Edenton was one of the colonial

capitals of North Carolina. The inn consists of three houses providing elegant accommodations within walking distance of town. A guided walking tour from the Visitor's Center provides an opportunity to see museum homes.
Location: Main street of town.
Rates: $45-$65. All year.
Innkeeper(s): Arch & Jane Edwards.
17 Rooms. 17 Private Baths. Guest phone in room. TV in room. Beds: KQTC. Meals: Full breakfast. Conference room. Pool.
"One of the happiest things in the whole wide world is to go visiting in a beautifully appointed home where you receive a gracious welcome, and everything possible is done for your comfort and ease."

Greensboro

College Hill B&B
922 Carr St
Greensboro NC 27403
(919) 274-6829
Circa 1901. Each guest room in this two-story frame house has a wood-burning fireplace, and a quilt pattern dictates the name of the room. White wicker furniture and collectibles decorate the sun room. Break-

fast is served from an English oak trolley and the beverage is poured from the silver service.
**Rates: $30-$55. June 15 - Sept.
Innkeeper(s): Tom & Ann Martin.
4 Rooms. 1 Private Baths. Guest phone available. TV available. Beds: QTD. Meals: Full breakfast. Fireplaces. CCs: Visa, MC. Tennis, golf, swimming, hiking.
Seen in: *Greensboro News & Record*.
"Like our favorite B&B in Scotland."

Colonial Inn
See: Hillsborough, NC

Greenwood B&B
205 N Park Dr
Greensboro NC 27401
(919) 274-6350
Circa 1905. Greenwood is a fully restored, stick-style chalet on the park in the historic district. Presi-

dent Hayes was once a guest here. The inn is decorated with wood carvings and art from around the world. The living room boasts two fireplaces. Air-conditioning and a swimming pool in the backyard are among the amenities.
Location: Central Greensboro in the historic district.
Rates: $30-$55. All year.
Innkeeper(s): JoAnne Green.
5 Rooms. 3 Private Baths. Guest phone in room. TV available. Beds: KQTD. Meals: Full breakfast, continental plus. Fireplaces. Pool. CCs: Visa, MC, AE. Swimming, tennis, hiking, golf, water park.
"Marvelous renovation. Courteous, helpful, knowledgeable hostess and per-

fectly appointed room and bath. Interesting fine art interior decorating."

Hendersonville

Claddagh Inn at Hendersonville
755 N Main St
Hendersonville NC 28739
(704) 697-7778 (800) 225-4700

Circa 1900. Claddagh has been host for 85 years to visitors staying in Hendersonville. The wide, wraparound porch is filled with inviting

rocking chairs. Many of North Carolina's finest craft and antique shops are just two blocks from the inn. Carl Sandburg's house and the Biltmore Estate are nearby, and within a short drive are spectacular sights in the Great Smoky Mountains and the Blue Ridge Parkway.
Location: One-half block north from 7th Avenue (US 64 W) & Main St.
**Rates: $35-$59. June to Oct.
Innkeeper(s): Marie & Fred Carberry.
18 Rooms. 14 Private Baths. Guest phone available. TV available. Beds: KQTC. Meals: MAP, full breakfast. Conference room. Fireplaces. CCs: Visa, MC, AE, DS. Tennis, golf all nearby.
Seen in: *New York Times.*
"Excellent food, clean, home atmosphere."

The Waverly Inn
783 N Main St
Hendersonville NC 28739
(704) 693-9193 (800)537-8195

Circa 1890. In the National Register, this three-story colonial Revival has welcomed travelers for more than 90 years. In all this time there have been only two cooks, and the current cook has been at the inn for 47 years. In the Thirties the Waverly Inn housed the area's schoolteachers, with men staying on the third floor, and women on the second. There are cozy, comfortable

rooms and many rockers line the long front veranda. The inn often hosts storytelling weekends.
Location: Corner of 8th Avenue & Main Street (Rt. 25 North)
**Rates: $45-$79. All year.
Innkeeper(s): John & Diane Sheiry.
20 Rooms. 20 Private Baths. Guest phone available. TV available. Beds: KQTDC. Meals: Full breakfast. Fireplaces. CCs: Visa, MC, AE, DS. Tennis, golf, murder mystery weekends. Biltmore Estates, Flatrock Playhouse.
Seen in: *The New York Times.*

Hertford

Gingerbread Inn
103 S Church St
Hertford NC 27944
(919) 426-5809

Circa 1904. In a colonial Revival style this yellow and white house has a wraparound porch with paired

columns and turned balusters. There are gables and leaded glass windows, and the spacious rooms are furnished comfortably. The hallmark of the inn is freshly baked gingerbread.
Rates: $35-$40.
Innkeeper(s): Jenny Harnisch
3 Rooms. 3 Private Baths. Guest phone available. TV in room. Beds: KQT. Meals: Full breakfast. CCs: Visa, MC. On the historical walking tour.

Hillsborough

Colonial Inn
153 W King St
Hillsborough NC 27278
(919) 732-2461

Circa 1759. This historic inn is said to be one of the oldest continuously operating inns in the United States. The original section was built on the site of a tavern constructed in 1752 but destroyed by fire in 1758. Cornwallis stayed at the inn and

used it as his headquarters. Aaron Burr, who fought a duel with Alexander Hamilton and was Vice President of the United States, was also a guest.
**Rates: $48-$65. All year.
Innkeeper(s): Carolyn B. Welsh & Evelyn B. Atkins.
10 Rooms. 6 Private Baths. Guest phone available. TV available. Beds: QTC. Meals: Full breakfast, restaurant. Conference room. CCs: Visa, MC, AE.

Kill Devil Hills

Ye Olde Cherokee Inn
500 N Virginia Dare Trail
Kill Devil Hills NC 27948
(919) 441-6127

Circa 1940. Originally a hunting and fishing lodge, this large pink beach house is just across the road from the ocean. Guest rooms are paneled in knotty cypress creating a rustic cabin atmosphere. Behind the inn is the Wright Brothers Memorial, and nearby, the spot where they made their first flight.
Location: Outer banks of North Carolina.
**Rates: $45-$65. April to Nov.
Innkeeper(s): Phyllis & Robert Combs.
6 Rooms. 6 Private Baths. Guest phone available. TV in room. Beds: D. Meals: Continental plus. CCs: Visa, MC, AE. Swimming, fishing, sailing, golf, tennis, hang gliding, hiking.
Seen in: *The North Carolina Independent.*
"Thanks for another wonderful visit! It gets harder to leave each time we come."

Lake Junaluska

Providence Lodge
1 Atkins Loop
Lake Junaluska NC 28745
(704) 456-6486

This is a simple and very rustic lodge in the Blue Ridge Mountains 26 miles from Asheville. Dinner is available and the inn is noted for its dining.

Rates: $60-$80.

16 Rooms. 8 Private Baths. Guest phone available. Meals: MAP. Handicap access provided. Fireplaces. Pool.

Sunset Inn
21 N Lakeshore Dr
Lake Junaluska NC 28745
(704) 456-6114

This rambling old mountain home overlooks the lake. Family-style meals are served in the dining room. Summer activities include concerts, tennis, canoeing, and religious services.

Location: Twenty-six miles west of Asheville.

Rates: $40 and up.

Innkeeper(s): Lillian Roberts.

Mt. Airy

Pine Ridge Inn
2893 W Pine St
Mt. Airy NC 27030
(919) 789-5034

Circa 1949. Pine Ridge is a grand English-style mansion set on eight acres at the foot of the Blue Ridge Mountains. This 10,000 square-foot country inn prides itself on providing many of the amenties found in large hotels such as its wood-paneled library, Nautilus-equipped exercise room and hot tub. An old barn remains on the property.

Rates: $50-$85.

Innkeeper(s): Ellen & Manford Haxton.

7 Rooms. 5 Private Baths. Guest phone in room. TV in room. Beds: QDT. Meals: Continental breakfast. Jacuzzi. Handicap access provided. Conference room. Pool. CCs: Visa, MC, AE.

"The Haxtons have updated all the facilities without destroying its grandeur. Their attitude is one of warmth and charm, openness and pleasantness."

New Bern

Harmony House Inn
215 Pollock St
New Bern NC 28560
(919) 636-3810

Circa 1850. This two-story Greek Revival was sawed in half and the west side moved nine feet to accom-

modate new hallways, additional rooms and a staircase. A wall was then built to divide the house into

two sections. The rooms are decorated with antiques, family heirlooms, and collectibles. Offshore breezes sway blossoms in the lush garden. Cross the street to an excellent restaurant or take a picnic to the water.

Location: Walk to Tryon Palace.

Innkeeper(s): Diane & A.E. Hansen.

9 Rooms. 9 Private Baths. Beds: KQD. Meals: Full breakfast. Conference room. CCs: Visa, MC, AE. Complimentary juices and sodas.

Seen in: *Americana*.

We feel nourished even now, six months after our visit to Harmony House."

New Berne House
709 Broad St
New Bern NC 28560
(919) 636-2250

Circa 1921. Using bricks salvaged from Tryon Palace, this stately red brick colonial Revival replica was

built by the Taylor family, known for their historic preservation work in North Carolina. Located in the historic district, it is one block to the governor's mansion, Tryon Palace, now a Williamsburg-style living museum. The splendidly refurbished formal parlor is the setting for afternoon tea, and a graceful sweeping staircase leads to guest rooms with canopy beds and antique furnishings.

**Rates: $50-$68. All year.

Innkeeper(s): Joel & Shan Wilkins.

6 Rooms. 6 Private Baths. Guest phone in room. TV in room. Beds: QTC. Meals: EP. Conference room. Fireplaces. CCs: Visa, MC, AE. Sailing, golf, swimming, tennis, boating.

"In six months of traveling around the country with the Roads to Liberty tour, New Berne House was our favorite stop!"

Pittsboro

Fearrington House
Fearrington Village Ctr
Pittsboro NC 27312
(919) 542-2121 (919) 967-7770

Circa 1927. The Fearrington is an old dairy farm. Several of the original outbuildings, including the silo and barn, have been converted

into a village with a potter's shop, needlepoint and jewelry shop, and a southern garden shop. The original homestead houses an award-winning restaurant, and an exact replica of the old farmhouse now contains the guest rooms.

Rates: $95-$175. All year.

Innkeeper(s): Richard & Debbie Delany.

14 Rooms. 14 Private Baths. Guest phone in room. TV available. Beds: Q. Meals: Continental. Handicap access provided. Conference room. Fireplaces. Pool. CCs: Visa, MC. Swimming, bicycling, golf and tennis nearby.

"There is an aura of warmth and caring that makes your guests feel like royalty in a regal setting!"

Raleigh

Colonial Inn
See: Hillsborough, NC

Fearrington House
See: Pittsboro, NC

The Oakwood Inn
411 N Bloodworth St
Raleigh NC 27604

(919) 832-9712

Circa 1871. Presiding over Raleigh's Oakwood Historic District, this lavender and gray Victorian beauty is in the National Register. A formal parlor is graced by rosewood and red velvet, while guest rooms exude an atmosphere of vintage Victoriana.

**Rates: $60-$80. All year.
Innkeeper(s): Diana Newton.
6 Rooms. 6 Private Baths. Guest phone available. TV available. Beds: KQD. Meals: Full breakfast. CCs: Visa, MC, AE.
Seen in: *Connoisseur*.

"Resplendent and filled with museum-quality antique furnishings." Kim Devins, Spectator.

Southport

Dosher Plantation House B&B

Rt 5 Box 100
Southport NC 28461
(917) 457-5554

Circa 1927. Dr. Dosher, founder of the local hospital, built this three-story plantation house with a two-story veranda and three dormer windows on the third floor. Most of the rooms have ceiling fans and a fireplace graces the parlor. Full home-style breakfasts are known to have inspired many a guest to skip lunch.
Location: On Highway 133.
Rates: $49-$54.
Innkeeper(s): George & Ola Inman.
5 Rooms. 5 Private Baths. Guest phone available. TV in room. Beds: QD. Meals: Full breakfast. Jacuzzi. Fireplaces. CCs: Visa, MC, AE.

Tarboro

Little Warren

304 E Park Ave
Tarboro NC 27886
(919) 823-1314

Circa 1913. The wide, wraparound front porch of this gracious family home overlooks the Town Common, said to be one of two originally chartered commons remaining in the United States. The house is in the historic district and is designated with a National Register plaque.
Location: Within city historic district.

Rates: $58-$65. All year.
Innkeeper(s): Patsy & Tom Miller.
3 Rooms. 3 Private Baths. Guest phone in room. TV available. Beds: DT. Meals: EP, full breakfast, continental. Fireplaces. CCs: Visa, MC, AE. Tennis. English & American Southern breakfast.

Washington

Pamlico House

400 E Main St
Washington NC 27889
(919) 946-7184

Circa 1906. This gracious Greek Revival home once served as the rectory for St. Peter's Episcopal

Church. A two-story veranda wraps around the house in a graceful curve. The parlor is furnished in Victorian antiques. Nearby is the city's quaint waterfront. Washington is on the Historic Albemarle Tour Route and within easy driving distance to the Outer Banks.
Location: Eastern North Carolina.
Rates: $45-$65. All year.
Innkeeper(s): Jeanne & Lawrence Hervey.
4 Rooms. 4 Private Baths. Guest phone available. TV available. Beds: KQT. Meals: Full breakfast. Fireplaces. CCs: Visa, MC. Tennis, fishing, sailing.

Waynesville

Hallcrest Inn

299 Halltop Rd
Waynesville NC 28786
(704) 456-6457

Circa 1880. This simple white frame farmhouse was the home of the owner of the first commercial apple orchard in western North Carolina. Atop Hall Mountain, it commands a breathtaking view of Waynesville and Balsam Mountain Range. A gathering room, a dining room, and eight guest rooms are fur-

nished with family antiques. The side porch features four rooms with balconies. Family-style dining is offered around lazy-susan tables.
Location: US 276N from Waynesville, left on Mauney Cove Road.
Rates: $40-$60. May to Oct.
Innkeeper(s): Russell & Margaret Burson.
12 Rooms. 12 Private Baths. Guest phone available. TV available. Beds: D. Meals: MAP. Golf, hiking, horseback riding, whitewater rafting.

"Country charm with a touch of class."

The Palmer House B&B

108 Pigeon St
Waynesville NC 28786
(704) 456-7521

Circa 1885. This rambling old inn reflects the small-town charm so often found in the mountains. A full breakfast is served and suppers are available. The hosts are booklovers as is evidenced by the stocked library and the bookstore at the rear of the inn. Nearby activities include hiking, golfing and skiing.
Rates: $41-$49. All year.
Innkeeper(s): Kris Gillet & Jeff Minick.
7 Rooms. 7 Private Baths. Guest phone available. Meals: Full breakfast, continental plus. Hiking, golfing, skiing all nearby.

Weaverville

Dry Ridge Inn

26 Brown St
Weaverville NC 28787
(704) 658-3899

Circa 1849. This three-story house was built as the parsonage for the Salem Campground, an old religious revival camping area. Because of the high altitude and pleasant weather, it was used as a camp hospital for Confederate soldiers suffering from pneumonia during the Civil War. The area was called Dry Ridge by

the Cherokee Indians before the campground was established.
Rates: $40-$45. All year.
Innkeeper(s): John & Karen Vander-Elzen.
5 Rooms. 5 Private Baths. Guest phone available. Beds: DC. Meals: Full breakfast. Dinner available. Fireplaces. CCs: Visa, MC. Bicycling, hiking.
"Best family vacation ever spent."

Wilmington

Anderson Guest House
520 Orange St
Wilmington NC 28401
(919) 343-8128
Circa 1851. The main house, a brick Italianate, features cherry woodwork, stained glass, and gas-electric lights. The gas lights still work. The guest house, built from the remnants of an old children's playhouse and shed, has its own fireplace and overlooks the lawn and garden. Breakfast is served in the main house.
Location: Wilmington's Historic District.
Rates: $60. All year.
Innkeeper(s): Landon & Connie Anderson.
2 Rooms. 2 Private Baths. Guest phone available. TV available. Beds: Q. Meals: EP, gourmet. Golfing, water skiing.
Seen in: *Star-News*.
"We agree with the gentleman who said you were the most gracious hostess in the state."

Dosher Plantation
See: Southport, NC

Wilson

Pilgrims Rest
600 W Nash St
Wilson NC 27893
(919) 243-4447
Circa 1858. This Italianate house is on Nash Street which was once described as one of the ten most beautiful streets in the world. It was

built by the grandson of the state's first printer. Twelve-foot ceilings in the parlor are accentuated with borders. Victorian wallpapers and antiques are featured in the guest rooms.
Location: Central North Carolina, near I-95 highway.
**Rates: $39-$59. All year.

Innkeeper(s): June & Doug Stewart.
4 Rooms. 2 Private Baths. Guest phone available. TV in room. Beds: DT. Meals: Full breakfast. Fireplaces. CCs: Visa, MC. Bicycling.

Winston-Salem

Colonel Ludlow Inn
Summit & W 5th
Winston-Salem NC 27101
(919) 777-1887
Circa 1887. This Queen Anne house features graceful porches and a hipped and gabled roof. In view of the ornate entrance are several stained-glass windows bordering the stairway window. The dining room has a gold-plated chandelier and reproduction wallpaper. The guest rooms feature antique beds and more stained glass windows, and some have whirlpool tubs.
Location: Off highway I-40.
**Rates: $45-$125. All year.
Innkeeper(s): Terri Jones, Manager.
12 Rooms. 12 Private Baths. Guest phone in room. TV in room. Beds: KQD. Meals: Continental plus. Jacuzzi. Fireplaces. CCs: Visa, MC, AE, DC.
Seen in: *The Charlotte Observer, Daily Record*.
"I have never seen anything like the meticulous and thorough attention to detail in Col. Ludlow's, a splendiferous Victorian spa." Dannye Romine, *The Charlotte Observer*.

North Dakota

Medora

The Rough Riders
Medora ND 58645
(701) 623-4444
Circa 1865. This old hotel has the branding marks of Teddy Roosevelt's cattle ranch as well as other brands stamped into the rough-board facade out front. A wooden sidewalk helps to maintain the turn-of-the-century cow town feeling. Guest rooms are above the restaurant and are furnished with antiques. In the summer an outdoor pageant is held complete with stagecoach and horses.
Rates: $45-$55. May to October.
9 Rooms. 9 Private Baths. Meals: Continental breakfast. CCs: Visa, MC, AE.

Ohio

Cincinnati

Amos Shinkle Townhouse
See: Covington, KY

Cleveland

Private Lodging
PO Box 18590
Cleveland OH 44118
(216) 321-3213
   Circa 1920. Private Lodgings is a reservation agency that has several historic homes in the Greater Cleveland area. Private apartments for short-term stays are also available. They list a historic Tudor home and several others near Case Western Reserve, John Carroll, and Cleveland State universities.
Rates: $30-$65.
Beds: QDT. Meals: Full breakfast.

Columbus

Slavka's Bed & Breakfast
180 Reinhard Ave
Columbus OH 43206
(614) 443-6076
   Circa 1888. This house is in German Village, a restored historic community. A patio looks out over the garden. Yugoslavian recipes are featured and the hostess speaks Serbo-Croatian in addition to English.
Location: One-half mile from I-70.
Rates: $45.
Innkeeper(s): Gloria Slavka.
3 Rooms. Meals: Full breakfast.

The Russell-Cooper House
See: Mount Vernon, OH

Danville

The White Oak Inn
29683 Walhonding Rd
Danville OH 43014
(614) 599-6107
   Circa 1915. Begonias hang from the wide front porch of this three-story farmhouse situated on 13 green

acres. It is adjacent to the Indian trail and pioneer road that runs along the Kokosing River, and was constructed from timber cut and milled on the property. The inn's woodwork is all original white oak and guest rooms are furnished in antiques. Visitors often shop for maple syrup, cheese and handicrafts at nearby Amish farms.
Location: North central Ohio.
Rates: $50-$90. All year.
Innkeeper(s): Joyce & Jim Acton.
7 Rooms. 7 Private Baths. Guest phone available. TV available. Beds: QDC. Meals: Full breakfast. Conference room. Fireplaces. CCs: Visa, MC. Fishing, hunting, hiking, canoeing, cross-country skiing, bicycles
Seen in: *Ladies Home Journal.*
   "We are moving, but we would go well out of our way to stay with the Acton's. It was lovely."

Granville

Buxton Inn
313 E Broadway
Granville OH 43023
(614) 587-0001
   Circa 1812. The Buxton Inn claims to be Ohio's oldest continuously operating inn. In the cellar is a popular tavern where stagecoach drivers once stabled their horses and meats were hung to smoke. The inn is noted for its fine dining and 18th-century furnishings.
Rates: $60.
15 Rooms. 15 Private Baths. Guest phone available. TV available. CCs: Visa,, MC, AE.
Seen in: *A "Top Ten" country inn chosen by Uncle Ben's Country Rice.*

Granville Inn
314 E Broadway
Granville OH 43023
(614) 587-3333
   Circa 1924. The Granville Inn is an English Tudor style inn that was constructed of sandstone quarried nearby. It features a fireplace in the common room and a coal flagstone patio for summer relaxing.
Rates: $55.
31 Rooms. 31 Private Baths. TV available.

Kelleys Island

The Beatty House
South Shore Dr, PO Box 402
Kelleys Island OH 43438
(419) 746-2379
   Circa 1861. In the National Register, this 14-room limestone house was built by Ludwig Bette, a

Russian immigrant who became a grape-grower and winemaker.

Large, cave-like wine cellars beneath the house stored more than 75,000 gallons of wine. Antiques include those of the original owner and the innkeepers. Guest rooms and parlors have both the views and breezes of Lake Erie. Vineyards, a winery, and a state park are also on this three-by-five-mile island.
Location: Twenty-minute ferry ride from Marblehead.
Rates: $50-$55. April to Nov.
Innkeeper(s): Martha & Jim Seaman.
3 Rooms. Beds: DC. Meals: Full breakfast.
"Wonderful stay, warm friendly hosts."

Lebanon

Golden Lamb
27 South Broadway
Lebanon OH 45036
(513) 932-5065
Circa 1803. Jonas Seaman obtained a license to operate a house of public entertainment and created the Golden Lamb. Most of the furnishings are Shaker, and the collection is so large that two museum-style rooms are set aside to house it. Eleven presidents and Charles Dickens stayed at the Golden Lamb.
Rates: $60.
Innkeeper(s): Jackson Reynolds
19 Rooms. 19 Private Baths. Guest phone available. Meals: EP. CCs: All.

Loudonville

Blackfork Inn
303 North Water St, PO Box 149
Loudonville OH 44842
(419) 994-3252
Circa 1865. A Civil War businessman, Philip Black brought the railroad to town and built the

Blackfork. Its well-preserved Second Empire style has earned it a place in the National Register. Noted preservationists have restored the inn with care and it is filled with a collection of Ohio antiques. Located in a scenic Amish area, the three-course breakfasts feature local produce.
Rates: $72.
Innkeeper(s): Sue & Al Gorisek.
6 Rooms. 6 Private Baths. Guest phone available. Meals: Continental-plus breakfast. CCs: Visa, MC.

Marblehead

Old Stone House Inn
133 Clemons St
Marblehead OH 43440
(419) 798-5922
Circa 1861. Built by Alexander Clemons, owner of the first stone quarry in the area, the Stone House

overlooks Lake Erie. Now a guest room, the enclosed Captain's Tower features a 15-foot ceiling, spindled railings around the staircase, and the best view of the lake and shoreline. The inn's green lawns and gardens slope to the shore where guests may fish from the rocks or swim.
Location: Marblehead Peninsula.
Rates: $55-$85.
Innkeeper(s): Dorothy Bright and Pat Whiteford Parks.
14 Rooms. 1 Private Baths. Guest phone available. TV available. Beds: DT. Meals: Continental-plus breakfast. Conference room. CCs: Visa, MC. Winter ice fishing, cross-country skiing, lake swimming.

Mount Vernon

The Russell-Cooper House
115 E Gambier St
Mount Vernon OH 43050
(614) 397-8638

Circa 1829. Dr. John Russell and his son-in-law Colonel Cooper modeled a simple brick Federal

house into a unique Victorian. Its sister structure is the Wedding Cake House of Kennebunk, Maine. There is a hand-painted plaster ceiling in the ballroom, and a collection of Civil War items and antique medical devices. Woodwork is of cherry, maple and walnut, and there are etched and stained-glass windows. Hal Holbrook called the town America's Hometown.
Rates: $60. All year.
Innkeeper(s): Tim & Maureen Tyler.
6 Rooms. 6 Private Baths. Guest phone available. Beds: QT. Meals: Full breakfast. Gourmet. Conference room. Fireplaces. CCs: Visa, MC. Downhill & cross-country skiing, fishing, canoeing, golf. Mystery weekends.
"A salute to the preservation of American history and culture. Most hospitable owners!"

Old Washington

Zane Trace Bed & Breakfast
Main St, PO Box 115
Old Washington OH 43768
(614) 489-5970
Circa 1859. An Italianate Victorian, Zane Trace Inn is on the Old National Trail in Zane Grey country. It is a two-story brick building with tall, many-paned windows and louvered shutters. Inside are 14-foot ceilings, a wide sweeping staircase, several fireplaces, an elegant parlor, and crystal chandeliers.
Rates: $35-$60. May to mid-Nov.
Innkeeper(s): Ruth Wade.
4 Rooms. 2 Private Baths. Meals: Continental-plus breakfast. Pool.

Poland

Inn at the Green
500 S Main St
Poland OH 44514
(216) 757-4688

Circa 1876. Main Street in Poland has a parade of historic houses including Connecticut Western Reserve Colonials, Federal and Greek Revival houses. The Inn at the Green is a Victorian Baltimore townhouse. All the common rooms including a greeting room, parlor, sitting room and library have working marble fireplaces. Interiors evoke an authentic turn-of-the-century atmosphere with antiques that enhance the moldings, twelve-foot ceilings and poplar floors.
Location: Seven miles southeast of Youngstown, Ohio.
Rates: $30-$45. All year.
Innkeeper(s): Ginny & Steve Meloy.
4 Rooms. 2 Private Baths. TV available. Beds: DT. Meals: Continental. CCs: Visa, MC. Cross-country skiing, golf, tennis, fly fishing, canoeing, sailing

Powell

Buckeye B&B
PO 130
Powell OH 43065
(614) 548-4555

Circa 1880. This reservation service lists 52 homes throughout Ohio, many of them historic. One home on the outskirts of Columbus is a restored 1847 Federal house while other homes near the city center are in German Village and include a studio apartment.
Rates: $45-$60.
52 Rooms. Beds: QDT. Meals: Full breakfast.

Sandusky

Old Stone House Inn
See: Marblehead, OH

Tipp City

Willowtree Inn
1900 W State, Rt 571
Tipp City OH 45371

(513) 667-2957

Circa 1827. This Federal-style mansion is a copy of a similar house in North Carolina, former home of the builders. Antique period furnishings and polished wood floors add to the atmosphere of this rambling homestead.
Rates: $55-$65.
Innkeeper(s): Mrs. John DeBold.
6 Rooms. 1 Private Baths. TV available. Beds: DT. Meals: Full breakfast. CCs: Visa, MC, AE.

Toledo

Mansion View
2035 Collingwood Blvd
Toledo OH 43620
(419) 244-5676

Circa 1887. This corbeled brick Queen Anne house, in the National Register, was built for Fred Reynolds, a wealthy grain merchant. The Secor family later spent many years here. There is a gargoyle at the top of the house and an unusual gabled roof. Stained and beveled glass, a massive oak entryway, and a carved mahogany ceiling are special features.
Rates: $35-$55.
Meals: Continental breakfast. CCs: Visa, MC.

Worthington

Worthington Inn
649 High St
Worthington OH 43085
(614) 885-2600

Circa 1831. The Worthington Inn was originally built as a stagecoach stop by R. D. Coles, a local entrepreneur. It was restored as a Victorian in 1983, but the original ballroom, main entry, dining and upper sitting rooms remain. The door from an old courthouse and ceiling rosettes from a local train station were added during reconstruction. Period wallpapers, stenciling, and Victorian furnishings are used throughout.
Rates: $69-$125.
26 Rooms. 26 Private Baths. Meals: B&B. CCs: All.

Youngstown

Inn at the Green
See: Poland, OH

Zoar

Cider Mill
PO Box 441
Zoar OH 44697
(216) 874-3133

Circa 1863. Originally built as a steam-operated mill, the citizens of Zoar, a religious commune, maintained a cabinet shop in the mill during the winter. Exposed ceiling beams highlight the guest rooms and a massive brick wall dominates the living room. Zoar has a museum complex with seven buildings and nearby are bicycle paths along the Erie Canal. River trips can be arranged at the canoe livery.
Rates: $45.
Innkeeper(s): Ralph & Judy Kraus.
2 Rooms. Guest phone available. Beds: D. Meals: Full breakfast. Fireplaces. CCs: Visa, MC, AE.

Zoar Village

Cobbler Shop Inn
Corner of 2nd and Main St
Zoar Village OH 44697
(216) 874-2600

Circa 1828. The original structure, a cobbler shop, was enlarged to twice its size in 1860. It is in the center of the historic district, where a

Christian communal society had been established in 1817. A favorite at the inn is the waist-high rope bed, spread with an 1835 coverlet.
Rates: $40-$50.
4 Rooms. 2 Private Baths. Guest phone available. TV available. Meals: B&B. CCs: Visa, MC, AE.

Your kindness and generosity was outstanding. I gained ten pounds, but what the heck!

Oklahoma

Guthrie

Harrison House
124 W Harrison
Guthrie OK 73044
(405) 282-1000

Circa 1890. This is the old Guthrie Savings Bank building. Totally res-

tored, Harrison House is Oklahoma's first bed and breakfast inn. The rooms are named after famous citizens such as Tom Mix, a Guthrie bartender who became a Hollywood cowboy star. The original vault is still in the inn, now completely furnished with Victorian antiques. Patchwork quilts, lace curtains and antique washstands are featured in each room. Guthrie, the original capital of Oklahoma, has a turn-of-the-century downtown.
Location: Thirty minutes north of Oklahoma.
**Rates: $50-$100.
Innkeeper(s): Phyllis Murray.
23 Rooms. 23 Private Baths. Guest phone in room. TV available. Beds: KT. Meals: B&B. CCs: Visa, MC, AE. Pollar Theater, Lazy E Ranch nearby.
Seen in: *Country Inns, The Tulsa Tribune.*

"I'd been in 10 different hotels in 10 days and couldn't remember a thing about the other nine or where they were. Harrison House, I'll remember forever."

Oklahoma City

The Grandison
1841 NW 15th
Oklahoma City OK 73507
(405) 521-0011

Circa 1896. This brick and shingled three-story house is situated on lawns and gardens shaded by pecan, apple and fig trees, and there is a pond and gazebo. Original Belgian stained glass remains and the decor is an airy country Victorian. The bridal suite includes a working fireplace, white lace curtains and a claw-foot tub.
Rates: $40-$90.
Innkeeper(s): Bob & Claudia Wright.
5 Rooms. 5 Private Baths. Guest phone available. Beds: QDT. Meals: Continental. Fireplaces.
Seen in: *The Daily Oklahoman, Oklahoma Pride.*

"Like going home to Grandma's!"

Oregon

Ashland

Chanticleer B&B Inn
120 Gresham St
Ashland OR 97520
(503) 482-1919

Circa 1920. This gray clapboard, Craftsman-style house has been totally renovated and several rooms added. The inn is light and airy and decorated with antiques. Special features include the open hearth fireplace and bricked patio garden.
Rates: $79 & up.
Innkeeper(s): Jim & Nancy Beaver
7 Rooms. 7 Private Baths. Guest phone available. Beds: Q. Meals: Full breakfast.

Cowslip's Belle
159 N Main St
Ashland OR 97520
(503) 488-2901

Circa 1913. Cowslip's Belle is a Craftsman bungalow, the simple

design a rebellion against the ornate and often over-decorated Victorian. The inn is named for a flower mentioned in *A Midsummer Night's Dream*, and each of the guest rooms is named for one of Shakespeare's favorite flowers.
Rates: $58-$68. All year.
Innkeeper(s): Jon & Carmen Reinhardt.
4 Rooms. 4 Private Baths. Guest phone available. Beds: QT. Meals: Full breakfast. CCs: Visa, MC.

"The atmosphere was delightful, the decor charming, the food delicious and

the company grand. Tony says he's spoiled forever."

Edinburgh Lodge B&B
586 E Main St
Ashland OR 97520
(503) 488-1050

Circa 1908. The Edinburgh, built by a miner, became the J. T. Currie Boarding House for teachers and

railroad workers. Handmade quilts and period furnishings adorn each guest room and afternoon tea is served at 5:00 p.m. The country garden features hollyhocks and delphiniums.
Rates: $49-$65. All year.
Innkeeper(s): Ann Rivera.
6 Rooms. 6 Private Baths. Guest phone available. Beds: QT. Meals: Full breakfast. CCs: Visa, MC.

"The rooms are so warm and quaint... like visiting family. Breakfast was delicious. I'm sure there's an Edinburgh Cookbook on its way. I want a copy!"

Hersey House
451 N Main St
Ashland OR 97520
(503) 482-4563

Circa 1904. A saltbox Victorian built with leaded-glass windows, the inn also features an L-shaped

staircase. James Hersey, Ashland city councilman, was the first of five generations of Herseys to occupy the house.
Rates: $65. May to Nov.
Innkeeper(s): Gail E. Orell & K. Lynn Savage.
4 Rooms. 4 Private Baths. Guest phone available. Beds: Q. Meals: Full breakfast. Bicycling, tennis, horseback riding, fishing, swimming.
Seen in: *The World*.

"Delicious breakfasts and thoughtful social hour. We couldn't have asked for anything more. Your house and gardens are beautiful."

Lawnridge House
See: Grants Pass, OR

Royal Carter House
514 Siskiyou Blvd
Ashland OR 97520
(503) 482-5623

Circa 1909. Listed in the National Register, the Royal Carter House is surrounded by tall trees and lovely gardens. The inn has a secluded deck and two guest rooms.
Location: Four blocks from the Shakespeare theater.
Rates: $45-$65.
Innkeeper(s): Roy & Alyce Levy.

"Thank you! I really feel special here!"

Astoria

Rosebriar Inn
636 14th St
Astoria OR 97103
(503) 325-7427

Circa 1902. Commanding a spectacular view of the harbor, the Rosebriar is a neoclassical clapboard

house on a hill overlooking the village. Built by banker Frank Patton, it grew to 7,000 square feet when it housed the Holy Name Convent. The house features hand stenciling, carved ceilings, leaded glass and polished woodwork. Astoria is the oldest American settlement west of the Rockies, dating from a fur trading post established in 1811.
Location: Near the mouth of the Columbia River, 100 miles from Portland.
Rates: $40-$76. All year.
Innkeeper(s): Ann Leenstra & Judith Papendick.
9 Rooms. 3 Private Baths. Guest phone available. Beds: QT. Meals: Full breakfast. Conference room. CCs: Visa, MC. Fishing, parks, beaches.

Cloverdale

Sandlake Country Inn
8505 Galloway Rd
Cloverdale OR 97112
(503) 965-6745

Circa 1894. This two-story farmhouse was built of 3 x 12 bridge timbers from a Norwegian sailing vessel that was shipwrecked on the beach south of Cape Lookout on Christmas Day 1890. On two acres adjacent to the Suislaw National Forest, the inn's garden is occasionally host to deer and other wildlife. Both the guest rooms fea-

ture canopied beds, down comforters and fresh flowers.
Location: On the Oregon Coast.
Rates: $35-$50.
Innkeeper(s): Margo Underwood.
2 Rooms. Guest phone available. Beds: Q. Meals: Full breakfast. Creekside hammock, croquet.

Eugene

House in the Woods
814 Lorane Hwy
Eugene OR 97405
(503) 343-3234

Circa 1910. This handsome Craftsman house on two landscaped acres was built by a Minnesota

lawyer. It was originally accessible by streetcar. Antiques include a rosewood, square grand piano with a collection of antique wedding photos. This house is attractively furnished and surrounded by a flower gardens.
**Rates: $38-$55. All year.
Innkeeper(s): Eunice & George Kjaer.
2 Rooms. 1 Private Baths. Guest phone available. TV available. Beds: QTDC. Meals: Full breakfast. Conference room. Fireplaces. Golf, tennis, hiking, bicycling, swimming, fishing.
Seen in: *The Register-Guard.*
"In our 50 plus years of marriage and travels all over the world we have never stayed at a more charming spot with more hospitable folks."

Grants Pass

Lawnridge House
1304 NW Lawnridge
Grants Pass OR 97526
(503) 479-5186

Circa 1909. This graceful gabled clapboard house is shaded by a tall old oak tree. There is a bridal suite and the house features air conditioning. Breakfast often includes quiche

or baked salmon and croissants. Nearby, the Rogue River provides

kayaking, river rafting and salmon and steelhead fishing.
**Rates: $40-$65. All year.
Innkeeper(s): Barbara Head.
2 Rooms. 2 Private Baths. Guest phone in room. TV in room. Beds: KQ. Meals: Full breakfast. Fireplaces. Tennis, golf, horseback riding, hiking, skiing.
"Thank you for your incredible friendliness, warmth, and energy expended on our behalf! I've never felt so nestled in the lap of luxury - what a pleasure!"

Jacksonville

Livingston Mansion Inn
4132 Livingston Rd, PO Box 1476
Jacksonville OR 97530
(503) 899-7107

Circa 1915. This stately shingled manor was built for Charles Connor, orchardist. The inn features spacious

rooms including a suite with a fireplace, two sofas and a sleeping area for children. The town of Jacksonville was founded in 1851 following the discovery of gold in Rich Gulch, and is now a National Historic Landmark.
Rates: $70 & up.
Innkeeper(s): Sherry Lossing.
3 Rooms. 3 Private Baths. Guest phone available. Beds: KQT. Meals: B&B. Fireplaces. Pool. CCs: Visa, MC.

Joseph

Wallowa Lake Lodge

Rt 1 Box 320
Joseph OR 97846
(503) 432-4082

Circa 1923. Originally called the Wallowa Lake Wonderland Lodge,

this inn was built in the National Park Service architectural style with unique patterns of wood siding. The furniture is original with antiques added. The lodge was restored in 1988.
Location: Wallowa Lake.
**Rates: $37-$85. May to Nov.
Innkeeper(s): Joanne M. Harrison.
32 Rooms. 16 Private Baths. Guest phone available. Beds: QT. Meals: Restaurant. Fireplaces. Horseback riding, boating, fishing, hiking. Gondola to 8,200 ft. 1920's menu.

La Grande

Wallowa Lake Lodge

See: Joseph, OR

Medford

Lawnridge House

See: Grants Pass, OR

Under the Greenwood Tree

3045 Bellinger Lane
Medford OR 97501
(503) 776-0000

Circa 1861. Orchards, acres of pasture and lawn, rose gardens and huge old oaks provide a lush green setting for the inn. The name Under the Greenwood Tree is a line taken from Shakespeare's *As You Like It* referring to a country farm setting. Hand-hewn buildings on the property include an old barn, grainery and Bedford weigh station. Elegantly appointed guest rooms, classical music, leatherbound volumes and afternoon tea are among the amenities.
Rates: $65-$85.
4 Rooms. 4 Private Baths. Meals: Three-course gourmet breakfast. CCs: Visa, MC.

Portland

General Hooker's House

125 SW Hooker
Portland OR 97201
(503) 222-4435

Circa 1900. This turn-of-the-century, Queen Anne townhouse has been exquisitely restored by a

fourth-generation Portlander. From the roof garden guests enjoy a view of the city below, the river, bridges and Mount Hood. Convenient to everything, the inn includes a business suite with private entrance and sitting room. The host's cat General Hooker sleeps here.
**Rates: $50-$70. All year.
Innkeeper(s): Lori Hall.
4 Rooms. 1 Private Baths. Guest phone in room. TV in room. Beds: KQ. Meals: Continental plus.
Seen in: *Yellow Brick Road*
"What a pleasure to walk into your bright and airy house with its engaging mix of the best of two centuries. Your welcoming home is Portland at its best!"

House in the Woods

See: Eugene, OR

John Palmer House

4314 N Mississippi Ave
Portland OR 97217
(503) 284-5893

Circa 1890. In a redevelopment area, this Queen Anne house features five gables, elaborate spool

and spindle work, and roof cresting. It was once the Multnomah Conservatory of Music and the owners, Oskar and Lotta Hoch, were founders of the Portland Symphony. Inside, a total of 37 splendid silk-screened and gold-leafed Victorian wallpapers adorn the walls and ceilings, often with five papers to a room. Polished woodwork and lavish antiques add to an opulence not easily forgotten.
Location: City Center.
Rates: $30-$95. All year.
Innkeeper(s): Mary & Richard Sauter.
7 Rooms. 2 Private Baths. Guest phone in room. TV available. Beds: Q. Meals: Continental. Jacuzzi. Handicap access provided. Conference room. CCs: Visa, MC. Horse drawn carriage tours.
Seen in: *The Oregonian.*
"We stayed a whole week, a wonderful week! Can't believe breakfast could be so fantastic each day."

Salem

State House B&B

2146 State St
Salem OR 97301
(503) 588-1340

Circa 1920. This three-story house sits on the banks of Mill Creek where ducks and geese meander past a huge old oak down to the water. (A baby was abandoned here because the house looked "just right" and "surely had nice people there." The baby grew up to become a circuit judge and legal counsel to Governor Mark Hatfield.) The inn is close to everything in Salem.
Location: One mile from the I-5 Santiam turn-off.
Rates: $40-$60. All year.
Innkeeper(s): Mike Winsett & Judy Uselman.
4 Rooms. 2 Private Baths. Beds: Q. Meals: Full breakfast. CCs: MC, Visa.

The Dalles

Williams House Inn
608 W 6th St
The Dalles OR 97058
(503) 296-2889

Circa 1899. This handsome, green-and-white gingerbread Victorian possesses a veranda, gazebo and belvedere. Lush green lawns, trees and shrubs slope down to Mill Creek. The popular Harriet's Room overlooks Klickitat Hills and the Columbia River, and has a canopied four-poster bed, chaise lounge and period writing desk. Each spring the hosts harvest their 25-acre cherry orchard. They are active in the historic preservation of the area.
**Rates: $45-$65. All year.

Innkeeper(s): Don & Barbara Williams.
3 Rooms. 1 Private Baths. Guest phone available. TV in room. Beds: QC. Meals: Full breakfast. CCs: Visa, MC, AE. Hiking, surfing, skiing, rafting.
Seen in: *Country Inns.*

"*A fantasy come true, including the most gracious, delightful company in conversation, Barb and Don Williams!*"

Pennsylvania

Airville

Spring House
Muddy Creek Forks
Airville PA 17302
(717) 927-6906

Circa 1798. Spring House, always the prominent house in this pre-

Revolutionary War village, was built by state legislator Robert Tuner. It was constructed of massive stones over a spring that supplies water to most of the village. The walls are either whitewashed or retain their original stenciling. The house is filled with memories of a simpler rural life.
**Rates: $60-$95. All year.
Innkeeper(s): Ray Constance Hearne.
5 Rooms. 2 Private Baths. Guest phone available. Beds: Q. Meals: Full breakfast. Fireplaces. Fishing, hiking, bicycling, horseback riding.
Seen in: *Woman's Day, Country Decorating.*
"What a slice of history! Thank you for your hospitality. We couldn't have imagined a more picturesque setting."

Allentown

Salisbury House
910 East Emmaus Ave
Allentown PA 18103

(215) 791-4225
Circa 1810. Built in the plantation style, this enchanting stone house was operated as an inn for more

than a century and then became a private home. A formal boxwood garden and lotus pond are framed by pleasant woodlands. Spacious rooms include an elegant dining room and a well-stocked, paneled library warmed with a fireplace. Family heirlooms, plank floors, wallpapers and more fireplaces fill the guest rooms.
Location: Three miles from Route 309.
Rates: $85-$95. All year.
Innkeeper(s): Judith & Ollie Orth.
5 Rooms. 1 Private Baths. Guest phone available. TV available. Beds: T. Meals: Full breakfast. Conference room. CCs: Visa, MC, AE.
Seen in: *The Morning Call.*

Bedford

Newry Manor
See: Everett, PA

Bethlehem

Salisbury House
See: Allentown, PA

Bloomsburg

The Inn at Turkey Hill
991 Central Rd
Bloomsburg PA 17815
(717) 387-1500

Circa 1839. Turkey Hill is an elegant, white brick farmhouse. All the guest rooms are furnished with handcrafted reproductions from Habersham Plantation in Georgia, and all have views of the duck pond and the gazebo. In the dining room are hand-painted scenes of the rolling Pennsylvania countryside.
Location: Two miles north of Bloomsburg at Exit 35 on Interstate 80.
**Rates: $50-$130. All year.
Innkeeper(s): Elizabeth E. & Andrew B. Pruden.
18 Rooms. 18 Private Baths. Guest phone in room. TV in room. Beds: KQC. Meals: EP, continental plus, restaurant. Jacuzzi. Handicap access provided. Conference room. Fireplaces. CCs: All. Golf, tennis, fishing, hunting.
Seen in: *The Baltimore Sun, Tempo Magazine.*
"How nice to find an enclave of good taste and class, a special place that seems to care about such old-fashioned virtues as quality and the little details that mean so much." Art Carey, *Philadelphia Inquirer.*

Canadensis

Brookview Manor B&B Inn
Rt 1 Box 365
Canadensis PA 18325
(717) 595-2541

Circa 1911. By the side of the road, hanging from a tall evergreen is the welcoming sign to this forest retreat. There are brightly decorated com-

mon rooms, and four fireplaces. The carriage house has three bedrooms and is suitable for small groups. The innkeepers like to share a "secret waterfall" that is a 20-minute walk from the inn.
Location: On scenic route 447, Pocono Mountains.
Rates: $50-$85. All year.
Innkeeper(s): Jane & Jim McKeon.
8 Rooms. 7 Private Baths. Guest phone available. TV available. Beds: QTD. Meals: Full breakfast. Fireplaces. CCs: Visa, MC, AE. Cross-country skiing, fishing, hiking.
Seen in: *Mid-Atlantic Country.*
   "Thanks for a great wedding weekend. Everything was perfect."

Carlisle

Field & Pine B&B
See: Shippensburg, PA

Churchtown

Churchtown Inn
Rt 23
Churchtown PA 17555
(215) 445-7794
   Circa 1735. This handsome, stone Federal house with its panoramic

views was once known as the Edward Davies Mansion, but was also once a tinsmith shop and rectory. It has heard the marching feet of Revolutionary troops and seen the Union Army during the Civil War. Tastefully furnished with antiques and collectibles, the inn features canopy, pencil-post and sleigh beds. There is music everywhere since the

innkeeper directed choruses appearing at Carnegie Hall and the Lincoln Center. By prior arrangement, guests may dine in an Amish home.
Location: Five miles from Pennsylvania Turnpike.
Rates: $49-$75. All year.
Innkeeper(s): Hermine & Stuart Smith, Jim Kent.
8 Rooms. 6 Private Baths. Guest phone available. TV in room. Beds: QT. Meals: Full breakfast. Conference room. Fireplaces. CCs: Visa, MC. Swimming, hiking, bicycling.
   "Magnificent atmosphere. Outstanding breakfasts. Our favorite B&B."

Danville

The Pine Barn Inn
1 Pine Barn Place
Danville PA 17821
(717) 275-2071
   Circa 1860. The inn is a restored Pennsylvania German barn. Original stone walls and beams accent the

restaurant and a large stone fireplace warms the tavern. It was the first all-electric residence in the state.
Rates: $35-$60.
Innkeeper(s): Susan Dressler.
51 Rooms. 45 Private Baths. TV available. Meals: EP. Conference room. CCs: All.
   "For four years we have stayed at the Pine Barn Inn. I thought then, and still think, it is truly the nicest inn I have been in and I've been in many."

Doylestown, Bucks Co

The Inn at Fordhook Farm
105 New Britain Rd
Doylestown, Bucks Co PA 18901
(215) 345-1766
   Circa 1760. Three generations of Burpees (Burpee Seed Company) have dispensed hospitality on this 60-acre farm. Guest rooms are in the family's 18th-century fieldstone house and Victorian carriage house.

The inn is filled with family heirlooms and guests can sit at the famous horticulturist's desk in the secluded study where Mr. Burpee wrote his first seed catalogs.
Location: Two miles west of Doylestown on route 202, Bucks County.
Rates: $75-$175. All year.
Innkeeper(s): Laurel & Dan Raymond, Blanche Burpee Dohan.
6 Rooms. 4 Private Baths. Guest phone available. TV available. Beds: KQ. Meals: Full breakfast. Conference room. CCs: Visa, MC, AE. Cross-country skiing, hiking.
Seen in: *Bon Appetit, Mid-Atlantic Country.*
   "The inn is absolutely exquisite. If I had only one night to spend in Bucks County, I'd do it all over again at Fordhook Farms!"

East Berlin

Bechtel Mansion Inn
400 West King St
East Berlin PA 17316
(717) 259-7760
   Circa 1897. The town of East Berlin, near Lancaster and Gettysburg,

was settled by Pennsylvania Germans prior to the American Revolution. William Leas, a wealthy banker, built this many-gabled Queen Anne mansion, now listed in the National Register. The inn is furnished with an abundance of Victorian antiques and collections.
**Rates: $72-$125. All year.

Innkeeper(s): Ruth Spangler & Mary Doyle.
7 Rooms. 7 Private Baths. Guest phone available. TV available. Beds: QTD. Meals: Full breakfast. Conference room. CCs: Visa, MC, AE. Skiing.
Seen in: *The Washington Post.*

"Ruth was a most gracious hostess and took time to describe the history of your handsome museum-quality antiques and the special architectural details."

Ephrata

Covered Bridge Inn
990 Rettew Mill Rd
Ephrata PA 17522
(717) 733-1592

Circa 1814. This Federal-style limestone farm house features original hand-carved woodwork, rare Indian

doors, corner cupboard floorboards, and old glass panes. Three herb gardens and views of the covered bridge, old mill, and barn all add to the rustic setting guests enjoy from the summer porch.
Rates: $55-$58. All year.
Innkeeper(s): Betty Lee Maxcy.
4 Rooms. Guest phone available. TV available. Beds: QD. Meals: Full Pennsylvania Dutch breakfast. Badminton, croquet.
Seen in: *Los Angeles Times, The Post.*

"We've been to quite a few B&B's and by far yours out ranks them all. You both are as special as the inn is. We loved the place so much we're not sure we want to share it with anyone else!"

The Smithton Inn
900 W Main St
Ephrata PA 17522
(717) 733-6094

Circa 1763. Henry Miller opened this inn and tavern on a hill overlooking the Ephrata Cloister, a religious society known as Seventh Day Baptists, of which he was a member. Several of their medieval-style German buildings are now a

museum. The inn's candlelit rooms have working fireplaces, canopy beds, and nightshirts for each guest.
Location: Lancaster County.
Rates: $55-$105. All year.
Innkeeper(s): Dorothy Graybill.
7 Rooms. 7 Private Baths. Guest phone in room. Beds: KQTC. Meals: Full breakfast, MAP. Jacuzzi. Fireplaces. CCs: Visa, MC, AE.

"After visiting over 50 inns in four countries Smithton has to be one of the most romantic picturesque inns in America. I have never seen its equal!"

Erwinna

Golden Pheasant Inn
River Rd
Erwinna PA 18920
(215) 294-9595

Circa 1857. Originally built to serve the mule barge workers and travelers, the Golden Pheasant is located between the Pennsylvania

Canal and the Delaware River. Features of the inn include fieldstone walls, exposed beams, and hardwood floors. There is a greenhouse dining room with views of the historic canal, in the evenings lit with spotlights. The cuisine here is highly rated.
Location: Bucks County.
Rates: $95-$125. All year.
Innkeeper(s): Barbary & Michel Faure.
5 Rooms. 1 Private Baths. Guest phone available. Beds: QT. Meals: Restaurant, gourmet. Conference room. Horseback riding, hiking, swimming, bicycling, cross-country skiing.
Seen in: *The Philadelphia Inquirer.*

"A more stunningly romantic spot is hard to imagine. A taste of France on the banks of the Delaware."

Everett

Newry Manor
Rt 1 Box 475
Everett PA 15537
(814) 623-1250

Circa 1805. Newry Manor and the adjacent stone woolen mill are both in the National Register. Four

generations of the Lutz family expanded the house into its current blend of stone, brick and log. The inn is filled with family heirlooms and antiques and there is a beautiful Prussian blue fireplace mantel in the keeping room. On quiet days guests can hear the trickle of the Raystown Branch of the Juniata River flowing past the old mill.
Location: Lutzville Road, 1 mile south of U.S. Route 30, near Everett.
Rates: $30-$60. April to Nov.
Innkeeper(s): Rosie & Carl Mulert.
3 Rooms. 3 Private Baths. Guest phone available. TV available. Beds: QT. Meals: Continental plus. Fireplaces. Canoeing.

"You are wonderful people. We will always remember this as our honeymoon home!"

Gardners

Goose Chase
200 Blueberry Rd
Gardners PA 17324
(717) 528-8877

Circa 1762. Originally a settler's log cabin, Goose Chase evolved as clapboard siding and stone facings were applied over the years. It is situated on 25 acres. Comfortable interiors include polished wide floor-

boards, stenciled walls, rag rugs and antiques. Across the way is a newly planted vineyard.
Location: Fourteen miles north of Gettysburg.
Rates: $55-$65. All year.
Innkeeper(s): Marsha & Rich Lucidi.
3 Rooms. 1 Private Baths. TV available. Beds: KDT. Meals: Full breakfast, gourmet. Fireplaces. Pool. CCs: Visa, MC. Cross-country & downhill skiing, fishing, golf, horseback riding. Afternoon wine/tea.
Seen in: *Gettysburg Times.*
  "Everything was just perfect. We were amazed at your fine decor."

Gettysburg

Bechtel Mansion Inn
See: East Berlin, PA

Beechmont Inn
See: Hanover, PA

Goose Chase
See: Gardners, PA

Hickory Bridge Farm
See: Ortanna, PA

Keystone Inn B&B
231 Hanover St
Gettysburg PA 17325
(717) 337-3888
  Circa 1913. Furniture-maker Clayton Reaser constructed this three-story brick Victorian with a

wide-columned porch hugging the north and west sides. Large-cut stone graces every door and win-

dowsill each with a keystone. A chestnut staircase ascends the full three stories, and the interior is decorated with comfortable furnishings, ruffles and lace.
Location: Route 116 East of Gettysburg.
Rates: $65. All year.
Innkeeper(s): Wilmer & Doris Martin.
4 Rooms. 2 Private Baths. Beds: QT. Meals: Full breakfast. Fireplaces. CCs: Visa, MC. Tennis, bicycling.
  "We slept like lambs...This home has a warmth that is soothing."

Spring Bank Inn
See: Frederick, MD

The Brafferton Inn
44 York St
Gettysburg PA 17325
(717) 337-3423
  Circa 1786. The earliest deeded house in Gettysburg, the inn was designed by James Gettys, and is listed in the National Register of Historic Places. The walls of this

huge brownstone range from 18 inches to two-and-one-half-feet thick. There are skylights in all the guestrooms and a primitive mural of famous scenes in the area painted on the four dining room walls.
Location: Ninety miles north of Washington, D.C.
**Rates: $65-$75. All year.
Innkeeper(s): Mimi & Jim Agard
8 Rooms. 4 Private Baths. Guest phone available. Beds: DT. Meals: Full breakfast. Handicap access provided. CCs: Visa, MC. Horseback riding, skiing, hiking, biking, swimming, golf.
Seen in: *Early American Life, Country Living.*
  "Your house is so beautiful - every corner of it - and your friendliness is icing on the cake. It was fabulous!"

The Doubleday Inn
104 Doubleday Ave
Gettysburg PA 17325
(717) 334-9119
  Circa 1929. Located directly on the Gettysburg Battlefield and bordered by original stone breastworks, this

restored colonial is furnished with Victorian sofas and period antiques. Available to guests is one of the largest known Civil War libraries with 200 volumes devoted ex-

clusively to the Battle of Gettysburg. On selected evenings, guests can participate in discussions with a Civil War historian who brings the battle alive with accurate accounts and authentic memorabilia and weaponry.
Location: On the Gettysburg Battlefield.
**Rates: $65-$90.
Innkeeper(s): Joan & Sal Chandon with Olga Krossick.
11 Rooms. 6 Private Baths. Guest phone available. Beds: Q. Meals: Full breakfast. Fireplaces. CCs: Visa, MC. Horseback riding, skiing, golfing, battlefield touring. Afternoon tea, hor d'oeuvres.
  "Thank you for a wonderful weekend. You have a terrific inn and a great location."

Glen Moore

Conestoga Horse B&B
Hollow Rd, PO Box 256
Glen Moore PA 19343
(215) 458-8535
  Circa 1750. This picturesque stone house was named for the six-bell teams of Conestoga horses and

wagons that passed on their journeys between Philadelphia and points west. Quiet horse pastures, old farmhouses, barns, and beautiful Chester County countryside provide the setting. Guest rooms are located

in the oldest part of the farmhouse or in the tenant's cottage, now furnished with antiques and period furniture.
Location: Northwestern Chester County.
Rates: $45-$80.
Innkeeper(s): Richard & Patricia Moore.
5 Rooms. 2 Private Baths. Guest phone available. Beds: DT. Meals: B&B.

Gordonville

The Osceola Mill House
313 Osceola Mill Rd
Gordonville PA 17529
(717) 768-3758
Circa 1766. This limestone millhouse rests on the banks of Pe-

quea Creek, surrounded by Amish farms in a quaint historic setting. Fireplaces in the keeping room and in the bedrooms provide warmth and charm.
Location: Lancaster County, 15 miles east of Lancaster near Intercourse.
Rates: $50-$65. All year.
Innkeeper(s): Barry & Joy Sawyer.
3 Rooms. Guest phone available. Beds: Q. Meals: Full breakfast.
Seen in: *The Journal.*
"One for my book of memories, charming, beautiful place, beautiful people."

Hanover

Beechmont Inn
315 Broadway
Hanover PA 17331
(717) 632-3013
Circa 1834. This gracious Georgian was a witness to the Civil War's first major battle on free soil, the Battle of Hanover. Decorated in pre-Victorian antiques, several guest rooms are named for the battle's commanders. The romantic Diller Suite contains a marble fireplace

and queen canopy bed. The inn is noted for elegant breakfasts often served by candlelight.
Rates: $55-$85.
Innkeeper(s): Terry & Monna, Glenn & Maggie Hormel.
7 Rooms. 3 Private Baths. Guest phone available. Beds: Q. Meals: Full breakfast. Handicap access provided. Fireplaces. CCs: Visa, MC. Boating, horseback riding, wineries. Dutch Days, Gettysburg National Park.

Holicong

Ash Mill Farm
PO Box 202
Holicong PA 18928
(215) 794-5373
Circa 1800. This estate includes a Federal addition completed in 1830. The finish on the house is 18th-cen-

tury plaster over stone, and the original section has a five-foot walk-in fireplace with a beehive oven and original cooking crane. Breakfast is served here and afternoon tea is also available. Grazing sheep dot the farm pastures.
Location: Route 202 located midway between Lahaska and Buckingham.
Rates: $60-$70. All year.
Innkeeper(s): Carolyn & Jeff Rawes.
5 Rooms. 3 Private Baths. Guest phone available. TV available. Beds: QD. Meals: Full breakfast, continental plus.

Fireplaces. CCs: Visa, MC. Horseback riding, canoeing, biking, hiking.
"The home's appointments are lovely and the quaint characteristics of the house itself a pleasure to look at."

Barley Sheaf Farm
Rt 202 Box 10
Holicong PA 18928
(215) 794-5104
Circa 1740. On part of the original William Penn land grant, this beautiful stone house with white

shuttered windows and mansard roof is set on 30 acres of farmland. Once owned by noted playwright George Kaufman, it was the gathering place for the Marx Brothers, Lillian Hellman, and S. J. Perlman. The bank barn, pond, and majestic old trees round out a beautiful setting.
Location: Fifty miles north of Philadelphia in Bucks County.
Rates: $100-$150. Feb. 13-Dec.20.
Innkeeper(s): Ann & Don Mills, Amy Donohoe.
10 Rooms. 10 Private Baths. Guest phone available. TV available. Beds: QT. Meals: Full breakfast. Handicap access provided. Pool.
Seen in: *Country Living.*

Intercourse

Churchtown Inn
See: Churchtown, PA

Jim Thorpe

Harry Packer Mansion
Packer Hill
Jim Thorpe PA 18229
(717) 325-8566
Circa 1874. This extravagant Second Empire mansion was constructed of New England sandstone, and local brick and stone trimmed in cast iron. Past ornately carved columns on the front veranda guests enter 400-lb., solid walnut doors.

The opulent interior includes marble mantels, hand-painted ceilings, and elegant antiques.
Location: Six miles south of Exit 34.
**Rates: $65-$110. All year.
Innkeeper(s): Bob & Pat Handwerr.
13 Rooms. 8 Private Baths. Guest phone available. Beds: QD. Meals: Full breakfast. Conference room. Fireplaces. CCs: Visa, MC. Downhill & cross-country skiing, swimming, rafting, fishing. Mystery weekends.

"The best B&B we have ever stayed at! We'll be back."

Kane

Kane Manor Country Inn
230 Clay St
Kane PA 16735
(814) 837-6522
Circa 1896. This Georgian Revival, on 250 acres of woods and trails, was built for Dr. Elizabeth Kane,

first female doctor to practice in the area. Many of the family's possessions dating back to the American Revolution and the Civil War remain. (Ask to see the attic.) Decor is a mixture of contemporary and old family items in an unpretentious homey style. Locals frequent the inn's pub.
Rates: $49-$79. All year.
Innkeeper(s): Laurie Anne.
10 Rooms. 6 Private Baths. Guest phone available. TV in room. Beds: DT. Meals: Full breakfast. CCs: Visa, MC, AE.

Cross-country skiing, fishing, hunting, swimming, bicycling, golf. Afternoon tea.
Seen in: *The Pittsburg Press.*

Kennett Square

Meadow Spring Farm
201 E St Rd
Kennett Square PA 19348
(215) 444-3903
Circa 1836. This working, 245-acre dairy farm has more than 300 holsteins grazing in pastures beside

the old red barn. The two-story, white brick house is decorated with old family pieces and collections of whimsical animals and antique wedding gowns. A Victorian doll collection fills one room. Breakfast is hearty country style and afterwards guests may see the milking operation, gather eggs or pick vegetables from the garden.
Location: Forty-five minutes from Philadelphia, 2 hours from New York.
**Rates: $45. All year.
Innkeeper(s): Anne Hicks.
4 Rooms. Guest phone available. TV available. Beds: QT. Meals: Full breakfast. Jacuzzi. Fireplaces. Pool. CCs: AE. Swimming, hiking, fishing all on premises.
Seen in: *Weekend GetAways.*

Lahaska

Golden Plough Inn
Rt 263-Rt 202
Lahaska PA 18913
(215) 794-7438
Circa 1750. This Early American house features French Colonial influences such as its mansard roof. It is located in Peddler's Village, the reproduction of an 18th-century colonial village five miles from New Hope and the Delaware River. There are high quality specialty shops here, and the Pearl Buck house,

Bucks County Playhouse and Dinner Theater are nearby.
Location: Peddler's Village, Route 263-Route 202.
**Rates: $75-$110. All year.
Innkeeper(s): Earl Jamison.
9 Rooms. 9 Private Baths. Guest phone available. TV in room. Beds: KQ. Meals: MAP, full breakfast, restaurant. Jacuzzi. Conference room. Fireplaces. CCs: Visa, MC, AE, DC. Horseback riding, hot air balloon, boating, tubing.

"We were very pleased with everything. It was great being here in the village, within walking distance of the shops and restaurants."

Lancaster

Bechtel Mansion Inn
See: East Berlin, PA

Churchtown Inn
See: Churchtown, PA

The Foreman House
See: Narvon, PA

Witmer's Tavern - Historic 1725 Inn
2014 Old Philadelphia Pike
Lancaster PA 17602
(717) 299-5305
Circa 1725. This authentic pre-Revolutionary War inn still lodges

travelers and is the sole survivor out of 62 inns that once lined the old Lancaster to Philadelphia turnpike. Located in the middle of the Penn-

sylvania Dutch area, it is a National Landmark. Highlights are original hand-carved stone, woodwork, stairs and cupboards. Guest rooms look out onto farmland and feature antiques, original fireplaces, and old quilts.
Location: One mile east of Lancaster on Route 340.
Rates: $55-$75. All year.
Innkeeper(s): Brant Hartung & his sister Pamela Hartung.
5 Rooms. Beds: D. Meals: Continental. Canoeing.
"Your personal attention and enthusiastic knowledge of the area and Witmer's history made it come alive and gave us the good feelings we came looking for."

Manheim

Herr Farmhouse Inn
Rt 7 Box 587
Manheim PA 17545
(717) 653-9852
Circa 1738. One of the earliest in Lancaster County, this stone farmhouse sits on 11 1/2 acres of

rolling farmland. All woodwork including moldings, doors, cabinets and pine flooring is original and there are six working fireplaces.
Location: Nine miles west of Lancaster off Route 283 (Mt. Joy 230 exit).
Rates: $65-$85. All year.
Innkeeper(s): Barry & Ruth Herr.
4 Rooms. 2 Private Baths. Guest phone available. TV available. Beds: QTD. Meals: Continental plus. Fireplaces. CCs: Visa, MC.

Maytown

Three Center Square Inn
PO Box 428
Maytown PA 17550
(717) 653-4338
Circa 1768. This old inn was originally built as a tavern and later

an annex was added to house a general store. The floors above the store were used for the manufacture of cigars but now house Victorian guest rooms.
**Rates: $69-$79. All year.
Innkeeper(s): Harry & Pachel Rebman.
16 Rooms. 14 Private Baths. Guest phone available. TV available. Beds: QT. Meals: Restaurant, gourmet. CCs: Visa, MC, AE.

Mercer

Magoffin Guest House B&B
129 S Pitt St
Mercer PA 16137
(412) 662-4611
Circa 1884. Dr. Magoffin built this house for his Pittsburgh bride Henrietta Bouvard. The Queen Anne

style is characterized by patterned brick masonry, gable detailing, bay windows and a wraparound porch. The technique of marbleizing was used on six of the nine fireplaces. Homemade cinnamon rolls are featured each morning and from Monday through Saturday a lunchroom is open.
Location: Near I-79 and I-80.
Rates: $60-$75. All year.
Innkeeper(s): Jacque McClelland, Gene Slagle.
7 Rooms. 7 Private Baths. Guest phone in room. TV in room. Beds: DTC. Meals: Full breakfast. Conference room. Fireplaces. CCs: Visa, MC, AE. Swimming, golf, tennis, fishing.
Seen in: *Western Reserve Magazine, Youngstown Vindicator.*
"While in Arizona we met a family from Africa who had stopped at the Magoffin House. After crossing the United States they said the Magoffin House was quite the nicest place they had stayed."

Mertztown

Longswamp B&B
RD 2 PO Box 26
Mertztown PA 19539
(215) 682-6197
Circa 1789. Country gentleman Colonel Trexler added a mansard roof to this stately Federal mansion in 1860. Inside is a magnificent walnut staircase and pegged wood floors. As the story goes, the colonel discovered his unmarried daughter having an affair and shot her lover. He escaped hanging but it was said that after his death his ghost could be seen in the upstairs bedroom watching the road. In 1905 an exorcism was reported to have sent his spirit to a nearby mountaintop.
Rates: $60-$65. All year.
Innkeeper(s): Elsa Dimick.
9 Rooms. 5 Private Baths. Guest phone available. TV available. Beds: Q. Meals: Gourmet. CCs: Visa, MC. Horseback riding, biking.
Seen in: *Weekend Travel, The Sun.*
"The warm country atmosphere turns strangers into friends."

Montoursville

The Carriage House At Stonegate
RD 1 Box 11A
Montoursville PA 17754
(717) 433-4340
Circa 1830. President Herbert Hoover was a descendant of the original settlers of this old homestead in the Loyalsock Creek Valley. Indians burned the original house but the present farmhouse and numerous outbuildings date from the early 1800s. The Carriage House is set next to a lovely brook.
Location: Six miles off I-180, north of Montoursville.
Rates: $45-$55. All year.
Innkeeper(s): Harold & Dena Mesaris.
4 Rooms. 2 Private Baths. Guest phone in room. TV available. Beds: QTC. Meals: Full breakfast, continental plus. Conference room. Hiking, golf, cross-country skiing, canoeing.
"A very fine B&B - the best that can be found. Gracious hosts."

Mount Joy

Cameron Estate Inn
RD 1 Box 305
Mount Joy PA 17552
(717) 653-1773

Simon Cameron, Abraham Lincoln's first Secretary of War, entertained his guests in this Federal-period estate situated on 15 acres of towering oaks with an old stone bridge and trout stream. There are oriental rugs, antiques, and working fireplaces.
Rates: $55-$95.
Innkeeper(s): Betty & Abe Groff.
18 Rooms. 16 Private Baths. Beds: KQD. Meals: Continental breakfast.
"Betty runs from pillar to post, filled with joy!" Sephanie Edwards, Los Angeles talk show host.

Narvon

The Foreman House B&B
RD 3 Box 161A
Narvon PA 17555
(215) 445-6713

Circa 1919. A prominent local farmer, Peter Foreman, built this house and then forbade all seven of his children to marry or they would lose their inheritance. Six obeyed. Surrounded by Amish farmlands, the inn provides views of horse-drawn carriages. A selection of the most sought after quilts in the country may be purchased in the parlors of farm ladies nearby.
Location: Lancaster County on Route 23.
Rates: $40-$50. All year.
Innkeeper(s): Jacqueline & Stephen Mitrani.
2 Rooms. Guest phone available. TV in room. Beds: DT. Meals: Full breakfast. Fireplaces.
Seen in: *Lancaster Daily Newspaper*.
"We couldn't have been happier staying anywhere else! You have a lovely home."

New Hope

Backstreet Inn
144 Old York Rd
New Hope PA 18939
(215) 862-9571

Circa 1750. Tucked away on a quiet street, this inn sits on three acres of park-like lawns that include a stream, an old wishing well, and a gurgling brook. Several rooms reveal the stone walls of the house and are decorated with antiques. A favorite is the Anne Frank Room down a small hallway hidden by a sliding bookcase.
Rates: $69-$125. All year.
Innkeeper(s): Karla Dolan.
7 Rooms. 2 Private Baths. Guest phone available. TV available. Beds: D. Meals: Full breakfast. Fireplaces. Pool. CCs: Visa, AE, DC. Horse and carriage rides.
"A great place to first see our first baby moving in the belly! Thanks for your tremendous hospitality."

The Inn at Fordhook Farm
See: Doylestown, PA

The Wedgwood Inn
111 W Bridge
New Hope PA 18938
(215) 862-2570

Circa 1870. A Victorian and a Classic Revival house sit side by side and compose the Wedgewood Inn. Twenty-six-inch walls are in the stone house. Lofty windows, hardwood floors and antique furnishings add to the warmth and style. Pennsylvania Dutch surreys arrive and depart from the inn for nostalgic carriage rides.
Rates: Call.
Innkeeper(s): Nadine Silnutzer & Carl Glassman.
10 Rooms. 8 Private Baths. Guest phone available. Meals: Continental plus.
"The Wedgewood has all the comforts of a highly professional accommodation yet with all the warmth a personal friend would extend."

North Wales

Joseph Ambler Inn
1005 Horsham Rd
North Wales PA 19454
(215) 362-7500

Circa 1734. This beautiful fieldstone-and-wood house was built over a period of three centuries. Originally, it was part of a grant that Joseph Ambler, a Quaker wheelwright, obtained from William Penn in 1688. A large stone bank barn and tenant cottage on 12 acres constitute the remainder of the property. Guests enjoy the cherry wainscoting and walk-in fireplace in the schoolroom.
Rates: $87-$140. All year.
Innkeeper(s): Steve & Terry Kratz.
28 Rooms. 28 Private Baths. Guest phone in room. TV in room. Beds: QD. Meals: Full breakfast, restaurant. Conference room. Fireplaces. CCs: Visa, MC, AE, DC. Golf, tennis.
Seen in: *Colonial Homes*.
"What a wonderful night my husband and I spent. It was special because of the great pains taken to make the inn quaint and unique. We are already planning to come back to your wonderful get-away."

Orrtanna

Hickory Bridge Farm
96 Hickory Bridge Rd
Orrtanna PA 17353
(717) 642-5261

Circa 1750. The oldest part of this farmhouse was constructed of mud bricks, and straw on land that once

belonged to Charles Carroll, father of a signer of the Declaration of Independence. Inside, there is an attractive stone fireplace for cooking. There are several country cottages in addition to the rooms in the

farmhouse. The host family have been innkeepers for nearly 20 years.
Location: Eight miles west of Gettysburg.
Rates: $59-$65. All year.
Innkeeper(s): Dr. & Mrs. James Hamett, Robert & Mary Lynn Marti.
7 Rooms. 6 Private Baths. TV available. Beds: Q. Meals: Continental. CCs: Visa, MC. Fishing, golfing, swimming, skiing.
Seen in: *Hanover Times, The Northern Virginia Gazzette.*
"*Beautifully decorated and great food!*"

Philadelphia

Ash Mill Farm
See: Holicong, PA

B&B of Valley Forge
See: Valley Forge, PA

Society Hill Hotel
301 Chestnut St
Philadelphia PA 19106
(215) 925-1919
Circa 1830. The small cozy rooms of this urban inn are decorated with brass beds, fresh flowers and other amenities expected by guests of the Society Hill group in Maryland. Breakfast is brought to the room and there is an outdoor cafe and a restaurant with nightly jazz piano.
**Rates: $90-$110.
Innkeeper(s): George Ambos & Howard Jacobs.
12 Rooms. 12 Private Baths. Guest phone in room. TV available. Beds: Q. Meals: B&B. CCs: Visa, MC, AE, DC.

Pittsburgh

The Priory
614 Pressley St
Pittsburgh PA 15212
(412) 231-3338
Circa 1888. The Priory, now a European-style hotel, was built to provide lodging for Benedictine priests traveling through Pittsburgh. It is adjacent to St. Mary's German Catholic Church in historic East Allegheny. The inn's design and maze of rooms and corridors give it a distinctly Old World flavor. All rooms are decorated with Victorian furnishings.
**Rates: $60-$115. All year.

Innkeeper(s): Mary Ann Graf.
27 Rooms. 27 Private Baths. Guest phone in room. TV in room. Beds: TC. Meals: Continental plus. Handicap access provided. Conference room. Fireplaces. CCs: All. Complimentary wine in sitting room.
Seen in: *The Pittsburg Press.*
"*Although we had been told that the place was elegant, we were hardly prepared for the richness of detail. We felt as though we were guests in a manor.*"

Pottstown

Fairway Farm B&B
Vaughn Rd
Pottstown PA 19464
(215) 326-1315
Circa 1734. This beautiful old fieldstone house is in a parklike setting that includes a spring-fed pool,

a tennis court, a pond and gazebo. The barn contains an internationally-known trumpet museum. The hosts' European tastes are reflected in the collection of hand-painted Bavarian furnishings and there are four posters and feather beds. Breakfast is served in the gazebo or on the terrace.
Location: Forty five miles southwest of Philadelphia.
Rates: $60.
Innkeeper(s): Katherine Streitwieser.

4 Rooms. 4 Private Baths. Guest phone available. TV available. Beds: KQ. Meals: Full breakfast. Jacuzzi. Sauna. Conference room. Fireplaces. Pool.
Seen in: *Today Show, Philadelphia Magazine.*

Red Lion

Red Lion B&B
101 South Franklin St
Red Lion PA 17356
(717) 244-4739
Circa 1920. A full country breakfast is served in this Twenties homestay in the breakfast room, parlor or dining room. Mr. B's Lunchbox is a restaurant on the property.
Rates: $50. May to October.
Innkeeper(s): Harry & Marilyn Brown.
2 Rooms. Guest phone available. Beds: TD. Meals: Full breakfast. Fireplaces.

Shippensburg

Field & Pine B&B
RD 5 Box 161
Shippensburg PA 17257
(717) 776-7179
Circa 1790. Local limestone was used to build this stone house located on the main wagon road to Baltimore and Washington. Originally, it was a tavern and weigh station, and the scales are still attached to the stagecoach barn on the property. The house is surrounded by stately pines, and sheep graze on the inn's 80 acres.
Location: Twelve miles south of Carlisle, on U.S. Route 11.
Rates: $40-$50. All year.
Innkeeper(s): Mary Ellen & Allan Williams.
3 Rooms. Guest phone available. TV in room. Beds: TD. Meals: Full breakfast. Fireplaces. Fly fishing, bicycles, horseback riding.
Seen in: *Valley Times-Star.*
"*Our visit in this lovely country home has been most delightful. The ambience of antiques and tasteful decorating exemplifies real country living.*"

Thornton

Pace One Restaurant and Country Inn

Thornton Rd
Thornton PA 19373
(215) 459-9784

Circa 1740. This beautifully renovated stone barn has two-and-a-half-foot thick walls, hand-hewn wood beams, and many small-paned windows. Just in front of the inn was the Gray family home used as a hospital during the Revolutionary War when Washington's army crossed nearby Chadd's Ford.
**Rates: $65-$75.
Innkeeper(s): Ted Pace.
8 Rooms. 7 Private Baths. Beds: Q. Meals: Continental breakfast. CCs: All.

"Dear Ted & Staff, we loved it here!! The accommodations were great and the brunch on Sunday, fantastic. Thanks for making it a beautiful weekend."

Valley Forge

Bed & Breakfast of Valley Forge

PO Box 562
Valley Forge PA 19481
(215) 783-7838

Circa 1692. Venerable boxwood hedges border this 15-room Pennsylvania stone farmhouse near Valley Forge. A flagstone path leads to a long, white-pillared facade overlooking acres of fields. Breakfast is served in the summer kitchen, the oldest part of the house. A tunnel that leads from the keep, a cold storage shed, allowed the owners to escape from the British during the Revolutionary War. Later, it was part of the Underground Railroad for slaves escaping to the North. Carolyn Williams represents seven private home bed and breakfasts, all rich in history, in the Valley Forge area.

Location: One half mile on Route 202, Exit 24.
Rates: $55-$85. All year.
Innkeeper(s): Carolyn J. Williams, Director.
3 Rooms. 3 Private Baths. Guest phone in room. TV in room. Beds: QTDC. Meals: Gourmet. Conference room. Fireplaces. Pool. CCs: Visa, MC, AE. Skiing, hunting, horses.
Seen in: *Suburban Business Review, Entertainment Magazine.*

"I'll never go back to a hotel. This is the way to get a real feel for the people and a chance to really discover the area. You often get the bonus of making lasting friends."

York

Bechtel Mansion Inn
See: East Berlin, PA

Beechmont Inn
See: Hanover, PA

Rhode Island

Block Island

New Shoreham House
PO Box 356, Water St
Block Island RI 02807
(401) 466-2651

Circa 1890. Complete with resident ghost and crooked stairs, the New Shoreham House maintains a fresh,

newly papered and painted Victorian seaside charm. A deck faces out to sea and there's a mystical herb garden in the backyard called the Sea Star. Afternoon tea and hors d'oeuvres are served.
Rates: $455-$115. All year.
Innkeeper(s): Robert & Kathleen Schleimer.
15 Rooms. Guest phone available. TV available. Beds: DC. Meals: Continental plus. CCs: Visa, MC. Bicycling, white sand beaches.

The Inn At Old Harbour
Water St, Box 994
Block Island RI 02807
(401) 466-2212 (401) 466-2932/2933

Circa 1882. This three-story Victorian with its gingerbread trim and double porch attracts many photographers. Recently renovated, all the rooms are appointed with period furnishings and most have views of the Atlantic. Block Island's inviting beaches and seaside cliffs are enjoyed by wind surfers, sailers, cyclists and those just sunning on

the sand. A noted wildlife sanctuary at Sandy Point is popular for bird-watchers.
Location: Overlooking the harbor and the Atlantic Ocean.
**Rates: $85-$140. May-Oct.
Innkeeper(s): Kevin & Barbara Butler.
10 Rooms. 5 Private Baths. Guest phone available. Beds: QTC. Meals: Continental plus. CCs: Visa, MC, AE.

"The most romantic enchanting inn we have stayed at and what gracious innkeepers!"

Bristol

The Joseph Reynolds House
956 Hope St, PO Box 5
Bristol RI 02809
(401) 254-0230 (401)254-0236

Circa 1693. The Joseph Reynolds house is a National Historic Landmark and is the only known 17th-century three-story structure in New England. It was the military headquarters of General Lafayette in 1778. Gradually being restored to its original elegance, guest rooms are on the second and third floors and the old summer kitchen is a self-contained apartment. Most of the common rooms have high ceilings and were painted to look like marble. There is a Jacobean stair-

case, a keeping room and a great room.
Location: Twenty-five minutes from Newport.
Rates: $55-$120.
Innkeeper(s): Richard & Wendy Anderson.
4 Rooms. Guest phone available. Beds: KDT. Meals: B&B.
Seen in: *American Design, The New England Colonial.*

Jamestown

Calico Cat Guest House
14 Union St
Jamestown RI 02835
(401) 423-2641

Circa 1860. This Victorian house is only 250 feet from East Harbour in Jamestown. The inn features high ceilings and spacious rooms. Children are welcome and the innkeeper stocks toys and games and will arrange for babysitting. Guests can walk to shops and restaurants and it's 10 minutes to Newport's shops and historic mansions across the bay.
**Rates: $40-$70. All year.
Innkeeper(s): Lori Lacaille.
10 Rooms. Guest phone available. TV available. Beds: KTW. Meals: Full breakfast, continental plus. Handicap access provided. Conference room. Fireplaces. CCs: Visa, MC. Water sports, horseback riding. Babysitting available.

"Jamestown is very quiet and the Calico Cat is like being home!"

Newport

Cliff View Guest House
4 Cliff Terrace
Newport RI 02840

(401) 846-0885

Circa 1871. This charming Victorian is cited in *Architectural History*

of *Newport, Rhode Island* as one of the "Seaview Cottages" formerly located on the Cliff Walk. It was moved half a mile to its present location on one of Newport's most beautiful tree-lined streets. Within a few minutes guests can walk to the beach along the Cliff Walk or to the wharves and shopping areas.
Rates: $55-$65. April to Oct.
Innkeeper(s): Pauline & John Shea.
4 Rooms. 2 Private Baths. Guest phone available. TV available. Beds: DTC. Meals: Continental plus. CCs: Visa, MC. Beach, shopping.
"I give it a 10! A happy house and great location."

Inn At Castle Hill
Ocean Dr
Newport RI 02840
(401) 849-3800

Circa 1874. The rambling Inn at Castle Hill was built as a summer home for scientist Alexander Agassiz and its architecture is reminiscent of the chalets of his native Switzerland. A laboratory included in the house was a forerunner of the Woods Hole Marine Laboratory. Many original furnishings remain and there are spectacular ocean views from most of the rooms.
Location: Five miles south of downtown.
Rates: $50-$225. All year.
Innkeeper(s): T. Paul McEnroe.
16 Rooms. 13 Private Baths. Guest phone available. Beds: DT. Meals: Continental, restaurant. Fireplaces. CCs: Visa, MC, AE. Swimming (private beach), tennis, golf.

Inn of Jonathan Bowen
29 Pelham St
Newport RI 02840

(401) 846-3324

Circa 1804. This three-story, square colonial is situated in the heart of Newport's Historic Hill. The inn is a half block to the water and there are views of the harbor and the sea from many of the guest rooms. Furnishings are primarily antiques. Off-street parking is provided.
Location: One half block from Newport harbor.
**Rates: $95-$175. All year.
Innkeeper(s): Sally Goddin.
9 Rooms. 7 Private Baths. Guest phone available. TV available. Beds: KQ. Meals: Full breakfast. Conference room. Fireplaces. CCs: Visa, MC, AE. Sail charters available.
"Thanks for making our stay so enjoyable. We have to come back very soon."

Jail House Inn
13 Marlborough St
Newport RI 02840
(401) 847-4638

Circa 1772. The owner of another B&B, the Yankee Peddler, has had a good bit of fun restoring and renovating the old Newport Jail. Prison-striped bed coverings, and tin cups and plates for breakfast express the jailhouse motif. Guests can stay in the "cell block", "maximum security" or "solitary confinement", each on a separate level of the inn. Nevertheless, since guests pay for their time here, there are luxuries in abundance.
Rates: $55-$125. All year.
Innkeeper(s): Beth Hoban & Carol Panaccione.
22 Rooms. 22 Private Baths. Guest phone in room. TV in room. Beds: Q. Meals: Full breakfast. Handicap access provided. CCs: Visa, MC, AE. Shopping.
Seen in: *The Providence Journal.*

Melville House
39 Clarke St
Newport RI 02840
(401) 847-0640

Circa 1750. This attractive two-story colonial once housed aides to

General Rochambeau during the American Revolution. Early American furnishings decorate the interior. There is also an unusual collection of old appliances including a cherry-pitter, mincer, and dough maker collected by Sam, a former household appliance designer. The inn is a pleasant walk to the waterfront and historic sites.
Location: In the heart of Newport's Historic Hill.
Rates: $65-$75. March to Jan.
Innkeeper(s): Rita & Sam Rogers.
7 Rooms. 5 Private Baths. Guest phone available. Beds: DT. Meals: Continental plus. Fireplaces. CCs: Visa, MC. Swimming, boating, fishing, tennis, golf.
"Comfortable with a quiet elegance."

Pilgrim House
123 Spring St
Newport RI 02840
(401) 846-0040

Circa 1900. This turn-of-the-century Victorian offers a panoramic view of Newport Harbor from its

third-floor deck, where breakfast is often served. The inn is in the wharf area, adjacent to historic Trinity Church and just a short walk to fine shops and restaurants. Newport's mansions and beaches are nearby and one can easily stroll to quaint antique shops on Spring Street.
Rates: $45-$120. All year.
Innkeeper(s): Pam & Bruce Bayuk & Donna Messerlian.
10 Rooms. 8 Private Baths. Guest phone available. TV available. Beds: QT. Meals: Continental. CCs: Visa, MC. Beach.
Seen in: *The Times.*
"Overwhelming view. Wonderful, warm hospitality."

The Admiral Fitzroy
398 Thames Street
Newport RI 02840
(401) 847-4459

Circa 1865. For 120 years this building, designed by architect Dudley Newton, was a convent located on Spring Street. To preserve it the

building was moved to Thames Street, restored, and converted to an inn. Guests now enjoy Victorian charm in the middle of Newport's wide array of shops and fine restaurants. The inn is air-conditioned.
Location: In the heart of Newport's Yachting Village.
Rates: $65-$135.
Innkeeper(s): Anita Gillin.
6 Rooms. 6 Private Baths. Guest phone in room. TV in room. Meals: Full breakfast.

The Brinley Victorian Inn
23 Brinley St
Newport RI 02840
(401) 849-7645
  Circa 1850. This is a three-story Victorian with a mansard roof and long porch. A cottage on the proper-

ty dates from 1850. There are two parlors and a library providing a quiet haven from the bustle of the Newport wharves. Each room is decorated with period wallpapers and furnishings and there are fresh flowers and mints on the pillows. The brick courtyard is planted with bleeding heart, peonies and miniature roses, perennials of the Victorian era.
Location: Newport Historic District.
Rates: $75-$95. May to October.
Innkeeper(s): Peter Carlisle & Donna Cinotti.

17 Rooms. 12 Private Baths. Guest phone available. TV available. Beds: D. Meals: Full breakfast. Conference room. Fireplaces. CCs: Visa, MC. Sailing, swimming.
Seen in: *New Hampshire Times, Boston Woman.*
  "Ed and I had a wonderful anniversary. The Brinley is as lovely and cozy as ever! The weekend brought back lots of happy memories."

The Old Dennis House
59 Washington St
Newport RI 02840
(401) 846-1324
  Circa 1740. Situated on the oldest residential street in Newport this

house was built by sea captain John Dennis and boasts the city's only flat widow's walk as well as an elaborate pineapple doorway. The house provides several inviting rooms with commanding views of Narragansett Bay.
**Rates: $55-190.
Innkeeper(s): Rev. Henry G. Turnbull.
10 Rooms. 9 Private Baths. Guest phone available. TV available.
  "Thank you for the wonderful weekend. The Luxury Suite was beautiful and very comfortable. It was like a home away from home!"

Yankee Peddler Inn
113 Touro St
Newport RI 02840
(401) 846-1323
  Circa 1830. This handsome Greek Revival inn is a five-minute walk from the harbor. Features include a deck on the third floor where guests enjoy views of the water. The inn is furnished in both contemporary and antique pieces. A garden and lounge are popular spots.
Rates: $60-$105. All year.
Innkeeper(s): Susan-Marie Beauchemin.

19 Rooms. 17 Private Baths. Guest phone available. TV available. Beds: QDT. Meals: Full breakfast. Conference room. Fireplaces. CCs: Visa, MC, AE.
  "So comfortable! We return four times each year, once per season. The Yankee Peddler is our home in Newport."

Providence

Perryville Inn
See: Rehoboth, MA

Westerly

Shelter Harbor Inn
Rt 1
Westerly RI 02891
(401) 322-8883
  Circa 1800. This farmhouse at the entrance to the community of Shelter Harbor has been renovated and transformed to create a handsome

country inn. Rooms, many with fireplaces, are in the main house, the barn and a carriage house. A third floor deck provides panoramic vistas of Block Island Sound. The dining room features local seafood and other traditional New England dishes. Nearby are secluded barrier beaches, stone fences and salt ponds.
**Rates: $72-$92. All year.
Innkeeper(s): Jim & Debbye Dey.
24 Rooms. 24 Private Baths. Guest phone in room. TV in room. Meals: Full breakfast, restaurant. Jacuzzi. Conference room. Fireplaces. CCs: Visa, MC, AE, DC. Table tennis, golf, tennis.

South Carolina

Aiken

Pine Knoll Inn
305 Lancaster St
Aiken SC 29801
(803) 649-5939
   Circa 1929. This winter colony home overlooks a golf course.

Unique plaster moldings are featured in the parlor and guest rooms are filled with antiques. Most rooms have views of the tall trees on the property. Bicycles are available to tour the historic district.
Location: Downtown historical district.
Rates: $55-$65. All year.
Innkeeper(s): Vicki & Jim McNair.
8 Rooms. 5 Private Baths. Guest phone available. TV available. Beds: QT. Meals: Full breakfast, continental plus. Fireplaces. Pool. CCs: Visa, MC, AE. Horseback riding, golf, tennis, swimming, nature trails. Complimentary golf.

The Cedars B&B Inn
See: Beech Island, SC

Willcox Inn
100 Colleton Ave At Whiskey Rd
Aiken SC 29801
(803) 649-1377
   Circa 1898. The Willcox was established by English valet Frederick Willcox and features a handsome, white columned facade. It is surrounded by horse farms and golf courses. Guest rooms often feature fireplaces, four poster beds and reproduction furnishings in keeping with the inn's National Register status. Fine dining is presented in the Pheasant Room.
Innkeeper(s): Stig Jorgensen.
30 Rooms. 30 Private Baths. Guest phone in room. TV in room. Beds: QTC. Meals: Restaurant, gourmet extra. Handicap access provided. Conference room. CCs: Visa, MC, AE. Tennis, golf, horseback riding.

Beaufort

Bay Street Inn
601 Bay St
Beaufort SC 29902
(803) 524-7720
   Circa 1850. Built by one of Beaufort's major cotton planters, the

inn is a fine example of Greek Revival architecture. Cracks remain on the front steps where trunks were thrown from the upper gallery when the Union fleet approached during the Civil War. There are 14-foot ceilings, marble fireplaces, and a two-story veranda. All the rooms have unobstructed water views and fireplaces. Joel Pointsett planted the original poinsettia plants while visiting the builder.
Location: On the water in the historic district.
Rates: $60-$65. All year.
Innkeeper(s): Gene & Kathleen Roc.
6 Rooms. 6 Private Baths. Guest phone available. TV available. Beds: QT. Meals: EP. Conference room. CCs: Visa, MC.

Old Point Inn
212 New St
Beaufort SC 29902
(803) 524-3177
   Circa 1898. In the historic district, this Queen Anne Victorian features two-story verandas where guests may often be found viewing boats on the Intercoastal Waterway. The innkeepers display fine collections of southern crafts and rooms are furnished in antiques and reproductions. A waterfront park, the marina, restaurants, and downtown shopping are a block and a half away.
Rates: $55. All year.
Innkeeper(s): Sandra & Charlie Williams.
3 Rooms. 3 Private Baths. Guest phone available. Beds: KQT. Meals: Continental plus. CCs: Visa, MC, AE. Beaches.
   "We are still cruising on our memories of a wonderful honeymoon. It certainly had a great start staying at the Old Point Inn. We couldn't have done better."

Rhett House Inn
1009 Craven St
Beaufort SC 29902
(803) 524-9030

Circa 1820. Most people cannot pass this stunning two-story clapboard without wanting to step up to the long veranda and try the hammock. Guest rooms are furnished in antiques with quilts and fresh flowers and many have fireplaces. Handsome gardens feature a fountain and are often the site for romantic weddings. Bicycles are available.
Location: In historic downtown.
**Rates: $60-$85. All year.
Innkeeper(s): Marianne & Steve Harrison.
8 Rooms. 8 Private Baths. Guest phone available. Beds: QT. Meals: Full breakfast. Fireplaces. CCs: Visa, MC. Bicycles, tennis, golf.

RSVP Savannah B&B Reservations
See: Savannah, GA

Beech Island

The Cedars B&B Inn
Box 117 1325 Williston Rd
Beech Island SC 29841
(803) 827-0248

Circa 1827. Three bay windows and the long front porch of this two-story inn overlook the lawns of the 12-acre homestead. The owner of The Cedars was General Henry Mayson of the South Carolina Home Guard. After hearing of Lee's surrender, he is reported to have said, *"General Lee may have surrendered but General Mayson has not."*
Location: Six miles east of Augusta on Route 278.
Rates: $42-$48. All year.
Innkeeper(s): Ralph & Maggie Zieger.
4 Rooms. 3 Private Baths. Guest phone available. TV in room. Beds: QT. Meals: Full breakfast, continental plus. CCs: Visa, MC. Lawn games, picnics.
Seen in: *Augusta Magazine.*
"The home and surroundings are lovely, food excellent, and hospitality plus. We have traveled over most of the U.S., Europe and England and have not yet found a more enjoyable atmosphere."

Charleston

1837 Bed & Breakfast
126 Wentworth St
Charleston SC 29401
(803) 723-7166

Circa 1800. Originally owned by a cotton planter, this three-story townhouse is situated in the historic district. Red cypress wainscoting, cornice molding and heart-of-pine floors adorn the formal parlor, while pine-beamed ceilings and red brick walls are features of the carriage house.
Location: In the historic district.
Rates: $39-$85. All year.
Innkeeper(s): Sherri Weaver Dunn & Richard Dunn.
7 Rooms. 7 Private Baths. Guest phone available. TV in room. Beds: QT. Meals: Full breakfast, restaurant. CCs: Visa, MC, AE.

Barksdale House Inn
27 George St
Charleston SC 29401
(803) 577-4800

Circa 1779. George Barksdale was a wealthy Charleston planter and a member of the South Carolina House of Representatives. The Barksdale family stayed in this gracious townhouse when they were not at their country residence, Younghall Plantation. Lavish interiors of the three stories include Scalamandre borders and 18th-and 19th-century fabrics. Gas-log fireplaces framed by marbleized or stenciled slate mantels are beside almost every bed.
10 Rooms. 10 Private Baths. Meals: Continental breakfast. Jacuzzi. CCs: Visa, MC. Bicycles available to rent.

Cannonboro Inn
184 Ashley Ave
Charleston SC 29403
(803) 723-8572

Circa 1840. The city of Charleston considered the Cannonboro irreplaceable because of its semi-circular two-story, columned piazzas. Shaded by crepe myrtles and palmettos, the inn is also air-conditioned. Rooms are appointed with period antiques such as four-poster beds and rice beds.
Location: Historic district.
**Rates: $59-$79. All year.

Innkeeper(s): Robert Warley & James Hare.
6 Rooms. 3 Private Baths. Guest phone available. TV in room. Beds: Q. Meals: Full breakfast. Conference room. Fireplaces. CCs: Visa, MC.
"Just wanted to tell you again what a great week I had in Charleston due to a large degree to the splendid atmosphere and treatment at the inn."

Charleston Society B&B
84 Murray Blvd
Charleston SC 29401
(803) 723-4948

Circa 1800. All the homes represented by this reservation service are located in the Charleston Historic District and include pre-Revolutionary, post-Revolutionary and antebellum homes. Handsome interiors include period furniture and all homes have air conditioning, and private baths.
Location: Historic district.
Rates: $50-$150. All year.
Innkeeper(s): Eleanor Rogers.
15 Rooms. 15 Private Baths. Guest phone available. TV available. Beds: QTC. Meals: Continental, some full breakfasts.

Elliott House Inn
78 Queen St
Charleston SC 29401
(803) 723-1855

Circa 1886. Located in the center of the Charleston Historic District, the

Elliott House was once a private single home. A renovation has

added a carriage house with shutters and flower boxes. Canopy beds are numerous as are balconies overlooking the garden.
**Rates: $98-$114.
26 Rooms. 26 Private Baths. Guest phone in room. TV in room. Beds: KQDT. Meals: Continental. Jacuzzi. CCs: Visa, MC, AE. Complimentary bicycles.
Seen in: *Innsider*.

Guilds Inn
See: Mt Pleasant, SC

Hayne House
30 King St
Charleston SC 29401
(803) 577-2633
  Circa 1770. Located one block from the Battery, this handsome three-story clapboard is joined by an 1840

addition and is surrounded by a wrought iron garden fence. The inn is furnished in antiques.
Rates: $55-$75. All year.
Innkeeper(s): Ben Chapman.
4 Rooms. 4 Private Baths. Guest phone available. TV available. Beds: DT. Meals: Continental. Fireplaces. Tennis, golf, beach.
"A fantasy realized. What a wonderful gift of hospitality."

Historic Charleston B&B
43 Legare St
Charleston SC 29401
(803) 722-6606
  Circa 1713. Listings in this reservation service include flamboyant Victorian mansions, narrow "single houses", pre-Revolutionary carriage houses and rooms overlooking the Battery. The oldest home open to guests was built in 1713. Some hosts are from old Charleston families that go back several generations. Family heirlooms, period antiques and silver tea service are often featured.
Location: Historic district.
Rates: $65-$100. All year.
Innkeeper(s): Many.
65 Rooms. 65 Private Baths. Guest phone in room. TV in room. Beds: KQTC.

Meals: Full breakfast, continental plus. Jacuzzi. Fireplaces. Pool. CCs: Visa, MC, AE. Swimming, bicycling.
Seen in: *The New York Times, Southern Living*.

Kings Courtyard Inn
198 King St
Charleston SC 29401
(803) 723-7000 (800) 845-6119
  Circa 1853. Architect Francis D. Lee designed this three-story building in the Greek Revival style with unusual touches of Egyptian detail. As

Charleston's oldest structure originally built as an inn, it catered to plantation owners. The atmosphere has been authentically restored and some rooms have fireplaces, canopied beds, and views of the two inner courtyards or the garden.
Location: In the historic district.
**Rates: $80-$120. All year.
Innkeeper(s): Laura Fox.
34 Rooms. 34 Private Baths. Guest phone in room. TV in room. Beds: KQT. Meals: Continental plus. Jacuzzi. Handicap access provided. Conference room. Fireplaces. CCs: Visa, MC, AE. Shopping.

Laurel Hill Plantation
See: McClellanville

Rutledge Museum Guest House
114 Rutledge Ave
Charleston SC 29401
(803) 722-7551
  Circa 1810. This Victorian house is situated in the Charleston Historic District. Newly opened to guests, the rooms are decorated in a quaint, antique decor and all are air conditioned. The focal point of this bed and breakfast is a beautiful front porch.

Rates: $25-$35. All year.
Innkeeper(s): B.J., Lisa, Mike, Jean & Janifer.
11 Rooms. Guest phone available. TV in room. Beds: DW. Meals: Continental plus. Fireplaces.

Sword Gate Inn
111 Tradd St
Charleston SC 29401
(803) 723-8518
  Circa 1800. This stately three-story inn is framed by a cobbled courtyard filled with magnolia trees, jasmine and azalea bushes. The

elegantly appointed interiors make it easy to visualize formally attired guests passing through a reception line when the house served as the British consulate. There is a finely carved Italian Carrara marble fireplace and two enormous rococo Revival mirrors in the ballroom. Some of the guest rooms are furnished with canopied beds and have fireplaces.
Location: In the historic district.
Rates: $89-$125. All year.
Innkeeper(s): Walter & Amanda Barton.
6 Rooms. 6 Private Baths. Guest phone in room. TV in room. Beds: QD. Meals: Full breakfast. Wine & cheese. Conference room. Fireplaces. CCs: Visa, MC, AE. Bicycles, sailing, boating, fishing.
Seen in: *Cover inn for American Historic Inns. Business Week*.

Two Meeting Street Inn
2 Meeting St
Charleston SC 29401
(803) 723-7322
  Circa 1890. Located directly on the Battery, horses and carriages carry visitors past the inn, perhaps the most photographed in Charleston. In the Queen Anne style, this Victorian has an unusual veranda graced by several ornate arches. The

same family has owned and managed the inn since 1946 with no

lapse in gracious southern hospitality. Among the elegant amenities are original Tiffany stained-glass windows, English oak paneling and exquisite collections of silver and antiques.
Location: On the Battery.
Rates: $55-$110. All year.
Innkeeper(s): David S. Spell.
8 Rooms. 6 Private Baths. Guest phone available. TV available. Beds: QD. Meals: Continental. Fireplaces. Water sports, beaches, tennis.
Seen in: *Innsider, Southern Bride.*
   "A magnificent Queen Anne mansion." Southern Bride.

Vendue Inn
19 Vendue Range
Charleston SC 29401
(803) 577-7970 (800) 845-7900
   Circa 1824. Built as a warehouse in the French Quarter, the inn is one short block from the historic waterfront. The bright lobby features fans and wicker furniture, and latticework screens, leather chairs, and writing tables fill the reading room. Afternoon wine and cheese and turn-down service are special features.
Location: In the historic district and near city market.
**Rates: $80-$180. All year.
Innkeeper(s): Evelyn & Morton Needle.
34 Rooms. 34 Private Baths. Guest phone in room. TV in room. Beds: KQT. Jacuzzi. Fireplaces. CCs: Visa, MC, AE. Bicycles.
   "Delightful. Excellent service."

Columbia

Claussen's Inn
2003 Green St
Columbia SC 29205
(800) 622-3382

Circa 1928. The Claussen bakery building, a 25,000-square-foot brick building, has been renovated to accommodate 29 king-size guest rooms. The three-story atrium features skylights and a fountain. All the guest rooms contain traditional furnishings and some feature four-poster beds.
Location: In Five Points adjacent to the University.
**Rates: $62-$88. All year.
Innkeeper(s): Dan Vance.
29 Rooms. 29 Private Baths. Guest phone in room. TV in room. Beds: KQT. Meals: Continental. Jacuzzi. Handicap access provided. Conference room. CCs: Visa, MC, AE.

McClellanville

Laurel Hill Plantation
8913 N Hwy 17, PO Box 182
McClellanville SC 29458
(803) 887-3708
   Circa 1850. Laurel Hill, although not an opulent plantation, is a good example of a practical, low country

farmhouse. It was built by Richard Morrison a co-founder of the village of McClellanville. In 1983, Dr. and Mrs. Richard Leland Morrison, III moved Laurel Hill more than a mile to its present location overlooking Cape Romain's lush marshes. Country and primitive collections are featured throughout the house and there is an antique shop on the lowest level. The lawn slopes down to the dock where the good doctor keeps a boat and occasionally takes guests out onto the Intercoastal Waterway to view pelicans.
Location: Thirty minutes north of Charleston on Hwy 17.
**Rates: $35-$45. All year.
Innkeeper(s): Jackie and Lee Morrison.
4 Rooms. Guest phone available. TV available. Beds: DTC. Meals: Full break-

fast. Fireplaces. Boating, fresh water fish pond, crabbing in creek.
Seen in: *Country Living Magazine.*
   "Southern hospitality at its best plus the charm and dignity of the old republic."

Mt Pleasant

Guilds Inn
101 Pitt St
Mt Pleasant SC 29464
(803) 881-0510
   Circa 1888. The Guilds Inn is located six miles from Charleston in a building that was purchased by the

innkeeper's grandfather. The family businesses conducted here have included a hardware store and grocery. The house has been restored and appointed in 18th-century reproduction furnishings. Supper at Seven is the dining room, with gleaming mahogany tables, sterling silver, and gold-rimmed china. Each table has an old-fashioned bell pull.
**Rates: $70-$100. All year.
Innkeeper(s): Guilds & Joyce Hollowell.
6 Rooms. 6 Private Baths. Guest phone in room. TV available. Beds: QT. Meals: Full breakfast. Jacuzzi. Handicap access provided. Conference room. Bicycles, tennis, both free.
   "Supper at Seven is the most outstanding restaurant I have ever visited in South Carolina." Ruth Achermann, *Travelhost.*

Pendleton

Liberty Hall Inn
Pendleton SC 29670
(803) 646-7500
   Circa 1840. On four acres of woods, lawns and gardens, this house is noted for the two-story columned verandas that stretch across the front. An elegant foyer

with a polished staircase greets guests as they enter the inn. All the rooms are furnished with antiques and original art, and there are wide-pine floorboards throughout. The Pendleton Historic District is one of the largest in the National Register and a short stroll brings guests to the town square.

Location: In the historic district.
**Rates: $50-$65. All year.
Innkeeper(s): Tom & Susan Jonas.
8 Rooms. 8 Private Baths. Guest phone available. TV in room. Beds: KDT.

Meals: Continental plus, restaurant. Conference room. CCs: Visa, MC, AE.
Seen in: *Country Home.*

"Elegant surroundings and excellent food! Best job of innkeeping we've seen."

South Dakota

Canova

Bed & Breakfast at Skoglund Farm
Rt 1 Box 45
Canova SD 57321
(605) 247-3445

Circa 1927. Spend a night on the South Dakota prairie. Ostriches and peacocks stroll around the farm along with cattle, chickens and horses. Guests can enjoy an evening meal with the family.
Location: Southeast South Dakota.
**Rates: $25. All year.
Innkeeper(s): Alden & Delores.
6 Rooms. Guest phone available. TV available. Beds: QDT. Meals: Full breakfast. Horseback riding, buggy rides.
"Thanks for the down home hospitality, good food, and antiques."

Tennessee

Clarksville

Hachland Hill Inn
1601 Madison St
Clarksville TN 37040
(615) 255-1727

Circa 1805. This log cabin contains a dining room and, in a stone-walled chamber, a place where pioneers sought refuge during Indian attacks. Three of Clarksville's oldest log houses have been reconstructed in the garden where old-fashioned barbeque suppers and square dances are held. Newly built rooms are available in the brick building, so request the log cabin if you want authentic historic atmosphere.
Location: Near Nashville.
Rates: $55. All year.
Innkeeper(s): Joe Hach and Phila Hach.
20 Rooms. 10 Private Baths. Guest phone available. TV available. Beds: QD. Meals: Continental. Handicap access provided. Conference room. Fireplaces. Pool. Horseback riding.

Gatlinburg

Big Spring Inn
See: Greenville, TN

Buckhorn Inn
Rt 3 Box 393
Gatlinburg TN 37738
(615) 436-4668

Circa 1937. Set high on a hilltop, Buckhorn is surrounded by more than 30 acres of woodlands and green lawns. There are inspiring mountain views and a spring-fed lake on the grounds. Paintings by area artists enhance the antique-filled guest rooms, most with working fireplaces.
Location: One mile from the Great Smoky Mountains National Park.
Innkeeper(s): John & Connie Burns.

Greenville

Big Spring Inn
315 N Main St
Greenville TN 37743
(615) 638-2917

Circa 1905. This brick manor features huge porches, leaded and stained glass windows and a grand entrance hall. Original wallpaper remains in the dining room and there is a 1790 Hepplewhite table. Franklin, for three years the smallest state in the union, was formed here when local pioneers seceded from North Carolina.
Rates: $65-$88.
Innkeeper(s): Jeanne Driese & Cheryl Van Dyck.
5 Rooms. 3 Private Baths. TV available. Beds: KT. Meals: B&B. Conference room. Pool. CCs: Visa, MC.

Knoxville

The Graustein Inn
8300 Nubbin Ridge Rd
Knoxville TN 37923
(615) 690-7007

Circa 1975. This enchanting European chateau, nestled on 20 wooded acres at the end of a quarter-mile driveway, is a reproduction of an 1870 German inn. Old World craftsmen used historic building methods and materials including 200 tons of lime-stone to create this graystone estate. Tongue and groove walnut walls,

and a circular three-story central staircase are features of the inn. The Great Smoky Mountain National Park is 30 minutes away.
Location: Twenty minutes west of downtown.
**Rates: $49-$90.
Innkeeper(s): Darlene & Jim Lara, Vanessa Gwin.
5 Rooms. 3 Private Baths. Guest phone in room. TV available. Beds: QT. Meals: Gourmet breakfast. Conference room. Fireplaces. CCs: Visa, MC, AE.
Seen in: *Knoxville News.*
"Almost overwhelmingly wonderful." Vicki Davis, *Huntsville Times.*

Loudon

River Road Inn
River Rd
Loudon TN 37774
(615) 458-4861

Circa 1857. River Road Inn, a Federal-style home, is in the National Register. Furnished with antiques, the inn features a teakwood circular staircase that winds up three floors.

Extensive gardens provide additional enjoyment as well as a bushy screen for fishing.
Location: Thirty miles southwest of Knoxville.
**Rates: $50.
Innkeeper(s): Dan, Dave & Kaky Smith.
7 Rooms. 4 Private Baths. Guest phone available. TV available. Beds: QC. Meals: Full breakfast. CCs: Visa, MC.

Memphis

Lowenstein-Long House
217 N Waldran-1084 Poplar
Memphis TN 38105
(901) 527-7174
Circa 1901. Department store owner Abraham Lowenstein built this Victorian mansion and it later became the Beethoven Music Club. In the Forties it was a boarding house, the Elizabeth Club for Girls, in the days before young ladies lived in their own apartments.
Innkeeper(s): Martha & Charles Long.
5 Rooms. 5 Private Baths. Guest phone available. TV available. Beds: Q. Meals: Continental plus. Conference room. CCs: Visa, MC, AE.
"We found it just lovely and enjoyed our stay very much."

Nashville

Host Homes Of Tennessee
PO Box 110227

Nashville TN 37222-0227
(615) 331-5244
Circa 1880. This reservation service, coordinated by Fredda Odom, features several historic homes in Nashville. One accommodation, a reconstructed log house, is situated on a shaded lot eight miles from the city center. Another is an 1859 house located one block from the Convention Center.
Rates: $75.
4 Rooms. Beds: DT. Meals: Continental. CCs: Visa, MC, AE.

Rogersville

Hale Springs Inn
110 W Main St
Rogersville TN 37857
(615) 272-5171
Circa 1824. On the town square, this is the oldest continually operat-

ing inn in the state. Presidents Andrew Jackson, James Polk, and Andrew Johnson stayed here. McKinney Tavern, as it was known

then, was Union headquarters during the Civil War. Canopy beds, working fireplaces, and an evening meal by candlelight in the elegant dining room all make for a romantic stay.
Location: Near Gatlinburg.
Innkeeper(s): Stan & Kim Pace.
10 Rooms. 10 Private Baths. Meals: Continental breakfast, restaurant. CCs: Visa, MC, AE.

Rugby

Newbury House at Historic Rugby
Hwy 52, PO Box 8
Rugby TN 37733
(615) 628-2441
Circa 1880. Mansard-roofed Newbury House first lodged visitors to this English village when author and social reformer Thomas Huges, founded Rugby. Filled with authentic Victorian antiques, the inn includes some furnishings that are original to the colony. There is also a restored three-bedroom cottage on the property.
Rates: $56. All year.
Innkeeper(s): Historic Rugby.
5 Rooms. 3 Private Baths. Guest phone available. Beds: D. Meals: Restaurant, evening tea. Conference room. Hiking, white water rafting, canoeing.
Seen in: *The Tennessean.*

Texas

Austin

Southard House
908 Blanco
Austin TX 78703
(512) 474-4731
 Circa 1900. This house, an Austin historic landmark, originally had a single story but was raised to accommodate an additional level at the turn of the century. There is an upper and lower parlor and 11-foot ceilings provide a background for antiques and paintings. A gazebo, porch and deck are popular spots. The University of Texas and the capitol are a mile and a half from the house.
Location: Downtown.
Rates: $49-$98.
Innkeeper(s): The Southards.
5 Rooms. 5 Private Baths. Guest phone available. TV available. Beds: QD. Meals: Continental plus. CCs: All.
 "A memory to be long cherished. We especially enjoyed the home atmosphere and the lovely breakfasts in the garden."

Big Sandy

Annie's Bed & Breakfast
106 N Tyler
Big Sandy TX 75755
(214) 636-4307
 Circa 1901. Annie's Attic, a well-known craft and pattern company, renovated this Victorian house, creating a showplace for fine antiques, imported rugs, outstanding handmade quilts and stitchery items. The inn is surrounded by a white picket fence and detailed gingerbread decorates the porches and balconies.
Location: Ten miles from I-20 in northeast Texas.
Rates: $38-$100.
Innkeeper(s): Les & Martha Lane.
13 Rooms. 8 Private Baths. Guest phone available. Meals: Full breakfast all days but Sat. Handicap access provided. CCs: Visa, MC, AE.

Dallas

Bed & Breakfast Texas Style, RSO
4224 W Red Bird Lane
Dallas TX 75237
(214) 298-8586
 The only state-wide bed and breakfast reservation service in Texas, this agency features more than 100 inspected and approved homes throughout the state. One home in Dallas, for instance, is a large, 1920 red brick, prairie style home in an area of restored mansions. Its three floors include a music room and an upstairs sunroom. A historic marker notes its significance.
Rates: $35-$85.
 Meals: Continental to full Texas spread. Each host home is individual and has special features.
Seen in: *Southern Bride.*

El Paso

Room with a View
821 Rim Rd
El Paso TX 79902
(915) 534-4400
 Circa 1929. This traditional Spanish-style mansion was built by architect William Wuehrmann who worked under the influence of Frank Lloyd Wright. The home provides views of two countries, three states and two cities. There is a parlor and library where afternoon tea is served.
Rates: $60-$85.
3 Rooms. 3 Private Baths. Guest phone available. TV available. Meals: Full breakfast. Pool.

Fort Worth

Medford House
2344 Medford Court East
Fort Worth TX 76109
(817) 924-2765
 Circa 1926. This English Tudor house was built for Texas oilman J. C. Maxwell. It is situated on top of a hill overlooking the park that surrounds the neighborhood. Art deco furnishings have been selected for the carriage apartment which is a non-smoking accommodation. Guests can walk to Log Cabin Village or Texas Christian University.
Location: Walled-in historic neighborhood.
Rates: $50.
Innkeeper(s): Maribeth Ashley.
1 Rooms. 1 Private Baths. Meals: Continental. Pool.

Fredericksburg

Country Cottage Inn
405 E Main St
Fredericksburg TX 78624
(512) 997-8549

Circa 1850. This house was built by blacksmith and cutler Friedrick

Kiehner. With two-foot-thick walls, it was the first two-story limestone house in town, and an outstanding example of the Fredericksburg "Sunday House." (Local farmers, mostly German, came to town for Saturday market day, and rather than go back home and return to church Sunday, they built small houses in town.) The Country Cottage holds a collection of Texas primitives and German country antiques, accentuated by Laura Ashley linens. Some of the baths include whirlpool tubs.
**Rates: $60-$85. All year.
Innkeeper(s): Jeff Webb, Jean & Mike Sudderth.
5 Rooms. 5 Private Baths. Guest phone available. TV in room. Beds: K. Meals: Full breakfast. Jacuzzi. Fireplaces. CCs: Visa, MC. Front porch swings.
Seen in: *Weekend Getaway.*
"Too good to be true! Heaven on earth."

Galveston

Dickens Loft
2021 The Strand
Galveston TX 77550
(409) 762-1653

Circa 1856. This former warehouse is constructed partially of Boston red brick which was found in some of Galveston's old ships. There are antiques and Turkish rugs. The inn is in the Strand Historic District.
Rates: $65-$150.
5 Rooms. Meals: Continental breakfast. Afternoon tea.

Houston

Sara's Bed & Breakfast Inn
941 Heights Boulevard
Houston TX 77008
(713) 868-1130

Circa 1900. This mauve and white, gingerbread Victorian is located in the Houston Heights, one of the first planned suburbs in Texas. A three-story stairway winds up to a cupola and there are handsome bay windows and a turret. Antiques fill the rooms, named after Texas cities.
Location: Four miles from downtown.
Rates: $46-$96.
Innkeeper(s): Donna & Tillman Arledge.
12 Rooms. 2 Private Baths. Beds: KQDT. Meals: Continental breakfast. Jacuzzi. CCs: All.
Seen in: *Houston Chronicle.*

Jefferson

Hotel Jefferson Historic Inn
124 W Austin
Jefferson TX 75657
(214) 665-2631

Circa 1851. This building was originally a cotton warehouse and was on the riverfront when Jefferson

was an inland port. Many Victorian homes and antique shops, museums and restaurants are nearby.
Rates: $45-$75.
23 Rooms. 23 Private Baths. Beds: KQ. Meals: EP. Handicap access provided. CCs: Visa, MC.

Pride House
409 Broadway
Jefferson TX 75657
(214) 665-2675

Circa 1888. Mr. Brown, a sawmill owner built this Victorian house using fine hardwoods, sometimes three layers deep. The windows are nine-feet tall on both the lower level and upstairs. The rooms are homey and comfortable and a wide veran-

da stretches around two sides of the house.
Rates: $75.
Innkeeper(s): Ruthmary Jordan.
8 Rooms. 8 Private Baths. Meals: Continental-plus breakfast. CCs: Visa, MC.

Navasota

The Castle
1403 E Washington
Navasota TX 77868
(409) 825-8051

Circa 1900. This Queen Anne Victorian boasts many bays, gables and turrets. The stained-glass windows had to be replaced after being destroyed by a storm in 1900. The guest rooms feature antique beds and other Victorian furnishings. Wine and cheese is served in the evening.
Location: Seventy miles north of Houston.
Rates: $75.
Innkeeper(s): Helen & Tim Urquhart.
4 Rooms. 4 Private Baths. Guest phone available. Beds: D. Meals: Continental breakast.
Seen in: *Southern Living, The Eyes of Texas.*

San Antonio

Country Cottage Inn
See: Fredericksburg, TX

The Bullis House Inn
PO Box 8059, 621 Pierce St
San Antonio TX 78208
(512) 223-9426

Circa 1906. A two-story portico supported by six massive columns accentuates the neo-classical architecture of this home built for General Bullis who was instrumental in the capture of Chief Geronimo. Features include stairways and paneling of dark oak and mahogany, marble fireplaces and parquet floors. There are contemporary and antique furnishings.
Rates: $36-$55.
8 Rooms. 1 Private Baths. Beds: DT.

Stephenville

The Oxford House
563 N Graham
Stephenville TX 76401
(817) 965-6885 (817)968-8171.

Circa 1898. A $3,000 lawyer's fee provided funds for construction of the Oxford House, and the silver

was brought to town in a buckboard by W. J. Oxford, Esq. The house was built of cypress with porches three-quarters of the way around. Hand-turned gingerbread trim and a carved wooden ridgerow are special features.
Rates: $60-$80.
Innkeeper(s): Paula & Bill Oxford.

Utah

Cedar City

Woodbury Guest House
237 S 300 W
Cedar City UT 84720
(801) 586-6696

Circa 1898. Roses line a driveway winding through a spacious lawn to this Victorian house. If you're not attending the Shakespeare Festival, there are other activities such as a drive to Dixie National Forest, Cedar Breaks National Monument or Brian Head Ski Resort. Excursions to Zion and Bryce National Parks are popular.
Location: Three-minute walk from the Utah Shakespeare Festival.
Rates: $45-$65. All year.
Innkeeper(s): Ben & Stephanie Whitney.
4 Rooms. 4 Private Baths. Meals: Full breakfast. CCs: Visa, MC. Near Zion and Bryce National Parks.

Midway

The Homestead
700 N Homestead Dr.
Midway UT 84049
(801) 654-1102

Circa 1886. Originally Simon Schneitter built this two-story brick house for his parents and the family soon began taking in guests when travelers began to appreciate the site's mineral springs. In the Fifties it was redeveloped as the Homestead. The Virginia House is the most historic part of the lodge.
**Rates: $59-$150.
Innkeeper(s): Jerry & Carole Sanders.
43 Rooms. 43 Private Baths. Guest phone in room. TV available. Beds: KQDT. Meals: EP. Jacuzzi. Sauna. Conference room. Fireplaces. Pool. CCs: Visa, MC, AE. Tennis, horseback riding, cross-country skiing, sleigh & hay rides. Kid camp.
Seen in: *Express-News*.
"The Homestead is the most romantic place Nicole and I have ever been."

Park City

505 Woodside
Box 2446
Park City UT 84060
(801) 649-4841

Circa 1929. This restored miner's bungalow in a historic mining town is one block from Main Street. It is

furnished beautifully in a mixture of styles. The inn is open from December 15 to April 15 and again from July 1 to October 31.
Location: Historic Old Town.
Rates: $55-$75. Seasonal.
Innkeeper(s): Carroll Horton.
3 Rooms. 3 Private Baths. Guest phone in room. TV in room. Beds: KQT. Meals: Full breakfast, afternoon tea. Jacuzzi. Fireplaces. CCs: Visa, MC. Helicopter skiing. Health club, restaurants nearby.
"Great breakfast, cheery atmosphere, charming wonderful hostess. We'll be back."

The Old Miner's Lodge, A B&B Inn
615 Woodside Ave, PO Box 2639
Park City UT 84060-2639
(801) 645-8068

Circa 1893. This was originally established as a miners' boarding house by E. P. Fetzay, owner of the Woodside-Norfolk silver mines. A

two-story Victorian with a western flavor, the lodge is a significant structure in the Park City National Historic District. Just on the edge of the woods beyond the house is a deck and a steaming hot tub.
Location: In the historic district.
**Rates: $40-$155. All year.
Innkeeper(s): Jeff Sadowsky, Susan Wynne & Hugh Daniels.
7 Rooms. 4 Private Baths. Guest phone available. Beds: KQT. Meals: Full breakfast. Jacuzzi. Conference room. Fireplaces. CCs: Visa, MC, AE, DS. Downhill & cross-country skiing, golf, tennis, ice skating, hiking
Seen in: *Boston Herald, Los Angeles Times*.
"This is the creme de la creme. The most wonderful place I have stayed at bar none including ski country in the U.S. and Europe."

Washington School Inn
544 Park Ave, PO Box 536
Park City UT 84060
(801) 649-3800

Circa 1889. This inn made of local limestone, was the former school house for Park City children. With its classic belltower, the four-story building is listed in the National Register. Luxuriously appointed guest rooms feature sitting areas and many have fireplaces. An inviting jacuzzi and sauna are on the property.
Location: Park City Historic District.
**Rates: $75-$225.
Innkeeper(s): Faye Evans & Delphine Covington.
15 Rooms. 15 Private Baths. Guest phone available. Meals: Full breakfast. Jacuzzi. Sauna. CCs: Visa, MC, AE.

Salt Lake City

Brigham Street Inn
1135 E South Temple
Salt Lake City UT 84102
(801) 364-4461

Circa 1896. This turreted Victorian is one of many historic mansions that dot South Temple Street

(formerly Brigham Street). The formal dining room features golden oak woodwork and a fireplace. With skylights, fireplaces or perhaps a jacuzzi, each of the nine rooms was created by a different designer for a showcase benefit for the Utah Heritage Foundation. The American Institute of Architects and several historic associations have presented the inn with architectural awards.

The inn also holds a Triple A four-diamond award.
**Rates: $65-$140. All year.
Innkeeper(s): Nancy & John Pace.
9 Rooms. 9 Private Baths. Guest phone in room. TV in room. Beds: QWC. Meals: Continental plus. Jacuzzi. Fireplaces. CCs: Visa, MC, AE. 40 minutes from 5 major ski areas.
Seen in: *Triple A four diamond award.*
"Your managers, pleasant, courteous, and helpful, uphold the high standards exemplified throughout your elegantly designed inn."

The Spruces B&B
6151 S 900 E
Salt Lake City UT 84121
(801) 268-8762

Circa 1903. This Gothic Victorian was built as a residence for cabinet-maker Martin Gunnerson and his

family. It is set amidst 16 tall spruce trees transplanted in 1915 from Big Cottonwood Canyon. The house is decorated with folk art and southwestern touches. The Cellar Suite includes a hydrobath and children enjoy its fruit cellar bedroom. A quarter horse breeding farm is adjacent.
**Rates: $40-$80. All year.
Innkeeper(s): Glen & Lisa Dutton.
7 Rooms. 4 Private Baths. Guest phone in room. TV in room. Beds: QDT. Meals: Continental plus. Jacuzzi. Conference room. CCs: Visa, MC. Skiing.
"We have never had a more peaceful, serene business trip. Thank you for your hospitality."

St George

Green Gate Village Historic B&B Inn
62-78 W Tabernacle

St George UT 84770
(801) 628-6999

Circa 1872. This is a cluster of four restored pioneer homes all located within one block. The Bentley House has an elegant Victorian decor while the Supply Depot is decorated in a style reflective of its origin as a shop for wagoners on their way to California. The Orson Pratt house and the Carriage House are other choices, all carefully restored.
16 Rooms. 14 Private Baths. Guest phone in room. TV in room. Beds: QTW. Meals: EP, gourmet extra. Jacuzzi. Conference room. Fireplaces. Pool. CCs: MC, AE. Tennis.
"You not only provided me with rest, comfort and wonderful food, but you fed my soul."

Seven Wives Inn
217 N 100 W
St George UT 84770
(801) 628-3737

Circa 1873. The inn is named after the innkeeper's great-grandfather Benjamin Johnson who served Joseph Smith, founder of the Mormon Church, as private secretary. Mr. Johnson had seven wives. The Melisssa room was named after his first wife and it features a fireplace and an oak-rimmed tin bathtub. The attic of the house, concealed by a secret door, is thought to have been a refuge for polygamists. It is now the Jane room and has a skylight and stenciling.
**Rates: $25-$65. All year.
Innkeeper(s): Donna & Jay Curtis; Alison & Jon Bowcutt.
15 Rooms. 15 Private Baths. Guest phone available. TV in room. Beds: QTC. Meals: Full breakfast. Jacuzzi. Handicap access provided. Conference room. Fireplaces. Pool. CCs: Visa, MC, DS. Golf, horseback riding. , tennis.
Seen in: *Salt Lake Tribune.*
"This was great! We want to return."

Vermont

Arlington

Hill Farm Inn
RR 2 Box 2015
Arlington VT 05250
(802) 375-2269

Circa 1790. One of Vermont's original land grant farmsteads, Hill Farm Inn has welcomed guests since

1905 when the widow Mettie Hill opened her home to summer vacationers. One section of the house was hauled by 40 yoke of oxen to its present location. The farm has recently benefited from a community conservancy group's efforts to save it from subdivision.
Location: One half mile from Historic Route 7A.
**Rates: $41-$52. All year.
Innkeeper(s): George & Joanne Hardy.
13 Rooms. 7 Private Baths. Guest phone available. TV available. Beds: KQTC. Meals: Full breakfast. CCs: Visa, MC, AE. Downhill and cross-country skiing, hiking, fishing, bicycles.
Seen in: *Providence Journal.*
"A superb location with lots to do indoors and out. Beautifully kept rooms and excellent home cooking."

Shenandoah Farm
Rt 313, Battenkill Rd
Arlington VT 05250
(802) 375-6372

Circa 1820. This old colonial has maintained a homey atmosphere

since the time it was a road house in 1930. Just across the front meadow

is the Battenkill River. The inn is furnished with colonial furniture and lovely antiques.
**Rates: $55-$65. March to July.
Innkeeper(s): Woody & Diana Masterson.
5 Rooms. 3 Private Baths. Guest phone available. TV in room. Beds: QTC. Meals: Full breakfast. Fireplaces. Skiing, golf, tennis, swimming, fishing, canoeing, tubing.
"A gracious home away from home."

The Arlington Inn
Historic Rt 7A
Arlington VT 05250
(802) 375-6532

Circa 1848. The Arlington Inn is one of Vermont's finest examples of

Greek Revival architecture. Set on lushly landscaped grounds, the inn boasts elegantly appointed guest rooms filled with period antiques. Norman Rockwell once used the carriage house as a studio.
Location: Intersection of Route 313.
**Rates: $58-$125. All year.
Innkeeper(s): Paul & Madeline Kruzel.

13 Rooms. 13 Private Baths. Guest phone available. TV available. Beds: DTC. Meals: Full breakfast, continental plus. Conference room. Fireplaces. CCs: Visa, MC, AE. Skiing, hiking, biking, canoeing.
Seen in: *New York, Bon Appetit.*
"What a romantic place and such outrageous food!!"

Barre

Woodruff House
13 East St
Barre VT 05641
(802) 476-7745

Circa 1883. This blue Queen Anne Victorian with cranberry shutters

was built by an area granite manufacturer. (Barre is the Granite Center of the World and has the world's largest granite quarries.) The Woodruff House has an eclectic atmosphere and friendly family.
Location: Halfway between Boston & Montreal.
Rates: $35-$45.
Innkeeper(s): Robert & Terry Somani.
2 Rooms. 1 Private Baths. Guest phone available. TV available. Beds: DT. Meals: Full breakfast.
"Friendly and warm. Like going home to Grandma's."

Belmont

The Parmenter House
Church St
Belmont VT 05730
(802) 259-2009

Circa 1874. This 12-room Victorian was the home of three generations of Parmenters. The living room is

decorated in the Eastlake style with paintings and screens by Alfred Rasmussen, grandfather of the hostess. Her mother carved the walnut dining room set and her uncles painted the trunk in which her grandmother brought her belongings from Denmark.
Rates: $65-$80. All year.
Innkeeper(s): Lester & Cynthia Firschein.
4 Rooms. 4 Private Baths. Guest phone available. Meals: B&B. CCs: Visa, MC.
It's the prettiest inn I've ever seen."

Bennington

The Arlington Inn
See: Arlington, VT

Bethel

Greenhurst Inn
River St
Bethel VT 05032
(802) 234-9474

Circa 1890. Greenhurst is a gracious Victorian mansion built for the

Harringtons of Philadelphia. Overlooking the White River, the inn's

opulent interiors include etched windows once featured on the cover of *Vermont Life*. There are eight masterpiece fireplaces and a north and south parlor.
Location: Route 107, 3 miles west of I-89.
**Rates: $40-$80. All year.
Innkeeper(s): Lyle & Claire Wolf.
13 Rooms. 7 Private Baths. Guest phone available. TV available. Beds: QTCD. Meals: Full breakfast, continental plus. Conference room. Fireplaces. CCs: Visa, MC. Tennis, horseback riding, fishing, hiking, biking, canoeing.
Seen in: *Los Angeles Times*.
"The inn is magnificent! The hospitality unforgettable."

Brandon

Beauchamp Place
31 Franklin St, US Rt 7
Brandon VT 05733
(802) 247-3905

Circa 1830. This elegant Victorian is a magnificently restored Second Empire mansard-style mansion. The

owner designed the metal ceilings and had them cast from original dies in Missouri. The inn is filled with Victorian and Second Empire furnishings and is in the National Register.
Location: Three hours from Albany.
Rates: $70-$85. All year.
Innkeeper(s): Georgia & Roy Beauchamp.
8 Rooms. Guest phone available. TV available. Beds: KQT. Meals: Full breakfast. CCs: Visa, AE. Tennis, bicycling, golf, hiking, skiing.
Seen in: *The Valley Voice*.

The Churchill House Inn
Rt 73 East
Brandon VT 05733
(802) 247-3300

Circa 1871. Caleb Churchill and his son Nathan first built a three-story lumber mill, a grist mill and a distillery here, all water powered.

Later, with their milled lumber, they constructed this 20-room house. Because of its location it became a stagecoach stop and has served generations of travelers with comfortable accommodations.
Location: Four miles east of Brandon.
Innkeeper(s): Roy & Lois Jackson.
9 Rooms. Guest phone available. Meals: MAP. Jacuzzi. Sauna. Pool. CCs: Visa, MC. Hiking, cross-country skiing.
"We felt the warm, welcoming, down-home appeal as we entered the front hall. The food was uncommonly good - home cooking with a gourmet flair!"

Brattleboro

Windham Hill Inn
See: West Townsend, VT

Brownsville

Mill Brook B&B
PO Box 410, Rte 44
Brownsville VT 05037
(802) 484-7283

Circa 1850. Once known as the House of Seven Gables, Mill Brook has been in constant use as a family home and for a while, a boarding house for mill loggers. Old German Fraktur paintings decorate the woodwork and there are three sitting rooms for guests. Antique furnishings are found throughout. Popular activities in the area include hang gliding, bike tours and canoeing.
Location: Fourteen miles from Woodstock, seven from Windsor.
**Rates: $40-$65.
Innkeeper(s): K. Carriere.
8 Rooms. 3 Private Baths. Guest phone available. TV available. Beds: QT. Meals: Gourmet breakfast. CCs: Visa, MC. Lawn games, hammock, fishing on premises. nearby horseback riding. Midweek specials. Afternoon tea.
"Splendid hospitality. Your B&B was beyond our expectation."

Burlington

Beaver Pond Farm Inn
See: Warren, VT

Mad River Barn
See: Waitsfield, VT

Strong House Inn
See: Vergennes, VT

Swift House Inn
See: Middlebury, VT

The Inn at Thatcher Brook Falls
See: Waterbury, VT

Chelsea

Shire Inn
PO Box 37
Chelsea VT 05038
(802) 685-3031
Circa 1832. This handsome Federal home is highlighted by massive

granite lintels over each window and the front door. Accentuated with a picket fence, the inn is on 17 acres of woods and fields, and a stream from the White River flows on the property. Wide-plank flooring is a fine backdrop for a collection of antiques and fireplaces.
Rates: $65-$95. All year.
Innkeeper(s): James & Mary Lee Papa.
6 Rooms. 6 Private Baths. Guest phone available. Beds: KD. Meals: Full breakfast, gourmet extra. Fireplaces. Swimming, bicycling, hiking, fishing, cross-country skiing.
Seen in: *Country Inn Review.*
"Max and I really enjoyed our stay in your wonderful inn and the meals were great."

Chester

Chester House
Box 708
Chester VT 05143
(802) 875-2205
Circa 1780. This Federal-style clapboard house situated on the village green has housed a variety of

enterprises including a hardware store and a millinery shop here.
Rates: $35-$70. All year.
Innkeeper(s): Irene & Norm Wright.
4 Rooms. 4 Private Baths. Guest phone available. TV available. Beds: KQTD. Meals: Full breakfast. Jacuzzi. Conference room. Fireplaces. Downhill & cross-country skiing, bicycling, hiking.
"The best hosts and the greatest of inns."

Henry Farm Inn
PO Box 646
Chester VT 05143
(802) 875-2674
Circa 1750. Fifty acres of scenic woodlands provide the setting for this handsomely restored stagecoach stop in the Green Mountains. There are original wide pine floors, eight fireplaces, and carefully selected early American furnishings. A pond and river are nearby.
Rates: $60-$70. All year.
Innkeeper(s): Jean Bowman.
7 Rooms. 7 Private Baths. Guest phone available. TV available. Beds: TW. Meals: Full breakfast. Fireplaces. CCs: Visa, MC, AE. Skating, antiquing, horseback riding, and skiing.

Old Town Farm Inn
See: Gassets, VT

The Inn at Long Last
PO Box 589
Chester VT 05143
(802) 875-2444
Circa 1923. Located on the green, this renovated inn reflects the personality of the owner Jack Coleman, former college president and author. Fulfilling a dream, he has created an inn for all seasons with fine cuisine and civilized surroundings. A library, tennis

courts, fishing stream, and personally designed guest rooms contribute to the atmosphere.
**Rates: $75-$95. All year.
Innkeeper(s): Jack Coleman.
30 Rooms. 28 Private Baths. Guest phone available. TV available. Beds: QTC. Meals: MAP, restaurant. Conference room. Fireplaces. Pool. CCs: Visa, MC, AE. Skiing, golf, hiking.
Seen in: *New York Times, Philadelphia Inquirer, Connoisseur.*
"For ambience and food combined, I would choose the...Inn at Long Last in Chester (the rooms also look lovely)." Carol Binzler, *Vogue*

The Stone Hearth Inn
Rt 11 West
Chester VT 05143
(802) 875-2525
Circa 1810. Exposed beams, wide-pine floors and Vermont stone

fireplaces are features of this restored country inn near Chester's historic Stone Village. Guests can relax in the parlor, library or attached barn that has been converted into a comfortable common room with a fieldstone fireplace. There is a fully stocked pub on the property.
Location: One mile west of Chester.
**Rates: $24-$66. All year.
Innkeeper(s): Janet & Don Strohmeyer.
10 Rooms. 8 Private Baths. Guest phone available. TV available. Beds: KQTC. Meals: Full breakfast, restaurant. Jacuzzi. Conference room. Fireplaces. CCs: Visa, MC, AE, DS. Bicycling, swimming, tennis, golf, fishing, skiing, snowmobiling.
"We love coming here and last time we brought the whole family. Good times, memories and friends were made here."

Chittenden

Mountain Top Inn
Box 493, Mountain Top Rd
Chittenden VT 05737
(800) 445-2100
Circa 1880. This secluded inn is situated in the Green Mountains of

Central Vermont and affords a spectacular view of the lake and surrounding mountains. Room selections include a few cottages with fireplaces or rooms with a view.

Location: Ten miles northeast of Rutland.
**Rates: $144-$935. All year.
Innkeeper(s): William P. Wolfe.
33 Rooms. 33 Private Baths. Guest phone in room. TV available. Beds: KQT. Meals: MAP. Jacuzzi. Sauna. Handicap access provided. Conference room. Fireplaces. Pool. CCs: Visa, MC, AE. Swimming, sailing, fishing, tennis, golf, cross-country skiing.

"*Twenty years ago we spent a very enjoyable week here with our daughter. The inn, the service and atmosphere were superior at that time and we are glad to report that it hasn't changed.*"

Tulip Tree Inn
Chittenden Dam Rd
Chittenden VT 05737
(802) 483-6213

Circa 1842. Thomas Edison was a regular guest here when the house was the country home of William

Barstow. The inn is surrounded by the Green Mountains on three sides with a stream flowing a few yards away. The guest rooms feature an antique decor.
**Rates: $60-$100. All year.
Innkeeper(s): Ed & Rosemary McDowell.
8 Rooms. 8 Private Baths. Guest phone available. Beds: QT. Meals: MAP. Jacuzzi. Fireplaces. CCs: Visa, MC. Hiking, bicycling, skiing, horseback riding.
Seen in: *New England Getaways.*
"*We had such a terrific time!*"

Craftsbury Common

Inn On The Common
Main St
Craftsbury Common VT 05827
(802) 586-9619

Circa 1795. Craftsbury Common is a classic Vermont village and the Inn On the Common, built by the Wil-

liam French family, is an integral part of this picturesque town. With its white picket fence and graceful white clapboard exterior the inn provides a quietly elegant retreat. Pastoral views are framed by the inn's famous perennial gardens.
Rates: $80-$95. All year.
Innkeeper(s): Michael & Penny Schmitt.
18 Rooms. 18 Private Baths. Guest phone available. TV available. Beds: QTC. Meals: MAP. Conference room. Fireplaces. Pool. CCs: Visa, MC. Tennis, hiking, croquet, golf.
Seen in: *The New York Times, Craftsbury Common.*

"*The closest my wife and I came to fulfilling our fantasy of a country inn was at the Inn on the Common.*" Paul Grimes, *In Search of the Perfect Vermont Inn, New York Times.*

Danby

Silas Griffith Inn
RR 1 Box 66F, S Main St
Danby VT 05739
(802) 293-5567

Circa 1891. Originally on 55,000 acres, this stately Queen Anne Vic-

torian mansion features solid cherry, oak, and birdseye maple woodwork. Considered an architechural marvel, an eight-foot round solid cherry

pocket door separates the original music room from the front parlor.
**Rates: $65-$75. All year.
Innkeeper(s): Paul & Lois Dansereau.
17 Rooms. 11 Private Baths. Guest phone available. TV available. Beds: QT. Meals: EP, restaurant. Conference room. Fireplaces. Pool. CCs: Visa, MC, AE. Hiking, bicycling, skiing.
Seen in: *The Vermont Weathervane, Rutland Business Journal.*

"*The warm welcome of antiques and beautiful country surroundings made the inn an ideal place.*"

Dorset

Cornucopia Of Dorset
Rt 30 Box 307
Dorset VT 05251
(802) 867-5751

Circa 1800. The newly renovated Cornucopia is a comely 19th century colonial set on a peaceful green lawn. All the inn's guest rooms have poster or canopy beds. A handsome cottage tucked in the trees has its own living room with fireplace and cathedral ceiling. Dorset summer theater is a five minute walk.
Rates: $90-$145. All year.
Innkeeper(s): Bill & Linda Ley.
5 Rooms. 5 Private Baths. Guest phone available. TV available. Beds: KQT. Meals: Full breakfast. Fireplaces. CCs: Visa, MC. Skiing, hiking, swimming, biking, tennis.

The Little Lodge at Dorset
Rt 30 Box 673
Dorset VT 05251
(802) 867-4040

Circa 1810. The Little Lodge at Dorset forms the northern boundary

of Dorset's historic district. The inn was built 16 miles away and was disassembled, moved and reassembled on a foundation of Dorset marble 60 years ago. Nestled against a backdrop of stately trees, the inn overlooks green lawns, a trout pond, and golf course.
Rates: $80-$90.
5 Rooms. 5 Private Baths. Guest phone available. TV available. Beds: KTC.

Meals: B&B. Handicap access provided. Fireplaces. CCs: AE.

"All my search for the perfect bed & breakfast paid off!"

East Middlebury

The Waybury Inn
Route 125
East Middlebury VT 05740
(802) 388-4015

Circa 1810. This is the famous Bob Newhart inn featured in the TV series. (And yes, Larry, Darryl and his brother Darryl have stayed here.) In continuous operation for more than 150 years, it was originally built as a stagecoach stop and tavern and there remains a fully licensed pub on the premises. Nearby is the local swimming hole, a natural gorge in a rocky river.
Rates: $100-$115.
Innkeeper(s): Kimberly Smith.
14 Rooms. 14 Private Baths. TV available. Beds: KQD. Meals: Full breakfast. CCs: Visa, MC.

Fair Haven

Maplewood Inn
Rt 22A, South
Fair Haven VT 05743
(802) 265-8039

Circa 1850. Maplewood is a classic Greek Revival with a gable and

detailed cornice over the front door. The porch wing is thought to have been a tavern once located down the road. Overlooking three acres of lawn, garden, and stream, the inn offers an idyllic setting.
Location: One mile south of Fair Haven village.
Rates: $60-$95. All year.
Innkeeper(s): Cindy & Paul Soder.
5 Rooms. 3 Private Baths. Guest phone available. TV available. Beds: QD. Meals: Full breakfast. Fireplaces. CCs: Visa, MC. Horseback riding, skiing, boating, waterskiing.

"Your inn is perfection. Leaving under protest."

Gassets

Old Town Farm Inn
Rt 10
Gassets VT 05143
(802) 875-2346

Circa 1861. This comfortable New England inn with its elegant spiral staircase was called the Town Farm

because anyone who needed food and lodging were provided for, in return for a day's work on the farm. The inn has a pond and features vegetables from its own garden. Maple syrup taken from the surrounding trees is served and the family sells its popular Country Inn Spring Water in Boston.
Rates: $45-50. All year.
Innkeeper(s): Ruth F. Lewis.
10 Rooms. 2 Private Baths. Guest phone available. TV available. Beds: QTC. Meals: EP, Full breakfast. CCs: Visa, MC, AE. Skiing, hunting, fishing, hiking, golf, swimming, horses.

"A warm haven! Very friendly and comfortable."

Gaysville

Cobble House Inn
PO Box 49
Gaysville VT 05746
(802) 234-5458

Circa 1864. This Victorian mansion is one of the grandest houses

around and commands a breathtaking view of the Green Mountains.

The White River flows just below the inn enticing the sporting set to fish for salmon and trout. Canoeing and tubing are popular also.
**Rates: $65-$95. All year.
Innkeeper(s): Beau, Phil & Sam Benson.
6 Rooms. 6 Private Baths. Guest phone available. Beds: QF. Meals: Full breakfast, restaurant. Fireplaces. CCs: Visa, MC. Cross-country skiing, swimming, fishing.

"My favorite place!"

Goshen

Blueberry Hill Inn
RD 3
Goshen VT 05733
(802) 247-6735

Circa 1813. Originally built for loggers this colonial clapboard inn has operated full-time since 1940. The *Blueberry Hill Cookbook* was written by a previous owner in the 1940s and the current English innkeeper is known for *"involving guests in things only mad dogs and Englishmen might ordinarily consider." Chicago Tribune,* Andrew Nemethy.
Location: On the Goshen-Ripton Road.
Rates: $68-$95 pp.
Innkeeper(s): Tony Clark.
12 Rooms. 12 Private Baths. Guest phone available. Beds: QD. Meals: MAP. Sauna. Handicap access provided. Conference room. Fireplaces. CCs: Visa, MC. Cross-country, skiing, hiking.
Seen in: *Ski-XC, Chicago Tribune, Better Homes and Gardens, Self.*

Killington

Inn at Long Trail
Rt 4 Box 267
Killington VT 05751
(802) 775-7181

Circa 1939. The inn was the first ski lodge in Vermont. It has a pub

with a 22-foot log bar and an enormous boulder incorporated into the decor. The lobby features sofas and tables constructed from tree trunks. Most of the rooms are decorated in a country style and there are several fireplace suites.

Location: Nine miles east of Rutland.
**Rates: $26-$36. June to Sept.
Innkeeper(s): Kyran & Rosemary McGrath.
20 Rooms. 20 Private Baths. Guest phone available. TV available. Beds: QT. Meals: Full breakfast, MAP, restaurant. Jacuzzi. Fireplaces. CCs: Visa, MC. Skiing, hiking, golf, tennis, swimming.
Seen in: *The Mountain Times.*

"We enjoyed our honeymoon for five days at the inn and we loved your Guiness stew after a cold, snowy day."

Salt Ash Inn
See: Plymouth, VT

The Silver Fox Inn
See: West Rutland, VT

The Vermont Inn
Rt 4
Killington VT 05751
(802) 775-0708 (800)541-7795
  Circa 1840. Surrounded by mountain views, this rambling red and

white farmhouse has provided lodging for many years. Exposed beams add to the atmosphere in the living and game rooms. The inn boasts an indoor sauna and hot tub. The award-winning dining room provides candle-lit tables beside a huge fieldstone fireplace.
**Rates: MAP.
Innkeeper(s): Susan & Judd Levy.
16 Rooms. 12 Private Baths. Guest phone available. TV available. Beds: QC. Meals: Full breakfast. Jacuzzi. Sauna. Fireplaces. Pool. CCs: Visa, MC, AE. Tennis, shuffleboard. canoeing and horseback riding nearby. The inn closes Nov., April & May.

"We had a wonderful time. The inn is breathtaking. Hope to be back to see you again."

Lower Waterford

Rabbit Hill Inn
Lower Waterford VT 05848
(802) 748-5168
  Circa 1825. Above the Connecticut River overlooking the White Mountains, Samuel Hodby opened this

tavern and provided a general store and inn to travelers. As many as 100 horse teams a day traveled by the inn. The ballroom, constructed in 1855, was supported by bentwood construction that gave the dance floor a spring effect. The classic Greek Revival exterior features solid pine Doric columns.
Rates: $55-$90.
18 Rooms. 18 Private Baths. Guest phone available. TV available. Beds: KQT. Meals: Full breakfast, restaurant, MAP. Conference room. Fireplaces. CCs: Visa, MC. Swimming, fishing, hiking, cross-country skiing, sleigh rides.
Seen in: *Today Show.*

"For the most loving, heartfelt service, I vote for Rabbit Hill Inn." C. Dragonwagon, *Uncommon Lodgings.*

Ludlow

The Governor's Inn
86 Main St
Ludlow VT 05149
(802) 228-8830
  Circa 1890. Governor Stickney built this house for his bride, Elizabeth

Lincoln, and it retains the intimate feeling of an elegant country house

furnished in the Victorian fashion. The Governor would have been pleased to know that *The Governor's Inn* has been elected to the prestigious Master Chefs Institute of America and was awarded first prize for "Best in American Country Inn Cooking" by Uncle Ben's Rice.
Rates: $160 MAP/2. All year.
Innkeeper(s): Charlie, Deedy & Jennifer Marble.
8 Rooms. 8 Private Baths. Guest phone available. Meals: Full breakfast, gourmet, MAP. Fireplaces. CCs: Visa, MC. Skiing, golf, tennis, sleigh rides, horses.
Seen in: *The Washington Post, Los Angeles Times, Mature Outlook.*

"As Rolls Royce is to cars... it is the standard by which all other inns can be judged." Ed Oakie.

Manchester

Birch Hill Inn
West Rd, Box 346
Manchester VT 05254
(802) 362-2761
  Circa 1790. It's rare to meet a Vermont innkeeper actually from Vermont but at Birch Hill the hostess is the fourth generation to live in this old farmhouse. The bedrooms are elegantly furnished and some have mountain views and fireplaces. There are eight miles of groomed, picturesque cross-country trails that lead past a small pond and flowing brook.
Rates: $48-$62. All year.
Innkeeper(s): Jim & Pat Lee.
6 Rooms. 6 Private Baths. Guest phone available. Beds: KQT. Meals: Full breakfast, MAP. Fireplaces. Pool. CCs: Visa, MC. Cross-country skiing, hiking, fishing.
Seen in: *The Rye Chronicle.*

"Without a doubt the loveliest country inn it has ever been my pleasure to stay in. I. Pastarnack, *Rye Chronicle.*

Manchester Highlands Inn
PO Box 1754, Highland Ave
Manchester VT 05255
(802) 362-4565
  Circa 1898. From the three-story turret of this Victorian mansion guests can look out over Mt. Equinox, the Green Mountains and the valley below. Guest rooms are homey and comfortable, and a large

veranda is provided with rocking chairs.

**Rates: $38-$43. All year.
Innkeeper(s): Robert & Patricia Eichorn.
15 Rooms. 12 Private Baths. Guest phone available. TV available. Beds: KQTD. Meals: Full breakfast. Fireplaces. Pool. CCs: Visa, MC, AE. Downhill and cross-country skiing, golf, tennis, cycling, fishing.

"We couldn't believe such a place existed. Now we can't wait to come again."

Reluctant Panther Inn

Box 678, West Rd
Manchester VT 05254
(802) 362-2568

Circa 1850. Elm trees line a street of manicured lawns and white clapboard estates. Suddenly, a muted purple clapboard house appears, the

Reluctant Panther. Rooms have recently been renovated and some include fireplaces, whirlpool tubs, and cable TV.

Rates: $80-$180. All year.
Innkeeper(s): Loretta & Edward Friihauf.
13 Rooms. 13 Private Baths. Guest phone available. TV in room. Beds: KQT. Meals: Full breakfast, restaurant. Jacuzzi. Handicap access provided. Fireplaces. CCs: Visa, MC, AE.
Seen in: *Vermont Summer, Sunday Republican.*

"We enjoyed our stay so much that now we want to make it our yearly romantic getaway."

The Arlington Inn

See: Arlington, VT

The Inn at Manchester

Box 41, Historic Rt 7A
Manchester VT 05254
(802) 362-1793

Circa 1880. This restored Victorian and its carriage house are in the National Register. There is an extensive

art collection of old prints and paintings. Guest rooms have French doors, bay windows, or alcoves furnished with antiques restored by the innkeepers.

**Rates: $55-$90. All year.
Innkeeper(s): Harriet & Stan Rosenberg.
20 Rooms. 16 Private Baths. Guest phone available. TV available. Beds: KQT. Meals: Full breakfast. Conference room. Fireplaces. Pool. CCs: Visa, MC, AE. Skiing, golf, tennis, swimming, bicycling.

"Spectacular! Bob Newhart - eat your heart out."

White Rocks Inn

See: Wallingford, VT

Wilburton Inn

Box 468, River Rd
Manchester VT 05254
(802) 362-2500 (800) 648-4944

Circa 1902. Shaded by tall maples, this three-story brick mansion sits high on a hill overlooking the Bat-

tenkill Valley set against a majestic mountain backdrop. Carved moldings, mahogany paneling, oriental carpets, and leaded glass windows are complemented with carefully chosen antiques. The inn's 17 acres provide three tennis courts, a pool and green lawns.
**Rates: $75-$145. All year.

Innkeeper(s): Georgette & Albert Levis, Stanley Holton.
30 Rooms. 30 Private Baths. Guest phone in room. TV available. Beds: KQTC. Meals: MAP. Gourmet restaurant. Conference room. Fireplaces. Pool. CCs: Visa, MC, AE. Skiing, tennis, swimming, golf.
Seen in: *Great Escapes TV, Travelhost, Getaways For Gourmets.*

"I have traveled extensively in Europe and the United States...if there is a more romantic and peaceful setting in the world, then I am not aware of its existence."

Manchester Village

1811 House

Historic Rt 7A
Manchester Village VT 05254
(802) 362-1811

Circa 1775. Since 1811 the historic Lincoln Home has been operated as

an inn, except for a time when it was the private residence of Mary Lincoln Isham, granddaughter of President Lincoln. It has been authentically restored to the Federal period with antiques and canopy beds. The gardens look out over a golf course and it's just a short walk to tennis or swimming.
Location: Center of Manchester Village.
Rates: $80-$120. All year.
Innkeeper(s): John & Mary Hurst, Pat & Jeremy David.
14 Rooms. 14 Private Baths. Guest phone available. TV available. Beds: KQ. Meals: Full breakfast. Fireplaces. CCs: Visa, MC, AE. Skiing, tennis, golf, hiking.

Village Country Inn

PO Box 408
Manchester Village VT 05254
(802) 362-1792

Circa 1889. The Kellogg cereal family built this as a summer house. The present owners have renovated and redecorated in a French colonial style, creating soft country vignettes

in each room. A French country breakfast is served.
**Rates: $150-$200. All year.
Innkeeper(s): Anne & Jay Degen.
30 Rooms. 30 Private Baths. Guest phone available. TV available. Beds: KQT. Meals: MAP, gourmet extra. Pool. CCs: Visa, MC. Swimming, tennis, golf.
Seen in: *Country Inn Magazine*.
"An inn for choosy guests." *Albany Times Union*.

Marlboro

Longwood, A Country Inn at Marlboro
Rt 9 Box 86
Marlboro VT 05344
(802) 257-1545

Circa 1800. This rambling colonial includes four studios in the Carriage House each accommodating 3-6 people. The ice skating pond is stocked with rainbow trout (and bullfrogs) each spring. Activities vary with the season and include sleigh rides, skiing, horseback riding and walking through the woods.
Location: Nine miles west of Route 91.
Rates: $85-$175. All year.
Innkeeper(s): Thomas & Janet Durkin.
15 Rooms. 13 Private Baths. Guest phone available. TV available. Beds: KQT. Meals: Full breakfast, restaurant, MAP. Jacuzzi. Handicap access provided. Conference room. Fireplaces. Pool. CCs: Visa, MC.
Seen in: *Boston Globe*.

Middlebury

Historic Brookside Farms
See: Orwell, VT

Strong House Inn
See: Vergennes, VT

Swift House Inn
25 Stewart Lane
Middlebury VT 05753
(802) 388-9925

Circa 1815. Former governor of Vermont, John Stewart, bought the elegant Swift House in 1875 from

Jonathan Swift. The governor's daughter, philanthropist Jessica Swift was born in the mansion and lived there for 110 years, till 1981. Elaborately carved walnut and marble fireplaces, and window seats grace the sitting rooms of the inn. The spacious lawns and formal gardens can be enjoyed from terraces and guest rooms.
Rates: $55-$99. All year.
Innkeeper(s): John & Andrea Nelson.
14 Rooms. 14 Private Baths. Guest phone in room. TV available. Beds: KQTC. Meals: Full breakfast, restaurant. Jacuzzi. Conference room. Fireplaces. CCs: Visa, MC, AE, DC. Skiing, bicycling, swimming.
Seen in: *Valley Voice, Uncommon Lodgings*.
"Fabulous wine list, great food, comfortable and relaxing atmosphere, friendly staff."

Middletown Springs

Middletown Springs Inn
Box 1068, On The Green
Middletown Springs VT 05757
(802) 235-2198

Circa 1879. This Italianate Victorian mansion on the green was built

when the bubbling springs of Middletown rivaled those of Saratoga. The inn is decorated in middle to late Victorian antiques with mahogany and cherry furniture, rich wallpapers and lace curtains. A staircase with an ornate newel post sweeps upstairs to the guest rooms. There are additional rooms in the

carriage house, once the village blacksmith shop.
Location: Fourteen miles from Rutland on Route 133.
Rates: $40-$75. All year.
Innkeeper(s): Steve & Jane Sax.
10 Rooms. 6 Private Baths. TV available. Beds: QTD. Meals: Full breakfast, MAP. Conference room. CCs: Visa, MC. Skiing, hiking, swimming, sailing, golf, bicycles, horses.
Seen in: *The Pittsburgh Press, Rutland Business Journal*.
"The charm of the inn, Steve's exquisite cuisine and the ambience you both provide blend wonderfully."

Montpelier

The Inn at Thatcher Brook Falls
See: Waterbury, VT

Newfane

The Country Inn at Williamsville
See: Williamsville, VT

North Hero

North Hero House
Rt 2 PO 106
North Hero VT 05474
(802) 372-8237

Circa 1891. This three-story inn stands on a slight rise overlooking Lake Champlain and Vermont's highest peak, Mt. Mansfield. Three other houses, including the Wadsworth store located at the City Dock, also provide accommodations for the inn's guests. Rooms hang over the water's edge and feature waterfront porches.
Rates: $41-$95. June to Oct.
23 Rooms. 21 Private Baths. Guest phone available. TV available. Beds: TC. Meals: EP, restaurant. Sauna. Handicap access provided. Fireplaces. Fishing, swimming, tennis, canoeing, sailing, bicycling, boating.
"We have visited many inns and this house was by far the best, due mostly to the staff!"

Orleans

Valley House Inn
4 Memorial Sq
Orleans VT 05860
(802) 754-6665

Circa 1800. There has been a Valley House in existence since 1833 though the present structure was built in 1873. A small dining room serves a hearty Vermont breakfast and there is a tavern with live entertainment on the weekends.
Location: On Route 5, off I-91, exit 26.
Innkeeper(s): David & Louise Bolduc.
21 Rooms. 9 Private Baths. CCs: Visa, MC, AE. Golf, hiking, bicycling, fishing, hunting.

Orwell

Historic Brookside Farms
Rt 22A Box 036
Orwell VT 05760
(802) 948-2727

Circa 1789. Nineteen stately Ionic columns grace the front of this neo-classical Greek Revival farmhouse,

redesigned by James Lamb. This is a working farm with Hereford cattle, Hampshire sheep, maple syrup production and poultry. There are 300 acres of lush country landscape including a 26-acre pond. Murray is a concert violinist and speaks seven languages.
**Rates: $35-$75. All year.
Innkeeper(s): Joan & Murray Korda & Family.
7 Rooms. 2 Private Baths. Guest phone available. Beds: TDC. Meals: Full breakfast, MAP, gourmet. Handicap access provided. Fireplaces. Cross-country skiing, fishing, hiking, tennis, golf, horses.

Plymouth

Salt Ash Inn
Jct 100 & 100A
Plymouth VT 05056
(802) 672-3748

Circa 1830. In the mid-1800s, the Woodstock to Ludlow Stagecoach would likely have stopped here at

the Union House as it was known. Most of the antiques featured at Salt Ash were in use when the building was a post office, general store and inn. Pine beds piled with homemade quilts or plaid blankets provide pleasant comfort, and an English pub and circular fireplace are welcome spots.
**Rates: $68-$120. All year.
Innkeeper(s): Glen & Ann Stanford.
15 Rooms. 13 Private Baths. Guest phone available. TV available. Beds: Q. Meals: Full breakfast. Jacuzzi. Fireplaces. CCs: Visa, MC, AE. Skiing, bicycling.

Poultney

Stonebridge Inn
Rt 30
Poultney VT 05764
(802) 287-9849

Circa 1808. The inn's land was part of a grant from Lord Poultney, first

Earl of Bath. In 1841, an addition was added with a five-foot-thick foundation, designed as the vault of the First Bank of Poultney. The house was built in the Federal style and a later addition added the Greek Revival front.
Rates: $54-$84.

Innkeeper(s): Jane Davidson & Lenore Lyons.
5 Rooms. 2 Private Baths. Beds: QD. Meals: Full breakfast. CCs: Visa, MC.

Proctorsville

Castle Inn
Rt 103 & 131, PO Box 157
Proctorsville VT 05153
(802) 226-7222

Circa 1904. The Fletcher family settled in the Ludlow area in the 1700s. Allen Fletcher grew up in Indiana but returned to Vermont, tearing

down a Victorian house to build this English-style mansion overlooking the Okemo valley. It features an oval dining room, a mahogany-paneled library, and spacious guest accommodations complete with individual sitting areas. In 1911, Mr. Fletcher became governor of Vermont.
Rates: $70-$120. All year.
Innkeeper(s): Michael & Sheryl Fratino.
13 Rooms. 9 Private Baths. Guest phone available. TV available. Beds: QD. Meals: MAP, restaurant. Conference room. CCs: Visa, MC, AE. Bicycling, tennis, swimming, cross-country skiing.
"Castle Inn has to be the very best place in Vermont."

The Golden Stage Inn
Depot St, PO Box 218
Proctorsville VT 05153
(802) 226-7744

Circa 1780. The Golden Stage Inn was a stagecoach stop shortly after Vermont's founding. It became a link in the Underground Railroad

and the home of Cornelia Otis Skinner. Extensive gardens surround the wraparound porch as well as the

swimming pool. The innkeepers were flavor experts for a New York company but now put their tasting skills to work for their guests.
Location: Near Ludlow.
Rates: $65-$75. All year.
Innkeeper(s): Kirsten Murphy & Marcel Perret.
10 Rooms. 6 Private Baths. Guest phone available. Beds: QT. Meals: MAP. Pool. CCs: Visa. Swimming, golf, bicycling, hiking, cross-country skiing, tennis.
Seen in: *Journal Inquirer.*
   "The essence of a country inn!"
   "The food is so good, it's a sin!"

Rochester

Harvey's Mountain View Inn
Rochester VT 05767
(802) 767-4273
   Circa 1809. The Harvey family has owned and operated this homestead as a farm for more than 180 years. During the summer, gathering eggs and watching the milking provide entertainment when guests are not enjoying the pool. Sunset hayrides are popular and there are rental horses nearby. A cottage is available for a weekly rate.
Rates: $26-$42. All year.
9 Rooms. 1 Private Baths. Guest phone available. TV in room. Beds: KQTDC. Meals: Full breakfast. Handicap access provided. Fireplaces. Golf, swimming, hiking, cross-country skiing, fishing, hunting.
Seen in: *The New York Times.*
   "Children are right at home here. They don't fight. They don't fuss. They're too busy. And when the children are happy, the parents are happy."

Rutland

Maplewood Inn
See: Fair Haven, VT

Shrewsbury

Buckmaster Inn
Lincoln Hill Rd, RR 1 Box 118
Shrewsbury VT 05738
(802) 492-3485
   Circa 1801. John Buckmaster's tavern was licensed in 1820, and the inn soon became well-known on the Woodstock Road. Standing majesti-

cally on a knoll, the Buckmaster overlooks a picturesque red barn

and valley scene. Its center hall, grand staircase and wide-pine floors are accentuated with family heirlooms. There are wood-burning fireplaces, a library, and large porches.
Rates: $35-$55. All year.
Innkeeper(s): Sam & Grace Husselman.
4 Rooms. 1 Private Baths. Guest phone available. TV available. Beds: KQTD. Meals: Full breakfast. Fireplaces. CCs: Travelers checks. Hiking, swimming, fishing.
   "I've been in many B&B's but the accommodations and hospitality are best here."

South Londonderry

Londonderry Inn
PO Box 3018
South Londonderry VT 05155
(802) 824-5226
   Circa 1826. For almost one hundred years the Melendy Home-

stead, overlooking the West River and the village, was a dairy farm. In 1940 it became an inn. A tourist brochure promoting the area in 1881 said, "Are you overworked in the office, counting room or workshop and need invigorating influences? Come ramble over these hills and mountains and try the revivifying effects of Green Mountains oxygen."

Location: Route 100.
**Rates: $56-$69. All year.
Innkeeper(s): Jim & Jean Cavanagh.
25 Rooms. 20 Private Baths. Guest phone available. TV available. Beds: KQTC. Meals: Full breakfast, restaurant. Handicap access provided. Conference room. Fireplaces. Pool. Hiking, cross-country skiing.
   "A weekend in a good country inn, such as the Londonderry, is on a par with a weekend on the ocean in Southern Maine, which is to say that it's as good as a full week nearly any place else." The Hornet.

South Strafford

Watercourse Way B&B
Rt 132 Box 101
South Strafford VT 05070
(802) 765-4314
   Circa 1850. Watercourse Way is a traditional white clapboard Cape with classic post-and-beam con-

struction solid to this day. A striking red barn and goat pasture are just beyond the house. During World War II, Strafford was the site of the country's largest copper mine and many geologists from Harvard and MIT made this house their home.
Location: North of White River Junction.
**Rates: $25-$50. All year.
Innkeeper(s): Anna & Lincoln Alden.
3 Rooms. Guest phone available. Beds: QTC. Meals: Full breakfast. Fireplaces. Bicycling, fishing, kayak.
   "Watercourse Way is a real gem - thanks for the great time!"

South Wallingford

Green Mountain Tea Room
Rt 7 Box 400
South Wallingford VT 05773
(802) 446-2611

Circa 1792. Originally a stagecoach stop, this colonial house possessed a barn large enough to hold the twelve horses needed for a complete change on the journey from Bennington to Rutland. The three upstairs bedrooms were originally a ballroom that saw many a gala affair when the house was known as Miller's Hall.
Rates: $40-$50. All year.
Innkeeper(s): Tracy & Ed Crelin.
4 Rooms. Guest phone available. TV available. Beds: D. Meals: Full breakfast, gourmet. Fireplaces. CCs: Visa, MC. Hiking, fishing, hunting, cross-country & downhill skiing.

South Woodstock

Kedron Valley Inn
Rt 106 Box 145
South Woodstock VT 05071
(802) 457-1473
Circa 1822. This inn has served the traveling public for more than 150 years. One of the guest buildings

has a secret attic passageway and is rumored to have been a stop on the Underground Railway during the Civil War. There is a 32-piece quilt collection that includes 100-year-old quilts made by great grandmothers of the hostess. Outdoors are a white sand beach and swimming lake, and nearby is a stable with horses for trail rides or inn-to-inn excursions.
Rates: $120-$176. All year.
Innkeeper(s): Max & Merrily Comins.
28 Rooms. 28 Private Baths. Guest phone available. TV in room. Beds: KQTC. Meals: Full breakfast, MAP. Handicap access provided. Conference room. Fireplaces. CCs: Visa, MC, AE. Horses, golf, tennis, cross-country & downhill skiing.
Seen in: *Oprah Winfrey Show, Good Housekeeping.*
"It's what you dream a Vermont country inn should be and the most im-

pressive feature is the innkeepers...outgoing, warm and friendly."

Stowe

Edson Hill Manor
RR 1 Box 2480
Stowe VT 05672
(802) 253-7371
Circa 1939. The springs, brooks and ponds on Edson Hill Manor are filled with native brook and rainbow trout. Guests are surrounded with majestic views of the Green Mountains as well as rolling hills, pastures and woods. Beams from Ethan Allen's barn are now part of the living room, and exterior brick was taken from the old Sherwood Hotel in Burlington. Some accommodations are in newly built carriage houses.
**Rates: $59-$99. All year.
Innkeeper(s): Anita & Larry Heath.
27 Rooms. 23 Private Baths. Guest phone available. TV available. Beds: KQ. Meals: Full breakfast, EP, gourmet. Handicap access provided. Conference room. Fireplaces. Pool. CCs: Visa, MC, AE. Horseback riding, sleigh rides, cross-country skiing, hiking.
"The best setting, close to the village but far enough to be secluded. Loved every minute."

The 1860 House
School St, PO Box 276
Stowe VT 05672
(802) 253-7351
Circa 1860. This charming National Register house is an Italianate style

with an intersecting gable. All the windows are topped with peaked lintel boards, and paired scroll brackets adorn the roof cornices. The interior is furnished in period furnishings.
**Rates: $75-$100. All year.
Innkeeper(s): Richard M. Hubbard & Rose Marie Matulionis.
5 Rooms. 5 Private Baths. Guest phone in room. TV available. Beds: KQTC. Meals: Full breakfast. Jacuzzi. Sauna.

Conference room. Fireplaces. Pool. CCs: Visa, MC. Skiing, skating, hiking, fishing, golf, tennis, horseback riding.
"A memorable place to visit...You do a great job!"

The Inn at Thatcher Brook Falls
See: Waterbury, VT

Sunderland

The Inn at Sunderland
Historic Rt 7A
Sunderland VT 05250
(802) 362-4213
Circa 1840. Farmer and merchant William Bradley built this house as

a wedding present for his wife, and heart medallions are incorporated into the roof trim and under each window. Chestnut trim and doors, and a polished walnut staircase are features of the interior where guests are surrounded with luxury and comfort.
Rates: $65-$95. May to March.
Innkeeper(s): Tom & Peggy Wall.
10 Rooms. 8 Private Baths. Beds: QDTC. Meals: Full breakfast. Handicap access provided. CCs: Visa, MC, AE. Fishing, golf, tennis, bicycling.
Seen in: *Country Living, Bennington Banner.*
"We've traveled many inns, this is the best!"

Vergennes

Strong House Inn
RD 1 Box 9, Rt 22A
Vergennes VT 05491
(802) 877-3337
Circa 1834. Samuel Paddock Strong, banker and railroad man, built this Federal-style house with Greek Revival influences. It is situated on a rise commanding views of the Green Mountains and the Adirondacks. Chartered in 1788, Vergennes is said to be the third

oldest city in the United States and with its 1200 acres is the smallest city in the United States.

Location: One mile west of Vergennes on 22A.

Rates: $45-$70. All year.

Innkeeper(s): Michelle & Ron Bring.

6 Rooms. 4 Private Baths. Guest phone available. TV available. Beds: D. Meals: Full breakfast. Fireplaces. CCs: Visa, MC. Bicycling, cross-country & downhill skiing.

"Blissful stay...Glorious breakfast!"

Waitsfield

Lareau Farm Country Inn
PO Box 563, Rt 100
Waitsfield VT 05673
(802) 496-4949

Circa 1832. This Greek Revival house was built by Simeon Stod-

dard, the town's first physician. Old-fashioned roses, lilacs, delphiniums, iris and peonies fill the gardens, and the inn sits in a wide meadow next to the crystal-clear Mad River. A canoe trip or a refreshing swim are possibilities here.

Location: Central Vermont, Sugarbush Valley.

**Rates: $30-$55. All year.

Innkeeper(s): Dan & Susan Easley.

10 Rooms. 6 Private Baths. Guest phone available. TV available. Beds: QTDC. Meals: Full breakfast. Handicap access provided. CCs: Visa, MC. Downhill & cross-country skiing, sleigh rides, hiking.

Seen in: *The Pittsburgh Press, The Philadelphia Inquirer.*

"Hospitality is a gift. Thank you for sharing your gift so freely with us."

Mad River Barn
Rt 17 Box 88
Waitsfield VT 05673

(802) 496-3310

Circa 1800. The "Annex" farmhouse dates to 1800 and was recently remodeled to contain a two-story lounge, game room, bar and restaurant. Just beyond the barn is a path to the mountain, and old stone walls and lumber trails run through the property.

**Rates: $33-$56. All year.

Innkeeper(s): Betsy Pratt.

16 Rooms. 15 Private Baths. Guest phone available. TV in room. Beds: QTC. Meals: MAP, Full breakfast, restaurant. Conference room. CCs: Visa, MC, AE. Cross-country skiing, golf, tennis, hiking, swimming.

"My favorite lounge, one with a massive stone fireplace and deep leather chairs." Christina Tree, *Boston Globe.*

Millbrook
RFD Box 62
Waitsfield VT 05673
(802) 495-2405

Circa 1840. Guests enter Millbrook through the warming room where

an antique Glenwood parlor stove is usually roaring. This classic Cape-style farmhouse is known for its individually stenciled guest rooms, Green Mountain views, and one of the valley's best dining rooms.

**Rates: $25-$65. All year.

Innkeeper(s): Joan & Thom Gorman.

7 Rooms. 4 Private Baths. Guest phone available. Beds: TD. Meals: MAP. Fireplaces. CCs: Visa, MC, AE, DC. Skiing, horseback riding, golf, hiking, bicycling.

"A gem of a country inn.." Boston Globe.

Round Barn Farm
RR Box 247
Waitsfield VT 05673
(802) 496-2276

Circa 1810. The Bates family built this farmhouse and in 1910, added a round barn that was a working dairy barn for almost 60 years. One of the few remaining in Vermont, it

has 12 sides and is capped with a windowed cupola. Eighty-five acres of ponds, meadows, fields and woods surround the inn, and spring and summer courses are offered in wildflower design and quilting.

**Rates: $85-$125. All year.

Innkeeper(s): Doreen, Jack & Anne Marie Simko.

6 Rooms. 6 Private Baths. Guest phone available. TV available. Beds: KQTD. Meals: Full breakfast. Jacuzzi. Conference room. Fireplaces. CCs: Visa, MC, AE. Horseback riding, biking, tennis, skiing, swimming.

Seen in: *Vermont Life.*

"Felt like home. Appreciate the champagne, flowers, love poems and mostly the warm, welcomed feeling. Perfect honeymoon spot."

The Inn at Thatcher Brook Falls
See: Waterbury, VT

Wallingford

White Rocks Inn
RR 1 Box 297, Rt 7
Wallingford VT 05773
(802) 446-2077

Circa 1840. Both the barn and farmhouse are listed in the National

Register. The barn is a fine example of Gothic architecture. The house was built by Israel Munson whose name is still engraved on the front doorbell. Furnished with antiques, oriental rugs, and canopied beds,

the inn provides views of White Rocks Mountain.
Location: Eleven miles south of Rutland.
Rates: $60-$85. All year.
Innkeeper(s): June & Alfred Matthews.
5 Rooms. 5 Private Baths. Guest phone available. TV available. Beds: KQTDC. Meals: Full breakfast. CCs: Visa, MC. Horseback riding, hiking, canoeing, skiing.

"Excellent on all counts! We enjoyed every minute. Breakfasts were delightful as were our hosts."

Warren

Beaver Pond Farm Inn
RD Box 306, Golf Course Rd
Warren VT 05674
(802) 583-2861

Circa 1860. Formerly a working dairy and sheep farm, this Vermont farmhouse is situated in a meadow

overlooking several beaver ponds. It has been tastefully and graciously restored by its present owners, with antiques and Laura Ashley wallpapers adding to the decor. Mrs. Hansen holds cooking classes here.
**Rates: $32-$45. All year.
Innkeeper(s): Betty & Bob Hansen.
5 Rooms. 3 Private Baths. Guest phone available. TV available. Beds: QT. Meals: Full breakfast. Conference room. Fireplaces. CCs: Visa, MC, AE. Skiing, golf, tennis.
Seen in: *Los Angeles Times, New Woman Magazine.*

"The inn is simply magnificent. I have not been in a nicer one on three continents. Breakfast was outrageous."

Waterbury

The Inn at Thatcher Brook Falls
RD 2, Box 62
Waterbury VT 05676

(802) 244-5911
Circa 1899. Framed by tall trees, this Victorian belonged to Stedman Wheeler, owner and operator of the local sawmill. Across the street, be-

hind the Colby Mansion, are two beautiful waterfalls that powered the mill. Mr. Wheeler used bird's-eye maple, quarter-sawn maple, cherry, oak and birch, and the fireplace and stairway are hand-carved. There is a front porch gazebo and Bailey's Fireside Tavern is in the oak room.
**Rates: $75-$115. All year.
Innkeeper(s): Peter Varty & Kelly Fenton.
12 Rooms. 12 Private Baths. Guest phone available. TV available. Beds: KQTD. Meals: Full breakfast, restaurant. Handicap access provided. Conference room. Fireplaces. CCs: Visa, MC. Skiing, bicycling, hiking, swimming, canoeing, golf, tennis.

"I'd have to put on a black tie in Long Island to find food as good as this and best of all it's in a relaxed country atmosphere. Meals are underpriced."

Weathersfield

The Inn at Weathersfield
Rt 106
Weathersfield VT 05151
(802) 263-9217

Circa 1795. Built by Thomas Prentis, a Revolutionary War veteran,

this was originally a four-room farmhouse set on 237 acres of wilderness. Two rooms were added in 1796 and a carriage house in 1830. During the Civil War the inn served as a station on the Underground Railroad. Six pillars give the inn a southern colonial look, and there are 11 fireplaces, a beehive oven, wide-plank floors and period antiques throughout.
**Rates: $65-$88. All year.
Innkeeper(s): Mary Louise & Ron Thorburn.
12 Rooms. 12 Private Baths. Guest phone available. TV available. Beds: KQT. Meals: MAP, restaurant, gourmet. Sauna. Handicap access provided. Conference room. Fireplaces. CCs: Visa, MC, AE. Sleigh rides, cycling, hiking, skiing, horseback riding, canoeing. Thanksgiving in colonial dress.

"There isn't one thing we didn't enjoy about our weekend with you and we are constantly reliving it with much happiness."

West Rutland

The Silver Fox Inn
Rt 133 Box 1222
West Rutland VT 05777
(802) 438-5555

Circa 1768. One of the first houses built in the area, this was the home

of Captain John Smith for whose head the governor of a neighboring state once offered the sum of 40 pounds. The inn is furnished with Queen Anne cherrywood and oak, and the Clarendon River runs along the property.
**Rates: $60-$65. All year.
Innkeeper(s): Frank Kranich.
8 Rooms. 8 Private Baths. Guest phone available. TV in room. Beds: KQD. Meals: MAP, restaurant, gourmet. Handicap access provided. Conference room. Fireplaces. CCs: Visa, MC. Bicycling, cross-country skiing, golf, tennis, fishing, hiking.

"We never expected dinner could be so imaginative. We used to stay at a ski condo but breakfast in bed is my idea of a great getaway."

West Townsend

Windham Hill Inn
RR 1 Box 44
West Townsend VT 05359
(802) 874-4080
  Circa 1825. Windham Hill was originally a working dairy farm

owned by William Lawrence. It was sold at auction but most of the existing furniture, silverware, rugs, and quilts belonged to the Lawrence family. Surrounded by 150 acres in a secluded hillside setting, the inn was selected by Uncle Ben's Country Rice as one of the top ten in the country.
Rates: $70-$105. May to March.
Innkeeper(s): Ken & Linda Busteed.
15 Rooms. 15 Private Baths. Guest phone available. TV available. Beds: KQTD. Meals: MAP. Handicap access provided. Fireplaces. CCs: Visa, MC, AE. Hiking, cross-country skiing.
  "The inn lived up to the expectations of any New Yorker or Bostonian who conjures up a romantic vision of a Vermont country inn. It also lived up to a Vermonter's expectation of a country inn." Madeleine Kunin, Governor of Vermont.

Weston

1830 Inn on the Green
Main St, Rt 100 Box 104
Weston VT 05161
(802) 824-6789
  Circa 1830. Originally a wheelwright's shop, the building

was later a town hall and an undertaker's parlor. Moved to its

present site, it became a private home graced with a beautiful curving staircase from the house of Hetty Green, "The Witch of Wall Street." Situated in the Weston Historic District and tucked in a hollow of the Green Mountains, the inn is across the village green from the oldest summer theater in the state.
Rates: $55-$70. All year.
Innkeeper(s): Sandy & Dave Grangers.
4 Rooms. 2 Private Baths. Beds: KT. Meals: Full breakfast. CCs: Visa, MC. Skiing, bicycling, hiking, golf, tennis, fishing, canoeing.
Seen in: *Yankee Homes.*

Williamsville

The Country Inn
at Williamsville
Grimes Hill Rd, Box 166
Williamsville VT 05362
(802) 348-7148
  Circa 1795. Overlooking 115 acres, this Federal-style house once

presided over a dairy and apple farm. The sugar house served as the

village auction house. The inn is filled with English and Victorian antiques collected in London.
**Rates: $72-$156. All year.
Innkeeper(s): Bill & Sandra Cassill.
6 Rooms. 6 Private Baths. Guest phone available. TV available. Beds: KQTD. Meals: Full breakfast, MAP, gourmet. Fireplaces. CCs: Visa, MC, AE. Hiking, cross-country skiing, bicycling, swimming.
Seen in: *Southern Vermont Magazine.*
  "Four stars. Ideal setting, memorable dining and most gracious hosts."

Woodstock

Kedron Valley Inn
See: South Woodstock, VT

The Charleston House
21 Pleasant St
Woodstock VT 05091
(802) 457-3843
  Circa 1835. This Greek Revival townhouse has been authentically restored and is listed in the National Register. It is furnished with an-

tiques, an art collection and oriental rugs. The picturesque village of Woodstock has been called one of the most beautiful villages in America by *National Geographic Magazine.*
Rates: $92-$115. All year.
Innkeeper(s): Barbara & Bill Hough.
7 Rooms. 7 Private Baths. Guest phone available. TV available. Beds: QT. Meals: Full breakfast. CCs: Visa, MC. Cross-country skiing, tennis, fishing, hiking.
  "I felt like I was a king, elegant but extremely comfortable."

Virginia

Arlington

Memory House
6404 N Washington Blvd
Arlington VA 22205
(703) 534-4607

Circa 1899. This vintage Victorian, built by a former mayor of Falls Church, was restored by the owners

over a period of several years. Terracotta, cream, and green highlight the gingerbread and shingled gables of the house. Inside are stenciled borders, polished hardwood floors, and antique furnishings. Restaurants are within eight blocks and the East Falls Church subway station is one block away.
Location: Two blocks from I-66 via exit 22.
**Rates: $65. All year.
Innkeeper(s): John & Marlys McGrath.
2 Rooms. 1 Private Baths. Guest phone in room. TV in room. Beds: QT. Meals: Full breakfast, Continental plus. Tennis, bicycling.
Seen in: *The Washington Post.*

"We feel so fortunate to have stayed in Memory House. It is charming and comfortable and so many things to look at!"

Charles City

Edgewood Plantation
Rt 5 Historic
Charles City VA 23030
(804) 829-2962

Circa 1849. This Carpenter Gothic plantation was built by northerner

Spencer Rowland. Romantic guest rooms are furnished with antiques and old-fashioned country artifacts. There are 10 fireplaces and a winding three-story staircase. A few yards from the inn is a three-story mill with an unusual inside mill wheel built in 1725.
Location: Halfway between Williamsburg and Richmond.
Rates: $88-$125. All year.
Innkeeper(s): Dot & Juilian Boulware.
6 Rooms. 2 Private Baths. Guest phone available. TV available. Beds: KQD. Meals: Full breakfast. Jacuzzi. Fireplaces. Pool. CCs: Visa, MC.

North Bend Plantation
Rt 1 Box 13A
Charles City VA 23030
(804) 829-5176

Circa 1801. The Copland family lived here for three generations. The present owner is twice great-grandson of noted agriculturist Ed-

mund Ruffin who is said to have fired the first shot of the Civil War at Fort Sumpter. Sheridan headquartered at North Bend and his desk is still here, one of many treasured family heirlooms.
Location: West of Colonial Williamsburg, 25 minutes.
Rates: $60.
Innkeeper(s): George & Ridgely Copland.
3 Rooms. Meals: Full breakfast.
Seen in: *The Washington Post.*

"Your hospitality, friendship and history lessons were all priceless. Your love of life embraced us in a warmth I shall never forget."

Piney Grove B&B
Rt 1 Box 148
Charles City VA 23030-9735
(804) 829-2480

Circa 1800. Piney Grove is located on Old Main Road among farms,

plantations, country stores and quaint churches. There is a rare Tidewater building with an original log portion on the property, and also a modest antebellum home called Lady Smith House. A unique collection of artifacts and antiques illustrates the history of the area.

Guests can tour the Main House, gardens and grounds.
Location: James River Plantation outside of Williamsburg.
Rates: $95-$125. All year.
Innkeeper(s): Brian E. Gordineer.
6 Rooms. 4 Private Baths. Guest phone available. TV available. Beds: D. Meals: Full breakfast. Conference room. Fireplaces. Pool. Bird-watching.

Charlottesville

200 South Street Inn
200 South St
Charlottesville VA 22901
(804) 979-0200

Circa 1853. This house was built for Thomas Jefferson Wertenbaker, son of Thomas Jefferson's partner at the University of Virginia. It is furnished with English and Belgian antiques and guests may choose rooms with whirlpool baths, fireplaces and canopy beds.
Location: Downtown historic district of Charlottesville.
**Rates: $80-$150. All year.
Innkeeper(s): Donna Deibert.
20 Rooms. 20 Private Baths. Guest phone in room. TV available. Beds: QT. Meals: Continental plus, restaurant. Jacuzzi. Handicap access provided. Conference room. Fireplaces. CCs: Visa, MC, AE.
Seen in: *New York Times, Gourmet, Vogue Magazine.*

"True hospitality abounds in this fine inn which is a neatly turned complement to the inspiring history surrounding it."

Guesthouses
PO Box 5737
Charlottesville VA 22905
(804) 979-7264

Circa 1750. Guesthouses, America's first reservation service for bed and breakfast accommodations, ap-

propriately originated in an area with a centuries-old tradition of out-

standing hospitality. Many of the homes are in the National Register. They are located in Charlottesville and throughout Albermarle County and have been inspected carefully to assure a pleasant stay.
Rates: $48-$150. All year.
CCs: Visa, MC. AE.

The Silver Thatch Inn
3001 Hollymead Rd
Charlottesville VA 22901
(804) 978-4686

Circa 1780. This rambling white colonial inn, shaded by tall elms,

originally began as a log house constructed by Hessian soldiers, Revolutionary War prisoners. Later it became a boys' school, melon farm and tobacco plantation. Its elegant life as an inn now provides guests with fine dining and guest rooms filled with country and English antiques.
Rates: $85-$105. All year.
Innkeeper(s): Joe & Mickey Geller.
7 Rooms. 7 Private Baths. Guest phone available. TV in room. Beds: QT. Meals: Full breakfast, Restaurant. Conference room. Fireplaces. Pool. CCs: Visa, MC, AE, DC. Swimming, tennis, canoeing, horse back riding.
Seen in: *The Washington Post, Washington Business Journal.*

"Charming rooms and delicious French cooking have made the Inn a Charlottesville favorite."

Woodstock Hall
Rt 3 Box 40
Charlottesville VA 22901
(804) 293-8977

Circa 1757. After leaving Thomas Jefferson's Monticello a French duke who stayed at Woodstock Hall tavern wrote, *"Mr. Woods Inn is so good and cleanly...I cannot forbear mentioning those circumstances with pleasure."* These standards remain at this national historic landmark. The two-story clapboard house contains hand-blown windowpanes, a

fireplace in each guest room, and many period antiques selected from the innkeeper's antique shop.
Location: Off I-64.
Rates: $95-$130.
Innkeeper(s): Jean Wheby & Mary Ann Elder.
4 Rooms. 4 Private Baths. Guest phone available. TV in room. Beds: KQ. Meals: B&B. Conference room. Fireplaces. Walking trail and gazebo.

Chincoteague

Miss Molly's Inn
113 N Main St
Chincoteague VA 23336
(804) 336-6686

Circa 1886. This Victorian was built by J. T. Rowley, the "Clam King of the World." His daughter Miss

Molly lived in it for 84 years. The house has been beautifully restored and furnished in period antiques. Marguerite Henry wrote *Misty of Chincoteague* here while rocking on the front porch with Miss Molly and Captain Jack.
Rates: $59-$95. April to Dec.
7 Rooms. 1 Private Baths. Guest phone available. Beds: KQT. Meals: Full breakfast. Conference room.

Culpeper

Fountain Hall B&B
609 S East St
Culpeper VA 22701
(703) 825-6708

Circa 1859. Culpeper was first surveyed by George Washington and this was Lot #3 of a subdivision of 33 acres. Fountain Hall was originally a Victorian house but in the Twenties was remodeled as a Colonial Revival. Most of the rooms are named after historic families in the community. The Frey Drawing Room displays old prints and a

library wall of books from the late 1800s.

**Rates: $45-$85. All year.
Innkeeper(s): Steve & Kathi Walker.
5 Rooms. 3 Private Baths. Guest phone in room. TV available. Beds: QTCD. Meals: Continental plus. Handicap access provided. Conference room. Fireplaces. CCs: Visa, MC, AE. Horse back riding, skiing, basketball, tennis, golf.
Seen in: *Culpeper Exponent.*
 "Liked the friendly greeting and atmosphere. Food was delicious."

Flint Hill

Caledonia Farm
Rt 1 Box 2080
Flint Hill VA 22627
(703) 675-3693
 Circa 1812. This Federal-style stone house is beautifully situated on 52 acres and was built by a Revolution-

ary War officer, Captain John Dearing. His musket is displayed over the mantel. The house has been restored and the colonial color scheme retained. The innkeeper is a retired broadcaster.
Location: Four miles north of Washington, Virginia.
**Rates: $70-$100. All year.
Innkeeper(s): Phil Irwin.
3 Rooms. 1 Private Baths. Guest phone available. TV available. Beds: D. Meals: Full breakfast. Handicap access provided. Conference room. Fireplaces. CCs: Visa, MC. Hiking, golf, tennis, swimming, fishing, canoeing, hay rides.
Seen in: *The Washington Post.*

 "Our first bed & breakfast was a delight!"

Fredericksburg

La Vista Plantation
4420 Guinea Station Rd
Fredericksburg VA 22401
(703) 898-8444
 Circa 1838. La Vista has a long and unusual past rich in Civil War history. Both Confederate and Union armies camped here, and this is where the Ninth Calvary was sworn in. A classical Revival with high ceilings and pine floors, the house sits on ten acres of pasture and woods, and there is a pond stocked with sunfish.
Rates: $65. All year.
Innkeeper(s): Michele & Edward Schiesser.
2 Rooms. 2 Private Baths. Guest phone in room. TV in room. Beds: KQDC. Meals: Full breakfast. Conference room. Fireplaces. CCs: Visa, MC. Fishing, hiking, bicycles, horseback riding.
 "Thanks for the best weekend we've ever had."

Gordonsville

Sleepy Hollow Farm
Rt 3 Box 43 on VA 231
Gordonsville VA 22942
(703) 832-5555
 Circa 1775. Many generations have added on to this brick farmhouse

with its 18th-century dining room and bedrooms. The pink and white room was frequently visited by a friendly ghost from Civil War days according to local stories. She hasn't been seen for several years since the innkeeper, a former missionary, had the house blessed. The grounds include an herb garden, a pond with gazebo, a chestnut slave cabin, terraces and abundant wildlife.
Location: Between Gordonsville & Somerset on Rt 231.

Rates: $50-$200. All year.
Innkeeper(s): Beverly Allison.
6 Rooms. 6 Private Baths. Guest phone available. TV available. Beds: QTC. Meals: Full breakfast. Conference room. Fireplaces. CCs: Visa, MC.
Seen in: *The Orange County Review.*
 "This house is truly blessed."

Lancaster

The Inn at Levelfields
Star Rt 3 Box 216
Lancaster VA 22503
(804) 435-6887
 Circa 1857. This hip-roofed Georgian colonial house stands a quarter

of a mile from the road bordered by hedges of 250-year-old English boxwood. Once the center of a large plantation, the mansion has been completely refurbished and filled with family antiques and oriental rugs, offering the finest in Virginia tradition.
Location: Three hours from Baltimore.
Rates: $55-$75. All year.
Innkeeper(s): Warren & Doris Sadler.
4 Rooms. 4 Private Baths. Guest phone available. TV available. Beds: KQT. Meals: Full breakfast, restaurant. Pool. CCs: Visa, MC.
 "Your hospitality far exceeds any we've experienced and truly made our stay one we'll treasure."

Leesburg

Norris House Inn
108 Loudoun St SW
Leesburg VA 22075
(703) 777-1806
 Circa 1806. The Norris brothers, Northern Virginia's foremost architects and builders, purchased this building in 1850 and began extensive renovations several years later. They used the finest wood and brick available remodeling the exterior to

an Eastlake style. Beautifully restored, the inn features built-in bookcases in the library and a cherry fireplace mantel.
Location: Laura Walton.
Rates: $60-$115.
Innkeeper(s): Forty miles west of Washington, DC.
7 Rooms. 2 Private Baths. Guest phone available. Beds: QT. Meals: Full breakfast
"Thank you for your gracious hospitality. We enjoyed everything about your lovely home, especially the extra little touches that really make the difference."

Lexington

Fassifern B&B
Rt 5 Box 87
Lexington VA 24450
(703) 463-1013
  Circa 1867. Fassifern, which draws its name from the seat of the

Cameron Clan in Scotland, was built on the site of an older dwelling just after the Civil War. Nestled in the Shenandoah Valley, the inn is on three-and-a-half acres surrounded by stately trees and graced with a pond.

Location: Route 39, 3/4 miles from I-64, Exit 13.
Rates: $37.50 - $68.50
Innkeeper(s): Pat & Jim Tichenor.
6 Rooms. 4 Private Baths. Guest phone available. Meals: Continental plus. CCs: Visa, MC, AE.
  "Excellent - best B&B ever. Exquisite room, excellent hospitality."

Llewellyn Lodge at Lexington
603 S Main St
Lexington VA 24450
(703) 463-3235
  Circa 1936. This brick colonial shaded by tall trees, features three

gables on the third story. It is decorated in antique and traditional furnishings. Nearby historic attractions include the home of Stonewall Jackson, the Natural Bridge and the Robert E. Lee house.
Location: Fifty miles north of Roanoke.
**Rates: $42-$65. All year.
Innkeeper(s): Ellen Thornber & John Roberts.
5 Rooms. 5 Private Baths. Guest phone available. TV in room. Beds: KQTD. Meals: Full breakfast. Conference room. Fireplaces. CCs: Visa, MC, AE. Swimming, golf, tennis, hiking, fishing, hunting.
Seen in: *The News-Gazette.*

Luray

Jordan Hollow Farm Inn
Rt 2 Box 375
Luray VA 22851
(703) 778-2209
  Circa 1790. Nestled in the foothills of the Blue Ridge Mountains, this delightful 45-acre horse farm is ideal for those who love riding and country living. The colonial farm house is decorated with antiques and country artifacts. On weekends there is live entertainment at the

Watering Trough Pub. Gentle trail horses are available for guests to ride for miles through the mountains and foothills.
Location: Shenandoah Valley, 6 miles south of Luray.
**Rates: $55-$65. All year.
Innkeeper(s): Jetze & Marley Beers.
16 Rooms. 16 Private Baths. Guest phone in room. TV available. Beds: QT. Meals: Restaurant. Handicap access provided. Conference room. CCs: Visa, MC, DC. Horseback riding, hiking, canoeing, fishing
  "I keep thinking of my day at your lovely inn and keep dreaming of that wonderful lemon mousse cake!"

The Ruffner House
Rt 4 Box 620
Luray VA 22835
(703) 743-7855 (312)278-1000
  Circa 1739. Situated on a farm nestled in the heart of the Shenandoah Valley, this stately manor was

built by Peter Ruffner, the first settler of Page Valley and Luray. Ruffner family members discovered a cavern opposite the entrance to the Luray Caverns which were found later. Pure bred Arabian horses graze in the pasture on this eighteen acre estate.
Location: Shenandoah Valley, South of Hwys. 211 and 340.
**Rates: $75-$95. All year.
Innkeeper(s): Vera Lushpinsky.
7 Rooms. 5 Private Baths. Guest phone available. TV available. Beds: QTD. Meals: Full breakfast. Conference room. Fireplaces. Pool. CCs: Visa, MC. Swimming, golf, canoeing, rafting, horses.
Seen in: *Page News and Courier.*
  "As a descendant of Peter Ruffner I am thrilled to see the house so beautifully restored and taken care of. We loved our visit and will return."

Mathews

Riverfront House B&B
Rt 14 East, PO Box 310
Mathews VA 23109

(804) 725-9975

Circa 1840. This farmhouse is situated on seven acres along Put In Creek and features a wraparound veranda. Guests use the dock for fishing, boating, and sunbathing. Mathews County is surrounded by the Chesapeake and Mobjack Bays, the East and Plankatank Rivers, and dozens of creeks, harbors and inlets. The landscape includes old sawmills, churches, farmlands and oystering boats.

**Rates: $50-$75. May-November.
Innkeeper(s): Annette Waldman Goldreyer.
6 Rooms. 6 Private Baths. Guest phone available. TV available. Beds: KQT. Meals: Continental plus breakfast. Crabbing, fishing on site, and a private dock. Biking, antiquing.

"A joyful relaxing experience."

Middleburg

Red Fox Inn & Tavern
PO Box 385, 2 E Washington St
Middleburg VA 22117
(703) 687-6301 (800)223-1728

Circa 1728. Originally Chinn's Ordinary, the inn was a popular stopping place for travelers between Winchester and Alexandria, and during the Civil War Colonel John Mosby and General Jeb Stuart met here. Guest rooms are furnished in 18-century decor and most feature four-poster canopy beds.
Location: Two miles east of Washington on Route 50.
**Rates: $85-$200.
Innkeeper(s): Turner Reuter, Jr.
28 Rooms. 28 Private Baths. Guest phone in room. TV in room. Beds: KQTC. Meals: Continental, restaurant. Handicap access provided. Conference room. Fireplaces. CCs: All. Foxhunting, horseback riding by arrangement. Vineyard tours.

Welbourne
Middleburg VA 22117
(703) 687-3201

Circa 1775. This seventh-generation mansion once presided over 10,000 acres. With family members starting their own estates, Welbourne now stands at 600 acres. Furnishing were collected during world travels over the past 200 years. Civil War stories fill the family history book and in the 1930s, F.

Scott Fitzgerald and Thomas Wolfe used the house as a setting for their writings.
Location: Fifty miles west of Washington, DC.
**Rates: $80-$100. All year.
Innkeeper(s): Mrs. N. H. Morison.
10 Rooms. 10 Private Baths. Guest phone available. TV available. Beds: QT. Meals: Full breakfast. Conference room. CCs: AE. Fox hunting.

"...furnishings portray a house and home that's been around for a long, long time. And none of it is held back from guests. Life today at Welbourne is quiet and unobtrusive. It's genteel..."
Philip Hayward, *Country Magazine*.

Mollusk

Greenvale Manor
PO Box 70
Mollusk VA 22517
(804) 462-5995

Circa 1840. Beautifully situated on the Rappahannock River and Greenvale Creek, Greenvale is a classic waterfront plantation. This land was patented to Anthony Stephens in 1651 but in 1607 Captain John Smith

said of Virginia's Northern Neck, *"Heaven and earth never agreed better to frame a place for men's habitation... rivers and brookes all running most pleasantly ... with fruitful and delightsome land."* The gracious manor lifestyle extends from tastefully furnished guest rooms to a licensed captain available for boat tours from the dock.
Location: Eight miles from Lancaster Courthouse off Route 3.
Rates: $60-$75. All year.
Innkeeper(s): Pam & Walt Smith.

9 Rooms. 5 Private Baths. Guest phone available. TV available. Beds: KTD. Meals: Full breakfast. Fireplaces. Pool. Swimming, boating bicycling, golf, tennis, badminton. Private beach.

"The inn and grounds are gorgeous, the water views breathtaking but the innkeepers make it really special."

Monterey

Highland Inn
PO Box 40
Monterey VA 24465
(703) 468-2143

Circa 1904. In the National Register, this clapboard Victorian

hotel has outstanding Eastlake wraparound verandas. Small-town life may be viewed from rocking chairs and swings. Guest rooms are furnished in country fashion with iron beds and antiques. Sheep outnumber people in a pastoral setting surrounded by three million acres of National Forest.
Location: Thirty-seven miles west of Staunton.
**Rates: $35-$55. All year.
Innkeeper(s): John & Joanne Crow.
17 Rooms. 17 Private Baths. Guest phone available. TV available. Beds: KQTWDC. Meals: Restaurant. Conference room. CCs: Visa, MC. Hiking, cross country skiing, fishing, golf.

Montross

The Inn at Montross
Courthouse Sq
Montross VA 22520
(804) 493-9097

Circa 1683. On the site of a 17th-century tavern, Montross was rebuilt in 1800. Operating as an "ordinary" since 1683, parts of the structure have been in continuous use for more than 300 years. It was visited by burgesses and Justices of the Court (Washington, Lee and Jefferson). The guest rooms feature

canopy beds and colonial furnishings.
Location: Seven miles from Stratford Hall.
Rates: $60-$75.
Innkeeper(s): Eileen & Michael Longman.
6 Rooms. 6 Private Baths. Guest phone in room. TV available. Beds: QT. CCs: All. Tennis on premises.

Mt Jackson

The Widow Kip's Country Inn

Rt 1 Box 117
Mt Jackson VA 22842
(703) 477-2400
   Circa 1830. This grand farmhouse is situated on seven acres just a

stone's throw from a fork of the Shenandoah River. During the Civil War the area was often a battlefield, but now life once again moves at a gentle pace. Often, the Widow Kip can be found making apple butter or preparing a split chicken for a picnic. Each guest room in the main house has a fireplace and a four-poster, Lincoln, sleigh or spindle bed topped with a handcrafted quilt.
Location: I-81 to Mt. Jackson. Exit 69 to Route 11, south to 263.
**Rates: $45-$65. All year.
Innkeeper(s): Rosemary Kip.
6 Rooms. 5 Private Baths. Guest phone available. TV in room. Beds: TD. Meals: Full breakfast. Sauna. Fireplaces. Pool. CCs: Visa, MC. Swimming, bicycling.
Seen in: *Americana*.
   "Its ambience, charm and warmth made our stay a memorable one. Decorated with flair and imagination..."

Orange

Hidden Inn

249 Caroline St
Orange VA 22960
(703) 672-3625
   Circa 1880. Gardens and five wooded acres can be seen from the veranda of this Victorian inn nestled in the Virginia countryside. Meticulous attention has been given to every detail of the restoration including the white lace and fresh flowers. The James Madison Museum is a short stroll from the inn. Montpelier, his home, Civil War sites and wineries are within five miles.
Rates: $59-$119.
Innkeeper(s): Ray & Barbara Lonick.
9 Rooms. 9 Private Baths. Guest phone available. TV available. Beds: KQTC. Meals: Full country breakfast and MAP. Jacuzzi. Fireplaces. CCs: Visa, MC.

Mayhurst Inn

US 15 South, PO Box 707
Orange VA 22960
(703) 672-5597
   Circa 1859. An extravagant Italianate Victorian villa, Mayhurst was built by the great-nephew of

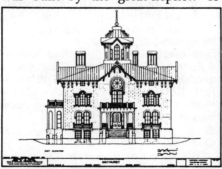

President James Madison, Col. John Willis. It is noted for its fanciful architecture and oval spiral staircase ascending four floors to a rooftop gazebo. It was once host to General Stonewall Jackson and during the Civil War served as the Northern Virginia army headquarters. Thirty-six acres of old oaks, cedars, and magnolias surround the inn.
Location: One mile south of Orange, 95 miles south of Washington, D.C.
**Rates: $85-$95. All year.
Innkeeper(s): Stephen & Shirley Ramsey.
7 Rooms. 7 Private Baths. Guest phone available. Beds: QTD. Meals: Full breakfast. Conference room. Fireplaces. CCs:

Visa, MC. A pond for fishing and swimming.
   "It's Victorian splendor at its highest."

Richmond

Bensonhouse of Richmond at Monument

2036 Monument Ave
Richmond VA 23220
(804) 648-7560
   Circa 1916. This graciously restored historic home is a showcase of

brightly colored walls, fireplaces, and detailed windows. The innkeepers have renovated five Richmond homes and love collecting antiques, art and new friends.
Rates: $72-$115. All year.
Innkeeper(s): Lyn M. Benson.
3 Rooms. 1 Private Baths. Guest phone available. TV available. Beds: QT. Meals: Full breakfast. CCs: Visa, MC, AE.
   "We loved the house and thoroughly enjoyed our stay. We have done quite a few B&Bs and your service rates a 10! Many thanks!"

Mr. Patrick Henry's Inn

2300 E Broad St
Richmond VA 23223
(804) 644-1322
   Circa 1858. Elegant Mr. Patrick Henry's is located in Richmond's oldest neighborhood Church Hill, an area of gaslit streets and beautifully restored townhouses. The inn is Greek Revival with a formal garden, carriage house, and an old bridal path. Most of the guest rooms have

a fireplace, kitchenette and private porch.
Rates: $75-$95. All year.
Innkeeper(s): Jim & Lynn News.
4 Rooms. 4 Private Baths. Guest phone in room. TV in room. Beds: KQT. Meals: Full breakfast. Restaurant. Conference room. Fireplaces. CCs: Visa, MC, AE, DC.
Seen in: *Roanoke Times, Mid-Atlantic Country.*

The Catlin-Abbott House
2304 E Broad St
Richmond VA 23223
(804) 780-3746
Circa 1845. This house was built for William Catlin by a slave, Wil-

liam Mitchell, a noted brick masons of the time. During the Reconstruction, a six-room addition was built to accommodate boarders and it now serves as innkeeper's quarters. This richly appointed inn is one block from St. John's Church, site of Patrick Henry's famous *Liberty or Death* speech.
**Rates: $82-$140. All year.

Innkeeper(s): Dr. & Mrs. James L. Abbott.
3 Rooms. 3 Private Baths. Guest phone available. TV available. Beds: QT. Meals: Full breakfast. Fireplaces. CCs: Visa, MC, AE.

Scottsville

High Meadows Inn
Rt 4 Box 6
Scottsville VA 24590
(804) 286-2218
Circa 1832. Minutes from Charlottesville on The Constitution Highway (Route 20) High Meadows

stands on 22 acres of gardens, forests, ponds, a creek and a vineyard. In the National Register, it is actually two historic homes joined together by a breezeway and furnished in Federal and Victorian styles. Guests are treated to gracious Virginia hospitality in an elegant and peaceful setting.
Location: Charlottesville area south.
Rates: $75-$85. All year.
Innkeeper(s): Peter & Jae Abbitt Sushka.
6 Rooms. 6 Private Baths. Guest phone available. Beds: QTF. Meals: Full breakfast, Restaurant. Jacuzzi. Fireplaces. Fishing, rafting, downhill skiing, horse back riding, croquet.
Seen in: *The Washington Times, The Cavalier Daily.*
"*We have rarely encountered such a smooth blend of hospitality and expertise in a totally relaxed environment.*"

Staunton

Frederick House
Frederick and New Streets
Staunton VA 24401
(703) 885-4220
Circa 1810. The three historic homes that comprise Frederick House appear as one. The oldest structure is believed to be a copy of a home designed by Thomas Jefferson and built on the campus of the University of Virginia. Original

staircases and woodwork are highlighted throughout.
Location: Downtown.
**Rates: $30-$50. All year.
Innkeeper(s): Joe & Evy Harman.
11 Rooms. 11 Private Baths. Guest phone in room. TV in room. Beds: KQTC. Meals: Full breakfast, Restaurant. Jacuzzi. Sauna. Conference room. Fireplaces. Pool. CCs: Visa, MC, AE, DC. Swimming, golf, tennis, skiing, hiking, horse back riding.
Seen in: *Richmond Times-Dispatch.*
"*Thanks for making the room so squeaky clean and comfortable! I enjoyed the Virginia hospitality. The furnishings and decor are beautiful.*"

Trevilians

Prospect Hill
Rt 613, RD 3 Box 430
Trevilians VA 23093
(703) 967-0844
Circa 1732. On a quarter of a mile of green lawn, nestled in the midst of an English garden, is the Manor House. Rare magnolias shade the inn and nearby is an old log cabin dating to 1699, now one of the guest accommodations. During the Civil War Mrs. Wilson stood on the landing and Union soldiers shot around her trying to discover where slaves were hidden. After the war, the owners began to take in guests and this hospitality has continued for more than 100 years.
Location: Fifteen miles east of Charlottesville near Zion Crossroads.
**Rates: $110-$140. All year.
Innkeeper(s): Mireille & Bill Sheehan.
11 Rooms. 11 Private Baths. Guest phone available. Beds: QDT. Meals: Full breakfast, MAP. Jacuzzi. Conference room. Fireplaces. Pool. CCs: Visa, MC. Swimming, jogging, walking.
"*We've been to many wonderful inns - this is the nicest!*"

Vesuvius

Sugar Tree Inn
Hwy 56
Vesuvius VA 24483
(703) 377-2197

Circa 1870. On twenty acres of woodland, Sugar Tree provides mountain views from its large front porch. Furnished in a rustic style, the inn has a library, greenhouse dining room, parlor, tavern and seven guest rooms.
Location: One mile west of Blue Ridge Parkway.
Rates: $80.
Innkeeper(s): Smoky & Geneva Schroeder.
7 Rooms. 7 Private Baths. Meals: Full breakfast.

Virginia Beach

The Picket Fence
209 43rd St
Virginia Beach VA 23451
(804) 428-8861

Circa 1939. This colonial-style home has only two guest rooms but there is a third in a separate cottage, popular with honeymooners. A four-course breakfast is served each morning. Comfortable furnishings include some antiques. Chairs and umbrellas can be borrowed for the beach.
Location: One block from the beach.
Rates: $65.
Innkeeper(s): Kathleen Hall.
3 Rooms. 3 Private Baths. Meals: Full breakfast.

Wachapreague

The Burton House
11 Brooklyn St
Wachapreague VA 23480
(804) 787-4560

Circa 1883. Located one block from the waterfront, The Burton House is

a good point from which to take day trips to Tangier Island, Chincoteague, Assateague and the Barrier Islands. Recently restored, the inn has an inviting screened gazebo with gingerbread trim and posts salvaged from the old Wachapreague Hotel. Baskets of red geraniums, wicker furniture, and a gentle breeze off the water entice guests to relax awhile.
Location: Midway between Norfolk, Virginia and Salisbury, Maryland.
Rates: $60. All year.
Innkeeper(s): Pat, Tom & Mike Hart.
7 Rooms. 1 Private Baths. Guest phone available. TV available. Beds: QTF. Meals: Full breakfast. Fireplaces. Bicycling, boating, tennis.
Seen in: Virginia Pilot.
"Staying here is like visiting with a favorite cousin."

Washington

The Foster-Harris House
PO 333
Washington VA 22747
(703) 675-3757

Circa 1901. This Victorian stands on a lot laid out by George Washington and is situated at the edge of the village. The streets of the

town are exactly as surveyed 225 years ago and the town is the first of more than 28 Washingtons in the United States. The village has many galleries and craft shops as well as the Inn at Little Washington, a five-star restaurant. The innkeeper is known in the area for her flower beds and floral arrangements.
Location: Fifty miles north of Charlottesville.
Rates: $60-$85. All year.
Innkeeper(s): Camille Harris & Pat Foster.
3 Rooms. 1 Private Baths. Guest phone available. TV available. Beds: Q. Meals: Full breakfast. Conference room.

Fireplaces. CCs: Visa, MC. Tennis, canoeing, fishing, cross country skiing, horseback riding.
Seen in: Culpepper News.

White Post

L'Auberge Provencale
PO Box 119
White Post VA 22663
(703) 837-1375

Circa 1753. This stone farmhouse was built with fieldstones gathered from the area. Hessian soldiers

crafted the woodwork of the main house, Mt. Airy. It contains three of the inn's dining rooms. Guest rooms are decorated in Victorian antiques.
Location: One mile south of Route 50 on Route 340.
Rates: $100-$140. Feb. to Dec.
Innkeeper(s): Alain & Celeste Borel.
6 Rooms. 6 Private Baths. Guest phone available. Beds: QD. Meals: Gourmet. Conference room. Fireplaces. CCs: Visa, MC, AE, DC. Horse back riding, hiking, canoeing.
Seen in: Washington Dossier, The Washington Post.
"Peaceful view and atmosphere, extraordinary food and wines. Honeymoon and heaven all in one!"

Williamsburg

Bensonhouse of Williamsburg
Contact Bensonhouse of Richmond
Williamsburg VA 23185
(804) 648-7560

Circa 1983. A copy of the 1760 Sheldon's Tavern in Litchfield, Connecticut, this home is located one mile from Colonial Williamsburg and the College of William and

Mary in a quiet, wooded area. A Palladian-style window, antique

heart-pine, wide-plank floors from Philadelphia, and oak paneling from an old Indiana church are special features. For reservations, contact Bensonhouse, 2036 Monument Avenue, Richmond, VA 23220.
Location: One block to Colonial Williamsburg.
Rates: $68-$85.
1 Rooms. 1 Private Baths. Guest phone available. Beds: QC. Meals: Full breakfast. Handicap access provided. CCs: Visa, MC, AE.

"You certainly chose wisely when you matched us with our hosts! You have a great thing going with the brochure, maps, and wonderful houses."

Liberty Rose Colonial B&B
1022 Jamestown Rd
Williamsburg VA 23185
(804) 253-1260

Circa 1929. This slate-roofed, two-story clapboard house is tucked

among tall trees a mile from Colonial Williamsburg. Constructed by the owner of Jamestown, much of the brick was brought from the Colony before it became a historic landmark. The entry porch is marked with the millstone from one of Williamsburg's old mills. The inn is lavishly decorated with antiques and collectables.

Rates: $68-$105. All year.
Innkeeper(s): Brad & Sandra Hirz.
4 Rooms. 3 Private Baths. Guest phone available. TV available. Beds: QTC. Meals: Full breakfast. Fireplaces.

"More delightful than we could possibly have imagined."

Newport House
710 South Henry St
Williamsburg VA 23185
(804) 229-1775

Circa 1988. This neo-Palladian house is a 1756 design by Peter Harrison architect of rebuilt Williamsburg. It features wooden rusticated siding. Colonial country dancing is held in the inn's

ballroom on Tuesday evenings and guests are welcome to participate. There are English and American antiques and reproductions include canopy beds in all the guest rooms. The host was a museum director and captain of a historic tall ship.
Location: Five minute walk from Colonial Williamsburg.
Rates: $75.
Innkeeper(s): John & Cathy Millar.
2 Rooms. 2 Private Baths. Guest phone available. TV available. Beds: QT. Meals: B&B. Conference room. Fireplaces. CCs: AE, DS. Scottish country dancing.

"I love the total colonial environment."

The Cedars
616 Jamestown Rd
Williamsburg VA 23185
(804) 229-3591

Circa 1930. This three-story brick house is one-half mile from colonial Williamsburg and directly across from William and Mary College. Traditional antiques and colonial reproductions are enhanced by

handmade quilts. Tucked behind the inn is a cottage for six.
**Rates: $45-$55. All year.
Innkeeper(s): Fred Strout.
9 Rooms. 3 Private Baths. Guest phone available. TV available. Beds: KQTC. Meals: Continental. Fireplaces.

Woodstock

The Inn at Narrow Passage
PO Box 608
Woodstock VA 22664
(703) 459-8000

Circa 1740. This log inn has been welcoming travelers since the time settlers took refuge here against the Indians. Later it served as a stagecoach inn on the old Valley

Turnpike, and in 1862 as Stonewall Jackson's headquarters. Many guest rooms feature fireplaces and views of the lawn as it slopes down to the Shenandoah River.
Location: On Shenandoah River and US 11, 2-1/2 miles south of Woodstock.
**Rates: $55-$80. All year.
Innkeeper(s): Ellen & Ed Markel.
12 Rooms. 8 Private Baths. Guest phone available. TV available. Beds: Q. Meals: Full breakfast. Conference room. Fireplaces. CCs: Visa, MC. Horse back riding, water skiing.
Seen in: *Capital Entertainment*.

"Just the setting I needed to unwind from my hectic civilized world."

Washington

Anacortes

Channel House
2902 Oakes Ave
Anacortes WA 98221
(206) 293-9382

Circa 1902. Built by an Italian count, the Channel House is desig-

nated as Krebs House by the Historical Home Tour. Guest rooms view Puget Sound and the San Juan Islands, and the ferry is minutes away. The inn has a Victorian flavor with a library, three fireplaces, and a dining room with French doors leading out to the garden.
Location: 85 miles north of Seattle.
**Rates: $55-$65.
Innkeeper(s): Dennis & Patricia Mc-Intyre.
4 Rooms. Guest phone available. Beds: D. Meals: Full breakfast. Jacuzzi. Fireplaces. CCs: Visa, MC. Boating, biking, swimming. Tulip festival.
Seen in: *Skagit Valley Herald.*

"The house is spectacular and your friendly thoughtfulness is the icing on the cake."

Hasty Pudding House
1312 8th Street
Anacortes WA 98221
(206) 293-5773

Circa 1913. This Edwardian Craftsman house is located in a quiet neighborhood near historic

downtown, the waterfront and Causland Park. The front porch solarium contains wicker furnishings, while the house is decorated with antiques, lace curtains and coordinated wallpapers.

"You and your beautiful bed and breakfast really made that trip for us."

Bainbridge Island

Bombay House
8490 Beck Rd NE
Bainbridge Island WA 98110
(206) 842-3926

Circa 1907. This Victorian captain's house is set high atop Blakely Hill, amidst beautiful unstructured gardens exploding with color. It boasts a quaint widow's walk and an old-fashioned gazebo overlooking picturesque sailboats and ferries cruising through Rich Passage.
Rates: $50-$78. All year.

Innkeeper(s): Bunny Cameron & Roger Kanchuk.
5 Rooms. 3 Private Baths. Guest phone available. TV available. Beds: KT. Meals: Continental plus. Conference room. CCs: AE.
"Your breakfast was marvelous! No lunch today!"

Bellingham

North Garden Inn
1014 N Garden
Bellingham WA 98225
(206) 671-7828

Circa 1897. In the National Register, this Queen Anne Victorian originally had bars on the basement windows to keep out the bears. Guestrooms feature views of Bellingham Bay and the surrounding islands. A mahogany Steinway piano is often played for guests. The inn is walking distance to Western Washington University.
**Rates: $40. All year.
Innkeeper(s): Frank & Barbara De-Freytas.
10 Rooms. 2 Private Baths. Guest phone available. Beds: Q. Meals: Continental plus. Conference room. Fireplaces. CCs: Visa, MC. Skiing, sailing, golfing.

Eastsound

Turtleback Farm Inn
Rt 1 Box 650, Crow Valley Rd Orcas
Eastsound WA 98245
(206) 376-4914

Circa 1890. This handsome farmhouse was considered one of the finest homes on Orcas Island in the early 1900s. The inn was restored and expanded from the ground up in 1985, with particular attention to authenticity and detail,

including bathroom fixtures purchased from the old Empress Hotel in Victoria. Cattle graze on the inn's eighty idyllic acres of meadows, pastures and woodlands.
Location: Six miles from ferry landing, 2 miles from Westsound.
Rates: $50-$90. All year.
Innkeeper(s): William & Susan Fletcher.
7 Rooms. 7 Private Baths. Guest phone available. TV available. Beds: KQT. Meals: Full breakfast. CCs: Visa, MC. Golf, kayaking, fishing, sailing, swimming.
Seen in: *Travel & Leisure, Contra Costa Sun.*

Greenbank

Guest House B&B & Cottages
835 E Christenson Rd
Greenbank WA 98253
(206) 678-3115
  Circa 1920. This cozy Whidbey Island home is located on 25 acres of forest and meadows, where deer wander by the wildlife pond and storybook cottages. Guest rooms have art deco touches, and there is a log house with a free-form jacuzzi and views over the pond to the sound. The Wildflower Suite and the Farm Guest Cottage are the most historic accommodations.
Location: On Whidbey Island.
**Rates: $70-$150. All year.
Innkeeper(s): Don & Mary Jane Creger.
3 Rooms. 3 Private Baths. Guest phone available. TV in room. Beds: KQTWD. Meals: EP, full breakfast. Jacuzzi. Fireplaces. Pool. CCs: Visa, MC, AE. Horseback riding, golf, fishing, hiking, clamming, boating. Exercise room, bathrobes provided.
Seen in: *Los Angeles Times.*
  "*Best B&B experience on the West Coast.*" Lewis Green, *Los Angles Times.*

Ilwaco

The Inn at Ilwaco
120 Williams St, NE
Ilwaco WA 98624
(206) 642-8686
  Circa 1926. A weathered, shingled New England-style building, the Inn at Ilwaco was originally the Community Presbyterian Church. The former sanctuary is now used for weddings, seminars, concerts and reunions. Some rooms have views of a stream that meanders by and the Columbia River seaport is two blocks away. Excursions include salmon fishing charters, clam digging, horseback riding, and visiting the cranberry bogs.
Rates: $45-$70.
Innkeeper(s): Jim Thorson.
10 Rooms. 4 Private Baths. Meals: Continental breakfast. Tour two lighthouses nearby.

Kirkland

Shumway Mansion
11410 99th Place NE
Kirkland WA 98033
(206) 823-2303
  Circa 1909. This resplendent 22-room, 10,000 square-foot mansion is situated on more than two acres overlooking Juanita Bay. With a large ballroom and veranda with water views, few could guess that a short time ago the building was hoisted on hydraulic lifts and pulled three miles across town to its present site, near the beach.
Location: West of I-405 at Juanita Bay.
**Rates: $52-$72. All year.
Innkeeper(s): Richard & Salli Harris, & daughter Julie.
7 Rooms. 7 Private Baths. Guest phone available. TV available. Beds: T. Meals: Full breakfast. Conference room. CCs: Visa, MC. Skiing, tennis. Athletic club.
Seen in: *Northgate Journal, Journal American.*
  "*Guests enjoy the mansion so much they don't want to leave.*" Northwest Living.

Langley

Country Cottage of Langley
PO Box 459, 215 6th St

Langley WA 98260
(206) 221-8709
  Circa 1926. Outstanding views of the Cascades, Saratoga Passage and the village can be seen from the three acres surrounding Country Cottage. An orchard, gazebo, outdoor hot tub, and wildflower garden add to the atmosphere. Rooms are decorated with Laura Ashley prints and one has French doors opening onto the garden.
Rates: $65-$85.
5 Rooms. 5 Private Baths. Guest phone available. TV available. Beds: QD. Meals: Full breakfast. Jacuzzi. Handicap access provided. Fireplaces. CCs: Visa, MC.
  "*Hospitality plus! Nicely decorated rooms. Beautiful breakfasts.*"

Orcas

Orcas Hotel
PO Box 155
Orcas WA 98280
(206) 376-4300
  Circa 1900. In the National Register, this three-story Victorian inn across from the ferry landing,

has been a landmark to travelers and boaters since the early 1900s. An open porch stretches around three sides and is filled with white wicker furniture. From this vantage point guests enjoy views of terraced lawns and flower beds of peonies, daffodils, iris and roses. A white picket fence and a vista of sea and islands complete the picture.
**Rates: $48-$75. All year.
Innkeeper(s): John & Barbara Jamieson.
12 Rooms. 3 Private Baths. Guest phone available. TV available. Beds: QTC. Meals: Full breakfast, gourmet. Conference room. CCs: Visa, MC, AE. Bicycling, sailing, golfing, horseback riding, fishing, hiking.
Seen in: *Los Angeles Times, Seattle Times, The New York Times.*

"Wonderful hospitality, super good food, pleasant surroundings, all provided a delightful experience."

Port Angeles

Tudor Inn
1108 S Oak
Port Angeles WA 98362
(206) 452-3138

Circa 1910. This English Tudor inn has been tastefully restored to display its original woodwork and fir

stairway. Guests enjoy stone fireplaces in the living room and study. A terraced garden with 100-foot oak trees graces the property.
Location: Eleven blocks south of the harbor with water & mountain views.
**Rates: $40-$70. All year.
Innkeeper(s): Jane & Jerry Glass.
5 Rooms. 1 Private Baths. Guest phone available. TV available. Beds: KQTD. Meals: Full breakfast. CCs: Visa, MC.

"Thanks for the warm,, gracious and delightful hospitality." Shelly (Fabera) and Mike Farrell (M*A*S*H).

Port Townsend

Arcadia Country Inn
1891 S Jacob Miller Rd
Port Townsend WA 98368
(206) 385-5245

Circa 1878. This red and white Craftsman-style house is situated on 80 acres of woodland and pasture. It is owned by the Flying Karamazov Brothers who sometimes practice in the barn where dances and theater were once held. Guest rooms are decorated with antiques and one room features views of the Olympic Mountains.
Location: Three-and-a-half miles north of town.
Rates: $45-$75.
Innkeeper(s): Yvonne Rose.
5 Rooms. 5 Private Baths. Guest phone available. Beds: QDT. Meals: Continental

breakfast. Jacuzzi. Conference room. CCs: Visa, MC.

Heritage House Inn
305 Pierce St
Port Townsend WA 98368
(206) 385-6800

Circa 1880. This stately Italianate in the National Register, was the home of Francis Pettygrove, a founder of

Port Townsend and Portland, Oregon. (He flipped a coin to name it Portland or Boston. Portland won.) The innkeepers have collected an array of unusual antiques, including a fold-down bathtub on wheels. Because of the mild climate and low rainfall, half that of Seattle, the town's elegant houses have withstood the ravages of time, and contain the best examples of Victorian architecture north of San Francisco.
Location: Across the street from the water.
Rates: $45-$79. All year.
Innkeeper(s): Pat & Jim Broughton, Bob & Carolyn Ellis.
6 Rooms. 3 Private Baths. Guest phone available. Beds: Q. Meals: Full breakfast, continental plus. Handicap access provided. CCs: Visa, MC, AE. Skiing, fishing, boating.

"You two provide the perfect balance between nurturing and unobtrusiveness, difficult to do!"

James House
1238 Washington
Port Townsend WA 98368
(206) 385-1238

Circa 1889. This Queen Anne mansion built by Francis James overlooks Puget Sound with views of the Cacades and Olympic mountain ranges. The three-story staircase was constructed of solid wild cherry brought around Cape Horn from Virginia. Parquet floors are comprised of oak, cherry, walnut and

maple. It is said to be the Northwest's first bed and breakfast, having opened in 1973.
Location: On the bluff overlooking Port Townsend Bay.
Rates: $47-$95. All year.
Innkeeper(s): Lowell & Barbara Bogart.
12 Rooms. 4 Private Baths. Guest phone available. TV available. Beds: D. Meals: Continental plus. Handicap access provided. Conference room. Fireplaces. CCs: Visa, MC. Fishing, tennis, golf, horseback riding, hiking, bicycling.
Seen in: *Washington Magazine.*

"We were enchanted by Victorian splendor and delicious breakfasts."

Lincoln Inn
538 Lincoln
Port Townsend WA 98368
(206) 385-6677

Circa 1888. This Victorian was faced in brick with cornerstones by local mason Elias Devoe as a showplace for his brick company. The original kerosene chandeliers were converted to electricity. The polished floors are covered with Persian rugs. Bicycles are available from the innkeeper for touring.
Rates: $60-$75. Feb. to Dec.
Innkeeper(s): Joan & Robert Allen.
6 Rooms. 6 Private Baths. Guest phone available. Beds: QD. Meals: Full breakfast, gourmet. Jacuzzi. Fireplaces. CCs: Visa, MC. Hiking, rafting, wind surfing, cross-country skiing, boating.
Seen in: *Daughters of Painted Ladies.*

"Exceeded our expectations. Thanks for a great honeymoon!"

Lizzie's
731 Pierce St
Port Townsend WA 98368
(206) 385-4168

Circa 1887. Named for Lizzie Grant, a sea captain's wife, this

Italianate Victorian is elegant and airy. In addition to the gracious interiors, the inn commands an outstanding view of Port Townsend Bay, Puget Sound, and the Olympic

and Cascade mountain ranges. Lizzie's is known for its elaborate breakfasts where guests are encouraged to help themselves to seconds.
Location: In uptown Historic District.
Rates: $45-$85. All year.
Innkeeper(s): Bill & Patti Wickline.
7 Rooms. 4 Private Baths. Guest phone available. Beds: KQT. Meals: Full breakfast. Fireplaces. CCs: Visa, MC. Hiking, boating, wind surfing, fishing.
Seen in: *Travel & Leisure.*
"*As they say in show biz, you're a hard act to follow.*"
"*A real place of taste and class amid the rough and tumble wilderness.*"

Manresa Castle
PO Box 564, 7th & Sheridan
Port Townsend WA 98368
(206) 385-5750 (800)732-1281 in Wash.

Circa 1892. This 30-room mansion was built by Charles Eisenbeis, a

merchant and the first mayor of Port Townsend. Later it was a school for priests and finally in 1973 was restored by the Smith family for overnight lodging. From the romantic guest rooms there are panoramic views of the Olympic Range, the Cascades, and the city. There is a full-service restaurant on the premises.
**Rates: $65-$100.
Innkeeper(s): Ronn & Carol Smith.
41 Rooms. 41 Private Baths. Guest phone in room. TV in room. Beds: KQDTC. Jacuzzi. Conference room. CCs: Visa, MC, AE.

Starrett House Inn
744 Clay St
Port Townsend WA 98368
(206) 385-3205

Circa 1889. George Starrett came from Maine to Port Townsend and became the major residential builder. By 1889, he had constructed one house a week, more than 350 houses. The Smithsonian believes the elaborate free-hung spiral stair-

case is the only one of its type in the United States. A frescoed dome atop

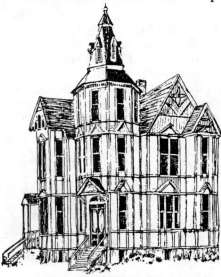

the octagonal tower depicts four seasons and four virtues. On the first day of each season, the sun causes a ruby light to point toward the appropriate painting.
Location: Three blocks from main business district.
Rates: $43-$83. All year.
Innkeeper(s): Bob & Edel Sokol.
8 Rooms. 3 Private Baths. Guest phone available. Beds: Q. Meals: Continental plus. CCs: Visa, MC. Fishing, wind surfing, golf, cross-country skiing, tennis. Cruises.
"*The Grande Bonbon of them all.*" Jan Halliday, *Pacific Northwest.*"

Seattle

Chambered Nautilus B&B Inn
5005 22nd NE
Seattle WA 98105
(206) 522-2536

Circa 1915. This blue Georgian colonial was built by an English

family. Three dormers and Palladian doors balance the front of the house.

Coved ceilings, fireplaces, and Persian rugs create an elegant counterpoint to country furnishings. Many of the guest rooms have French doors and balconies.
Location: In the University District.
Rates: $50-$80. All year.
Innkeeper(s): Deborah Sweet & Kate McDill.
6 Rooms. Guest phone available. Beds: Q. Meals: Full breakfast. Conference room. CCs: All. Jogging.
"*Food for the mind, body and spirit. Thank you.*"

Chelsea Station B&B Inn
4915 Linden Ave N
Seattle WA 98103
(206) 547-6077

Circa 1920. This Federal Colonial home is one of Seattle's finest examples of the bricklayer's art. It is located in a tranquil wooded setting in the midst of the city. A secluded hot tub is tucked away privately in one of the carriage houses. The inn has 29 varieties of its own special roses, including a Mint Julep. The Woodland Park Zoo and Rose Gardens are only a few steps away.
Location: At the Woodland Park Zoo and Rose Gardens.
**Rates: $59-$73. June to Oct.
Innkeeper(s): Dick & Marylou Jones.
5 Rooms. 5 Private Baths. Guest phone available. TV available. Beds: K. Meals: Full breakfast. Jacuzzi. Fireplaces. CCs: All. Swimming, boating, tennis, biking, golf.
Seen in: *Seattle Post-Intelligencer.*
"*What a wonderful fairyland room and hospitable hosts.*"

Country Cottage
See: Langley, WA

Galer Place
318 W Galer St
Seattle WA 98119
(206) 282-5339

Circa 1906. This two-story shingled house is located in South Queen Anne Hill and is walking distance to Seattle Center. The rooms are furnished in antiques and plants. The English innkeepers have made afternoon tea a tradition. An outside deck features a redwood hot tub overlooking the garden.
Rates: $50-$70. All year.
Innkeeper(s): Chris & Terry Giles.
4 Rooms. 2 Private Baths. Guest phone available. TV available. Beds: KQT.

Meals: Full breakfast. Jacuzzi. Conference room. CCs: Visa, MC, AE, DC.

Roberta's B&B
1147 16th Ave, E
Seattle WA 98112
(206) 329-3326

Circa 1900. This two-story Victorian home in Capitol Hill is near

Volunteer Park and the Seattle Art Museum. Polished hardwood floors glisten under comfortable furnishings. The Peach Room boasts a bay window, Franklin wood stove, love seat and brass bed. Knowledgeable about Seattle, the innkeepers can help you make the most of your time with suggestions on restaurants and touring.
Location: On Historic Capitol Hill near Volunteer Park.
Rates: $55-$75. All year.
Innkeeper(s): Roberta C. Barry.
4 Rooms. 1 Private Baths. Guest phone available. Beds: KQT. Meals: Full breakfast. Fireplaces. CCs: Visa, MC, AE, DC.

"Thanks for all the special touches. I'm afraid you've spoiled us."

Shumway Mansion
See: Kirkland, WA

The Old Tjomsland House
See: Vashon, WA

The Williams House
1505 Fourth Ave N
Seattle WA 98109
(206) 285-0810

Circa 1905. Built by a midwestern cart builder, the inn features much original woodwork and gaslight fixtures as well as an ornate gas

fireplace. A formal parlor is accentuated with Victorian furnishings arranged within a bay window. Many of the rooms have commanding views of mountains, lakes, Puget Sound, and the downtown Seattle skyline.
Location: Queen Anne Hill.
**Rates: $40-$70. All year.
Innkeeper(s): Susan, Doug & Danielle Williams.
5 Rooms. 1 Private Baths. Guest phone available. TV available. Beds: KQD. Meals: Full breakfast, continental plus. Conference room. CCs: Visa, MC, AE, DC.

Seaview

Shelburne Inn
PO Box 250, Pacific Hwy 103 & 45th
Seaview WA 98644
(206) 642-2442

Circa 1896. The Shelburne is known as the oldest continuously operating hotel in the state of Washington. The front desk at the

hotel is a former church altar. Art nouveau stained glass windows rescued from a church torn down in Morcambe, England, now sheds light and color on the dining room. The guest rooms are appointed in antiques. In between the Columbia River and the Pacific Ocean, the inn is situated on Long Beach Peninsula, a 28-mile stretch of seacoast that includes bird sanctuaries, lighthouses and Pacific Ocean views.
Location: Southwest Washington State.
**Rates: $67-$125. All year.
Innkeeper(s): David Campiche & Laurie Anderson.
16 Rooms. 13 Private Baths. Guest phone available. TV available. Beds: QTDC.

Meals: Full breakfast, restaurant, gourmet Handicap access provided. Conference room. Fireplaces. CCs: Visa, MC, AE. Horseback riding, fishing, beach walking, clamming.
Seen in: *Better Homes & Gardens*.

"Homey but elegant atmosphere. Hospitable service, like being a guest in an elegant home."

Tacoma

The Old Tjomsland House
See: Vashon, WA

Vashon

The Old Tjomsland House
99 Ave SW & 171st St, Box 913
Vashon WA 98070
(206) 463-5275

Circa 1890. A. T. Tjomsland, builder of the Methodist Church and Parsonage, constructed his farmhouse with a triangular gable

that is topped by a sunburst design. The front porch is accentuated by a diamond-patterned stained-glass door. The two guest rooms on the upper floor have a separate entrance. A family-style dinner may be arranged.
**Rates: $55. All year.
Innkeeper(s): Jan & Bill Morosoff.
2 Rooms. Guest phone available. TV available. Beds: QTC. Meals: Full breakfast. Bicycling, golf.

"Your house is neat as a pin, spotless. We have been at B&Bs all over the world and yours is outstanding."

Washington, D. C.

Washington

Adams Inn
1744 Lanier Pl NW
Washington DC 20009
(202) 745-3600

Circa 1908. This restored townhouse has fireplaces, a library, and parlor all furnished home-style

as are the guestrooms. Former residents of this neighborhood were Tallulah Bankhead, Woodrow Wilson, and Al Jolson. The Adams-Morgan area is home to diplomats, radio and television personalities and government workers. A notable firehouse across the street holds the record for the fastest response of a horse-drawn fire apparatus.
Location: Two miles from the White House, walking distance to major hotels.
**Rates: $40-$55.
Innkeeper(s): Gene & Nancy Thompson.
17 Rooms. 11 Private Baths. Guest phone available. TV available. Beds: DT. Meals: Continental-plus breakfast. Fireplaces. CCs: All.

"We enjoyed your friendly hospitality and the homelike atmosphere. Your sug-gestions on restaurants and helping plan our visit were appreciated."

Kalorama Guest House
1854 Mintwood Place NW
Washington DC 20009
(202) 667-6369

Circa 1900. This is a group of six Victorian townhouses decorated with period antiques and artwork. The inn features original wainscoting, fireplace mantles, and claw-footed tubs. Brass beds, plush comforters, oriental rugs, and sunny bay windows add to the charm. Each house is hosted year round and sherry is served by the fireplace each afternoon. The subway is a short walk as are the Chinese Embassy, the French Embassy, major hotels and stately Massachusetts Avenue diplomatic residences.
Location: Downtown residential area 10 minutes to the Mall and White House.
**Rates: $35-$75.
Innkeeper(s): Rick Fenstemaker.
31 Rooms. 12 Private Baths. Guest phone available. TV available. Beds: QDT. Meals: Continental-plus breakfast. Conference room. CCs: All.

Memory House
See: Arlington, VA

West Virginia

Caldwell

The Greenbrier River Inn
US 60
Caldwell WV 24925
(304) 647-5652

Circa 1824. The completely restored Greenbrier was built as a stagecoach stop and during the Civil

War it was almost burned by a Union commander. Inside the house, a woman too sick to be moved had to be checked by the Union doctor. He agreed she was ill and the house was left unscathed. Robert E. Lee and President Van Buren were guests. The inn is tucked behind a giant elm tree and provides a southern mansion experience for guests.
Location: Between Lewisburg and White Sulphur Springs.
Rates: $55. All year.
Innkeeper(s): Joan & Jim Jeter.
7 Rooms. 7 Private Baths. Guest phone available. TV available. Beds: KTC. Meals: Full breakfast. CCs: Visa, MC. Fishing, boat dock and tennis on the property.
Seen in: *The Charleston Gazette.*

Charlestown

Magnus Tate's Kitchen
201 E Washington St
Charlestown WV 25414
(304) 725-8052

Circa 1796. Magnus Tate, wealthy planter and business associate of George Washington's brother Charles, built his townhouse with a separate two-story brick building as the kitchen and servant's quarters. It is this building that has been restored. Recently featured in the Spring House and Garden Tour, it reflects a gracious 18th-century lifestyle.
Rates: $80-$95. All year.
Innkeeper(s): Louis & Katherine Santucci.
2 Rooms. 2 Private Baths. Guest phone available. TV in room. Beds: D. Meals: Full breakfast. Fireplaces. Horseracing, whitewater rafting, hiking, cross-country skiing.
"Thank you for making our honeymoon so wonderful. We enjoyed staying at such a lovely place and the breakfasts were unbelievable."

Davis

Bright Morning
William Ave, Rt 32
Davis WV 26260
(304) 259-5119

Circa 1898. This was originally constructed as a lumberjack boarding house. Handmade nails, exposed beams and wooden overlaid water pipes are still in evidence. Early American antiques are complemented by locally handcrafted quilts and rugs. The innkeepers also

manage Trans-Montane Outfitters across the road, offering expert guides for white-water rafting, skiing and spelunking.
Location: Thirty five miles from Elkins, 18 miles from Oakland.
**Rates: $55-$65. All year.
Innkeeper(s): George & Missy Bright.
11 Rooms. 8 Private Baths. Guest phone available. TV available. Beds: QT. Meals: MAP, full breakfast, restaurant. Handicap access provided. Conference room. Tennis, golf, hiking, rafting, canoeing. Two state parks nearby.

Gerrardstown

Prospect Hill
PO Box 135
Gerrardstown WV 25420
(304) 229-3346

Circa 1789. An 18th-century gentleman's home, this Georgian

mansion belonged to William Wilson, a member of Thomas Jefferson's cabinet. During the Civil War it is said that Mrs. Wilson stood on the landing while Union soldiers shot around her, trying to discover where the slaves had been hidden. A metal detector indicates bullets in the shape of a large inverted 'U' in the wall. A hand-painted wall mural of colonial scenes winds up the staircase wall to the third floor. There are

225 acres of woodlands, stocked ponds, orchard groves, and berry patches.
Location: Three-and-a-half miles West of I-81 on Route 51.
Rates: $75-$85. All year.
Innkeeper(s): Hazel & Charles Hudock.
2 Rooms. 2 Private Baths. Guest phone available. TV in room. Beds: QD. Meals: EP, restaurant. Fireplaces. Hiking, fishing.
Seen in: *The Daily Mail, the Washington Post.*
   "What a wonderful old house, full of history."

Harpers Ferry

Fillmore Street B&B
Box 34
Harpers Ferry WV 25425
(301) 377-0070 (304)535-2619
   Circa 1890. This two-story clapboard Victorian was built on the foundation of a Civil War structure on land deeded by Jefferson Davis,

Secretary of War. The surrounding acreage was an encampment for both the Union and Confederate soldiers (at different times). Within walking distance to the inn are the national park, museums, shopping, and dining.
Rates: $62. All year.
Innkeeper(s): Alden and James Addy
2 Rooms. 2 Private Baths. Guest phone available. TV in room. Beds: KQ. Meals: Full breakfast, gourmet. Fireplaces. Hiking, rafting, bicycling.
   "Delightful! What superb host and hostess you two are. We enjoyed ourselves luxuriously."

Spring Bank Inn
See: Frederick, MD

Lewisburg

The General Lewis
301 E Washington St
Lewisburg WV 24901
(304) 645-2600
   Circa 1834. Patrick Henry and Thomas Jefferson registered at the

inn's walnut desk retrieved from an old hot springs resort in the area. A stagecoach that traveled between the springs on the James River and Kanawha Turnpike rests under an arbor. Memory Hall displays household items and tools once used by local pioneers. The town has more than 50 historic houses.
Rates: $45-$70. All year.
Innkeeper(s): Rodney Fisher.
27 Rooms. 27 Private Baths. Beds: DTC. Meals: EP. Handicap access provided. Pool. CCs: All.
Seen in: *Southern Living.*
   "The staff is wonderful at making us feel at home, and we can be as much a part of the inn as we want."

Martinsburg

Boydville-
The Inn at Martinsburg
601 S Queen St
Martinsburg WV 25401
(304) 263-1448
   Circa 1812. This Georgian estate was saved from burning by Union

troups only by a specific proclamation from President Lincoln dated July 18, 1864. Tall maples line the long driveway leading up to the house. It is constructed of two-foot-thick stone walls covered with plaster. The entry hall retains the original wallpaper brought from England in 1812 and hand-painted murals, fireplaces, and antiques adorn the spacious guest rooms. Ivy-covered brick and stone walls enclose gardens surrounding the inn.
**Rates: $75-$105. All year.
Innkeeper(s): Owen Sullivan & Ripley Hotch.
7 Rooms. 4 Private Baths. Guest phone available. Beds: Q. Meals: Full breakfast. Fireplaces. Fishing, golf, hiking, skiing.
   "Your gracious home, hospitality and excellent amenities were enjoyed so much. Such a fine job of innkeeping."

Middleway

Gilbert House B&B
Rt 1 Box 160
Middleway WV 25430
(304) 725-0637
   Circa 1760. A magnificent greystone of early Georgian design, the Gilbert House boasts the state's oldest flagstone sidewalk. During restoration, graffiti found on the upstairs bedroom walls included a drawing of President James Polk and a child's growth chart from the 1800s. The inn is elegantly appointed with fine oriental rugs, tasteful art and antique furnishings. The village contains one of the country's most well-preserved collections of old stone homes.
Rates: $75-$125. All year.
Innkeeper(s): Jean & Bernie Heiler.
3 Rooms. 3 Private Baths. Guest phone available. TV available. Beds: Q. Meals: Full breakfast. Conference room. Fireplaces. CCs: Visa, MC.
   "We have stayed at inns for 15 years and yours is at the top of the list as Best Ever!"

Moorefield

Hickory Hill Farm
Rt 1 Box 355
Moorefield WV 26836
(304) 538-2511

Circa 1809. This working farm is situated on a bluff overlooking the river. The two-story brick Federal

house is considered to be one of the finest architectural gems in the South Branch Valley. Woodwork throughout the inn is hand carved, and the mantels and door frames are decorated with a repeated pattern of sunbursts. The porch contains a written history with several notes inscribed on the planks of the porch dating from 1819.
Location: On the South Branch of the Potomac River, 9 miles south of town.
Rates: $44-$65.
Innkeeper(s): Fran & Jack Welton.
2 Rooms. Guest phone available. TV available. Beds: DC.

"I have passed this place for years, and it is just as beautiful inside as out."

Shepherdstown

Thomas Shepherd Inn
Box 1162, German & Duke St
Shepherdstown WV 25443
(304) 876-3715

Circa 1868. Spreading oaks and maples shade the cobbled streets outside this stately two-story brick house, once a Lutheran parsonage. It was built on land owned by Thomas Shepherd a founder of Shepherdstown, West Virginia's oldest town. Furnishings are American antiques.
Location: In the beautiful eastern panhandle of West Virginia.
Rates: $60-$75. All year.
Innkeeper(s): Ed & Carol Ringoot.
6 Rooms. 4 Private Baths. Guest phone available. TV available. Beds: QTD. Meals: Full breakfast. Fireplaces. CCs: Visa, MC. Golf, rafting, canoeing, biking, tennis, cross-country skiing.
Seen in: *The Baltimore Sun, Herald Mail.*

"The elegance and tastefulness of the inn, the breakfast and the trip back into time that it affords can only be exceeded by the hospitality of Carol and Ed."

Wisconsin

Alma

The Gallery House
215 N Main St
Alma WI 54610
(608) 685-4975

Circa 1861. This quaint river town stretches along the bluffs of the Mississippi and is the setting for The Gallery House, an artist's gallery and home. Watercolors and prints decorate the inn which is furnished in antiques and traditional furnishings.
Location: On the Great River Road.
Rates: $40.00 All year.
Innkeeper(s): John & Joan Runions
3 Rooms. Meals: Full breakfast.

Appleton

The Parkside B&B
402 E North St
Appleton WI 54011
(414) 733-0200

Circa 1906. This three-story Richardson Romanesque house fea-

tures gables, bays and a partial center turret. The house is filled with sunlight filtered through windows of decorative leaded glass. It is situated near downtown and faces the park and Lawrence University campus, once the neighborhood home of Harry Houdini and Edna Ferber.
Rates: $51-$62. All year.
Innkeeper(s): Bonnie Riley
1 Rooms. 1 Private Baths. Guest phone available. TV in room. Beds: K. Meals: Full breakfast. Conference room. Fireplaces. Swimming.
Seen in: *Sunday Post-Crescent*.

"Thank you for making our visit so delightful! Everything was perfect."

Baraboo

The Barrister's House
226 9th Ave, PO Box 166
Baraboo WI 53913
(608) 356-3344

Circa 1932. Built by a prominent Baraboo attorney, this stately home

was designed by architect Frank Riley (builder of the governor's mansion) to replicate the warmth and grace of colonial New England homes. The fireplaces, crystal chandeliers, library and veranda are favorites with guests.
Location: In the heart of the Devil's Lake.
Rates: $45-$55. April to Nov.
Innkeeper(s): Glen & Mary Schulz.
4 Rooms. 4 Private Baths. Beds: QD. Meals: Continental plus. Skiing, hiking, fishing, swimming, boating.

"Your home is simply wonderful and we've enjoyed every moment. Lovely rooms, gracious hosts, delicious food! A special place to remember."

Bayfield

Old Rittenhouse Inn
301 Rittenhouse Ave, PO Box 584-1
Bayfield WI 54814
(715) 779-5111

Circa 1890. This rambling Queen Anne Victorian was built by Civil War General Allen Fuller, using

cedar shingles and the local brownstone for which Bayfield was famous. Antique furnishings abound throughout the inn, which has 12 working fireplaces. Underneath massive gables a wraparound veranda is filled with geraniums, petunias, and white wicker furnishings, and there is a spectacular view of Lake Superior.
Location: On Bayfield's main street, 5 blocks from Lake Superior shore.
Rates: $69-$109. April to Nov.
Innkeeper(s): Jerry & Mary Phillips.
9 Rooms. 9 Private Baths. Beds: KQC. Meals: Full breakfast, gourmet. Handicap access provided. Conference room. CCs: Visa, MC. Cross-country skiing, sailing, swimming.
Seen in: *Wisconsin Trails, The Magazine of Good Living*.

"The whole decor, the room, the staff, and the food were superb! Your per-

sonalities and talents give a great warmth to the inn."

Cedarburg

Stagecoach Inn B&B
W 61 N 520 Washington Ave
Cedarburg WI 53012
(414) 375-0208

Circa 1853. Restored by historian Brook Brown, this stone Greek Revival house was originally used as a stagecoach stop between Milwaukee and Greenbay. Authentically decorated with antiques, all the suites feature king-size whirlpools. There is a pub, chocolate shop and bookstore on the first floor.
Location: Downtown Cedarburg.
Rates: $45-$85. All year.
Innkeeper(s): Brook & Liz Brown.
12 Rooms. 12 Private Baths. Guest phone available. TV available. Beds: QTDC. Meals: Full breakfast, continental plus. Jacuzzi. Conference room. CCs: Visa, MC, AE, DC. Cross-country skiing, bicycling, tennis, golf, horseback riding.
Seen in: *News Graphic Pilot.*

The Washington House Inn
W 62 N 573 Washington Ave
Cedarburg WI 53012
(414) 375-3550

Circa 1886. Completely renovated, this original Cream-City-brick building is decorated in a light-hearted

country Victorian style featuring antiques as well as whirlpool baths. Some rooms have two fireplaces and there are brick and rough-stone walls with wood-plank floors. There is an original guest registry, over a hundred years old.
Location: In the heart of downtown Cedarburg.
**Rates: $49-$129. All year.
Innkeeper(s): Judith Drefahl.

29 Rooms. 29 Private Baths. Guest phone in room. TV in room. Beds: KQTC. Meals: Full breakfast. Jacuzzi. Sauna. Handicap access provided. Conference room. Fireplaces. CCs: All. Victorian interlude dinner package.
Seen in: *Country Home.*
"A piece of time lost to all but a fortunate few who will experience it. Please save it for my children."

Ellison Bay

The Griffin Inn
11976 Mink River Rd
Ellison Bay WI 54210
(414) 854-4306

Circa 1910. This New England-style country inn is situated on five acres of rolling lawns and maple

trees with a gazebo. There are verandas with porch swings, a gracious lobby with a stone fireplace, and a cozy library. Guest rooms are furnished with antique beds and dressers and feature handmade quilts. In addition to the main house there are four cottages.
Location: Two blocks east of Highway 42 on the Door County Peninsula.
Rates: $56-$62. All year.
Innkeeper(s): Jim & Laurie Roberts.
10 Rooms. Guest phone available. Beds: DT. Meals: Full breakfast. Cross-country skiing, golf, hiking, fishing, swimming.
Seen in: *Travel & Leisure, Ladies Circle.*
"A classic bed and breakfast inn."
Travel and Leisure Magazine.

Fish Creek

Thorp House Inn & Cottages
4135 Bluff Rd, PO Box 90
Fish Creek WI 54212
(414) 868-2444

Circa 1902. Freeman Thorp picked the site for this home because of its view of Green Bay and the village. Before his house was finished, however, he perished in the bay when the *Erie L. Hackley* sank. His wife

completed it as a guest house. Each room has a view of the harbor, cedar forest, or village. A stone fireplace is the focal point of the parlor and two of the cottages on the property have fireplaces.
Location: Heart of Door County, in the village of Fish Creek.
Rates: $49-$65. All year.
Innkeeper(s): Christine & Sverre Falck-Pedersen.
4 Rooms. Guest phone available. Beds: QD. Meals: Full breakfast, continental plus. Fireplaces. Swimming, fishing, bicycling, hiking, golf, tennis, horses.
Seen in: *Green Bay Press-Gazette.*
"Once upon a time, two travelers and their two fine friends happened upon a wonderful inn filled with love and hope and kindness. Thank you for decorating our lives and our memories with your thoughtfulness."

Kenosha

The Manor House
6536 3rd Ave
Kenosha WI 53140
(414) 658-0014

Circa 1928. This stately Georgian mansion overlooking Lake Michigan

was built for the daughter of the Nash Motor Company founder. There are Chippendale furnishings and antiques from Rothchild's Mentmore Manor in Buckinghamshire, England. The grounds feature a sunken pool, water fountain and gazebo. Across the street is an 11-acre wooded park with tennis courts, an art gallery and fishing pier.

Location: Thirty minutes between Milwaukee & Chicago.
Rates: $75-$110. All year.
Innkeeper(s): Ron & Mary Rzeplinski.
4 Rooms. 4 Private Baths. Guest phone available. TV in room. Beds: KQT. Meals: Continental plus. Conference room. CCs: Visa, MC. Tennis, bicycling, skiing nearby, fishing, swimming, golf.
Seen in: *Kenosha News*.
"Elegant, magnificent, beautiful beyond words. Absolutely superb."

Milwaukee

Ogden House
2237 N Lake Dr
Milwaukee WI 53202
(414) 272-2740
Circa 1916. Listed in the National Register, this white brick Federal house is located in the North Point-South Historic District. It was built for Miss Ogden, who lived to be 101 years old and was one of the founders of the Milwaukee County Historical Society. The house is set on a bluff overlooking Lake Michigan.
Location: One block from Lake Michigan, 1 mile north of downtown.
**Rates: $65-$75. All year.
Innkeeper(s): Mary Jane & John Moss.
2 Rooms. 2 Private Baths. Guest phone available. TV available. Beds: Q. Meals: Continental plus. Fireplaces.
"You made me feel as if I were staying with friends and at the same time added the details desired at a fine hotel. I'm ready to adopt my room."

Mineral Point

Wilson House Inn
110 Dodge St Hwy 151
Mineral Point WI 53565
(608) 987-3600
Circa 1853. One of Wisconsin's first attorney generals, Alexander Wilson, built this two-story brick house,

now on the Mineral Point Historic Tour. It has a wraparound veranda, and is currently undergoing restoration.
Rates: $45. All year.
Innkeeper(s): Bev & Jim Harris.
4 Rooms. 2 Private Baths. Guest phone available. Beds: T. Meals: Full breakfast. Fireplaces. CCs: Visa, MC. Fishing, swimming, skiing, bicycling.

Sister Bay

Renaissance Inn
414 Maple Dr
Sister Bay WI 54234
(414) 854-5107
Circa 1903. Before its debut as a B&B, this building was a bait and tackle shop, a boardinghouse, and a butcher shop. Renovations on the building, as well as the collection of all appointments took many months. Renaissance art is featured in the inn, a property in the National Register.
Location: Off Hwy 42.
Rates: $50-$70. Closed Dec & Ap
Innkeeper(s): John & Jodee Faller.
5 Rooms. 5 Private Baths. Guest phone available. TV available. Beds: D. Meals: Full breakfast. CCs: Visa, MC, AE.

Sturgeon Bay

White Lace Inn
16 N 5th Ave
Sturgeon Bay WI 54235
(414) 743-1105
Circa 1903. White Lace Inn is three Victorian houses, one an ornate

Queen Anne. It is adjacent to two districts listed in the National Register. Often the site for romantic wedding festivities, a favorite suite has a two-sided fireplace, magnificent walnut Eastlake Bed,

English country fabrics, and a two-person whirlpool tub.
Location: Door County, Lake Michigan on one side, Green Bay on the other.
Rates: $58-$125. All year.
Innkeeper(s): Dennis & Bonnie Statz.
15 Rooms. 15 Private Baths. Guest phone available. TV in room. Beds: Q. Meals: Continental. Jacuzzi. Handicap access provided. Fireplaces. CCs: Visa, MC. Cross-country skiing, beaches.
Seen in: *Wisconsin Trails*.
"Each guest room is such an overwhelming visual feast, such a dazzling fusion of colors, textures, and beautiful objects. It is one of these rare gems that established a tradition the day it opened." Wisconsin Trails.

Wausau

Rosenberry Inn
511 Franklin St
Wausau WI 54401
(715) 842-5733
Circa 1908. This stucco and brick house was built for Marvin Rosenberry, a judge on the Wisconsin Supreme Court. It is in the midwestern Prairie School style, with overhanging eaves and massive porch supports. Stained glass windows feature a water lily design and geometric motifs. The inn is decorated with handmade quilts and American antiques collected from the innkeepers' antique shop in the old Brokaw Depot.
Location: Downtown area.
Rates: $40-$45. All year.
Innkeeper(s): Gerald & Patricia Artz & son, Doug.
8 Rooms. 8 Private Baths. Guest phone available. TV available. Beds: TD. Meals: Continental. CCs: Visa, MC.
Seen in: *Wausau Herald*.

Wyoming

Cody

Pitcher Guest House
See: Red Lodge, MT

Savery

Boyer YL Ranch
PO Box 24
Savery WY 82332
(307) 383-7840

Circa 1889. This is a working sheep, cattle and horse ranch that has been taking in guests since the Twenties. In those days, visitors were met with horses at the top of the Continental Divide because cars couldn't make it. In addition to the rambling old ranch house there are guest cabins, barns, a saddle house, blacksmith shop, and corrals nestled among the cottonwood trees. Savery Creek has popular swimming holes in the summer. The ranch is known for exceptional riding horses and delicious meals.

Location: 9 miles north of Savery (population 25).
**Rates: $85-$105.
Innkeeper(s): Joyce B. Saer.
10 Rooms. 5 Private Baths. Guest phone available. Beds: KQDT. Meals: Full breakfast. Conference room. Fireplaces. Riding, fishing, tennis on the ranch. rodeos, picnics, cookouts. Bald eagles and wildlife.

"Marianne and I had a wonderful stay at your place (too short!)"

U.S. Territories

Condado, San Juan, PR

El Canario Inn
1317 Ashford Ave
Condado, San Juan PR 00907
(809) 722-3861

Circa 1938. This three-story inn is close to white sandy beaches. All the rooms are air-conditioned and there is a tropical patio with a swimming pool.
**Rates: $38-$75.
25 Rooms. 25 Private Baths. Meals: Continental breakfast. Pool. CCs: Visa, MC, AE.

Directory of American Historic Inns

The following directory contains the names, addresses, and phone numbers of Bed & Breakfast Inns, Country Inns, and guesthouses believed to be of historic significance. Every attempt has been made to be as comprehensive and as accurate as possible, however, there always remains the possibility of error, omission, or change. This list is presented for information purposes only and is offered without warranty of any kind. Although there are many fine inns in the list inclusion does not constitute a recommendation nor does non-inclusion indicate a nonrecommendation. Additions, corrections or changes, if any, and if brought to our attention, will be made in subsequent editions.

Inns listed in **bold type** are described in more detail in the main body of the book.

We suggest that if you are interested in making reservations with any of these that you drop them a postcard or give them a call. If you do, be sure to mention that you saw them in **The Official Guide to American Historic Inns.**

Alabama

Anniston
Victoria, 1604 Quintard Ave, 36201 ....(205)236-0503
Birmingham
B&B Birmingham, Box 31328, 35222 ....(205)933-2487
Decatur
Dancy-Polk House, 901 Railroad St NW, 35601 ....(205)353-3579
Fairhope
Mershond Court, 203 Fairhope Ave, 36532.......................(205)928-7398
Franklin
Rutherford Johnson House, PO Box 202, 36444 ....(205)282-4423
Mentone
Mentone Inn, Highway 117, PO Box 284, 35984, 1927 ...(205)634-4836
Millbrook
B&B B Montgomery, Box 886, 36054 ....(205)285-5421
Mobile
Kraft Korner, 90 Carlile Dr, 36619 ....(205)666-6819
Malaga Inn, 359 Church St, 36602, 1862...........................(205)438-4701
Vincent-Doan Home, 1664 Springhill Ave, 36604, 1827 (205)433-7121
Montrose
Seven Gables, 36559 ....(205)928-5454
Opelika
Under The Oaks, 707 Geneva St, 36801.............................(205)745-2449
Scottsboro
Brunton House, PO Box 1006, 112 College Ave, 35768,
    1921 ....(205)259-1298

Alaska

Anchorage
A Log Home B&B, 2440 Sprucewood St, 99508 ....(907)276-8527
Alaska Private Lodgings, PO Box 110135 South Station,
    99511 ....(907)345-2222
All The Comforts of Home, 12531 Turk's Turn St, 99516 (907)345-4279
Green Bough Inn, 3832 Young St, 99508 ....(907)562-4636
McCarthy Wilderness B&B, Box 111241, 99511, 1917 .....(907)277-6867
Angoon
Favorite Bay Inn, PO Box 101, 99820, 1937 ....(907)788-3123
Gustavus
Glacier Bay Country Inn, Box 5, Dub-Al-U Ranch,
    99826..(907)697-2288
Gustavus Inn, PO Box 31, 99826, 1928 ....(907)697-3311
Haines
Fort William Seward B&B, House-1, PO Box 5, 99827,
    1904 ....(907)766-2856
Homer
Driftwood Inn, 135-T W Bunnell Ave, 99603, 1920
Homer B&B/Seekins, Box 1264, 99603..............................(907)235-8996
Magic Canyon Ranch, Box 632, 99603 ....(907)235-6077
Juneau
Fifth & Franklin B&B, 505-TN Franklin, 99801
Mullins House, 526 Seward St, 99802, 1904 ....(907)586-2959
Palmer
Hatcher Pass Lodge, Box 2655, 99645 ....(907)745-5897
Petersburg
Scandia Haus, PO Box 689, 206 Nordic Dr, 99833 ....(907)772-4281
Seldovia
Annie McKenzie's Boardwalk Hotel, PO Box 72, 99663 ..(907)234-7816
Skagway
Golden North Hotel, PO Box 431, 99840, 1898 ....(907)983-2294
Irene's Inn, PO Box 543, 99840 ....(907)983-2520
Skagway Inn, PO 292, 99840, 1899 ....(907)983-2294
Talkeetna
Fairview Inn, PO Box 379, 99676, 1921 ....(907)733-2423
Tenakee Springs
Tanakee Inn, 167 S Franklin, 99801 ....(907)586-1000
Tok
1260 Inn, Mi 1260, Ak Hwy, 99780 ....(907)778-2205
Valdez
B&B Valdez, Box 442, 99686 ....(907)835-4211

Arizona

Bisbee
Bisbee Inn, 45 OK St, PO Box 1855, 85603 ....(602)432-5131
Inn At Castle Rock, Box 1161, 112 Tombstone Canyon,
    85603 ....(602)432-7195
Carefree
Adobe Inn-Carefree, Box 1081, Elbow Bend & Sidewinder,
    85377...(602)488-4444
Cochise
Cochise Hotel, PO Box 27, 85606, 1882 ....(602)384-3156
Flagstaff
Arizona Mountain Inn, 685 Lake Mary Rd, 86001 ....(602)774-8959
Dierker House B&B, 423 W Cherry, 86001, 1914 ....(602)774-3249
Rainbow Ranch, 2860 N Fremont, 86001, 1886 ....(602)774-3724
Walking L Ranch, RR 4, Box 721B, 86001 ....(602)779-2219
Fountain Hills
Villa Galleria B&B, 16650 E Hawk Dr, 85268 ....(602)837-1400
Pearce
Grapevine Canyon Ranch, PO Box 302, 85625 ....(602)826-3185
Phoenix
Squaw Peak Inn, 4425 E Horseshoe Rd, 85028, 1929......(602)990-0682
Westways Resort, PO 41624, 85080, 1939 ....(602)582-3868
Prescott
Ford's B&B, 212 S Pleasant, 86303, 1900 ....(602)776-1564
Marks House Inn, 203 E Union, 86303, 1894 ....(602)778-4632
Prescott Pines Inn, 901 White Spar Rd, 86303, 1902 ....(602)445-7270
Sasabe
Rancho De La Osa, PO Box 1, 85633, 1890 ....(602)823-4257
Scottsdale
Valley 'O the Sun B&B, PO Box 2214, 85252 ....(602)941-1281
Sedona
Briar Patch Inn, Star Rt 3, Box 1002, 86336 ....(602)282-2342
Garland's Oak Creek Lodge, PO Box 152, Hwy 89A, 86336,
    1930 ....(602)282-3343
Graham's B&B Inn, PO Box 912, 86336 ....(602)284-1425
Keyes' B&B, Box 1682, 2271 Roadrunner, 86336 ....(602)282-6008
L'Auberge de Sedona Resort, PO Box B, 301 Little Ln,
    86336 ....(602)282-7131
Moore's Music Museum B&B, 3085 W Hwy 89A, 86336.(602)282-3419
Rose Tree Inn, 376 Cedar St, 86336 ....(602)282-2065
Saddle Rock Ranch, 255 Rock Ridge Dr, 86336, 1939 ....(602)282-7640
Tempe
Mi Casa-Su Casa B&B, PO Box 950, 85281, 1882.............(602)990-0682
Tucson
Casa Suecia B&B, PO Box 36883, Ste 181, 86704
Desert Needlework Ranch, 1645 N Harrison Rd, 85715,
    1930 ....(602)885-6264
La Madera, 9061 E Woodland Rd, 8575111, 1888 ....(602)749-2773
La Posada Del Valle, 1640 N Campbell Ave, 85719,
    1920 ....(602)795-3840
Wickenburg
Kay El Bar Ranch, PO Box 2480, 85358, 1926 ....(602)684-7593
Rancho De Los Caballeros, Box 1148, 85358....................(602)684-5484

Arkansas

Brinkley
The Great Southern Hotel, 127 West Cedar, 72021,
    1913 ....(501)734-4955
Clarksville
May House, 101 Railroad Ave, 72830 ....(501)754-6851
Des Arc
The 5-B's, 210 S 2nd St, 72040 ....(501)256-4789
Eureka Springs
Bridgeford Cottage, 263 Spring St, 72632
Cabin On The Boardwalk, Box 492, 185 Spring St, 72632
Coach House Inn, 140A S Main, 72632.............................(501)253-8099
Crescent Cottage Inn, 211 Spring St, 72632, 1881 ....(501)253-6022
Crescent Hotel, Prospect St, 72632
Crescent Moon Townhouse, PO Box 429, 72632 ....(501)253-9463
Dairy Hollow House, Rt 4 Box 1, 72632, 1888..................(501)253-7444
Elmwood House, 110 Spring St #62b, 72632

Eureka Sprs & N. Ark. RW, PO Box 310, 72632 ....(501)253-9623
Heart of the Hills Inn, 5 Summit, 72632 ....(501)253-7468
Heartstone Inn, 35 King's Hwy, 72632 ....(501)253-8916
Johnson's Hilltop Cabin, Rt 1, Box 503, 72632 ....(501)253-9537
Lake Lucerne Resort, PO Box 441, 72632 ....(501)253-8085
Lookout Cottage, 12 Lookout Cir., 72632
Magnolia Guest Cottage, 180 Spring St, 72632 ....(501)253-9463
Main Street Inn, 217 N. Main St, 72632
Maplewood B&B, 4 Armstrong St, 72632 ....(501)253-8053
New Orleans Hotel, 63 Spring St, 72632, 1892 ....(501)253-8630
Oak Crest Cottages, Rt 2, Box 26, 72632 ....(501)253-9493
Palace Hotel, 135 Spring, 72632 ....(501)253-7474
Paul's Place Rose Room, 5 Ridgeway, 72632
Red Bud Valley Resort, RR 1, Box 500, 72632 ....(502)253-9028
Redbud Manor, 7 Kings Hwy, 72632
Riverview Resort, RR 2, Box 475, 72632 ....(501)253-8367
School House Inn, 15 Kansas St, 72632 ....(501)253-7854
Singleton House B&B, 11 Singleton, 72632, 1895 ....(501)253-9111
Sunnyside Cottage, 5 Ridgeway, 72632
Sweet Seasons Guest Cottages, 26 Spring St, 72632,
   1890 ....(501)253-7603
Tatman-Garrett House, Box 171, 72632
The Basin Park Hotel, Prospect St, 72632
The Heartstone Inn and Cottages, 35 King's Highway, 72632,
   1903 ....(501)253-8916
The Inn On Depot Grade, 75 Hillside Ave, 72632
The Old Homestead, 78-82 Armstrong St, 72632
The Palace Hotel, 135 Spring St, 72632
The Piedmont House, 165 Spring St, 72632, 1880 ......(501)253-9258
The School House Inn, 15 Kansas St, 72632
White Flower Cottage, 62 Kings Hwy, 72632 ....(501)253-9636

Everton
Corn Cob Inn, Rt 1 Box 183, 72633, 1910 ....(501)429-6545

Fort Smith
McCartney House, 500 S 19th St, 72901 ....(501)782-9057
Merry Go Round Cottage, 412 North 8th, 72901, 1895 ....(501)783-3472
Thomas Quinn Guest House, 815 N B St, 72901 ....(501)782-0499

Garfield
Dogwood Inn B&B, US 62, 72732 ....(604)287-4213

Gilbert
Anna's House, PO Box 58, 72636 ....(501)439-2888

Heber Springs
Oak Tree Inn, Vinegar Hill & 110 W, 72543 ....(501)362-8870

Helena
Edwardian Inn, 317 S Biscoe, 72342, 1904 ....(401)338-9155

Hot Springs
Stillmeadow Farm Reproduction, Rt 1 Box 434-d, 71913
Williams House Inn, 420 Quapaw St, 71901, 1890 ....(501)624-4275

Hot Springs National
Megan-Lorien House, 426 Spring St, 71901

Jasper
Cliff House Inn, Scenic Ark, Hwy 7, 72641 ....(501)446-2292

Morrilton
Tanyard Springs, Rt 3, Box 335, 72110 ....(501)727-5200

Mountain View
The Commercial Hotel, A Vintage Guesthouse, PO Box 72, 72560,
   1920 ....(501)269-4383

Pine Bluff
Margland 11 B&B Inn, PO Box 8594, 71611 ....(501)536-6000

Romance
Hammons Chapel Farm, 1 Mi of Ark 5, 72136 ....(501)849-2819

Washington
Old Country Jail, PO Box 157, 71862, 1872 ....(501)983-2178

Yellville
Red Raven Inn, PO Box 160, 72687 ....(501)449-5168

California

Alameda
Garratt Mansion, 900 Union St, 94501 ....(415)521-4779

Albion
Fensalden B&B, PO Box 99, 95410, 1860 ....(707)937-4042
Wool Loft, 32751 Navarro Ridge Rd, 95410 ....(707)937-0377

Alleghany
Kenton Mine Lodge, Box 942, 95910 ....(916)287-3212

Amador City
Mine House Inn, PO Box 245, S Hwy 49, 95601 ....(209)267-5900

Anaheim
Anaheim Country Inn, 856 South Walnut St, 92802,
   1910 ....(714)778-0150

Angels Camp
Cooper House, 1184 Church St, 95222, 1911 ....(209)736-2145

Aptos
Apple Lane Inn, 6265 Soquel Dr, 95003, 1870 ....(408)475-6868
Bayview Hotel, 8041 Soquel Dr, 95003 ....(408)688-1927
Mangels House, 570 Aptos Creek Rd, PO Box 302, 95001,
   1886 ....(408)688-7982
The Inn at Depot Hill, 134 Hyannis Ct, 95003

Arcata
Lady Ann, 902 14th St, 95521, 1888 ....(707)822-2797
Plough & the Stars Country Inn, 1800 27th St, 95521,
   1860 ....(707)822-8236

Arroyo Grande
Guest House, 120 Hart Lane, 93420, 1850 ....(805)481-9304

Auburn
Powers Mansion Inn, 164 Cleveland Ave, 95603, 1886 ....(916)885-1166

Avalon
Glenmore Plaza Hotel, 120 Sumner Ave, 90704 ....(213)510-0017
Island Inn, PO Box 467, 125 Metropole, 90704, 1906 ....(213)510-1623
The Inn On Mt. Ada, Box 2560, 207 Wrigley Rd, 90704, 1921(213)510-
   2030
The Old Turner Inn, PO Box 97, 90704, 1927 ....(213)510-2236
Zane Grey Pueblo Hotel, PO Box 216, 90704, 1926 ....(213)510-0966

Bakersfield
Helen Kay Inn, 2105 19th St, 93301, 1901 ....(805)325-5451

Ben Lomond
Fairview Manor, 245 Fairview Ave, 95005, 1920 ....(408)336-3355

Benicia
Captain Dillingham's Inn, 145 East D St, 94510 ....(707)746-7164
Union Hotel, 401 First St, 94510, 1882 ....(707)746-0100

Berkeley
Dolphin B&B, 1007 Leneve Pl, 94530 ....(415)527-9622
Gramma's Inn, 2740 Telegraph, 94705, 1905 ....(415)549-2145
Old Blue Hotel, 2740 Telegraph Ave, 94705-1131, 1900 ....(415)549-9281

Big Bear City
Gold Mountain Manor, 1117 Anita, PO Box 2027, 92314,
   1926 ....(714)585-6997

Big Bear Lake
Cathy's Cottage, PO Box 3706, 92314, 1949
Knickerbocker Mansion, 869 S Knickerbocker Rd, 92315,
   1917 ....(714)866-8221

Big Sur
Deetjen's Big Sur Inn, Hwy One, 93920, 1938 ....(408)667-2377

Bishop
Chalfant House, 213 Academy St, 93514, 1898 ....(619)872-1790

Bodega
Estero Vista Inn, 17699 Highway 1, Box 255, 94922 ....(707)876-3300

Bolinas
Bolinas Villa, PO Box 40, 23 Brighton Ave, 94924 ....(415)868-1650

Boonville
Bear Wallow Resort, PO Box 533, 95415 ....(707)895-3335
Toll House Inn, Box 268, 15301 Hwy 25, 95415, 1912 ......(707)895-3630

Buena Vista
Adobe Inn, Box 1560, 303 N Hwy 24, 81211 ....(303)395-6340
Blue Sky Inn, 719 Arizona St, 81211 ....(303)395-8865

Calistoga
Brannan Cottage Inn, 109 Wapoo Ave, 94515, 1860 ....(707)942-4200
Callistoga Inn, 1250 Lincoln Ave, 94515 ....(707)942-4101
Culver's, A Country Inn, 1805 Foothill Blvd, 94515,
   1875 ....(707)942-4535
Foothill House, 3037 Foothill Blvd, 94515, 1890
Larkmead Country Inn, 1103 Larkmead Ln, 94515, 1900
Mount View Hotel, 1457 Lincoln Ave, 94515, 1917
Pine Street Inn, 1202 Pine St, 94515 ....(707)942-6829
Scarlett's Country Inn, 3918 Silverado Trail N, 94515,
   1900 ....(707)942-6669

California (Continued)

Silver Rose Inn, 351 Rosedale Rd, 94515 .... (707)942-9581
The Pink Mansion, 1415 Foothill Boulevard, 94515, 1875 (707)942-0558
Trailside Inn, 4201 Silverado Tr, 94515, 1930 .... (707)942-4106
Wine Way Inn, 1009 Foothill Blvd, 94515, 1915 .... (707)942-0680

Cambria
Beach House, 6432 Charing Ln, 93428 .... (805)927-5865
J. Patrick House, 2990 Burton Dr, 93428 .... (805)927-3812
Olallieberry Inn, 2476 Main St, 93428 .... (805)927-3222
Pickford House B&B, 2555 MacLeod Way, 93428 .... (805)927-8619

Carmel
Cobblestone, PO Box 3185, 93921 .... (408)625-5222
Cypress Inn, 7th & Lincoln Streets, PO Box 7, 93921, 1929 .... (408)624-3871
Happy Landing Inn, Monte Verde between 5th & 6th, 93921, 1925 .... (408)624-7917
Holiday House, Box 782, Camino Real At 7th Ave, 93921, 1905
Lincoln Green Inn, Box 2747, 93921 .... (408)624-1880
Martin House B&B, 26270 Dolores St, 93921
Mission Ranch, 26270 Dolores, 93923 .... (408)624-6436
Pine Inn, Ocean & Monte Verde St, 93921
Sandpiper Inn-At-the Beach, 2408 Bay View Ave, 93923. (408)624-6433
Sea View Inn, Box 4318, 93921, 1910 .... (408)624-8778
Sundial Lodge, PO Box J, 93921 .... (408)624-8578
The Stonehouse Inn, Box 2517, 93921, 1906 .... (408)624-4569

Carmel Valley
Robles del Rio Lodge, 200 Punta Del Monte, 93924 .... (408)659-3705
Valley Lodge, PO Box 93, 93924 .... (408)659-2261

Cazadero
Cazanoma Lodge, PO Box 37, 1000 Kidd Creek Rd, 95421 .... (707)632-5255
Timberhill Ranch Resort, 35755 Hauser Bridge Rd, 95421 .... (707)847-3258

Chico
Bullard House, 256 E First Ave, 95926, 1902 ... (916)342-5912

Clio
White Sulphur Springs Ranch B&B, PO Box 136, Hwy 89 S, 96106 .... (916)836-2387

Cloverdale
Abrams House Inn, 314 N Main St, 95425, 1870 .... (707)894-2412
Vintage Towers Inn, 302 N Main St, 95425, 1900 .... (707)894-4535
Ye Olde Shelford House, 29955 River Rd, 95425, 1880 ..... (707)894-5956

Colfax
Bear River Mountain Farm, 21725 Placer Hills Rd, 95713

Coloma
Coloma Country Inn, PO Box 502, #2 High St, 95613, 1852 .... (916)622-6919
Sierra Nevada House, PO Box 268, 95613 .... (916)622-5856
Vineyard House, Cold Spring Rd, PO Box 176, 95613, 1878 .... (916)622-2217

Columbia
City Hotel, PO Box 1870, Main St, 95310 .... (209)532-1479
Fallon Hotel, PO Box 1870, Washington St, 95310, 1856 .. (209)532-1470

Colusa
O'Rourke Mansion, 1765 Lurline Rd, 95932, 1900 .... (916)458-5625

Coulterville
Jeffrey Hotel, PO Box 4, 95311 .... (209)878-3400

Crowley Lake
Rainbow Tarns, PO Box 1097, 93546, 1920 .... (619)935-4556

Davenport
New Davenport B&B, 31 Davenport Ave, 95017, 1902 .. (408)425-1818

Davis
The Partridge Inn, 521 First St, 95616, 1912 .... (916)753-1211

Del Mar
Rock Haus B&B, 410 15th St, 92014, 1910 .... (619)481-3764

Dinsmore
Dinsmore Lodge, Hwy 36, 95526, 1901 .... (707)574-6466

Downieville
Sierra Shangri-la, PO Box 285, 95936, 1939 .... (916)289-3455

Dulzura
Brookside Farm, 1373 Marron Valley Rd, 92017, 1928 ... (619)468-3043

Elk
Elk Cove Inn, PO Box 367, 95432, 1883 .... (707)877-3321
Green Dolphin Inn, PO Box 132, 6145 S Hwy 1, 95432, 1979 .... (707)877-3342
Greenwood Lodge, PO Box 172, 5910 S Hwy 1, 95432 .... (707)877-3422
Greenwood Pier Inn, Box 36, 5940 S Hwy 1, 95432 .... (707)877-9997
Harbor House, 5600 S Hwy 1, 95432, 1916 .... (707)877-3203

Etna
Scott Valley Inn, PO Box 261, 642 Main St, 96027, 1899 .. (916)467-3229

Eureka
Carter House, 1033 Third St, 95501, 1982 .... (707)445-1390
Eagle House, 139 Second St, 95501, 1886 .... (707)442-2334
Heuer's Victorian Inn, 1302 E St, 95501, 1890 .... (707)442-7334
Hotel Carter, 301 L St, 95501 .... (707)444-8062
Old Town B&B Inn, 1521 Third St, 95501, 1871 .... (707)445-3951
Steven's House, 917 Third St, 95501 .... (707)445-9080

Fairfield
Frietas House Inn, 744 Jackson St, 94533, 1925 .... (707)425-1366

Ferndale
Ferndale Inn, PO Box 887, 619 Main St, 95536, 1859 .... (707)786-4307
Gingerbread Mansion, 400 Berding St, 95536 .... (707)786-4000
Shaw House Inn, PO Box 250, 703 Main St, 95536, 1854 .... (707)786-9958

Fish Camp
Narrow Gauge Inn, 48571 Hwy 41, 93623 .... (209)683-7720

Fort Bragg
Avalon House, 561 Stewart St, 95437, 1905 .... (707)964-5555
Captain Capps, 32980 Gibney Lane, 95437, 1883 .... (707)964-1415
Colonial Inn, PO Box 565, 533 E Fir, 95437, 1912 .... (707)964-9979
Country Inn, 632 N Main St, 95437, 1890 .... (707)964-3737
Glass Beach B&B, 726 N Main St, 95437, 1900 .... (707)964-6774
Grey Whale Inn, 615 N Main St, 95437, 1915 .... (707)964-0640
Jughandle Beach Country B&B Inn, 32980 Gibney Ln, 95437 .... (707)964-1415
Noyo River Lodge, 500 Casa Del Noyo Dr, 95437, 1868 (707)964-8045
Pudding Creek Inn, 700 N Main St, 95437, 1889 .... (707)964-9529

Freestone
Green Apple Inn, 520 Bohemian Hwy, 95472, 1862 .... (707)874-2526

Fremont
Lord Bradley's Inn, 43344 Mission Blvd Mission San Jo, 94539, 1865 .... (415)490-0520

Fresno
The Victorian, 1003 S Orange Ave, 93702

Garberville
Benbow Inn, 445 Lake Benbow Dr, 95440, 1926 .... (707)923-2124

Georgetown
American River Inn, Orleans Street, PO Box 43, 95634, 1853 .... (916)333-4499

Geyserville
Campbell Ranch, 1475 Canyon Rd, 95441 .... (707)857-3476
Isis Oasis, 20889 Geyserville Ave, 95441, 1895
The Hope-Bosworth House, Box 42, 21238 Geyserville Ave, 95441, 1904
The Hope-Merrill House, Box 42, 21253 Geyserville Ave, 95441, 1870

Glen Ellen
Stone Tree Ranch, PO Box 173, 7910 Sonoma Mtn Rd, 95442 .... (707)996-8173

Goleta
Circle Bar B Ranch, 1800 Refugio Rd, 93117, 1940 .... (805)968-1113

Grass Valley
Annie Horan's, 415 W Main St, 95945, 1874 .... (916)272-2418
Domike's Inn, 220 Colfax Ave, 95945, 1894 .... (916)273-9010
Golden Ore House B&B, 448 S Auburn, 95945 .... (916)272-6870
Holbrooke Hotel & Purcell House, 212 W Main, 95945, 1851 .... (916)273-1353
Murphy's Inn, 318 Neal St, 95945 .... (916)273-6873
Swan-Levine House, 328 S Church St, 95945, 1880 .... (916)272-1873

Groveland
Hotel Charlotte, PO Box 884, 95321, 1918 .... (209)962-6455

Gualala
Gualala Hotel, PO Box 675, 95445, 1903 .... (707)884-3441
North Coast Country Inn, 34591 S Hwy, 95445 .... (707)884-4537
Old Milano Hotel, 38300 Hwy 1, 95445, 1905 .... (707)884-3256
St. Orres, PO Box 523, 95445, 1820 .... (707)884-3303

Whale Watch Inn, 35100 Hwy 1, 95445 ....(707)884-3667
Guerneville
Creekside Inn/crescione, PO Box 2185, 95446 ....(707)869-3623
Estate, 13555 Hwy 116, 95446 ....(707)869-9093
Ridenhour Ranch, 12850 River Rd, 95446, 1906 ....(707)887-1033
Santa Nella House, 12130 Hwy 116, 95466, 1870 ....(707)869-9488
Half Moon Bay
Mill Rose Inn, 615 Mill St, 94019, 1903 ....(415)726-9794
Old Thyme Inn, 779 Main St, 94019, 1890 ....(415)726-1616
San Benito House, 356 Main St, 94019, 1905 ....(415)726-3425
Hanford
The Irwin Street Inn, 522 North Irwin St, 93230, 1900 .....(209)584-9286
Victorian Inn, 322 N Irwin St, 93230, 1890.........................(209)584-9286
Healdsburg
Belle Du Jour Farm, 16276 Healdsburg Ave, 95448, 1870 (707)433-7892
Camellia Inn, 211 North St, 95448, 1869 ....(707)433-8182
Grape Leaf Inn, 539 Johnson St, 95448, 1900 ....(707)433-8140
Haydon House, 321 Haydon St, 95448, 1912 ....(707)433-5228
Healdsburg Inn On The Plaza, 116 Matheson St, PO Box 1196, 95448,
   1900 ....(707)433-6991
L'auberge Du Sans-souci, 25 West Grant, 95448, 1900 .....(707)431-1110
Madrona Manor, PO Box 818 1001 Westside, 95448,
   1881 ....(707)433-4231
Raford House, 10630 Wohler Rd, 95448 ....(707)887-9573
Homewood
Rockwood Lodge, 5295 W Lake Blvd, PO Box 544, 95718,
   1930 ....(916)525-4663
Hope Valley
Sorensen's Resort, Hwy 88, 96120 ....(916)694-2203
Idyllwild
Strawberry Creek Inn, PO Box 1818, 26370 Hwy 243,
   92349..(714)659-3202
Wilkum Inn, 26770 Hwy 243, PO Box 1115, 92349, 1939 (714)659-4087
Independence
Winnedumah Inn, PO Box 209, 211 N Edwards, 93526,
   1926 ....(619)878-2040
Inverness
Blackthorne Inn, PO Box 712, 94937 ....(415)663-8621
Manka's Inverness Lodge, PO Box 126, 30 Calender Way,
   94937..(415)669-1034
Ten Inverness Way, 10 Inverness Way, 94937, 1904 ....(415)669-1648
Ione
The Heirloom, 214 Shakeley Lane, PO Box 322, 95640,
   1863 ....(209)274-4468
Jackson
Ann Marie's, 410 Stasal St, 95642, 1892 ....(209)223-1452
Broadway Hotel, 225 Broadway, 95642 ....(209)223-3503
Court Street Inn, 215 Court St, 95642, 1872 ....(209)223-0416
Gate House Inn, 1330 Jackson Gate Rd, 95642, 1890 ....(209)223-3500
Wedgewood Inn, 11941 Narcissus Rd, 95642 ....(209)296-4300
Jamestown
National Hotel, Main Street, PO Box 502, 95327, 1859 .. (209)984-3446
Jenner
Murphy's Jenner-by-the-Sea, PO Box 69, Hwy 1, 95450 ..(707)865-2377
Stillwater Cove Ranch, 95450, 1900 ....(707)847-3227
Julian
Julian Gold Rush Hotel, 2032 Main St, PO Box 856, 92036,
   1897 ....(619)765-0201
Julian Lodge, PO Box 1430, 92036 ....(619)765-1420
Pine Hills Lodge, 2960 La Posada Way, PO Box 2260, 92036,
   1912 ....(619)765-1100
Kyburz
Strawberry Lodge, Hwy 50, 95720, 1935 ....(916)659-7030
La Jolla
Prospect Park Inn, 1110 Prospect St, 92037 ....(619)454-0133
The B&B Inn at La Jolla, 7753 Draper Ave, 92037, 1913 (619)456-2066
Laguna Beach
Carriage House, 1322 Catalina St, 92651, 1920 ....(714)494-8945
Casa Laguna, 2510 S Coast Hwy, 92651, 1930 ....(714)494-2996
Eiler's Inn, 741 S Coast Hwy, 92651, 1940 ....(714)494-3004
Lake Arrowhead
Eagles Landing, PO Box 1510, Blue Jay, 92317 ....(714)336-2642
Lakeview Lodge Victorian, Box 128, 92352 ....(714)337-6633

Lemon Cove
Lemon Cove B&B Inn, 33038 Sierra Hwy, 93244 ....(209)587-2555
Little River
Glendeven, 8221 N Hwy 1, 95456, 1867 ....(707)937-0083
Heritage House, 95456, 1877 ....(707)937-5885
Little River Inn, 95456, 1853 ....(707)937-5942
The Victorian Farmhouse, 7001 N Hwy 1, PO Box 357, 95456,
   1877 ....(707)937-0697
Long Beach
Appleton Place, 935 Cedar Ave, 90813, 1910 ....(213)432-2312
Los Alamos
Union Hotel, PO Box 616, 362 Bell St, 93440, 1900 ....(805)344-2744
Los Angeles
Eastlake Victorian Inn, 1442 Kellam Ave, 90026, 1887 ... (213)250-1620
Salisbury House, 2273 W 20th St, 90018, 1909 ....(213)737-7817
Terrace Manor, 1353 Alvarado Terr, 90006, 1902 ....(213)381-1478
West Adams B&B Inn, 1650 Westmoreland Blvd, 90006 ..(213)737-5041
Los Gatos
La Hacienda Inn, 18840 Saratoga Rd, 95030......................(408)354-9230
Los Gatos Hotel, 39 E. Main St #1, 95030-6907, 1890 ......(408)354-4440
Mammoth Lakes
Snow Goose Inn, PO Box 946, 93546, 1929 ....(619)934-2660
Tamarack Lodge, Tamarack Lodge Rd, 93546, 1924 ....(619)934-2442
Mariposa
Granny's Garden, 7333 Hwy 49 N, 95338, ...(209)377-8342
Meadow Creek Ranch B&B Inn, 2669 Triangle Rd, 95338,
   1858 ....(209)966-3843
Pelennor-B&B at Bootjack, 3871 Hwy 49 S, 95338 ....(209)966-2832
McCloud
McCloud Guest House, PO Box 1510, 606 W Colombero Dr, 96057,
   1907 ....(916)964-3160
Mendocino
Agate Cove Inn, PO Box 1150, 95460, 1860 ....(707)937-1551
Ames Lodge, PO Box 207, 95460, 1967 ....(707)937-0811
B.G. Ranch & Inn, 9601 N Hwy 1, 95460 ....(707)937-5322
Big River Lodge/Stanford Inn, PO Box 487, Hwy 1,
   95460..(707)937-4752
Blue Heron Inn, 390 Kasten St, 95460 ....(707)937-4323
Brewery Gulch Inn, 9350 Hwy 1, 95460 ....(707)937-4752
Headlands Inn, PO Box 132, 95460, 1868 ....(707)937-4431
Hill House Inn, PO Box 65, 10701 Palette Dr, 95410 ....(707)937-0554
Joshua Grindle Inn, 44800 Little Lake Rd, PO Box 647, 95460,
   1879 ....(707)937-4143
Kelly's Attic, PO Box 858, 699 Ukiah St, 95460, 1860 ....(707)937-5588
MacCallum House Inn, 45020 Albion St, 95460, 1882 .... (707)937-0289
Main Street Guest House, PO Box 108, 1021 Main St, 95460,
   1861 ....(707)937-5150
Mendocino Bay Trading Co., PO Box 817, 750 Albion St, 95460,
   1882 ....(707)937-5266
Mendocino Hotel, PO Box 587, 45080 Main St, 95460,
   1878 ....(707)937-0511
Mendocino Village Inn, 44860 Main St, PO Box 626, 95460,
   1882 ....(707)937-0246
Rachel's Inn, Box 134, 8200 N Hwy 1, 94560 ....(707)937-0088
Sea Gull Inn, PO Box 317, 95460, 1880 ....(707)937-5204
Sears House Inn, PO Box 844, 95460, 1870 ....(707)937-4076
Whitegate Inn, PO Box 150, 499 Howard St, 95460,
   1883 ....(707)937-4892
Middletown
Harbin Hot Springs, PO Box 782, 95461 ....(707)987-2477
Mill Valley
Mountain Home Inn, 810 Panoramic Hwy, 94941, 1912 (415)381-9000
Mokelumne Hill
Hotel Leger, PO Box 50, 95245, 1851 ....(209)286-1401
Monte Rio
Huckleberry Springs, PO Box 400, 8105 Old Beedle Rd,
   95462 ....(707)865-2683
Montecito
San Ysidro Ranch, 900 San Ysidro Ln, 93108
Monterey
Del Monte Beach Inn, 1110 Del Monte Ave, 93940............(408)649-4410
Merritt House, 386 Pacific St, 93940, 1830 ....(408)646-9640
Old Monterey Inn, 500 Martin St, 93940, 1929 ....(408)375-8284
The Jabberwock, 598 Laine St, 93940, 1911 ....(408)372-4777

California (Continued)

The Spindrift Inn, Box 3196, 652 Cannery Row, 93940
Muir Beach
Pelican Inn, 10 Pacific Way, 94965 .... (415)383-6000
Murphys
Dunbar House, 1880, PO Box 1375, 95247, 1880 .... (209)728-2897
Murphy's Hotel, 457 Main St, 95247, 1856 .... (209)728-3444
Napa
Arbor Guest House, 1436 G St, 94559 .... (707)252-8144
Beazley House, 1910 First St, 94559, 1902 .... (707)257-1649
Churchill Manor, 485 Brown St, 94559, 1889 .... (707)253-7733
Coombs Residence "Inn on the Park", 720 Seminary St, 94559,
  1852 .... (707)257-0789
Country Garden Inn, 1815 Silverado Tr, 94558 .... (707)255-1197
Gallery Osgood B&B Inn, 2230 First St, 94559, 1898 ...... (707)224-0100
Goodman House, 1225 Division St, 94558 .... (707)257-1166
Hennessey House B&B, 1727 Main St, 94559, 1889 .... (707)226-3774
Magnolia Hotel, PO Box M, 6529 Yount St, 94599 .... (707)944-2056
Napa Inn, 1137 Warren St, 94559, 1885 .... (707)257-1444
Old World Inn, 1301 Jefferson, 94559 .... (707)257-0112
Sybron House, 7400 St Helena Hwy, 94559 .... (707)944-2785
Yesterhouse Inn, 643 Third St, 94559, 1896 .... (707)257-0550
Napa Valley
Burgundy/Bordeaux House, PO Box 2776, 6600 Washington,
  94599 .... (707)944-2855
Rancho Caymus Inn, PO Box 78, 94573 .... (707)963-1777
National City
Dickinson Boal Mansion, 1433 East 24th St, 92050,
  1887 .... (619)477-5363
Nevada City
Downey House, 517 West Broad St, 95959, 1869 .... (916)265-2815
Grandmere's Inn, 449 Broad St, 95959 .... (916)265-4660
National Hotel, 211 Broad St, 95959, 1852 .... (916)263-4551
Piety Hill Inn, 523 Sacramento St, 95959, 1933 .... (916)265-2245
Red Castle Inn, 109 Prospect St, 95959, 1857 .... (916)265-5135
Newport Beach
Doryman's Inn, 2102 W Ocean Front, 92663, 1880 .... (714)675-7300
Little Inn on the Bay, 617 Lido Park Dr, 92663 .... (714)673-8800
Portofino Beach Hotel, 2306 W Oceanfront, 92663 .... (714)673-7030
Nipomo
The Kaleidoscope Inn, Box 1297, 130 E Dana St, 93444,
  1887 .... (805)929-5444
Nipton
Hotel Nipton, Rt 1, Box 357, 92364 .... (619)856-2335
North Fork
Ye Old South Fork Inn, 57665 Rd 225, 93643 .... (209)877-7025
North Hollywood
La Maida House, 11154 La Maida St, 91601 .... (818)769-3857
Oakland
Rockridge B&B, 5428 Thomas Ave, 94618 .... (415)655-1223
Ojai
Ojai Manor Hotel, 210 E Matilija, 93023, 1874 .... (805)646-0961
The Theodore Woolsey House, 1484 E Ojai Ave, 93023,
  1887 .... (805)646-9779
Wheeler Hot Springs, PO 250, 16825 Maricopa, 93023
Olema
Bear Valley Inn, PO Box 33, 88 Bear Valley, 94950, 1876 . (415)663-1777
Olympic Valley
Christy Hill, 1650 Squaw Valley Rd Box 2449, 95730 .... (916)583-8551
Orland
Inn at Shallow Creek Farm, Rt 3, Box 3176, 95963 .... (916)865-4093
Orosi
Valley View Citrus Ranch, 14801 Ave 428, 93647 .... (209)528-2275
Oroville
Jean's Riverside B&B, PO Box 2334, 95965 .... (916)533-1413
Pacific Grove
Centrella Hotel, PO Box 884, 612 Central, 93950, 1889 .... (408)372-3372
Gosby House Inn, 643 Lighthouse Ave, 93950, 1887 ...... (408)375-1287
Green Gables Inn, 104 5th St, 93950, 1888 .... (408)375-2095
House of Seven Gables, 555 Ocean View, 93950, 1886 .. (408)372-4341
Martine Inn, 255 Ocean View Blvd., 93950, 1899 .... (408)373-3388
Old St Angela Inn, 321 Central Ave, 93950, 1890 .... (408)372-3246

Roserox Country Inn By-The-Sea, 557 Ocean View Blvd, 93950,
  1904 .... (408)373-7673
Seven Gables Inn, 555 Ocean View Blvd, 93950 .... (408)372-4341
Palm Springs
Ingleside Inn, 200 W Ramon Rd, 92262, 1920 .... (619)325-0046
Villa Royale Inn, 1620 S Indian Tr, 92264 .... (619)327-2314
Palo Alto
The Victorian On Lytton, 555 Lytton Ave, 94301, 1890 .... (415)322-8555
Pasadena
Donneymac Irish Inn, 119 N Meridith, 91106 .... (818)440-0066
Petaluma
Barbara Welch, 524 Howard, 94952
Philo
Philo Pottery Inn, PO Box 166, 8550 Rt 128, 95466 .... (707)895-3069
Placerville
Fleming-Jones Homestead, 3170 Newton Rd, 95667,
  1883 .... (916)626-5840
Historic Combellack-Blair House, 3059 Cedar Ravine, 95667,
  1895 .... (916)622-3764
James Blair House, 2985 Clay St, 95667, 1901 .... (916)626-6136
River Rock Inn, PO Box 827, 1756 Georgetown Rd,
  95667 .... (916)622-7640
Point Reyes
Holly Tree Inn, Box 642, Pt Reyes St, 94956 .... (415)663-1554
Point Richmond
East Brother Light Station Inc., 117 Park Pt., 94801,
  1873 .... (415)233-2385
Princeton-By-The-Sea
Pillar Point Inn, PO Box 388 El Granada, 94018 .... (415)728-7377
Quincy
The Feather Bed, 542 Jackson St, PO Box 3200, 95971,
  1893 .... (916)283-0102
Rancho Cucamonga
Christmas House B&B Inn, 9240 Archibald Ave, 91730,
  1904 .... (714)980-6450
Red Bluff
Faulkner House, 1029 Jefferson St, 96080, 1890 .... (916)529-0520
Redlands
Morey Mansion, 190 Terracina Blvd., 92373 .... (714)793-7970
Reedley
Hotel Burgess, 1726 11th St, 93654, 1911 .... (209)638-6315
Riverside
Nelle Lethers, 4561 Orange Grove Ave, 92501 .... (714)683-3246
Rutherford
Rancho Caymus Inn, PO Box 78, 94573 .... (707)963-1777
Sacramento
Amber House, 1315 22nd St, 95816, 1905 .... (916)444-8085
Aunt Abigail's, 2120 G St, 95816, 1910 .... (916)441-5007
Bear Flag Inn, 2814 I St, 95816, 1906 .... (916)448-5417
Briggs House B&B, 2209 Capitol Ave, 95816, 1901 ...... (916)441-3214
Driver Mansion Inn, 2019 21st St, 95818 .... (916)455-5243
Hartley House Inn, 700 22nd St, 95816, 1906 .... (916)447-7829
Sterling Hotel, 1300 H St, 95814
Saint Helena
Ambrose Bierce House, 1515 Main St, 94574, 1870 .... (707)963-3003
Bell Creek B&B, 3220 Silverado Trail, 94574, 1900 .... (707)963-2383
Chalet Bernensis, 225 St Helena Hwy, 94574, 1884 .... (707)963-4423
Chestelson House, 1417 Kearny St, 94574, 1904 .... (707)963-2238
Cornerstone B&B Inn, 1308 Main St, 94574, 1891 .... (707)963-1891
Deer Run B&B, 3996 Spring Mtn Rd, 94574 .... (707)963-3794
Hotel Saint Helena, 1309 Main St, 94574 .... (707)963-4388
Ink House, 1575 St Helena Hwy, 94574, 1884 .... (707)963-3890
Oliver House B&B Country Inn, 2970 Silverado Tr,
  94574 .... (707)963-4089
Prager Winery B&B, 1281 Lewelling Ln., 94574 .... (707)963-3713
Shady Oaks Country Inn, 399 Zinfandel, 94574, 1880 .. (707)963-1190
The Cinnamon Bear, 1407 Kearney St, 94574, 1904 .... (707)963-4653
White Ranch, 707 White Ln, 94574, 1865 .... (707)963-4635
Wine Country Cottage, 400 Meadow Wood Ln., 94574 .... (707)963-4633
Wine Country Inn, 1152 Lodi Ln, 94574 .... (707)963-7077
San Andreas
Black Bart Inn, PO Box 576, 55 St Charles, 95249, 1893 ... (209)754-3808
Robin's Nest, PO Box 1408, 247 W St Charles, 95249 .... (209)754-1076

California (Continued)

San Diego
Balboa Park Inn, 3402 Park Blvd, 92130 .... (619)298-0823
Britt House, 406 Maple St, 92103, 1887 .... (619)234-2926
Carole's B&B, 3227 Grim Ave, 92104, 1904 .... (619)280-5258
Dickinson Boal Mansion, National City
Edgemont Inn, 1955 Edgemont St, 92102
Harbor Hill Guest House, 2330 Albatross St, 92101 .... (619)233-0638
Heritage Park B&B Inn, 2470 Heritage Park Row, 92110,
   1889 .... (619)295-7088
Keating House Inn, 2331 Second Ave, 92101 .... (619)239-8585
Surf Manor & Cottages, PO Box 7695, 92107, 1930 .... (619)225-9765

San Francisco
1818 California, 1818 California St, 94109, 1818 .... (415)885-1818
Alamo Square Inn, 719 Scott St, 94117, 1895 .... (415)922-2055
Albion House, 135 Gough St, 94102 .... (415)621-0896
Andrews Hotel, 624 Post St, 94109 .... (415)563-6877
Archbishop's Mansion, 1000 Fulton St, 94117 .... (415)563-7872
Art Center Wamsley B&B, 1902 Filbert St, 94123, 1857. (415)567-1526
B&B Inn, 4 Charlton Ct, 94123 .... (415)921-9784
B&B Near The Park, 1387 Sixth Ave, 94122 .... (415)753-3574
Casa Arguello, 225 Arguello Blvd, 94118 .... (415)752-9482
Edward II Inn, 3155 Scott St, 94123 .... (415)921-9776
Emperor Norton Inn, 615 Post St, 94109 .... (415)775-2567
Golden Gate Hotel, 775 Bush St, 94108 .... (415)392-3702
Grove Inn, 890 Grove St, 94117 .... (415)929-0780
Hermitage House, 2224 Sacramento St, 94115, 1901 .... (415)921-5515
Hotel Louise, 845 Bush St, 94108 .... (415)928-6000
Inn At Union Square, 440 Post St, 94102 .... (415)397-3510
Inn On Castro, 321 Castro St, 94114, 1910 .... (415)861-0321
Inn San Francisco, 943 S Van Ness, 94110, 1872 .... (415)641-0188
Jackson Court, 2198 Jackson St, 94115 .... (415)929-7670
Mansion Hotel, 2220 Sacramento, 94115 .... (415)929-9444
Marina Inn B&B, 431 Hugo St, 94123 .... (415)928-1000
Moffatt House, 431 Hugo St, 94122, 1910 .... (415)661-6210
Monte Cristo, 600 Presidio Ave, 94115, 1875 .... (415)931-1875
Obrero Hotel & Basque Restaurant, 1208 Stockton St,
   94133 .... (415)989-3960
Pacific Heights Inn, 1555 Union St, 94123 .... (415)776-3310
Pension San Francisco, 1668 Market St, 94102 .... (415)864-1271
Petite Auberge, 863 Bush St, 94108, 1919 .... (415)928-6000
Red Victorian B&B Inn, 1665 Haight St, 94117 .... (415)864-1978
Riley's B&B, 1234 Sixth Ave, 94122 .... (415)731-0788
Sherman House, 2160 Green St, 94123 .... (415)563-3600
Spencer House, 1080 Haight St, 94117, 1890 .... (415)626-9205
Spreckels Mansion, 737 Buena Vista West, 94117, 1887 (415)861-3008
Stanyon Park Hotel, 750 Stanyon St, 94117 .... (415)751-1000
The Inn San Francisco, 943 S Van Ness Ave, 94110, 1872 (415)641-0188
The Mansion Hotel, 2220 Sacramento St, 94115, 1887 ...... (415)929-9444
The Monte Cristo, 600 Presidio Ave, 94115, 1875 ...... (415)931-1875
The Red Victorian, 1665 Haight St, 94117 .... (415)864-1978
Union Street Inn, 2229 Union St, 94123, 1902 .... (415)345-0424
Victorian Inn On The Park, 301 Lyon St, 94117, 1889 ...... (415)931-1830
White Swan Inn, 845 Bush St, 94108, 1908 .... (415)775-1755
Willows B&B Inn, 710 14th St, 94114 .... (415)431-4770

San Francisco,
Washington Square Inn, 1660 Stockton St, 94117 .... (415)981-4220

San Juan Bautista
B&B San Juan, PO Box 613, 95045, 1858 .... (408)623-4101

San Juan Capistrano
Casa De La Vista, PO Box 388, 92693, 1928 .... (714)496-7050
Hospitality Plus, PO Box 388, 92693, 1910 .... (714)496-6953

San Luis Obispo
Heritage Inn, 978 Olive St, 93401, 1890 .... (805)544-7440

San Mateo
Stewart-Grinsell House, 410 Georgetown Ave, 94402-2252,
   1890 .... (415)346-0424

San Pedro
Grand Cottages, 809 S Grand Ave, 90731, 1920 .... (213)548-1240

San Rafael
Casa Soldavini, 531 "C" St, 94901, 1932 .... (415)454-3140
Panama Hotel, 4 Bayview St, 94901, 1910 .... (415)457-3993

Santa Ana
The Craftsman, 2900 N Flower St, 92706, 1910 .... (714)543-1168

Santa Barbara
Bath Street Inn, 1720 Bath St, 93101, 1875 .... (805)682-9680
Bayberry Inn, 111 W Valerio, 93101 .... (805)682-3199
Blue Quail Inn, 1908 Bath St, 93101, 1915 .... (805)687-2300
Cheshire Cat Inn, 36 W Valerio, 93101, 1892 .... (805)569-1610
Glenborough Inn, 1327 Bath St, 93101, 1880 .... (805)966-0589
Harbour Carriage House, 420 West Montecito Street, 93101,
   1900 .... (805)962-8447
Hitchcock House, 431 Corona Del Mar, 93103, 1920 .... (805)962-3989
Inn at Two Twenty Two, 222 W Valerio, 93101 .... (805)687-7216
Old Yacht Club Inn, 431 Corona Del Mar, 93103, 1912 . (805)962-1277
Olive House, 1604 Olive St, 93101, 1904 .... (805)962-4902
Red Rose Inn, 1416 Castillo St, 93101, 1886 .... (805)966-1470
Simpson House Inn, 121 East Arrellaga St, 93101, 1874 (805)963-7067
The Parsonage, 1600 Olive St, 93101, 1892 .... (805)962-9336
Tiffany Inn, 1323 De La Vina, 93101 .... (805)963-2283
Upham Hotel, 1404 De La Vina St, 93101, 1871 .... (805)962-0058
Villa d' Italia, 780 Mission Canyon Rd, 93105, 1919 ...... (805)687-6933
Villa Rosa, 15 Chapala St, 93101 .... (805)966-0851

Santa Clara
Madison Street Inn, 1390 Madison St, 95050, 1890 ...... (408)249-5521

Santa Cruz
Babbling Brook B&B Inn, 1025 Laurel St, 95060, 1909 .. (408)427-2437
Chateau Victorian, 118 First St, 95060, 1890 .... (408)458-9458
Cliff Crest, 407 Cliff St, 95060, 1887 .... (408)427-2609
Darling House, 314 W Cliff Dr, 95060, 1910 .... (408)458-1958

Santa Monica
Channel Road Inn, 219 West Channel Road, 90402,
   1912 .... (213)454-7577
Sovereign at Santa Monica Bay, 205 Washington Ave, 90403,
   1920 .... (800)331-0163

Santa Paula
Glen Tavern Inn, 134 N Mill St, 93060, 1910 .... (805)525-6658
The Lemon Tree Inn, 299 W Santa Paula St, 93060

Santa Rosa
Gee-Gee's B&B Home, 7810 Sonoma Hwy, 95405 .... (707)833-6667
Inn At The Belvedere, 727 Mendocino Ave, 95401, 1901 . (707)575-1857
Melitta Station Inn, 5850 Melita Rd, 95409 .... (707)538-7712
Pygmalion House, 331 Orange St, 95407, 1880 .... (707)526-3407
The Gables, 4257 Petaluma Hill Rd, 95404, 1877 .... (707)585-7777

Sausalito
Alta Mira Hotel, 125 Bulkley St, 94965, 1890 .... (415)332-1350
Casa Madrona Hotel, 801 Bridgeway, 94965, 1885 .... (415)332-0502
Sausalito Hotel, 16 El Portal, 94965, 1900 .... (415)332-4155

Sea Ranch
Sea Ranch Lodge, PO Box 44, 95497 .... (707)785-2371

Seal Beach
Seal Beach Inn & Gardens, 212 5th St, 90740, 1924 ...... (213)493-2416

Sierraville
Campbell Hot Springs Spiritual Retreat, Box 234 #1 Campbell Hot
   Springs Rd, 96126, 1850 .... (916)994-3737

Sky Forest
Storybook Inn, PO Box 362, 92385, 1939 .... (714)336-1483

Sonoma
Chalet B&B, 18935 5th St W, 95476 .... (707)938-3129
Overview Farm, 15650 Arnold Dr, 95476, 1880 .... (707)938-8574
Sonoma Hotel, 110 W Spain St Box 1326, 95476 .... (707)996-2996
The Hidden Oak, 214 E Napa St, 95476, 1913 .... (707)996-9863
Thistle Dew Inn, 171 W Spain St Box 1326, 95476, 1910.. (707)938-2909
Trojan Horse Inn, 19455 Sonoma Hwy, 95476 .... (707)996-2430
Victorian Garden Inn, 316 E Napa St, 95476, 1870 ..... (707)996-5339

Sonora
Barretta Gardens Inn, 700 S Barretta St, 95370, 1904 . (209)532-6039
Gunn House, 286 S Washington St, 95370, 1851 .... (209)532-3421
Jameson's, 22157 Feather River, 95370, 1972 .... (209)532-1248
Lulu Belle's, 85 Gold St, 95370, 1883 .... (209)533-3455
Serenity, PO Box 3484, 95370, 1860 .... (209)533-1441
Sonora Inn, 160 S. Washington, 95370, 1896 .... (209)532-7468
The Ryan House B&B, 153 S Shepherd St, 95370, 1855 (209)533-3445

Soulsbyville
Willow Springs Country Inn, 20599 Kings Ct., 95372,
   1880 .... (209)533-2030

South Lake Tahoe
Christiana Inn, PO Box 18298, 95706 .... (916)544-7337
Strawberry Lodge, Hwy 50, 95720 .... (916)659-7030

California (Continued)

Sunset Beach
Sunset B&B Inn, PO Box 1202, 90742 ....(213)592-1666
Sutter Creek
Botto Country Inn, 11 Sutter Hill Rd, 95685 ....(209)267-5519
Hanford House, PO Box 847, 95685 ....(209)267-0747
Nancy & Bob's 9 Eureka Street Inn, 55 Eureka Street, PO Box 386,
95685, 1916 ....(209)267-0342
Sutter Creek Inn, PO Box 385, 7 Main St, 95685 ....(209)267-5606
The Foxes, PO Box 159, 77 Main St, 95685, 1862 ....(209)267-5882
Tahoe City
Mayfield House, 256 Grove St, PO Box 5999, 95730,
1930 ....(916)583-1001
River Ranch, PO Box 197, Hwy 89, 95730 ....(916)583-4264
The Cottage Inn, PO Box 66, 95730, 1938
Templeton
Country House Inn, 91 Main St, 93465, 1886 ....(805)434-1598
Three Rivers
Cort Cottage, PO Box 245, 93271 ....(209)501-4671
Timbercove
Timberhill Ranch, 35755 Hauser Bridge Rd, 95421 ....(707)847-3477
Tomales
Byron Randall's Famous Tomales Guest Hse, 25 Valley St,
94971 ....(707)878-9992
Trinidad
Trinidad B&B, PO Box AU, 95570 ....(707)677-0840
Truckee
Alta Hotel, PO Box 2118, 95734, 1902 ....(916)587-6668
Bradley House, PO Box 2011, 95734, 1880 ....(916)587-5388
Mountain View Inn, PO Box 8579, Off Hwy 267, 95737 ..(916)587-2545
Tuolumne
Oak Hill Ranche, Box 307, 95379 ....(209)928-4717
Twain Harte
Twain Harte's B&B, PO Box 1718, 95383 ....(209)586-3311
Ukiah
Sanford House, 306 S Pine, 95482......................(707)462-1653
Valley Ford
Inn At Valley Ford, PO Box 439, 14395 Hwy 1, 94972,
1860 ....(707)876-3182
Venice
Venice Beach House, 15 30th Ave, 90291, 1911 ....(213)823-1966
Ventura
Bella Maggiore Inn, 67 S California St, 93001, 1925 ....(805)652-0277
La Mer, 411 Poli St, 93001, 1890 ....(805)643-3600
Volcano
St. George Hotel, PO Box 9, 95689 ....(209)296-4458
Watsonville
Warner Embassy Inn, 24 Sunset Dr, 95076-9651
Weaverville
Hocker-Bartlett House, PO Box 1511, 807 Main St, 96093,
1860 ....(916)623-4403
West Covina
Hendrick Inn, 2124 E Merced Ave, 91791 ....(818)919-2125
Westport
Bowen's Pelican Lodge & Inn, PO Box 35, 38921 N Hwy 1,
95488 ....(707)964-5588
Howard Creek Ranch, 40501 North Hwy, PO Box 121, 95488,
1871 ....(707)964-6725
Williams
Wilbur Hot Springs, 95987 ....(916)473-2306
Yosemite
Hotel Charlotte, Tr 120, 95321 ....(209)962-6455
Yountville
Magnolia Hotel, Drawer M, 6529 Yount St, 94599, 1870 ..(707)944-2056
Napa Valley Railway Inn, Box 2568, 6503 Washington, 94599
Oleander House, PO Box 2937, 7433 St Helena Hwy,
94599 ....(707)944-8315
The Webber Place, Box 2873, 94599, 1850
Yuba City
Harkey House B&B, 212 C St, 95991, 1864 ....(916)674-1942
The Wicks, 560 Cooper Ave, 95991 ....(916)674-7951

Colorado

Allenspark
Lazy H Ranch, Box 248, 80510
Aspen
Alpina Haus, 935 E Durant, 81611 ....(800)242-7736
Aspen Ski Lodge, 101 W Main St, 81611 ....(303)925-3434
Brass Bed Inn, 926 E Durant, 81611 ....(303)925-3622
Christmas Inn, 232 W Main St, 81611 ....(303)925-3822
Copper Horse House, 328 W Main St, 81611, 1886
Fireside Inn, 130 W Cooper, 81661 ....(303)925-6000
Hearthstone House, 134 E Hyman St, 81611
Hotel Lenado, 200 S Aspen St, 81611 ....(303)925-6246
Innsbruck Inn, 233 W Main St, 81611
Little Red Ski Haus, 118 E Cooper, 81611, 1888
Molly Gibson Lodge, 120 W Hopkins, 81611
Pomegranate Inn, Box 1368, 81612 ....(800)525-4012
Sardy House, 128 E Main St, 81611, 1892 ....(303)920-2525
Snow Queen Lodge, 124 E Cooper, 81611
Tipple Inn, 747 S Galena St, 81611
Ullr Lodge, 520 W Main St, 81611
Bayfield
Deer Valley Resorts, PO Box 796, 81122 ....(303)884-2600
Boulder
B&B Colorado, Ltd, PO Box 6061, 80306 ....(303)442-6664
Briar Rose B&B, 2151 Arapahoe, 80302, 1897 ....(303)442-3007
Pearl Street Inn, 1820 Pearl St, 80302 ....(303)444-5584
Pearl's Place, 497 Pearl St, 80302, 1875 ....(303)442-2242
Breckenridge
Fireside Inn, 212 Wellington PO Box 2252, 80424
Buena Vista
Adobe Inn B&B, Hwy 24 #2 Sterling, 81211 ....(303)395-6340
Blue Sky Inn, 719 Arizona St, 81211 ....(303)395-8865
Carbondale
Crystal River Inn, Hell Roaring Ranch, 12954 Hwy 133., 81657,
1895 ....(303)963-3902
Central City
Golden Rose Hotel, 80427 ....(303)582-5060
Two Ten Casey, PO Box 154, 80427
Clark
Home Ranch, Box 822, 80428 ....(303)879-1780
Colorado Springs
B&B Rocky Mountains, PO Box 804, 80901 ....(719)630-3433
Hearthstone Inn, 506 N Cascade Ave, 80903, 1885 ....(719)473-4413
Holden House-1902, 1102 W Pikes Peak Ave, 80904,
1902 ....(719)471-3980
Crested Butte
Brumber Hearth, PO Box 1152, 81224 ....(303)349-6253
Claim Jumper Inn, 704 Whiterock, Box 1181, 81224 ....(303)349-6471
Forest Queen Hotel, Box 127 2nd/Elk Ave, 81224 ....(303)349-5336
Nordic Inn, PO Box 939, 81224
Purple Mountain Lodge, PO Box 897, 714 Gothic Ave, 81224,
1927 ....(303)349-5888
Cripple Creek
Imperial Hotel, 123 N Third St, 80813, 1896 ....(719)689-2922
Del Norte
Balloon Ranch, Box 41, 81132 ....(303)754-2533
The Windsor Hotel, 605 Grande Ave, Box 762, 81132,
1872 ....(719)657-2668
Denver
Cambridge Club Hotel, 1560 Sherman, 80203 ....(303)831-1252
Queen Anne Inn, 2147 Tremont Place, 80205, 1879 ......(303)296-6666
Sheets Residence, 577 High St, 80218 ....(303)329-6170
The Oxford Alexis, 1600 17th St, 80202, 1891 ....(800)228-5838
Victoria Oaks Inn, 1575 Race St, 80218, 1894 ....(303)355-1818
Dillon
Silverheels, Box 367, 81 Buffalo Dr, 80435 ....(303)468-2926
Durango
B&B Durango, PO Box 544, 81301, 1878.................(303)247-2223
River House B&B, 495 County Rd 203, 81301 ....(303)247-4775
Tall Timber, Box 90G, 81301 ....(303)259-4813
Victorian Inn, 2117 W Second Ave, 81301, 1880
Empire
The Peck House, PO Box 423, 80438, 1860 ....(303)569-9870

Estes Park
Aspen Lodge, Longs Peak Rte, 80517, 1915 .... (303)586-4241
Tommer Hus B&B, 1060 Mary's Lake Rd, 80517 .... (303)586-6200
Wind River Ranch, PO Box 3410, 80517 .... (303)586-4212
Fort Collins
Elizabeth Street Guesthouse, 202 E Elizabeth, 80524,
  1905 .... (303)493-2337
Emerald Manor, 3213 Crockett St, 80526 .... (303)223-1396
Helmshire Inn, 1204 S College, 80524
Georgetown
The Hardy House, 605 Brownell St, Box 0156, 80444,
  1877 .... (303)569-3388
Glenwood Springs
Hideout, 1293 117 Rd, 81601 .... (303)945-5621
Talbott House, 928 Colorado Ave, 81601 .... (303)945-1039
Golden
The Dove Inn, 711 14th St, 80401, 1889 .... (303)278-2209
Granby
Drowsy Water Ranch, Box 147A, 80446 .... (303)725-3456
Grand Junction
The Gatehouse, 2502 N 1st St, 81501, 1889 .... (303)242-6105
Grant
Tumbling River Ranch, 80448 .... (303)838-5981
Green Mountain Falls
Columbine Lodge, Box 267, 80819, 1895
Outlook Lodge, Box 5, 80819, 1889 .... (719)684-2303
Gunnison
Waunita Hot Springs Ranch, 8007 Country Rd 877,
  81230 .... (303)641-1266
Gypsum
7-W Guest Ranch, 3412 County Rd 151, 81637 .... (303)524-9328
Sweetwater Creek Guest Ranch, 2650 Sweetwater Rd,
  81637 .... (303)524-9301
Hesperus
Blue Lake Ranch, 16919 Hwy 140, 81326, 1900 .... (303)385-4537
Ignacio
Ute Creek Ranch, 2192 County Rd 334, 81137 .... (303)563-4464
La Veta
1899 B&B Inn, 314 S Main, 81055, 1899 .... (303)742-3576
Lake City
Crystal Lodge, 81235.. (303)944-2201
Leadville
Hilltop House, 100 W 9th St, 80461, 1907 .... (303)486-2362
Limon
Midwest Country Inn, Box X, 795 Main St, 80828 .... (303)775-2373
Manitou Springs
Billy's Cottage, 117 Deer Path, 80829, 1909 .... (303)685-1828
Nippersink, 106 Spencer Ave, 80829, 1885
Meredith
Diamond J Guest Ranch, 26604 Frying Pan Rd, 81642 .... (303)927-3222
Minturn
Eagle River Inn, PO Box 100, 145 N Main St, 81645 .... (303)827-5761
Nathrop
Deer Valley Ranch, Box Y, 81236 .... (303)395-2353
Nederland
Goldminer Hotel, Eldora Star Rt, 80466, 1897
Ouray
Baker's Manor, 317 Second St, 81427, 1881
House Of Yesteryear, Box 440, 81427
St. Elmo Hotel, 426 Main St, 81427, 1897
Weisbaden Spa & Lodge, Box 349, 81427, 1895
Pagosa Springs
Davidson's Country Inn B&B, Box 87, Hwy 160, 81147 .. (303)264-5863
Parshall
Bar Lazy J Guest Ranch, Box N, 80468 .... (303)725-3437
Poncha Springs
Jackson Hotel, 220 S Main St, 81242, 1878
Redstone
Historic Redstone Inn, 82 Redstone Blvd, 81623
Ridgway
MacTiernan's San Juan Ranch, 2882 Hwy 23, 81432 .... (303)626-5360
Pueblo Hostel & Cantina, PO Box 346, 81432................... (303)626-5939

Rifle
Coulter Lake Guest Ranch, PO Box 906, 81650 .... (303)625-1473
Salida
Poor Farm Country Inn, 8495 Co Rd 160, 81201
Shawnee
North Fork Ranch, Box B, 80475.. (303)838-9873
Silver Plume
Brewery Inn, 246 Main St, PO Box 473, 80476, 1890 ...... (303)571-1151
Silverton
Alma House, PO Box 780, 81433, 1898
Fool's Gold, 1069 Snowden, 81433, 1883 .... (303)387-5879
Grand Imperial Hotel, 1219 Green St, 81433, 1882 .... (303)387-5527
Teller House Hotel, 1250 Greene St, 81433 .... (303)387-5423
Steamboat Springs
Bear Pole Ranch, Star Rt 1 Box Bb, 80487
Crawford House, 1184 Crawford Ave, Box 775062, 80477,
  1894 .... (303)879-1859
Harbor Hotel, PO Box 4109, 80477 .... (800)543-8888
Inn at Steamboat, 3070 Columbine Dr, 80477 .... (303)879-2600
The House On The Hill, PO Box 770598, 80477
Vista Verde Guest Ranch, Box 465, 80477 .... (303)879-3858
Steamboat Village
Scandinavian Lodge, Box 5040, 80449 .... (303)879-0517
Telluride
Dahl House, PO Box 695, 81435, 1890
Johnstone Inn, PO Box 546, 81435
New Sheridan Hotel, 231 W Colorado Ave, 81435, 1895
Skyline Guest Ranch, 7214 Hwy 145, 81435 .... (303)728-3757
Victorian Inn, PO Box 217, 81435 .... (303)728-3684
Victor
The Portland Inn, 412 W Portland Ave, PO Box 32, 80860,
  1900 .... (303)689-2102
Woodland Park
Woodland Hills Lodge, PO Box 276, 80863 .... (800)621-8386

Connecticut

Bolton
Jared Cone House, 25 Hebron Rd, 06043, 1775 .... (203)643-8538
Bridgewater
Sanford/pond House, PO Box 306, 06752
Bristol
Chimney Crest Manor, 5 Founders Dr, 06010, 1930 .... (203)582-4219
Brooklyn
Tannerbrook, 329 Pomfret Rd, 06234
Chester
Inn At Chester, 318 W Main St, 06412, 1776 .... (203)526-4961
Clinton
Captain Dibbell House, 21 Commerce St, 06413, 1865 .. (203)669-1646
Harbor View On Holly Place, 63 Pratt Rd, 06413
Cornwall Bridge
Turning Point Farm, Rt 45, 06754, 1787
Cos Cob
Harbor House Inn, 50 River Rd, 06807, 1860 .... (203)661-5845
Coventry
Maple Hill Farm B&B, 365 Goose Ln, 06423, 1731 .... (203)742-0635
Deep River
Riverwind, 209 Main St, 06417, 1850 .... (203)526-2014
Selden House, 20 Read Rd, 06417, 1900
E Haddam
Whispering Winds Inn, 93 River Rd, 06423 .... (203)526-3055
East Haddam
Bishop's Gate, Goodspeed Landing, 06423, 1818 .... (203)873-1677
Gelston House,Inn At Goodspeed's Landing, Rt 9 Ex 7, 06423
Stonecroft Inn, 17 Main St, 06423, 1830
East Lyme
The Red House, 365 Boston Post Rd, 06333, 1760
East Windsor
Stephen Potwine House, 84 Scantic Rd, 06088, 1831 ..... (203)623-8722
Essex
Griswold Inn, 06426, 1775

Connecticut (Continued)

Glastonbury
Butternut Farm, 1654 Main St, 06033, 1720 ....(203)633-7197
Greenwich
Homestead Inn, 420 Field Point Rd, 06830, 1799 ....(203)869-7500
Stanton House, 76 Maple Ave, 06830 ....(203)869-2110
Groton Long Point
Shore Inne, 54 East Shore Rd, 06340, 1915 ....(203)536-1180
Higganum
Simeon Platt B&B, 365 Old Saybrook Rd, 06441, 1823
Ivoryton
Copper Beach Inn, Main St, 06442, 1800
Ivoryton Inn, Main St, 06442, 1838 ....(203)767-0422
Kent
1741 Saltbox Inn, PO Box 677, 06757, 1741
Constitution Oak Farm, Beardsley Rd, 06757, 1830 ....(203)354-6495
The Country Goose B&B, RFD 1 Box 276, 06757
Killingworth
Killingworth Inn, 249 Rt 81, 06417
Lakeville
Wake Robin Inn, Rt 41, 06039, 1898 ....(203)435-2515
Ledyard
Applewood Farms Inn, 528 Colonel Ledyard Hwy,
   06355 ....(203)536-2022
Applewood Farms Inn, 520 Col Ledyard Hwy, 06339,
   1826 ....(203)536-2022
Litchfield
Tollgate Hill Inn, Route 202 and Tollgate Rd, 06759,
   1745 ....(203)567-4545
Madison
Dolly Madison Inn, 73 W Wharf Rd, 06443 ....(203)245-7377
Madison Beach Hotel, 94 W Wharf Rd, 06443 ....(203)245-1404
Middlebury
Tucker Hill Inn, 96 Tucker Hill Rd, 06762, 1923 ....(203)758-8334
Montville
1841 House, 1851 Rt 32, 06382, 1841
Moodus
Fowler House, PO Box 432, 06469, 1890
Mystic
Adams House, 382 Cow Hill Road, 06355, 1790
Adams House, PO Box 4, 382 Cow Hill Rd, 06355 ....(203)572-9551
Comolli's Guest House, 36 Bruggeman Pl., 06355
Harbour Inne and Cottage, Edgemont Street, 06355,
   1898 ....(203)572-9253
Inn At Mystic, Jct Rt 1 & 27, 06355, 1904 ....(203)536-9604
Red Brook Inn, PO Box 237, 06372, 1740 ....(203)572-0349
Whalers Inne, PO Box 488t, 06355, 1900 ....(203)536-1506
Mystic - Noank
Palmer Inn, 25 Church St, 06340, 1907 ....(203)572-9000
New Canaan
Maples Inn, 179 Oenoke Ridge, 06840, 1908
Roger Sherman Inn, 195 Oenoke Ridge, 06840, 1740 ....(203)955-4541
New Hartford
Cobble Hill Farm, Steel Rd, 06057, 1796 ....(203)379-0057
Highland Farms B&B, Highland Ave, 06057, 1879 ....(203)379-6029
New Haven
The Inn at Chapel West, 1201 Chapel St, 06511, 1847 ....(203)777-1201
New London
Lighthouse Inn, 6 Guthrie Place, 06320, 1902 ....(203)443-8411
Queen Anne, 265 Williams St, 06320
New Milford
Homestead Inn, 5 Elm St, 06776, 1853 ....(203)354-4080
New Preston
Birches Inn, West Shore Rd, 06777, 1920 ....(203)868-0229
Boulders Inn, Rt 45, 06777, 1895 ....(203)868-7918
Hopkins Inn, Hopkins Rd, 06777
Inn on Lake Waramaug, North Shore Rd, 06777, 1795 ..(203)868-0563
Newton
Hawley Manor Inn, 19 Main St, 06470, 1780 ....(203)426-4456
Norfolk
Blackberry River Inn, Rt 44, 06058, 1763

Greenwoods Gate, Greenwoods Rd E, 06058, 1797
Manor House, Maple Ave, Box 447, 06058, 1898 ....(203)542-5690
Mountain View Inn, Rt 272, 06058, 1875 ....(203)542-5595
Weaver's House, Rt 44, 06058 ....(203)542-5108
North Stonington
Randall's Ordinary Inn, PO Box 243, 06359
Norwalk
Silvermine Tavern, Silvermine & Perry Aves, 06850,
   1786 ....(203)847-4558
Old Greenwich
Harbor House Inn, 165 Shore Rd, 06850 ....(203)637-0145
Old Lyme
Bee And Thistle Inn, 100 Lyme St, 06371, 1756
Old Lyme Inn, 85 Lyme St, 06371, 1850 ....(203)434-2600
Old Saybrook
Castle Inn-Cornfield Pointe, Hartland Dr, 06475, 1900
Plainsfield
Lemuel Cleveland House, Rt 12 Box 153, 06374, 1900
Pomfret
Cobbscroft, Routes 169 & 44, 06258, 1780
Grosvenor Place, Rt 97, 06258, 1700
Wintergreen, Rt 44 & 169, 06259, 1800 ....(203)928-5741
Pomfret Center
Colonel Angell House, Wrights Crossing Rd, 06259, 1773
Inn at Gwyn Careg, Rt 44, 06230 ....(203)928-9352
Selah Farm, Rt 44 & 169, PO Box 43, 06259
Portland
The Croft B&B, 7 Penny Corner Road, 06480
Putnam
Feishaw Tavern, Five Mile River Road, 06260, 1742 ....(203)928-3467
Ridgefield
Stonehenge, Rt 7, 06877
The Elms Inn, 500 Main St, 06877, 1760
West Lane Inn, 22 West Ln., 06877, 1890
Riverton
Old Riverton Inn, Rt 20 Box 6, 06065, 1796
Salisbury
Ragamont Inn, Main St, 06068, 1702 ....(203)435-2372
Under Mountain Inn, Rt 41, 06068, 1710 ....(203)435-0242
White Hart Inn, Village Green, 06068, 1800
Yesterday's Yankee B&B And Rso, Rt 44 E, 06068, 1744 ..(203)435-9539
Simsbury
Simsbury House, 731 Hopmeadow St, 06070, 1820
Somersville
The Old Mill Inn, 63 Maple St, 06072, 1850 ....(203)763-1473
South Woodstock
General Sameul Mcclellan House, Stonebridge Rd, 06267, 1769
Inn at Woodstock Hill, Box 98, Plaine Hill Rd, 06267 ......(203)928-0528
Stafford Springs
Winterbrook Farm, Beffa Rd, 06076
Stonington
Farnan House, 10 Mcgrath Ct, 06378
Stonington Village
Lasbury's B&B, 24 Orchard St, 06378 ....(203)535-2681
Storrs
Altnaveigh Inn, 957 Storrs Rd, 06268, 1734 ....(203)429-4490
Farmhouse On The Hill, 418 Gurleyville Rd, 06268
Thompson
Hedgerow House, 1020 Quaddick Rd, 06277
Samuel Watson House, Rt 193 Box 86, 06277, 1767 ....(203)923-2491
Tolland
Old Babcock Tavern, 484 Mile Hill Rd, 06084, 1720
Tolland Inn, 63 Tolland Green, Box 717, 06084, 1800 .....(203)872-0800
Uncasville
Hillcrest House, 2351 Norwich New London Tpke, 06382
Washington
Mayflower Inn, Rt 47, 06793, 1894 ....(203)868-0515
Waterbury
The House On The Hill, 92 Woodlawn Terrace, 06710
The Parsonage, 18 Hewlett St, 06710, 1900 ....(203)574-2855
West Woodstock
Ebenezer Stoddard House, Rt 171 & Perrin Rd, 06267 ....(203)974-2552

Westbrook
Captain Stannard House, 138 S Main St, 06498, 1850 .... (203)399-7565
Westport
Cotswold Inn, 76 Myrtle Ave, 06880 ....(203)226-3766
Longshore Inn, 280 Compo Rd S, 06883, 1890 ....(203)226-3316
Winsted
Provincial House, 151 Main St, 06098, 1890
Woodbury
Curtis House, Main St, 06798, 1754 .... (203)263-2101
Woodstock
Inn at Woodstock Hill, Plaine Hill Rd, 06267, 1816 .... (203)928-0528

Delaware

Bethany Beach
166 Ocean View, PO Box 275, 166 Ocean View Pkwy, 19930,
   1909 ....(302)539-3707
Homestead Guests, 721 Garfield Pkwy., 19930, 1909
Sea-vista Villas, Box 62, 19930
The Addy Sea, Box 275, 19930, 1900
The Sandbox, Box 62, 19930 ....(302)539-3354
Camden
Jonathan Wallace House, 9 South Main St, 19934, 1785 .. (302)697-2921
Dover
Biddles B&B, 101 Wyoming Ave, 19901 ....(302)736-1570
Nobel Guest House, 33 S Bradford St, 19901, 1880 ....(302)674-4048
The Inn at Meeting House Square, 305 S Governors Ave, 19901,
   1850 ....(302)678-1242
Laurel
Spring Garden, Rt 1 Box 283-A, 19956, 1780 ....(302)875-7015
Lewes
Savannah Inn, 330 Savannah Rd, 19958..............................(302)645-5592
Milford
The Towers, 101 Northwest Front St, 19963, 1783 ....(302)422-3814
New Castle
David Finney Inn, 216 Delaware St, 19720, 1683 ....(302)322-6367
The Jefferson House B&B, The Strand at the Wharf, 19720,
   1800 ....(302)323-0999
William Penn Guest House, 206 Delaware St, 19720,
   1682 ....(302)328-7736
Odessa
Cantwell House, 107 High St, 19730, 1840 ....(302)378-4179
Rehoboth Beach
Beach House Bedroom, Box 138, 19971 ....(302)227-0937
Corner Cupboard Inn, 50 Park Ave, 19971, 1932
Gladstone Inn, 3 Olive Ave, 19971 ....(302)227-2641
Lord Baltimore Lodge, 16 Baltimore Ave, 19971, 1875 .... (302)227-2855
Pleasant Inn Lodge, 31 Olive Ave, 19971, 1928 ....(302)227-7311
Sea Lodge, 15 Hickman St, 19971
The Abbey, 31 Maryland Ave, 19971, 1900 ....(302)227-7023
Wilmington
The Boulevard B&B, 1909 Baynard Blvd., 19802, 1913 .... (302)656-9700

Florida

Amelia Island
1735 House, 584 S Fletcher Ave, 32034, 1928 ....(904)261-5878
Apalachicola
Gibson Inn, PO Box 221, 32320, 1907 ....(904)653-2191
Big Pine Key
Barnacle, Rt 1 Box 780A, 33043..(305)872-3298
Boca Grande
Gasparilla Inn, 33921 ....(813)964-2201
Bokeelia
Cabbage Key Inn, PO Box 489, 33922..................................(813)283-2278
Bradenton
Banyan House, 624 Fontana Ln., 33529
Carrabelle
Pelican Inn, PO Box 301, 32322..(904)697-2839
Cedar Key
Historic Island Hotel, Box 460, 32625, 1849.....................(904)543-5111
Coral Gables
Hotel Place St. Michel, 162 Alcazar Ave, 33134, 1926 .... (305)444-1666

Daytona Beach
Captain's Quarters Inn, 3711 S Atlantic Ave, 32019 ....(904)767-3119
Englewood
Lemon Bay B&B, 12 S Wind Dr, 33533 ....(813)474-7571
Everglades City
Rod & Gun Club, PO Box G, 33929, 1883
Fernandina Beach
Bailey House, PO Box 805, 32034, 1895.............................(904)261-5390
Greyfield Inn, Box 878 Cumberland Isl., 32034, 1904
Seaside Inn, 1998 South Fletcher Ave, 32034
Fort Myers
Wind Song Garden, 5570-4 Woodrose Ct, 33907 ....(813)936-6378
Ft Lauderdale Beach
Casa Alhambra B&B Inn, 3029 Alhambra St, 33304,
   1930 ....(305)467-2262
Hawthorne
Yearling Cabins, Rt 3, Box 123, 32640 ....(904)466-3033
Holmes Beach
Harrington House B&B, 5626 Gulf Dr, 34217, 1925........(813)798-9933
Indianatown
Seminole Country Inn, 15885 Warfield, 33456, 1925
Inverness
Crown Hotel, 109 N. Seminole Ave, 32650, 1880
Jacksonville
House on Cherry St, 1844 cherry St, 32205, 1912.............(904)384-1999
Key West
Alexander's, 1118 Fleming St, 33040 ....(305)294-9919
Artist House, 534 Eaton St, 33040, 1880 ....(305)296-3977
Author's, 725 White At Petronia, 33040, 1900 ....(305)294-7381
Chelsea House, 707 Truman, 33040, 1906............................(305)296-2211
Coconut Grove Guest House, 817 Fleming St, 33040 ....(305)296-5107
Colours Key West, 410 Fleming St, 33040, 1889........(305)294-6977
Cypress House, 601 Caroline St, 33040, 1887 ....(305)294-6969
Duval House, 815 Duval St, 33040, 1880 ....(305)294-1666
Eaton Lodge, 511 Eaton St, 33040, 1886 ....(305)294-3800
Eden House, 1015 Fleming, 33040, 1924
Ellie's Nest, 1414 Newton St, 33040 ....(305)296-5757
Garden House, 329 Elizabeth St, 33040 ....(305)296-5368
Gideon Lowe House, 409 William St, 33040 ....(305)294-5969
Heron House, 512 Simonton St, 33040, 1856 ....(305)294-9227
Hollinsed House, 611 Southard St, 33040 ....(305)296-8031
Island City House, 411 William St, 33040, 1880 ....(305)294-5702
Island House, 1129 Fleming St, 33040 ....(305)294-6284
Key West B&B, Popular House, 415 William St, 33040,
   1890 ....(305)296-7274
Marquesa Hotel, 600 Fleming St, 33040 ....(305)292-1919
Merlinn Guest House, 811 Simonton St, 33040 ....(305)296-3336
Oasis Guest House, 823 Fleming St, 33040, 1867 ....(305)296-2131
Palms Of Key West, 820 White St, 33040, 1889 ....(305)294-3146
Pines of Key West, 521 United St, 33040 ....(305)296-7467
Simonton Court, 320 Simonton St, 33040 ....(305)294-6386
Sunrise Sea House B&B, 39 Bay Dr, 33040 ....(305)745-2875
Sweet Caroline Guest House, 529 Caroline St, 33040 ....(305)296-5173
The Hollinsed House, 609-11 Southard St, 33040 ....(305)296-8031
Walden Guest House, 223 Elizabeth, 33040, 1890 ....(305)296-7161
Watson House, 525 Simonton, 33040, 1860 ....(305)294-6712
Wicker Guest House, 913 Duval St, 33040 ....(305)296-4275
Kissimee
Beaumont House, 206 S Beaumont Ave, 32741, 1900 ....(305)846-7916
Kissimmee
Unicorn Inn, 8 S Orlando Ave, 31724 ....(305)846-1200
Lake Wales
Chalet Suzanne, 319 W Starr Ave, Drawer AC, 33859-9003,
   1928 ....(813)676-6011
Marathon
Hopp-Inn Guest House, 5 Man-O-War Dr, 33050 ....(305)743-4118
Mayo
Jim Hollis' River Rendezoux, Rt 2, Box 60, 32066
Miami
B&B Company, PO Box 262, 33243, 1900.........................(305)661-3270
Micanopy
Herlong Mansion, Cholakka Blvd., 32667

Florida (Continued)

Mount Dora
Lakeside Inn, Box 1390, 32757, 1920 .... (800)556-5016
Naples
Feller House, 2473 Longboat Dr, 33942 .... (813)774-0182
Ocala
Doll House B&B, 719 SE 4th St, 32671 .... (904)351-1167
Orange Springs
Orange Springs, 1 Main St, Box 550, 32682 .... (904)546-2052
Orlando
Avonelle's, 4755 Anderson Rd, 32806 .... (305)275-8733
Brown's B&B, 529 W Dartmouth St, 32804, 1926 .... (305)423-8858
Fugate House, Box 2009, 32802, 1920 .... (305)423-8382
Meadow Marsh, 940 Tildenville School Rd, 32787, 1877. (305)656-2064
Spencer Home B&B, 313 Spencer St, 32809 .... (305)855-5603
The Norment-Parry Inn, 211 N Lucerne Circle E, 32801,
     1900 .... (305)648-5188
Pensacola
Homestead Inn, 7830 Pine Forest Rd, 32506 .... (904)944-4816
North Hill Inn, 422 N Baylen St, 32501, 1904
Sunshine, 508 Decatur Ave, 32507 .... (904)455-6781
Saint Augustine
Carriage Way B&B, 70 Cuna St, 32084, 1883
Casa De La Paz, 22 Avenida Menendez, 32084, 1915 .... (904)829-2915
Casa de Solana, 21 Aviles St, 32084, 1763 .... (904)824-3555
Kenwood Inn, 38 Marine St, 32084, 1865 .... (904)824-2116
Sailor's Rest, 298 St George St, 32084 .... (904)824-3817
St. Francis Inn, 279 St George St, 32084, 1791 .... (904)824-6068
Victorian House B&B, 11 Cadiz St, 32084 .... (904)824-5214
Westcott House, 146 Avenida Menendez, 32084, 1889 ..... (904)824-4301
Saint Petersburg
Bayboro House on Old Tampa Bay, 1719 Beach Dr, SE, 33701,
     1904 .... (813)823-4955
Sanibel
Kona Kai Motel, 1539 Periwinkle Way, 33957 .... (813)472-1001
Siesta Key, Sarasota
Cresent House, 459 Beach Rd, 34242, 1918 .... (813)346-0857
Tampa
Bayshore Terrace, 214 Hyde Park Place, 33606, 1903 .... (813)877-3649
Tarpon Springs
Spring Bayou Inn, 32 W Tarpon Ave, 34689 .... (813)938-9333
Umatilla
Umatilla Hotle, 8 South Central/ PO 1670, 32784, 1920.. (904)669-1088
Wakulla Springs
Wakulla Springs Lodge, 1 Spring Dr, 32305, 1930 .... (904)640-7011
West Palm Beach
Hibiscus House, PO Box 2612, 33402

Georgia

Athens
The Serpentine Inn, 1416 S Milledge Ave, 30606, 1921 .... (404)353-8548
Atlanta
Beverly Hills Inn, 65 Sheridan Dr NE, 30305, 1929 .... (404)233-8520
Shellmont B&B Lodge, 821 Piedmont NE, 30308 .... (404)872-9290
Augusta
Augusta House, PO Box 40069, 30904 .... (404)738-5122
Peach Blossom Inn, 1119 Green St, 30901
Telfair Inn, 326 Greene St, 30901, 1888 .... (404)724-3315
Barnesville
Bird In A Bush, 722 Thomaston St, 30204
Blairsville
1880 Victorian Inn, Box 2901 Town Creek Rd, 30512
Blakely
Layside, 611 River St, 31723, 1900
Clarkesville
Burns-Sutton House, 124 S Washington St, Box 992, 30523,
     1901 .... (404)754-5565
Charm House Inn, Box 392, Hwy 441, 30523 .... (404)754-9347
Glen-Ella Springs Hotel, Rt 3, Bear Gap Rd, 30523 .... (404)754-7295
Laprade's, Rt 1, Hwy 197, 30523, 1916
The Charm House, Box 392, 30523 .... (404)754-9347

Cleveland
McCollum House, Rt 4 Box 309, Rt 255, 30528
Ru Sharon, Box 273, 30528
Towering Oaks, Rt 4 Box 457bb, 30528
Columbus
De Loffre House, 812 Broadway, 31901, 1863
Dahlonega
Forest Hills Mt. Resort, Rt 3, 30533
Mountain Top Lodge, Rt 3, Box 173, 30533 .... (404)864-5257
Smith House, 202 S. Chestatee St, 30533 .... (404)864-2348
Worley Homestead Inn, 410 W Main, 30533, 1845 .... (404)864-7002
Dalton
Amy's Place, 217W Cuyler, 30720
Dillard
Dillard House Inn, PO Box 10, 30537 .... (404)746-5349
Forsyth
A Country Place, Route 3, Box 290, 31019
Fort Oglethorpe
Captain's Quarters, Barnhardt Circle, 30742, 1903 .... (404)858-0624
Gainesville
Dunlap House, 635 Green St, 30501
Greenville
Samples Plantation, Rt 1 Box 735, 30222
Hartwell
Hartwell Inn, 504 W Howell St, 30643
Helen
Derdenhof Inn, PO Box 405, 30545
Helendorf Inn, PO Box 305, 30545 .... (404)878-2271
Lakemont
Anapauo Farm, Star Rt, Box 13C, 30522 .... (404)782-6442
Lake Rabun Hotel, Rt 1 Box 101, 30552, 1922 .... (404)782-4946
Macon
1842 Inn, 353 College St, 31201, 1842 .... (912)741-1842
Hutnick House, 273 Orange St, 31201
La Petite Maison, 1165 Dures Ln, 31201 .... (912)742-4674
Marietta
Arden Hall, 1052 Arden Dr SW, 30060 .... (404)422-0780
The Marlow & Stanley House, 192 Church St, 30060, 1900
Mcdonough
D.P. Cook House, 69 Keys Ferry St, 30253, 1900 .... (404)957-7562
Montezuma
Olena's Guest House, Rt 26, 31063 .... (912)472-7620
Mountain City
York House, Box 126, 30562, 1896 .... (404)746-2068
Saint Mary's
Riverview Hotel, 105 Osborne St, 31558, 1916 .... (912)882-3242
Saint Simons Island
Little St. Simons Island, PO Box 1078 G, 31522, 1917 ... (912)638-7472
Sautee
Stovall House, Rt 1 Box 152, 30571, 1837
Woodhaven Chalet, Rt 1, Box 39, 30571 .... (404)878-2580
Savannah
"417" The Haslam-Fort House, 417 East Charlton St, 31401,
     1872 .... (912)233-6380
17hundred90 Inn, 307 E. President, 31401, 1790 .... (912)236-7122
B&B Inn, 117 W Gordon St, 31401 .... (912)238-0518
Ballastone Inn, 14 E Oglethorpe Ave, 31401, 1835 .... (912)236-1484
Barrister House, 25 W Perry St, 31401
Charlton Court, 403 E. Charlton St, 31401, 1860 .... (912)236-2895
Comer House, 2 East Taylor St, 31401, 1880
East Bay Inn, 225 E Bay St, 31401, 1800 .... (912)238-1225
Eliza Thompson House, 5 W. Jones St, 31401, 1847
Foley House Inn, 14 W Hull St, 31401, 1896 .... (912)232-6622
Forsyth Park Inn, 102 W Hall St, 31401 .... (912)233-6800
Gastonian, 220 E.gaston St, 31401, 1868
Greystone Inn, 214 E. Jones St, 31401
Haslam-Fort House, 417 E Charlton St, 31401 .... (912)233-6380
Jesse Mount House, 209 W Jones St, 31401, 1854 .... (912)236-1774
Liberty Inn 1834, 128 W Liberty St, 31401, 1834 .... (912)233-1007
Magnolia Place Inn, 503 Whitaker St, 31401, 1876
Mary Lee's House, PO Box 607, 31402, 1854
Morel House, 117 W Perry St, 31401, 1818 .... (912)234-4088
Mulberry Inn, 601 E. Bay St, 31402

Oglethorpe Inn, PO Box 9803, 31412 .... (912)232-2700
Olde Harbour Inn, 508 E Factors Walk, 31401, 1892 ...... (912)234-4100
Presidents' Quarters, 225 E President St, 31401, 1885 ...... (912)233-1600
Pulaski Square Inn, 203 W Charlton, 31401, 1853
Remshart-Brooks House, 106 W Jones St, 31401, 1853 .. (912)234-6928
Royal Colony Inn, 29 Abercorn St, 31401 .... (912)232-5678
RSVP Savannah B&B Reservation Service, 417 E Charlton St, 31401,
    1848 .... (912)232-7787
Stoddard-Cooper House, 19 W Perry St, 31401, 1854
The Forsyth Park Inn, 102 W Hall St, 31401, 1893 .... (912)233-6800
Timmons House, 407 E Charlton St, 31401 .... (912)233-4456

Senoia
Culpepper House, Corner Of Broad At Morgan, PO Box 4, 30276,
    1871 .... (404)599-8182
The Veranda - (Hollberg Hotel), 252 Seavy St, 30276-0177,
    1907 .... (404)599-3905

Statesboro
Statesboro Inn B&B, 301 South, 30458 .... (912)489-8628

Swainsboro
Edenfield House Inn, Box 556, 358 Church St, 30401 ...... (912)237-3007

Thomaston
The Guest House, 318 W Main St, 30286, 1900 .... (404)647-1203

Thomasville
Neel House, 502 S Broad St, 31792 .... (912)228-6000
Susina Plantation Inn, Rt 3 Box 1010, 31792, 1841

Toccoa
Habersham Manor House, 326 Doyle St, 30577

Washington
Liberty Street, 108 W Liberty St, 30673
Water Oak Cottage, 211 S Jefferson St, 30673

Winterville
Old Winterville Inn, 108 S Main St, 30683, 1870 .... (404)742-7340

Hawaii

Aiea
Alohaland Guest House, 98-1003 Oliwa St, 96701 .... (808)487-0482
Captain Cook
Manago Hotel, Box 145, 96704 .... (808)323-2642
Haiku, Maui
Haikuleana B&B Inn, 69 Haiku Rd, 96708, 1850 .... (808)575-2890
Hana
Kaia Ranch & Co, PO Box 404, Ulaino Rd, 96713 .... (808)248-7725
Hana, Maui
Heavenly Hana Inn, PO Box 146, 96713 .... (808)248-8442
Hawi
Aha Hui Hawaiian Plantation, PO Box 10, 96719 .... (808)889-5523
Honolulu
B&B Waikiki Beach, PO Box 89080, 96830 .... (808)923-5459
Hale O Kahala, 4614 Kilauea Ave #565, 96816 .... (808)732-5889
Hawaii Kai, 876 Ka'ahue St, 96825 .... (808)395-8153
John Guild Inn, 2001 Vancouver Dr, 96822, 1919 .... (808)947-6019
Manoa Valley Inn, 2001 Vancouver Dr, 96822, 1919 .... (808)947-6019
Kalapana
Kalani Honua, Box 4500, Ocean Hwy 137, 96778 .... (808)965-7828
Kaneohe, Oahu
Emma's Guest Rooms, 47-600 Hui Ulili St, 96744 .... (808)239-7248
Kaunakakai, Molokai
Pau Hana Inn, PO Box 546, 96748 .... (800)367-8047
Koloa, Kauai
Poipu B&B Inn, 2720 Hoonani Rd, 96756, 1933 .... (808)742-1146
Kula, Maui
Kula Lodge & Restaurant, Inc., RR1 Box 475, 96790 .... (808)878-1535
Lahaina
Plantation Inn, 174 Lahainaluna Rd, 96761 .... (800)433-6815
Lahaina, Maui
The Lahaina Hotel, 127 Lahainaluna Road, 96761,
    1963 .... (808)661-0577
Napili, Maui
Coconut Inn, PO Box 10517, 96791 .... (800)367-8006
Volcano
My Island B&B, Box 100, 96785

Idaho

Boise
Sunrise, 2730 Sunrise Rim Rd, 83705 .... (208)345-5260
Bonner's Ferry
Deep Creek Inn, 83805 .... (208)267-2373
Coeur D'alene
Blackwell House, 820 Sherman Ave, 83814 .... (208)664-0656
Greenbriar B&B, 315 Wallace, 83814, 1908 .... (208)667-9660
Grangeville
Tulip House, 403 S Florence St, 83530 .... (208)983-1034
Hailey
Comfort Inn, Box 984, 83333 .... (208)788-2477
Ellsworth Inn, 715 3rd Ave S, 83333
Harrison
MaryAnne's, HCR 1, Box 43E, 83833 .... (208)245-2537
Peg's B&B Place, PO Box 144, 83833 .... (208)689-3525
Horseshoe Bend
Old Riverside Depot, Rt 1 Box 14a, 83629 .... (208)793-2408
Idaho City
Idaho City Hotel, PO Box 70, 83631, 1935 .... (208)392-4290
Irwin
McBride's B&B, PO Box 166, 83428 .... (208)483-4221
Kellogg
Dorsett House, 305 S Division, 83837 .... (208)786-2311
Ketchum
Busterback Ranch, Star Rt, 83340 .... (208)774-2217
Lift Haven Inn, Box 21, 100 Lloyd Dr, 83340 .... (208)726-5601
Powderhorn Lodge, Box 3970, 83340 .... (208)726-3107
River Street Inn, PO Box 182, 83353 .... (208)726-3611
Kooskia
Looking Glass Ranch, HC-75, Box 32, 83539 .... (208)926-0855
Meridian
Home Place, 415 W Lake Hazel Rd, 83642 .... (208)888-3857
Northfork
Indian Creek Ranch, Rt 2 Box 105, 83466, 1905
Pocatello
Holmes Retreat, 178 N Mink Creek Rd, 83204
Saint Mraies
Knoll Hus, PO Box 572, 83861 .... (208)245-4137
Sandpoint
Whitaker House, 410 Railroad Ave #10, 83466
Stanley
Idaho Rocky Mtn. Ranch, HC 64 Box 9934, 83278, 1935
Redfish Lake Lodge, PO Box 9, 83278, 1935 .... (208)774-3536
Wallace
Jameson B&B, 304 Sixth St, 83873 .... (208)556-1554
Pine Tree Inn, 177 King St, Box 1023, 83873 .... (208)752-4391

Illinois

Carthage
Wright Farmhouse, RR3, 62321 .... (217)357-2421
Casey
Cumberland Trail B&B, 201 W Main St, 62420, 1800 .... (217)932-5522
Champaign
Davidson Place B&B, 1110 Davidson Dr, 61820 .... (217)356-5915
Chicago
Burton House B&B Inn, 1454 N Dearborn Pkwy, 60610,
    1877 .... (312)787-9015
Cisco
Country House, Rt 1 Box 61, 61803, 1888 .... (217)669-2291
Collinsville
Maggie's B&B, 2102 N Keebler Rd, 62234, 1890 .... (618)344-8283
Dallas City
1850's Guest House, Rt 1, 62330, 1850 .... (217)852-3652
Decatur
Hamilton House, 500 W Main St, 62522, 1892 .... (217)429-1669
Dixon
Colonial Inn, Rt 3 Grand Detour, 61021, 1890 .... (815)652-4422
River View Guest House, 507 E Everett, 61021 .... (815)288-5974

Illinois (Continued)

Eldred
Hobson's Bluffdale, Rt 1, Hillview Rd, 62027, 1828 .... (217)983-2854
Elsah
Corner Nest B&B, 3 Elm St, PO Box 22, 62028 .... (618)374-1892
Green Tree Inn, 15 Mill St, Box 96, 62028 .... (618)374-2821
Maple Leaf Cottage Inn, 12 Selma St, PO Box 156, 62028,
    1891 .... (618)374-1684
Evanston
Homestead, 1625 Hinman Ave, 60201 .... (312)475-3300
Galena
Aldrich Guest House, 900 Third St, 61036
Avery Guest House, 606 S Prospect St, 61036, 1859 .... (815)777-3883
Bedford House, Rt 20 W, 61036, 1850
Belle Aire Mansion, 11410 Rt 20 W, 61036, 1834 .... (815)777-0893
Captain Harris Guest House, 713 S Bench St, 61036, 1836
Chestnut Mountain Resort, 8700 W Chestnut Rd, 61036. (800)435-2914
Colonial Guest House, 1004 Park Ave, 61036, 1826 .... (815)777-0336
Comfort Guest House, 1000 Third St, 61036
Creekside Guest House, 3825 West Miner Rd, 61036
Farmer's Home Hotel, 334 Spring St, 61036, 1867
Farster's Executive Inn, 305 N Main St, 61036, 1845
Felt Manor, 125 S Prospect St, 61036, 1840 .... (815)777-9093
Gallery Guest Suite, 204 1/2 S Main St, 61036 .... (815)777-1222
Grandview Guest Home, 113 S Prospect St, 61036, 1870
Hellman Guest House, 318 Hill St, 61036
Homestead, 1022 Fourth St, 61036 .... (815)774-6963
Log Cabin Guest House, 11661 W Chetlain Ln, 61036
Mars Avenue Guest House, 515 Mars Ave, 61036, 1854 (815)777-3880
Mother's Country Inn, 349 Spring St, 61036
Pillsbury's Guest House, 713 S Bench St, 61036, 1836 ...... (815)777-1611
Renaissance Vintage Suites, Box 291, 61036
Ryan Mansion Inn, Rt 20 W, 61036, 1876
Spring Street Guest House, 418 Spring S, 61036, 1876
Stillman's Country Inn, 513 Bouthillier, 61036, 1858 ..... (815)777-0557
Temperly Tourist Home, 401 Broadway, 61036
The Desoto House Hotel, 230 S Main St, 61036, 1855
Victorian Mansion Guest House, 301 S High St, 61036,
    1861 .... (815)777-0675
Geneva
The Oscar Swan Country Inn, 1800 W State St, 60134,
    1902 .... (312)232-0173
Gibson City
Stolz Home, RR 2, Box 27, 60936 .... (217)784-4502
Golconda
Riverview Mansion Hotel, Columbus Ave, PO Box 56, 62938,
    1894 .... (618)638-3001
The Mansion Of Golconda, Bed & Breakfast, 62938
Goodfield
Brick House Inn, Box 301, Conklin Ct, 61742 .... (309)965-2545
Grand Detour
Colonial Inn, Rock & Green Sts, 61021 .... (815)652-4422
Gratt Park
Bennett-Curtis House, 302 W Taylor, 60940
Harden
Wittmond Hotel, C/o Calhoun Herald, 62017 .... (818)883-2345
Jacksonville
Rosalee Mckinley, 840 W Walnut, 62650 .... (217)245-2697
The Gable Inn, 258 W Monton, 62650, 1845
Lake Forest
Deer Path Inn, 255 E Illinois Rd, 60045 .... (312)234-2280
Lanark
Standish House, 540 W Carroll St, 61046, 1882 .... (815)493-2307
Lockport
Hotel President, 933 State St, 60441
Mundelein
Round-Robin Guesthouse, 231 Maple Ave, 60060 .... (312)566-7664
Nauvoo
Hotel Nauvoo, Rt 96 Town Center PO 398, 62354, 1840 .. (217)453-2211
Oakland
Inn-on-the-Square, 3 Montgomery St, 61943 .... (217)346-2289

Oregon
Pinehill B&B, 400 Mix St, 61061, 1874 .... (815)732-2061
Polo
Barber House Inn, 410 W Mason, 61064 .... (815)946-2607
Rock Island
Top O' The Morning, 1505 19th Ave, 61201 .... (309)786-3513
Rockford
Victoria's B&B, 201 N 6th St, 61107, 1900
Springfield
Corinne's B&B Inn, 1001 S Sixth St, 62703, 1883 .... (217)527-1400
Mischler House, 718 S 8th St, 62703, 1880 .... (217)523-3714
Stockton
Herrings Maple Lane Farm, 3114 Rush Creek Rd, 61085
Maple Lane, 3115 Rush Creek Rd, 61085 .... (815)947-3773
Memory Lane Lodge, 409 N Canyon Park Rd, 61085 ...... (815)947-2726
Sycamore
Country Charm B&B, Rt 2 Box 154, 60178, 1900
Urbana
Gray Goose B&B, 1206 S Vine, 61801
Wheaton
Wheaton Inn, Roosevelt Rd & Wheaton Ave, 60187,
    1895 .... (312)690-2600
Winnetka
Chateau des Fleurs, 552 Ridge Rd, 60093, 1936 .... (312)256-7272
Wuincy
The Kaufman House, 1641 Hampshire, 62301, 1888 .... (217)223-2502

Indiana

Auburn
Auburn Inn, 225 Touring Dr, 46707 .... (219)925-6363
Batesville
Sherman House Restaurant & Inn, 35 S Main Street, 47006,
    1852 .... (812)934-2407
Berne
Schug House Inn, 206 W Main St, 46711, 1907 .... (219)589-2303
Beverly Shores
Dunes Shore Inn, Box 807, Lakeshore County Rd, 46301 (219)879-9029
Bloomingdale
Ewbank-Loudermilk House, RR 1, Box 104, 47832, 1883 (317)597-2579
Bloomington
The Bauer House B&B, 4595 N Maple Grove Rd, 47401,
    1868 .... (812)336-4383
Bristol
Open Hearth B&B, 56782 SR 15, 46507 .... (219)825-2417
Chesterton
Wingfield's Inn B&B, 526 Indian Oak Mall, 46304 .... (702)348-0766
Churubusco
Sycamore Spring Farm, Box 224, 46723 .... (219)693-3603
Columbus
Lafayette Street B&B, 723 Lafayette St, 47201 .... (812)372-7245
The Columbus Inn, 445 Fifth St, 47501, 1895 .... (812)378-4289
Crawfordsville
Davis House, 1010 W Wabash Ave, 47933, 1870 .... (317)364-0461
Decatur
Cragwood Inn, 303 N Second St, 46733 .... (219)728-9388
Evansville
Brigadoon B&B Inn, 1201 SE Second St, 47713, 1892 .... (812)422-9635
Fort Wayne
The Candlewyck B&B, 331 W Washington Blvd, 46802,
    1914 .... (219)424-2643
Goshen
Checkerberry Inn, 62644 Country Rd 37, 46526
Hagerstown
Teetor House, 300 W Main St, 47346 .... (317)489-4422
Hartford City
De'Coy's B&B, 1546 W 100 N, 47348 .... (317)348-2164
Indianapolis
Barn House, 10656 E 63rd St, 46236

Hollingsworth House Inn, 6054 Hollingsworth Road, 46254,
1854 .... (317)299-6700
Le Chateau Delaware, 1456 N Delaware St, 46202, 1906 (317)636-9156
Osborne House, 1911 N Delaware, 46202, 1899 .... (317)924-1777
Pairadux Inn, 6363 N Guilford Ave, 46220 .... (317)259-8005
Stewart Manor, 612 E 13th St, 46202, 1870 .... (317)634-1711

Knightstown
Old Hoosier House, Rt 2 Box 299-I, 46148, 1836 .... (317)345-2969

La Grange
The 1886 Inn, PO Box 5, 212 W Factory St, 46761 .... (219)463-4227

Leavenworth
Ye Olde Scotts Inn, RR 1, Box 5, 47137 .... (812)739-4747

Madison
Millwood House, 512 West St, 47250, 1870 .... (812)265-6780
The Cliff House, 122 Fairmount Dr, 47250, 1885 .... (812)265-5272

Metamora
The Publick House, PO Box 219, 47030, 1850 .... (317)647-6235
The Thorpe House, Clayborne St, 47030 .... (317)647-5425

Michigan City
Creekwood Inn, Rt 20-35, 46460 .... (219)872-8357
Duneland Beach Inn, 3311 Potawatomi, 46360, 1920
Nutcracker Inn, 220 W 10th St, 46360, 1900 .... (219)872-3237
Plantation Inn, RR 2 Box 296-s, 46360 .... (219)874-2418

Middlebury
Patchwork Quilt, 11748 Cr 2, 46540

Mishawaka
The Beiger Mansion Inn, 317 Lincoln Way E, 46544,
1903 .... (219)256-0365

Morgantown
The Rock House, 380 W Washington St, 46160, 1894 .... (812)597-5100

Muncie
Old Franklin House, 704 East Washington St, 47305,
1896 .... (317)286-0277

Nashville
Allison House, 90 S Jefferson St, 47448 .... (812)988-6664
McGinley's Cabins, Rt 3, Box 332, 47448 .... (812)988-7337
Seasons, PO Box 187, 47448 .... (812)988-2284
Story Inn, PO Box 64, 47448 .... (812)988-6516
Sunset House, RR 3, Box 127, 47448 .... (812)988-6118

New Harmony
New Harmony Inn, North St, 47631 .... (812)682-4491

Paoli
Braxtan House Inn B&B, 210 N Gospel St, 47454, 1893 (812)723-4677

Richland
Country Homestead, Rt 1, Box 353, 47634 .... (812)359-4870

Rising Sun
Jelly House Country Inn, 222 S Walnut St, 47404 .... (812)438-2319

Roachdale
Victorian House, RR 1 Box 27, 46172

Rockport
The Rockport Inn, Third At Walnut, 47635, 1855 .... (812)649-2664

Shipshewana
Green Meadow, Rt 2 Box 592, State Rd 5, 46565

South Bend
Jamison Inn, 1404 N Ivy Rd, 46637 .... (219)277-9682
Queen Anne Inn, 420 W Washington, 46601, 1893 .... (219)234-5959
The Queen Anne Inn, 420 W Washington, 46601, 1893 ... (219)234-5959

Vincennes
Mayor Wilhelm's Villa, 428 N Fifth St, 47591, 1887 .... (812)882-9487

Wabash
Hilltop House B&B, 88 W Sinclair St, 46992 .... (219)563-7726

Wappanee
Amish Acres, Inc., 160 W Market, 46550 .... (219)773-4188

Warsaw
Candlelight Inn, 503 E Fort Wayne St, 46580 .... (219)267-2906

Iowa

Adel
Walden Acres B&B, RR 1, Box 30, 50003 .... (515)987-1567

Amana
Guest House Motor Inn Motel, 52203 .... (319)622-3599

Amana Colonies
Die Heimat Country Inn, Main St, 52236, 1854 .... (319)622-3937

Bellvue
Mont Rest, 300 Spring St, 52031, 1893 .... (319)872-4220

Brooklyn
Hotel Brooklyn, 154 Front St, 52211, 1895 .... (515)522-9229

Calmar
Calmar Guesthouse, RR 1 Box 206, 52132 .... (319)562-3851

Clear Lake
Budget Inn, Box 102, 50428

Council Bluffs
Robin's Nest Inn B&B, 327 9th Ave, 50501 .... (712)323-1649

Davenport
River Oaks Inn, 1234 E River Dr, 52803, 1850 .... (319)326-2629

Decorah
Montgomery Mansion, 812 Maple Ave, 52101 .... (319)382-5088
Orval & Diane Bruvold, Rt 1, 52101 .... (319)382-4729

Dubuque
Redstone Inn, 504 Bluff St, 52001, 1894 .... (319)582-1894
Stout House, 1105 Locust, 52001, 1890 .... (319)582-1890

Elk Horn
Rainbow H. Lodging House, RR 1, Box 89, 51531 .... (712)764-8272
The Travelling Companion B&B, 4314 Main St, 51531,
1909 .... (712)764-8932

Elkader
Little House Vacations, 52043 .... (319)783-7774

Fort Atkinson
Cloverleaf Farm, Rt 2, Box 140A, 52144 .... (319)534-7061
LaVerne/Alice Hageman, Rt 1, Box 104, 52144 .... (319)534-7545

Fort Dodge
Larson House, 300 N 9th St, 50501 .... (515)573-5733

Fort Madison
The Morton House, 7 Highpoint, 52627, 1920 .... (319)372-9517

Keosauqua
Hotel Manning, 100 Van Buren St, 52565, 1854 .... (319)293-3232
Mason House Inn, RR 2 - Bentonsport, 52565 .... (319)592-3133

Lansing
Fitzgerald's Inn, 106 3rd St, 52151 .... (319)538-4872
Lansing House, Box 97, 291 N Front St, 52151 .... (319)538-4263

Leighton
Heritage House, RR 1, 50143 .... (515)626-3092

Maquoketa
Decker Hotel, 128 N Main, 52060, 1874 .... (319)652-6654

Missouri Valley
Apple Orchard Inn, RR 3, Box 129, 51555 .... (712)642-2418

Morengo
Loy's B&B, RR 1, 52301 .... (319)642-7787

Pella
Strawtown Inn, LIll Washington St, 50219 .... (515)628-2681

Spencer
The Hannah Marie Country Inn, Rt 1, Hwy 71 S, 51301,
1910 .... (712)262-1286

Spillville
Old World Inn, 331 S Main St, 52168, 1871 .... (319)562-3739

Swisher
Terra Verde Farm, Rt 1, Box 86, 52338 .... (319)846-2478

Tipton
Victorian House Tipton, 508 E 4th St, 52772 .... (319)886-2633

Webster City
Centennial Farm, RR 2 Box 40, 50595 .... (515)832-3050

Kansas

Ashland
Hardesty House, 712 Main St, 67831, 1900 .... (316)635-2911

Cimarron
The Cimarron Hotel, 203 N Main, 67835, 1886 .... (316)855-2244

Council Grove
The Cottage House, 25 N Neosho, 66846, 1876 .... (316)767-6828

Fort Scott
Country Quarters, Rt 5, Box 80, 66701 .... (316)223-2889

Kansas (Continued)

Lawrence
Halcyon House, 1000 Ohio, 66044, 1886 ....(913)841-0314
Manhattan
Kimble Cliff, Rt 1 Box 139, 66502
Melvern
Schoolhouse Inn, 106 E Beck, PO Box 175, 66510, 1870 (913)549-3473
Peabody
Jones Sheep Farm B&B, RR 2, 66866, 1930 ....(316)983-2815
Rogersville
Anchor Hill Lodge, Rt 1, 65742
Saint Marys
Morning Star Inn, 110 W Bertrand, 66536, 1902 ....(913)437-6851
Tonganoxie
Almeda's B&B, 220 S Main, 66086, 1917 ....(913)845-2295
Topeka
Heritage House, 3535 SW Sixth St, 66606
Valley Falls
The Barn B&B, RR 2 Box 87, 66088
Wakefield
B&B On Our Farm, Rt 1 Box 132, 67487 ....(913)461-5596
Wichita
Max Paul...an inn, 3910 E Kellogg, 67218 ....(316)689-8101

Kentucky

Bardstown
Bruntwood 1802, Mrs. Bare, 714 N 3 St, 40004
Jailer's Inn, 111 W Stephen Foster Ave, 40004, 1819 ......(502)348-5551
Old Talbott Tavern, Court Square, 107 W Stephen Foster, 40004,
    1779 ....(502)348-3494
Berea
Boone Tavern Hotel, Main St CPO 2345, 40403, 1909 ....(606)986-9358
Bowling Green
Bowling Green B&B, 659 E 14th Ave, 42101, 1939 ....(502)781-3861
Brandenburg
Doe Run Inn, Rt 2, 40108, 1820
Covington
Amos Shinkle Townhouse, 215 Garrard St, 41011, 1854(606)431-2118
Cynthiana
Broadwell Acres, Rt 6 Box 58, 41031 ....(606)234-4255
Frankfort
Olde Kentucke, 210 E Fourth St, 40601 ....(502)227-7389
Georgetown
Log Cabin B&B, 350 N Broadway, 40324, 1809 ....(502)863-3514
Grays Knob
Three Deer Inn, PO Drawer 299, 40829 ....(504)892-1952
Harrodsburg
Beaumont Inn, 638 Beaumont Dr, 40330, 1835 ....(606)734-3381
Shakertown At Pleasant Hill, Rt 4, 40330, 1805 ....(606)734-5411
Independence
Ohio Valley B&B Service, 6876 Taylor Mill Rd, 41051 .....(606)356-7865
Lexington
547 B&B, 547 N Broadway, 40508 ....(606)255-4152
Rokeby Hall, 318 S Mill St, 40508, 1880 ....(606)252-2368
Murray
The Diuguid House, 603 Main St, 42071, 1895 ....(502)753-5470
Paducah
Ehrhardts B&B, 285 Springwell Dr, 42001 ....(502)554-0644
Richmond
Jordan Hill Farm, 722 Walker Parks Rd, 40475................(606)623-8114
Simpsonville
The Old Stone Inn, Rt 5, 40065 ....(502)722-8882
Versailles
Bluegrass B&B, Rt 1 Box 263, 40383 ....(606)873-3208
Peacham, Rt 1 Box 263, 40383, 1829
Springdale, Rt 1 Box 263, 40383, 1800
Welcome Hall, Rt 1 Box 263, 40383, 1792

Louisiana

Baton Rouge
Mount Hope Plantation, 8151 Highland Rd, 70808, 1817 (504)766-8600
Brittany
Rosewood Manor, 10254 Hwy 431, Box 127, 70718 ....(504)675-5781
Clinton
Brame-bennet House, 227 S Baton Rouge St, 70722,
    1839 ....(504)683-5241
Convent
Tezcuco Plantation, Rt 1 Box 157, 70723, 1855
Covington
Plantation Bell Guest House, 204 W 24th Ave, 70433, 1809
Darrow
Tezcuco Plantation Village, 313 Hwy 44, 70725 ....(504)562-3929
Jackson
Asphodel Plantation, Rt 2 Box 89, 70748, 1820 ....(504)654-6868
Milbank, 102 Bank St, 70748 ....(504)634-5901
Jeanerette
Albania Plantation Mansion, Hwy 182, 70544, 1837 ....(318)276-4816
Patout's Guest House, Rt 1, Box 288, 70544 ....(318)364-0644
Lafayette
Ti Frere's House, 1905 Verot School Rd, 70508
Napoleonville
Madewood Plantation, Rt 2 Box 478, 70390, 1848 ....(504)369-7151
New Iberia
Mintmere Plantation, 1400 E Main, 70560, 1857
New Orleans
A Creole House, 1013 St Ann St, 70116, 1820 ....(504)524-8076
A Hotel, the Frenchman, 417 Frenchman St, 70116,
    1860 ....(504)948-2166
Andrew Jackson Hotel, 919 Royal St, 70166, 1880 ....(504)561-5881
Burgundy Inn, 911 Burgundy St, 70116, 1780 ....(504)524-0141
Chimes Cottages, 1360 Moss St, Box 52257, 70152...........(504)525-4640
Club La Pension, 501 Canal St, 70130, 1821
Columns Hotel, 3811 St Clarles Ave, 70115 ....(504)899-9308
Cornstalk Hotel, 915 Royal St, 70116, 1805 ....(504)523-1515
Dauzat House, 337 Burgandy St, 70130, 1788 ....(504)524-2075
Dusty Mansion, 2231 General Pershing, 70115, 1913 .....(504)891-6061
French Quarter Maisons, 1130 Chartres St, 70116
Grenoble House, 329 Dauphine, 70112, 1854 ....(504)522-1331
Hansel And Gretel House, 916 Burgundy St, 70116,
    1880 ....(504)524-0141
Hedgewood, 2427 St Charles Ave, 70130, 1840
Hotel Maison De Ville & Audubon Cottages, 727 Rue Toulouse,
    70130 ....(504)561-5858
Hotel Villa Convento, 616 Ursulines St, 70116, 1820
Jensen's B&B, 1631 Seventh St, 70115 ....(504)897-1895
Josephine Guest House, 1450 Josephine St, 70130 ....(504)524-6361
Lafitte Guest House, 1003 Bourbon St, 70116, 1849........(504)581-2678
Lamothe House, 621 Esplanade Ave, 70116, 1840 ....(504)947-1161
Longpre Garden's Guest House, 1726 Prytania, 70130 ....(504)561-0654
Maison Chartres, 508 Chartres St, 70130, 1835 ....(504)529-2172
Maison De Ville, 727 Toulouse St, 70130, 1742 ....(504)561-5858
Marquette Hostel, 2253 Carondelet St, 70130
Mazant Street Guest House, 906 Mazant St, 70117, 1882.(504)944-2662
Nine-O-Five Royal Hotel, 905 Rue Royal St, 70116,
    1890 ....(504)523-0219
Noble Arms Inn, 1006 Royal St, 70116, 1820
Old World Inn, 1330 Prytania, 70130
Park View, 7004 St Charles St, 70118, 1884
Prince Conti Hotel, 830 Conti St, 70112.............................(504)529-4172
Prytania Inn, 1415 Prytania St, 70130 ....(504)566-1515
Soniat House, 1133 Chartres St, 70116, 1830 ....(504)522-0570
St. Charles Guest House, 1748 Prytania St, 70130, 1850 (504)523-6556
St. Peter House, 1005 St Peter St, 70116, 1850 ....(504)524-9232
Stone Manor Hotel, 3800 St Charles Ave, 70115, 1908 ...(504)899-9600
Terrell House, 1441 Magazine St, 70130
The Columns Hotel, 3811 St Charles Ave, 70115, 1883.....(504)899-9308
The Frenchman, 417 Frenchmen St, 70116, 1860 ....(504)948-2166
The Hedgewood Hotel, 2427 Saint Charles Ave, 70130 ...(504)895-9708
The Prytania Park Hotel, 1525 Prytania St, 70130, 1834 (800)862-1984
New Roads
Bondy House & Claiborne House, Box 386, 304 Court St, 70760
Pointe Coupee B&B, 605 E Main St, 70760, 1850 ....(504)638-6254

Opelousas
Estorge House, 427 N. Market St, 70570, 1827
Ruston
Twin Gables, 711 N Vienna St, 71270, 1882 .... (318)255-4452
Saint Francisville
Barrow House, 524 Royal St, 70775, 1809 .... (504)635-4791
Cottage Plantation, Rt 5 Box 425, 70775, 1795 .... (504)635-3674
Myrtles Plantation, PO Box 1100, 70775 .... (504)635-6277
Myrtles Plantation, PO Box 387, 70775, 1796
St. Francisville Inn, 118 N Commerce St, PO Drawer 1369, 70775,
   1880 .... (504)635-6502
Saint Martinville
Evangeline Oak Corner, 215 Evangeline Blvd, 70582,
   1879 .... (318)394-7675
Shreveport
Fairfield Place, 2221 Fairfield Ave, 71104, 1890 .... (318)222-0048
The Columns on Jordan, 615 Jordan, 71101, 1898 .... (318)222-5912
Vacherie
Oak Alley Plantation, Rt 2 Box 10 Hwy 18, 70090, 1880
Vinton
Old Lyons House, 1335 Horridge St, 70668
Viroqua
Viroqua Heritage Inn, 220 E Jefferson Inn, 54665 .... (608)637-3306
Wakefield
Wakefield Plantation, PO Box 41, 70784, 1834
White Castle
Nottoway, PO Box 160, Mississippi River Road, 70788,
   1859 .... (504)545-2409
Wilson
Glencoe Plantation, PO Box 178, 70789, 1903

Maine

Alfred
The Olde Berry Inn, Kennebunk Rd, 04002 .... (207)324-0603
Annaolis
Jonah Williams House, 101 Severn Ave, 21403 .... (301)267-7005
Augusta
Crosby's B&B, 51 Green St, 04330
Bailey Island
Cloverleaf Cottage B&B, RFD 1 Box 326, 04003
Driftwood Inn, 04003
The Lady & The Loon, PO Box 98, 04003 .... (207)833-6871
Bar Harbor
Atlantean Inn, 11 Atlantic Ave, Dept B, 04609 .... (207)288-3270
Bayview Inn & Hotel, 111 Eden St, 04609
Black Friar Inn, 10 Summer St, 04609........................... (207)288-5091
Central House, 60 Cottage St, 04609
Clefstone Manor, 92 Eden St, 04609, 1880
Dow Cottage Inn, 227 Main St, 04609, 1830
Graycote Inn, 40 Holland Ave, 04609, 1881 .... (207)288-3044
Hearthside Inn, 7 High St, 04609, 1907 .... (207)288-4533
Holbrook House, 74 Mount Desert, 04609, 1880 .... (207)288-4970
Ledgelawn Inn, 66 Mount Desert, 04609, 1904 .... (207)288-4596
Manor House Inn, W St Historic District, 04609, 1887 . (207)288-3759
Mira Monte Inn, 69 Mt Desert St, 04609, 1864 .... (207)288-4263
Primrose Cottage Inn, 73 Mt Desert St, 04609 .... (207)288-4031
Shady Maples, RD 1 Box 360, 04609
Stratford House Inn, 45 Mount Desert St, 04609, 1900 . (207)288-5189
The Atlantean Inn, 11 Atlantic Ave, 04609
The Inn On High, 15 High St, 04609
The Maples, 16 Roberts Ave, 04609, 1903 .... (207)288-3443
The Tides, 119 West St, 04609 .... (207)288-4968
Thornhedge, 47 Mt. Desert St, 04609, 1900
Town Guest House, 12 Atlantic Ave, 04609, 1894
Bar Mills
Royal Brewster B&B, Box 307, Corner Rt 202 & 112, 04004,
   1805 .... (207)929-3012
Baring
Moosehorn B&B, Rt 1, Box 322, 04694 .... (207)454-8883
Bas Harbor
Bass Harbor Inn, Shore Rd, 04653.................................... (207)244-5157

Bass Harbor
Bass Harbor Cottages, Rt 102A, 04653 .... (207)244-3460
Pointy Head Inn, Rt 102A, 04653
Bath
Elizabeth's B&B, 360 Front St, 04530, 1820 .... (207)443-1146
Fairhaven Inn, RR 2 Box 85, N Bath Rd, 04530, 1790..... (207)443-4391
Glad II, 60 Pearl St, 04530
Grane's Fairhaven Inn, N Bath Rd, 04530 .... (207)443-4391
Levitt Family B&B, 50 Pearl St, 04530
Belfast
Hiram Alden Inn, 19 Church St, 04915, 1840 .... (703)338-2151
Horatio Johnson House, 36 Church St, 04915 .... (207)338-5153
Londonderry Inn, Rt 3, Belmont Ave, 04915 .... (207)338-3988
Northport House B&B, City One, Mounted Rt, US Rt. 1, 04915,
   1873 .... (207)338-1422
Penobscot Meadows, Rt 1, 04915
The Jeweled Turret Inn, 16 Pearl St, 04915, 1898 .... (207)338-2304
Bethel
Bakers B&B, RFD 2 Box 2090, 04217
Bethel Inn & Court, PO Box 26, 04217 .... (800)654-0125
Chapman Inn, PO Box 206, 04217
Douglass Place, Rt 2, Box 9, 04217 .... (207)824-2229
Four Seasons Inn, Upper Main St, 04217 .... (207)824-2755
Hammons House, Broad St, 04217, 1859 .... (207)824-3170
L'Auberge Country Inn, PO Box 21, 04217 .... (207)824-2774
Norseman Inn, Rt 2 Rumford Rd, 04217, 1800 .... (207)824-2002
Sudbury Inn, Lower Main St, 04217 .... (207)824-2174
Sunday River Inn, Sunday River Rd, 04217 .... (207)824-2410
The Pointed Fir, PO Box 745, 04217 .... (207)824-2251
Biddefordpool
Lodge, 19 Yates, 04006 .... (617)284-7148
Bingham
Mrs. G's B&B, PO Box 389, Meadow St, 04920 .... (207)672-4034
Blue Hill
Altenhofen House, Peters Point, 04614, 1810
Arcady Down East, South St, 04614, 1810 .... (207)374-5576
Blue Hill Farm Country Inn, Rt 15 Box 437, 04614,
   1832 .... (207)374-5126
John Peters Inn, PO Box 916, 04614 .... (207)374-2116
Boothbay
Kenniston Hill Inn, Rt 27, 04537, 1786 .... (207)633-2159
Boothbay Harbor
Admiral's Quarters, 105 Commercial St, 04538, 1820 ..... (207)633-2474
Boothbay Harbor Inn, 37 Atlantic Ave, Box 446, 04538 ... (207)633-6302
Captain Sawyer's Place, 87 Commercial St, 04538 .... (207)633-2290
Green Shutters Inn, PO Box 543, 04538
Harbour Towne Inn, 71 Townsend Ave, 04538 .... (207)633-4300
Hilltop House, 44 Mckown Hill, 04538, 1830
Howard House, Route 27, 04538
Seafarer Guest House, 38 Union St, 04538
The Anchor Watch, PO Box, 04538 .... (207)366-2284
The Atlantic Ark Inn, 64 Atlantic Ave, 04538 .... (207)633-5690
Thistle Inn, PO Box 176, 04538, 1850
Topside, Mckown Hill, 04538
Welch House, 36 Mckown St, 04538, 1840
Westgate Guest House, 18 West St, 04538, 1903
Bowdoinham
The Maples, RR 1 Box 75, 04008 .... (207)666-3012
Bridgton
Mountainside B&B, PO Box 290, 04009
Noble House, PO Box 180, 04009, 1903 .... (207)647-3733
North Woods B&B, 55 N High St, 04009
Tarry-a-While Resort, Box A, 04009 .... (207)647-2522
The 1859 Guest House, 60 S. High St, 04009, 1859 .... (207)647-2508
Bristol
Middlefield Farm, PO Box 4, 04539
Brooksville
Breezemere Farm, Box 290, 04617, 1850
Brunswick
Aaron Dunning House, 76 Federal St, 04011 .... (207)729-4486
Brunswick B&B, 165 Park Row, 04011, 1860 .... (207)729-4914
Harborgate B&B, RD 2-2260, 04011 .... (207)725-5894
Lookout Point House, PO Box 806, 04074 .... (207)833-5509
Samuel Newman House, 7 South St, 04011, 1821 .... (207)729-6959
Stowe House, 63 Federal St, 04011 .... (207)725-5543

Maine (Continued)

Bryant Pond
The Glen Mountain House, PO Box 176, 04219
Bucksport
Jed Prouty Tavern, Box 550, 04416
L'ermitage, 219 Main St, 04416, 1830 ....(207)469-3361
The Old Parsonage Inn, PO Box 1577, 190 Franklin St, 04415,
    1800 ....(207)469-6477
The River Inn, 210 Main St, 04416, 1830 ....(207)469-3783
Camden
Blackberry Inn, 82 Elm St, 04843 ....(207)236-6060
Blue Harbor House, 67 Elm St, Rt 1, 04843, 1835 ....(207)236-3196
Camden Harbour Inn, 83 Bayview St, 04843, 1874 ....(207)236-4200
Chestnut House, 69 Chestnut St, 04843
Edgecombe-Coles House, 64 High St, HCR 60 Box 3010, 04843,
    1830 ....(209)236-2336
Goodspeeds Guest House, 60 Mountain St, 04843
Hartstone Inn, 41 Elm St, 04843 ....(207)236-4259
Hawthorne Inn, 9 High St, 04843, 1890 ....(207)236-8842
High Tide Inn, 04843, 1940
J. Sloan Inn, 49 Mountain St, 04843
Lord Camden Inn, 24 Main St, 04843
Maine Stay B&B, 22 High St, 04843, 1813 ....(207)236-9636
Norumbega Inn, 61 High St, 04843
Owl And The Turtle, 8 Bay View, 04843
Park Street Inn, 90 Mechanic St, 04843
The Elms, 84 Elm St, Rt 1, 04843, 1806 ....(207)236-6250
The Swan House, 49 Mountain St, 04843
Whitehall Inn, 52 High St, 04843
Windward House, 6 High St, 04843 ....(207)236-9656
Cape Elizabeth
Crescent Beach Inn, Rt 77, 04107
Cape Neddick
Cape Neddick House, Rt 1 Box 70, 03902
Sea Chimes B&B, Shore Rd, 03902
Wooden Goose Inn, Rt 1 Box 195, 03902
Cape Newagen
Newagen Seaside Inn, Box H, 04552 ....(207)633-5242
Carrabassett Valley
Sugarloaf Inn, Carrabasset Vly, 04947 ....(207)237-2701
Casco
Maplewood Inn, Rt 302 Box 627, 04015 ....(207)655-7586
Castine
Castine Inn, PO Box 41, 04421, 1898 ....(207)326-4365
Pentagoet Inn, PO Box 4, 04421, 1894
The Manor, Battle Ave, PO Box 276, 04421, 1895 ....(207)326-4861
Center Lovell
Center Lovell Inn, Rt 5, 04016, 1805 ....(207)925-1575
Westways On Kezar Lake, Rt 5, 04016
Chebeague Island
Chebeague Inn, 04017 ....(207)967-3118
Chebeague Island Inn, Box 492-MBB, 04107 ....(207)846-5155
Cherryfield
Ricker House, Box 256, 04622
Clark Island
Craignair Inn, Clark Island Rd, 04859, 1930 ....(207)594-7644
Coopers Mills
Claryknoll Farm, Rt 215, Box 751, 04341 ....(207)549-5250
Cornish
Cornish Country Inn, Box 206, 04020
The Cornish Inn, Rt 25 Box 266, 04020, 1826 ....(207)625-8501
Damariscotta
The Brannon Bunker, PO Box 045, HCR 64, 04543,
    1820 ....(207)563-5941
Yellow House B&B, Water St, Box 732, 04543 ....(207)563-1388
Deer Isle
Eggemoggin Inn, RFD Box 324, 04650 ....(207)348-2540
Pilgrim's Inn, Main St, 04627, 1793
Dennysville
Lincoln House Country Inn, Rts 1 & 86, 04628, 1787 .....(207)726-3953
Dixmont
Ben-loch Inn, RFD 1 Box 1020, 04932 ....(207)257-4768

Dover-Foxcroft
The Foxcroft, 25 W Main St, 04426
East Boothbay
Linekin Village B&B, Ocean Point Rd, Rt 96, 04544,
    1882 ....(207)633-3681
Ocean Point Inn, Shore Rd, 04544 ....(207)633-4200
East Machias
East River B&B, PO Box 205, High St, 04630 ....(207)255-8467
East Waterford
Waterford Inne, Box 49, 04233
Eastport
Artists Retreat, 29 Washington St, 04631, 1846 ....(207)853-4239
The Inn At Eastport, 13 Washington St, 04631 ....(207)853-4307
Todd House, Todd's Head, 04631, 1775 ....(207)853-2328
Weston House, 26 Boynton Street, 04631, 1810 ....(207)853-2907
Eliot
Ewenicorn Farm B&B, 116 Goodwin Rd, Rt 101, 03903 ...(207)439-1337
High Meadows B&B, Rt 101, 03903, 1736 ....(207)439-0590
Ellsworth
Mrs. Bancroft's, Box 693, 04605, 1878 ....(207)667-4696
Victoria's B&B, 58 Pine St, 04605
Enfield
Inn At Cold Stream Pond, PO Box 76, 04433
Five Islands
Grey Havens Inn, Box 82, 04546
Freeport
181 Main St, 181 Main St, 04032, 1840 ....(207)865-1226
Captain Josiah Mitchell House, 188 Main St, 04032,
    1779 ....(207)865-3289
Harraseeket Inn, 162 Main St, 04032, 1850 ....(207)865-9377
Holbrook Inn, 7 Holbrook St, 04032 ....(207)865-6693
Isaac Randall House, Independence Drive, 04032,
    1823 ....(207)865-9295
Maple Hill B&B, 18 Maple Ave, 04032 ....(207)865-3730
Nathan Nye Inn, 11 Nathan Nye St, 04032, 1800 ....(207)865-9606
Old Red Farm, Rr2 Box 242 Desert Rd, 04032 ....(207)865-4550
The Bagley House, RR 3 Box 269C, 04032, 1772 ....(207)865-6566
Fryeburg
The Oxford House Inn, 105 Main St, 04037
Gorham
Country Squire B&B, Box 178 Mighty St Rt1, 04038
Gouldsboro
Sunset House, HCR #60, Box 62, 04607 ....(207)963-7156
Greenville
Greenville Inn, PO Box 1194, 04441, 1895 ....(207)695-2206
Guilford
Trebor Inn, PO Box 299, 04443
Hancock
Crocker House, 04640, 1884
LeDomaine Restaurant & Inn, US 1, Box 496, 04640 ......(207)422-3395
Harpswell Center
Lookout Point House, Lookout Point Rd, 04079 ....(207)833-5509
Harrison
Tolman House Inn, PO Box 551, Tolman Rd, 04040 ....(207)583-4445
Hartford
Green Acres Inn, RFD #112, Green Acres Rd, 04221 ....(207)597-2333
Houlton
The Mallard Inn, 48 North St, 04730, 1917 ....(207)532-4377
Hulls Cove
Inn at Canoe Point, Rt 3 Box 216A, 04644, 1889 ....(207)288-9511
Isle Au Haut
The Keeper's House, PO Box 26, 04645 ....(207)677-3678
Isleford
Island B&B, Box 275, 04646 ....(207)244-9283
Islesboro
Dark Harbor House Inn, Box 185, 04848
Gablewood, Main Road, 04848
Islesboro Inn, 04848 ....(207)734-2222
Jonesboro
Chandler River Lodge, Rt 1, 04648, 1800 ....(201)679-2778
Jonesport
Tootsie's B&B, Trynor Sq, RFD 1, Box 252, 04649

Kennebunk
Alewife House, 1917 Alewive Rd, Rt 35, 04043, 1756 ...... (207)985-2118
Arundel Meadows Inn, PO Box 1129, 04043 .... (207)985-3770
Captain Littlefield Inn, 26 Fletcher St, 04043
Kennebunk Inn 1799, 45 Main St, 04043, 1799
Kennebunkport
1802 House, Box 646A Locke St, 04046, 1802 .... (207)967-5632
Breakwater, PO Box 1160, 04046
Bufflehead Cove, Box 499, Gornitz Ln, 04046 .... (207)967-3879
Captain Fairfield House, PO Box 202, 04046
Captain Jefferds Inn, Box 691, 04046, 1804
Captain Lord Mansion, Pleasant & Green, PO Box 800, 04046,
     1812 .... (207)967-3141
Chetwynd House, PO Box 130, 04046, 1840
Dock Square Inn, PO Box 1123, 04046
English Meadows, Rt 35, 04046
English Robin, Rt 1 Box 194, 04046
Farm House, RR 1, Box 656, 04046 .... (207)967-4169
Flakeyard Farm, RFD 2, 04046
Green Heron Inn, Drawer 151, 04046 .... (207)967-3315
Harbor Inn, PO Box 538A, 04046, 1903 .... (207)967-2074
Inn at Harbor Head, RR 2 Box 1180, 04046, 1898 .... (207)967-5564
Inn on South Street, PO Box 478A, South St, 04046,
     1807 .... (207)967-5151
Kennebunkport Inn, Box 111, Dock Sq, 04046 .... (207)967-2621
Kilburn House, PO Box 1309, 04046 .... (207)967-4762
Kylemere House 1818, South Street, PO Box 1333, 04046,
     1818 .... (207)967-2780
Lake Brook Guest House, RR3, Box 1333, 04046 .... (207)967-4069
Maine Stay Inn and Cottages, Maine St, PO Box 500A, 04046,
     1860 .... (207)967-2117
North Street Guest House, Box 1229, 04046
Old Fort Inn, Old Fort Ave, PO Box M 24, 04046, 1880 (207)967-5353
Port Gallery Inn, PO Box 1367, 04046, 1891 .... (207)967-3728
Schooners Inn & Restaurant, PO Box 1121 Ocean Ave,
     04046 .... (207)967-5333
Seaside Inn, Gooch's Beach, 04046
Sundial Inn, PO Box 1147, 04043, 1891 .... (207)967-3850
The Green Heron Inn, Ocean Ave, 04046, 1908
The White Barn Inn, Beach Street, RR 3 Box 387,
     04046 .... (207)967-2321
Tides Inn By The Sea, Goose Rock Beach, 04046, 1900
Village Cove Inn, PO Box 650, 04046 .... (207)967-3993
Welby Inn, Ocean Ave, PO Box 774, 04046, 1900 .... (207)967-4655
Kingfield
Herbert Inn, PO Box 67, 04947
Three Stanley Avenue, PO Box 169, 04947
Witner's Inn, Box 44, 04947, 1800
Kittery
Melfair Farm B&B, 365 Wilson Rd, 03904
Kittery Point
Harbor's Watch, RFD 1 Box 42, 03905
Whaleback Inn, Pepperrell Rd, Box 162, 03905 .... (207)439-9570
Lincolnville
Cedarholm Cottages, Star Rt, 04849 .... (207)236-3886
Green Woods, RFD #2, 04849 .... (207)338-3187
Longville, PO Box 75, 04849 .... (207)236-3785
Red House, HC 60, Box 540, 04849 .... (207)236-4621
Sign of the Owl, Rt 1, Box 85, 04849 .... (207)338-4669
Youngtown Inn, Rt 52, 04849, 1810 .... (207)763-3037
Lincolnville Beach
North House 1792, Box 165, 04849
Litchfield
Old Tavern Inn, PO Box 445, 04350
Little Deer Isle
Eggemoggin Inn, 04650, 1906
Lubec
Breakers-by-the-bay, 37 Washington, 04652, 1888 .... (207)733-2487
Due East, Bailey's Mistake, 04652, 1800 .... (207)733-2413
Home Port Inn, 45 Main Street, 04652, 1862 .... (207)733-2077
Hugel Haus B&B, 55 Main St, 04652 .... (207)733-4965
Overview, RD 2, Box 106, 04652 .... (207)733-2005
Machias
Clark Perry House, 59 Court St, 04654, 1868 .... (207)255-8458

Manset
The Moorings, 04679, 1780
Martinsville
Mill Pond House, Mrs. Korpinen, 04860
Milbridge
Bayside Inn, Rt 1, 04658, 1900 .... (207)546-7852
Monhegan
Monhegan House, 04852 .... (207)594-7983
Monhegan Island
Island Inn, Shore Rd, 04852, 1850
Shinning Sails Inc, Box 44, 04852 .... (207)596-0041
Mount Vernon
Feather Bed Inn, Box 65, 04352, 1856
Naples
Charmwoods, 04055
Songo B&B, Songon Locks Rd, 04055 .... (207)693-3960
The Augustus Bove House, RR 1 Box 501, 04055
The Epicurean Inn, PO Box Aq, 04055 .... (207)693-3839
The Inn at Long Lake, Lake House Road, PO 806, 04055,
     1906 .... (207)693-6226
New Harbor
Bradley Inn, 361 Pemaquid Pt., 04554, 1890
Gosnold Arms, Northside Road, Rt 32, 04554, 1870 .... (207)677-3727
Southside-By The Harbor, Southside Rd, 04554, 1857 ..... (207)677-2991
Newcastle
Elfinhill, 20 River Rd, PO Box 497, 04553, 1851 .... (207)563-1886
Glidden House, Glidden St, RR 1 Box 740, 04553, 1850 .. (207)563-1859
Mill Pond Inn, RFD 1 Box 245, 04553, 1780 .... (207)563-8014
The Captain's House, PO Box 516, 04553, 1840 .... (207)563-1482
The Markert House, PO Box 224, Glidden St, 04553 .... (207)563-1309
The Newcastle Inn, River Road, 04553, 1860 .... (207)563-5685
Nobleboro
Oliver Farm Inn, Old Rt 1, Box 136, 04555, 1795 .... (207)563-1527
Norridgewock
Norridgewock Colonial Inn, RFD 1 Box 1190, 04957
North Edgecomb
Channelridge Farm, 358 Cross Pt Rd, 04556
North Haven
Pulpit Harbor Inn, Crabtree Point Rd, 04853
North Waterford
Olde Rowley Inn, Rt 35 N, 04267, 1790 .... (207)583-4143
Northeast Harbor
Grey Rock Inn, 04662
Harbourside Inn, 04662, 1888
Ogunquit
Berwick, Box 261, 03907 .... (207)646-4062
Blue Shutters, 6 Beachmere Pl., 03907
Blue Water Inn, Beach St, 03907
Channing Hall, 3 Pine Hill Rd, 03907
Clipper Ship Guest House, 46 N Main St, 03907
Gazebo, Rt 1 Box 668, 03907
Hartwell House, 116 Shore Rd, 03907 .... (207)646-7210
Hillcrest Inn Resort, Shore Rd, 03907 .... (207)646-7776
Inn At 77 Shore Road, 77 Shore Rd, 03907, 1840
Juniper Hill Inn, Rt 1 N, 03907 .... (207)646-4501
Leisure Inn, 19 School St, 03907 .... (207)646-2737
Lemon Tree Inn, Box 564, 03907
Marimor Motor Inn, 66 Shore Rd, 03907 .... (207)646-7397
Morning Dove B&B, 5 Bourne Ln, PO Box 1940, 03907,
     1865 .... (207)646-3891
Ogunquit House, PO Box 1883, 03907
Old Village Inn, 30 Main St, 03907 .... (207)646-7088
Sea Chambers-The Sea Bell, 37 Shore Rd, 03907, 1800 .... (207)646-9311
Seafair Inn, 24 Shore Rd Box 1221, 03907, 1890
Strauss Haus, Shore Rd, 03907 .... (207)646-7756
Terrace By the Sea, 11 Wharf Ln, 03907 .... (207)646-3232
Trellis House, Box 2229, 2 Bearhmere Pl, 03907 .... (207)646-7909
Yardarm Village Inn, PO Box 773, 03907
Yellow Monkey Guest House, 44 Main St, 03907 .... (207)646-9056
Oquossoc
Oquossoc's Own B&B, PO Box 27, 04964 .... (207)864-5584
Peaks Island
Moonshell Inn, Island Ave, 04081 .... (207)766-2331

Maine (Continued)

Pemaquid
Little River Inn, Rt 130, 04588
Phippsburg Center
The Captain Drummond House, PO Box 72, 04562,
    1792 ....(207)289-1394
Port Clyde
Copper Light, PO Box 67, 04855 ....(207)372-8510
Ocean House, Box 66, 04855
Portland
Carleton Gardens, 43 Carleton St, 04102 ....(207)772-3458
Inn At Carleton, 46 Carleton St, 04102
Inn at Parkspring, 135 Spring St, 04101, 1845 ....(207)774-1059
The Inn At Park Spring, 135 Spring St, 04101, 1835 ....(207)774-1059
Prospect Harbor
Oceanside Meadows Inn, Box 85, 04669, 1900 ....(207)963-5557
Rangeley
Farmhouse Inn, PO Box 173, 04970
Raymond
North Pines Health Resort, 04071......................(207)655-7624
Robinhood
Benjamin Riggs House, PO Box 440, 04530 ....(207)371-2256
Rockland
Old Granite Inn, 546 Main St, 04841 ....(207)594-7901
Rockport
Bread & Roses B&B, Corner US Rt 1 & Beech St, 04856 ..(207)236-6116
Rosemary Cottage, Russell Ave, 04856 ....(207)236-3513
Sign Of The Unicorn, 191 Beauchamp Ave, 04856
Sanford
Allen's Inn, 279 Main St, 04073
Sargentville
Oakland House, Herricks Rd, 04673 ....(207)359-8521
Searsport
Carriage House Inn, Rt 1 E Main St, 04974, 1849
Homeport Inn, Rt 1 East main St, 04974, 1862 ....(207)548-2259
House Of Three Chimneys, Rt 1 Box 397, 04974, 1838 .....(207)548-6117
McGilvery House, PO Box 588, 04974, 1860 ....(207)548-6289
Sunrise Lodge B&B, PO Box 330, 04974, 1795 ....(207)548-6575
The Hannah Nickels House, Rt 1 Box 38, 04974, 1830 .....(207)548-6691
Sebasco Estates
Rock Gardens Inn, 04565 ....(207)389-1161
Skowhegan
Brick Farm B&B, RFD 1, Box 1500, 04976 ....(207)474-3949
South Brooksville
Breezemere Farm Inn, PO Box 390, Breezemore Rd,
    04617 ....(207)326-8628
Buck's Harbor Inn, Rt 176 Box 268, 04617
South Casco
Migis Lodge, Rt 302, 04077 ....(207)655-4524
Thomas Inn & Playhouse, PO Box 128, 04077, 1850
South Harpswell
Alfred M. Senter B&B, Box 830, 04079 ....(207)833-2874
Senter B&B, Rt 123, 04079 ....(207)833-2874
South Thomaston
The Weskeag Inn, PO Box 213, 04858, 1800 ......(207)596-6676
Southport
Albonegon Inn, Capitol Island, 04538
Southwest Harbor
Claremont, 04676, 1884 ....(207)244-9828
Harbor Lights Home, Rt 102, 04679, 1880
Island House, Box 1006, 04679 ....(207)244-5180
Island Watch B&B, Box 1359, Freeman Ridge Rd, 04679 .(207)244-7229
Kingsleigh Inn, PO Box 1426, 100 Main St, 04679 ....(207)244-5302
Lindenwood Inn, PO Box 1328, 04679, 1906 ....(207)244-5335
Penury Hall, Main St Box 68, 04679, 1830 ....(207)244-7102
The Island House, Box 1006, 04679, 1830 ....(207)244-5180
The Kingsleigh Inn, PO Box 1426, 04679, 1904 ....(207)244-5302
Stonington
Rosehip, Box 346, 04681
Stratton
Widow's Walk, Box 150, 04982, 1897

Sullivan
Sullivan Harbor Farm, Rt 1, 04682 ....(207)422-3591
Sunset
Goose Cove Lodge, Deer Isle, 04683
Surry
Surry Inn, PO Box 25, 04684, 1834 ....(207)667-5091
Time & Tide B&B, RR1 Box 275B, 04684 ....(207)667-3382
Tenants Harbor
Church Hill B&B, Box 126, 04860, 1858 ....(207)372-6256
East Wind Inn & Meeting House, PO Box 149, 04680, 1860
Mill Pond House, Box 640, 04860 ....(207)372-6209
The Forks
Crab Apple Acres, Rt 201, 04985, 1835
Thomaston
Bedside Manor Guest House, HCR 35, Box 100, 04861 ...(207)354-8862
Captain Frost's B&B, 241 W Main St, 04861 ....(207)354-8217
Gracie's B&B, 52 Main St, 04861
River House B&B, HCR 35, Box 119, 04861 ....(207)354-8936
The Belvedere, 163 Main St, 04861
Topsham
Captain Purinton House, 64 Elm St, 04086, 1797 ....(207)729-3603
Middaugh B&B, 36 Elm St, 04086 ....(207)725-2562
The Walker Wilson House, 2 Melcher Place, 04086
Union
Shepard Hill B&B, PO Box 338, 04862
Vinalhaven
Fox Island Inn, Carver St, 04863
Vinnehaven
Old Granite Inn, PO Box 570, 04863-0570
Waldoboro
Broad Bay Inn & Gallery, Main Street, PO Box 607, 04572,
    1905 ....(207)832-6668
James & Lobby Hopkins, Main St, 04572
Le Vatout, Rt 32, Box 375, 04572 ....(207)832-4552
Letteney Farm Vacations, RFD 2, Box 166A, 04572 ......(207)832-5143
Medomark House, PO Box 663, Friendship St, 04572 ......(207)832-4971
The Roaring Lion, Box 756, 04572
Tide Watch Inn, PO Box 94, Pine St, 04572, 1850 ....(207)832-4987
Walpole
The Bittersweet Inn, Hcr 64, PO Box 013, 04573, 1840 .....(207)563-5552
Washington
Windward Farm, Young's Hill Rd, 04574
Waterford
Artemus Ward House, 04088, 1805
Kedarburn Inn, Rt 35 Box A-1, 04088
Lake House, Rts 35 & 37, 04088
Weld
Kawanhee Inn Lakeside Lodge, Lake Webb, 04285,
    1930 ....(207)585-2243
Weld Inn, Box 8, 04285, 1893
Wells
Bayview Inn B&B, Rt 1-2131, 04090
Grey Gull Inn, 321 Webhannet Dr, 04090, 1893
Purple Sandpiper Guest House, RR 3, Box 226, 04090.....(207)646-7990
Wells Beach
The Haven, Church St, 04090 ....(207)646-4194
West Bath
Bakke B&B, RD 1, Box 505A, 04530 ....(207)442-7185
New Meadows Inn, Bath Rd, 04530 ....(207)443-3921
West Bethel
King's Inn, PO Box 92, 04286
Winter Harbor
Main Stay Inn, PO Box 459, 04693......................(207)963-5561
Wiscasset
The Squire Tarbox Inn, RR 2 Box 620, 04578, 1765 ....(207)882-7693
The Stacked Arms, RR 2 Box 146, 04578 ....(207)882-5436
Twenty-Two Federal B&B, PO Box 57, 04578
Yarmouth
Homewood Inn, PO Box 196, 04096......................(207)846-3351
York
A Summer Place, D 1 Box 196, 03909
Dockside Guest Quarters, PO Box 205, Harris Island, 03909,
    1885 ....(207)363-2868

Hutchins House, 173 Organug Rd, 03909 .... (207)363-3058
Scotland Bridge Inn, PO Box 521, 03909 .... (207)363-4432
Summer Place, RFD 1 Box 196, 03909, 1790 .... (207)363-5233
The Wild Rose Of York, 78 Long Sands Rd, 03909, 1814 (207)363-2532

York Beach
Jo-Mar B&B on the Ocean, Box 838, 41 Freeman St,
    03910 .... (207)363-4826
Lighthouse Inn, Box 249, Nubble Rd, 03910 .... (207)363-6072
Lilac Inn, Box 1325 3 Ridge Rd, 03910 .... (207)363-3930
Nautilus B&B, 7 Willow Ave, Box 916, 03910 .... (207)363-6496
The Benetts, 3 Broadway, 03910
The Katahdin Inn "on The Ocean", PO Box 193, 03910 .. (207)363-2759

York Harbor
Edwards' Harborside Inn, Stage Neck Rd, 03911 .... (207)363-3037
The Inn At Harmon Park, York St, 03911
York Harbor Inn, Rt 1A Box 573, 03911, 1637 .... (207)363-5119

Maryland

Annapolis
Charles Inn, 74 Charles St, 21401, 1860 .... (301)268-1451
Gibson's Lodging, 110-114 Prince George, 21401, 1786. (301)268-5555
Green Street B&B, 161 Green St, 21401 .... (301)268-9549
Maryland Inn, 16 Church Circle, 21401 .... (301)263-2641
Prince George Inn, 232 Prince George St, 21401, 1884 .. (301)263-6418
Reynolds Tavern, 4 Church Circle, 21401 .... (301)263-2641
Robert Johnson House, 23 State Circle, 21401 .... (301)263-2641
State House Inn, 15 State Circle, 21401 .... (301)263-2641

Baltimore
Admiral Fell Inn, 888 S Broadway, 21231, 1850 .... (301)522-7377
Betsy's B&B, 1428 Park Ave, 21217, 1895 .... (301)383-1274
Bolton Hill B&B, 1534 Bolton St, 21217 .... (301)669-5356
Eagles Mere B&B, 102 E Montgomery, 21230 .... (301)332-1618
Harborview, 112 E Montgomery St, 21230 .... (301)528-8692
Mulberry House, 111 West Mulberry St, 21201, 1830 ... (301)576-0111
Society Hill Government House, 1125 N Calvert St, 21202,
    1827 .... (301)752-7722
Society Hill Hotel, 58 W Biddle St, 21201, 1890 .... (301)837-3630
Society Hill Hopkins, 3404 St Paul St, 21218, 1920 ...... (301)235-8600
The Shirley-Madison Inn, 205 W Madison St, 21201,
    1880 .... (301)728-6550
Twin Gates, 308 Morris Ave, 21093, 1857 .... (301)252-3131

Bethesda
Winslow Home, 8217 Caraway St, 20818

Betterton
Ye Lantern Inn, PO Box 310, 21610 .... (301)348-5809

Buckeystown
Inn At Buckeystown, 3521 Buckeystown Pike, 21717, 1890

Cabin John
Winslow Home, 8217 Caraway St, 20818 .... (301)229-4654

Cambridge
Sarke Plantation, Rt 3 Box 139, 21613

Cascade
Inwood Guest House, Box 378, Rt 1, 21719 .... (301)241-3467

Chestertown
Flyway Lodge, Rt 1, Box 660, 21620 .... (301)778-5557
Great Oak Manor, Rt 2 Box 766, 21620 .... (301)778-5796
Hill's Inn, 114 Washington Ave, 21620 .... (301)778-4667
Imperial Hotel, 208 High St, 21620 .... (301)778-5000
Inn At Mitchell House, RD 2 Box 329, Rt 21, 21620,
    1743 .... (301)778-6500
Radcliffe Cross, Quaker Neck Rd, Rt 3 Box 360, 21620 ... (301)778-5540
White Swan Tavern, 231 High St, 21620, 1730 .... (301)778-2300

Denton
Sophie Kerr House, Rt 3 Box 7-B, Kerr & 5th Aves, 21629,
    1861 .... (301)479-3421

Easton
Hynson Tourist Home, 804 Dover Rd, 21601 .... (301)822-2777
Tidewater In, Dover & Harrison St, 21601 .... (301)822-1300

Ellicott City
Hayland Farm, 500 Sheppard Ln, 21043 .... (301)531-5593

Flintstone
Trailside Country Inn, US 40, 21530 .... (301)478-2032

Frederick
Spring Bank Inn, 7945 Worman's Mill Rd, 21701, 1881 (301)694-0440
Tran Crossing, 121 E Patrick St, 21701, 1877 .... (301)663-8449
Turning Point Inn, 3406 Urbana Pike, 21701, 1910 .... (301)874-2421

Freeland
Freeland Farm, 21616 Middletown Rd, 21053 .... (301)357-5364

Georgetown
Kitty Knight House, Rt 213, 21930 .... (301)648-5305

Hagerstown
Lewrene Farm B&B, RD 3 Box 150, 21740 .... (301)582-1735

Harwood
Oakwood, 4566 Solomons Island Rd, 20776, 1840 .... (301)261-5338

Havre De Grace
Vandiver House, 301 S Union Ave, 21078 .... (301)939-5055

Manokin
Hunters Cove, Box 4, 21836 .... (301)651-9664

Mc Henry
Country Inn, PO Box 397, 21541 .... (301)387-6694

Middletown
Fountaindale Inn, 4253 Old National Pike, 21769

Mount Savage
Castle, PO Box 578, Rt 36, 21545 .... (301)759-5946

New Market
National Pike Inn, 9 W Main St, 21774, 1796 .... (301)865-5055
Strawberry Inn, 17 Main St, PO Box 237, 21774, 1860 ... (301)865-3318

North Beach
Westlawn Inn, 7th St, 20714 .... (301)855-8410

Oakland
Red Run Inn, Rt 5, Box 268, 21550, 1940 .... (301)387-6606

Oxford
1876 House, 110 N. Morris St, 21654
The Robert Morris Inn, Box 70, On The Tred Avon,
    21654 .... (301)226-5111

Princess Anne
Elmwood C. 1770 B&B, Locust Point, PO Box 220, 21853,
    1770 .... (301)651-1066
Washington Hotel & Inn, Somerset Ave, 21853, 1744

Rising Sun
Chandlee House, 168 Chandlee Rd, 21911, 1712 .... (301)658-6958

Saint Leonard
Matoaka Cottages, PO Box 124, 20685 .... (301)586-0269

Saint Michaels
Hambleton Inn/Harbor, 202 Cherry St, Box 299, 21663 .. (301)245-3350
Kemp House Inn, 412 S Talbot St, 21663, 1805 .... (301)745-2243
Parsonage Inn, 210 N Talbot St, 21663 .... (301)745-5519
The Inn At Perry Cabin, 21663, 1810
Two Swan Inn, PO Box 727, 21663 .... (301)745-2929

Scotland
St Michael's Manor B&B, St Michael's Manor, 20687, 1805 ... (301)872-4025

Sharpsburg
Inn At Antietam, PO Box 119, 21782, 1908 .... (301)432-6601
Piper House On Antietam Battlefield, Box 100, 21782 ..... (301)797-1862

Snow Hill
Snow Hill Inn, 104 E Market St, 21863, 1790 .... (301)632-2102

Solomons
Capt. & Ms. J's Guest House, Calvert & A St, 20688
Locust Inn, Box 254, 20688, 1860

Solomons Island
Davis House, PO Box 759, 20688 .... (301)326-4811

Stevenson
Mensana Inn, 1718 Greenspring Valley Rd, 21153,
    1900 .... (301)653-2403

Sykesville
Long Way Hill, 7406 Springfield Ave, 21782, 1900 .... (301)795-8129

Taneytown
Glenburn, 3515 Runnymede Rd, 21787

Tilghman
Harrison's Country Inn, PO Box 310, 21671 .... (301)886-2123

Vienna
Governor's Ordinary, Church & Water Box 156, 21869
Nanticoke Manor House, Church St & Water Box 248, 21869, 1700

Maryland (Continued)

Tavern House, 111 Water St, PO Box 98, 21869, 1760 ..... (301)376-3347
Westminster
Judge Thomas House, 195 Willis St, 21157 .... (301)876-6686
Winchester House, 430 S Bishop St, 21157, 1760 .... (301)867-7373
Woodsboro
Rosebud Inn, 4 N. Main St, 21798, 1920

Massachusetts

Amherst
The Amity House, 194 Amity St, 01002 .... (413)549-6446
Ashfield
Ashfield Inn, Main St, 01330, 1919 .... (413)628-4571
Bull Frog B&B, Box 210, Star Rt, 01330 .... (413)628-4493
Gold Leaf Inn, Box 477, 01330 .... (413)628-3392
Attleboro
Colonel Blackinton Inn, 203 N Main St, 02703 .... (617)222-6022
Auburn
Captain Samuel Eddy House Inn, 609 Oxford St, 01501,
    1765 .... (508)832-5282
Barnstable
Ashley Manor, 3660 Olde Kings Highway, PO Box 856, 02630,
    1699 .... (508)362-8044
Cobbs Cove, PO Box 208, Rt 6a, 02630, 1643 .... (508)362-9356
Goss House B&B, 61 Pine Ln, 02630 .... (617)362-8559
Thomas Huckins House, 2701 Main St, Rt 6A, 02630,
    1705 .... (508)362-6379
Barnstable Village
Beechwood, 2839 Main St, 02630, 1853 .... (508)362-6618
Charles Hinckley House, Olde Kings Highway, PO Box 723, 02630,
    1809 .... (508)362-9924
Bass River
Anchorage, 122 S Shore Dr, 02664 .... (617)398-8265
Belvedere B&B Inn, 167 Main St, 02664, 1820 .... (508)398-6674
Captain Isaiah's House, 33 Pleasant St, 02664
Old Cape Inn, 108 Old Main St, 02664, 1815
The Anchorage, 122 South Shore Dr, 02664 .... (508)398-8265
Becket
Canterbury Farm, Fred Snow Rd, 01223, 1780 .... (413)623-8765
Berlin
Stonehedge, 119 Sawyer Hill Rd, 01503, 1735 .... (617)838-2574
Bernardston
Bernardston Inn, Church St, 01337, 1905 .... (413)648-9282
Blandford
Tirnanoag-McKenna Place, Chester Rd, 01008 .... (413)848-2083
Boston
Host Homes of Boston, PO Box 117, Waban Branch, 02168,
    1864 .... (617)244-1308
Laura Felton, PO Box 93, 02117 .... (617)353-1111
The Federal House, 48 Fayette, 02116, 1836 .... (617)350-6657
The Terrace Townhouse, 60 Chandler St, 02116, 1870 .... (617)350-6520
Victorian B&B, 35 Greenwich Park, 02118 .... (617)247-1599
Boylston
Frenches' B&B, 5 Scar Hill Rd, 01505
Brewster
Bramble Inn, Rt 6a 2019 Main St, 02631, 1861 .... (508)896-7644
Captain Freeman Inn, 15 Breakwater Rd, 02631 .... (617)896-7481
Isaiah Clark House, 1187 Old King's Hwy, 02631, 1780 .. (508)896-2223
Old Manse Inn, 1861 Main St, PO 839, 02631, 1800 .... (508)896-3149
Old Sea Pines Inn, 2553 Main St, 02631, 1900 .... (508)896-6114
Brookline
Beacon Inns, 1087 & 1750 Beacon St, 02146 .... (617)566-0088
Beacon Plaza, 1459 Beacon St, 02146 .... (617)232-6550
Beacon Street Guest House, 1047 Beacon St, 02146,
    1900 .... (800)872-7211
Brookline Manor House, 32 Centre St, 02146 .... (617)232-0003
Buckland
1797 House, Charlemont Rd, 01338, 1797 .... (413)625-2975
Scott House, Hawley Rd, 01338 .... (413)625-6624

Cambridge
A Cambridge House, B&B Inn, 2218 Massachusetts Ave, 02140,
    1892 .... (617)491-6300
Cambridge House, PO Box 211, 02140 .... (617)491-6300
Harvard Square B&B Of Cambridge, Box 211, 02140 .... (617)491-6300
Cape Cod-Chatham
Captains House Inn of Chatham, 369 Old Harbor Rd,
    02633 .... (617)945-0127
Cape Cod-Eastham
Over Look Inn, PO Box 771, 02642 .... (508)255-1886
Whalewalk Inn, 169 Bridge Rd, 02642, 1830 .... (617)255-0617
Cape Cod-Harwick Prt
Harbor Walk Guest House, 6 Freeman St, 02646 .... (617)432-1675
Centerville
Carver House, 638 Main St, 02632 .... (617)775-9414
Copper Beech Inn, 497 Main St, 02632, 1820 .... (508)771-5488
Terrace Gardens Inn, 539 Main St, 02632 .... (617)775-4707
The Old Hundred House, 1211 Craigville Beach Rd,
    02632 .... (508)775-6166
Charlemont
Forest Way Farm, Rt 8a (heath), 01339 .... (413)337-8321
Charlton
Gingerbread B&Brunch Hospitality, RR 2 Box 542A,
    01507 .... (617)248-7940
The Mower Homestead, Aux #2, RR Box 86, 01507, 1756
Chatham
Bow Roof House, 59 Queen Anne Rd, 02633 .... (617)945-1346
Chatham Bars Inn, Shore Rd, 02633 .... (617)945-0096
Cyrus Kent House, 63 Cross St, 02633
Queen Anne Inn, 70 Queen Anne Rd, 02633, 1840 .... (617)945-0394
Seafarer Motel, Main St, 02633 .... (617)432-1739
Ship's Inn at Chatham, PO Box 468, 02659, 1839 .... (617)945-5859
Chatham, Cape Cod
Chatham Town House Inn, 11 Library Lane, 02633,
    1881 .... (508)945-2180
Chestnut Hill
The Pleasant Pheasant, 296 Heath St, 02167 .... (617)566-4178
Colrain
Grandmother's House, Rt 1 Box 37 Rte 112n, 01340 .... (413)624-3771
Concord
Anderson-Wheeler Homestead, 154 Fitchburg Turnpike, 01742,
    1890 .... (617)369-3756
Colonel Roger Brown House, 1694 Main St, 01742,
    1775 .... (508)369-9119
Colonial Inn, 48 Monument Sq, 01742, 1716 .... (617)369-9200
Hawthorne Inn, 462 Lexington Rd, 01742, 1870 .... (508)369-5610
Conway
Hilltop B&B, Truce Rd, 01341 .... (413)369-4928
Poundsworth B&B, Old Cricket Hill Rd, 01341
Cotuit
Allen's B&B, 60 Nickerson Ln Box 222, 02635 .... (617)428-5702
Salty Dog B&B, 451 Main St, 02635 .... (617)428-5228
Cummington
Cumworth Farm, Rt 112, RR 1 Box 110, 01026 .... (413)634-5529
Hill Gallery, Cole St, 01026 .... (413)238-5914
Windfields Farm, Rt 1 Box 170 Bush Rd, 01026, 1850 ...... (413)684-3786
Cuttyhunk
Allen House Inn & Restaurant, PO Box 27, 02713 .... (617)996-9292
Dalton
Dalton House, 955 Main St, 01226 .... (413)684-3854
Danvers
Salem Village B&B, 34 Centre St, 01923 .... (617)774-7851
Deerfield
Deerfield Inn, The Street, 01342, 1885 .... (413)774-5587
Dennis
Four Chimneys Inn, 946 Main St, Rt 6A, 02638, 1881 .... (508)385-6317
Isaiah Hall B&B Inn, 152 Whig St, 02638, 1857 .... (508)385-9928
Dennisport
By-the-Sea Guests, 57 Chase Ave, Box 507, 02639 .... (617)398-8685
Dorchester
The Emma James House, 47 Ocean St, 02124, 1894 .... (617)288-8867
Thomas Jones, 373 Adams St, 02122 .... (617)825-7676

Duxbury
Black Friar Brook Farm, 636 Union Street, 02332, 1708. (617)834-8528
Winsor House Inn, PO Box 387 Shs 390 Washington St, 02331

East Brewster
Ocean Gold Cape Cod B&B, 74 Locust Lane Rt 2, 02631 (617)255-7045

East Orleans
Nauset House Inn, 143 Beach Rd PO 774, 02643, 1810 .... (508)255-2195
Parsonage, 202 Main St, PO Box 1016, 02643, 1770 .... (508)255-8217
Ships Knees Inn, Beach Rd, 02643, 1817 .... (508)255-1312
The Farmhouse At Nauset Beach, 163 Beach Rd, 02653,
   1900 .... (508)255-6654
The Nauset House Inn, Box 774, 02643, 1830

East Sandwich
Wingscorton Farm Inn, 11 Wing Blvd, 02537, 1757 .... (617)888-0534

Eastham
The Penny House, Rt 6, Box 238, 02651, 1751 .... (508)255-6632
Whalewalk Inn, 169 Bridge Rd, 02642, 1830

Edgartown
Ashley Inn, 129 Main St, 02539, 1860 .... (508)627-9655
Chadwick Inn, 67 Winter St, 02539, 1840 .... (508)627-4435
Charlotte Inn, S Summer St, 02539, 1860 .... (508)627-4751
Colonial Inn, Box 668, 02539 .... (617)627-4711
Daggat House, PO 1333 59 N. Water St, 02539
Daggett House, PO Box 1333, 02539 .... (617)627-4600
Dr. Shiverick House, Pent Lane, PO Box 640, 02539,
   1840 .... (508)627-8497
Edgartown Heritage Hotel, 227 Upper Main St, 02539,
   1798 .... (508)627-5161
Edgartown Inn, 56 N Water, 02539, 1798 .... (508)627-4794
Governor Bradford Inn, 128 Main St, 02539 .... (508)627-9510
Harborside Inn, Box 67, 02539 .... (617)627-4321
Katama Guest House, RFD 108, 166 Katama Rd, 02539 .. (617)627-5158
Kelly House, PO Box 1637, 02539, 1742 .... (508)627-4394
Point Way Inn, 104 Main St, Box 128, 02539, 1840 .... (508)627-8633
Shiretown Inn, N Water St, Box 921, 02539 .... (800)541-0090
The Arbor, 222 Upper Main St, 02539, 1890 .... (508)627-8137
Victorian Inn, S Water St, PO Box 947, 02539, 1890 .... (508)627-4784

Fairhaven
Edgewater B&B, 2 Oxford St, 02719, 1760 .... (508)997-5512

Falmouth
Amherst, 30 Amherst Ave, 02540 .... (617)548-2781
Captain Tom Lawrence House, 75 Locust St, 02540,
   1861 .... (508)540-1445
Elm Arch Inn, Elm Arch Way, 02540 .... (617)548-0133
Gladstone Inn, 219 Grand Ave S, 02540 .... (617)548-9851
Grafton Inn, 261 Grand Ave S, 02540
Hastings By the Sea, 28 Worcester Ave, 02540 .... (617)548-1628
Mostly Hall, 27 Main St, 02540, 1849 .... (508)548-3786
Palmer House Inn, 81 Palmer Ave, 02540, 1901 .... (508)548-1230
The Inn At One Main Street, One Main St, 02540,
   1892 .... (508)540-7469
The Moorings Lodge, 207 Grand Ave, 02540 .... (508)540-2370
Village Green Inn, 40 W Main St, 02540, 1804 .... (508)548-5621
Wyndemere House at Sippewissett, 718 Palmer Ave, 02193,
   1797 .... (508)540-7069

Fiskdale
Commonwealth Inn, PO Box 251, 01518 .... (617)347-7603

Gloucester
Blue Shutters Inn, 1 Nautilus Rd, 01930, 1900 .... (617)281-2706
Gray Manor, 14 Atlantic Rd, 01930, 1925 .... (617)283-5409
Williams Guest House, 136 Bass Ave, 01930

Goshen
The Whale Inn, Rt 9, Main St, 01032, 1799 .... (413)268-7246

Great Barrington
Bread And Roses, Star Rt 65 Box 50, 01230, 1810 .... (413)528-1099
Littlejohn Manor, Newsboy Monument Rt 23, 01230 .... (413)528-2882
Red Bird Inn, Box 592, 01230 .... (413)229-2433
Round Hill Farm, 17 Round Hill Rd, 01230 .... (413)528-3366
Seekonk Pines Inn, 142 Seekonk Cross Rd, 01230,
   1832 .... (413)528-4192
Thornewood, Rt. 7 & Rt. 183, 01230
Turning Point Inn, RD 2 Box 140 3 Lake Buel Rd, 01230
Windflower Inn, Egremont Star Rt, PO 25 Rt 23, 01230,
   1860 .... (413)528-2720

Harwich Center
Victorian Inn At Harwich, Box 340 102 Parallel St,
   02645 .... (508)432-8335

Harwich Port
Captain's Quarters, 85 Bank St, 02646, 1850 .... (508)432-0337
Country Inn, 86 Sisson Rd, 02646 .... (508)432-2769
Dunscroft By the Sea, 24 Pilgrim Rd, 02646, 1922 .... (508)432-0810
Harbor Breeze, 326 Lower County Rd, 02646 .... (508)432-0337
Harbor Walk, 6 Freeman St, 02646 .... (617)432-1675
The Inn On Bank Street, 88 Bank St, 02646 .... (508)432-3206

Heath (Charlemont)
Forestway Farm, Rt 8A, 01339 .... (413)337-8321

Holland
Alpine Haus, Mashapaung Rd, Box 782, 01550 .... (413)245-9082

Holyoke
Yankee Pedler Inn, 1866 Northampton St, 01040, 1875 . (413)532-9494

Hopkinton
The Laurels, 18 Ash St, 01748 .... (617)435-5410

Huntington
Paulson B&B, Allen Coit Rd, 01050 .... (413)667-3208

Hyannis
Acorn House, 240 Sea St, 02601 .... (617)771-4071
Captain Sylvester Baxter House, Park Square Village, 156 Main St,
   02601, 1855 .... (508)775-5611
Elegance By-The-Sea, 162 Sea St, 02601 .... (617)775-3595
Inn on Sea Street, 358 Sea St, 02601 .... (617)775-8030
Park Square Village, 156 Main St, 02601 .... (617)775-5611
Sea Breeze By The Beach, 397 Sea St Cape Cod, 02601
The Acorn House, 240 Sea St, 02601 .... (508)771-4071

Lakeville
Pistachio Cove, 229 County Rd, 02347 .... (617)763-2383

Lanesboro
AMC-Bascom Lodge, PO Box 686, 01237 .... (413)743-1591

Lee
1777 Greylock House, 58 Greylock St, 01238
Haus Andreas, RR 1 Box 605 B, 01238, 1928
Morgan House, 33 Main St, 01238 .... (413)243-0181
Ramsey House, 203 W Park St, 01238 .... (413)243-1598
The Donahoes, Fairview St Box 231, 01238 .... (413)243-1496

Lenox
Amity House, 15 Cliffwood St, 01240 .... (413)637-0005
Apple Tree Inn, 224 West St, 01240, 1885 .... (413)637-1477
Birchwood Inn, 7 Hubbard St, Box 2020, 01240, 1764 .... (413)637-2600
Blantyre, 01240, 1903 .... (413)637-3556
Brook Farm Inn, 15 Hawthorne St, 01240, 1890 .... (413)637-3013
Candlelight Inn, 53 Walker St, 01240, 1885 .... (413)637-1555
Cliffwood Inn, 25 Cliffwood St, 01240, 1904 .... (413)637-3330
Cornell House, 197 Pittsfield Rd, 01240, 1890
East Country Berry Farm, 830 East St, 01240, 1798 ...... (413)442-2057
Garden Gables Inn, 141 Main St, 01240, 1770 .... (413)637-0193
Gateways Inn, 71 Walker St, 01240 .... (413)637-2532
Rookwood Inn, 19 Stockbridge Rd, 02140, 1830 .... (413)637-9750
Strawberry Hill, PO Box 718, 01240, 1800 .... (413)637-3381
The Gables Inn, 103 Walker St, Rt 183, 01240, 1885 ..... (413)637-3416
The Quincy Lodge, 19 Stockbridge Rd, 01240 .... (413)637-9750
Underledge Inn, 76 Cliffwood St, 01240, 1876 .... (413)637-0236
Village Inn, 16 Church St, 01240, 1771 .... (413)637-0020
Walker House, 74 Walker St, 01240, 1804 .... (413)637-1271
Wheatleigh, PO Box 824, 01240 .... (413)637-0610
Whistler's Inn, 5 Greenwood St, 01240, 1820 .... (413)637-0975

Lexington
Ashley's B&B, 6 Moon Hill Rd, 02173 .... (617)862-6488
Halewood House, 2 Larchmont Ln, 02173 .... (617)862-5404

Littleton
Hideaways International, PO Box 1270, 01460 .... (800)843-4433

Lowell
Sherman-Berry House, 163 Dartmouth St, 01851, 1893 . (617)459-4760

Manchester
Old Corner Inn, 2 Harbor St, 01944, 1865 .... (617)526-4996

Marblehead
10 Mugford Street B&B, 10 Mugford St, 01945 .... (617)631-5642
Harborside House, 23 Gregory St, 01945 .... (617)631-1032
Lindsey's Garrett, 38 High St, 01945 .... (617)631-2653
Spray Cliff on the Ocean, 25 Spray Ave, 01945, 1910 .... (617)631-6789

Massachusetts (Continued)

Tidecrest, Spray Ave, 01945, 1830 ....(617)631-4515

Martha's Vineyard
Arbor, PO Box 1628, 02539 ....(617)627-8137
Ashley Inn, PO Box 650, 129 Main St, 02539, 1800 ...(617)627-9655
Captain Dexter House, Box 2457, 02568, 1843 ....(617)693-6564
Farmhouse, State Rd, 02568 ....(617)693-5354
Thorncroft Inn, 278 Main St, 02568 ....(617)693-3333

Menemsha
Beach Plum Inn, Box 98, 02552 ....(617)645-9454

Middleboro
Myra & Dick Wilmot, 115 North St, 02346, 1740 ....(617)947-2356

Middlefield
Strawberry Banke Farm, Skyline Tr, 01243 ....(413)623-6481

Monument Beach
Bay Breeze, PO 307, 02553

Nantucket
1739 House, 43 Centre St, 02554 ....(508)228-0120
76 Main Street, 76 Main St Box E, 02554, 1883 ....(508)228-2533
Anchor Inn, 66 Centre St, 02554 ....(508)228-0072
B&B, One Cottage Ct, 02554, 1830 ....(508)228-2486
Brant Point Inn, 6 North St, 02554 ....(508)228-5442
Brass Lantern Inn, 11 N Water St, 02554 ....(617)228-4064
Carlisle House, 26 N Water St, 02554
Carriage House, 4 Ray's Ct, 02554, 1865 ....(508)228-0326
Centerboard, 8 Chester St, 02584 ....(617)228-9696
Century House, 10 Cliff Rd Box 603, 02554, 1833 ...(508)228-0530
Cliff House, 34 Cliff Rd, 02554 ....(508)228-2154
Cliff Lodge B&B, 9 Cliff Rd, 02554 ....(617)228-9480
Cliffside Beach Club, PO Box 449, 02554 ....(617)228-0618
Corner House, Box 1828, 49 Center St, 02554 ....(617)228-1530
Dolphin Guest House, 10 N Beach St, 02554, 1850 ...(508)228-4028
Easton House, 17 N Water St, 02554, 1812 ....(508)228-2759
Eighteen Gardner Street, 18 Gardner St, 02554, 1835
Fair Gardens, 27 Fair St, 02554 ....(617)228-4258
Fair Winds, 4 Ash St, 02554, 1885 ....(508)228-4899
Four Ash Street, 4 Ash St, 02554, 1795
Four Chimneys, 38 Orange St, 02554, 1835 ....(617)228-1912
Four Seasons Guest House, 2 Chestnut St, 02554, 1850 .. (508)228-0326
Halliday's Nantucket House, 2 East York St Box 165, 02554,
   1820 ....(508)228-9450
Hawthorne House, 2 Chestnut St, 02554, 1849 ....(508)228-1468
House of Seven Gables, 32 Cliff Rd, 02554 ....(617)228-4706
Hussey House, 15 N Water St, 02554, 1795 ....(508)228-0747
India House, 37 India St, 02554, 1803 ....(508)228-9043
Ivy Lodge, 2 Chester St, 02554, 1790 ....(508)228-0305
Jared Coffin House, 29 Broad St, 02554, 1845 ....(508)228-2400
Le Languedoc Inn, 24 Broad St, 02554 ....(508)228-2552
Martin's Guest House, 61 Centre St PO 743, 02554, 1803 (508)228-0678
Nantucket Landfall, 4 Harbor View Way, 02554 ....(508)228-0500
Parker Guest House, 4 East Chestnut St, 02554 ....(508)228-4625
Paul West House, 5 Liberty St, 02554, 1748 ....(508)228-2495
Periwinkle Guest House, 9 N Water St, 02554, 1846
Phillips House, 54 Fair St, 02554, 1786 ....(508)228-9217
Quaker House, 5 Chestnut St, 02554 ....(508)228-0400
Roberts House, 11 India St, 02554, 1846 ....(508)228-9009
Ruben Joy Homestead, 107 Main St, 02554, 1720 ....(508)228-1703
Seven Sea Street, 7 Sea St, 02554 ....(617)228-3577
Ships Inn, 13 Fair St, 02554, 1812 ....(508)228-0040
Stumble Inne, 109 Orange St, 02554, 1704 ....(508)228-4482
Ten Hussey, 10 Hussey St, 02554, 1786 ....(508)228-9552
Ten Lyon Street Inn, 10 Lyon St, 02554, 1850 ....(508)228-0072
The Beachside, North Beach St, 02554 ....(508)228-2241
The Chestnut House, 3 Chestnut St, 02554 ....(508)228-0049
The Harbor House, South Beach St, 02554 ....(508)228-1500
The House At Ten Gay Street, 10 Gay St, 02554, 1830 .....(508)228-4425
The Hungry Whale, 8 Derrymore Rd, 02554, 1900 ....(508)228-0793
The Island Reef, 20 North Water St, 02554 ....(508)228-2156
The Wauwinet, An Inn by the Sea, PO Box 2580, 02584,
   1853 ....(800)426-8718
The Woodbox, 29 Fair St, 02554, 1709 ....(508)228-0587
Tuckernuck Inn, 60 Union St, 02554 ....(508)228-4886
Wake Up On Pleasant Street, 31 Pleasant St, 02554 ....(617)228-0673
West Moor Inn, Off Cliff Rd, 02554, 1917 ....(508)228-0877
Woodbox, 29 Fair St, 02554, 1709 ....(617)228-0587

Nantucket Island
Beachside, N Beach St, 02554 ....(617)228-2241
Brant Plantation Inn, 6 N Beach St, 02554 ....(617)228-5442
Carriage House, 4 Ray's Ct, 02554 ....(617)228-0326
Chestnut House, 3 Chestnut St, 02554 ....(617)228-0049
Corner House, 49 Centre St, PO Box 1828, 02554, 1723 .(508)228-1530
Easton House, 17 N Water St, 02554 ....(617)228-2759
Four Chimneys, 38 Orange St, 02554, 1839 ....(508)228-1912
LaPetite Mansion, 132 Main St, 02554 ....(617)228-9242
Martin's Guest House, 61 Centre St, 02554 ....(617)228-0678
Nesbitt Inn, 21 Broad St, 02554 ....(617)228-0156
Roberts House, India & Centre St, 02554 ....(617)228-9009
Seven Sea Street, 7 Sea St, 02554 ....(617)228-3577
Stumble Inne, 109 Orange St, 02554 ....(617)228-4482
Wharf Cottages, New Whale St, 02554 ....(617)228-4620

Nantucket-Siasconset
The Summer House, Box 313, 02564 ....(617)257-9976

New Marlborough
Old Inn On The Green, Star Rt 70, 01230
Red Bird Inn, Rt 57 & Grosby Rd, 01230, 1791 ....(413)229-2433

Newburyport
Benjamin Choate House, 25 Tyng St, 01950, 1794
Essex Street Inn, 7 Essex St, 01950 ....(617)465-3145
Garrison Inn, On Brown Square, 01950, 1809 ....(617)465-0910
Morrill Place Inn, 209 High St, 01950
Windsor House, 38 Federal St, 01950

North Billrtivs
Ted Barbour, 88 Rogers St, 01862 ....(617)667-7317

North Eastham
The Penny House, Rt 6 Box 238, 02651, 1751 ....(508)255-6632

North Falmouth
Wingate Crossing, R 28a/190 N Falmouth Hwy, 02556,
   1800 ....(508)540-8723

North Scituate
Rasberry Ink, 748 Country Way, 02060, 1900 ....(617)545-6629

Northfield
Centennial House, 94 Main St, 01360, 1811 ....(413)498-5921
Northfield Country House, School St RR 1 Box 79a, 01360, 1901

Northhampton
The Knoll, 230 N Main, 01060 ....(413)584-8164

Oak Bluffs
Attleboro House, 11 Lake Ave Box 1564, 02557 ....(508)693-4346
Nashua House, 30 Kennebec Ave, 02557, 1873 ....(508)693-0043

Orleans
Farmhouse, 163 Beach Rd, 02653 ....(617)255-6654

Osterville
East Bay Lodge, East Bay Rd PO Box N, 02655, 1800 ......(508)428-6961
Osterville Fairways Country Inn, 105 Parker Rd, 02655 ..(617)428-2747

Petersham
Winterwood at Petersham, North Main St, 01366, 1842 (508)724-8885

Pittsfield
Greer B&B, 193 Wendell Ave, 01201 ....(413)443-3669
The Captains House 1840, 8 Nichils St, 04967-1612 ....(207)354-6738

Plymouth
Another Place Inn, 240 Sandwich St, 02360 ....(617)746-0126
Colonial House Inn, 207 Sandwich St, 02360, 1855
Morton Park Place, 1 Morton Park Rd, 02360 ....(617)747-1730

Princeton
Country Inn At Princeton, 30 Mountain Rd, 01540, 1890
Harrington Farm, 178 Westminster Rd, 01541, 1763 ....(617)464-5600
Hill House, PO Box 276, 105 Merriam Rd, 01541 ....(617)464-2061

Provincetown
1807 House, 54 Commercial St, 02657
Asheton House, 3 Cook St, 02657, 1806 ....(508)487-9966
Bradford Gardens Inn, 178 Bradford St, 02657, 1820
Cape Codder Guest House, 570 Commercial St, 02657 ...(508)487-0131
Captain Lysander Inn, 96 Commercial St, 02657, 1850 ....(508)487-2253
Elephant Walk Inn, 156 Bradford St, 02657, 1917 ....(508)487-2543
Fairbanks Inn, 90 Bradford St, 02657, 1776 ....(508)487-0386
Fiddle Leaf, 186 Commercial St, 02657 ....(508)487-1443
Hargood House, 493 Commercial St, 02657, 1820 .....(508)487-1324
Land's End Inn, 22 Commercial St, 02657, 1908 ....(508)487-0706
Ocean's Inn, 386 Commercial St, 02657 ....(508)487-0358
Rose And Crown, 158 Commercial St, 02657, 1780

Somerset House, 378 Commercial St, 02657, 1850 .... (508)487-0383
Victoria House, 5 Standish St, 02657 .... (508)487-1319
White Wind Inn, 174 Commercial St, 02657, 1840 .... (508)487-1526
Windamar House, 568 Commercial St, 02657, 1840 .... (508)487-0599
Rehoboth
Gilbert's B&B, 30 Spring St, 02769 .... (508)252-6416
Perryville Inn, 157 Perryville Rd, 02769, 1824 .... (508)252-9239
Richmond
Cogswell Guest House, Rt 41, 01254 .... (413)698-2750
Pierson Place, Rt 41, 01254 .... (617)698-2750
Westgate, Rt 295, 01254 .... (413)698-2657
Rockport
Addison Choate Inn, 49 Broadway, 01966, 1851
Cable House, Norwood Ave, 01966, 1882 .... (508)546-6383
Eden Pines Inn, Eden Rd, 01966 .... (508)546-2505
Inn on Cove Hill, 37 Mt Pleasant St, 01966, 1791 .... (508)546-2701
Old Farm Inn, 291 Granite St, 01966, 1799 .... (508)546-3237
Ralph Waldo Emerson Inn, Phillips Ave, 01966, 1846 ...... (508)546-6321
Rocky Shores Inn, Eden Rd, 01966, 1905 .... (508)546-2823
Sally Webster Inn, 34 Mt Pleasant St, 01966, 1832 .... (508)546-9251
Seacrest Manor, 131 Marmion Way, 01966 .... (508)546-2211
Seaward Inn, 62 Marmion Way, 01966, 1912 .... (508)546-3471
Tuck Inn, 17 High St, 01966, 1785 .... (508)546-6252
Yankee Clipper Inn, Box 2399, 99 Granite St, 01966, 1840
Rutland
The General Rufus Putnam House, 344 Main St, 01543,
1750 .... (508)886-4256
Salem
Amelia Payson Guest House, 16 Winter St, 01970,
1845 .... (508)744-8304
Coach House Inn, 284 Lafayette St, 01970, 1879 .... (508)744-4092
Salem Inn, 7 Summer St, 01970, 1834 .... (508)741-0680
Stephen Daniels House, 1 Daniels St, 01970, 1667 .... (508)744-5709
Suzannah Flint House, 98 Essex St, 01970 .... (508)744-5281
Sandisfield
New Boston Inn, Jct Rt 8 & 57, 01255-0120, 1737 .... (413)258-4477
Sandwich
Captain Ezra Nye House, 152 Main St, 02563, 1829 .... (508)888-6142
Quince Tree, 164 Main St, 02563
The Daniel Webster Inn, 149 Main St, 02563, 1800 .... (508)888-3622
The Summer House, 158 Main St, 02563, 1835 .... (508)888-4991
Seedbury
Checkerberry Corner, 5 Checkerberry Cir, 01776 .... (617)443-8660
Seekonk
Simeon's Mansion House, 940 County St, 02771, 1798 .... (508)336-6674
Sheffield
Centuryhurst B&B, Box 486 Main St, 01257, 1800 .... (413)229-8131
Colonel Ashley Inn, Bow Wow Road, RR 1, PO Box 142, 01257,
1814 .... (413)229-2929
Ivanhoe Country House, Rt 41 Undermountain Rd,
01257 .... (413)229-2143
Stagecoach Hill Inn, Rt 41, 01257 .... (413)229-8585
Staveleigh House, PO 608, South Main St, 01257, 1821 (413)229-2129
Shelburne Falls
Parson Hubbard House, Old Village Rd, 01370 .... (413)625-9730
South Egremont
Egremont Inn, Old Sheffield Rd, 01258, 1780 .... (413)528-2111
Weathervane Inn, PO Box 388, 01258, 1785 .... (413)528-9580
South Lee
Federal House Inn, Rt 102 Main St, 01260 .... (413)243-1824
Historic Merrell Tavern Inn, Rt 102 Main St, 01260,
1794 .... (413)243-1794
South Sudbury
Longfellow's Wayside Inn, Wayside Inn Rd, 01776,
1702 .... (617)443-8846
South Yarmouth
River Street Guest House, 9 River St, 02664 .... (508)398-8946
Sterline
Sterling Inn, Rt 12 Box 609, 01564
Stockbridge
Inn At Stockbridge, Rt 7 Box 2033, 01262 .... (413)298-3337
The Red Lion Inn, 01262 .... (413)298-5545
Sturbridge
Chamberlain House, PO Box 187, 01566 .... (617)347-3313

Colonel Ebenezer Craft's, PO 187, 01566, 1786
Commonwealth Inn, 11 Summit Ave, 01566, 1890 .... (617)347-7603
Publick House Historic Inn, On The Common, 01566,
1771 .... (617)347-3313
Sudbury
Checkerberry Corner, 5 Checkerberry Circle, 01776 .... (617)443-8660
Sudbury B&B, 3 Drum Ln, 01776 .... (617)443-2860
Townsend
B&B At Wood Farm, 40 Worchester Rd, 01469, 1716 .... (617)597-5019
Wood Farm, 40 Worcester Rd, 01469
Uxbridge
Capron House, 2 Capron St, 01569 .... (617)278-2214
Vineyard Haven
Bayberry, RFD 1 Box 546 Old Courthouse Rd, 02568, 1968
Captain Dexter House, 100 Main St, PO Box 2457, 02568,
1843 .... (508)693-6564
Geyer's Heritage House, 16 Greenwood Ave Box 2475,
02568 .... (508)693-5977
Lothrop Merry House, Owen Park Box 1939, 02568,
1790 .... (508)693-1646
Thorncroft Inn, 278 Main St, PO Box 1022, 02568, 1918 ... (508)693-3333
Tuckerman House, 45 William St Box 194, 02568 .... (508)693-0417
Ware
The Wildwood Inn, 121 Church St, 01082, 1880 .... (413)967-7798
Wildwood Inn, 121 Church St, 01082
Wareham
Little Harbor Guest House, 20 Stockton Shortcut, 02571,
1703 .... (508)295-6329
Wellfleet
Holden Inn, Commercial St, PO Box 816, 02667, 1840 ..... (508)349-3450
Inn At Duck Creeke, PO Box 364, 02667
West Barnstable
Honeysuckle Hill, 591 Main St, 02668, 1825 .... (508)362-8418
West Boylston
The Old Rose Cottage, 24 Worcester St, 01583 .... (617)835-4034
West Dennis
Beach Side Lodge, The Edwards, 140 Lower County Rd, 02670
West Dennis, Cape Co
The Beach House, 61 Uncle Stephen's Rd, 02670
West Falmouth
Elms, PO 895, 02574
Sjoholm B&B Inn, 17 Chase Rd Box 430, 02574 .... (508)540-5706
West Harwich
Barnaby Inn, PO Box 151, 02671 .... (508)432-6789
Cape Cod Sunny Pines B&B Inn, 77 Main St, 02671,
1900 .... (508)432-9628
Lion's Head Inn, 186 Belmont Rd PO 444, 02671, 1804 . (508)432-7766
West Newton
Withington House, 274 Otis St, 02165, 1830 .... (617)332-8422
West Stockbridge
Westbridge Inn, Main St PO Box 378, 01266 .... (413)232-7120
West Tisbury
Old Parsonage B&B, Box 137 State Rd, 02575 .... (508)693-4289
West Yarmouth
Manor House, 57 Maine Ave, 02673, 1920
Westborough
Heywood House, 207 W Main St, 01581 .... (617)366-2161
Westhampton
Outlook Farm, Rt 66, 01027 .... (413)527-0633
Outlook Farm, David & Mary Lee Morse, Rt 66, 01060,
1781 .... (413)527-0633
Whitinsville
The Victorian, 583 Linwood Ave, 01588 .... (617)234-2500
Williamsburg
Twin Maples B&B, 106 South St, 01096, 1788 .... (413)268-7925
Woods Hole
Grey Whale Inn, 565 Woods Hole Rd, 02543, 1804 .... (508)548-7692
Marlborough, 320 Woods Hole, 02543
Worcester
The General Rufus Putnam House, Rutland, MA

Michigan

Adrian
Briaroaks Inn, 2980 N Adrian Hwy, 49221, 1934 ....(517)263-1659
Rosewood Country Inn, 3325 S Adrian Hwy (M-52),
49221 ....(517)263-5085
Albion
D's B&B, 110 Park, 49224 ....(517)629-2976
Smith-White House, 401 E Porter St, 49224, 1867 ....(517)629-2220
Alden
Torch Lake B&B, Box 165, 49612 ....(616)331-6424
Allegan
Winchester Inn, 524 Marshall St, 49010, 1863 ....(616)673-3621
Alma
Granny's Garrett Guest Rooms, 910 Vassar St, 48801 ......(517)463-3961
Ann Arbor
The Urban Retreat, 2759 Canterbury Rd, 48104, 1950 ......(313)971-8110
Wood's Inn, 2887 Newport Rd, 48103, 1859 ....(313)665-8394
Au Gres
Point Au Gres Hotel, 3279 S Point Ln, 48703, 1939 ....(517)876-7217
Battle Creek
The Old Lamp-Lighter's Homestay, 276 Capital Ave NE,
49017 ....(616)963-2603
Bay City
Stonehedge Inn, 924 Center Ave, 48708 ....(517)894-4342
William Clements Inn, 1712 Center Ave, 48708, 1886 ....(517)894-4600
Bay View
Terrace Inn, 216 Fairview Ave, 49770, 1910 ....(616)347-2410
The Gingerbread House, 205 Bluff, PO Box 1273, 49770 . (616)348-2829
Belding
The Rose Garden B&B, 322 E Washington St, 48809,
1900 ....(616)794-3844
Beulah
Brookside Inn, 115 N Michigan, 49617 ....(616)882-7271
Windermere Inn, 747 Crystal Dr, 49617 ....(616)882-7264
Big Bay
Big Bay Lighthouse B&B, 3 Lighthouse Rd, 49808,
1896 ....(906)345-9957
Big Rapids
Taggart House, 371 Maple St, 49307, 1902 ....(616)796-1713
Black River
Silver Creek, 4361 S US-23, 48721 ....(517)471-2198
Blaney Park
Celibeth House, Rt 1 Box 58A, M-77 Blaney Park Rd, 49836, 1890
Blissfield
H. D. Ellis Inn, 415 W Adrian St, 49228, 1883 ....(517)486-3155
Boyne Falls
The Arman House, PO Box 195, 49713 ....(616)549-2764
Brooklyn
Chicago Street Inn, 219 Chicago St, PO Box 546, 49230, 1886 (517)592-
3888
Buckley
A Wicklow House, 9270 M-37, 49620 ....(616)269-4212
Calumet
The Calumet House, 1159 Calumet Ave, 49913, 1895
Caro
Garden Gate B&B, 315 Pearl St, 48723, 1985 ....(517)673-2696
Caseville
Carkner House, 6766 Pine St, PO Box 843, 48725, 1880 ... (517)856-3456
Country Charm Farm, 5048 Conkey Rd, 48725 ....(517)856-3110
Cedar
Hillside B&B, Rt 1-A W Lakeshore Rd, 49621, 1898 ....(616)228-6106
Center Line
The Meares House, 8250 Warren Blvd, 48015, 1964 ....(313)756-8250
Central Lake
Bridgewalk B&B, 2287 S Main, PO Box 577, 49622, 1900 (616)544-8122
Lamplight Inn, 2535 Main St, PO Box 778, 49622, 1924 ... (616)544-6443
Charlevoix
Aaron's Windy Hill Guest Lodge, 202 Michigan, 49720 .. (616)547-2804
Bay B&B, Rt 1, Box 136-A, 49720 ....(616)599-2570
Belvedere House, 306 Belvedere Ave, 49720, 1888 ....(616)547-4501

Boar's Head Inn, 306 Belvedere Ave, 49720, 1887 ....(616)547-2251
Bridge Street Inn, 113 Michigan Ave, 49720 ....(616)547-6606
Channelview Inn, 217 Park Ave, 49720 ....(616)547-6180
Charlevoix Country Inn, 106 W Dixon Ave, 49720, 1896. (616)547-5134
Patchwork Parlour B&B, 109 Petoskey Ave, 49720 ....(616)547-5788
Chassell
Palosaari's Rolling Acres B&B, Rt 1, Box 354, 49916,
1940 ....(906)523-4947
Clare
Doherty Hotel, 604 McEwan, 48617, 1924 ....(800)525-4115
Clio
Chandelier Guest House, 1567 Morgan Rd, 48420 ....(313)687-6061
Columbiaville
Redwing, 3176 Shady Oak Dr, 48421 ....(313)793-4301
Conklin
Miller School Inn, 2959 Roosevelt Rd, 49403 ....(616)677-1026
Davison
Oakbrook Inn, 7256 E Court St, 48423 ....(313)653-1744
De Tour Village
Hubbard's Boonevue Lodge, 206 S Huron Box 65, 49725,
1912 ....(906)297-2391
Dearborn
The Dearborn Inn, 20301 Oakwood Blvd, 48124, 1931 .....(313)271-2700
Detroit
B&B in Michigan, 1905 ....(313)561-6041
The Blanche House Inn, 506 Parkview Dr, 48214, 1805 ... (313)822-7090
Dimondale
Bannicks B&B, 4608 Michigan Rd (M-99), 48821 ....(517)646-0224
Douglas
Rosemont Inn, 83 Lake Shore Dr, 49406, 1886 ....(616)857-2637
Eagle Harbor
The Lake Breeze, Lake Breeze Rd, 49950, 1850 ....(906)289-4514
East Jordan
Easterly Inn, 209 Easterly, PO Box 0366, 49727, 1906 ....(616)536-3434
Jordan Inn, 228 Main St, PO Box 687, 49727, 1881 ....(616)536-2631
East Lansing
Coleman Corners B&B, 7733 M-78, 48823 ....(517)339-9360
Eastmanville
The Eastman House, 6754 W Leonard, 49404, 1841 ....(616)837-6474
Eastport
Sunrise B&B, PO Box 52, 49627 ....(616)599-2706
Edwardsburg
Glenda's B&B, 68699 M-62, 49112 ....(616)663-7905
Ellsworth
The House On The Hill, Lake St Box 206, 49729 ....(616)588-6304
Empire
Clipper House Inn, 10085 Front St, PO Box 35, 49630 ..... (616)326-5518
Escanaba
The House of Ludington, 223 Ludington St, 49829 ....(906)786-4000
Evart
Lynch's Dream, 22177 80th Ave, 49631 ....(616)734-5989
Farmington Hills
The Botsford Inn, 28000 Grand River, 48024, 1836 ....(313)474-4800
Fennville
Crane House & Cider Mill, 6051 124th Ave, 49408, 1880 (616)561-6931
Heritage Manor, 2253 Blue Star Hwy, 49408 ....(616)543-4384
Hiatus House, 2125 Lakeshore Dr, 49408, 1800 ....(616)543-4530
Hidden Pond Farm, 5975 128th Ave, 49408, 1973 ....(616)561-2491
J. Paules' Fenn Inn, 2254 S 58th St, 49408, 1900 ....(616)561-2836
The Porches, 2297 70th St, 49408, 1897 ....(616)543-4162
Fenton
Pine Ridge, N-10345 Old US-23, 48430 ....(313)629-8911
Flint
Avon House, 518 Avon St, 48503
Frankenmuth
B&B at the Pines, 327 Ardussi St, 48734 ....(517)652-9019
Bender's Haus, 337 Trinklein St, 48734 ....(517)652-8897
Johnson Haus B&B, 242 S Franklin, 48734, 1920 ....(517)652-8870
Kueffner's Haus, 176 Parker, 48734 ....(517)652-8897
Lewis Haus, 337 Trinklein St, 48734 ....(517)652-3133
Parlberg's Place, 8180 Roedel, 48734 ....(517)652-8134

Frankfort
Hotel Frankfort, Main St, 49635, 1933 .... (616)882-7271
Galesburg
Old Memories Farm, PO Box 98, 49053 .... (616)665-9516
Gaylord
Heritage House, 521 E Main St, 49735 .... (517)732-1199
Norden Hem, PO Box 623, 49735 .... (517)732-6794
Gladwin
Sullivan's B&B, PO Box 585, 48624 .... (517)426-6426
The Riverside B&B, 66 Lockwood Dr, 48624 .... (517)426-1206
Glen Arbor
The Sylvan Inn, PO Box 309, 49636, 1885 .... (616)334-4333
White Gull Inn, PO Box 351, 49636 .... (616)334-4486
Grand Blanc
The Country Inn of Grand Blanc, 6136 S Belsay Rd,
　　48439 .... (313)694-6749
Grand Haven
Highland Park Hotel B&B, 1414 Lake St, 49417, 1889 ..... (616)842-6483
Shifting Sands, 19343 N Shore Dr, 49456 .... (616)842-3594
Washington Street Inn, 608 Washington St, 49417, 1902.. (616)842-1075
Grand Marais
Lakeview Inn of Grand Marais, PO Box 297, 49839,
　　1887 .... (906)494-2612
Grand Rapids
B&B of Grand Rapids, 455 College Ave SE, 49503 .... (616)451-4849
Downtown B&B, 311 Lyon St NE, 49503, 1901 .... (616)454-6622
Fountain Hill, 222 Fountain NE, 49503 .... (616)458-6621
Greenville
Winter Inn, 100 N Lafayette, 48838 .... (616)754-7108
Harbor Beach
The Wellock Inn, 404 S Huron Ave, 48441, 1928 .... (517)479-3645
Harbor Springs
Main Street B&B, 403 E Main St, 49740, 1847 .... (616)526-7782
Harrisville
Red Geranium Inn, 508 E Main, PO Box 613, 48740 .... (517)724-6153
The Widow's Watch B&B, 401 Lake St, PO Box 271, 48740,
　　1866 .... (517)724-5465
Hart
Rooms at "The Inn" B&B, 515 State St, PO Box 214, 49420,
　　1880 .... (616)873-2448
Holland
Dutch Colonial Inn, 560 Central Ave, 49423, 1930 .... (616)396-3664
McIntyre B&B House, 13 E 13th St, 49423, 1906 .... (616)392-9886
Old Wing Inn, 5298 E 147th Ave, 49423, 1844 .... (616)392-7362
The Old Holland Inn, 133 W 11th St, 49423, 1900 .... (616)396-6601
The Parsonage, 6 E 24th St, 49423, 1908 .... (616)396-1316
The Witt House, 283 Fallen Leaf Ln, 49424 .... (616)399-0877
Homer
Grist Mill Guest House, 310 E Main, 49245, 1905 .... (517)568-4063
Hansen's Guest House, 102 W Adams, 49245 .... (517)568-3001
Hudson
The Sutton-Weed Farm, 18736 Quaker Rd, 49247, 1873 .. (517)547-6302
Indian River
Tuscarora Historical Society B&B, 6024 Prospect St, PO Box 807,
　　49749, 1900 .... (616)238-9072
Ithaca
Chaffin Farms B&B, 3239 W St Charles Rd, 48847 .... (617)463-4081
Jonesville
Munro House B&B, 202 Maumee St, 49250, 1840 .... (517)849-9292
Kalamazoo
Bartlett-Upjohn House, 229 Stuart Ave, 49007, 1886 .... (616)342-0230
Hall House, 106 Thompson St, 49007, 1923 .... (616)343-2500
Kalamazoo House, 447 W South St, 49007 .... (616)343-5426
Stuart Avenue B&B, 405 Stuart Ave, 49007
The Touch of Dutch, 7062 S Sixth St, 49009 .... (616)375-4527
Laingsburg
Seven Oaks Farm, 7891 Hollister Rd, 48848, 1888 .... (517)651-5598
Lakeside
The Pebble House, 15093 Lakeshore Rd, 49116, 1912 .... (616)469-1416
Lamont
The Stagecoach Stop, 4819 Leonard Rd W Box 18, 49430,
　　1859 .... (616)677-3940

Lansing
Cherry Hill B&B, 306 E Lenawee St, 48933, 1874 .... (517)372-9545
Maplewood, 15945 Wood St, 48906, 1890 .... (517)485-1426
Lawrence
Oak Cove Resort, 58881 46th St, 49064 .... (616)674-8228
Lawton
Springbrook B&B, 8143 Springbrook Dr, 49065 .... (616)624-6359
Leland
Snowbird Inn, PO Box 1021, 49653 .... (616)256-9462
The Highlands, 612 N Lake St, 49654 .... (616)256-7632
The Riverside Inn, 302 River St, 49654, 1902 .... (616)256-9971
Leslie
Hampton's Guest House, 112 Washington St, PO Box 123,
　　49251 .... (517)589-9929
Lexington
Governor's Inn, 7277 Simons St, 48450, 1859 .... (313)359-5770
The Crow's Nest, 5696 Main, 48450, 1850 .... (313)359-8500
Vicki Van's B&B, 5076 S Lakeshore Rd, 48450 .... (313)369-5533
West Wind B&B, 7156 Huron Ave, 48450, 1874 .... (313)359-5772
Ludington
1880 Inn on the Hill, 716 E Ludington Ave, 49431, 1880 . (616)845-6458
B&B at Ludington, 2458 S Beaune Rd, 49431 .... (616)843-9768
The Ludington House, 501 E Ludington Ave, 49431,
　　1878 .... (616)845-7769
Victorian Inn, 701 E Ludington Ave, 49431, 1889 .... (616)845-7055
White Rose Country Inn, 6036 Barnhart Rd, 49431
Mackinac Island
Bogan Lake Inn, Box 482, 49757 .... (906)847-3439
Chippewa Hotel, PO Box 250, 49757 .... (906)847-3341
Grand Hotel, 49757, 1887 .... (906)847-3331
Haan Cottage B&B, Box 1268, 49757
Iroquois Hotel-On-the-Beach, 49757, 1900 .... (906)847-3321
Lake View Hotel, 49757, 1858 .... (906)847-3384
Metivier Inn, Box 285, 49757 .... (906)847-6234
Murray Hotel, Main St, 49757, 1882 .... (906)847-3361
Pine Cottage, PO Box 519, 49757 .... (906)847-3820
The Island House, 49757, 1848 .... (906)847-3347
Thuya B&B Cottage, Box 459, 49757 .... (906)847-3400
Manistee
E E Douville House, 111 Pine St, 49660 .... (616)723-8654
Inn Wick-A-Te-Wah, 3813 Lakeshore Dr, 49660, 1902 ...... (616)889-4396
Manistee Country House, 1130 Lake Shore Rd, 49660,
　　1901 .... (616)723-2367
Manistique
Marina Guest House, PO Box 344, 49854 .... (906)341-5147
Maple City
Country Cottage B&B, 135 E Harbor Hwy, 49664 .... (616)228-5328
Leelanau Country Inn, 149 E Harbor Hwy, 49664, 1891 . (616)228-5060
Marquette
Greenwood Estates, 18 Oakridge Dr, 49855 .... (906)249-9246
Marshal
National House Inn, 102 S. Parkview, 49068, 1835
Marshall
McCarthy's Bear Creek Inn, 15230 C Drive N, 49068,
　　1940 .... (616)781-8383
Mcmillan
Helmer House Inn, Rt 3 Country Rd 417, 49853, 1881
Mears
Duneland Inn-Foster's B&B, PO Box 53, 49436 .... (616)873-5128
Mecosta
Blue Lake Lodge, 9765 Blue Lake Lodge Ln Box 1,
　　48823 .... (616)972-8391
Mendon
The Mendon Country Inn, 440 W Main St, 49072, 1873 (616)496-8132
Midland
Jay's B&B, 4429 Bay City Rd, 48640 .... (517)496-2498
Montague
Country Haven B&B, 9691 Sikkenga Rd, 49437, 1862 ...... (616)894-4977
Morning Glory Inn, 8709 Old Channel Trail, 49437 .... (616)894-8237
Old Channel Inn, 6905 Old Channel Tr, 49437 .... (616)893-3805
Mount Pleasant
Country Chalet, 723 S Meridian Rd, 48858 .... (517)772-9259

Michigan (Continued)

Muskegon
Blue Country B&B, 1415 Holton Rd, 49445, 1920 .... (616)744-2555
New Buffalo
Little Bohemia, 115 S Whittaker, 49117 .... (616)469-1440
Sans Souci B&B, 19265 S Lakeside Rd, 49117 .... (616)756-7206
Tall Oaks Inn B&B, Box 6, Grand Beach, 49117 .... (616)469-0097
Niles
Woods & Hearth B&B, 950 S Third St, 49120 .... (616)683-0876
Yesterdays Inn, 518 N 4th, 49120, 1875 .... **(616)683-6079**
Northport
Apple Beach Inn, 617 Shabwasung, PO Box 2, 49670 ...... (616)386-5022
Hutchinson's Garden, PO Box 661, 49670 .... (616)386-5534
North Shore Inn, 12794 Country Rd 640, 49670 .... (616)386-7111
Old Mill Pond Inn, 202 W Third St, 49670, 1895 .... **(616)386-7341**
Plum Lane Inn, Box 74, 49670 .... (616)386-5774
Vintage House B&B, 102 Shabwasing, PO Box 424, 49670,
   1884 .... (616)386-7228
Wood How Lodge, Rt 1 Box 44, 49670
Nunica
Stonegate Inn, 10831 Cleveland, 49448 .... (616)837-9267
Olivet
Ackerman's B&B Inn, 243 Kalamo St, 49076 .... (616)749-9422
Omena
Haus Austrian, 4626 Omena Point Rd, 49674 .... (616)386-7338
Omena B&B, PO Box 75, 49674 .... (616)386-7274
Owosso
Archer's Castle, 203 E King, 48867 .... (517)723-2572
Merkel Manor, 623 N Park St, 48867 .... (517)725-5600
Mulberry House, 1251 N Shiawassee St, 48867 .... (517)723-4890
R & R Farm-ranch, 308 E Hibbard Rd, 48867 .... (517)723-2553
Sylverlynd, 3452 McBride Rd, 48867 .... (517)723-1267
The J B Cain's, 4650 Waugh Rd, 48867 .... (517)723-4708
Victorian Splendor B&B, 426 N Washington St, 48867,
   1884 .... (517)725-5168
Paw Paw
Carrington's Country House, 43799 Sixtieth Ave, 49079. (616)657-5321
Pentwater
Pentwater Inn, 180 E Lowell Box 98, 49449, 1880 .... (616)869-5909
Petoskey
Bear & The Bay, 421 Charlevoix Ave, 49770 .... (616)347-6077
Gull's Way, 118 Boulder Lane, 49770 .... (616)347-9891
Perry Hotel, Bay & Lewis Sts, 49770, 1899 .... (616)347-2516
Stafford's Bay View Inn, Box 3, 49770, 1886
The Chapman House, 618 E Lake St, 49770, 1880 .... (616)347-1338
The Cozy Spot, 1145 Kalamazoo, 49770 .... (616)347-3869
Petosky
Apple Tree Inn, 915 Spring St, PO Box 574, 49770 .... (616)347-2900
Bed 'N' Breakfast, 212 Arlington, 49770 .... (616)347-6145
Plymouth
Mayflower B&B Hotel, Main & Ann Arbor Tr, 48170,
   1927 .... (313)453-1620
Port Austin
Garfield Inn, 8544 Lake St, 48467 .... (517)738-5254
Lake Street Manor, 8569 Lake St, 48467, 1884 .... (517)738-7720
Questover Inn, 8510 Lake St, 48467 .... (517)738-5253
Port Huron
Victorian Inn, 1229 Seventh St, 48060, 1896 .... (313)984-1437
Port Sanilac
Raymond House Inn, M-25, 111 S Ridge St, 48469,
   1871 .... (313)622-8800
Portland
Weber House, 527 James, 48875 .... (517)647-4671
Reed City
Osceola Inn, 110 E Upton, 49677, 1892 .... (616)832-5537
Romeo
Country Heritage B&B, 64707 Mound Rd, 48065, 1840 ... (313)752-2879
Saginaw
Montague Inn, 1581 S Washington Ave, 48601 .... (517)752-3939
The Heart House, 419 N Michigan, 48602, 1860 .... (517)753-3145
Saint Clair
Murphy Inn, 505 Clinton, 48079, 1836 .... (313)329-7118

Saint Ignace
Colonial House Inn, 90 N State St, 49781
Saint James
McCann House B&B, PO Box (Beaver Island), 49782,
   1899 .... (616)448-2387
Saint Joseph
South Cliff Inn, 1900 Lakeshore Dr, 49055, 1900 .... (616)983-4881
Saline
The Homestead B&B, 9279 Macon Rd, 48176, 1851 .... **(313)429-9625**
Saugatuck
Fairchild House, 606 Butler St, 49453 .... (616)857-5985
Jann's Guest House, 132 Mason St, 49453 .... (616)857-8851
Kemah Guest House, 633 Pleasant St, 49453, 1906 .... (616)857-2919
Maplewood Hotel, 428 Butler St Box 1059, 49453, 1860 (616)857-2788
The Kirby House, 294 W Center St, PO Box 1174, 49453,
   1890 .... (616)857-2904
The Newnham Inn, 131 Griffith St, PO Box 1106, 49453 . (616)857-4249
The Park House, 888 Holland St, 49453, 1857 .... **(616)857-4535**
Twin Gables Country Inn, Box 881, 49453, 1900 .... (616)857-4346
Wickwood Inn, 510 Butler St, 49453, 1929 .... (616)857-1097
Sault Saint Marie
Ojibway Hotel, 240 W Portage St, 49783, 1927 .... (906)632-4100
Schoolcraft
Grand Street B&B, 330 S Grand St, PO Box 454, 49087,
   1800 .... (616)679-5697
Sebewaing
Tree Haven, 41 N Beck, 48759, 1878 .... (517)883-2450
South Haven
A Country Place B&B, Rt 5, Box 43, 49090 .... (616)637-5523
Last Resort, 86 North Shore Dr, 49090
The Ross, 229 Michigan Ave, 49090 .... (616)637-2256
Victoria Resort, 241 Oak, 49090
Sparta
Morton House, 11 Pleasant St, 49345, 1800 .... (616)887-7073
Spring Lake
Alberties Waterfront B&B, 18470 Main St, 49456 .... (616)846-4016
Seascape B&B, 20009 Breton, 49456 .... (616)842-8409
Stanton
Clifford Lake Hotel, 561 Clifford Lake Dr, 48888
Stockbridge
Ballacraine B&B, E Cooper Rd, 49285, 1930 .... (517)851-7437
Suttons Bay
Garthe Guest House, 504 St Joseph, PO Box 82, 49682 .... (616)271-3776
Swartz Creek
Pink Palace Farms, 6095 Baldwin Rd, 48473 .... (313)655-4076
Tecumseh
Boulevard Inn, 904 W Chicago Blvd, 49286, 1854 .... **(517)423-5169**
Traverse City
Cedar Creek, 12666 W Bayshore Dr, 49684 .... (616)947-5643
Cider House B&B, 5515 Barney Rd, 49684 .... (616)947-2833
Hannah Beach House, 743 Munson Ave, 49684, 1930 ...... (616)947-8778
Linden Lea, 279 S Long Lake Rd, 49684 .... (616)943-9182
Neahtawanta Inn, 1308 Neahtawanta Rd, 49684 .... (616)223-7315
Painted Pony Inn, 8392 W M-72, 49684, 1885 .... (616)947-9117
Rafael's B&B, 325 Wellington, 49684, 1913 .... (616)946-4106
Tall Ship Malabar, 13390 W Bay Shore Dr, 49684, 1975 .. (616)941-2000
The Hemlocks on Long Lake, 8939 Gilbert Tr, 49684,
   1972 .... (616)946-2869
The Stonewall Inn, 17898 Smokey Hollow Rd, 49684,
   1865 .... (616)223-7800
The Victoriana, 622 Washington St, 49684, 1898 .... (616)929-1009
The Wooden Spool, 316 W Seventh St, 49684, 1890 .... (616)947-0357
Thomas' Broadbrick Inn, 6369 Secor Rd, 40794 .... (616)946-0650
Warwickshire Inn, 5037 Barney Rd, 49684, 1902 .... **(616)946-7176**
Union City
Victorian Villa, 601 N Broadway, 49094, 1876
Union Pier
Gordon Beach Inn, 16240 Lakeshore Rd, 49129
Inn at Union Pier, Box 222, 9708 Berrien St, 49129 .... (616)469-4700
Wakefield
The Medford House, PO Box 149, 49968, 1968 .... (906)224-5151
West Branch
Green Inn, 4045 W M-76, 48661 .... (517)345-0334

White Cloud
Shack Country Inn, 2263 W 14th St, 49349, 1947 .... (616)924-6683
White Pigeon
River Haven, 9222 St Joseph River Rd, 49099 .... (616)483-9104
Whitehall
Bunk 'N' Galley B&B, 1411 Mears Ave, 49461, 1900 .... (616)894-9851
Williamston
Williamston B&B, 3169 S Williamston Rd, 48895, 1916 ... (517)655-1061

Minnesota

Afton
The Afton House Inn, 3291 St Croix Tr Ave S, 55001,
    1867 .... (612)436-8883
Annandale
Thayer Hotel, Highway 55, 55302, 1895 .... (612)274-3371
Askov
The Governor's House, Box 252, 55704, 1917 .... (612)838-3296
Bloomington
Fitger's Inn, 1500 E 79th St, 55420, 1800 .... (612)854-2906
Brainerd
Grand View Lodge, Rt 6 Box 22, 56401
Pleasant Acres, Rt 6 Box 313, 56401, 1918 .... (218)963-2482
Cannon Falls
Quill & Quilt, 615 W Hoffman St, 55009, 1897 .... (507)263-5507
Chaska
Bluff Creek Inn, 1161 Bluff Creek Dr, 55318, 1864 .... (612)445-2735
Chatfield
Lund's Guest House, 500 Winona St SE, 55923, 1920 ...... (507)867-4003
Crookston
Wilkinson-Thorson B&B, 327 Houston Ave, 56716, 1891 (218)281-1601
Dodge Center
Eden B&B, Rt 1 Box 215, 55927, 1898 .... (507)527-2311
Duluth
Fitger's Inn, 600 E Superior St, 55082 .... (218)722-8826
The Mansion, 3600 London Rd, 55804
Elmare
Kuchenbecker Farm, PO Box 107, 56027
Excelsior
Christopher Inn, 201 Mill St, 55331, 1887 .... (612)474-6816
Faribault
Hutchinson House B&B, 305 NW Second St, 55021,
    1892 .... (507)332-7519
Grand Marais
Cascade Lodge, PO Box 693, 55604, 1938 .... (218)387-1112
Clearwater Lodge, Gunflint Tr (CR31B), 55604, 1926....... (218)388-2254
East Bay Hotel, 55604, 1909 .... (218)387-2800
Gunflint Lodge, PO 100 Gt, 55604 .... (218)388-4487
Naniboujou Lodge, HC 1 Box 505, 55604, 1928 .... (218)387-2688
Pincushion Mountain B&B, PO Box 181, 55604 .... (218)387-1276
Young's Island, Gunflint Tr 67-1, 55604
Harmony
Michel Farm Vacations, Rt 1 Box 914, 55939, 1889 .... (507)886-5392
Hastings
Thorwood, 4th & Pine, 55033
Herman
Lawndale Farm, Rt 2 Box 50, 56248, 1880
Kalispell
Huckleberry Inn, 1028 3rd Ave W, 55901 .... (406)755-4825
Lake City
Evergreen Knoll Acres, Rt 1 Box 145, 55041, 1920 .... (612)345-2257
Red Gables Inn, 403 N High St, 55041, 1865 .... (612)345-2605
The Rahilly House, 304 S Oak St, 55041
The Victorian B&B, 620 S High St, 55041, 1896 .... (612)345-2167
Lanesboro
Carrolton Country Inn, RR 2 Box 139, 55949 .... (507)467-2257
Mrs. B's Historic Lanesboro Inn, 101 Pkwy, 55949, 1872 (507)467-2154
Scanlan House, 708 Park Ave S, 55949, 1890 .... (507)467-2158
Lesueur
The Cosgrove, 228 S Second St, 56058, 1893 .... (612)665-2763
Little Falls
Pine Edge Inn, 308 First St SE, 56345, 1823

Mantorville
Grand Old Mansion, 501 Clay St, 55955, 1899 .... (507)635-3231
Marine On St Croix
Asa Parker House, 17500 St Croix Tr N, 55047, 1856 .... (612)433-5248
Minneapolis
Evelo's B&B, 2301 Bryant Ave S, 55405, 1897
Whitney Hotel, 150 Portland, 55401
Morris
The American House, 410 E Third St, 56267, 1900 .... (612)589-4054
Northfield
Archer House, 212 Division St, 55057
Nw Prague
Schumacher's New Prague Hotel, 212 W Main St,
    56071 .... (612)758-2133
Old Frontenac
Lowell House B&B, 531 Wood St, 55026, 1856
Olivia
Sheep Shedde Inn, Hwy 212 & 71 W, 56277, 1938
Owatonna
The Northrop House, 358 E Main St, 55060, 1890 .... (507)451-4040
The Tudor On Bridge, 473 W Bridge St, 55060, 1921 .... (507)451-8567
Pipestone
The Calumet, PO Box 111, 56164, 1883 .... (507)825-5658
Red Wing
Pratt-Taber Inn, 706 W Fourth, 55066, 1876 .... (612)388-5945
Rochester
Canterbury Inn B&B, 723 2nd St SW, 55902, 1890 .... (507)289-5553
Rush City
Grant House, Fourth & Bremer (Box 87), 55069, 1896 ..... (612)358-3661
Saint Cloud
Rachael Corrigan, Box 399, 56302........................... (612)252-6262
Saint Paul
Chatsworth B&B, 984 Ashland, 55104, 1902 .... (612)227-4288
University Club of St. Paul, 420 Summit Ave, 55102,
    1912.. (612)222-1751
Yoerg House, 215 W Isabel, 55107
Sauk Centre
Palmer House Hotel, 500 Sinclair Lewis Ave, 56378, 1901
Shafer
Country B&B, 32030 Ranch Tr., 55074, 1880 .... (612)257-4773
Spicer
Spicer Castle, 11600 Indian Beach Rd, 56288, 1893 .... (612)796-5870
Spring Valley
Chase's, 508 N Huron Ave, 55975, 1879 .... (507)346-2850
Stillwater
Driscolls For Guests, 1103 South 3rd St, 55082, 1869 .... (612)439-7486
Lowell Inn, 102 N Second St, 55082, 1930 .... (612)439-1100
Rivertown Inn, 306 W Olive St, 55082 .... (612)430-2955
The Overlook Inn, 210 E Laurel, 55082, 1859 .... (612)439-3409
Taylors Falls
Historic Taylor Falls Jail, 102 Government Rd, 55084
Wabasha
Anderson House, 333 Main St, PO Box 262, 55981, 1856 (612)565-4524
Walker
Chase On The Lake Lodge, PO Box 206, 56484 .... (218)547-1531
Weaver
Noble Studio & Galleries, Rt 1 Box 28, 55910, 1875 .... (507)767-2244
Winona
Carriage House B&B, 420 Main St, 55987, 1870 .... (507)452-8256
The Hotel, 129 W Third St, 55987, 1892 .... (507)452-5460

Mississippi

Aberdeen
Rosemont B&B, 407 S Meridian, 39730, 1909 .... (601)369-9434
Brookhaven
Edgewood, 412 Storm Ave, 39601, 1890 .... (601)833-2001
Chatham
Mount Holly, Box 140, 38731, 1855 .... (601)827-2652
Columbus
Alexander's Inn, 408 7th S, 39701, 1828 .... (601)327-4259

Mississippi (Continued)

Cartney-Hunt House, 408 S 7th St, 39701 ....(601)327-4259
Liberty Hall, Rt 4, Armstrong Rd, 39701
Rosewood Manor, 719 7 St, 39701
Temple Heights, 515 9 St N, 39701
Fayette
Historic Springfield Plantation, Hwy 553, 39069, 1791 ....(601)786-3802
Fillmore
Generals Quarters, 924 Fillmore St, 38834, 1890 ....(601)286-3325
Holly Springs
Hamilton Place, 105 E Mason Ave, 38635, 1838................(601)252-4368
Jackson
Fairview, 734 Fairview St, 39202
Judy Fenter, 1851 Drecon Dr, 39211
Millsaps-Buie House, 628 N State St, 39202, 1888 ....(601)352-0221
Lorman
Rosswood Plantation, Hwy 552, 39096, 1857 ....(601)437-4215
Natchez
Burn, 712 N Union St, 39120, 1832 ....(601)445-8566
Dixie, 211 S Wall St, 39120, 1795 ....(601)442-2525
Dunleith, 84 Homochitto, 39120, 1856 ....(601)446-8500
Guest House Of Natchez, 210 N Pearl St, 39120, 1840 ...(601)445-6000
Hope Farm, 147 Homochitto St, 39120
Linden, 1 Linden Place, 39120, 1800 ....(601)445-5472
Monmouth Plantation, 36 Melrose, 39120, 1818 ....(800)828-4531
Ravennaside, 601 S. Union St, 39120, 1870
Silver Street Inn, 1 Silver St, 39120, 1840
Texada, 212 S. Wall St, 39120, 1792...............................(601)445-4283
The Briars, PO Box 2180, 39120, 1818 ....(601)442-7210
The Burn, 712 N. Union St, 39120, 1832
Oxford
Oliver-Britt House, 512 Van Buren Ave, 38655
Port Gibson
Oak Square, 1207 Church St, 39150, 1850 ....(601)437-4350
Vicksburg
Anchuca, 1010 First East, 39180, 1830............................(601)636-4931
Balfour House, 1002 Crawford St, 39180
Cedar Grove Mansion Inn, 2200 Oak St, 39180, 1840 ....(601)636-1605
Gray Oaks, 4142 Rifle Range Rd, 39180
Manor House, 2011 Cherry St, 39180, 1906 ....(601)638-0683
Old Feld Home, 2108 Cherry St, 39180
The Corners, 601 Klein St, 39180, 1872............................(601)636-7421
The Duff Green Mansion, 1114 First East St, 39180,
    1856 ....(601)636-6968
Tomil Manor, 2430 Drummond St, 39180, 1906 ....(601)638-8893
Woodville
Square Ten Inn, 242 Depot St, 39669, 1830 ....(601)888-3993

Missouri

Arrow Rock
Borgman's B&B, 65320 ....(816)837-3350
Bonne Terre
The Lamplight Inn, 207 E School St, 63628, 1915 ....(314)358-4222
Branson
Branson House, 120 4th St, 65616, 1920 ....(417)334-0959
Carthage
Maple Lane Farms, RR 1, 64836, 1904 ....(417)358-6312
Gallatin
Gallatin B&B Inn, 200 E Grand, 64640
Hannibal
Fifth St Mansion B&B, 213 S Fifth St, 63401 ....(314)221-0445
Garth Woodside Mansion, RR 1, 63401, 1871 ....(314)221-2789
The Fifth Street Mansion B&B, 213 S Fifth St, 63401,
    1865 ....(314)221-0445
Victorian Guest House, 3 Stillwell, 63401
Hartville
Frisco House, PO Box 118, 65667, 1895 ....(417)741-7304
Hermann
Birk's Goethe St Gauthaus, 700 Goethe St, 65041 ....(314)486-2911
Der Klingerbau Inn, 108 E 2nd St, 65041, 1878 ....(314)486-2030
William Klinger Inn, 108 E 2nd St, 65041 ....(314)486-3528

Jamesport
Richardson House B&B, PO 227, 64648, 1900 ....(816)684-6664
Kansas City
Doanleigh Wallagh, 217 E 37th St, 64111, 1900 ....(816)753-2667
Lebanon
Historic Oakland Mansion, Rt 1 Box 179, 65536, 1887 .....(417)588-3291
Macon
Wardell Guest House, 1 Wardell Rd, 63552, 1890
Parkville
Down to Earth Lifestyles, Rt 22, 64152..............................(816)891-1018
Platte City
Basswood Country Inn B&B, Rt 1 Box 145B, 64079 ....(816)431-5556
Rocheport
School House B&B, Third And Clark St, 65279, 1914.......(314)698-2022
Saint Charles
Boone's Lick Trail Inn, 1000 South Main St, 63301,
    1840 ....(314)947-7000
Saint Genevieve
The Inn St. Gemme Beauvais, 78 N Main, PO Box 231, 63670,
    1848 ....(314)883-5744
Saint Joseph
Harding House, 219 N 20th St, 64501, 1903 ....(816)232-7020
McNally House B&B, 1105 S 15, 64503
Schuster-Rader Mansion, 703 Hall St, 64501, 1881
Saint Louis
Lafayette House, 2156 Lafayette Ave, 63104, 1876...........(314)772-4429
Seven Gables Inn, 26 N Meramec, 63105 ....(314)863-8400
The Coachlight B&B, 1 Grandview Heights, 63131,
    1904 ....(314)965-4328
Springfield
Walnut Street B&B, 900 E Walnut St, 65806, 1894 ....(417)864-6346
St Louis
Coach Light B&B, 4612 Mc Pherson, 63108, 1904 ....(314)367-2449
Washington
Schwegmann House, 438 West Front, 63090
Zachariah Foss Guest House, 4 Lafayette, 63090, 1846 ...(314)239-6599

Montana

Big Fork
O'Duachain Country Inn, 675 Ferndale Dr, 59911 ....(406)837-6851
Big Sky
Lazy K Bar Ranch, Box 550, 59011, 1888 ....(406)537-4404
Lone Mountain Ranch, PO Box 145, 59716, 1920 ....(406)995-4644
Bozeman
Hillard's Guest House, 11521 Axtell Gateway Rd, 59715 (406)463-4696
Lehrkind Mansion, 719 N Wallace, 59715
Silver Forest Inn, 15325 Bridger Canyon Rd, 59715
Voss Inn, 319 S Willson, 59715, 1883 ....(406)587-0982
Butte
Copper King Mansion, 219 West Granite, 59701, 1884 .....(406)782-7580
Essex
Izaak Walton Inn, PO Box 653, 59916, 1939 ....(406)888-5700
Gallatin Gateway
Gallatin Gateway, 59730, 1920 ....(406)763-4672
Great Falls
Three Pheasant Inn, 626 5th Ave N, 59401, 1910 ....(406)453-0519
Helena
Sanders Inn, 328 Ewing, 59601 ....(406)442-3309
Nevada City
Nevada City Hotel, 59755 ....(406)843-5377
Red Lodge
Pitcher Guest House, 2 S Platt PO 1148, 59068, 1910 .....(406)446-2859
Stevensville
Country Caboose, 852 Willoughby Rd, 59870, 1923 ....(406)777-3145
White Sulphur Spring
Foxwood Inn, Box 404, 59645

Nebraska

Alliance
Prairie House, 602 Box Butte, 69301, 1903 ....(308)762-1461

Bartley
Pheasant Hill, HC 68 Box 12, 69020, 1937 .... (308)692-3278
Crawford
Fort Robinson Inn, Box 392, 69339, 1909
Dixon
The Georges, Rt 1 Box 50, 68732 .... (402)584-2625
Lincoln
Rogers House, 2145 B St, 68502, 1914 .... (402)476-6961
North Platte
Watson Manor Inn, 410 S Sycamore, PO Box 458, 69103,
1880 .... (308)532-1124
Omaha
Offutt House, 140 N 39th St, 68131, 1894 .... (402)553-0951

Nevada

Carson City
Elliot-Chartz House, 412 N Nevada St, 89701
Winters Creek Ranch, 1201 US 395 North, 89701, 1865. (702)849-1020
Genoa
Orchard House, Box 77, 89411
Gold Hill
Gold Hill Hotel, Box 304, 89440
Imlay
Old Pioneer Garden, Star Rt, Unionville #79, 89418,
1861 .... (702)538-7585
Incline Village
Haus Bavaria, PO Box 3308, 89450 .... (702)831-6122
Silver City
Hardwicke House, Box 96, 89429
Virginia City
Edith Palmer's Country Inn, South B Street, PO Box 756, 89440,
1862 .... (702)847-0707
Winnemucca
Stauffer House, 82 Lay St, 89445
Yerington
Robric Ranch, Box 2, 89447

New Hampshire

Alton Bay
Oak Birch Inn, Rt 28a (23), 03810
Andover
The English House, PO Box 162, 03216
Antrim
Breezy Point Inn, RD 1 Box 302, 03440
Maplehurst Inn, Rt 202, 03440
Steele Homestead Inn, RR 1 Box 78, Rt 9, 03440, 1810
Uplands Inn, Miltimore Rd, 03440, 1840
Ashland
Cheney House, PO Box 683, 03217, 1895
Country Options, PO 443, 03217
Bartlett
Notchland Inn, Hart's Location, 03812 .... (603)374-6131
Bedford
Bedford Village Inn, 2 Old Bedford Road, 03102, 1810 (603)472-2001
Bennington
David's Inn, Bennington Sq., 03442, 1788
Bethlehem
Shepherd's Inn, PO Box 70, 03574, 1892 .... (603)823-8777
The Bells, Strawberry Hill, PO Box 276, 03574, 1892..... (603)869-2647
The Highlands Inn, PO 118 C, 03574
The Mulburn Inn, Main St, 03574, 1913 .... (603)869-3389
Bradford
Andrew Brook Lodge, RFD 1 Box 62, 03221
Bradford Inn, Main St, 03221, 1898 .... (603)938-5309
Mountain Lake Inn, Rt 114, 03221, 1760 .... (603)938-2136
Bridgewater
Pasquaney Inn On Newfound Lake, Star Rt 1 Box 1066, 03222,
1840 .... (603)744-2712
Bristol
Victorian, 16 Summer St, 03222 .... (603)744-6157

Campton
Mountain Fare Inn, Mad River Rd, 03223, 1850 .... (603)726-4283
The Campton Inn, Rt 175 N Box 282, 03223, 1835 .... (603)726-4449
Village Guest House, PO Box 222, 03223, 1825 .... (603)726-4449
Canaan
Inn On Canaan Street, The Kremzners, 03741 .... (603)523-7310
The Towerhouse Inn, 1 Parker St, 03741 .... (603)523-7244
Center Harbor
Dearborn Place, Box 997, 03226 .... (603)253-6711
Kona Mansion Inn, Box 458, 03226, 1900 .... (603)253-4900
Center Ossipee
Hitching Post Inn, Old Rt 16, 03814, 1850 .... (603)539-4482
Center Sandwich
Corner House Inn, Main St PO 204, 03227
Centre Harbor
Red Hill Inn, RD 1 Box 99M, 03226, 1904 .... (603)279-7001
Charlestown
Indian Shutters Inn, Rt 12, 03603, 1791 .... (603)826-4445
Chichester
Hitching Post B&B, Dover Rd #2, 03263, 1786 .... (603)798-4951
Chocorua
Staffords-in-the-field, 03817
The Farmhouse, PO 14 Page Hill Rd, 03817, 1840 .... (603)323-8707
Claremont
The Poplars, 13 Grandview St, 03743 .... (603)543-0858
Concord
Hitching Post-B&B, Dover Rd, RD #2, 03263, 1787 .... (603)798-4951
Wyman Farm, Rt 8 Box 437, 03301 .... (603)783-4467
Conway
Darby Field Inn, Bald Hill, PO Box D, 03818, 1826 .... (603)447-2181
Merrill Farm Resort, PO Box 2070, 03818, 1790 .... (603)447-3866
Cornish
Chase House B&B, Rt 12 A, RR 2 Box 909, 03745, 1775 (603)675-5391
Danbury
Inn At Danbury, Rt 104, 03230
Dover
Silver Street Inn, 03820 .... (603)749-6524
Dublin
Trinitarian Parsonage, Main St, 03444, 1837 .... (603)563-8889
Durham
Country House, 2 Stagecoach Rd, 03824
East Hebron
Six Chimneys, Star Rt Box 114, 03232, 1791
East Sullivan
Delford Inn, Centre St, 03445
Eaton Center
Inn At Crystal Lake, Rt 163, 03832
Palmer House Inn, Rt 153, 03832, 1884
Rockhouse Mountain Farm, 03832, 1900 .... (603)447-2880
Elkins
Limner Haus, Box 126, 03233, 1786
Enfield
Kluge's Sunset Hill Inn, Masacoma Lake, 03748, 1850 .... (603)632-4335
Epping
Haley House Farm, RFD 1, N River Rd, 03042, 1770
Etna
Moose Mountain Lodge, Moose Mountain, 03750,
1938 .... (603)643-3529
Exeter
The "G" Clef, Ashbrook Rd, 03833 .... (603)772-8850
Fitzwilliam
Amos Parker House, 119 West, 03447
Barntique, Sugar Hill Rd, 03447
Fern Hill, PO Box 13, 03447, 1790 .... (603)585-6672
Fitzwilliam Inn, 03447, 1796 .... (603)585-9000
Francestown
Inn At Crotched Mountain, Mountain Rd, 03043 .... (603)588-6840
Francestown Village
The Francestown B&B, Box 236, 03043
Franconia
Franconia Inn, Easton Rd, 03580, 1936 .... (603)823-5542

New Hampshire (Continued)

Horse and Hound Inn, Cannon Mt, 03580 .... (603)823-5501
Lovett's Inn, Rt 18, Profile Rd, 03580, 1784 .... **(603)823-7761**
Pinestead Farm Lodge, Rt 116 RD 1, 03580, 1899
Shepherd's Inn, PO Box 534, 03580, 1890 .... (603)823-8777
Sugar Hill Inn, Rt 117, 03580, 1748

Franklin
Webster Lake Inn, Webster Ave, 03235 .... (603)934-4050

Freedom
Freedom House, PO Box 338, 1 Maple St, 03836 .... (603)539-4815

Freedon
Knob Hill B&B, Rt 153, 03836 .... (603)539-6576

Gilford
Cartway House Inn, 83 Old Lake Shore Rd, 03246,
1771 .... **(603)528-1172**
Kings Grant Inn, RD 5 Box 385, 03246 .... (603)293-4431

Gilmonton
The Historic Tavern Inn, Box 365, 03237, 1793 .... (603)267-7349

Glen
Bernerhof Inn, Box 381 Rt 302, 03838, 1890 .... **(603)383-4414**

Gorham
The Gables, 139 Main St, 03581 .... (603)466-2875
The Gorham House Inn, 55 Main St, 03581 .... (603)466-2271

Goshen
Cutter's Loft, Rt 31, 03752 .... (603)863-5306

Grafton
Grafton Inn, Rt 4 Box 445, 03240

Greenfield
The Greenfield Inn, Box 156, 03047, 1817 .... **(603)547-6327**

Hampton
Blue Heron Inn, 124 Landing Rd, 03842 .... (603)926-9666

Hampton Beach
Boar's Head, 12 Dumas, 03842 .... (603)926-3911
Century House, 552 Ocean Blvd., 03842, 1803
The Grayhurst, 11 F St, 03842, 1890

Hancock
John Hancock Inn, Main St, 03449, 1789 .... (603)525-3318

Hanover
Trumbull House, Box C29, 03755 .... (603)643-1400

Haverhill
Haverhill Inn, Box 95, 03765, 1810 .... (603)989-5961

Henniker
Colby Hill Inn, Box 778, 03242, 1800
Hanscom House B&B, 03242
The Meeting House Inn & Restaurant, 35 Flanders Rd, 03242,
1850 .... **(603)428-3228**

Hillsborough
Stonebridge Inn, Rt 9 Box 82, 03244, 1830

Holderness
Manor On Golden Pond, Rt 3 Box T, 03245, 1903 .... **(603)968-3348**
The Inn on Golden Pond, Rt 3 Box 680, 03245, 1879 ..... **(603)968-7269**

Intervale
New England Inn, Rte. 16a, 03845, 1815 .... (603)356-5541
Riverside, An Elegant Country Inn, Rt 16A, 03845, 1906 (603)356-9060
The Forest-A Country Inn, PO Box 37, 03845, 1890 .... (603)356-9772

Jackson
Blake House, Pinkham Notch Rd, PO Box 246, 03846 ..... (603)383-9057
Christmas Farm Inn, Rt 16 Box 176, 03846, 1780
Dana Place Inn, Rt 16, Pinkham Notch Rd, 03846 .... (603)383-6822
Ellis River House, Rt 16 Box 656, 03846, 1890 .... (603)383-9339
Inn At Thorn Hill, PO Box A, Thorn Hill Road, 03846,
1895 .... (603)383-4242
Nestlenook Inn, PO Box Q, Dinsmore Rd, 03846 .... (603)383-9443
The Inn at Jackson, PO Box H, 03846, 1900 .... **(603)383-4321**
Village House, Rt 16A Box 359, 03846, 1860 .... **(603)383-6666**
Whitney's Village Inn, Rt 16B Box W, 03846, 1842 .... (603)383-6886
Wildcat Inn, Main St, PO Box T, 03846 .... (603)383-4245

Jackson Village
Nestlenook Inn, PO Box Q, 03846

Jaffrey
Benjamin Prescott Inn, Rt 124 East, 03452, 1853 .... **(603)532-6637**

Lilac Hill Farm, 5 Ingalls Rd, 03452 .... (603)532-7278
Woodbound Inn, Woodbound Rd, 03452, 1892 .... (603)532-8341

Jaffrey Center
Monadnock Inn, Main St Box 103, 03454, 1840

Jefferson
Davenport Inn, RFD 1 Box 93A, 03583 .... (603)586-4320
The Country Inn On Jefferson Hill, Rt 2, 03583, 1896 ...... (603)586-7998
The Jefferson Inn, Rt 2, 03583, 1896 .... **(603)586-7998**

Keene
Carriage Barn Guest-House, 358 Main St, 03431

Laconia
Ferry Point House, Rt 1 Box 335, 03246, 1838 .... **(603)524-0087**
Hickory Stick Farm, RFD 2, 03246
Mackissock House, 1047 Union Ave, 03246
Parade Rest Inn, Parade Rd, 03269 .... (603)524-3152
Perry Point House, Lower Bay Rd, 03269 .... (603)524-0087
The Tin Whistle Inn, 1047 Union Ave, 03246 .... (603)528-4185

Lincoln
Charpentier B&B, Box 562, 03251 .... (603)745-8517
Inn of the White Mountains B&B, PO Box 562, Pollard Rd,
03251 .... (603)745-8517

Lisbon
Ammonoosuc Inn, Bishops Rd, 03585, 1888 .... (603)838-6118

Littleton
1895 House, 74 Pleasant St, 03561, 1895
Beal House Inn, 247 West Main St, 03561, 1833 .... **(603)444-2661**
Edencroft Manor, Rt 135, 03561, 1890 .... (603)444-6776
Thayers Inn, 136 Main St, 03561, 1843 .... **(603)444-6469**

Lyme
Loch Lyme Lodge, Rt 10 RFD 278, 03768, 1784 .... (603)795-2141
Lyme Inn, Route 10, 03768, 1809
Marjorie's House, Rt 10, 03768, 1772 .... (603)795-4641

Manchester
Manor on the Park, 503 Beech St, 03104 .... (603)669-8600

Marlborough
Thatcher Hill Inn, Thatcher Hill Rd, 03455
Tolman Pond, PO RFD, 03455

Meredith
Hathaway Inn, RFD 4, Red Gate Ln, 03253 .... (603)279-5521

Milford
Ram In The Thicket, Off Rt 101, Maple St, 03055
Victoria Place, 88 Nashua St Rt 101-a, 03055

Milton
Thirteen Colonies Farm, RFD Rt 16, 03887, 1841 .... (603)652-4458

Moultonboro
Olde Orchard Inn, Box 256, 03254 .... (603)476-5004

Mount Sunapee
Backside Inn, PO Box 171, 03772 .... (603)863-5161

New London
Maple Hill Farm, RR 1 Box 1620, 03257, 1824
New London Inn, Box 8 Main St, 03257, 1792 .... **(603)526-2791**
Pleasant Lake Inn, PO Box 1030, N Pleasant St, 03257,
1790 .... (603)526-6271

Newmarket
Haley House Farm, Rt 1 N River, 03857 .... (603)679-8713

Newport
Backside Inn, RFD 2 Box 213, 03773, 1835 .... (603)863-5161
The Inn at Coit Mountain, HCR 63, PO 3 Rt 10, 03773,
1790 .... (603)863-3583

North Conway
Buttonwood Inn, Mt Surprise Rd, PO Box 3297, 03860,
1820 .... (603)356-2625
Center Chimney - 1787, PO Box 1220, River Rd, 03860 ... (603)356-6788
Cranmore Inn, PO Box 885, 03860 .... (603)356-5502
Cranmore Mt Lodge, Kearsarge Rd, PO Box 1194, 03860,
1850 .... **(603)356-2044**
Foothills Farm B&B, PO Box 1904, 03860 .... (207)935-3799
Nereledge Inn & White Horse Pub, River Rd Off Main St, 03860
Old Red Inn & Cottages, Rt 16 Box 467, 03860, 1819
Peacock Inn, PO Box 1012, 03860, 1773 .... **(603)356-9041**
Scottish Lion Inn, Rt 16, Main St, 03860 .... (603)356-6381
Stonehurst Manor, Rt 16, 03860, 1876 .... **(603)356-3271**
Sunny Side Inn, Seavey St, 03860 .... (603)356-6239
The 1785 Inn, Rt 16 at The Scenic Vista, 03860, 1785 ..... **(603)356-9025**

Wildflowers Guest House, Box 597, 03860
North Sutton
Follansbee Inn, PO Box 92, Keyser St, 03260, 1840 .... (603)927-4221
North Woodstock
Cascade Lodge, 222 Main St, 03262 .... (603)745-2722
Mt. Adams Inn, Rt 3, South Main St, 03262, 1875 .... (603)745-2711
Woodstock Inn, Rt 3 Box 118, Main St, 03262 .... (603)745-3951
Northfield
Haus Alpenrose, 28 Summer St, 03276
Northwood
Lake Shore Farm, Jeness Pond Rd, 03261, 1848 .... (603)942-5521
Meadow Farm B&B, Jenness Pond Rd, 03261, 1770 .... (603)942-8619
Ossipee
Acorn Lodge, PO Box 144, Duncan Lake, 03864 .... (603)539-2151
Kimberwick Farm, 03864
Oxford
White Goose Inn, PO Box 17, 03777 .... (603)353-4812
Peterborough
Salzburg Inn, Gov. Steele Estate, 03458
Willows Inn, PO Box 527, 03458, 1830
Plymouth
Crab Apple Inn, RFD 2 Box 200B, Rt 25, 03264, 1835 .... (603)536-4476
Northway House, RFD 1 US Rt 3 North, 03264 .... (603)536-2838
The Glynn House, 1-93 On Rt 3, 03264
Portsmouth
Inn At Christian Shore, 335 Maplewood, PO Box 1474, 03801,
  1800 .... (603)431-6770
Leighton Inn, 69 Richards Ave, 03801, 1809 .... (603)433-2188
Martin Hill Inn, 404 Islington St, 03801, 1820 .... (603)436-2287
Sheafe Street Inn, 3 Sheafe St, 03801, 1815 .... (603)436-9104
Sise Inn, 40 Court St, 03801, 1881 .... (603)433-1200
The Inn at Strawbery Banke, 314 Court St, 03801,
  1790 .... (603)436-7242
Rindge
Grassy Pond House, 03461
Rye
Rock Ledge Manor B&B, 1413 Ocean, 03870, 1880 .... (603)431-1413
Sanbornton
Ferry Point House, Lower Bay Road, 03269
Shelburne
Philbrook Farm Inn, North Rd, 03581, 1861 .... (603)466-3831
Snowville
Snowvillage Inn, Box 83, Foss Mt. Rd, 03849, 1850 .... (603)447-2818
Springfield
Hide-Away Lodge, PO Box 6, 03257 .... (603)526-4861
Stoddard
Stoddard Inn, Rt 123, 03464, 1830 .... (603)446-7873
Strafford
Province Inn, PO Box 309, Bow Lake, 03884, 1800 .... (603)664-2457
Sugar Hill
Ledgeland, 03585, 1926 .... (603)823-5341
Sunset Hill House, Sunset Rd, 03585, 1880 .... (603)823-5522
The Homestead, 03585, 1802 .... (603)823-5564
Sunapee
Dexter's Inn, Stagecoach Rd, PO Box 5, 03782 .... (603)763-5571
Haus Edelweiss, Box 609, 03782 .... (603)763-2100
Inn At Sunapee, Box 336, 03782 .... (603)763-4444
Old Governor's House, Lower Main & Myrtle, 03782 .... (603)763-9918
Seven Hearths Inn, Old Rt 11, 03782 .... (603)763-5657
Times Ten Inn, Rt 103b, PO Box 572, 03782, 1820 .... (603)763-5120
Suncook
Suncook House, 62 Main St, 03275, 1920 .... (603)485-8141
Sutton Mills
Village House At Sutton Mills, Box 151, 03221 .... (603)927-4765
Tamworth
Tamworth Inn, Main St, 03886, 1833 .... (603)323-7721
Temple
Birchwood Inn, Rt 45, 03084, 1800 .... (603)878-3285
Tilton
Country Place, RD 2 Box 342, Rt 132 N., 03276 .... (603)286-8551
The Black Swan Inn, 308 W Main St, 03276 .... (603)286-4524
Tilton Manor, 28 Chestnut St, 03276 .... (603)268-3457

Troy
Charlie Napoli's Headmasters Inn, 03465
Twin Mountain
Thimbleberry B&B, Parker Rd, 03595 .... (603)846-2211
Wakefield
Wakefield Inn, Mountain Laurel Rd, Rt 1 Box 2185, 03872,
  1803 .... (603)522-8272
Walpole
The 1801 House, Box 35, 03608, 1801
Waterville Valley
Silver Squirrel Inn, PO Box 363, Show's Brook Rd,
  03223 .... (603)236-8325
Snowy Owl Inn, Waterville Valley Resort, 03215 .... (603)236-8371
Wentworth
Hobson House, Town Common, 03282 .... (603)764-9460
Wentworth Inn & Art Gallery, Ellsworth Hill Rd, Off Rt 25,
  03282 .... (603)764-9923
West Chesterfield
Chesterfield Inn, 03466, 1780 .... (603)256-3211
West Franklin
Maria Atwood Inn, RFD 2, Rt 3a, 03235 .... (603)934-3666
Westmoreland
Partridge Brook Inn, Hatt Rd, PO Box 151, 03467, 1790 .. (603)399-4994
Whitefield
Kimball Hill Inn, Kimball Hill Rd, PO Box 03264, 03598 (603)837-2284
The 1875 Mountain Inn, The Dieterichs, 03598, 1875 .... (603)837-2220
Wilmont Flat
Limner Haus, Box 126, 03233 .... (603)526-6451
Wolfeboro
Lakeview Inn, Rt 109 N Main St, 03894
Tuc'Me Inn, PO 657, 03894, 1880 .... (603)569-5702

New Jersey

Avon-By-The-Sea
Cashelmara Inn, 22 Lakeside Ave, 07717, 1902 .... (201)776-8727
Sands Of Avon, 42 Sylvania Ave, 07717, 1890 .... (201)776-8386
Bay Head
Bay Head Sands, 2 Twilight Rd, 08742, 1920 .... (201)899-7016
Conover's Bay Head Inn, 646 Main Ave, 08742, 1912 ...... (201)892-4664
Beach Haven
Barque, 117 Centre St, 08008, 1900 .... (609)492-5539
Magnolia House, 215 Centre St, 08008 .... (609)492-0398
St. Rita Hotel, 127 Engleside, 08008 .... (609)492-9192
Cape May
Abbey, Columbia & Gurney, 08204 .... (609)884-4506
Abigail Adams B&B, 12 Jackson St, 08204, 1888 .... (609)884-1371
Albert G. Stevens Inn, 127 Myrtle Ave, 08204, 1903 .... (609)884-4717
Barnard-Good House, 238 Perry St, 08204, 1865 .... (609)884-5381
Bedford Inn, 805 Stockton Ave, 08204 .... (609)884-4158
Bell Shields House, 501 Hughes St, 08204 .... (609)884-8512
Brass Bed Inn, 719 Columbia Ave, 08204 .... (609)884-8075
Captain Mey's Inn, 202 Ocean St, 08204, 1881 .... (609)884-7793
COLVMNS by the Sea, 1513 Beach Dr, 08204, 1905 .... (609)884-2228
Dormer House, International, 800 Columbia Ave, 08204,
  1899 .... (609)884-7446
Duke of Windsor Inn, 817 Washington St, 08204, 1896 (609)884-1355
Gingerbread House, 28 Gurney St, 08204, 1869 .... (609)884-0211
Hanson House, 111 Ocean St, 08204
Heirloom B&B, 601 Columbia Ave, 08204, 1876 .... (609)884-1666
Holly House, 20 Jackson St, 08204, 1888 .... (609)884-7365
Humphrey Hughes House, 29 Ocean St, 08204, 1903 .... (609)884-4428
Mainstay Inn, 635 Columbia Ave, 08204, 1872 .... (609)884-8690
Mason Cottage, 625 Columbia Ave, 08204, 1871 .... (609)884-3358
Mooring, 801 Stockton Ave, 08204 .... (609)884-5425
Poor Richard's Inn, 17 Jackson St, 08204 .... (609)884-3536
Queen Victoria, 102 Ocean St, 08204, 1881 .... (609)884-8702
Sand Castle Guest House, 829 Stockton Ave, 08204,
  1873 .... (609)884-5451
Seventh Sister Guesthouse, 10 Jackson St, 08204, 1888 (609)884-2280
Springside, 18 Jackson St, 08204, 1888 .... (609)884-2654
Summer Cottage Inn, 613 Columbia Ave, 08204, 1867 .... (609)884-4948
The Abbey, Columbia Ave & Gurney St, 08204, 1869 ...... (609)884-4506
The Chalfonte, 301 Howard St, 08204, 1878 .... (609)884-8409

New Jersey (Continued)

The Manor House, 612 Hughes St, 08204 ....(609)884-4710
The Wooden Rabbit, 609 Hughes St, 08204, 1838 ....(609)884-7293
Victorian Rose, 719 Columbia Ave, 08204 ....(609)884-2497
White House Inn, 831 Beach Dr, 08204, 1888 ....(609)884-5329
Windward House, 24 Jackson St, 08204, 1890 ....(609)884-3368
Chester
Publick House Inn, 111 Main St, 07930 ....(201)879-6878
Dennisville
Henry Ludlum Inn, RD 3 Box 298, 08270, 1804 ....(609)861-5847
Flemington
Jerica Hill B&B Inn, 96 Broad St, 08822 ....(201)782-8234
Frenchtown
Hunterdon House, 12 Bridge St, 08825 ....(201)996-3632
National Hotel, 31 Race St, 08825, 1851 ....(201)996-4871
Old Hunterdon House, 12 BridgeSt, 08825 ....(201)996-3632
Island Heights
Studio Of John F. Peto, 102 Cedar Ave, 08732, 1889 ....(201)270-6058
Lambertville
Chimney Hill Farm, 08530, 1820 ....(609)397-1516
Coryell House, 44 Coryell St, 08530 ....(609)397-2750
York Street House, 42 York St, 08530
Lyndhurst
The Jeremiah J. Yereance House, 410 Riverside, 07071,
   1841 ....(201)438-9457
Milford
Chesnut Hill, PO Box N, 63 Church St, 08848, 1860 ....(201)995-9761
Montclair
Marboro Inn, 334 Grove St, 07042, 1866 ....(201)783-5300
Ocean Grove
Cordova, 26 Webb Ave, 07756, 1886 ....(201)774-3084
Keswick Inn, 32 Embury Ave, 07756 ....(201)775-7506
Pine Tree Inn, 10 Main Ave, 07756, 1880 ....(201)775-3264
Ocean View
Major Gandy's, 180 Shore Rd, 08230
Princeton
Peacock Inn, 20 Bayard Ln, 08540, 1775 ....(609)924-1707
Seagirt
Holly Harbor Guest House, 112 Baltimore Blvd., 08750,
   1900 ....(201)449-9731
Spring Lake
Ashling Cottage, 106 Sussex Ave, 07762 ....(201)449-3553
Chateau, 500 Warren Ave, 07762, 1888 ....(201)974-2000
Johnson House, 25 Tuttle Ave, 07762 ....(201)449-1860
Kenilworth, 1505 Ocean Ave, 07762, 1882 ....(201)449-5327
Sandpiper Hotel, 7 Atlantic Ave, 07762, 1888 ....(201)449-6060
Stone Post Inn, 115 Washington Ave, 07762, 1882 ....(201)449-1212
The Normandy Inn, 21 Tuttle Ave, 07762, 1888 ....(201)449-7172
Victoria House, 214 Monmouth Ave, 07762 ....(201)974-1882
Stanhope
Whistling Swan Inn, Box 791, 110 Main Street, 07874,
   1900 ....(201)347-6369
Stockton
Colligan's Stockton Inn, Rt 29, 08559 ....(609)397-1250
Woolverton Inn, 6 Woolverton Rd, 08559, 1793 ....(609)397-0802
Woodbine
Henry Ludlam Inn, 124 S Delsea Dr, RD 3 Box 298, 08270,
   1760 ....(609)861-5847

New Mexico

Albuquerque
Casita Chamisa, 850 Chamisal Rd NW, 87107, 1850 ....(505)897-4644
W.E. Mauger Estate, 701 Roma Ave NW, 87102, 1897 ....(505)242-8755
Chimayo
Hacienda Rancho De Chimayo, Box 11 State Rd 520,
   87522 ....(505)351-2222
La Posada De Chimayo, Box 463, 87522 ....(505)351-4605
Cloudcroft
The Lodge, PO Box 497, 88317, 1899 ....(505)682-2566

Corrales
Corrales Inn B&B, PO Box 1361, 87048 ....(505)897-4422
Galisteo
Galisteo Inn, Box 4, 87540, 1760 ....(505)982-1506
Las Cruces
Inn Of The Arts, 618 S Alameda Blvd, 88005, 1900 ....(505)526-3327
Llewellyn House, 618 S Alameda, 88005 ....(505)526-3327
Las Vegas
Plaza Hotel, 230 Old Town Plaza, 87701 ....(505)425-3591
Pilar
The Plum Tree, Box 1-a, Rt 68, 87571, 1900 ....(505)758-4696
Ranchos De Taos
Two Pipes, Box 52, Talpa Rt, 87557, 1713 ....(505)758-4770
San Juan Pueblo
Chinguague Compound, Box 1118, 87566 ....(505)852-2194
Santa Fe
El Paradero, 220 W Manhattan, 87501, 1912 ....(505)988-1177
Grant Corner Inn, 122 Grant Ave, 87501, 1905 ....(505)983-6678
Preston House, 106 Faithway St, 87501, 1886 ....(505)982-3465
Pueblo Bonito, 138 W Manhattan, 87501, 1883 ....(505)984-8001
Rancho Encantado, Rt 4, Box 57-C, 87501 ....(505)982-3537
Sunrise Springs, Rt 2, Box 203, 87501 ....(505)471-3600
The Rim House, Box 1537, 87501
Silver City
Bear Mtn. Guest Ranch, PO Box 1163, 88062 ....(505)538-2538
Talpa
Blue Door B&B, La Maranda Rd, Box 1168, 87571, 1889 .(505)758-8360
Taos
Gallery House West, East Kit Carson Rd, PO 2983, 87571,
   1920 ....(505)758-8001
Hacienda del Sol, Box 177, 87571, 1800 ....(505)758-0287
La Posada De Taos, 309 Juanita Lane, Box 1118, 87571,
   1900 ....(505)758-8164
Las Palomas Conf. Center, Box 6689, 87571 ....(505)758-9456
Plum Tree, Box A-1, Hwy 68, 87571 ....(505)758-4696
The Taos Inn, 125 Paseo del Pueblo Norte, 87571, 1660 (505)758-2233

New York

Afton
Jericho Farm Inn, 155 E Main St, 13730, 1788
Akron
Providence Farm, 11572 Hiller Rd, 14001
Altamont
Appel Inn, Rte 146, 12009, 1765 ....(518)861-6557
Amagansett
Mill Garth Mews, PO Box 700, 11930 ....(516)267-3757
Amenia
Marshfield, Box 432, 12501
Troutbeck, Box 26, Leedsville Rd, 12501, 1918 ....(914)373-9681
Ashville
Green Acres, RD1, 14710
Auburn
Springside Inn, Box 520, 13021 ....(315)252-7247
Aurora
Aurora Inn, Main St
Averill Park
The Gregory House, PO Box 401, 12018, 1837 ....(518)674-3774
Avon
Mulligan Farm, 5403 Barber Rd, 14414, 1852
Bainbridge
Berry Hill Farm, Box 128, RD #1, 13733, 1820
Barryville
All Breeze Guest Farm, Haring Rd, 12719 ....(914)557-6485
Bath
Wheeler B&B, RD 2 Box 455, 14810, 1865 ....(607)776-6756
Beaver Dams
Vrede Langoed, Dug Rd, 14812
Bellport, Long Islan
The Great South Bay Inn, 160 S County Rd, 11713 ....(516)286-8588

Bengali
Beaverbrook, Duell Rd, 12546
Big Moose Lake
Big Moose, 13331 .... (315)357-2042
Blue Mountain Lake
Hedges, 12812
Boicerille
Cold Brook Inn, PO Box 251, 12412
Bolton
Hilltop Cottage, Box 186, 12814
Boonville
Greenmeadow, RD 3, 13309, 1900
Branchport
Four Seasons B&B, 470 W Lake Rd, 14418 .... (607)868-4686
Buffalo
Linwood House, 242 Linwood, 14209, 1880 .... (716)882-6116
Burdett
The Red House Country Inn, Picnic Area Rd, 14818,
    1844 .... (607)546-8566
Cairo
Glen Durham, Rt 2 Box 816, 12413
Canaan
Inn At Shaker Mill Farm, Cherry Ln, 12029, 1824 .... (518)794-9345
The Lace House, Rt 22 At Tunnel Hill Rd, 12029, 1806 ... (518)781-4669
Canandaigua
Inn At Still Woode, 131 East St, 14424, 1857 .... (716)394-0504
Wilder Tavern B&B, 5648 N Bloomfield Rd, 14424, 1829 (716)394-8132
Canaseraga
The Country House, 37 Mill St, 14822, 1888 .... (607)545-6439
Candor
Edge Of Thyme, 6 Main St, 13743, 1900 .... (607)659-5155
Canoga
Locustwood Inn, 3563 Rt 89, 13148
Castile
Eastwood House, 45 S Main, 14427
Cayuga
Ludwig, Box 866, 13034
Cazenovia
Brae Loch Inn, 5 Albany St, 13035, 1805 .... (315)655-3431
Lincklaen House, 79 Albany St, 13035, 1835 .... (315)655-8171
Central Valley
Gasho Inn, Rt 32, 10917
Chateaugay Lake
Banner House, 12920
Chautauqua
Longfellow Inn, 11 Roberts Ave Box Y, 14722, 1888 .... (716)357-2285
Chestertown
Balsam House Inn, Atateka Dr,rr1,box 365, 12817 .... (518)494-2828
The Friends Lake Inn, Friends Lake Rd, 12817, 1860 .... (518)494-4251
Chichester
Maplewood, PO Box 40, 12416
Clarence
Asa Ransom House, 10529 Main St, 14031 .... (716)759-2315
Clayton
Thousand Islands Inn, 335 Riverside Dr, 13624, 1897 ...... (315)686-3030
Clinton
Lewago Hall, 68 College St, 13323, 1840
Victorian Carriage House, 46 Williams St, 13323, 1840
Clintondale
Green's Victorian B&B, Rt 44 & 55, 12515, 1860
Cobleskill
The Gables, 62 W Main, 12043, 1900
Cold Brook
Grand Inn, Stormy Hill Rd, 13324 .... (315)826-7677
Cold Spring
Hudson House, 2 Main St, 10516, 1832 .... (914)265-9355
One Market Street, 1 Market St, 10516, 1810
Pig Hill, 73 Main St, 10520 .... (914)265-9247
The Old Post Inn, 43 Main St, 10516
Colden
Back of the Beyond, 7233 Lower E Hill Rd, 14033 .... (716)652-0427

Cooperstown
Angelholm, PO Box 705, 14 Elm St, 13326, 1815 .... (607)547-2483
Cooper Inn, PO Box 311, 13326 .... (607)547-2567
Creekside B&B, RD 1 Box 206, 13326, 1788 .... (607)547-8203
Hickory Grove Inn, Rt 80 At Six Mile Pt, 13326 .... (607)547-8100
Hill & Hollow Farm, RD3 Box 70, 13326 .... (607)547-2129
Inn at Cooperstown, 16 Chestnut St, 13326, 1874 .... (607)547-5756
The Inn At Brook Willow Farm, RD 2 Box 514, Middlefield Center,
    13326 .... (607)547-9700
The Inn At Mill Pond, PO Box 167, 13326, 1890 .... (315)858-1654
The J. P. Sillhouse, 63 Chestnut St, 13326
Tunnicliff Inn, 34 Pioneer St, 13326
Coopertown
Inn at Brook Willow Farm, Rt 33, RD2, Box 514, 13326
Corning
Cecce Guest House, 166 Chemung St, 14830, 1900 .... (607)962-5682
Rosewood Inn, 134 E First St, 14830, 1855 .... (607)962-3253
Victoria House, 222 Pine St, 14830, 1900 .... (607)962-3413
White Birch, 69 E First, 14830, 1865 .... (607)962-6355
Cuba
33 South, 33 South St, 14727, 1902 .... (716)968-1387
Dandee
1819 Red Brick Inn, Box 57A, 14837 .... (607)243-8844
Davenport
The Davenport Inn, Stewart Wohirab, 13750, 1819 .... (607)278-5068
Dryden
Sarah's Dream, 49 W Main St, 13050, 1828
Dundee
Country Manor B&B, 4798 Dundee-Himrod Rd, 14837 .. (607)243-8628
Willow Cove, 77 South Glenora Rd, RD 1 Box 8, 14837,
    1888 .... (607)243-8482
East Aurora
Roycroft Inn, 40 S Grove St, 14052 .... (716)652-9030
East Bloomfield
Holloway House, Rt 5 & 20, 14443
East Concord
Highland Springs, Allen Rd, 14055
East Hampton
1770 House, 143 Main St, 11937 .... (516)324-1770
Bassett House, 128 Montauk Hwy, 11937
Hedges House, 74 James Ln, 11937 .... (516)324-7100
Huntting Inn, 94 Main St, 11937, 1751 .... (516)324-0410
Maidstone Arms, 207 Main St, 11937 .... (516)324-5006
East Quogue
Caffrey House, Squires Ave, 11942
Elka Park
Redcoat's Return, Dale Ln, 12427 .... (518)589-6379
Windswept, County Rd 16, 12427, 1890 .... (518)589-6275
Ellicotville
Ellicottville Inn, 4-10 Washington St, 14731
Fairport
Woods Edge, PO Box 444, 14450
Falconer
Mansard Inn, Rd 1, Box 633, 14733
Fleischmanns
Runaway Inn, Main St, 12430, 1900 .... (914)254-5660
Fly Creek
Litco Farms, PO Box 148, 13337 .... (607)547-2501
Forestburgh
Inn At Lake Joseph, PO Box 81, 12777 .... (914)791-9506
Frankfort
B&B Leatherstocking, 399 Brockway Rd, 13340
Blueberry Hill, 389 Brockway Rd, 13340, 1828 .... (315)733-0040
Franklinville
1870 House, 20 Chestnut St, 14734, 1870 .... (716)676-3571
Fulton
Battle Island Inn, RD 1 Box 176, 13069, 1840 .... (315)598-3985
Garrison
Bird & Bottle Inn, Rt 9, 10524, 1761
Garrison's Landing
The Golden Eagle Inn, 10524, 1848

New York (Continued)

Geneseo
American House, 39 Main St, 14454, 1897 ....(716)243-5483
Geneva
Geneva On The Lake, 1001 Lochland Rd, 14456, 1910.....(315)789-7190
Inn at Belhurst Castle, PO 609, 14456, 1895 ....(315)781-0201
The Cobblestones, Rt 2, 14456, 1848
Gilbertsville
Leatherstocking Trails, RD 1 Box 40, 13776 ....(607)783-2757
Glens Falls
The Crislip's B&B, RD 1 Box 57, Ridge Rd, 12801,
    1820 ....(518)793-6869
Greenport
Randy Wade, Box 5, 11944
Greenville
Greenville Arms, South St, 12083, 1889 ....(518)966-5219
Groton
Benn Conger Inn, 206 W Cortland, 13073, 1921 ....(607)898-5817
Hadley
Highclere Inn, PO Box 179, 12835 ....(518)696-2861
Hammondsport
Laufersweller, 11 William St, 14840, 1843 ....(607)569-3402
Hampton Bays
House on the Water, Box 106, 11946 ....(516)728-3560
Hancock
Sunrise Inn, RD1 Box 232, 13856 ....(607)865-7254
Hempstead
Duvall B&B, 237 Cathedral Ave, 11550 ....(516)292-9219
Henderson Harbor
Gill House Inn, 13651, 1860
Herkimer
Bellinger Woods, 611 W German St, 13350, 1860
High Falls
Brodhead House, Rt 213, 12440, 1900
Captain Schoonmaker's House, Rt 2 Box 37, 12440,
    1760 ....(914)687-7946
House On The Hill, Box 86, 12440, 1825
Highland
Monica Hunter, Pancake Hollow Rd, RD 2 Box 561, 12528
Hillsdale
L'hostellerie Bressane, Corner Rts 22 & 23, 12529, 1780
Howes Cave
Cavern View, RD 1, Box 23, 12092, 1870
Ilion
Chesham Place, 317 W Main, 13357, 1872
Irvington-on-Hudson
Shadowbrook B&B, 821 N Broadway, 10533, 1850 ....(914)591-9291
Ithaca
Buttermilk Falls, 110 E Buttermilk Falls Rd, 14850, 1825.(607)273-3947
Glendale Farm, 224 Bostwick Rd, 14850 ....(607)272-8756
Peregrine House, 140 College Ave, 14850, 1874 ....(607)272-0919
Rose Inn, 813 Auburn Rd, Rt 34 N, Box 6576, 14851-6576,
    1851 ....(607)533-7905
Keene
The Bark Eater, Alstead Mill Rd, 12942, 1830 ....(518)576-2221
Kingston
Rondout B&B, 88 W Chester St, 12401, 1905
Lake George
East Lake George House, 492 Glen St, 12801 ....(518)656-9452
Lake Luzerne
Lamplight Inn, PO Box 70, 2129 Lake Ave (9n), 12846,
    1890 ....(518)696-5294
Lake Placid
Highland House Inn, 3 Highland Place, 12946, 1910 .....(518)523-2377
South Meadow Farm, Cascade Rd, 12946.................(518)523-9369
The Stagecoach Inn, Old Military Rd, 12946, 1830
Lansing
The Federal House B&B, 175 Ludlowville Rd, 14882
Lewiston
The Peter House, 175 S Fourth St, 14092, 1838 ....(716)754-8877

Little Valley
Napoli Stagecoach Inn, 14755, 1830
Livingston Manor
Lanza's Country Inn, RD 2 Box 446, Shandelee Rd, 12758,
    1901 ....(914)439-5070
Lockport
Chestnut Ridge Inn, 7205 Chestnut Ridge, 14094, 1826 ...(716)439-9124
Macedon
Iris Farm, 162 Hook Rd, 14502, 1860 ....(315)986-4536
Marathon
Merryhart Victorian Inn, 12 Front St, PO Box 363, 13803,
    1895 ....(607)849-3951
Margaretville
Margaretville Mountain Inn, Margaretville Mountain Rd,
    12455 ....(914)586-3933
Mayville
Plumbush B&B at Chautauqua, Chautauqua — Stedman RD2,
    14757, 1860 ....(716)789-5309
Mcgraw
Tinell's Hathaway House, Rt 41, Box 621 Solon, 13101
Milford
Maple Shade B&B, Rt 1 Box 105, 13807
Millerton
Simmon's Way Village Inn, Main St, Route 44, 12546,
    1856 ....(518)789-6235
Mohawk
Country Hills, 3289 Vickerman Hill, 13407, 1860
Mount Tremper
Mt. Tremper Inn, Rt 212 & Wittenberg Rd, 12457, 1850
Mumford
Genesee Country Inn, 948 George St, 14511, 1833
Naples
Maxfield Inn, 105 N Main, 14512, 1814
Nelliston
The Historian, Rt 5, Box 224, 13410, 1842
New Lebanon
New Lebanon Guest House, Rt 20, 12125, 1853
New Paltz
Ujjala's B&B, 2 Forest Glen, 12561, 1910 ....(914)255-6360
White House Farm, 211 Phillies Bridge Rd, 12561
New Rochelle
Rose Hill, 44 Rose Hill Ave, 10804 ....(914)632-6464
New York
Adobe B&B, PO Box 20022, 10028
B&B, 35 W 92nd St, 10025
New York City
Incentra Village House, 32 8th Ave, 10014, 1841 ....(212)206-0007
Newfield
The Historic Cook House B&B, 167 Main St, 14867 ....(607)564-9926
Newport
Roesler's B&B, RD 1, 13416
Niagara Falls
Rainbow Hospitality, 9348 Hennepin Ave, 10011, 1839.(716)754-8877
North Hudson
Pine Tree Inn, PO Box 555, 12855, 1920 ....(518)532-9255
North River
Garnet Hill Lodge, 13th Lake Rd, 12856 ....(518)251-2821
Ogdensburg
Maple Hill, Riverside Dr, 13669
Olcott
Bayside Guest House, Box 34, 14126
Oneida
The Pollyanna, 302 Main St, 13421, 1860 ....(315)363-0524
Painted Post
Dannfield, 50 Canada Rd, 14870, 1828
Palmyra
Canaltown, 119 Canandaigua St, 14522, 1850
Penfield
Strawberry Castle B&B, 1883 Penfield Rd, Rt 441, 14526,
    1875 ....(716)385-3266

Penn Yan
Fox Run Vineyards B&B, 670 Rte 14 RD 1, 14527
Pine Hill
Pine Hill Arms, 12462, 1900
Pittsford
Oliver Loud's Inn, 1474 Marsh Rd, 14534, 1812................ (716)248-5200
Portageville
Genesee Falls Hotel, Rt 436, 14536 .... (716)493-2484
Poughkeepsie
Inn At The Falls, 50 Red Oaks Mill Rd, 12603
Pulaski
The Way Inn, 7377 Salina St, 13142, 1840 .... (315)298-6073
Purling
Shepherd's Croft, HC Box 263, 12470
Red Hook
The Red Hook Inn, 31 S Broadway, 12571, 1838 .... (914)758-8445
Rensselaer
The Tibbitts House, 100 Columbia Turnpike, 12144, 1860
Rhinebeck
Beekman Arms, Rt 9, 12572, 1766 .... (914)876-7077
Village Victorian Inn, 31 Center St, 12572, 1860 .... (914)876-8345
Richfield Springs
Jonathan House, 39 E Main, 13439, 1880
Summerwood B&B, PO Box 388, 13439 .... (315)858-2024
Riverhead
The Libby House, Box 343, 11901
Rochester
The Rose Mansion & Gardens, 625 Mt Hope Ave, 14620
Rosendale
Astoria Hotel, 25 Main St, 12472
Roxbury
Scudder Hill House, Scudder Hill Rd, 12474, 1858 .... (607)326-4215
Rushville
Lakeview Farm, 4761 Rt 364, 14544 .... (716)554-6973
Sandy Creek
Pink House Inn, 9125 S Main St, 13145, 1872 .... (315)387-3276
Saranac Lake
The Point, Star Route, 12983, 1930 .... (518)891-5678
Saratoga Springs
Adelphi Hotel, 365 Broadway, 12866.. (518)587-4688
Saratoga B&B, Out Church St, 12866
The Westchester House, 102 Lincoln Ave, PO Box 944, 12866,
   1880 .... (518)587-7613
Saugerties
High Woods Inn, 7472 Glasco Turnpike, 12477
Secret Garden, 6071 Malden Tpk, 12477
Schuylerville
Inn on Bacon Hill, RD 1 Box 114, 12871 .... (518)695-3693
The Schmids, Rt 1 Box 1114, 12871
Seneca Falls
Locustwood Country Inn, 3568 Rt 89, 13148, 1820
Shandaken
Two Brooks B&B, Rt 42, 12480
Shelter Island
Chequit Inn, 23 Grand Ave, 11965, 1871 .... (516)749-0018
The Bowditch House, 166 N Ferry Rd, 11965
Skaneateles
Sherwood Inn, 26 W Genesee St, 13152, 1807 .... (315)685-3405
Sodus
Maxwell Creek Inn, 7563 Lake Rd, 14551, 1840 .... (315)483-2222
Southampton
Country Inn, 200 Hill St, 11968, 1880
The Old Post House Inn, 136 Main St, 11968, 1684 .... (516)283-1717
Village Latch, 101 Hill St, 11968 .... (503)283-2160
Southold
Goose Creek Guesthouse, 1475 Waterview Dr, 11971,
   1860 .... (516)765-3356
Spencertown
Spencertown Guests, Box 122, Elm St & Rt 203, 12165 ... (518)392-2358
Stephentown
Kirkmead, Box 169A, 12168, 1767 .... (518)733-5420

Millhof Inn, Rt 43, 12168, 1930
Stone Ridge
Baker's B&B, Rt 2 Box 80, 12484, 1780
Hasbrouck House Inn, PO Box 76, 12484, 1800 .... (914)687-0055
Stony Brook
Three Village Inn, 150 Main St, 11790, 1800 .... (516)751-0555
Syracuse
Ivy Chimney, 143 Didama St, 13224 .... (315)446-4199
Tannersville
The Eggery Inn, County Rd 16, 12485..................................... (518)589-5363
Trumansburg
Sage Cottage, Box 121, 14886, 1855
Taughannock Farm, Rt 89 & Gorge Rd, 14886................... (607)387-7711
Vernon
Lavender Inn, RD #1, Box 325, 13476, 1799
Warrensburg
Country Road, Box 227, 12885
White House Lodge, 53 Main St, 12885 .... (518)623-3640
Waterloo
The Historic James R. Webster Mansion, 115 E Main St - Rts 5 & 20,
   13165, 1845 .... (315)539-3032
Waterville
B&B in Waterville, 211 White St, 13480
Westfield
The William Seward Inn, RD 2, S Portage Rd, Rt 394, 14787,
   1821 .... (716)326-4151
Westfield House, E Main Rd, PO Box 505, 14787, 1840. (716)326-6262
Westhampton Beach
1880 Seafield House, 2 Seafield Lane, 11978, 1880 .... (516)288-1559
Windham
Albergo Allegria B&B, Rt 296, 12496, 1876 .... (518)734-5560

North Carolina

Asheville
Cedar Crest Victorian Inn, 674 Biltmore Ave, 28803,
   1890 .... (704)252-1389
Cornerstone Inn, 230 Pearson Dr, 28801 .... (704)253-5644
Flint Street Inn, 100 & 116 Flint St, 28801, 1915 .... (704)253-6723
Heritage Hill, 64 Linden Ave, 28801, 1909 .... (704)254-9336
Ray House, 83 Hillside St, 28801, 1891 .... (704)252-0106
Reed House B&B, 119 Dodge St, 28803, 1892 .... (704)274-1604
Richmond Hill Inn, 87 Richmond Hill Dr, 28806, 1889 (919)273-9409
The Grove Park Inn & Country Club, 290 Macon Ave, 28804,
   1913 .... (704)252-2711
The Lion & The Rose, 276 Montford Ave, 28801 .... (704)255-7673
The Old Reynolds Mansion, 100 Reynolds Hgts, 28804,
   1855 .... (704)254-0496
Ashville
Blake House Inn, 150 Royal Pines Dr, 28704 .... (704)684-1847
Balsam
Balsam Lodge, Box 279, Valley Dr, 28707, 1906 .... (704)456-6528
Banner Elk
Archers Inn, Rt 2 Box 56-a, 28604 .... (704)898-9004
Bat Cave
Old Mill Inn, PO Box 252, Hwy 64/74, 28710 .... (701)625-4256
Stonehearth Inn, Rte 74, PO Box 9, 28710, 1940 .... (704)625-9990
Bath
Bath Guest House, S Main St, 27808
Beaufort
Belford House B&B, 129 Craven St, 28516 .... (919)728-6031
Captains' Quarters, Bed & Biscuit, 315 Ann St, 28516,
   1902.. (919)728-7711
Cedars at Beaufort, 305 Front St, 28516, 1768 .... (919)728-7036
Langdon House, 135 Craven St, 28516, 1733 .... (919)728-5499
The Cedars at Beaufort, 305 Front St, 28516, 1768 .... (919)728-7036
The Shotgun House, 406 Ann St, Box 833, 28516
Black Mountain
Red Rocker Inn, 3888 40 Way S., 28711, 1894
The Blackberry Inn, Box 965, 28711, 1930 .... (704)669-8303
Blowing Rock
Gideon Ridge Inn, PO Box 1929, 28605 .... (704)295-3644
Maple Lodge, PO Box 66, Sunset Drive, 28605 .... (704)295-3331

North Carolina (Continued)

Meadowbrook Inn, Box 2005, 28605 ....(704)295-9341
Ragged Garden B&B, Box 1927, 28605, 1900 ....(704)295-9703
Sunshine Inn, Box 528, 28605
Brevard
Pines Country Inn, 719 Hart Rd, 28768, 1883 ....(704)877-3131
Red House Inn, 412 W Probart St, 28712, 1851 ....(704)884-9349
The Inn At Brevard, 410 E Main St, 28712, 1890 ....(704)884-2105
Womble Inn, 301 W Main St, 28712 ....(704)884-4770
Bryson City
Folkestone Inn, 767 W Deep Creek Rd, 28713, 1926 ......(704)488-2730
Fryemont Inn, PO Box 459, 28713 ....(704)488-2159
Randolph House, PO Box 816, 28713, 1937 ....(704)488-3472
Burnsville
Nu-Wray Inn, PO Box 156, 28714, 1830 ....(704)682-2329
Chapel Hill
Fearrington House, Fearrington Village Ctr, 27312 ....(919)542-2121
The Inn At Bingham School, PO Box 267, 27514, 1791
Charleston
Olde Towne Inn, 184 Ashley Ave, 29403 ....(803)723-8572
Charlotte
Hampton Manor, 3327 Carmel Rd, 28211
Inn On Providence, 6700 Providence Rd, 28105 ....(704)366-6700
Morehead Inn, 1122 E. Morehead St, 28204
Overcarsh House, 326 W Eighth St, 28202 ....(704)334-8477
The Homeplace B&B, 5901 Sardis Rd, 28226, 1902 ....(704)365-1936
Chimney Rock
Gingerbread Inn, PO Box 187, Hwy 74, 28720 ....(704)625-4038
Clemmons
Tanglewood Manor, PO Box 1040, 27012, 1859 ....(919)766-0591
Clinton
The Shield House, 216 Sampson St, 28328 ....(919)592-2634
Dillsboro
Jarrett House, PO Box 219, 28725, 1884 ....(704)586-9964
Squire Watkins Inn, Haywood Road, Box 430, 28725 ......(704)586-5244
Durham
Arrowhead Inn, 106 Mason Rd, 27712, 1775 ....(919)477-8430
Edenton
Mulberry Hill, R7 D4, 27923 ....(919)482-4175
The Lords Proprietors' Inn, 300 N Broad St, 27932,
    1787 ....(919)482-3641
Trestle House Inn, Rt 4 Box 370, 27932 ....(919)482-2282
Flat Rock
Woodfield Inn, PO Box 98, 28731, 1852 ....(704)693-6016
Franklin
Buttonwood Inn, 190 Georgia Road, 28734 ....(704)369-8985
Franklin Terrace, 67 Harrison Ave, 28734, 1880 ....(704)524-7907
Poor Richards Summit Inn, PO Box 511, 28734, 1898 ......(704)524-2006
Glendale Springs
Glendale Springs Inn, 28629 ....(919)982-2102
Mountain View Lodge, PO Box 90, 28629 ....(919)982-2233
Glenville
Mountain High, Big Ridge Rd, 28736 ....(704)743-3094
Graham
Leftwich House, 215 E Harden St, 27253 ....(919)226-5978
Greensboro
College Hill B&B, 922 Carr St, 27403, 1901 ....(919)274-6829
Greenwood B&B, 205 N Park Dr, 27401, 1905 ....(919)274-6350
Julia Parks, Box 9753, 27408
Powhatan Condominiums, 906 W Market St, 27401, 1925
The Erwin & Clark House, 214 S Mendenhall St, 27401, 1900
Henderson
La Grange Plantation Inn, Rt 3 Box 610, 27536, 1770 ....(919)438-2421
Hendersonville
Claddagh Inn at Hendersonville, 755 N Main St, 28739,
    1900 ....(704)697-7778
Echo Mountain Inn, 2849 Laurel Park Hwy, 28739, 1896
The Waverly Inn, 783 N Main St, 28739, 1890 ....(704)693-9193
Hertford
Gingerbread Inn, 103 S Church St, 27944, 1904 ....(919)426-5809

Hickory
The Hickory B&B, 464 7th St Sw, 28602, 1908 ....(704)324-0548
High Point
Premier B&B Inn, 1001 Johnson St, 27262, 1915
Highlands
Colonial Pines Inn, Hickory St, PO Box 2309, 28741,
    1930 ....(704)526-2060
Highlands Inn, PO Box 1030, 28741, 1880 ....(704)526-9380
Old Edwards Inn, 4th & Main St, 28741, 1870 ....(704)526-5036
Hillsborough
Colonial Inn, 153 W King St, 27278, 1759 ....(919)732-2461
Inn At Teardrop, West King St, 27278, 1888 ....(919)732-1120
Kill Devil Hills
Ye Olde Cherokee Inn, 500 N Virginia Dare Trail, 27948,
    1940 ....(919)441-6127
Lake Junaluska
Brookside Lodge, 7 Lakeshore Dr, 28745 ....(704)456-8897
Providence Lodge, 1 Atkins Loop, 28745 ....(704)456-6486
Sunset Inn, 21 N. Lakeshore Dr, 28745 ....(704)456-6114
Lake Lure
Lodge On Lake Lure, Rt 1 Box 529, 28746 ....(704)625-2789
Lake Toxaway
Greystone Inn, Greystone Lane, 28747 ....(704)966-4700
Maggie Valley
Cataloochee Ranch, Rt 1 Box 500, 28751 ....(704)926-1401
Mars Hill
Baird House, 121 S Main St, 28754 ....(704)689-5722
Marshall
Marshall House, Box 606, 28753, 1902 ....(704)649-2999
Milton
Woodside Inn, Box 197, 28305, 1838
Morehead
Morehead Manor, 107 North 10th Street, 28557, 1909
Mount Airy
Pine Ridge Inn, 2893 W Pine St, 27030, 1949 ....(919)789-5034
Nags Head
Carefree Cottages, Rt 1 Box 748, 27959 ....(919)441-5340
Colony Beach Inn, PO Box 87, 27959 ....(919)441-3666
New Bern
Aerie, an Inn of Distinction, 509 Pollock St, 28560 ....(919)636-5553
Harmony House Inn, 215 Pollock St, 28560, 1850 ....(919)636-3810
King's Arms Inn, 217 Pollock St, 28560, 1848 ....(919)638-4409
New Berne House, 709 Broad St, 28560, 1921 ....(919)636-2250
Ocracoke
Berkley Country Inn, Box 220, 27960
Boyette House, PO Box 39, 27960 ....(919)928-4261
Island Inn, Box 9, 27960, 1901
Ships Timbers B&B, Box 10, 27960, 1902 ....(919)928-6141
The Beach House, Box 443, 27960
Oriental
The Tar Heel Inn, 205 Church Street, 28571 ....(818)325-2592
Pilot Mountain
Pilot Knob-A B&B Inn, PO Box 1280, 27041, 1863
Pittsboro
Fearrington House, Fearrington Village Ctr, 27312,
    1927 ....(919)542-2121
Raleigh
The Oakwood Inn, 411 N Bloodworth St, 27604, 1871 ..(919)832-9712
Robbinsville
Blue Boar Lodge, 200 Santeetlah Rd, 28771 ....(704)479-8126
Snowbird Mountain Lodge, 275 Santeetlah Rd, 28771 .....(704)479-3433
Salisbury
Rowan Oak House, 208 S.fulton St, 28144, 1902 ....(704)633-2086
Saluda
Orchard Inn, PO Box 725, 28773, 1900 ....(704)749-5471
Smithfield
Eli Olive's, 3719 US 70 W, 27577
Southern Pines
Jefferson Inn, 150 W New Hampshire Ave, 28387, 1902
Southport
Dosher Plantation House B&B, Rt 5 Box 100, 28461,
    1927 ....(917)457-5554

Spruce Pine
Fairway Inn, 110 Henry Lane, 28777 .... (704)765-4917
The Richmond Inn, 101 Pine Ave, 28777, 1939 .... (704)765-6993
Tarboro
Little Warren, 304 E Park Ave, 27886, 1913 .... (919)823-1314
Tryon
Melrose Inn, 211 Melrose, 28782, 1880
Mill Farm Inn, PO Box 1251, 28782 .... (704)859-6992
Pine Crest Inn, PO Box 1030, 200 Pine Crest Ln., 28982.. (704)859-9135
Stone Hedge Inn, Howard Gap Road, PO Box 366, 28782,
   1932 .... (704)859-9114
Valle Crucis
Mast Farm Inn, PO Box 704, 28691 .... (704)963-5857
Wanchese
C.W. Pugh's B&B, PO Box 427, 27981 .... (919)473-5466
Warsaw
The Squire's Vintage Inn, Rt 2 Box 130r, 28398 .... (919)473-5466
Washington
Pamlico House, 400 E Main St, 27889, 1906 .... (919)946-7184
Waynesville
Hallcrest Inn, 299 Halltop Rd, 28786, 1880 .... (704)456-6457
Haywood Street Inn, 409 Haywood St, 28786
Heath Lodge, 900 Donlan Rd, 28786 .... (704)456-3333
Piedmont Inn, 630 Eagle's Nest Rd, 28786
The Palmer House B&B, 108 Pigeon St, 28786, 1885 ..... (704)456-7521
The Swag, Rt 2 Box 280-a, 28786, 1971 .... (704)926-0430
Weaverville
Dry Ridge Inn, 26 Brown St, 28787, 1849 .... (704)658-3899
Wilmington
Anderson Guest House, 520 Orange St, 28401, 1851 ..... (919)343-8128
Five Star Guest House, 14 N 7th St, 28401 .... (919)763-7581
Grayston Guesthouse, 100 S Third St, 28401
Worth House, 412 S Third St, 28401 .... (919)762-8562
Wilson
Pilgrims Rest, 600 W Nash St, 27893, 1858 .... (919)243-4447
Winston-salem
Brookstown Inn B&B, 200 Brookstown Ave, 27101, 1837
Colonel Ludlow Inn, Summit & W 5th, 27101, 1887 ..... (919)777-1887

North Dakota

Grassy Butte
Long X Trail Ranch, Box 157, 58634 .... (701)842-2128
Medora
The Rough Riders, 58645, 1865 .... (701)623-4444

Ohio

Akron
Portage House, 601 Copley Rd, 44320, 1917 .... (216)535-9236
Archbold
Murbach House, 504 N Defiance St, 43502, 1800 .... (419)445-5195
Ashtabula
Michael Cahill B&B, PO Box 3024, 1106 Walnut Blvd, 44004, 1887
Bellville
Frederick Fitting House, 72 Fitting Ave, 44813 .... (419)886-4283
Belmont
Victorian B&B, 121 West Main St, Box 233, 43718, 1850 .. (614)484-4872
Chillicothe
Chillicothe B&B, 202 S Paint St, 45601, 1867 .... (614)772-6848
Vanmeter B&B, 178 Church St, 45601, 1830 .... (614)774-3510
Cleveland
Private Lodging, PO Box 18590, 44118, 1920 .... (216)321-3213
Tudor House, PO Box 18590, 44118 .... (216)321-3213
Columbus
Slavka's B&B, 180 Reinhard Ave, 43206, 1888 .... (614)443-6076
Danville
The White Oak Inn, 29683 Walhonding Rd, 43014,
   1915 .... (614)599-6107
Dellroy
Litt's Country Inn, 2196 Lodge Rd, Box 41, 44620, 1887 . (216)735-2035

Pleasant Journey Inn, 4247 Roswell Rd SW, 44620 .... (216)735-2987
Granville
Buxton Inn, 313 E Broadway, 43023, 1812 .... (614)587-0001
Granville Inn, 314 E Broadway, 43023, 1924 .... (614)587-3333
Kelleys Island
Cricket Lodge, Kelleys Island, Lakeshore Dr Box 323, 43438,
   1850 .... (419)746-2263
Southaven, PO Box 442, 43438 .... (419)746-2784
Sweet Valley Inn, PO Box 733, Division St, 43438, 1892 .. (419)746-2750
The Beatty House, South Shore Dr, PO Box 402, 43438,
   1861 .... (419)746-2379
The Inn On Kelleys Island, Box 11, 43438, 1876 .... (419)746-2258
Kinsman
Hidden Hollow, 9340 Rt 5 NE, 44428 .... (216)876-8686
Lakeville
Quite Country, 14758 Tr 453, 44638 .... (216)378-3882
Lebanon
Golden Lamb, 27 South Broadway, 45036, 1803 .... (513)932-5065
Lexington
The White Fence Inn, 8842 Denman Rd, 44904 .... (419)884-2356
Logan
Bartholomew, 7657 Twp Rd, 234, 43138, 1830 .... (614)385-8363
Loudonville
Blackfork Inn, 303 North Water St, PO Box 149, 44842,
   1865 .... (419)994-3252
Lucas
Pleasant Valley Lodge, Pleasant Valley Rd, Rt 1 Box 522, 44843,
   1898 .... (419)892-2443
Marblehead
Old Stone House Inn, 133 Clemons St, 43440, 1861 .... (419)798-5922
Marietta
House Of Seven Porches, 331 Fifth St, 45750, 1835 .... (614)373-1767
Medina
Oakwood B&B, 226 N Broadway, 44256 .... (216)723-1162
Millersburg
Inn At Honey Run, 6920 Country Rd 203, 44654, 1982.... (216)674-0011
Morrow
Locust Hill, 1659 East US 22-3, 45152 .... (513)899-2749
Mount Vernon
The Russell-Cooper House, 115 E Gambier St, 43050,
   1829 .... (614)397-8638
Oberlin
The Oberlin College Inn, 44074, 1960 .... (216)775-1111
Old Washington
Zane Trace B&B, Main St, PO Box 115, 43768, 1859 .... (614)489-5970
Peebles
The Bayberry Inn, 25675 State Rt 41 N, 45660 .... (513)587-2221
Peninsula
Centennial House, 5995 Center St, 44264, 1876 .... (216)657-2506
Fleder's B&B, 5964 Center St, 44264, 1835 .... (216)657-2284
Poland
Inn at the Green, 500 S Main St, 44514, 1876 .... (216)757-4688
Pomeroy
Holly Hill Inn, 114 Butternut Ave, 45769, 1836 .... (614)992-5657
Port Clinton
Old Island House Inn, Box K, 102 Madison St, 43452, 1886
Put-in-bay
The Vineyard, Box 283, 43456, 1858 .... (419)285-6181
Sagamore Hills
Inn At Brandywine Falls, 8230 Brandywine Rd, 44067,
   1848 .... (216)467-1812
Sandusky
Bogart's Corner B&B, 1403 E Bogart, 44870 .... (419)627-2707
Pipe Creek, 2719 Columbus Ave, 44870, 1885 .... (419)626-2067
Spring Valley
3 B's B&B, 103 Race St, 45370, 1900 .... (513)862-4241
Tipp City
Willowtree Inn, 1900 W State, Rt 571, 45371, 1827 .... (513)667-2957
Toledo
Mansion View, 2035 Collingwood Blvd, 43620, 1887 ..... (419)244-5676

Ohio (Continued)

Waverly
Governor's Lodge, Lake White, 45690 ....(614)947-2266
West Milton
Locust Lane Farm, 5590 Kessler Cowlesville Rd, 45383 ..(513)698-4743
Wooster
The Howey House, 340 N Bever St, 44691, 1851 ....(216)264-8231
Worthington
Worthington Inn, 649 High St, 43085, 1831 ....(614)885-2600
Xenia
Hattle House, 502 N King St, 45385, 1887 ....(513)372-2315
Zoar
Cider Mill, PO Box 441, 44697, 1863.........................(216)874-3133
Cowger House #9, 9 Fourth St, 44697, 1817 ....(216)874-3542
Haven at 4th & Park, PO Box 467, 44697, 1830 ....(216)874-4672
Weaving Haus, C/o Zoar Community Assoc. Box 621, 44697,
  1825 ....(216)874-2646
Zoar Village
Cobbler Shop Inn, Corner of 2nd and Main St, 44697,
  1828 ....(216)874-2600

Oklahoma

Clayton
Clayton Country Inn, Rt 1 Box 8, 74536
Grove
Edgewater B&B, Box 1746, 74344
Guthrie
Harrison House, 124 W Harrison, 73044, 1890 ....(405)282-1000
Stone Lion Inn, 1016 W Warner, 73044
Oklahoma City
Chisolm Springs, 824 Evan Hale Rd, 73127, 1948 ....(405)942-5193
The Grandison, 1841 NW 15th, 73507, 1896..................(405)521-0011

Oregon

Ashland
Ashland's Main Street Inn, 142 W Main St, 97520 ....(503)488-0969
Chanticleer B&B Inn, 120 Gresham St, 97520, 1920 ......(503)482-1919
Coach House Inn, 70 Coolidge St, 97520, 1890 ....(503)482-2257
Cowslip's Belle, 159 N Main St, 97520, 1913 ....(503)488-2901
Edinburgh Lodge B&B, 586 E Main St, 97520, 1908 ....(503)488-1050
Hersey House, 451 N Main St, 97520, 1904..................(503)482-4563
Iris Inn, 59 Manzanita St, 97520, 1905
McCall House, 153 Oak St, 97520, 1883 ....(503)482-9296
Morical House, 688 N Main St, 97520, 1880
Oak Street Station, 239 Oak St, 97520 ....(503)482-1726
Romeo Inn, 295 Idaho St, 97520 ....(503)488-0884
Royal Carter House, 514 Siskiyou Blvd, 97520, 1909 .....(503)482-5623
Scenic View B&B, 467 Scenic Dr, 97520, 1910 ....(503)482-2315
Winchester Inn, 35 S 2nd St, 97520, 1886
Astoria
Franklin Street Station, 1140 Franklin, 97103, 1900 ....(503)325-4314
Rosebriar Inn, 636 14th St, 97103, 1902 ....(503)325-7427
The Collins House, 682 34th St, 97103, 1890 ....(503)325-3292
Brookings
Sea Dreamer Inn, 15167 Mcvay Ln, 97415 ....(503)469-6629
Cloverdale
Sandlake Country Inn, 8505 Galloway Road, 97112,
  1894 ....(503)965-6745
The Hudson House, 37700 Hwy 101 S, 97112 ....(503)472-4814
Coos Bay
Captain's Quarters B&B, PO Box 3231, 97420, 1890 ....(503)888-6895
Corvallis
Madison Inn, 660 SW Madison Ave, 97333 ....(206)757-1274
Depoe Bay
Channel House, PO Box 56, 97341 ....(503)765-2140
Eugene
Campus Cottage, 1136 E 19th Ave, 97403, 1922
Country Garden B&B Inn, 245 Pearl St, 97401, 1909 ....(503)345-7417
House in the Woods, 814 Lorane Hwy, 97405, 1910........(503)343-3234

Florence
The Johnson House, 216 Maple St, PO 1892, 97439, 1892 (503)997-8000
Frenchglen
Frenchglen Hotel, 97736, 1914 ....(503)493-2565
Gardiner
Guest House At Gardiner By The Sea, 401 Front St,
  97441 ....(503)271-4005
Gold Beach
Endicott Gardens, 95768 Jerry's Flat Rd, 97444 ....(503)247-6513
Tu Tu Tun Lodge, 96550 N Bank Rogue, 97444 ....(503)247-6664
Grants Pass
Ahlf House, 762 NW 6th St, 97526, 1902.....................(503)474-1374
Lawnridge House, 1304 NW Lawnridge, 97526, 1909 ....(503)479-5186
Paradise Ranch Inn, 7000 Monument Dr, 97526 ....(503)479-4333
The Washington Inn, 1002 Washington Blvd., 97526,
  1883 ....(503)476-1131
Halfway
Clear Creek Farm B&B, Rt Box 138, 97834 ....(503)742-2238
Hood River
Barkheimer House/Lakecliff Estate, 3820 Westcliff Dr,
  97031 ....(503)386-5918
Columbia Gorge Hotel, 4000 W Cliff Dr, 97031, 1921 ......(503)386-5566
Independence
Davidson House, 887 Monmouth St, 97351 ....(503)838-3280
Out of the Blue B&B, 386 Monmouth St, 97351, 1880 ......(503)838-3636
Jacksonville
Farmhouse B&B, 755 E California St, 97530
Livingston Mansion Inn, 4132 Livingston Road, PO Box 1476,
  97530, 1915 ....(503)899-7107
McCully House Inn, 240 E California, 97530, 1861 ....(503)899-1656
Joseph
Wallowa Lake Lodge, Rt 1 Box 320, 97846, 1923 ....(503)432-4082
Madras
Madras, 343 C Street At Hwy 26, 97741 ....(503)475-2345
McMinnville
Mattey House, 10221 NE Mattey Ln, 97128 ....(503)434-5058
Medford
Under the Greenwood Tree, 3045 Bellinger Lane, 97501,
  1861 ....(503)776-0000
Myrtle Creek
Sonka's Sheep Station Inn, 901 NW Chadwick, 97457 .....(503)863-5168
Newport
Ocean House B&B, 4920 NW Woody Way, 97365 ....(503)265-6158
North Bend
Sherman House B&B, 2380 Sherman Ave, 97459, 1903 ....(503)756-3496
Oakland
Pringle House, Locust & 7th Sts, 97462 ....(503)459-5038
Port Orford
Home by the Sea, PO Box 606, 444 Jackson St, 97465 ......(503)332-2855
Madelaine's, 735 8th Box 913, 97465 ....(503)332-4373
Portland
Corbett House B&B, 7533 SW Corbett, 97219, 1920 ....(503)245-2580
General Hooker's House, 125 SW Hooker, 97201, 1900. (503)222-4435
John Palmer House, 4314 N Mississippi Ave, 97217,
  1890 ....(503)284-5893
Old Portland Estate, 1870 SE Exeter Dr, 97202 ....(503)236-6533
Peninsula Guest House, 2911 N Russet, 97217 ....(503)289-9141
Portland's White House, 1914 NE 22, 97212, 1912 ....(503)287-7131
Salem
Harbison House, 1845 Commercial St, 97302...................(503)581-8118
State House B&B, 2146 State St, 97301, 1920 ....(503)588-1340
Seal Rock
Blackberry Inn, 6575 NW Pacific Coast Hwy, 97376,
  1938 ....(503)563-2259
Seaside
The Boarding House, 208 N Holladay Dr, 97138 ....(503)738-9055
The Gilbert House, 341 Beach Dr, 97138 ....(503)738-9770
Steamboat
Steamboat Inn, 97447 ....(503)496-3495
The Dalles
Bigelow B&B, 606 Washington, 97058 ....(503)298-8239
Williams House Inn, 608 W 6th St, 97058, 1899 ....(503)296-2889

Tillamook
Blue Haven Inn, Box 1034, 97141, 1926 .... (503)842-2265
Yamhill
Flying M Ranch, 23029 NW Flying M Rd, 97148 .... (503)662-3222

Pennsylvania

Airville
Spring House, Muddy Creek Forks, 17302, 1798 .... (717)927-6906
Allentown
Coachaus, 107-111 N 8th St, 18102
Salisbury House, 910 East Emmaus Ave, 18103, 1810 .... (215)791-4225
Annville
Horseshoe Farm, Rt 1 Box 228, 17003
Atglen
Umble Rest, RD 1 Box 79, 19310, 1700 .... (215)593-2274
Avondale
Springs Valley Inn, RD 1 Box 532, 19311 .... (215)268-2597
Beach Lake
Beach Lake Hotel, PO Box 144, 18405, 1850 .... (717)729-8239
East Shore House B&B, Box 12, 18405
Bear Creek
Bischwind, One Coach Rd, 18602, 1887 .... (717)472-3820
Bedford
Jean Bonnet Tavern, Rt 2 Box 188, 15522
Bendersville
Historic Paul Sourss Plantation House, PO Box 238, 17306,
   1802 .... (717)677-6688
Benton
Grandmaws, Rt 3 Box 239, 17814
Berlin
Ogline's B&B, 1001 E Main St, 15530
Bernville
Sunday's Mill Farm, Rt 2 Box 419, 19506
Bird-in-hand
Greystone Motor Lodge, 2658 Old Philadelphia Pike, 17505,
   1883 .... (717)393-4233
Bloomsburg
The Inn at Turkey Hill, 991 Central Rd, 17815, 1839 ..... (717)387-1500
Blue Ridge Summit
The Greystone, 17214
Boiling Springs
The Garmanhaus, 217 Front St, 17007, 1860 .... (717)258-3980
Canadensis
Brookview Manor B&B Inn, Rt 1 Box 365, 18325, 1911. (717)595-2541
Dreamy Acres, PO Box 7, Seese Hill Rd & Rt 44, 18325,
   1888 .... (717)595-7115
Laurel Grove, Pocono Vacationland, 18325 .... (717)595-7262
Overlook Inn, Dutch Hill Rd, 18325
Pine Knob, Rt 447, 18325 .... (717)595-2532
Pump House Inn, Sky Top Rd, 18325
Cedar Run
Cedar Run Inn, Rt 414, 17727 .... (717)353-6241
Central City
Noah's Ark, Rt 1 Box 425, 15926
Chadds Ford
Hill House, Creek Rd, 19317
Christiana
Winding Glen Farm, PO Box 160, 17509, 1770 .... (215)593-5535
Churchtown
Churchtown Inn, Rt 23, 17555, 1735 .... (215)445-7794
Clark
Tara, Box 475, 3665 Valley View, 16113
Cooksburg
Clarion River Lodge, River Rd, 16217, 1962 .... (814)744-8171
Gateway Lodge & Cabins, Rt 36 PO Box 125, 16217,
   1934 .... (814)744-8017
Cowansville
Garrott's B&B, RD 1 Box 73, 16218, 1888 .... (412)545-2432

Cranberry Township
Cranberry B&B, Box 1009, 16033 .... (412)776-1198
Cresco
La Anna Guest House, RD 2 Box 1051, 18326 .... (717)676-4225
Danville
The Pine Barn Inn, 1 Pine Barn Place, 17821, 1860 .... (717)275-2071
Delaware Water Gap
Mountain House, Mountain Rd, 18327, 1870 .... (717)424-2254
Downington
Duck Hill Farm, Rt 1, 19335
Doylestown
Doylestown Inn, 18 W State St, 18901 .... (215)345-6610
Doylestown, Bucks Co
The Inn at Fordhook Farm, 105 New Britain Rd, 18901,
   1760 .... (215)345-1766
Dushore
Cherry Mills Lodge, PO 6525, 19610 .... (717)928-8978
Eagles Mere
Eagles Mere Inn, PO Box 356, 17731
Shady Lane Lodge, Allegheny Av., 17731
East Berlin
Bechtel Mansion Inn, 400 West King St, 17316, 1897 .... (717)259-7760
East Stroudsburg
Inn at Meadowbrook, RD 7 Box 7651, 18301 .... (717)629-0296
Elm
Elm Country Inn, Box 37, 17521, 1860 .... (717)664-3623
Elverson
Rocky Side Farm, RD 1, 19520, 1919 .... (215)286-5362
Ephrata
Covered Bridge Inn, 990 Rettew Mill Rd, 17522, 1814 .. (717)733-1592
Gerhart House B&B, 287 Duke St, 17522, 1926 .... (717)733-0263
Guesthouse at Doneckers, 318-324 N State St, 17522 .... (717)733-8696
The Smithton Inn, 900 W Main St, 17522, 1763 .... (717)733-6094
Erie
Royal Acre Retreat, 5131 Lancaster Rd, 16506, 1900 .... (814)838-7928
Erwinna
Evermay-on-the-Delaware, River Rd, 18920 .... (215)294-9100
Golden Pheasant Inn, River Rd, 18920, 1857 .... (215)294-9595
Isaac Stover House, PO Box 68, 18920, 1837 .... (215)294-8044
Everett
Newry Manor, Rt 1 Box 475, 15537, 1805 .... (814)623-1250
Exton
Duling Kurtz House, 146 S. Whitford Rd, 19341
Fairfield
Historic Fairfield Inn, Box 96, 17320
Fogelsville
Glasbern, RD 1 Box 250, 18051-9743 .... (215)285-4723
Fort Washington
Quaker Manor House, 1165 Pinetown Rd, 19034
Freeport
Hobby House B&B, 174 Srader Grove Rd, 16229
Gardners
Goose Chase, 200 Blueberry Rd, 17324, 1762 .... (717)528-8877
Gettysburg
Abraham Spangler Inn, 264 Baltimore St, 17325, 1870 ..... (717)337-3997
Gettystown Inn, 89 Steinwehr Ave, 17325
Keystone Inn B&B, 231 Hanover St, 17325, 1913 .... (717)337-3888
Swinn's Lodging, 31 E Lincoln Ave, 17325
The Brafferton Inn, 44 York St, 17325, 1786 .... (717)337-3423
The Doubleday Inn, 104 Doubleday Ave, 17325, 1929 .. (717)334-9119
The Old Appleford Inn, 218 Carlisle St, 17325
Twin Elms, 228 Buford Ave, 17325 .... (717)334-4520
Glen Mills
Sweetwater Farm, PO Box 86, Sweetwater Rd, 19342,
   1758 .... (215)459-4711
Gordonville
The Osceola Mill House, 313 Osceola Mill Rd, 17529,
   1766 .... (717)768-3758
Hallstead
Log Cabin B&B, Rt 11 Box 393, 18822
The Corner Inn, Box 777, 18822

Pennsylvania (Continued)

Hanover
Beechmont Inn, 315 Broadway, 17331, 1834 .... (717)632-3013
Country View Acres, 676 Beaver Creek Road, 17331 .... (717)637-8992
Hawley
Academy Street B&B, 528 Academy St, 18428, 1865 .... (717)226-3430
Settlers Inn, 4 Main Ave, 18428
Hershey
Gibson's B&B, 141 W Caracas Ave, 17033, 1938 .... (717)534-1035
Hesston
Aunt Susie's Country Vacations, Rt 1 Box 225, 16647
Hickory
Shady Elms Farm B&B, Rt 1 Box 188, 15340
Holicong
Ash Mill Farm, PO Box 202, 18928, 1800 .... (215)794-5373
Barley Sheaf Farm, Rt 202 Box 10, 18928, 1740 .... (215)794-5104
Hollidaysburg
Brun Run Estate, 132 Logan Blvd., 16648
Honesdale
Hotel Wayne, 1202 Main St, 18431 .... (717)253-3290
Jamestown
Das Tannen-Lied, Rt 1, 16134, 1872
Jersey Shore
Ye Olde Library B&B, 310 S Main St, 17740
Jim Thorpe
Harry Packer Mansion, Packer Hill, 18229, 1874 .... (717)325-8566
Kane
Kane Manor Country Inn, 230 Clay St, 16735, 1896 .... (814)837-6522
Kennet Square
Longwood Inn, 815 E Baltimore Pike, 19348 .... (215)444-3515
Kennett Square
Buttonwood Farm, 231 Pemberton Rd, 19348, 1804 .... (215)444-0278
Meadow Spring Farm, 201 E St Rd, 19348, 1836 .... (215)444-3903
Kintnersville
Bucksville House, Rt 2 Box 146, 18930
Kinzer
Bethania Farm, PO Box 228, 17535 .... (717)442-4939
Groff Tourist Farm, RD 1 Box 36, 17353
Kunkletown
The Koller's, Rt 2 Box 400, 18058
Lahaska
Bucks County Inn, Street Rd, Peddlers Village, 18931,
    1860 .... (215)794-7055
Golden Plough Inn, Rt 263-Rt 202, 18913, 1750 .... (215)794-7438
The Buttonwood Inn, Rt 202, 18931, 1792 .... (215)794-7438
Lampeter
Walkabout Inn, 837 Village Rd, 17537 .... (717)464-0707
Lancaster
Buena Kotte B&B, 2020 Marietta Ave, 17603
Hollinger House, 2336 Hollinger Rd, 17602, 1876 .... (717)464-3050
Witmer's Tavern - Historic 1725 Inn, 2014 Old Philadelphia Pike,
    17602, 1725 .... (717)299-5305
Langhorne
Gertrude Garber, 1768 Highland Ave, 19047
The Waln House, 1242 Brownsville Rd, 19047, 1682 .... (215)757-2921
Laughlintown
Ligonier Country Inn, PO Box 46 Rt 30 E, 15655
Leesport
The Loom Room, RD 1 PO Box 1420, 19533, 1812 .... (215)926-3217
Leola
Turtle Hill Road B&B, Rt 1, 111 Turtle Hill Rd, 17540
Lewisburg
Pineapple Inn, 439 Market St, 17837
Ligonier
Grant House B&B, 244 W Church St, 15658, 1875 .... (412)238-5135
Lititz
General Sutter Inn, 14 E Main St, 17543, 1764 .... (717)626-2115
The Alden House, 62 E Main St, 17543, 1850 .... (717)627-3363
Lumberville
1740 House, River Rd, 18933, 1740 .... (215)297-5661

Black Bass Hotel, River Rd, 18933
Malvern
The Great Valley House, 110 Swedesford Rd RD 3,
    19355 .... (215)644-6759
Manheim
Herr Farmhouse Inn, Rt 7 Box 587, 17545, 1738 .... (717)653-9852
Maytown
Three Center Square Inn, PO Box 428, 17550, 1768 .... (717)653-4338
Mcelhatten
Restless Oak B&B, Box 241, 17748
Mcknightstown
New Salem House, 275 Old Rt 30, PO Box 24, 17343,
    1875 .... (717)337-3520
Mercer
Magoffin Guest House B&B, 129 S Pitt St, 16137, 1884 (412)662-4611
Stranahan House B&B, 117 E Market St, 16137
Mercerburg
The Mercerburg Inn, 405 S Main St, 17236 .... (717)328-5231
Mertztown
Blair Creek Inn & Lodging, 19539 .... (215)682-6700
Longswamp B&B, RD 2 PO Box 26, 19539, 1789 .... (215)682-6197
Milfor
The Vines, 107 E Ann St, 18337, 1864 .... (717)296-6775
Milford
Black Walnut Inn, 509 Fire Tower Rd, 18337
Cliff Park Inn, Cliff Park Rd, 18337 .... (717)296-6491
Millersville
Walnut Hill B&B, Rt 1 Box 113, 17551
Montoursville
The Carriage House At Stonegate, RD 1 Box 11A, 17754,
    1830 .... (717)433-4340
Mount Bethel
Elvern Country Lodge, Box 177, 18343 .... (215)588-7922
Mount Gretna
Mt Gretna Inn, Kaufman & Pine, 17064, 1921 .... (717)964-3234
Mount Joy
Cameron Estate Inn, RD 1 Box 305, 17552 .... (717)653-1773
Rocky Acre Farm, RD 3, 17552 .... (717)653-4449
Muncy
The Bodine House B&B, 307 S Main St, 17756
Myerstown
Tulpehocken Manor Inn, 650 W Lincoln Ave, 17067
Narvon
The Foreman House B&B, RD 3 Box 161A, 17555, 1919 (215)445-6713
New Albany
Waltman's B&B, Rt 1 Box 87, 18833
New Hope
Backstreet Inn, 144 Old York Rd, 18939, 1750 .... (215)862-9571
Centre Bridge Inn, Rts. 32 & 263, 18938
Hotel Du Village, N River Rd, 18938 .... (215)862-9911
Inn At Phillips Mill, N River Rd, 18938 .... (215)862-2984
Logan Inn, 10 W Ferry St, 18938
Pineapple Hill, 1324 River Rd, 18938, 1800
Whitehall Inn, Pineville Rd, RD 2 Box 250, 18938, 1794 .. (215)598-7945
Newfoundland
White Cloud Sylvan Retreat, RD 1 Box 215, 18445
North East
Windward Inn, 51 Freeport Rd, 16428
North Wales
Joseph Ambler Inn, 1005 Horsham Rd, 19454, 1734 .... (215)362-7500
Orbisonia
Salvino's Guest House, PO Box 116, 17243 .... (814)447-5616
Orrtanna
Hickory Bridge Farm, 96 Hickory Bridge Rd, 17353,
    1750 .... (717)642-5261
Paradis
The Rose And Crown, 44 Frogtown Rd, 17562, 1760 .... (717)768-7684
Paradise
Maple Lane Farm, 505 Paradise Ln., 17562
Neffdale Farm, 604 Strasburg Rd, 17562 .... (717)687-7837
Rayba Acres Farm, 183 Black Horse Rd, 17562 .... (717)687-6729

Peach Bottom
Lofty Acres, RD 1 Box 331, 17563, 1788 ....(717)548-3052
Pleasant Grove Farm, Rt 1 Box 132, 17563

Perkasie
The Benfield Mill #302, 624 E Walnut St, 18944

Philadelphia
La Reserve, 1804 Pine St, 19103, 1836..........................(215)735-0582
Society Hill Hotel, 301 Chestnut St, 19106, 1830 ....(215)925-1919
The Independence Park Inn, 235 Chestnut St, 19106 ....(215)922-4443

Pittsburgh
The Priory, 614 Pressley St, 15212, 1888 ....(412)231-3338

Plumsteadville
Plumsteadville Inn, Box 40, 18949..................................(215)766-7500

Point Pleasant
Inn Of Innisfree, Box 108, 18950
Tattersall Inn, PO Box 569, 18950

Pottstown
Coventry Forge Inn, RD 2, 19464
Fairway Farm B&B, Vaughn Rd, 19464, 1734 ....(215)326-1315

Quakertown
Sign Of Sorrel Horse, RD 3, 18951

Reading
El Shaddai, 229 Madison Ave, Hyde Villa, 19605 ....(215)929-1341

Red Lion
Red Lion B&B, 101 S Franklin St, 17356, 1920 ....(717)244-4739

Ridgway
Bogert House, 140 Main St, 15853
The Bogert House, 140 Main St, 15853

Riegelsville
Riegelsville Hotel, 10-12 Delaware Rd, 18077

Scenery Hill
Century Inn, Rt 40, 15360

Schellsburg
Millstone Inn, PO Box 279, 15559, 1922 ....(814)733-4864

Scottdale
Pine Wood Acre, Rt 1 Box 278, 15683-9567

Selinsgrove
The Blue Lion Inn, 350 S Market St, 17870

Shartlesville
Haag's Hotel, Main St, 19554

Shippensburg
Field & Pine B&B, RD 5 Box 161, 17257, 1790..................(717)776-7179

Smoketown
Smoketown Village Tourist Home, 2495 Old Phila. Pike, 17576

Solebury
Rambouillet at Hollyhedge Estate, Box 213, 6987 Upper York Rd,
18963 ....(215)862-3136

South Sterling
The French Manor Inn, PO Box 39, 18460, 1932................(717)676-3244

Spring House
Charles Bauerlein, Box 369, 19477

Starlight
Inn At Starlight Lake, 18461, 1909 ....(717)798-2519

Strasburg
Limestone Inn B&B, 33 E Main St, 17579, 1786 ....(717)687-8392
Siloan, Village Rd Box 82, 17579
Strasburg Village Inn, 1 W Main St, 17579
The Decoy, 958 Eisenberger Rd, 17579 ....(717)687-8585

Sumneytown
Kaufman House, Box 183, Rt 63, 18084, 1850 ....(215)234-4181

Thompson
Jefferson Inn, Rt 2 Box 36, 18465

Thornton
Pace One Restaurant and Country Inn, Thornton Rd, 19373,
1740 ....(215)459-9784

Towanda
Victorian Guest House, 118 York Ave, 18848

Tyler Hill
Tyler Hill B&B, Rt 371, PO Box 62, 18469, 1847 ....(717)224-6418

Upper Black Eddy
Bridgeton House, PO Box 167, 18972

Tara, 1 Bridgeton Hill, 18972
Upper Black Eddy Inn, Rt 32 River Rd, 18972

Valley Forge
B&B of Valley Forge, PO Box 562, 19481, 1692..........(215)783-7838

Warren
Bennett's B&B, 1700 Pennsylvania Ave E, 16365...............(814)723-7358
Willows, 40 Kinzua Rd, 16365

Washington Crossing
Woodhill Farms Inn, 130 Glenwood Dr, 18977

Waterford
Altheim B&B, Box 2081, 104 Walnut St, 16441

Waterville
The Point House, Church St, 17776, 1800 ....(717)299-5305

Wellsboro
Jesse Robinson Manor, 141 Main St, 16901

West Chester
Crooked Winsor, 409 S. Church St, 19382
Quarry House, RD 5, Street Rd, 19382, 1884.......................(215)793-1725
The Barn, 1131 Grove Rd, 19380, 1800................................(215)436-4544

Wexford
The Coreys, 2522 Wexford Run Rd, 15090

Williamsport
Reighard House, 1323 E Third St, 17701

Willow Street
Apple Bin Inn, 2835 Willow St Pike, 17584 ....(717)464-5881
Green Gables B&B, 2532 Willow St Pike, 17584

Woodward
Woodward Inn, Box 177, 16882

Wrightsville
Roundtop B&B, RD #2, Box 258, 17368, 1880 ....(717)252-3169

Wycombe
Wycombe Inn, PO Box 204, 18980

York
Fairhaven, RD 12 Box 445, 17406
Inn At Mundis Mill, Rt 1 Box 15, Mundis Race Rd, 17402

Rhode Island

Block Island
1661 Inn, PO Box 1, 02807, 1661 ....(401)466-2421
Blue Dory Inn, Dodge St, 02807 ....(401)466-2254
Hotel Manisses, PO Box 1, 02807, 1872 ....(401)466-2836
New Shoreham House, PO Box 356, Water St, 02807,
1890...(401)466-2651
Seacrest Inn, 207 High St, 02807 ....(401)466-2882
Sheffield House, PO Box 836, 02807, 1886 ....(401)466-2494
The Inn At Old Harbour, Water St, Box 994, 02807,
1882...(401)466-2212
The White House, Box 447, 02807 ....(401)466-2653
Willow Grove, Corn Neck Rd PO Box 156, 02807, 1778 ..(401)466-2896

Bristol
The Joseph Reynolds House, 956 Hope St, PO Box 5, 02809,
1693...(401)254-0230

Charlestown
General Stanton Inn, Rt 1 Box 222, 02813 ....(401)364-8888

Jamestown
Bay Voyage Inn, 02835 ....(401)423-0540
Calico Cat Guest House, 14 Union St, 02835, 1860.........(401)423-2641

Middletown
Stone Towers, 152 Tuckerman Ave, 02840 ....(401)846-3227

Narragansett
Four Gables, 12 S. Pier Rd, 02882, 1898 ....(401)789-6948
Ilverthorpe Cottage, 41 Robinson St, 02882, 1896 ....(401)789-2392
Louis Sherry Cottage, 59 Gibson Ave, 02882 ....(401)783-8626
Mon Reve, 41 Gibson Ave, 02882, 1890 ....(401)783-2846
Murphy's B&B, 43 S Pier Rd, 02882.....................................(401)789-1824
Narragansett Pier Inn, 7 Prospect Ave, 02882 ....(401)783-8090
Richards' Guest House, 104 Robinson St, 02882 ....(401)789-7746
Sea Gull Guest House, 50 Narragansett Ave, 02882,
1906 ....(401)783-4636
Starr Cottage, 68 Caswell St, 02882, 1883 ....(401)783-2411
Summer House Inn, 87 Narragansett Ave, 02882 ....(401)783-0123
The House Of Snee, 191 Ocean Rd, 02882, 1888 ....(401)783-9494

Rhode Island (Continued)

Newport

Aboard Commander's Quarters, 54 Dixon St, 02840, 1885 ....(401)849-8393
Admiral Benbow Inn, 93 Pelham St, 02840, 1855 ....(401)846-4256
Admiral Farragut Inn, 8 Fair St, 02840, 1702 ....(401)849-0006
Bellevue House, 14 Catherine St, 02840, 1825 ....(401)847-1355
Brinley Victorian Inn, 23 Brinley St, 02840, 1870 ....(401)849-7645
Cliff View Guest House, 4 Cliff Terrace, 02840, 1871 ....(401)846-0885
Cliff Walk Manor, 82 Memorial Blvd, 02840, 1855 ......(401)847-1300
Cliffside Inn, 2 Seaview Ave, 02840 ....(401)847-1811
Covell Guest House, 43 Farewell St, 02840, 1810 ....(401)847-8872
Dennis Guest House, 59 Washington St, 02840
Easton's Inn On The Beach, 30 Wave Ave, 02840 ....(401)846-0310
Ellery Park House, 44 Farewell St, 02840, 1900 ....(401)847-6320
Harborside Inn, Christie's Landing, 02840 ....(401)846-6600
Inn At Castle Hill, Ocean Dr, 02840, 1874 ....(401)849-3800
Inn of Jonathan Bowen, 29 Pelham St, 02840, 1804 ......(401)846-3324
Inntowne, 6 Mary St, 02840 ....(401)846-9200
Jail House Inn, 13 Marlborough St, 02840, 1772 ....(401)847-4638
Melville House, 39 Clarke St, 02840, 1750 ....(401)847-0640
Merritt House Guest, 57 2nd St, 02840 ....(401)847-4289
Moulton-Weaver House, 4 Training Station Rd, 02840, 1805 ....(401)847-0133
Oceancliff, Ocean Dr, 02840 ....(401)847-7777
Pilgrim House, 123 Spring St, 02840, 1900 ....(401)846-0040
Queen Anne Inn, 16 Clarke St, 02840, 1890 ....(401)846-5676
Queen Anne Inn, 16 Clarke St, 02840 ....(401)846-5676
Spring Street Inn, 353 Spring St, 02840 ....(401)847-4767
Sunnyside Mansion, 25 Old Beach Rd, 02840, 1886 ....(401)849-3114
The Admiral Fitzroy, 398 Thames Street, 02840, 1865 ....(401)847-4459
The Brinley Victorian Inn, 23 Brinley St, 02840, 1850 ....(401)849-7645
The Old Dennis House, 59 Washington St, 02840, 1740 (401)846-1324
The Pilgrim House, 123 Spring St, 02846, 1900 ....(401)846-0040
The Thames Street Inn, 400 Thames St, 02840, 1865 ......(401)847-4459
The Victorian Ladies, 63 Memorialblvd, 02840, 1899 ......(401)849-9960
The Wallett House, 91 Second St, 02840, 1930 ....(401)849-5177
Wayside, Bellevue Ave, 02840, 1876
William Fludder House, 30 Bellevue Ave, 02840 ....(401)849-4220
Willows of Newport, 8-10 Willow St, 02840 ....(401)846-5486
Yankee Peddler Inn, 113 Touro St, 02840, 1830 ....(401)846-1323
Yellow Cottage, 82 Gibbs Ave, 02840, 1900 ....(401)847-6568

Portsmouth

Twin Spruce Tourist Houme, 515 Turnpike Ave, 02871 ...(401)682-0673

Providence

Old Court B&B, 144 Benefit St, 02906 ....(401)757-2002

Wakefield

B&B At Highland Farm, 4145 Tower Hill Rd, 02879, 1800 ....(401)783-2408
Larchwood Inn, 176 Main St, 02879, 1831 ....(401)783-1709

Watch Hill

Watch Hill Inn, 50 Bay St, 02891 ....(401)348-8912

Weekapaug

J. Livingston's Guest House By The Sea, 39 Weekapaug Rd, 02891 ....(401)322-0249

Westerly

Inn On The Hill, 29 Summer St, 02891 ....(401)596-3791
Longvue Guest House, 311 Shore Rt 1, 02891 ....(401)322-0465
Shelter Harbor Inn, Rt 1, 02891, 1800 ....(401)322-8883

South Carolina

Abbeville

Belmont Inn, 106 E Pickens St, 29620 ....(803)459-9625

Aiken

Holley Inn, 235 Richland Ave, 29801 ....(803)648-4265
Pine Knoll Inn, 305 Lancaster St, 29801, 1929 ....(803)649-5939
The Brodie Residence, 422 York St, 29801 ....(803)648-1445
Willcox Inn, 100 Colleton Ave At Whiskey Rd, 29801, 1898 ....(803)649-1377

Anderson

Evergreen Inn, 1109 S Main, 29621, 1834 ....(803)225-1109

Beaufort

Bay Street Inn, 601 Bay St, 29902, 1850 ....(803)524-7720

Old Point Inn, 212 New St, 29902, 1898 ....(803)524-3177
Rhett House Inn, 1009 Craven St, 29902, 1820 ....(803)524-9030
Twelve Oaks Inn, PO Box 4126, Rt 2 Box 293, 29902 ......(803)525-1371

Beech Island

The Cedars B&B Inn, Box 117 1325 Williston Rd, 29841, 1827 ....(803)827-0248

Bluffton

Fripp House Inn, Bridge & Boundary, Box 857, 29910, 1835

Camden

Aberdeen, 1409 Broad St, 29020 ....(803)432-2524
The Carriage House, 1413 Lyttleton St, 29020 ....(803)432-2430
The Inn, 1308 19 Broad St, 29020, 1800 ....(803)425-1806

Charleston

1837 B&B, 126 Wentworth St, 29401, 1800 ....(803)723-7166
Ann Harper's B&B, 56 Smith St, 29401, 1870 ....(803)723-3947
Ansonborough Inn, 21 Hasell St, 29401 ....(803)732-1655
B&B, 36 Meeting St, 29401 ....(803)722-1034
Barksdale House Inn, 27 George St, 29401, 1779 ....(803)577-4800
Battery Carriage House, 20 S Battery St, 29401, 1845 ....(803)723-9881
Belvedere B&B, 40 Rutledge Ave, 29401, 1900 ....(803)722-0973
Cannonboro Inn, 184 Ashley Ave, 29403, 1840 ....(803)723-8572
Charleston Society B&B, 84 Murray Blvd, 29401, 1800 .(803)723-4948
Church Street Inn, 177 Church St, 29401, 1890 ....(800)845-7638
Coach House, 39 E Battery Pl, 29401, 1810 ....(803)722-8145
Elliott House Inn, 78 Queen St, 29401, 1186 ....(803)723-1855
Hayne House, 30 King St, 29401, 1770 ....(803)577-2633
Historic Charleston B&B, 43 Legare St, 29401, 1713 ....(803)722-6606
Jasmine House, 64 Hasell St, 29401, 1843 ....(803)577-5900
Kings Courtyard Inn, 198 King St, 29401, 1853 ....(803)723-7000
Maison Du Pre, 317 E Bay St, 29401, 1830 ....(803)723-8691
Meeting Street Inn, 173 Meeting St, 29401, 1870 ....(803)723-9881
Palmer Home, 5 East Battery, 29401 ....(803)723-1574
Planters Inn, 112 N Market St, 29401, 1840 ....(803)722-2345
Rutledge Museum Guest House, 114 Rutledge Ave, 29401, 1810 ....(803)722-7551
Sweet Grass Inn, 23 Vendue Range, 29401, 1800 ....(803)723-9980
Sword Gate Inn, 111 Tradd St, 29401, 1800 ....(803)723-8518
The Kitchen House, 126 Tradd St, 29401, 1732 ....(803)577-6362
The Lodge Alley Inn, 195 E Bay St, 29401, 1773 ....(803)722-1611
Two Meeting Street Inn, 2 Meeting St, 29401, 1890 ......(803)723-7322
Vendue Inn, 19 Vendue Range, 29401, 1824 ....(803)577-7970

Cheraw

Spears B&B, 501 Kershaw St, 29520 ....(803)537-7733

Columbia

Claussen's Inn, 2003 Green St, 29205, 1928 ....(800)622-3382

Dale

Coosaw Plantation, 29401 ....(803)846-8225

Edgefield

Adams House, 212 Augusta Rd, 29824
The Village Inn, Court House Sq, 29824 ....(803)637-3789

Estill

The John Lawton House, 159 Third St E, 29918 ....(803)625-3240

Fort Mill

Pleasant Valley B&B Inn, 160 East At Blackweider, 29715, 1874 ....(803)548-5671

Georgetown

Shaw House, 8 Cypress Ct, 29440 ....(801)546-9663

Greenwood

The Inn On The Square, 104 Court St, 29646 ....(803)223-4488

Johnston

The Cox House Inn, 602 Lee St, PO Box 486, 29832, 1910 ....(803)275-3234

Little River

Stella's Guest House, PO Box 564, 29566 ....(803)249-1871

McClellanville

Laurel Hill Plantation, 8913 N Hwy 17, PO Box 182, 29458, 1850 ....(803)887-3708

Mt Pleasant

Guilds Inn, 101 Pitt St, 29464, 1888 ....(803)881-0510

Mullins

Webster Manor, 115 E James St, 29574 ....(803)464-9632

Myrtle Beach

Serendipity, An Inn, 407 71st Ave N, 29577 ....(803)449-5268

Orangeburg
Russell Street Inn, 491 Russell St, 29115 ....(803)531-2030
Pendleton
Liberty Hall Inn, 29670, 1840 ....(803)646-7500
Sullivan's Island
The Palmettos, 2014 Middle St, PO Box 706, 29482 ....(803)883-3389
Summerville
B&B In Summerville, 304 S Hamilton St, 29483, 1865 ......(803)871-5275
Gadsden Manor Inn, Box 1710, 29483, 1906 ....(803)875-1710
Switzer
Nicholls-Crook Plantation House, PO Box 5812, 29304 ...(803)583-7337
Union
Forest Hill Manor, Rt 2 Box 725, 29379 ....(803)427-4525

South Dakota

Canova
B&B at Skoglund Farm, Rt 1 Box 45, 57321, 1927 ....(605)247-3445
Yankton
The Mulberry Inn, 512 Mulberry St, 57078, 1873 ....(605)665-7116

Tennessee

Allardt
Charlo B&B, Box 69, 38504, 1880 ....(615)879-8056
Bolivar
Magnolia Manor, 418 N Main St, 38008, 1849
Brentwood
Eileen Herbert's B&B, 9318 Old Smyrna Rd, 37027,
    1917 ....(615)373-9300
Chattanooga
Lookout Mountain Guest House, 4415 Guild Tr, 37409,
    1927 ....(615)821-8307
The Chattanooga Choo-Choo Hilton Inn, 1400 Market St,
    37402 ....(615)266-5000
Clarksville
Hachland Hill Inn, 1601 Madison St, 37040, 1805 ....(615)255-1727
Clifton
Hidden Hollow Farm-Log Cabin B&B, Beech Creek Rd, Hwy 228,
    38424, 1840 ....(615)676-5295
Cookeville
Scarecrow Country Inn, 1720 E Spring St, 38501, 1788 ....(615)526-3434
Fayetteville
The Magnolias, Box 806, 37334 ....(615)433-3351
Gatlinburg
Buckhorn Inn, Rt 3 Box 393, 37738, 1937 ....(615)436-4668
Leconte Lodge, PO Box 350, 37738, 1930 ....(615)436-4473
Moon Mountain Lodge, 964 River Rd, 37738, 1831 ....(615)436-2131
Windhover, Rt 4, Box 371, 37738 ....(615)436-4068
Wonderland Hotel, Rt 2, 37738 ....(615)436-5490
Greeneville
East Tennessee B&B Inns and Lodges Assoc, 315 N Main St,
    37743 ....(615)638-2917
Greenville
Big Spring Inn, 315 N Main St, 37743, 1905 ....(615)638-2917
Hendersonville
Monthaven, 1154 W Main, 37075, 1810 ....(615)824-6319
Jonesborough
Jonesborough, 100 Woodrow Ave, 37659 ....(615)753-9223
Knoxville
The Graustein Inn, 8300 Nubbin Ridge Rd, 37923,
    1975 ....(615)690-7007
Three Chimneys, 1302 White Ave, 37916, 1896 ....(615)521-4970
Limestone
Snapp Inn B&B, Rt 3 Box 102, 37681, 1815 ....(615)257-2482
Loudon
River Road Inn, River Road, 37774, 1857 ....(615)458-4861
Lyles
Silver Leaf 1815-Country Inn, Rt 1 Box 122, 37098, 1815 (615)670-3048
Lynchburg
Lynchburg B&B, PO Box 34, 37532 ....(615)759-7158

Memphis
Lowenstein-Long House, 217 N Waldran-1084 Poplar, 38105,
    1901 ....(901)527-7174
The Peabody, 149 Union Ave, 38103, 1869
Monteagle
Edgeworth Inn, PO Box 365, 37356, 1888 ....(615)924-2669
Monterey
Walnut House, Rt 2, 38574
Murfreesboro
Clardy's Guest House, 435 E Main St, 37130, 1898 ....(615)893-6030
Nashville
Host Homes Of Tennessee, Box 110227, 37222-0227,
    1880 ....**(615)331-5244**
Normandy
Parish Patch Farm & Inn, PO Box 27, 37360 ....(615)857-3441
Paris
The Oaks, 1001 Memorial Dr, 38242
Pickwick Dam
Homestead House Inn, Box 79, 38365, 1843
Pickwick Dam, Box 76, 38365
Red Boiling Springs
Donoho Hotel, Box 36, 37150 ....(615)699-3141
Red Boiling Inn, Box 40, 37150 ....(615)699-2180
Rogersville
Hale Springs Inn, 110 W Main St, 37857, 1824 ....(615)272-5171
Rugby
Newbury House at Historic Rugby, Hwy 52, PO Box 8, 37733,
    1880 ....**(615)628-2441**
Sevierville
Blue Mountain Mist Country Inn, Rt 3 Box 490, 37862 ...(615)428-2335
Shiloh
Leawood-Williams Estate, PO Box 24, 38376 ....(901)689-5106
Wartrace
Ledford Mill And Museum, Rt 2 Box 152, 37183, 1880....(615)298-5674
Waverly
Nolan House Inn, Rt 4 Box 164, 37185, 1870 ....(615)296-2511

Texas

Austin
Brook House, 609 W 33rd St, 78705, 1920 ....(512)459-0534
Southard House, 908 Blanco, 78703, 1900 ....(512)474-4731
The McCallum House, 613 W 32nd, 78705 ....(512)451-6744
Big Sandy
Annie's B&B, 106 N Tyler, PO Box 928, 75755, 1901 ......(214)636-4307
Chappell Hill
Browning Plantation, Rt 1, Box 8, 77426 ....(409)836-6144
Cleburne
Cleburne House, 201 N Anglin, 76031, 1886 ....(817)641-0085
Comfort
Gast Haus Lodge, 944 High St, 78013 ....(512)995-2304
Cuero
Reiffert-Mugge Inn, 304 W Prairie, 77954, 1886 ....(512)275-2626
Dallas
Frank Lloyd Wright B&B Home, Rso Address: 4224 W Red Bird Lane,
    75237, 1920 ....(214)298-8586
El Paso
Room with a View, 821 Rim Rd, 79902, 1929 ....(915)534-4400
Fayetteville
Lickskillet Inn, PO Box 85, Fayette St, 78940, 1850...........(409)378-2846
Fort Davis
Indian Lodge, PO Box 786, 79734, 1933 ....(915)426-3254
Fort Worth
Medford House, 2344 Medford Court East, 76109, 1926 (817)924-2765
Fredericksburg
Baron's Creek Inn, 110 E Creek St, 78624 ....(512)997-9398
Country Cottage Inn, 405 E Main St, 78624, 1850 ....(512)997-8549
J Bar K Ranch B&B, Mason Rt Box 53-A, 78624 ....(512)669-2471
The Historic Hotel Association of Texas ....(512)997-5616

Texas (Continued)

Galveston
Dickens Loft, 2021 The Strand, 77550, 1856 .... (409)762-1653
Tremont House, 2300 Ship's Mechanic Row, 77550 .. (409)763-0300
Victorian Inn, 511 17th St, 77550 .... (409)762-3235
Glen Rose
Inn on the River, PO Box 1417, 76043 .... (817)897-2101
Graham
Louise Witkowski, 800 Third St, 76046
Granbury
Nutt House, Town Square, 76048, 1893 .... (817)573-5612
Houston
La Colombe D'or, 3410 Montrose Blvd, 77006 .... (713)524-7999
Sara's B&B Inn, 941 Heights Blvd, 77008, 1900 .... (713)868-1130
Jefferson
Excelsior House, 211 W Austin, 75657, 1850 .... (214)665-2513
Gone With the Wind Inn, 412 Soda St, 75657, 1851
Hale House, 702 South Lee, 75657
Hotel Jefferson Historic Inn, 124 W Austin, 75657,
    1851 .... (214)665-2631
McKay House, 306 E Delta St, 75657, 1851 .... (214)665-7322
New Jefferson Inn, 124 Austin St, 75657 .... (214)665-2631
Pride House, 409 Broadway, 75657, 1888 .... (214)665-2675
Queen Anne's Lace, 304 N Alley, 75657, 1888 ...... (214)665-2483
Stillwater Inn, 203 E Broadway, 75657, 1890 .... (214)665-8415
The Cottage in Jefferson, 307 Soda, 75657, 1880 .. (214)665-8572
The Magnolias, 209 Broadway, 75657, 1867 .... (214)665-2754
William Clark House, 201 W Henderson, 75657, 1855 ..... (214)665-8880
Wise Manor, 312 Houston St, 75657, 1874 .... (214)665-2386
Marshall
Ginocchio Hotel, 707 N Washington, 75670, 1896 .. (214)935-7635
Three Oaks, 609 N Washington Ave, 75670 .... (214)938-6123
Mcallen
La Posada, 100 N Main, 78501 .... (800)292-5659
Mount Vernon
Dutton-Teague B&B Inn, 110 Roach St, 75457 .... (214)537-2603
Nacogdoches
Haden Edwards Inn, 106 N Nanana, 75961, 1843 .... (409)564-9999
Tol Barret House, Rt 4, Box 9400, 75961, 1840 .... (409)569-1249
Navasota
The Castle, 1403 E Washington, 77868, 1900 .... (409)825-8051
New Braunfels
Prince Solms Inn, 295 E San Antonio, 78130 .... (512)625-9169
Rio Grande City
La Borde House, 601 E Main St, 78582, 1897 .... (512)487-5101
Salado
Inn At Salado, N Main At Pace Park, 76571 .... (817)947-8200
San Antonio
Belle Of Monte Vista, 505 Belknap Pl, 78212, 1890 .... (512)732-4006
Bullis House Inn, PO Box 8059, 78208, 1909 .... (512)223-9426
Menger Hotel, 204 Alamo Plaza, 78205 .... (512)223-4361
Terrell Castle, 950 E Grayson St, 78208, 1894 .... (512)271-9145
The Bullis House Inn, PO Box 8059, 621 Pierce St, 78208,
    1906 .... (512)223-9426
San Marcos
Aquarena Springs Inn, 1 Aquarena Dr, 78666, 1929 .... (512)396-8901
Crystal River Inn, 326 West Hopkins, 78666 .... (512)396-3739
Stephenville
The Oxford House, 563 N Graham, 76401, 1898 .... (817)965-6885
Tyler
Rosevine Inn B&B, 415 S Vine, 75702 .... (214)592-2221
Weimar
Weimar Country Inn, Jackson Sq, 78962 .... (409)725-8888

Utah

Bluff
Bluff B&B, PO Box 158, 84512 .... (801)672-2220
Castle Valley
Sistelita, Box 1905 CVSR, 84532 .... (801)259-6012

Cedar City
Meadeau View Lodge, Box 356, 84720 .... (801)682-2495
Paxman's Summer House, 170 N 400 W, 84720, 1900 ...... (801)586-3755
Woodbury Guest House, 237 S 300 W, 84720, 1898 .... (801)586-6696
Logan
Center Street B&B, 169 E Center St, 84321, 1879 .... (801)752-3443
The Birch Trees B&B, 315 Blvd, 84321 .... (801)753-1331
Manti
Yardley's Inn, 190 W 200 S, 84642 .... (801)835-1861
Midway
The Homestead, 700 N. Homestead Dr, 84049, 1886 ...... (801)654-1102
Mt Pleasant
Mansion House B&B, 298 S State St, 84647 .... (801)462-3031
Park City
505 Woodside, Box 2446, 84060, 1929 .... (801)649-4841
The Imperial Hotel, 221 Main St, PO Box 1628, 84060,
    1904 .... (801)649-1904
The Old Miner's Lodge, A B&B Inn, 615 Woodside Ave, PO Box
    2639, 84060-2639, 1893 .... (801)645-8068
Washington School Inn, 544 Park Ave, PO Box 536, 84060,
    1889 .... (801)649-3800
Provo
The Pullman, 415 S University Ave, 84601 .... (801)374-8141
Salina
Burr House, 195 W Main St, 84654 .... (801)529-7320
Salt Lake City
Brigham Street Inn, 1135 E South Temple, 84102, 1896. (801)364-4461
Eller B&B, 123 2nd Ave #202, 84103-4712, 1903 .... (802)375-2272
Pinecrest B&B Inn, 6211 Emigration Canyon Rd, 84108,
    1915 .... (801)583-6663
Saltair B&B, 164 S 9th E, 84102 .... (801)533-8184
The National Historic B&B, 936 E 1700 South, 84105,
    1891 .... (801)485-3535
The Spruces B&B, 6151 S 900 E, 84121, 1903 .... (801)268-8762
Sandy
Mountain Hollow B&B Inn, 10209 S Dimple Dell Rd,
    84092 .... (801)942-3428
St George
Green Gate Village Historic B&B Inn, 62-78 W Tabernacle, 84770,
    1872 .... (801)628-6999
Seven Wives Inn, 217 N 100 W, 84770, 1873 .... (801)628-3737

Vermont

Alburg
Auberge Alburg, RD 1, Box 3, 05440, 1920 .... (802)796-3169
Arlington
Arlington's West Mountain Inn, PO Box 481, 05250,
    1850 .... (802)375-6516
Hill Farm Inn, RR 2 Box 2015, 05250, 1790 .... (802)375-2269
Inn at Sunderland, RR 2 Box 2440, 05250 .... (802)362-4213
Shenandoah Farm, Rt 313, Battenkill Rd, 05250, 1820 ... (802)375-6372
Sycamore Inn, Rt 7 Box 2485, 05250, 1786 .... (802)362-2284
The Arlington Inn, Historic Rt 7A, 05250, 1848 .... (802)375-6532
The Evergreen, Sandgate Rd, 05250, 1830 .... (802)375-2272
Barnard
Silver Lake, Box 13, North Rd, 05031, 1810 .... (802)234-9957
The Silver Lake House, PO Box 13, North Rd, 05081 ...... (802)234-9957
Barnet
Innwood Manor, Lower Waterford Rd, 05821, 1925 .... (802)633-4047
Old Homestead Inn, PO Box 35, 05821 .... (802)633-4100
Barre
Woodruff House, 13 East St, 05641, 1883 .... (802)476-7745
Barton
The Barton Inn, PO Box 67, Main St, 05822, 1856 .... (802)525-4721
Bellows Falls
Horsefeathers B&B and Antique Shop, 16 Webb Terr, 05101,
    1897 .... (802)463-9776
Belmont
The Parmenter House, Church St, 05730, 1874 .... (802)259-2009
Bennington
Bennington Hus, 208 Washington Ave, 05201 .... (802)447-7972

Four Chimneys Inn & Restaurant, 21 West Rd, 05201,
1912 .... (802)447-3500
Mt. Anthony Guest House, 226 Main St, 05201 .... (802)447-7396
South Shire Inn, 124 Elm St, 05201, 1887 .... (802)447-3839
Bethel
Eastwood House, Rt 2 Rt 107, 05032, 1816 .... (802)234-9686
Greenhurst Inn, River St, 05032, 1890 .... (802)234-9474
Poplar Manor, Rt 2, 05032, 1810 .... (802)234-5426
Bondville
Alpenrose Inn, Winhall Hollow Rd, 05340, 1870 .... (802)297-2750
Bradford
Village Inn of Bradford, PO Box 354, 05033, 1828 .... (802)222-9303
Brandon
Beauchamp Place, 31 Franklin St, US Rt 7, 05733, 1830 (802)247-3905
Moffett House, 69 Park St, 05733 .... (802)247-3843
Norlo Inn, 25 Grove St, 05733, 1880 .... (802)247-3235
Old Mill Inn, 05773, 1788 .... (802)247-8002
The Arches, 53 Park St, 05733, 1910 .... (802)247-8200
The Churchill House Inn, Rt 73 East, 05733, 1871 .... (802)247-3300
The Inn at Tiffany Corner, Rt 7 & Country Club Rd, 05733,
1831 .... (802)247-6571
Bridgewater Corners
October Country Inn, PO Box 66, 05035 .... (802)672-3412
Bristol
Long Run Inn, RD 1, Box 560, 05443, 1799 .... (802)453-3233
Maplewood Farm B&B, Rt 17, RD2, Box 520, 05443,
1820 .... (802)453-2992
Brookfield
Green Trails Country Inn, Pond Village, 05036, 1750 .... (802)276-3412
Brownesville
Mill Brook B&B, PO Box 410, Rte 44, 05037, 1850 .... (802)484-7283
Brownsville
Inn At Mt. Ascutney, Brook Rd, 05037, 1802 .... (802)484-7725
The Mill Brook B&B & Gallery, PO Box 410, Rt 44, 05037,
1870 .... (802)484-7283
Burlington
Howden Cottage B&B, 32 N Champlain St, 05401, 1825 (802)864-7198
Charlotte
Green Meadows B&B, Box 1300, Mount Philo Rd, 05445,
1864 .... (802)425-3059
Chelsea
Shire Inn, PO Box 37, 05038, 1832 .... (802)685-3031
Chester
Chester House, Main St, Box 708, 05143, 1780 .... (802)875-2205
Greenleaf Inn, PO Box 188, 05143, 1860 .... (802)875-3171
Henry Farm Inn, PO Box 646, 05143, 1750 .... (802)875-2674
Hugging Bear Inn & Shoppe, Main St, Box 32, 05143,
1850 .... (802)875-2412
Karen & Brian Morris, RR 2 Box 48, Stone Village, 05143
Night with A Native: B&B, PO Box 327, Rt 103, 05143,
1931 .... (802)875-2616
Old Town Farm Inn, RD 4, Box 383B, 05143, 1861 .... (802)875-2346
Rowell's Inn, RR 1, Box 269, 05143, 1820 .... (802)875-3658
The Inn at Long Last, PO Box 589, 05143, 1923 .... (802)875-2444
The Stone Hearth Inn, Rt 11 West, 05143, 1810 .... (802)875-2525
Chittenden
Mountain Top Inn, Box 493, Mountain Top Rd, 05737,
1880 .... (800)445-2100
Tulip Tree Inn, Chittenden Dam Rd, 05737, 1842 .... (802)483-6213
Colchester
On the Lamb B&B, 60 Depot Rd, 05446, 1905 .... (802)862-2144
Craftsbury
Craftsbury Inn, 05826, 1850 .... (802)586-2848
Gary Meadow Dairy Farm, RR 1 Box 11, 05826, 1884 ..... (802)586-2536
Craftsbury Common
Craftsbury B&B on Wylie Hill, 05827, 1860 .... (802)586-2206
Craftsbury B&B On Wylie Hill, Wylie Hill, 05827, 1860 . (802)586-2206
Inn On The Common, Main St, 05827, 1795 .... (802)586-9619
Cuttingsville
Maple Crest Farm, Box 120, 05738 .... (802)492-3367
Danby
Quail's Nest B&B, PO Box 221, Main St, 05739 .... (802)293-5099
Silas Griffith Inn, RR 1 Box 66F, S Main St, 05739,
1891 .... (802)293-5567

Derby Line
Derby Village Inn, 46 Main St, 05830, 1899 .... (802)873-3604
Dorset
Barrows House, 05251, 1784 .... (802)867-4455
Cornucopia Of Dorset, Rt 30 Box 307, 05251, 1800 .... (802)867-5751
Dorset Inn, 05251, 1796 .... (802)867-5500
Dovetail Inn, Rt 30 Box 976, 05251, 1820 .... (802)867-5747
Little Lodge At Dorset, Rt 30 Box 673, 15251 .... (802)867-4040
Maplewood Colonial Inn, Rt 30 Box 1019, 05251, 1788 ... (802)867-4470
Marble West Inn, PO Box 22, 05251 .... (802)867-4155
The Little Lodge at Dorset, Rt 30 Box 673, 05251, 1810. (802)867-4040
Village Auberge, Rt 30 Box 970, 05251 .... (802)867-5715
East Barnet
Inwood Manor, Lower Waterford Rd, 05821 .... (802)633-4047
East Burke
Burke Green, RR 1 Box 81, 05832, 1840 .... (802)467-3472
The Old Cutter Inn, RR 1 Box 62, 05830, 1845 .... (802)626-5152
East Hardwick
Brick House Guests, Box 128, Brick House Rd, 05836,
1830 .... (802)472-5512
East Middlebury
October Pumpkin B&B, Rt 125 E, PO Box 226, 05740,
1850 .... (802)388-9525
The Waybury Inn, Rt 125, 05740, 1810 .... (802)388-4015
East Poultney
Eagle Tavern on the Green, PO Box 587, 05741, 1785 ...... (802)287-9498
Enosburg Falls
Berkson Farms, 05450 .... (802)933-2522
Essex Junction
Varnum's, 143 Weed Rd, 05452, 1792 .... (802)899-4577
Fair Haven
Fair Haven Inn, 5 Adams St, 05743, 1837 .... (802)254-4907
Maplewood Inn, Rt 22A, South, 05743, 1850 .... (802)265-8039
The Vermont Marble Inn, 12 W Park Dr, 05743 .... (802)265-8383
Fairfax
Foggy Hollow Farm, Rt 104, 05454, 1857
Fairfield
Tetreault's Hillside View Farm, South Rd, 05455, 1880 ... (802)827-4480
Fairlee
Aloha Manor, Lake Morey, 05045, 1785 .... (802)333-4478
Silver Maple Lodge & Cottages, S Main St, 05045, 1855. (802)333-4326
Franklin
Fair Meadow Dairy Farm, Rt 235 Box 430, 05457, 1853... (802)285-2132
Gassets
Old Town Farm Inn, Rt 10, 05143, 1861 .... (802)875-2346
Gaysville
Cobble House Inn, PO Box 49, 05746, 1864 .... (802)234-5458
Goshen
Blueberry Hill Inn, RD 3, 05733, 1813 .... (802)247-6735
Grafton
Stronghold Inn, HCR 40 Rt 121, 05146, 1820 .... (802)843-2203
The Hayes House, 05146, 1803 .... (802)843-2461
The Inn At Woodchuck Hill Farm, Middletown Rd, 05146,
1780 .... (802)843-2398
The Old Tavern at Grafton, Main St, 05146, 1801 .... (802)843-2231
Greensboro
Highland Lodge, Caspian Lake, 05841, 1860 .... (802)533-2647
Guildhall
Guildhall Inn, Box 129, 05905, 1800 .... (802)676-3720
Hancock
Kincraft Inn, Rt 100 Box 96, 05748 .... (802)767-3734
Hardwick
Carolyn's B&B, 15 Church St, 05843, 1890 .... (802)472-6338
Kahagon At Nichols Pond, Box 728, Nichols Pond, 05843,
1890 .... (802)472-6446
Hartford
The House of Seven Gables, 221 Main St, Box 526, 05047,
1891 .... (802)295-1200
Hyde Park
Fitch Hill Inn, RFD 1 Box 1879, 05655, 1800 .... (802)888-5941
Jamaica
Three Mountain Inn, Box 180 Bbi, 05343, 1780 .... (802)874-4140

Vermont (Continued)

Jay
The Jay Village Inn, Rt 242, 05859, 1901 ....(802)988-2643
Jeffersonville
Jefferson House B&B, PO Box 288, Main St, 05464, 1910 (802)644-2030
Windridge Inn, Main St, 05464, 1860 ....(802)644-8281
Jericho
Milliken's, RD 2 Box 397, 05465, 1867 ....(802)899-3993
Killington
Inn at Long Trail, Rt 4 Box 267, 05751, 1939 ....(802)775-7181
Mountain Meadows Lodge, Rt 1 Box 3, 05751, 1856 ....(802)775-1010
Sherburne Valley Inn, Rt 4, 05751, 1900 ....(802)422-9888
The Vermont Inn, Rt 4, 05751, 1840 ....(802)775-0708
Troutbrook Lodge, PO Box 212, 05751, 1883 ....(802)672-3716
Londonderry
The Highland House, RR 1 Box 107, 05148, 1842 ....(802)842-3019
The Village Inn At Londgrove, RD Box 215, Landgrove, 05148,
1830 ....(802)824-6673
Lower Waterford
Rabbit Hill Inn, Pucker St, 05848, 1825 ....(802)748-5168
Ludlow
Black River Inn, 100 Main St, 05149, 1835 ....(802)228-5585
Combes Family Inn, RFD 1 Box 275, 05149, 1888 ....(802)228-8799
Echo Lake, PO Box 142, 05149 ....(802)228-8602
Governor's Inn, 86 Main St, 05149, 1890 ....(802)228-8830
Jewell Brook Inn, 82 Andover St, Rt 100, 05149, 1800 ......(802)228-8926
Okemo Inn, RFD 1 Box 133, 05149, 1810 ....(802)228-8834
The Governor's Inn, 86 Main St, 05149, 1890 ....(802)228-8830
Lyndonville
The Wildflower Inn, Star Rt, 05851, 1796 ....(802)626-8310
Manchester
Birch Hill Inn, West Rd, Box 346, 05254, 1790 ....(802)362-2761
Manchester Highlands Inn, PO Box 1754, Highland Ave, 05255,
1898 ....(802)362-4565
Reluctant Panther Inn, Box 678, West Rd, 05254, 1850 ..(802)362-2568
The Inn at Manchester, Box 41, Historic Rt 7A, 05254,
1880 ....(802)362-1793
Wilburton Inn, Box 468, River Rd, 05254, 1902 ....(802)362-2500
Manchester Center
River Meadow Farm, PO Box 822, 05255, 1829 ....(802)362-3700
Manchester Village
1811 House, Historic Rt 7A, 05254, 1775 ....(802)362-1811
Village Country Inn, PO Box 408, 05254, 1889 ....(802)362-1792
Marlboro
Longwood-"A Country Inn at Marlboro", Rt 9 Box 86, 05344,
1800 ....(802)257-1545
Whetstone Inn, 05344
Mendon
Red Clover Inn, Woodward Rd, 05701, 1840 ....(802)775-2290
Middlebury
Middlebury Inn, Courthouse Sq, 05753, 1827 ....(800)842-4666
Swift House Inn, 25 Stewart Lane, 05753, 1815 ....(802)388-9925
Middletown Springs
Middletown Springs Inn, Box 1068, On The Green, 05757,
1879 ....(802)235-2198
Montgomery
Eagle Lodge, Box 900, 05471, 1900 ....(802)326-4518
Montgomery Center
The Inn On Trout River, The Main St, 05471, 1895 ....(802)326-4391
Montgomery Village
Black Lantern Inn, Route 118, 05470, 1803 ....(802)326-4507
Moretown
Camel's Hump View Farm, Rt 100b, 05660, 1831 ....(802)496-3614
Schultzes' Village Inn, PO Box 465, 05660, 1860 ....(802)496-2366
Morgan
Seymour Lake Lodge, Rt 111, 05853, 1842 ....(802)895-2752
Morrisville
Lepine's Inn By The Brook, PO Box 27, 05661, 1833 ....(802)888-5862
Mount Holly
Austria Haus, Box 2 Austria Haus Rd, 05758 ....(802)259-2441
Hound's Folly, Box 591, 05758, 1810 ....(802)259-2718

The Hortonville Inn, RD 1 Box 14, 05758 ....(802)259-2587
New Haven
The Horn Farnsworth House B&B, Rt 7 & River Rd, RR1 Box 170A,
05472, 1793 ....(802)388-2300
Newbury
Century Past, Rt 5 Box 186, 05051, 1790 ....(802)266-3358
Newfame
Four Columns Inn, 05345, 1830 ....(802)365-7713
Newfane
Old Newfane Inn, PO Box 101, 05345 ....(802)365-4427
West River Lodge, RR 1 Box 693, 05354, 1850 ....(802)365-7745
Newport
Memphre Manor B&B, 9 Prospect St, 05855, 1900 ....(802)334-5646
North Hero
Charlie's Northland Lodge, Box 88, 05474, 1850 ....(802)372-8822
North Hero House, Rt 2 PO 106, 05474, 1891 ....(802)372-8237
North Thetford
Stone House Inn, Rt 5 Box 47, 05054, 1835 ....(802)333-9124
North Troy
Rose Apple Acres Farm, RR 1, Box 300, E Hill Rd, 05859,
1910 ....(802)988-4300
Norwich
The Inn At Norwich, 225 Main St, 05055, 1797 ....(802)649-1143
Orleans
Valley House Inn, 4 Memorial Sq, 05860, 1800 ....(802)754-6665
Orwell
Historic Brookside Farms, Rt 22A Box 036, 05760, 1789 (802)948-2727
Perkinsville
Peregrine's Rest, Upper Falls Rd, 05151, 1830 ....(802)263-5784
Peru
Russell Inn, 05152, 1840 ....(802)824-6631
The Wiley Inn, PO Box 37, 05152, 1835 ....(802)842-6600
Pittsfield
Pittsfield Inn, PO Box 526c, 05762, 1835 ....(802)746-8943
Swiss Farm Lodge, Rt 100n, 05762, 1825 ....(802)746-8341
Plainfield
Yankees' Northview B&B, RD 2 Box 1000, 05667 ....(802)454-7191
Plymouth
Salt Ash Inn, Jct 100 & 100A, 05056, 1830 ....(802)672-3748
The Hawk Inn, Rt 100, 05056 ....(802)672-3811
Post Mills
Lake House Inn At Lake Fairlee, Rt 244 Box 65, 05058,
1871 ....(802)333-4025
The Lake House Inn, Rt 244, PO Box 65, 05058, 1871 ......(802)333-4025
Poultney
Lake St. Catherine Inn, PO Box 129, 05764, 1920 ....(802)287-9347
Stonebridge Inn, Rt 30, 05764, 1808 ....(802)287-9849
Proctorsville
Castle Inn, Rt 103 & 131, PO Box 157, 05153, 1904 ....(802)226-7222
Okemo Lantern Lodge, PO Box 247, 05153, 1800 ....(802)226-7770
The Golden Stage Inn, Depot St, PO Box 218, 05153,
1780 ....(802)226-7744
Putney
Hickory Ridge House, RFD 3 Box 1410, 05346, 1808 ....(802)387-5709
Mapleton Farm B&B, RD 2, Box 510, 05346, 1803 ....(802)257-5252
Putney Inn, Depot Rd, 05346, 1830 ....(802)387-6617
Quechee
Quechee B&B, Rt 4 Box 0080, 05059, 1795 ....(802)295-1776
Quechee Inn At Marshland Farm, Clubhouse Rd, Box 104, 05059,
1800 ....(802)295-3133
Randolph
The Three Stallion Inn, RD 2, Stock Farm Rd, 05060,
1820 ....(802)728-5575
Reading
The Peeping Cow B&B, Rt 106 Box 47, 05062, 1800 ....(802)484-5036
Readsboro
Old Coach Inn, RR 1 Box 260, 05350, 1783 ....(802)423-5394
Ripton
Chipman Inn, Rt 125, 05766, 1828 ....(802)388-2390
Peaceful Acres, PO Box 114, 05466 ....(802)388-2076
Rochester
Harvey's Mountain View Inn, 05767, 1809 ....(802)767-4273

Liberty Hill Farm, 05767 .... (802)767-3926
The New Homestead, PO Box 25, 05767, 1900 .... (802)767-4751
Tupper Farm Lodge, RR 1 Box 149, 05767, 1820 .... (802)767-4243
Royalton
Fox Stand Inn & Restaurant, Rt 14, 05068, 1818 .... (802)763-8437
Rutland
Hillcrest Guest House, RR 1 Box 4459, 05701, 1838 .... (802)775-1670
Saint Johnsbury
Echo Ledge Farm Inn, Rt 2 Box 77, 05838, 1793 .... (802)748-4750
Sandgate
The Evergreen, 05250, 1935 .... (802)375-2272
Saxtons River
Red Barn Guest House, Hatfield Ln, 05154, 1910 .... (802)869-2566
Saxtons River Inn, Main St, 05154, 1900 .... (802)869-2110
Shaftsbury
Munro Hawkins House, Historic Rt 7A, 05262 .... (802)447-2286
Shoreham Village
Shoreham Inn & Country Store, On The Village Green, 05770,
1790 .... (802)897-5081
Shrewsbury
Buckmaster Inn, Lincoln Hill Rd, RR 1 Box 118, 05738,
1801 .... **(802)492-3485**
Simonsville
Rowell's Inn, RR 1 Box 269, 05143, 1820 .... (802)875-3658
South Burlington
Lindenwood-A Country Inn, 916 Shelburne Rd, 05404,
1930 .... (802)862-2144
South Londonderry
Londonderry Inn, PO Box 3018, 05155, 1826 .... (802)824-5226
South Newfame
The Inn At South Newfane, Dover Rd, 05351, 1900 .... (802)348-7191
South Strafford
Watercourse Way B&B, Rt 132 Box 101, 05070, 1850 ...... (802)765-4314
South Wallingford
Green Mountain Tea Room, Rt 7 Box 400, 05773, 1792. (802)446-2611
South Woodstock
Kedron Valley Inn, Rt 106 Box 145, 05071, 1822 .... (802)457-1473
Springfield
Hartness House Inn, 30 Orchard St, 05156, 1903 .... (802)885-2115
Starksboro
North Country B&B, Rt 116, PO Box 1, 05487, 1850 .... (802)453-3911
Stockbridge
Scarborough Inn, Rt 100 HC65 #23, 05772 .... (802)746-8141
Stowe
Bittersweet Inn, Rt 100 S, 05672 .... (802)253-7787
Edson Hill Manor, RR 1 Box 2480, 05672, 1939 .... (802)253-7371
Fiddler's Green Inn, Mountain Rd Rt 108, 05672, 1820 ... (802)253-8124
Fountain House, RR2, Box 2480, 05672, 1926 .... (802)253-9285
Foxfire Inn, RD 2 Rt 100, 05672 .... (802)253-4887
Gables Inn, Mountain Rd, 05672 .... (802)253-7730
Golden Kitz Lodge, RD 1 Box 2980, 05672 .... (802)253-4217
Grey Fox Inn, Route 108, 05672 .... (802)253-8921
Mountain Brook Inn, 1505 Mountain Rd, 05672, 1859 ..... (800)553-3035
Nichols Lodge, Box 1098, 05672 .... (802)253-7683
Spruce Pond Inn, 05672, 1827 .... (802)253-4828
Stowe-Away Lodge, RR 1 Box 1360, 05672, 1793 .... (802)253-7574
Stowe-Bound Lodge, RR 2 Box 2890, 05672, 1830 .... (802)253-4515
The 1860 House, School St, PO Box 276, 05672, 1860 .... (802)253-7351
The Charda Inn, RR 2 Box 2610, 05672, 1800 .... (802)253-4598
The Yodler, Rt 1 Box 10, 05672, 1797 .... (802)253-4836
Wood Chip Inn, RR 1, Box 1618, 05672 .... (802)253-9080
Ye Olde England Inne, Mountain Rd, 05672, 1890 .... (802)253-7558
Sunderland
Eastbrook B&B, River Rd, 05250, 1850 .... (802)375-6509
The Inn at Sunderland, Historic Rt 7A, 05250, 1840 ...... **(802)362-4213**
Swanton
Royale Swans Country Inn & Motel, RD 2 Box 83, 05488,
1750 .... (802)868-2010
Townshend
Boardman House, On the Green, 05353, 1800 .... (802)365-4086
Townshend Country Inn, RR 1, Box 3100, 05353, 1776 .... (802)365-4141
Vergennes
Basin Harbor Club, Basin Harbor Rd, 05491, 1880 .... (802)475-2311

Emersons' Guest House, 82 Main St, 05491 .... (802)877-3293
Strong House Inn, RD 1 Box 9, Rt 22A, 05491, 1834 ...... **(802)877-3337**
Waitsfield
Finchingfield Farm B&B, Rt 100, Box 159, 05673, 1824 .... (802)496-7555
Honeysuckles Inn, PO Box 828, 05673, 1799 .... (802)469-6200
Hyde Away, Rt 17, 05673, 1830 .... (802)496-2322
Knoll Farm Country Inn, Bragg Hill Rd, 05673 .... (802)496-3939
Lareau Farm Country Inn, PO Box 563, Rt 100, 05673,
1832 .... **(802)496-4949**
Mad River Barn, Rt 17 Box 88, 05673, 1800 .... **(802)496-3310**
Millbrook, RFD Box 62, 05673, 1840 .... (802)495-2405
Mountain View Inn, Rt 17 RFD Box 69, 05673 .... (802)496-2426
Olde Tymes Inn, Rt 100, PO Box 165, 05673, 1850 .... (802)196-3875
Round Barn Farm, RR Box 247, 05673, 1810 .... **(802)496-2276**
The Valley Inn, Rt 100 Box 8, 05673 .... (802)496-3450
Wallingford
Dunham House, 7 S Main St, 05773, 1856 .... (802)446-2600
Wallingford Inn, Box 404, 05773, 1876 .... (802)446-2849
White Rocks Inn, RR 1 Box 297, Rt 7, 05773, 1840 .... (802)446-2077
Warren
Beaver Pond Farm Inn, RD Box 306, Golf Course Rd, 05674,
1860 .... **(802)583-2861**
Pitcher Inn, PO Box 408, 05674, 1860 .... (802)496-3831
South Hollow Farm, RR1, Box 287, 05674, 1837 .... (802)496-5627
Waterbury
Blush Hill House, Blush Hill Rd, 05676, 1818 .... (802)244-7529
The Inn at Thatcher Brook Falls, RD 2, Box 62, 05676,
1899 .... (802)244-5911
Waterbury Center
The Black Locust Inn, RR 1, Box 715, 05677, 1830 .... (802)244-7490
Weathersfield
The Inn at Weathersfield, Rt 106, PO Box 165, 05151,
1795 .... **(802)263-9217**
West Arlington
Four Winds Country Inn, River Rd, 05250, 1850 .... (802)375-6734
The Inn on Covered Bridge Green, RD 1, Box 3550, River Rd, 05250,
1792 .... (802)375-9489
West Brattleboro
Captain Henry Chase House, Rt 4 Box 788, 05301
West Dover
Doveberry Inn, Rt 100, 05356 .... (802)464-5652
Inn At Sawmill Farm, Box 8, 05356, 1788 .... (802)464-8131
Snow Den Inn, Rt 100, 05356, 1885 .... (802)464-9355
West Dover Inn, Rt 100 Box 506, 05356 .... (802)464-5207
West Rutland
The Silver Fox Inn, Rt 133 Box 1222, 05777, 1768 .... (802)438-5555
West Townsend
Windham Hill Inn, RR 1 Box 44, 05359, 1825 .... (802)874-4080
West Woodstock
Lincoln Covered Bridge Inn, Rt 4, 05091 .... (802)457-3312
Weston
1830 Inn on the Green, Main St, Rt 100 Box 104, 05161,
1830 .... **(802)824-6789**
Darling Family Inn, Rt 100, 05161 .... **(802)824-6286**
Inn At Weston, Rt 100 Box 56bb, 05161, 1848 .... (802)824-5804
The 1830 Inn on the Green, Rt 100, 05161, 1830 .... (802)824-6789
The Colonial House, Rt 100 Box 138, 05161, 1790 .... (802)824-6286
The Wilder Homestead Inn, RR 1 Box 106d, 05161, 1827 (802)842-8172
Williamstown
Autumn Crest Inn, Clark Rd, 05679 .... (802)433-6627
Rosewood Inn, Rt 14 Box 31, 05679, 1898 .... (802)433-5822
Williamsville
The Country Inn at Williamsville, Grimes Hill Rd, Box 166, 05362,
1795 .... **(802)348-7148**
Wilmington
Darcroft's Schoolhouse, Rt 100, 05363, 1837 .... (802)464-2631
Hermitage Inn, Coldbrook Rd, 05363, 1875 .... (802)464-3511
Misty Mountain Lodge, Stowe Hill Rd, Box 114, 05363, 1803 (802)464-3961
Nordic Hills Lodge, 179 Coldbrook Rd, 05363 .... (802)464-5130
Nutmeg Inn, Rt 9W, Molly Starke Tr, 05363, 1780 .... (802)464-3351
The Red Shutter Inn, Box 636, Rt 9, 05363, 1894 .... (802)464-3768
The White House: A Cross-country Inn, Rt 9, 05363,
1914 .... (802)464-2136

Vermont (Continued)

Windsor
Juniper Hill Inn, Juniper Hill Rd, RR 1 Box 79, 05089,
1900 ....(802)464-2135
Woodstock
Cambria House, 43 Pleasant St, 05091, 1880 ....(802)457-3077
Carriage House of Woodstock, Rt 4 W, 05091, 1850 ....(802)457-4322
Deer Brook Inn, HCR 35, Box 189, 05091, 1820 ....(802)672-3713
Lincoln Covered Bridge Inn, RR 2, Box 40, 05091, 1800 ..(802)457-3312
The Charleston House, 21 Pleasant St, 05091, 1835 ....(802)457-3843
The Jackson House At Woodstock, Rt 4 W, 05091
The Winslow House, #38, Rt 4 W, 05091, 1872 ....(802)457-1820
The Woodstock Inn, Fourteen The Green, 05091 ....(802)457-1000
Three Church Street, 3 Church St, 05091, 1830 ....(802)457-1925
Village Inn Of Woodstock, 41 Pleasant St, 05091, 1899 ....(802)457-1255
Woodstock House B&B, Rt 106 Box 361, 05091, 1860 ....(802)457-1758

Virginia

Abingdon
Litchfield Hall, 247 E Valley St, 24210 ....(703)628-9317
Martha Washington Inn, 150 W Main St, 24210, 1830 ......(703)628-3161
Mason Place B&B, 243 Mason Place, NW, 24210 ....(703)628-2887
Summerfield Inn, 101 W Valley St, 24210, 1830 ....(703)628-5905
Aldie
Little River Inn, PO Box 116, 22001, 1819 ....(703)327-6742
Alexandria
Alexandria Lodgings, PO Box 416, 22313 ....(703)836-5575
Princely B&B, Ltd., 819 Prince St, 22314 ....(703)683-2159
Arlington
Memory House, 6404 N Washington Blvd, 22205, 1899 (703)534-4607
Banco
Olive Mill B&B, Rt 231, 22711 ....(703)923-4664
Bassett
Annie's Country Inn, Rt 5 Box 562, 24055 ....(703)629-1517
Bedford
Elmo's Rest, Rt 2 Box 198, 24523, 1890 ....(703)586-3707
Bowling Green
The Old Mansion, 22427
Bridgewater
Bear & Dragon B&B, 401 N Main St, 22812 ....(703)828-2807
Burkeville
Hyde Park Farm, Rt 2 Box 38, 23922, 1752 ....(804)645-8431
Charles City
Edgewood Plantation, Rt 5 Historic, 23030, 1849 ....(804)829-2962
North Bend Plantation, Rt 1 Box 13A, 23030, 1801 ....(804)829-5176
Piney Grove B&B, Rt 1 Box 148, 23030-9735, 1800 ....(804)829-2480
Charleston
Benedict Haid Farm, N 8 Hale St, 25301, 1872 ....(304)346-1054
Charlottesville
200 South Street Inn, 200 South St, 22901, 1853 ....(804)979-0200
Carrsbrook, Guesthouses, PO Box 5737, 22905, 1794 ......(804)979-7264
English Inn, 316 14th St NW, 22903, 1920 ....(804)295-7707
Franklin-Halifax House, Guesthouses, PO Box 5737, 22905,
1750 ....(804)979-7264
Guesthouses, PO Box 5737, 22905, 1750 ....(804)979-7264
Longhouse, Guesthouses, PO Box 5737, 22905, 1812 ....(804)979-7264
Silver Thatch Inn, PO Box 6370, 22906, 1780 ....(804)978-4686
The Silver Thatch Inn, 3001 Hollymead Rd, 22901,
1780 ....(804)978-4686
Westbury, Guesthouses, PO Box 5737, 22905, 1820 ....(804)979-8327
Woodstock Hall, Rt 3 Box 40, 22901, 1757 ....(804)293-8977
Chatham
Sims Mitchell House, Box 846, 242 Whittle St SW, 24531
Chincoteague
Channel Bass Inn, 100 Church St, 23336, 1871 ....(804)336-6148
Little Traveller Inn, 112 N Main St, 23336 ....(804)336-6686
Miss Molly's Inn, 113 N Main St, 23336, 1886 ....(804)336-6686
Year Of The Horse Inn, 600 S Main St, 22336
Churchville
Buckhorn Inn, Star Rt Box 139, 24421 ....(703)337-6900

Culpeper
Fountain Hall B&B, 609 S East St, 22701, 1859 ....(703)825-6708
Flint Hill
Caledonia Farm, Rt 1 Box 2080, 22627, 1812 ....(703)675-3693
Floyd
Brookfield Inn B&B, PO Box 341, 24091 ....(703)763-3363
Fredericksburg
Fredericksburg Inn, 1707 Princess Anne St, 22401, 1928 .(703)371-8300
Kenmore Inn, 1200 Princess Anne St, 22401, 1790 ....(703)371-7622
La Vista Plantation, 4420 Guinea Station Rd, 22401,
1838 ....(703)898-8444
Richard Johnston Inn, 711 Caroline St, 22401 ....(703)642-5330
The McGrath House, 225 Princess Anne St, 22401, 1900 .(703)371-4363
Front Royal
Constant Spring Inn, 413 S Royal Ave, 22630 ....(703)635-7010
Gordonsville
Sleepy Hollow Farm, Rt 3 Box 43 on VA 231, 22942,
1775 ....(703)832-5555
Harrisonburg
Joshua Wilton House, 412 S Main St, 22801, 1896 ....(703)434-4464
Haywood
Shenandoah Springs Country Inn, 22722 ....(703)923-4300
Hillsville
Tipton House B&B, 1043 N Main St, 24343 ....(703)728-2351
Hot Springs
Vine Cottage Inn, Rt 220, 24445, 1900 ....(703)839-2422
Irvington
King Carter Inn, PO Box 425, 22480, 1890 ....(804)438-6053
Lancaster
The Inn at Levelfields, Star Rt 3 Box 216, 22503, 1857 ..(804)435-6887
Leesburg
Laurel Brigade Inn, 20 W Market St, 22075, 1759 ....(703)777-1010
Norris House Inn, 108 Loudoun St SW, 22075, 1806 ......(703)777-1806
Lexington
Alexander-Withrow House, 3 W Washington, 24450,
1789 ....(703)463-2044
Fassifern B&B, Rt 5 Box 87, 24450, 1867 ....(703)463-1013
Historic Country Inn, 11 N Main St, 24450 ....(703)463-2044
Llewellyn Lodge at Lexington, 603 S Main St, 24450,
1936 ....(703)463-3235
Maple Hall, 11 N Main St, 24450
McCampbell Inn, 11 N Main St, 24450, 1809 ....(703)463-2044
Luray
Jordan Hollow Farm Inn, Rt 2 Box 375, 22851, 1790 ......(703)778-2209
Mountain View House B&B, 151 S Court St, 22835 ....(703)743-3723
Shenandoah Countryside B&B, Rt 2 Box 377, 22835 ......(703)743-6434
The Ruffner House, Rt 4 Box 620, 22835, 1739 ....(703)743-7855
Mathews
Ravenswood Inn, PO Box 250, 23109 ....(804)725-7272
Riverfront House B&B, Rt 14 E, PO Box 310, 23109,
1840 ....(804)725-9975
McGaheysville
Shenandoah Valley Farm & Inn, Rt 1 Box 142, 22840 .....(703)289-5402
Meadows Of Dan
Dr. & Mrs. Spangler, Virginia Hwy 602, 24120 ....(703)952-2454
Middleburg
Briar Path At Middleburg, PO Box 803, 22117 ....(703)327-4455
Red Fox Inn & Tavern, PO Box 385, 2 E Washington St, 22117,
1728 ....(703)687-6301
Welbourne, 22117, 1775 ....(703)687-3201
Middletown
Wayside Inn Since 1797, 7783 Main St, 22645, 1797 ....(703)869-1797
Millwood
Brookside, 22646, 1780 ....(703)837-1780
Mollusk
Greenvale Manor, PO Box 70, 22517, 1840 ....(804)462-5995
Monterey
Highland Inn, PO Box 40, 24465, 1904 ....(703)468-2143
Montross
The Inn at Montross, Courthouse Sq, 22520, 1683 ....(804)493-9097
Mt Crawford
Pumpkin House Inn, Ltd, Rt 2, Box 155, 22841, 1847 ......(703)434-6963

Mt Jackson
The Widow Kip's Country Inn, Rt 1 Box 117, 22842,
    1830 .... (703)477-2400
Natural Bridge
Burger's County Inn B&B, Rt 1 Box 564, 24578 .... (703)291-2464
Occoquan
Rockledge B&B, 410 Mill St, 22125, 1758 .... (703)690-3377
Onacock
Colonial Manor Inn, PO Box 94, Market St, 23417, 1890. (804)787-3521
Orange
Hidden Inn, 249 Caroline St, 22950, 1880 .... (703)672-3625
Mayhurst Inn, US 15 South, PO Box 707, 22960, 1859 ... (703)672-5597
Paris
The Ashby Inn, Rt 1 Box 2a, 22130 .... (703)592-3900
Petersburg
The High Street Inn, 405 High St, 23803 .... (804)733-0505
Rappahannock
Bunree, PO Box 53, 22002 .... (703)937-4133
Meadowwood B&B, PO Box 29, 22713 .... (703)547-3851
Richmond
Abbie Hill B&B, PO Box 4503, 23220, 1904 .... (804)355-5855
B&B On The Hill, 2304 E Broad St, 23223 .... (804)780-3746
Bensonhouse of Richmond at Monument, 2036 Monument Ave,
    23220, 1916 .... (804)648-7560
Duncan Lee House, PO Box 15131, 22314 .... (804)321-6277
Mr. Patrick Henry's Inn, 2300 E Broad St, 23223, 1858 .. (804)644-1322
The Carrington Row Inn, 2309 E Broad St, 23223 .... (804)343-7005
The Catlin-Abbott House, 2304 E Broad St, 23223,
    1845 .... (804)780-3746
The Leonine Experience, PO Box 4772, 23220 .... (804)349-1952
Roanoke
The Mary Blandon House B&B, 381 Washington Ave Old SW,
    24016 .... (703)344-5361
Scottsville
Guesthouse Of Chester, PO Box 5737, Charlottesville 22905, 24590,
    1847 .... (804)979-7264
High Meadows Inn, Rt 4 Box 6, 24590, 1832 .... (804)286-2218
Smith Mountain Lake
Holland-Duncan House, Rt 3 Box 681, 24121 .... (703)721-8510
Manor at Taylor's Store, Rt 1 Box 533, 24184 .... (703)721-3951
Sperryville
Conyers House, Slate Mills Rd, 22740, 1770 .... (703)987-8025
Staunton
Belle Grae Inn, 515 W Frederick St, 24401 .... (703)886-5151
Frederick House, Frederick and New Streets, 24401,
    1810 .... (703)885-4220
Thornrose House At Gypsy Hill B&B, 531 Thornrose Ave,
    24401 .... (703)885-7026
Steele's Tavern
The Osceola Mill Country Inn, 24476 .... (703)377-6455
Strasburg
Hotel Strasburg, 201 Holliday St, 22657 .... (703)465-9191
Swoope
Lambsgate B&B, Rt 1 Box 63, 24479, 1816 .... (703)337-6929
Tangier
Sunset Inn, Box 156, 23440 .... (804)891-2535
Trevilians
Prospect Hill, Rt 613, RD 3 Box 430, 23093, 1732 .... (703)967-0844
Upperville
1763 Inn, Rt 1 Box 19, 22176 .... (703)592-3848
Gibson Hall Inn, PO Box 225, Rt 50, 22176 .... (703)592-3514
Urbanna
The Town House, 1880 Prince George St, Box 757,
    23175 .... (804)758-3521
Vesuvius
Sugar Tree Inn, Hwy 56, 24483, 1870 .... (703)377-2197
Virginia Beach
The Picket Fence, 209 43rd St, 23451, 1939 .... (804)428-8861
Wachapreague
The Burton House, 11 Brooklyn St, 23480, 1883 .... (804)787-4560
Warenton
Rosemont Farm Inn, Rt 3 Box 240, 22186, 1850 .... (703)347-5422

Warm Springs
Inn At Gristmill Square, PO Box 229, 24484 .... (703)839-2231
Meadow Lane Lodge, Star Rt A Box 110, 24484 .... (703)839-5959
Washington
Heritage House B&B, PO Box 90, 22747 .... (703)675-3207
The Foster-Harris House, PO 333, 22747, 1901 .... (703)675-3757
Waterford
The Pink House, 22190 .... (703)882-3453
White Post
L'Auberge Provencale, PO Box 119, 22663, 1753 .... (703)837-1375
Williamsburg
Fox Grape Of Williamsburg, 701 Monunental Ave,
    23185 .... (804)229-6914
Governor's Trace, 303 Capitol Landing Rd, 23185 .... (804)229-7552
Liberty Rose Colonial B&B, 1022 Jamestown Rd, 23185,
    1929 .... (804)253-1260
The Cedars, 616 Jamestown Rd, 23185, 1930 .... (804)229-3591
War Hill Inn, 4560 Long Hill Rd, 23185, 1790 .... (804)565-0248
Woodstock
Schlisselsmith, 22664, 1898 .... (703)459-5369
The Candlewick Inn, 127 N Church St, 22664 .... (703)459-8008
The Inn at Narrow Passage, PO Box 608, 22664, 1740 ... (703)459-8000

Washington

Anacortes
Channel House, 2902 Oakes Ave, 98221, 1902 .... (206)293-9382
Hasty Pudding House, 1312 8th Street, 98221, 1913 ...... (206)293-5773
Nantucket Inn, 3402 Commercial Ave, 98221, 1925 .... (206)293-6007
Anohomish
Countryman B&B, 11 Cedar, 98290, 1896 .... (206)568-9622
Ashford
Alexander's Country Inn, Highway 706, 98304 .... (206)569-2300
National Park Inn, Mt Ranier Guest Services, Star Rt, 98304,
    1920 .... (206)569-2563
Bainbridge Island
Bombay House, 8490 Beck Rd NE, 98110, 1907 .... (206)842-3926
Bellingham
North Garden Inn, 1014 N Garden, 98225, 1897 .... (206)671-7828
The Castle B&B, 1103 15th & Knox Sts, 98225, 1889 .... (206)676-0974
Bingen
The Grand Old House, Hwy 14 PO Box 667, 98605,
    1860 .... (509)493-2838
Chelan
Em's B&B, PO Box 206, 304 Wapato, 98816 .... (509)682-4149
Coupeville
Captain Whidbey, 2072 W Captain Whidbey Inn Rd, 98239,
    1907 .... (206)678-4097
Victorian House, PO Box 761, 602 N Main, 98239 .... (206)678-5305
Eastsound
Kangaroo House, 5 North Beach Rd, Orcas Island,
    98245 .... (206)376-2175
Outlook Inn, Box 210 Main St, 98245, 1888 .... (206)376-2200
Turtleback Farm Inn, Rt 1 Box 650, Crow Valley Rd Orcas, 98245,
    1890 .... (206)376-4914
Eatonville
Old Mill House B&B, PO Box 543, 98328 .... (206)832-6506
Edmonds
Pinkham's Pillow, Dayton St & 3rd Ave, 98020 .... (206)774-3406
Ferndale
Anderson House B&B, 2140 Main St, 98248, 1897 .... (206)384-3450
Freeland
Pillars By The Sea, 1367 E Bayview, 98249 .... (205)221-7736
Friday Harbor
Blair House B&B, 345 Blair Ave, 98250, 1900 .... (206)378-5907
Olympic Lights, 4531A Cattle Point Rd, 98250, 1895 ...... (206)378-3186
San Juan Inn, PO Box 776, 98250, 1873 .... (206)378-2070
Tucker House B&B, 260 B St, 98250 .... (206)378-2783
Gig Harbor
Olde Glencove Hotel, 9418 Glencove Rd, 98335 .... (206)884-2835
Gold Bar
Bush House, PO Box 863, 5th & Index Aves, 98251,
    1898 .... (206)363-1244

Washington (Continued)

Greenbank
Guest House B&B & Cottages, 835 E Christenson Rd, 98253,
1920 ....(206)678-3115
Ilwaco
The Inn at Ilwaco, 120 Williams St, NE, 98624, 1926 ..... (206)642-8686
Kirkland
Shumway Mansion, 11410 99th Place NE, 98033, 1909 .. (206)823-2303
La Conner
Katy's Inn, PO Box 304, 503 S 3rd, 98257 .... (206)466-3366
La Conner Country Inn, PO Box 573, 2nd & Morris,
98257 ....(206)466-3101
Rainbow Inn, PO Box 1600, 98257, 1900 .... (206)466-4578
Langley
Country Cottage of Langley, PO Box 459, 215 6th St, 98260,
1926 ....(206)221-8709
Sally's B&B Manor, PO Box 459, 98260, 1929 .... (206)221-8709
Saratoga Inn, 4850 South Coles Rd, 98260, 1892 .... (206)221-7526
The Orchard, 619 3rd St, 98260, 1905 .... (206)221-7880
Whidbey House, PO Box 156, 106 First St, 98260, 1934 ... (206)221-7115
Leavenworth
Edel Haus B&B, 320 Ninth St, 98826, 1930 .... (509)548-4412
Haus Rohrback, 12882 Ranger Rd, 98826 .... (206)548-7024
Lopez Island
Inn at Swifts Bay, Rt 2 Box 3402, 98261 .... (206)468-3636
Mount Vernon
White Swan Guest House, 1388 Moore Rd, 98273 .... (206)445-6805
North Bend
Apple Tree Inn, 43317 S North Bend Way, 98045 .... (206)888-3672
Olympia
Harbinger Inn, 1136 E Bay Dr, 98506 .... (206)754-0389
Puget View Guesthouse, 7924 61st NE, 98506 .... (206)459-1676
Sylvester House, 1803 Capitol Way, 98501, 1907 .... (206)786-8582
Orcas
Orcas Hotel, PO Box 155, 98280, 1900 .... (206)376-4300
Port Angeles
Tudor Inn, 1108 S Oak, 98362, 1910 .... (206)452-3138
Port Townsend
Arcadia Country Inn, 1891 S Jacob Miller Rd, 98368,
1878 ....(206)385-5245
Bishop Victorian Suites, 714 Washington St, 98368, 1892 (206)385-6122
Hastings House, 313 Walker St, 98368 .... (206)385-3553
Heritage House Inn, 305 Pierce St, 98368, 1880 .... (206)385-6800
Irish Acres, PO Box 466, 780 Arcadia W., 98368 .... (206)385-4485
James House, 1238 Washington, 98368, 1889 .... (206)385-1238
Lincoln Inn, 538 Lincoln, 98368, 1888 .... (206)385-6677
Lizzie's, 731 Pierce St, 98368, 1887 .... (206)385-4168
Manresa Castle, PO Box 564, 7th & Sheridan, 98368,
1892 ....(206)385-5750
Palace Hotel, 1004 Water St, 98368, 1889 .... (206)385-0773
Starrett House Inn, 744 Clay St, 98368, 1889 .... (206)385-3205
Poulsbo
Manor Farm Inn, 26069 Big Valley Rd, 98370 .... (206)779-4628
Roche Harbor
Hotel De Haro, PO Box 1, 98250, 1886 .... (206)378-2155
Roche Harbor Resort, 98250 .... (206)378-2155
Seattle
Beech Tree Manor, 1405 Queen Anne Ave N, 98109,
1904 ....(206)281-7037
Burton House, PO Box 9902, 98109 .... (206)285-5945
Challenger, 809 Fairview Place N, 98109 .... (206)340-1201
Chambered Nautilus B&B Inn, 5005 22nd NE, 98105,
1915 ....(206)522-2536
Chelsea Station B&B Inn, 4915 Linden Ave N, 98103,
1920 ....(206)547-6077
College Inn Guest House, 4000 University Way NE, 98105,
1908 ....(206)633-4441
Galer Place, 318 W Galer St, 98119, 1906 .... (206)282-5339
Mildred's B&B, 1202 15th Ave E, 98112, 1890 .... (206)325-6072
Roberta's B&B, 1147 16th Ave E, 98112, 1900 .... (206)329-3326
The Williams House, 1505 Fourth Ave N, 98109, 1905 .. (206)285-0810

Seaview
Shelburne Inn, PO Box 250, Pacific Hwy 103 & 45th, 98644,
1896 ....(206)642-2442
South Cleelum
Moore House B&B Country Inn, PO Box 2861, 98943 ...... (509)674-5939
Spokane
Fotheringham House B&B, 2128 W 2nd Ave, 99204 .... (509)838-4363
Tacoma
Keenan House, 2610 N Warner, 98407, 1890 .... (206)752-0702
Tokeland
Tokeland Hotel, PO Box 117, 98590, 1854 .... (206)267-7700
Usk
River Bend Inn, Rt 2 Box 943, 99180 .... (509)445-1476
Vashon
The Old Tjomsland House, 99 Ave SW & 171st St, Box 913, 98070,
1890 ....(206)463-5275
Walla Walla
Rees Mansion Inn, 260 E Birch St, 99362 .... (509)529-7845
White Salmon
Inn Of The White Salmon, PO Box 1446, 172 SE Jewett,
98672 ....(509)493-2335
Orchard Hill Inn, Rt 2 Box 130, 98672 .... (509)493-3024

Washington, D. C.

Washington
Adams Inn, 1744 Lanier Pl NW, 20009, 1908 .... (202)745-3600
Connecticut-Woodley, 2647 Woodley Rd NW, 20008,
1890 ....(202)667-0218
Kalorama Guest House, 1854 Mintwood Place NW, 20009,
1900 ....(202)667-6369
Kalorama Guest House/Woodley Park, 2700 Cathedral Ave NW,
20008 ....(202)328-0860
Meg's International Guest House, 1315 Euclid St NW, 20009,
1894 ....(202)232-5837
Morrison-Clark Inn, Massachusetts And Eleventh St Nw, 20001,
1900 ....(202)898-1200
Reeds B&B, PO Box 12011, 20005 .... (202)328-3510
Tabard Inn, 1739 N St NW, 20036 .... (202)785-1277

West Virginia

Athens
Concord Church Inn, 304 Vermillion St, 24712, 1896 .... (304)384-5084
Berkeley Springs
Folkestone B&B, Rt 2 Box 404, 25411, 1929 .... (304)258-3743
Highlawn Inn, 304 Market St, 25411 .... (304)258-5700
Maria's Garden & Inn, 201 Independence St, 25411,
1929 ....(304)258-2021
Oak Lee B&B, 501 Johnson Mill Rd, 25411
The Country Inn, 25411 .... (304)258-2210
The Manor, 415 Fairfax St, 25411 .... (304)258-1552
Bramwell
The Bluestone Inn, 1 Main St, 24715 .... (304)248-7402
Three Oaks & A Quilt, Duhring St, 24715 .... (304)248-8316
Caldwell
The Greenbrier River Inn, US 60, 24925, 1824 .... (304)647-5652
Cass
Shay Inn, General Delivery, 24927 .... (304)456-4652
Charles Town
The Cottonwood Inn, Rt 2 Box 615, 25414 .... (304)725-3371
Charlestown
Hillbrook Inn, Rt 2 Box 152, 25414
Magnus Tate's Kitchen, 201 E Washington St, 25414,
1796 ....(304)725-8052
The Carriage Inn, 417 E Washington St, 25414, 1836 .... (304)728-8003
Chloe
Pennbrooke Farm B&B, Granny-she Run, 25235 .... (304)655-7367
Crawley
Oak Knoll B&B, General Delivery, 24931, 1900 .... (304)392-6903
Davis
Bright Morning, William Ave, Rt 32, 26260, 1898 .... (304)259-5119
The Twisted Thistle B&B, Box 480, 26260 .... (304)259-5389

Elkins
Lincoln Crest B&B, Box 408, 26241 .... (304)636-8460
Marian's Guest House, 731 Harrison Ave, 26241, 1917 ... (304)636-9883
The Retreat, 214 Harpertown Rd, 26241 .... (304)636-2960
The Wayside Inn, 201 Sycamore St, 26241 .... (304)636-1985

Fairmont
Tichnell's Tourist Home, 1367 Locust Ave, 26554, 1939 ... (304)366-3811

Gauley Bridge
Three Rivers Inn, PO Box 231, 25085, 1929 .... (304)632-2121

Gerrardstown
Prospect Hill, PO Box 135, 25420, 1789 .... (304)229-3346

Glen Ferris
Glen Ferris Inn, 25090, 1853 .... (304)632-1111

Harpers Ferry
Fillmore Street B&B, Box 34, 25425, 1890 .... (301)377-0070
Spangler Manor, 55 High St, Rt 3 Box 1402, 25425
The View B&B, Box 286, 25425 .... (304)535-2688

Helvetia
Beekeeper Inn, 26224 .... (304)924-6435

Hillsboro
The Current, Box 135, 25945

Huntington
Heritage Station, 11th St & Veterns Mem Blvd, 25701 ..... (304)523-6373

Jane Lew
West Fork Inn, Rt 2 Box 212, 26378 .... (304)745-4893

Lewisburg
Lynn's Inn B&B, Rt 4 Box 40, 24901 .... (304)645-2003
Minnie Manor, 403 E Washington St, 24901 .... (304)647-4096
The General Lewis, 301 E Washington St, 24901, 1834 . (304)645-2600

Lost Creek
Crawford's Country Corner, Box 112, 26385 .... (304)745-3017

Martinsburg
Boydville-The Inn at Martinsburg, 601 S Queen St, 25401,
     1812 .... (304)263-1448
The Dunn Family Farm, Rt 3, 25401, 1850 .... (304)263-8646

Mathias
Valley View Farm, PO Box 467, 26812 .... (304)897-5229

Middleway
Gilbert House B&B, Rt 1 Box 160, 25430, 1760 .... (304)725-0637

Moorefield
Hickory Hill Farm, Rt 1 Box 355, 26836, 1809 .... (304)538-2511
McMechen House Inn, 109 N Main St, 26836 .... (304)538-2417

Morgantown
Chestnut Ridge School B&B, 1000 Stewartstown Rd,
     26505 .... (304)598-2262

Orlando
Kilmarnock Farms, Rt 1 Box 91, 26412, 1900 .... (304)452-8319

Pence Springs
Riverside Inn, Rt 3, 24962 .... (304)445-7469

Prosperity
Prosperity Farmhouse, Box 393, 25909 .... (304)255-4245

Quicksburg
Mccoy's Mill, Rt 1 Box 94, 22847 .... (304)358-7893

Saint Albans
The Chilton House, 2 Sixth Ave, 25177 .... (304)722-2918

Shepherdstown
Bavarian Inn & Lodge, Rt 1 Box 30, 25443 .... (304)876-2551
Mecklenburg Inn, 128 E German St, 25443 .... (304)876-2126
The Little Inn, PO Box 219, Princess At German St,
     25443 .... (304)876-2208
Thomas Shepherd Inn, Box 1162, German & Duke St, 25443,
     1868 .... (304)876-3715

Sinks Grove
Morgan Orchard, Rt 2 Box 114, 24976 .... (304)772-3638

Sistersville
Cobblestone Inn B&B, 103 Charles St, 25175 .... (304)652-1206
Wells Inn, 316 Charles St, 26175, 1893 .... (304)652-3111

Slatyfork
Fassiferns Farms, Rt 219 N, 26291 .... (304)572-4645
Willis Farm, Rt 219, 26291 .... (304)572-3771

Snowshoe
Whistlepunk Inn, Box 70, 26209 .... (800)624-2757

Summerville
Old Wilderness Inn, 1 Old Wilderness Rd, 26651 .... (304)872-3481
Summit Point
Countryside, PO Box 57, 25446, 1930 .... (304)725-2614
Wellburg
Dovers Inn, 1001 Washington Pike, 26070 .... (304)737-0188
Wheeling
Yesterdays, Ltd., 614 Main St, 26003 .... (304)232-0864
White Sulphur Spring
The Greenbrier, 24986 .... (304)536-1110
Winona
Garvey House, Box 98, 25942 .... (304)574-3235

Wisconsin

Alma
Lane House, 1111 S Main, 54610, 1863 .... (608)685-4923
The Gallery House, 215 N Main St, 54610, 1861 .... (608)685-4975
Appleton
The Parkside B&B, 402 E North St, 54011, 1906 .... (414)733-0200
Baraboo
Frantiques Showplace, 704 Ash St, 53913, 1863 .... (608)356-5273
House Of Seven Gables, PO Box 204, 215 6th St, 53913. (608)356-8387
The Barrister's House, 226 9th Ave, PO Box 166, 53913,
     1932 .... (608)356-3344
Bayfield
Chez Joliet, PO Box 768, Bayfield, 54814, 1890 .... (715)779-5480
Cooper Hill House, 33 S Sixth St Box 5, 54814 .... (715)779-5060
Greunke's Inn, 17 Rittenhouse, 54184, 1863 .... (715)779-5480
Le Chateau Boutin, PO Box 584, 54814, 1920 .... (715)779-5111
Old Rittenhouse Inn, 301 Rittenhouse Ave, PO Box 584-1, 54814,
     1890 .... (715)779-5111
Cedarburg
Stagecoach Inn B&B, W 61 N 520 Washington Ave, 53012,
     1853 .... (414)375-0208
The Washington House Inn, W 62 N 573 Washington Ave, 53012,
     1886 .... (414)375-3550
Chippewa Falls
Wilson House, 320 Superior St, 54729, 1887 .... (715)723-0055
Delavan
The Allyn House, 511 E Walworth, 53115 .... (414)728-9090
Ellison Bay
The Griffin Inn, 11976 Mink River Rd, 54210, 1910 ...... (414)854-4306
Ephraim
Eagle Harbor Inn, PO Box 72 B, 54211 .... (414)854-2121
Hillside Hotel, PO Box 17, 54211 .... (414)854-2417
Fish Creek
Proud Mary, PO Box 193, 54212, 1870 .... (414)868-3442
Thorp House Inn & Cottages, 4135 Bluff Rd, PO Box 90, 54212,
     1902 .... (414)868-2444
Whistling Swan Inn, Main St Box 193, 54212 .... (414)868-3442
White Gull Inn, PO Box 175, 54212, 1896 .... (414)868-3517
Green Bay
La Baye House, 803 Oregon, 54303 .... (414)437-5081
Green Lake
Strawberry Hill B&B, Rt 1 Box 524-d, 54941 .... (414)294-3450
Hartland
Monches Mill House, W 301 N 9430 Hwy E, 53029 .... (414)966-7546
Hazel Green
Wisconsin House Stagecoach Inn, 2105 Main, 53811,
     1846 .... (608)854-2233
Jamesville
Sessler's Guest House, 210 S Jackson St, 53545
Kenosha
The Manor House, 6536 3rd Ave, 53140, 1928 .... (414)658-0014
Lake Mills
Midwest Fargo Mansion Inn, 406 Mulberry St, 53551 ..... (414)648-3654
Lewis
Seven Pines Lodge, 54851, 1903 .... (715)653-2323
Madison
Chesterfield Inn, 20 Commerce St, 53565, 1834 .... (608)987-3682
Mansion Hill Inn, 424 N Pinckney, 53703, 1858 .... (608)255-3999
Plough Inn B&B, 3402 Monroe St, 53711, 1850 .... (608)238-2981

Wisconsin (Continued)

The Collins House, 704 E Gorham, 53703, 1911 .... (608)255-4230
Milwaukee
Ogden House, 2237 N Lake Dr, 53202, 1916 .... (414)272-2740
Mineral Point
The Duke Guest House B&B, 618 Maiden St, 53565 .... (608)987-2821
Wilson House Inn, 110 Dodge St Hwy 151, 53565, 1853 (608)987-3600
Montello
Westmont Farms, Rt 3, Box 556, 53959 .... (414)293-4456
Mount Horeb
H.B. Dahle House, 200 N 2nd St, 53572
New Lisbon
The Evansen House, Rt 1 Box 18, 53950
Oconomowoc
The Inn at Pine Terrace, 351 Lisbon Rd, 53066 .... (414)567-7463
Oxford
Halfway House, Rt 2 Box 80, 53952, 1800 .... (608)586-5489
Plymouth
Irish Guest House, 52 Staffrord, 53073
Portage
Breese Waye B&B, 816 Macfarlane Rd, 53901, 1888 .... (608)742-5281
Poynette
Jamieson House, 407 N Franklin, 53955, 1883 .... (608)635-4100
Prescott
Yankee Bugler Inn, 506 Oak St, 54021, 1854 .... (715)262-3019
Soldiers Grove
Page's Old Oak Inn, Hwy 131 S, 54655, 1901 .... (608)624-5217
Spring Green
Hardyns House, 250 N Winstead, 53588 .... (608)588-7007
Strum
Lake House, RR 2 Box 217, 54770 .... (715)693-3519
Sturgeon Bay
Inn at Cedar Crossing, 336 Louisiana St, 54235, 1884 ...... (414)743-4200
The Scofield House, 908 Michigan St, PO Box 761, 54235,
   1900 .... (414)743-7727
White Lace Inn, 16 N 5th Ave, 54235, 1903 .... (414)743-1105
Viroqua
Viroqua Heritage Inn, 220 E Jefferson St, 54665, 1890 ...... (608)637-3306
Wausau
Rosenberry Inn, 511 Franklin St, 54401, 1908 .... (715)842-5733
White Lake
Wolf River Lodge, 54491, 1920 .... (715)882-2182
Whitewater
Green House B&B, RR 2, Box 214, 53190, 1840 .... (414)495-8771
Wisconsin Dells
House On River Road, 922 River Rd, 53965 .... (608)253-5573

Wyoming

Cody
Shoshone Lodge Resort, PO Box 790bb, 82414 .... (307)587-4044
The Lockhart Inn, 109 West Yellowstone Ave, 82414 .... (307)587-6074
Valley Ranch, 100 Valley Ranch Rd, 82414 .... (307)587-4661
Evanston
Pine Gables B&B, 1049 Center St, 82930, 1883 .... (307)789-2069
Glenrock
Hotel Higgins, 416 W Birch, 82637, 1900 .... (307)436-9212
Jackson Hole
Captain Bob Morris, PO Box 261 Teton Village, 83025 .... (307)733-4413
Lander
Miner's Delight Inn, Atlantic City Rt, PO Box 205, 82520,
   1899 .... (307)332-3513
Laramie
Annie Moore's Guest House, 819 University, 82070 .... (307)721-4177
Moran
Jenny Lake Lodge, PO Box 240, 83013 .... (307)733-4677
Rawlins
Ferris Mansion, 607 W Maple St, 82301, 1903 .... (307)324-3961
Saratoga
Wolf Hotel, PO Box 1298, 101 E Bridge, 82331 .... (307)326-5525

Savery
Boyer YL Ranch, PO Box 24, 82332, 1889 .... (307)383-7840
Wilson
Heck Of A Hill Home-stead, PO Box 105, 83014 .... (307)733-8023
Snow Job, PO Box 371, 83014 .... (307)739-9695

U.S. Territories

Puerto Rico

Condado, San Juan
El Canario Inn, 1317 Ashford Ave, 00907, 1938 .... (809)722-3861
Maricao
Parador Hacienda Juanita, PO Box 838, 00706 .... (809)838-2550
Patillas
Caribe Playa Resort, B. 2730 Guardamaya, 00723
San German
Parador Oasis, PO Box 144, 00753 .... (809)892-1175
Vieques
La Casa Del Frances, PO Box 458, Esperanza, 00765 .... (809)741-3751

Virgin Islands

Saint Croix
Pink Fancy, 27 Prince St, Christiansted, 00820, 1780 .... (809)773-8460
Saint Thomas
Galleon House, PO Box 6577, 00801 .... (809)774-6952
Hotel 1829, PO Box 1567, 00801 .... (809)774-1829

Reservation Services

Alabama

Bed and Breakfast, Birmingham, Inc., PO Box 31328, Birmingham AL 35222 .... (205) 591-6406

Bed and Breakfast Montgomery, PO Box 886, Milbrook AL 36054 .... (205) 285-5421

Bed and Breakfast Mobile, PO Box 66261, Mobile AL 36606 .... (205) 473-2939

Alaska

Alaska Bed and Breakfast, 526 Seward St, Juneau AK 99801 .... (907) 586-2959

Alaska Guest Homes, 1941 Glacier Hwy, Juneau AK 99801 .... (907) 586-1840

Anchorage B'B, PO Box 110135, South Station, Anchorage AK 99511 .... (907) 345-2222

Fairbanks B&B, PO Box 74573, Fairbanks AK 99707 .... (907) 452-4967

Ketchikan B'B, Box 7814, Ketchikan Ak 99901
.... (907) 225-6044
.... (907) 247-8444

Stay With a Friend, 3605 Arctic Blvd #173, Anchorage AK 99503 .... (907) 274-6445

Arizona

Barbara's B&B, PO Box 13603, Tucson AZ 85732-3603
.... (602) 886-5847

Bed and Breakfast in Arizona, (8433 N Black Canyon Ste 160, Phoenix AZ 85021 .... (602) 995-2831

Bed & Breakfast-Scottsdale, PO Box 624, Scottsdale AZ 85252 .... (602) 998-7044

Mi Casa Su Casa, Bed & Breakfast, 1456 N Scottsdale Rd, Ste 110, Tempe AZ 85281 .... (602) 990-0682

Arkansas

Bed & Breakfast in the Arkansas Ozarks, RT 1 PO Box 38, Calico Rock AR 72519 .... (501) 297-8764

Bed & Breakfast Reservations, 11 Singleton, Eureka Springs AR 72632 ....(501) 253-9111

B&B of Eureka Springs, PO Box 27, Eureka Springs AR 72632 .... (501) 253-6767

California

America Family Inn B&B, Box 349, San Francisco CA 94101 .... (415) 931-3083

American Historic Homes B&B, PO Box 336-C, Dana Point CA 92629, National reservations .. (714) 496-6953

Bed and Breakfast Hospitality, PO Box 2407, Oceanside CA 92054 .... (619) 722-6694

B&B International, 151 Ardmore Rd, Kensington CA 94707 .... (415) 525-4569

B&B of Los Angeles, 32127 Harborview Ln, Westlake Village CA 91361 .... (818) 889-7325
.... (818) 889-8870

B&B of Southern California, Box 218, Fullerton CA 92632 .... (714) 738-8361

B&B Approved Hosts, 10890 Galvin, Ventura CA 93004
.... (805) 647-0651

California Houseguests International, 6051 Lindley Ave #6, Tarzana CA 91356 .... (818) 344-7878

California Coast B&B, 25624 Monte Nido Dr, Calabasas CA 91302 .... (213) 999-3130

California Sunshine B&B, 22704 Ventura Blvd, Woodland Hills CA 91364 .... (818) 992-1984

Carolyn's B&B Homes in San Diego, 416 Third Ave #25, Chula Vista CA 92010 .... (619) 422-7009

Christian B&B of America, Box 388-B, San Juan Capistrano CA 92693, United States, Britain .... (714) 496-7050

Co-Host, America's B&B, 11715 S Circle Dr, Whittier CA 90601 .... (213) 699-8427

Dig's West, 8191 Crowley Cir, Buena Park CA 90621 .... (714) 739-1669

Educators' Vacation Alternatives, 317 Piedmont Rd, Santa Barbara CA 93105, Membership organization for teachers .... (805) 687-2947

El Camino Real Bed & Breakfast, PO Box 7155, Northridge CA 91327-7155 .... (818) 363-6753

Eye Openers B&B, Box 694, Altadena CA 91001 .... (818) 684-4428 .... (818) 797-2055

B&B Homestay, Box 326, Cambria CA 93428 .... (805) 927-4613

Hospitality Plus, Box 388-B, San Juan Capistrano CA 92693, California coastal cities and Yosemite .... (714) 496-7050

Megan's Friends B&B Reservations, PO Box 4835, San Luis Obispo CA 93403 .... (805) 544-4406

Napa B&B Reservations, 1834 First St, Napa CA 94559 .... (707) 224-4667

New Age Travel, 839 Second St Ste 3, Encinitas CA 92024 .... (619) 436-9977

Rent-A-Room International, 11531 Varna St, Garden Grove CA 92640 .... (714) 638-1406

Traveler's Bed & Breakfast, PO Box 1368, Chino CA 91710 .... (714) 627-7971

University B&B, 1387 Sixth Ave, San Francisco CA 94122 .... (415) 661-8940

Wine Country B&B, Box 3211, Santa Rosa CA 95403 .... (707) 578-1661

Colorado

Bed & Breakfast Colorado, PO Box 20596, Denver CO 80306 .... (303) 442-6664

B&B Rocky Mountains, Box 804, Colorado Springs CO 89901 .... (303) 630-3433

Vail B&B, Box 491, Vail CO 81658 .... (303) 949-1212

Connecticut

Bed & Breakfast, Ltd in New Haven, PO Box 216, New Haven CT 06518 .... (203) 469-3260

Covered Bridge B&B, West Cornwall CT 06796 .... (203) 542-5944

Nautilus B&B, 133 Phoenix Dr, Groton CT 06340 .... (203) 448-1538

Nutmeg B&B, 222 Girard Ave, Hartford CT 06105 .... (203) 236-6698

Seacoast Landings, 133 Neptune Dr, Groton CT 06340 .... (203) 442-1940

Delaware

Bed & Breakfast of Delaware, 1804 Breen Lane, Wilmington DE 19810 .... (302) 479-9500

Florida

A&A B&B of Florida, Box 1316, Winter Park FL 32790 .... (305) 628-3233

B&B Company, Box 262, S Miami FL 33243 .... (305) 661-3270

B&B of the Keys, 5 Man-O-War Dr, Marathon FL 33050 .... (305) 743-4118

B&B of the Palm Beaches, 5 Man-O-War Drive, Marathon FL 33050 .... (305) 743-4118

B&B Suncoast Accommodations, 8690 Gulf Blvd, St Petersburg Beach FL 33706 .... (813) 360-1753

Open House B&B Registry, PO Box 43025, Palm Beach FL 33480 .... (305) 842-5190

Georgia

Atlanta Home Hospitality, 2472 Lauderdale Dr NE, Atlanta GA 30345 .... (404) 493-1930

B&B Atlanta, 1801 Piedmont Ave NE, #208, Atlanta GA 30324 .... (404) 875-0525

Quail Country Bed & Breakfast Ltd, 1104 Old Monticello Rd, Thomasville GA 31792 .... (912) 226-6882

Savannah Historic Inns & Guesthouses, 1900 Lincoln St, Savannah GA 31401 .... (912) 226-7218

Hideaway B'B, PO Box 300, Blue Ridge GA 30513 .... (404) 632-2411

Hawaii

B&B Hawaii, Box 449, Kapaa HI 96746 .. (808) 822-7771

Pacific-Hawaii B&B, 19 Kai Nani Place, Kailua, Oahu
HI 96734 .... (808) 262-6026

B&B Honolulu, 3242 Kaohinani Dr, Honolulu HI 96817
(808) 595-7533

Go Native - Hawaii, PO Box 13115, Lansing MI 48901
.... (517) 349-9598

Idaho

B&B of Idaho, PO Box 7323, BoiseID 83707
.... (208) 336-5174

Illinois

B&B Chicago, Inc, 3500 N Lake Shore Dr, Suite 17-D,
Chicago IL 60657 .... (312) 472-2294

B&B of Chicago, Box 14088, Chicago IL 60614
.... (312) 951-0085

Bed and Board America Inc, 7308 W Madison St, Forest
Park IL 50130 .... (312) 771-8100

Indiana

Indiana Amish Country Bed & B'fast Amish Acres, Inc,
1660 W Market St, Nappanee IN 46550 .. (219) 773-4188

Iowa

Bed & Breakfast in Iowa, Box 430, Preston IA 52069
.... (319) 689-4222

Kansas

Kansas City B&B, Box 14781, Lenexa KS 66215
.... (913) 888-3636

Kentucky

Kentucky Homes B&B, 1431 St James Court, Louisville
KY 40208 .... (502) 635-7341
.... (502) 452-6629

Bluegrass B&B, Route 1, Box 263, Versailles KY 40383
.... (606) 873-3208

Louisiana

B&B Inc, 1360 Moss St, New Orleans LA 70152-2257
.... (504) 525-4640
.... (800) 228-9711 dialtone 184

New Orleans B&B and Bed & Breakfast of Louisiana &
Tours, PO Box 8128, New Orleans LA 70182
.... (504) 822-5038
.... (504) 822-5046

Southern Comfort B&B Reservation Service, 2856
Hundred Oaks, Baton Rouge LA 70808 .. (504) 346-1928

Bed, Bath & Breakfast, Box 52466, New Orleans LA
70152 .... (504) 897-3867
.... (504) 891-4862

Louisiana Hospitality Services, Box 80717, Baton Rouge
LA 70898 .... (504) 769-0366

Peggy Lindsay Enterprises Bed, Bath & Breakfast, PO
Box 15843, New Orleans LA 70175 ...... (504) 897-3867

Maine

B&B Down East, Box 547, Eastbrook ME 04634
.... (207) 565-3517

B&B of Maine, 32 Colonial Village, Falmouth ME 04105
.... (207) 781-4528

Chamber of Commerce, 142 Free St, Portland ME 04101

The Maine Publicity Bureau, 97 Winthrop St, Hallowell
ME 04347

Maryland

Armanda's B&B, 1428 Park Ave, Baltimore, MD 21217-
4230 .... (301) 225-0001

Sweet Dreams & Toast, Inc, PO Box 9490, Washington
DC 20016 .... (202) 363-7767

The Traveller in Maryland, 33 West St, Annapolis, MD
21401 .... (301) 269-6232
.... (301) 261-2233

Massachusetts

Around Plymouth Bay, PO Box 6211, Plymouth MA
02360 .... (617) 747-5075

B&B Agency of Boston, 47 Commercial Wharf, Boston
MA 02110 .... (617) 720-3540

B&B Associates Bay Colony LTD, Box 166 Babson Park,
Boston MA 02157 .... (617) 449-5302

B&B Brookline/Boston, Box 732, Brookline MA 02146
.... (617) 277-2292

B&B Cambridge & Greater Boston, Box 665 Kirkland St,
Cambridge MA 02140 .... (617) 576-1492

B&B Cape Cod, Box 341, West Hyannisport MA 02672
.... (617) 775-2772

B&B Folks, 73 Providence Rd, Westford MA 01886
.... (617) 692-3232
.... (617) 692-2700

B&B in Minuteman Country, 8 Carriage Dr, Lexington
MA 02173 .... (617) 861-7063

Be Our Guest B&B, Box 1333, Plymouth MA 02360
.... (617) 837-9867

Berkshire Bed & Breakfast, PO Box 211, Main St, Williamsburg MA 01096-0211 .... (413) 268-7244

Christian Hospitality, 636 Union St, Duxbury MA 02332
.... (617) 834-8528

Folkstone B&B, PO Box 931, Boylston MA 01505
.... (617) 869-2687

Greater Boston Hospitality, Box 1142, Brookline MA 02146 .... (617) 277-5430

Host Homes of Boston, Box 117, Newton MA 02168
.... (617) 244-1308

House Guests, Cape Cod, Box 8-A, Dennis MA 02638
.... (617) 398-0787

Mayflower B&B, Box 172, Belmont MA 02178
.... (617) 484-0068

New England B&B, 1045 Centre St, Newton Centre MA 02159 .... (617) 244-2112
.... (617) 498-9819

Orleans B&B Associates, Box 1312, Orleans MA 02653
.... (617) 255-3824

Pineapple Hospitality Inc, 47 N Second St, Ste 3A, New Bedford MA 02740 .... (617) 990-1696

Michigan

Betsy Ross B&B in Michigan, PO Box 1731, Dearborn MI 48121 .... (313) 561-6041

Frankenmuth Area B&B, 337 Trinklein St, Frankenmuth MI 48734 .... (517) 652-8897

Minnesota

B&B Registry, Box 8174, St Paul MN 55108
.... (612) 646-4238

Mississippi

Lincoln, Ltd, Bed & Breakfast, PO Box 3479, Meridian, MS 39303 .... (601) 482-5483

Natchez Pilgrimage Tours, Box 347, Natchez MS 39120
.... (601) 446-6631
.... (800) 647-6742

Missouri

B&B St Louis, 4418 West Pine St, St Louis MO 63108
.... (314) 533-9299

Lexington B&B, 115 N 18th St, Lexington MO 64067
.... (816) 259-4163

B&B of St Louis - River Country, #1 Grandview Heights, St Louis MO 63131 .... (314) 965-4328

Kansas City B&B, PO Box 14781, Lenexa KS 66215
.... (913) 888-3636

Ozark Mountain Country B&B, Box 295, Branson MO 65616
.... (417) 334-4720
.... (417) 334-5077

Truman Country B&B, 424 N Pleasant, Independence MO 64050 .... (816) 254-6657

Montana

Western B&B Hosts, Box 322, Kalispell MT 59901
.... (406) 257-4476

B&B-Rocky Mountains-Montana, PO Box 804, Colorado Springs CO 80901 .... (303) 630-3433

Nebraska

B&B of Nebraska, 1464 28th Ave, Columbus NE 68601
.... (402) 564-7591

B&B of the Great Plains, PO Box 2333, Lincoln NE 68502 .... (402) 423-3480

Swede Hospitality B&B, 1617 Ave A, Gothenburg NE 69138 .... (308) 537-2680

New Hampshire

New Hampshire Bed & Breakfast, RFD 3, Box 53, Laconia NH 03246 .... (603) 279-8348

New Jersey

Bed and Breakfast of New Jersey, Suite 132, 103 Godwin Ave, Midland Park NJ 07432 .... (201) 444-7409

B&B of Princeton, PO Box 571, Princeton NJ 08540
.... (609) 924-3189

Town & Country Bed & Breakfast, PO Box 301, Lambertville NJ 08530 .... (609) 397-8399

Northern NJ Bed & Breakfast, 11 Sunset Trail, Denville NJ 07834 .... (201) 625-5129

New Mexico

Bed and Breakfast Santa Fe, Inc, 218 E Buena Vista, Santa Fe NM 87501 .... (505) 982-3332

New York

Alternate Lodgings, Inc, PO Box 1782, East Hampton NY 11937 .... (516) 324-9449

The American Country Collection of B&B Homes, 984 Gloucester Place, Schenectady NY 12309   (518) 370-4948

A Reasonable Alternative, 117 Spring St, Port Jefferson NY 11777 . . . . (516) 928-4034

B&B of Greater Syracuse, 143 Didama St, Syracuse NY 13224 . . . . (315) 446-4199

Bed & Breakfast of Long Island, PO Box 392, Old Westbury NY 11568 . . . . (516) 334-6231

Bed & Breakfast Reservation Service of Greater New York, PO Box 1015, Pearl River NY 10965

Bed & Breakfast Rochester, Box 444, Fairport NY 14450 . . . . (716) 223-8510
. . . . (716) 223-8877

Bed & Breakfast, USA, Ltd, PO Box 606, Croton-on-Hudson NY 10520 . . . . (914) 271-6228

Cherry Valley Ventures, 6119 Cherry Valley Turnpike, Lafayette NY 13084 . . . . (315) 677-9723

City Lights Bed & Breakfast, Ltd, PO Box 20355, Cherokee Station, New York NY 10028 . . (212) 877-3235

Guest Quarters International Club, 207 E 85th St, Suite 166, New York NY 10028 . . . . (212) 249-1014

Hampton Bed & Breakfast, PO Box 378, East Moriches NY 11940 . . . . (516) 878-8197

Leatherstocking B&B, 389 Brockway Rd, Frankfort NY 13340 . . . . (315) 733-0040

New World Bed & Breakfast, Ltd, 150 Fifth Ave, Suite 711, New York NY 10011 . . . . (212) 675-5600

North Country Bed & Breakfast, PO Box 286, Lake Placid NY 12946 . . . . (518) 523-3739

Rainbow Hospitality Bed & Breakfast, 9348 Hennepin Ave, Niagara Falls NY 14304 . . . . (716) 283-4794
. . . . (716) 754-8877

Traveler's Retreat, RD 3, Melvin Lane, Baldwinsville NY 13027 . . . . (315) 638-8664

Urban Ventures, PO Box 426, New York NY 10024
. . . . (212) 594-5650

North Carolina

Bed & Breakfast of Asheville, 217-B Merrimon Ave, Asheville NC 28801 . . . . (704) 255-8367

B&B in the Albemarle, PO Box 248, Everetts NC 27825
. . . . (919) 792-4584

Charlotte Bed & Breakfast, 1700-2 Delane Ave, Charlotte NC 28211 . . . . (704) 366-0979

North Dakota

The Old West B&B, Box 211, Regent ND 58650
. . . . (701) 563-4542

Ohio

Buckeye Bed & Breakfast, PO Box 130, Powell OH 43065 . . . . (614) 548-4555

Columbus Bed & Breakfast Group, 769 S Third St, Columbus OH 43206 . . . . (614) 443-3680

Ohio Valley B&B, 6876 Taylor Mill Rd, Independence KY 41051 . . . . (606) 356-7865

Private Lodgings, PO Box 18590, Cleveland OH 44118-0590 . . . . (216) 321-3213

Oklahoma

Redbud Reservations/B&B for Oklahoma, PO Box 23954, Oklahoma City OK 73123 . . . . (405) 720-0212

Oregon

Bed & Breakfast Accommodations - Oregon Plus, 5733 SW Dickinson, Portland OR 97219 . . . . . . (503) 245-0642

Northwest Bed and Breakfast Travel Unlimited, 610 SW Broadway, Portland OR 97205 . . . . (503) 243-7616

Pennsylvania

Bed & Breakfast Center City, 1804 Pine St, Philadelphia PA 19103 . . . . (215) 735-1137

Bed & Breakfast of Chester County, PO Box 825, Kennett Square PA 19348 . . . . (215) 444-1367

Bed & Breakfast of Lancaster County, PO Box 19, Mountville PA . . . . (717) 285-5956

Bed & Breakfast of Philadelphia, PO Box 630, Chester Springs PA 19425 . . . . (215) 827-9650

B&B of Valley Forge, Valley Forge PA 19481-0562
. . . . (215) 783-7838

Bed & Breakfast of Southeast Pennsylvania, Box 278, RD1, Barto PA 19504 . . . . (215) 845-3526

The B&B Traveler, PO Box 21, Devon PA 19333
. . . . (215) 687-3565

Harvest Time Services, Boxx 48, RD 3, Parker PA 16049
. . . . (412) 791-2061

Hershey B&B, PO Box 208, Hershey PA 17033-0208
. . . . (717) 533-2928

Guesthouses B&B Reservations, RD 9, West Chester PA 19380 . . . . (215) 692-4575

Pittsburgh Bed & Breakfast, 2190 Ben Franklin Dr, Pittsburgh PA 15237 .... (412) 367-8080

Rest & Repast, PO Box 126, Pine Grove Mills PA 16868 .... (814) 238-1484

Rhode Island

Bed & Breakfast of Rhode Island, Inc, PO Box 3291, Newport RI 02840 .... (401) 849-1298

Castle Keep Bed & Breakfast, 44 Everett St, Newport RI 02804 .... (401) 846-0362

Guest House Association of Newport, 23 Brinley St, Newport RI 02840 .... (401) 849-7645

South Carolina

Charleston Society Bed & Breakfast, 84 Murray Blvd, Charleston SC 29401 .... (803) 723-4948

Bay Street Accommodations, 601 Bay St, Beaufort SC 29902 .... (803) 524-7720

Historic Charleston Bed & Breakfast, 43 Legare St, Charleston SC 29401 .... (803) 722-6606

South Dakota

South Dakota Bed & Breakfast, PO Box 80137, Sioux Falls SD 57116 .... (605) 528-6571

Tennessee

Bed & Breakfast in Memphis, PO Box 41621, Memphis TN 38104 .... (901) 726-5920

Hospitality at Home, Rt 1, Box 318, Lenior City TN 37771 .... (615) 693-3500

B&B Host Homes of Tennessee, PO Box 110227, Nashville TN 37222-0227 .... (615) 331-5244

Nashville Bed & Breakfast, PO Box 150651, Nashville TN 37215 .... (615) 298-5674
.... (615) 269-6555

River Rendezvous, PO Box 240001, Memphis TN 38124 .... (901) 767-5296

Texas

Bed & Breakfast Hosts of San Antonio, 166 Rockhill, San Antonio TX 78209 .... (512) 824-8036

Bed & Breakfast Society, Intl, 407-D Cora St, Fredericksburg TX 78624 .... (512) 997-7150

Bed & Breakfast Society of Texas, 921 Heights Blvd, Houston TX 77008 .... (713) 868-4654

Bed & Breakfast Texas Style, 4224 W Red Bird Lane, Dallas TX 75237 .... (214) 298-5433
.... (214) 298-8586

Gasthaus Bed & Breakfast Lodging Services, 330 W Main St, Fredericksburg TX 78624 ...... (512) 997-4712

Sand Dollar Hospitality B&B, 3605 Mendenhall, Corpus Christi TX 78415 .... (512) 853-1222

Utah

B&B Homestay, PO Box 335, Salt Lake City UT 84110
.... (801) 532-7076

Vermont

American Bed & Breakfast in New England, Box 983, St Albans VT 05478 .... (802) 524-4731

Vermont Bed & Breakfast, Box 1, East Fairfield VT 05448 .... (802) 827-3827

Virginia

Bed & Breakfast of Tidewater, PO Box 3343, Norfolk VA 23514 .... (804) 627-1983
.... (804) 627-9409

Bensonhouse of Richmond and Williamsburg, 2036 Monument Ave, Richmond VA 23220 ... (804) 648-7560

Blue Ridge Bed & Breakfast, Rocks & Rills, Rt2, Box 3895, Berryville VA 22611 .... (703) 955-1246

Guesthouses - B&B, Inc, PO Box 5737, Charlottesville VA 22905 .... (804) 979-7264
.... (804) 979-8327

Princely B&B, Ltd, 819 Prince St, Alexandria VA 22314 .... (703) 683-2159

Rockbridge Reservations, PO Box 76, Brownsburg VA 24415 .... (703) 348-5698

Shenandoah Valley Bed & Breakfast, PO Box 305, Broadway VA 22815 .... (703) 896-9702
.... (703) 896-2579

Sojourners Bed & Breakfast, PO Box 3587, Lynchburg VA 24503 .... (804) 384-1655

The Travel Tree, PO Box 838, Williamsburg VA 23187
.... (804) 253-1571

Washington

(BABS) Bed & Breakfast Service, PO Box 5025, Bellingham WA 98227 .... (206) 733-8642

INNterlodging Co-op, PO Box 7044, Tacoma WA 98407
.... (206) 756-0343

Pacific Bed & Breakfast, 701 NW 60th St, Seattle WA 98107 .... (206) 784-0539

Travellers' Bed & Breakfast, PO Box 492, Mercer Island WA 98040 .... (206) 232-2345

Washington, DC

Bed 'n Breakfast Ltd of Washington DC, PO Box 12011, Washington DC 20005 .... (202) 328-3510

The Bed & Breakfast League, Ltd, PO Box 9490, Washington DC 20016 .... (202) 363-7767

Sweet Dreams & Toast Inc, PO Box 9490, Washington DC 20016............................ (202) 363-7767

Wisconsin

Bed & Breakfast Guest-Homes, Route 2, Algoma WI 54201 .... (414) 743-9742

Bed & Breakfast of Milwaukee, 320 E Buffalo St, Milwaukee WI 53202 .... (414) 271-2337

Wyoming

Bed & Breakfast Rocky Mountains-Wyoming, PO Box 804, Colorado Springs CO 80901 ....(307) 630-3433

State Tourism Information

- Bureau of Publicity and Information, 532 South Perry St, Montgomery AL 36104

- Alaska Division of Tourism, Pouch E-445, Juneau AK 99811

- Arizona Office of Tourism, 307 North Central Ave Ste 506, Phoenix AZ 85012

- Department Parks & Tourism ,1 Capitol Mall, Little Rock AR 72201

- Office of Tourism, 1121 L St First Floor, Sacramento CA 95814

- Tourism Board, 5500 S Syracuse #267, Englewood CO 80111

- Vacations, Department of Economic Development, 210 Washington St, Hartford CT 06106

- State Travel Service, PO Box 1401, 99 Kings Hwy, Dover DE 19903

- Division of Tourism, Visitor Inquiry Section, 126 Van Buren St, Tallahassee FL 32301

- Tour Georgia, PO Box 1776, Atlanta GA 30301

- Visitors Bureau, Waikiki Business Plaza, 2270 Kalakaua Ave #801, Honolulu HI 96815

- Tourism, Statehouse, Room 108, Boise ID 83720

- Tourist Information Center, 310 S Michigan Ave #108, Chicago IL 60604

- Tourism Development Division, 1 N Capitol Ave #700, Indianapolis IN 46204

- Development Commission, Tourism Division, 600 E Court Ave Ste A, Des Moines IA 50309

- Department of Economic Development, Travel and Tourism Division, 503 Kansas Ave 6th Floor, Topeka KS 66603

- Kentucky Department of Travel Development, Capitol Plaza Tower, Frankfort KY 40601

- Office of Tourism, Inquiry Dept, PO Box 44291, Baton Rouge LA 70804

- Publicity Bureau, 97 Winthrop St, Hallowell ME 04347

- Office of Tourist Development, 45 Calvert St, Annapolis MD 21401

- Division of Tourism, Department of Commerce & Development, 100 Cambridge St 13th Floor, Boston MA 02202

- Travel Bureau, Department of Commerce, PO Box 30226, Lansing MI 48909

- Office of Tourism, 240 Bremer Building, 419 N Robert St, St Paul MN 55101

- Division of Tourism, Department of Economic Development, PO Box 22825, Jackson MS 39205

- Division of Tourism, Truman Building, PO Box 1055, Jefferson City MO 65102

- Promotion Division, Department of Commerce, 1424 Ninth Ave, Helena MT 59620

- Division of Travel & Tourism, Department of Economic Development, PO Box 94666, 301 Centennial Mall South, Lincoln NE 68509

- Commission on Tourism, Capitol Complex, 600 E Williams St, Carson City NV 89710

- Office of Vacation Travel, PO Box 856, Concord NH 03301

- Division of Travel and Tourism, CN-826, Trenton NJ 08625

- Travel Division, Economic Development & Tourism Department, Bataan Memorial Building, Room 751, Santa Fe NM 87503

- State Department of Commerce, Division of Tourism, 1 Commerce Plaza, Albany NY 12245

- Travel & Tourism Division, Department of Commerce, Raleigh NC 27611

- Tourism Promotion, Liberty Memorial Building, State Capitol Grounds, Bismarck ND 58505

- Office of Travel and Tourism, PO Box 1001, Columbus OH 43216

- Tourism and Recreation Department, Literature Distribution Department, 215 NE 28th, Oklahoma City OK 73105

- Economic Development Department, Tourism Division, 595 Cottage St, NE, Salem OR 97310

- Bureau of Travel Development, Department of Commerce, 416 Forum Building, Harrisburg PA 17120

- Department of Economic Development, 7 Jackson Walkway, Providence RI 02903

- Department of Parks, Recreation, and Tourism, PO Box 71, Columbia SC 29202

- Tourism, Box 1000, Pierre SD 57501

- Department of Tourist Development, PO Box 23170, Nashville TN 37202

- Department of Highways & Public Transportation, Travel & Information Division, PO Box 5064, Austin TX 78763

- Travel Council, Council Hall, Capitol Hill, Salt Lake City UT 84114

- Travel Division, 134 State St, Montpelier VT 05602

- Division of Tourism, 202 North 9th St #500, Richmond VA 23219

- State Department of Commerce & Economic Development, Tourism Development Division, General Administration Building, Olympia WA 98504

- Washington Convention and Visitors Association, 1575 Eye St, NW #250, Washington DC 20005

- Division of Tourism, PO Box 7606, Madison WI 53707

- Travel West Virginia, Capitol Complex, Charleston WV 25305

- Travel Commissions, Frank Norris Jr. Travel Center, Cheyenne WY 82002

Inn Associations

Alaska

Alaska B&B Association, 3-6500 Seward St #169,
Juneau, 99802 . . . .(907)586-2959

Arkansas

Association of B&B of Eureka Springs, 82 Armstrong St,
Eureka Springs, 72632

California

Association of American Historic Inns, PO Box 336,
Dana Point 92629 . . . .(714)496-6953

B&B Inns of the Auburn Area, 512 Auburn Ravine Rd,
Auburn, 95603 . . . .(916)885-5616

B&B Innkeepers of Northern California, PO Box 7150,
Chico, 95927 . . . .(800)284-4667

B&B Inns of Humbolt County, PO Box 40, Ferndale,
95536 . . . .(707)786-4000

Wine Country Inns of Sonoma County, PO Box 51,
Geyserville, 95441 . . . .(707)533-4667

B&B of Amador County, 215 Court St, Jackson, 95642
. . . .(209)223-0416

B&B Innkeepers of Southern California, PO Box 15425,
Los Angeles, 90015

Mendocino Coast B&B Association, PO Box 1141, Men-
docino, 95460 . . . .(707)877-3321

Monterey Peninsula B&B Association, 500 Martin St,
Monterey, 93940 . . . .(408)375-5284

El Dorado County Innkeepers Association, PO Box 106,
Placerville, 95667

Historic Country Inns of the Mother Lode, PO Box 106,
Placerville, 95667 . . . .(916)626-5840

Inns of Point Reyes, PO Box 145, Point Reyes, 94956
. . . .(415)662-1420

California B&B in Sacramento, PO Box 1551, Sacramento, 95814

Sacramento Innkeepers Association, 2209 Capitol,
Sacramento, 95816 . . . .(916)441-3214

Association of B&B Innkeepers, 737 Buena Vista W, San
Francisco, 94117 . . . .(415)861-3008

B&B Innkeepers Guild of Santa Barbara, PO Box 20246,
Santa Barbara, 93120

B&B Innkeepers of Santa Cruz, PO Box 464, Santa
Cruz, 95061 . . . .(408)425-8212

B&B Inn of the Gold Country, PO Box 462, Sonora,
95370 . . . .(916)626-6136

Gold Country Inns of Toulomne County, PO Box 462,
Sonora, 95370 . . . .(209)553-1845

Colorado

Small B&B Inns of Colorado, 1102 W Pikes Peak Ave,
Colorado Springs, 80904 . . . .(719)471-3980

Assoc of Historic Hotels of Rocky Mntns, 3391 S Race
St, Englewood, 80110 . . . .(303)757-6556

Western Slope B&B Association, PO Box 43,
Wheatridge, 80033

Delaware

Biking Inn to Inn on the Eastern Shore, Rt 1, Box 283A,
Laurel, 19956 . . . .(302)875-7015

Georgia

Savannah Inn Association, 29 Abercorn St, Savannah,
31401

Illinois

Illinois B&B Association, 500 W Main St, Decatur, 62522
. . . .(217)429-1669

Indiana

Indiana B&B Association, 420 W Washington, South Bend, 46601 ....(219)234-5959

Iowa

Iowa B&B Association, Box 359, North Liberty, 52317 ....(319)324-6843

Maine

Maine Farm Vacation and B&B Association, PO Box 4, Bristol Mills, 04539

Maine Innkeepers Association, 142 Free St, Portland, 04101

Maryland

Annapolis Assoc of Licensed B&B Owners, PO Box 744, Annapolis, 21404 ....(301)263-6418

B&B Inns of the Eastern Shore, 1500 Hambrooks Blvd, Cambridge, 21613 ....(301)228-0575

Chesapeake Inns, PO Box 609, Chestertown, 21620 ....(301)778-4667

Inns of the Blue Ridge, 19 E Church St, Frederick, 21701 ....(301)663-8703

Massachusetts

In the Country B&B, PO Box 5, Buckland, 01338

Assoc of Massachusetts Reservation Svcs, PO Box 1312, Orleans, 02653 ....(508)255-3824

Independent Innkeepers Association, Box CI, Stockbridge, 01262 ....(413)298-3636

Pioneer Valley B&B Association, PO Box 307, Williamsburg, 01096 ....(413)737-7953

Michigan

Heartland Triangle, PO Box 546, Brooklyn, 49230

Lake to Lake B&B Association, 405 Stuart Ave, Kalamazoo, 49007 ....(616)342-0230

B&B Saugatuck, PO Box 1123, Saugatuck, 49453

Holland Heritage B&B Association, Old Wine Inn, PO Box 1142, Saugatuck, 49453 ....(616)392-7362

Minnesota

Minnesota Historic B&B Association, 4th & Pine, Hastings, 55033 ....(612)437-3297

Minnesota B&B Association, 306 W Olive, Stillwater, 55082 ....(612)430-2955

Missouri

Missouri B&B Association, PO Box 31246, Saint Louis, 63131

Nevada

Northern Nevada B&B Guild, 1201 Hwy 395N, Carson City, 89701 ....(702)849-1020

New Hampshire

New England Innkeepers Association, 47 A Winnacunnet Rd, PO Box 1997, Hampton, 03842

Inns and B&Bs of Monadnock Region, PO Box 236, Jaffrey, 03452

Traditional B&B Assoc Of New Hampshire, PO Box 6104, Lakeport, 03246

New Mexico

New Mexico B&B Association, PO Box 2925, Santa Fe, 87504

New York

Finger Lakes B&B Association, PO Box 862, Canandaigua, 14424 ....(607)962-3253

B&B of New York State, Rt 1, Box 206, Cooperstown, 13326 ....(607)547-8203

B&B Leatherstocking, Central NY, 389 Brockway Rd, Frankfort, 13340 ....(315)733-0040

North Carolina

North Carolina B&B Association, PO Box 11215, Raleigh, 27604 ....(704)477-8430

Ohio

Ohio B&B Association, PO Box 265, Oxford, 45056 ....(513)523-5935

Oregon

Ashland B&B Network, PO Box 1051, Ashland, 97520 ....(503)482-2337

Unique Northwest Inns, 4000 Westcliff Dr, Hood River, 97031 ....(503)386-5566

Pennsylvania

B&B Association of Delaware River Valley, 125 Swamp
Rd, Doylestown, 18901 . . . .(215)345-4552

Rhode Island

Guest House Association of Newport, PO Box 981,
Newport, 02840 . . . .(401)847-7455

South Dakota

Old West & Badlands B&B Association, Box 728, Philip,
57567 . . . .(605)859-2040

Tennessee

East Tennessee B&B Inns & Lodges Assoc, 315 N Main
St, Creeneville, 37743

Texas

Historic Hotel Association, 3600 Commerce, Ste E, Dal-
las, 75226 . . . .(214)822-0100

B&B of Wimberley, PO Box 589, Wimberley, 78676
. . . .(512)847-9666

Utah

B&B Inns of Utah, PO Box 2639, Park City, 84060
. . . .(801)645-8068

Vermont

Historic Inns of Norman Rockwell's VT, PO Box 203,
Arlington, 05250 . . . .(802)375-2269

Virginia

Hist Inns of Charlottesville & Albemarle, PO Box 5737,
Charlottesville, 22905

Virginia Inns of Shenandoah, PO Box 918, Hot Springs,
24445

Inns of the Northern Neck, Box 425, Irvington, 22480
. . . .(804)438-6053

Virginia B&B Association, PO Box 15416, Richmond,
23227

Rappahannock B&B Guild, Conyers House, Sperryville,
22740

Washington

B&B Bellingham-Whatcom County, 4421 Lakeway Dr,
Bellingham, 98226 . . . .(206)733-0055

Columbia George Country Inns, PO Box 797, Bingen,
98605

B&B Association of San Juan Island, 4531 Cattle Point
Rd, Friday Harbor, 98250 . . . .(206)378-3186

Whidbey Island B&B Association, PO Box 259, Langley,
98260 . . . .(206)678-3115

Leavenworth Country Inns, PO Box 417, Leavenworth,
98826 . . . .(800)572-7753

Island B&B Inns of Distinction, Rt 1, Box 1940, Lopez Is-
land, 98261 . . . .(206)468-2253

Olympic Peninsula B&B Association, Port Townsend,
98368 . . . .(206)385-6800

Seattle B&B Association, 5005 22nd Ave NE, Seattle,
98105 . . . .(206)522-2536

Washington B&B Guild, 4915 Linden N, Seattle, 98103
. . . .(206)547-6077

West Virginia

B&B Network of West Virginia, 710 Ann St,
Parkersburg, 26101 . . . .(304)485-1458

Awards

Each year the Association of American Historic Inns presents Outstanding Achievement Awards to innkeepers who have made significant contributions to the preservation of historic properties. These individuals go beyond the confines of their own inn and reach out to the community encouraging historic preservation and restoration locally, statewide and even nationally. Nominations for future awards should be sent to **The Association of American Historic Inns, PO Box 336, Dana Point, CA 92629.**

We congratulate the winners and are pleased to honor them with these awards.

Past recipients of the award:
Kit Sargent, Casita Chamisa, Albuquerque, New Mexico
Tom Carroll, Mainstay Inn, Cape May, New Jersey

The Association of American Historic Inns
Outstanding Achievement Award for 1989
Tim Tyler
Russell-Cooper House B&B
Mount Vernon, Ohio

In 1987 Tyler and his wife Maureen moved from New York City to this historic Ohio town and restored the Russell-Cooper House to a Bed & Breakfast Inn. But Tyler's vision carried him beyond the B&B. He expressed it this way, "We love Ohio's Colonial City for what it is and for what it could be!" He serves the community as president of the Knox County Renaissance Foundation, writes a column for the local newspaper, is active in the Chamber of Commerce, and was active in the 1988 Dan Emmett Music and Arts Festival, and — among other things — is undertaking projects to restore the Memorial Theater and Woodward Opera House in Mount Vernon. The opera house dates back 150 years and is one of the only remaining music halls with a horseshoe shaped balcony. Tyler was recently honored by the Senate of the State of Ohio for outstanding, unselfish dedication to community service, to Knox County and to the Colonial City — Mount Vernon, Ohio.

Tim Tyler's dream to put his beloved city on the map and to preserve it as one of this country's finest towns — "the best little city we know ... a place where people respect each other, where it is safe to walk the streets at night" — may quickly come to pass. To him the key to preserving the past lies in making it accessible to the present. Historic preservation and tourism are inseparable. We feel the strength of his vision and commend him for his service and achievements.

Inns of Interest

Inns associated with the Revolutionary War

Ashley Manor
Barnstable, MA

The Village Green
Falmouth, MA

Spring House
Airville, PA

Churchtown Inn
Churchtown, PA

Pace One Restaurant and Country Inn
Thornton, PA

Bed & Breakfast of Valley Forge
Valley Forge, PA

Melville House
Newport, RI

The Silver Thatch Inn
Charlottesville, VA

Caledonia Farm
Flint Hill, VA

The Inn at Weathersfield
Weathersfield, VT

Inns associated with the Civil War

Historic Island Hotel
Cedar Key, FL

Culpepper House
Senoia, GA

Cornstalk Hotel
New Orleans, LA

Elmwood C. 1770
Princess Anne, MD

Rosswood Plantation
Lorman, MS

Dunleith
Natchez, MS

Oak Square
Port Gibson, MS

Cedar Grove Mansion Inn
Vicksburg, MS

Langdon House
Beaufort, NC

Dry Ridge Inn
Weaverville, NC

The Russell-Cooper House
Mount Vernon, OH

Churchtown Inn
Churchtown, PA

The Doubleday Inn
Gettysburg, PA

Beechmont Inn
Hanover, PA

Kane Manor Country Inn
Kane, PA

Bay Street Inn
Beaufort, SC

Hale Springs Inn
Rogersville, TN

North Bend Plantation
Charles City, VA

La Vista Plantation
Fredericksburg, VA

Red Fox Inn & Tavern
Middleburg, VA

Welbourne
Middleburg, VA

The Widow Kip's Country Inn
Mt Jackson, VA

Mayhurst Inn
Orange, VA

Prospect Hill
Trevilians, VA

Old Rittenhouse Inn
Bayfield, WI

The Greenbrier River Inn
Caldwell, WV

Prospect Hill
Gerrardstown, WV

Fillmore St B&B

Harpers Ferry, WV

Boydville - The Inn at Martinsburg
Martinsburg, WV

Black history and Underground Railroad

A Hotel, the Frenchman
New Orleans, LA

Cornstalk Hotel
New Orleans, LA

Dauzat House
New Orleans, LA

Isaac Randall
Freeport, ME

Old Manse Inn
Brewster, MA

Wingscorton Farm Inn
East Sandwich, MA

Ships Inn
Nantucket, MA

Colonel Ashley Inn
Sheffield, MA

Rosswood Plantation
Lorman, MS

The Wooden Rabbit
Cape May, NJ

Troutbeck
Amenia, NY

Bed and Breakfast Valley Forge
Valley Forge, PA

Sleepy Hollow Farm
Gordonsville, VA

The Catlin-Abbott House
Richmond, VA

Prospect Hill
Trevilians, VA

Kedron Valley Inn
South Woodstock, VT

The Inn at Weathersfield
Weathersfield, VT

The Golden Stage Inn
Proctorsville, VT

Inns connected to literary figures

Robert Louis Stevenson
Brannan Cottage
Calistoga, California

Pearl Buck
Historic Island Hotel
Cedar Key, Florida

Harriet Beecher Stowe, Uncle Tom's Cabin
Cornstalk Hotel
New Orleans, Louisiana

Replica of Shakespeare's birthplace
Stratford House Inn
(built by the publisher of Little Women
Bar Harbor Maine

Longfellow's The Courtship of Miles Standish
Isaac Randall House
Freeport Maine

Sophie Kerr House
Denton, Maryland

Ralph Waldo Emerson, Louisa Mae Alcott, Nathaniel Hawthorne
Hawthorne Inn
Concord, Massachusetts

Nathaniel Hawthorne
Edgartown Inn
Edgartown, Massachusetts

Edith Wharton
The Gables Inn
Lenox, Massachusetts

The Yankee Bodleys, Naomi Babson
Old Farm Inn
Rockport Massachusetts

Longfellow's Wayside Inn
South Sudbury, Massachusetts

Mark Twain
Garth Woodside Mansion
Hannibal, Missouri

Becky Thatcher
The Fifth Street Mansion
Hannibal, Missouri

Marguerite Henry, Misty of Chincoteague
Miss Molly's Inn
Chincoteague, Virginia

F. Scott Fitzgerald, Thomas Wolfe

Welbourne
Middleburg, Virginia

Who slept here

Wrigley chewing gum family
The Inn on Mt. Ada
Avalon, Catalina, California

Scripps family
Britt House
San Diego, California

Spreckels Mansion
San Francisco, California

Marilyn Monroe, Arthur Miller
Homestead Inn
New Milford, Connecticut

George Washington
David Finney Inn
New Castle, Delaware

William Penn Guest House
New Castle, Delaware

Susan B. Anthony
The Park House
Saugatuck, Michigan

John Phillip Souza
The B&B Inn at La Jolla
La Jolla, California

Jefferson Davis, Henry Clay, Governor of Mexico & Mississippi
Monmouth Plantation
Natchez, Mississippi

Samuel Clemens
Garth Woodside Mansion
Hannibal, Missouri

The Woolworth family, Barbara Hutton & Cary Grrant
The Mulburn Inn
Bethlehem, New Hampshire

Salmon Chase, Chief Justice, and on Lincoln's cabinet
Chase House B&B
Cornish, New Hampshire

Architect Stanford White
The Inn at Jackson
Jackson, New Hampshire

Babe Ruth
Cranmore Mountain Lodge
North Conway, New Hampshire

Bigelow family
Stonehurst Manor
North Conway, New Hampshire

Robert E. Lee
The Wooden Rabbit

Cape May, New Jersey

Presidents Wilson, Cleveland and Roosevelt
Cordova
Ocean Grove, New Jersey

Teddy Roosevelt
Troutbeck
Amenia, New York

Newberry family
Shadowbrook B&B
Irvington-on-Hudson, New York

Aaron Burr, William Jennings Bryan, Horace Greeley, Franklin Roosevelt
Beekman Arms
Rhinebeck, New York

William Rockefeller
The Point
Saranac Lake, New York

William Seward Inn
Westfield, New York

Cornwallis, Aaron Burr
Colonial Inn
Hillsborough, North Carolina

Burpee family
The Inn at Fordhook Farm
Doylestown, Pennsylvania

Marx Brothers, Lillian Hellman, S. J. Perlman
Barley Sheaf Farm
Holicong, Pennsylvania

General Lafayette
Joseph Reynolds House
Bristol, Rhode Island

"Bob Newhart" Inn
The Waybury Inn
East Middlebury, Vermont

Kellogg family
Village Country Inn
Manchester Village, Vermont

Cornelia Otis Skinner
The Golden Stage
Proctorsville, Vermont

General Stonewall Jackson
Mayhurst Inn
Orange, Virginia

Inn at Narrow Passage
Woodstock, Virginia

Robert E. Lee and President Van Buren
The Greenbrier River Inn
Caldwell, West Virginia

Inns by Name

The following is a list of inns by name. It lists only those described in the main body of this book.

"417" The Haslam-Fort House .... Savannah GA
1735 House .... Amelia Island FL
The 1785 Inn .... North Conway NH
1802 House .... Kennebunkport ME
1811 House .... Manchester Village VT
1830 Inn on the Green .... Weston VT
1837 B&B .... Charleston SC
1842 Inn .... Macon GA
The 1860 House .... Stowe VT
1880 Seafield House .... Westhampton Beach NY
200 South Street Inn .... Charlottesville VA
33 South .... Cuba NY
505 Woodside .... Park City UT
A Cambridge House, B&B Inn .... Cambridge MA
A Hotel, the Frenchman .... New Orleans LA
Abigail Adams B&B .... Cape May NJ
Abrams House Inn .... Cloverdale CA
Adams Inn .... Washington DC
Admiral Fell Inn .... Baltimore MD
The Admiral Fitzroy .... Newport RI
Admiral's Quarters .... Boothbay Harbor ME
Alaska Private Lodgings .... Anchorage AK
Amber House .... Sacramento CA
Amelia Payson Guest House .... Salem MA
American House .... Geneseo NY
The American House .... Morris MN
American River Inn .... Georgetown CA
Amos Shinkle Townhouse .... Covington KY
Anaheim Country Inn .... Anaheim CA
Anderson Guest House .... Wilmington NC
Anderson-Wheeler Homestead .... Concord MA
Annie Horan's .... Grass Valley CA
Annie's B&B .... Big Sandy TX
Inn at Antietam .... Sharpsburg MD
Appel Inn .... Altamont NY
Apple Lane Inn .... Aptos CA
The Arbor .... Edgartown MA
Arcadia Country Inn .... Port Townsend WA
The Arlington Inn .... Arlington VT
Arrowhead Inn .... Durham NC
Art Center Wamsley B&B .... San Francisco CA
Artists Retreat .... Eastport ME
Ash Mill Farm .... Holicong PA
Ashfield Inn .... Ashfield MA
Ashley Manor .... Barnstable MA
Asphodel Plantation .... Jackson LA
Avery Guest House .... Galena IL
B&B at Skoglund Farm .... Canova SD
B&B Company .... Miami FL
B&B in Michigan .... Detroit MI
The B&B Inn at La Jolla .... La Jolla CA
B&B of Valley Forge .... Valley Forge PA
B&B Texas Style, RSO .... Dallas TX

Babbling Brook B&B Inn .... Santa Cruz CA
Backstreet Inn .... New Hope PA
The Bagley House .... Freeport ME
Bailey House .... Fernandina Beach FL
Ballastone Inn .... Savannah GA
The Bark Eater .... Keene NY
Barksdale House Inn .... Charleston SC
Barley Sheaf Farm .... Holicong PA
Barnard-Good House .... Cape May NJ
The Barrister's House .... Baraboo WI
Barrow House .... Saint Francisville LA
Bay Street Inn .... Beaufort SC
Bayboro House on Old Tampa Bay .... St. Petersburg FL
Beacon Street Guest House .... Brookline MA
Beal House Inn .... Littleton NH
The Beatty House .... Kelleys Island OH
Beauchamp Place .... Brandon VT
Beaver Pond Farm Inn .... Warren VT
Bechtel Mansion Inn .... East Berlin PA
Bedford Village Inn .... Bedford NH
Beechmont Inn .... Hanover PA
Beechwood .... Barnstable Village MA
Beekman Arms .... Rhinebeck NY
The Beiger Mansion Inn .... Mishawaka IN
Inn at Belhurst Castle .... Geneva NY
Belle Aire Mansion .... Galena IL
The Bells .... Bethlehem NH
Benbow Inn .... Garberville CA
Benjamin Prescott Inn .... Jaffrey NH
Benn Conger Inn .... Groton NY
Bensonhouse of Williamsburg .... Williamsburg VA
Bensonhouse of Richmond at Monument .... Richmond VA
Bernardston Inn .... Bernardston MA
Bernerhof Inn .... Glen NH
Betsy's B&B .... Baltimore MD
Beverly Hills Inn .... Atlanta GA
Big Bay Lighthouse B&B .... Big Bay MI
Big Spring Inn .... Greenville TN
Birch Hill Inn .... Manchester VT
Birchwood Inn .... Lenox MA
Black Friar Brook Farm .... Duxbury MA
Blackfork Inn .... Loudonville OH
Blue Harbor House .... Camden ME
Blue Hill Farm Country Inn .... Blue Hill ME
Blue Lake Ranch .... Hesperus CO
Blue Quail Inn .... Santa Barbara CA
Blueberry Hill Inn .... Goshen VT
Bluff Creek Inn .... Chaska MN
Bombay House .... Bainbridge Island WA
Boone Tavern Hotel .... Berea KY
Boone's Lick Trail Inn .... Saint Charles MO
Boulevard Inn .... Tecumseh MI
Boydville-The Inn at Martinsburg .... Martinsburg WV
Boyer YL Ranch .... Savery WY
Bradford Inn .... Bradford NH
Brae Loch Inn .... Cazenovia NY
The Brafferton Inn .... Gettysburg PA
Bramble Inn .... Brewster MA
Brannan Cottage Inn .... Calistoga CA

The Brannon Bunker	Damariscotta ME
Branson House	Branson MO
Braxtan House Inn B&B	Paoli IN
Brewery Inn	Silver Plume CO
Briar Rose B&B	Boulder CO
Brigadoon B&B Inn	Evansville IN
Briggs House B&B	Sacramento CA
Brigham Street Inn	Salt Lake City UT
Bright Morning	Davis WV
The Brinley Victorian Inn	Newport RI
Britt House	San Diego CA
Broad Bay Inn & Gallery	Waldoboro ME
Brook Farm Inn	Lenox MA
Brookside Farm	Dulzura CA
Brookview Manor B&B Inn	Canadensis PA
Buckeye B&B	Powell OH
Buckhorn Inn	Gatlinburg TN
Buckmaster Inn	Shrewsbury VT
Bullard House	Chico CA
The Bullis House Inn	San Antonio TX
The Burton House	Wachapreague VA
Burton House B&B Inn	Chicago IL
Butternut Farm	Glastonbury CT
Buttonwood Inn	North Conway NH
Buxton Inn	Granville OH
Caledonia Farm	Flint Hill VA
Calico Cat Guest House	Jamestown RI
Camellia Inn	Healdsburg CA
Cameron Estate Inn	Mount Joy PA
The Candlewyck B&B	Fort Wayne IN
Cannonboro Inn	Charleston SC
Inn at Canoe Point	Hulls Cove ME
Canterbury Inn B&B	Rochester MN
Cape Cod Sunny Pines B&B	West Harwich MA
Captain Dexter House	Vineyard Haven MA
Captain Dibbell House	Clinton CT
Captain Ezra Nye House	Sandwich MA
Captain Lord Mansion	Kennebunkport ME
Captain Mey's Inn	Cape May NJ
Captain Samuel Eddy House Inn	Auburn MA
Captain Stannard House	Westbrook CT
Captain Sylvester Baxter House	Hyannis MA
Captain Tom Lawrence House	Falmouth MA
Captain's Quarters	Harwich Port MA
Captains' Quarters, Bed & Biscuit	Beaufort NC
Carriage House	Laguna Beach CA
The Carriage House At Stonegate	Montoursville PA
Carter House	Eureka CA
Cartway House Inn	Gilford NH
Casa de Solana	St. Augustine FL
Casa Laguna	Laguna Beach CA
Casa Madrona Hotel	Sausalito CA
Casa Soldavini	San Rafael CA
Casita Chamisa	Albuquerque NM
The Castle	Navasota TX
Inn at Castle Hill	Newport RI
Castle Inn	Proctorsville VT
The Catlin-Abbott House	Richmond VA
Cedar Crest Victorian Inn	Asheville NC
Cedar Grove Mansion Inn	Vicksburg MS
The Cedars	Williamsburg VA
The Cedars B&B Inn	Beech Island SC
Centennial House	Northfield MA
Center Lovell Inn	Center Lovell ME
Century House	Nantucket MA
Centuryhurst B&B	Sheffield MA
Chadwick Inn	Edgartown MA
Chalet Suzanne	Lake Wales FL
The Chalfonte	Cape May NJ
Chambered Nautilus B&B Inn	Seattle WA
Channel House	Anacortes WA
Channel Road Inn	Santa Monica CA
Chanticleer B&B Inn	Ashland OR
Inn at Chapel West	New Haven CT
Charles Hinckley House	Barnstable Village MA
The Charleston House	Woodstock VT
Charleston Society B&B	Charleston SC
Charlotte Inn	Edgartown MA
Chase House B&B	Cornish NH
Chase's	Spring Valley MN
Chateau	Spring Lake NJ
Chateau des Fleurs	Winnetka IL
Chateau Victorian	Santa Cruz CA
Chatham Town House Inn	Chatham, Cape Cod MA
Chatsworth B&B	Saint Paul MN
Chelsea Station B&B Inn	Seattle WA
Cheshire Cat Inn	Santa Barbara CA
Chester House	Chester VT
Chichester House B&B	Placerville CA
Chimney Crest Manor	Bristol CT
Christmas House B&B Inn	Rancho Cucamonga CA
The Churchill House Inn	Brandon VT
Churchtown Inn	Churchtown PA
Cider Mill	Zoar OH
Claddagh Inn at Hendersonville	Hendersonville NC
Claussen's Inn	Columbia SC
Cliff Crest	Santa Cruz CA
Cliff View Guest House	Newport RI
Cliffwood Inn	Lenox MA
Coach House Inn	Salem MA
The Coachlight B&B	Saint Louis MO
Cobble Hill Farm	New Hartford CT
Cobble House Inn	Gaysville VT
Cobbler Shop Inn	Zoar Village OH
Inn at Coit Mountain	Newport NH
College Hill B&B	Greensboro NC
Coloma Country Inn	Coloma CA
Colonel Ashley Inn	Sheffield MA
Colonel Ludlow Inn	Winston-Salem NC
Colonel Roger Brown House	Concord MA
Colonial Inn	Hillsborough NC
Colours Key West	Key West FL
The Columns on Jordan	Shreveport LA
COLVMNS by the Sea	Cape May NJ
The Commercial Hotel	Mountain View AR
Commonwealth Inn	Sturbridge MA
Conestoga Horse B&B	Glen Moore PA
Coombs Residence "Inn on the Park"	Napa CA
Cooper House	Angels Camp CA
Inn at Cooperstown	Cooperstown NY
Copper Beech Inn	Centerville MA
Cordova	Ocean Grove NJ
Corner House	Nantucket MA
The Corners	Vicksburg MS
Cornerstone B&B Inn	Saint Helena CA
Cornstalk Hotel	New Orleans LA
Cornucopia Of Dorset	Dorset VT
The Cottage House	Council Grove KS
Country Cottage Inn	Fredericksburg TX
Country Cottage of Langley	Langley WA
Country House Inn	Templeton CA
Country Inn	Fort Bragg CA
The Country Inn at Williamsville	Williamsville VT
Country Roads Guesthouse	Westfield IN
Covered Bridge Inn	Ephrata PA
Cowslip's Belle	Ashland OR
Crab Apple Inn	Plymouth NH
The Craftsman	Santa Ana CA
Craignair Inn	Clark Island ME
Cranmore Mt Lodge	North Conway NH
The Crislip's B&B	Glens Falls NY
Culpepper House	Senoia GA
Curtis House	Woodbury CT
Cypress Inn	Carmel CA
Dairy Hollow House	Eureka Springs AR
Darby Field Inn	Conway NH
Dauzat House	New Orleans LA
David Finney Inn	New Castle DE
Davis House	Crawfordsville IN
Deerfield Inn	Deerfield MA
Deetjen's Big Sur Inn	Big Sur CA
Dickens Loft	Galveston TX
Dickinson Boal Mansion	National City CA
Die Heimat Country Inn	Amana Colonies IA
The Diuguid House	Murray KY
Doanleigh Wallagh	Kansas City MO

Dockside Guest Quarters .... York ME
Dormer House, International ....Cape May NJ
Doryman's Inn .... Newport Beach CA
Dosher Plantation House B&B .... Southport NC
The Doubleday Inn ....Gettysburg PA
The Dove Inn.................................Golden CO
Downey House .... Nevada City CA
Driftwood Inn .... Homer AK
Dry Ridge Inn ....Weaverville NC
The Duff Green Mansion .... Vicksburg MS
Duke of Windsor Inn ....Cape May NJ
Dunbar House, 1880 .... Murphys CA
Dunleith .... Natchez MS
Dunscroft By the Sea ....Harwich Port MA
Dusty Mansion ....New Orleans LA
East Brother Light Station .... Point Richmond CA
East Country Berry Farm ....Lenox MA
Eastlake Victorian Inn .... Los Angeles CA
Edgartown Inn .... Edgartown MA
Edgecombe-Coles House .... Camden ME
Edgewood Plantation .... Charles City VA
Edinburgh Lodge B&B ....Ashland OR
Edith Palmer's Country Inn .... Virginia City NV
Edson Hill Manor .... Stowe VT
Egremont Inn .... South Egremont MA
Eiler's Inn ....Laguna Beach CA
El Canario Inn .... Condado, San Juan PR
El Paradero .... Santa Fe NM
Elk Cove Inn ....Elk CA
Elliott House Inn .... Charleston SC
Ellis River House .... Jackson NH
Fairfield Place ....Shreveport LA
Fairhaven Inn .... Bath ME
Fairway Farm B&B ....Pottstown PA
Fassifern B&B ....Lexington VA
Faulkner House ....Red Bluff CA
Fearrington House .... Pittsboro NC
The Feather Bed ....Quincy CA
The Federal House .... Boston MA
Fensalden B&B .... Albion CA
Ferry Point House .... Laconia NH
Field & Pine B&B ....Shippensburg PA
The Fifth Street Mansion B&B .... Hannibal MO
Fillmore Street B&B .... Harpers Ferry WV
Fitzwilliam Inn ....Fitzwilliam NH
Flint Street Inn ....Asheville NC
Foley House Inn .... Savannah GA
Folkestone Inn .... Bryson City NC
Follansbee Inn .... North Sutton NH
Inn at Fordhook Farm ....Doylestown, Bucks Co PA
The Foreman House B&B .... Narvon PA
Forsyth Park Inn .... Savannah GA
The Foster-Harris House .... Washington VA
Fountain Hall B&B .... Culpeper VA
Four Chimneys .... Nantucket MA
Four Chimneys Inn .... Dennis MA
Franconia Inn .... Franconia NH
Frederick House .... Staunton VA
The Gables Inn ....Lenox MA
Galer Place .... Seattle WA
Galisteo Inn .... Galisteo NM
The Gallery House .... Alma WI
Garden Gables Inn ....Lenox MA
Garland's Oak Creek Lodge .... Sedona AZ
Garth Woodside Mansion .... Hannibal MO
General Hooker's House ....Portland OR
The General Lewis .... Lewisburg WV
The General Rufus Putnam House ....Rutland MA
Genesee Country Inn ....Mumford NY
Gibson Inn .... Apalachicola FL
Gibson's Lodging .... Annapolis MD
Gilbert House B&B .... Middleway WV
Gingerbread House ....Cape May NJ
Gingerbread Inn .... Hertford NC
Glenborough Inn ....Santa Barbara CA
Glendeven .... Little River CA
Gold Mountain Manor .... Big Bear City CA
Golden Lamb .... Lebanon OH

Golden Pheasant Inn ....Erwinna PA
Golden Plough Inn ....Lahaska PA
The Golden Stage Inn ....Proctorsville VT
Goose Chase ....Gardners PA
Gosby House Inn ....Pacific Grove CA
Gosnold Arms .... New Harbor ME
The Governor's Inn .... Ludlow VT
Gramma's Inn ....Berkeley CA
The Grandison ....Oklahoma City OK
Grant Corner Inn ....Santa Fe NM
Granville Inn .... Granville OH
Grape Leaf Inn .... Healdsburg CA
The Graustein Inn .... Knoxville TN
Graycote Inn ....Bar Harbor ME
The Great Southern Hotel .... Brinkley AR
Green Apple Inn .... Freestone CA
Green Gables Inn ....Pacific Grove CA
Green Gate Village Historic B&B Inn .... St George UT
Green Mountain Tea Room ....South Wallingford VT
Greenbriar B&B ....Coeur d'Alene ID
The Greenbrier River Inn .... Caldwell WV
The Greenfield Inn ....Greenfield NH
Greenhurst Inn .... Bethel VT
Greenvale Manor .... Mollusk VA
Greenville Arms .... Greenville NY
Greenville Inn .... Greenville ME
Greenwood B&B .... Greensboro NC
The Gregory House .... Averill Park NY
Grenoble House .... New Orleans LA
Grey Whale Inn .... Fort Bragg CA
The Griffin Inn ....Ellison Bay WI
Guest House .... Arroyo Grande CA
Guest House B&B & Cottages .... Greenbank WA
Guesthouses ....Charlottesville VA
Guilds Inn .... Mt Pleasant SC
Hachland Hill Inn ....Clarksville TN
Hacienda del Sol .... Taos NM
Haikuleana B&B Inn ....Haiku, Maui HI
Halcyon House .... Lawrence KS
Hale Springs Inn ....Rogersville TN
Hallcrest Inn ....Waynesville NC
Hammons House .... Bethel ME
The Hannah Marie Country Inn .... Spencer IA
Happy Landing Inn .... Carmel CA
Inn at Harbor Head .... Kennebunkport ME
Harbor House .... Elk CA
Harbor Inn .... Kennebunkport ME
Harbour Carriage House .... Santa Barbara CA
Harbour Inne and Cottage .... Mystic CT
Harmony House Inn ....New Bern NC
Harraseeket Inn .... Freeport ME
Harrington House B&B .... Holmes Beach FL
Harrison House ....Guthrie OK
Harry Packer Mansion ....Jim Thorpe PA
Hartley House Inn .... Sacramento CA
Harvey's Mountain View Inn .... Rochester VT
Hasty Pudding House ....Anacortes WA
Haverhill Inn ....Haverhill NH
Hawthorne Inn ....Concord MA
Hawthorne Inn .... Camden ME
Haydon House .... Healdsburg CA
Hayne House .... Charleston SC
Headlands Inn ....Mendocino CA
Hearthside Inn ....Bar Harbor ME
Hearthstone Inn ....Colorado Springs CO
The Heartstone Inn and Cottages .... Eureka Springs AR
The Heirloom .... Ione CA
Henry Farm Inn .... Chester VT
Henry Ludlam Inn .... Woodbine NJ
Heritage Hill .... Asheville NC
Heritage House Inn ....Port Townsend WA
Heritage Park B&B Inn .... San Diego CA
Heron House .... Key West FL
Herr Farmhouse Inn ....Manheim PA
Hersey House .... Ashland OR
Hickory Bridge Farm .... Orrtanna PA
Hickory Hill Farm .... Moorefield WV
Hidden Inn .... Orange VA

High Meadows B&B	Eliot ME
High Meadows Inn	Scottsville VA
Highland House Inn	Lake Placid NY
Highland Inn	Monterey VA
Hill Farm Inn	Arlington VT
Hilltop Inn	Sugar Hill NH
Historic Brookside Farms	Orwell VT
Historic Charleston B&B	Charleston SC
Historic Island Hotel	Cedar Key FL
The Historic James R. Webster Mansion	Waterloo NY
Historic Merrell Tavern Inn	South Lee MA
Holbrook House	Bar Harbor ME
Holden House-1902	Colorado Springs CO
Hollingsworth House Inn	Indianapolis IN
Holly House	Cape May NJ
The Homeplace B&B	Charlotte NC
Homeport Inn	Searsport ME
The Homestead	Sugar Hill NH
The Homestead	Saline MI
The Homestead	Midway UT
Homestead Inn	New Milford CT
Homestead Inn	Greenwich CT
Honeysuckle Hill	West Barnstable MA
Hospitality Plus	San Juan Capistrano CA
Host Homes of Boston	Boston MA
Host Homes Of Tennessee	Nashville TN
Hotel Jefferson Historic Inn	Jefferson TX
Hotel Place St. Michel	Coral Gables FL
House in the Woods	Eugene OR
House of Seven Gables	Pacific Grove CA
House on Cherry St	Jacksonville FL
Howard Creek Ranch	Westport CA
Hudson House	Cold Spring NY
Humphrey Hughes House	Cape May NJ
Inn at Ilwaco	Ilwaco WA
Imperial Hotel	Cripple Creek CO
Incentra Village House	New York City NY
Ink House	Saint Helena CA
Inn of Jonathan Bowen	Newport RI
Inn on Cove Hill	Rockport MA
The Inn on Golden Pond	Holderness NH
Inn on Lake Waramaug	New Preston CT
The Inn On Mt. Ada	Avalon CA
Inn on South Street	Kennebunkport ME
Inn On The Common	Craftsbury Common VT
Isaac Randall House	Freeport ME
Isaiah Hall B&B Inn	Dennis MA
Island City House	Key West FL
The Island House	Southwest Harbor ME
The Jabberwock	Monterey CA
Inn at Jackson	Jackson NH
Jail House Inn	Newport RI
Jailer's Inn	Bardstown KY
James Blair House	Placerville CA
James House	Port Townsend WA
Jared Coffin House	Nantucket MA
Jared Cone House	Bolton CT
The Jefferson House B&B	New Castle DE
The Jefferson Inn	Jefferson NH
The Jeremiah J. Yereance House	Lyndhurst NJ
Jesse Mount House	Savannah GA
The Jeweled Turret Inn	Belfast ME
John Palmer House	Portland OR
Jordan Hollow Farm Inn	Luray VA
Joseph Ambler Inn	North Wales PA
The Joseph Reynolds House	Bristol RI
Joshua Grindle Inn	Mendocino CA
The Kaleidoscope Inn	Nipomo CA
Kalorama Guest House	Washington DC
Kane Manor Country Inn	Kane PA
Kawanhee Inn Lakeside Lodge	Weld ME
Kedron Valley Inn	South Woodstock VT
Kemah Guest House	Saugatuck MI
Kemp House Inn	Saint Michaels MD
Kenilworth	Spring Lake NJ
Kenniston Hill Inn	Boothbay ME
Kenwood Inn	St. Augustine FL
Key West B&B, Popular House	Key West FL
Keystone Inn B&B	Gettysburg PA
Kings Courtyard Inn	Charleston SC
The Kingsleigh Inn	Southwest Harbor ME
The Kirby House	Saugatuck MI
Knickerbocker Mansion	Big Bear Lake CA
Kylemere House 1818	Kennebunkport ME
L'Auberge Provencale	White Post VA
La Mer	Ventura CA
La Posada De Taos	Taos NM
La Posada Del Valle	Tucson AZ
La Vista Plantation	Fredericksburg VA
Lafayette House	Saint Louis MO
Lafitte Guest House	New Orleans LA
The Lahaina Hotel	Lahaina, Maui HI
Lamothe House	New Orleans LA
Lamplight Inn	Lake Luzerne NY
Land's End Inn	Provincetown MA
Langdon House	Beaufort NC
Lanza's Country Inn	Livingston Manor NY
Lareau Farm Country Inn	Waitsfield VT
Laurel Hill Plantation	McClellanville SC
Lawnridge House	Grants Pass OR
Ledgeland	Sugar Hill NH
Ledgelawn Inn	Bar Harbor ME
Leighton Inn	Portsmouth NH
Inn at Levelfields	Lancaster VA
Liberty Hall Inn	Pendleton SC
Liberty Hill Inn	Yarmouth Port MA
Liberty Inn 1834	Savannah GA
Liberty Rose Colonial B&B	Williamsburg VA
Lincoln House Country Inn	Dennysville ME
Lincoln Inn	Port Townsend WA
Lindenwood Inn	Southwest Harbor ME
Linekin Village B&B	East Boothbay ME
Lion's Head Inn	West Harwich MA
The Little Lodge at Dorset	Dorset VT
Little St. Simons Island	Saint Simon's Island GA
Little Warren	Tarboro NC
Livingston Mansion Inn	Jacksonville OR
Lizzie's	Port Townsend WA
Llewellyn Lodge at Lexington	Lexington VA
The Lodge	Cloudcroft NM
Log Cabin B&B	Georgetown KY
Londonderry Inn	South Londonderry VT
Lone Mountain Ranch	Big Sky MT
Inn at Long Lake	Naples ME
Inn at Long Last	Chester VT
Inn at Long Trail	Killington VT
Longfellow's Wayside Inn	South Sudbury MA
Longswamp B&B	Mertztown PA
Longwood, A Country Inn at Marlboro	Marlboro VT
The Lords Proprietors' Inn	Edenton NC
Lothrop Merry House	Vineyard Haven MA
Lovett's Inn	Franconia NH
Lowell Inn	Stillwater MN
Lowenstein-Long House	Memphis TN
MacCallum House Inn	Mendocino CA
Mad River Barn	Waitsfield VT
Madewood Plantation	Napoleonville LA
Madison Street Inn	Santa Clara CA
Madrona Manor	Healdsburg CA
Maggie's B&B	Collinsville IL
Magnus Tate's Kitchen	Charlestown WV
Magoffin Guest House B&B	Mercer PA
Maine Stay B&B	Camden ME
Maine Stay Inn and Cottages	Kennebunkport ME
Mainstay Inn	Cape May NJ
Inn at Manchester	Manchester VT
Manchester Highlands Inn	Manchester VT
Mangels House	Aptos CA
Manoa Valley Inn	Honolulu HI
The Manor	Castine ME
Manor House	Norfolk CT
The Manor House	Kenosha WI
Manor House Inn	Bar Harbor ME
Manor On Golden Pond	Holderness NH
Manresa Castle	Port Townsend WA
Mansion View	Toledo OH

Maple Hill Farm B&B .... Coventry CT
The Maples .... Bar Harbor ME
Maplewood Hotel .... Saugatuck MI
Maplewood Inn .... Fair Haven VT
Marks House Inn ....Prescott AZ
Mars Avenue Guest House .... Galena IL
Martin Hill Inn ....Portsmouth NH
Mason Cottage .... Cape May NJ
Mayfield House ....Tahoe City CA
Mayhurst Inn .... Orange VA
McCarthy Wilderness B&B ....Anchorage AK
McGilvery House ....Searsport ME
Meadow Creek Ranch B&B Inn .... Mariposa CA
Meadow Farm B&B ....Northwood NH
Meadow Spring Farm .... Kennett Square PA
Medford House .... Fort Worth TX
The Meeting House Inn & Restaurant .... Henniker NH
Melville House .... Newport RI
Memory House ....Arlington VA
Mendocino Village Inn .... Mendocino CA
The Mendon Country Inn .... Mendon MI
Mensana Inn .... Stevenson MD
Mentone Inn .... Mentone AL
Merrill Farm Resort ....Conway NH
Mi Casa-Su Casa B&B ....Tempe AZ
Michel Farm Vacations .... Harmony MN
Middletown Springs Inn .... Middletown Springs VT
Mill Brook B&B ....Brownsville VT
Inn at Mill Pond .... Cooperstown NY
Mill Rose Inn .... Half Moon Bay CA
Millbrook .... Waitsfield VT
Millsaps-Buie House .... Jackson MS
Mira Monte Inn .... Bar Harbor ME
Miss Molly's Inn ....Chincoteague VA
Moffatt House ....San Francisco CA
Monmouth Plantation .... Natchez MS
Mont Rest ....Bellvue IA
Inn at Montross .... Montross VA
Moose Mountain Lodge .... Etna NH
Morning Star Inn .... St. Marys KS
Mostly Hall .... Falmouth MA
Mount Holly .... Chatham MS
Mountain Fare Inn .... Campton NH
Mountain Home Inn .... Mill Valley CA
Mountain Lake Inn .... Bradford NH
Mountain Top Inn .... Chittenden VT
Mountain View Inn ....Norfolk CT
Mr. Patrick Henry's Inn .... Richmond VA
Mt. Adams Inn .... North Woodstock NH
The Mulburn Inn .... Bethlehem NH
Murphy's Hotel .... Murphys CA
Nancy & Bob's 9 Eureka Street Inn .... Sutter Creek CA
Naniboujou Lodge .... Grand Marais MN
Napa Inn ....Napa CA
Inn at Narrow Passage ....Woodstock VA
Nashua House .... Oak Bluffs MA
National Hotel .... Jamestown CA
National Pike Inn .... New Market MD
New Berne House .... New Bern NC
New Davenport B&B ....Davenport CA
New London Inn .... New London NH
New Shoreham House ....Block Island RI
Newbury House at Historic Rugby ....Rugby TN
The Newcastle Inn .... Newcastle ME
Newport House .... Williamsburg VA
Newry Manor ....Everett PA
Nine-O-Five Royal Hotel ....New Orleans LA
Noble House .... Bridgton ME
The Normandy Inn .... Spring Lake NJ
Norris House Inn .... Leesburg VA
North Bend Plantation .... Charles City VA
North Garden Inn ....Bellingham WA
North Hero House .... North Hero VT
The Northrop House .... Owatonna MN
Nottoway .... White Castle LA
Noyo River Lodge .... Fort Bragg CA
Oak Square .... Port Gibson MS
Oakwood .... Harwood MD

The Oakwood Inn ....Raleigh NC
Offutt House ....Omaha NE
Ogden House ....Milwaukee WI
Ojai Manor Hotel ....Ojai CA
The Old Dennis House ....Newport RI
Old Farm Inn .... Rockport MA
Old Fort Inn .... Kennebunkport ME
Inn at Old Harbour .... Block Island RI
Old Hoosier House ....Knightstown IN
Old Lyme Inn .... Old Lyme CT
Old Manse Inn .... Brewster MA
The Old Mill Inn .... Somersville CT
Old Mill Pond Inn ....Northport ME
The Old Miner's Lodge, A B&B Inn .... Park City UT
Old Monterey Inn .... Monterey CA
Old Point Inn .... Beaufort SC
The Old Reynolds Mansion .... Asheville NC
Old Rittenhouse Inn ....Bayfield WI
Old Sea Pines Inn .... Brewster MA
Old St Angela Inn ....Pacific Grove CA
Old Stone House Inn ....Marblehead OH
Old Talbott Tavern .... Bardstown KY
The Old Tjomsland House .... Vashon WA
Old Town Farm Inn .... Gassets VT
Old Wing Inn ....Holland MI
Old World Inn .... Spillville IA
Old Yacht Club Inn .... Santa Barbara CA
Old Yarmouth Inn .... Yarmouth Port MA
Olde Harbour Inn ....Savannah GA
Olive House .... Santa Barbara CA
Inn at One Main Street ....Falmouth MA
Orcas Hotel .... Orcas WA
The Oscar Swan Country Inn .... Geneva IL
The Osceola Mill House .... Gordonville PA
Outlook Lodge .... Green Mountain Falls CO
Overview Farm ....Sonoma CA
The Oxford Alexis .... Denver CO
The Oxford House ....Stephenville TX
Pace One Restaurant and Country Inn ....Thornton PA
The Palmer House B&B ....Waynesville NC
Palmer House Inn .... Falmouth MA
Palmer Inn .... Mystic - Noank CT
Pamlico House ....Washington NC
The Park House ....Saugatuck MI
The Parkside B&B ....Appleton WI
The Parmenter House ....Belmont VT
Parsonage .... East Orleans MA
The Parsonage ....Holland MI
The Parsonage .... Santa Barbara CA
Pasquaney Inn On Newfound Lake .... Bridgewater NH
Peacock Inn ....North Conway NH
The Pebble House ....Lakeside MI
The Peck House .... Empire CO
The Penny House ....North Eastham MA
Peregrine House ....Ithaca NY
Perryville Inn .... Rehoboth MA
Petite Auberge .... San Francisco CA
The Picket Fence ....Virginia Beach VA
The Piedmont House ....Eureka Springs AR
Pilgrim House ....Newport RI
Pilgrims Rest .... Wilson NC
The Pine Barn Inn .... Danville PA
Pine Hills Lodge ....Julian CA
Pine Knoll Inn .... Aiken SC
Pine Ridge Inn .... Mt. Airy NC
Pine Tree Inn .... Ocean Grove NJ
Piney Grove B&B ....Charles City VA
Pitcher Guest House ....Red Lodge MT
Pleasant Inn Lodge .... Rehoboth Beach DE
Plumbush B&B at Chautauqua .... Mayville NY
The Point .... Saranac Lake NY
Point Way Inn .... Edgartown MA
Pointe Coupee B&B ....New Roads LA
Poipu B&B Inn ....Koloa, Kauai HI
The Pollyanna ....Oneida NY
Port Gallery Inn .... Kennebunkport ME
Pratt-Taber Inn ....Red Wing MN
Prescott Pines Inn ....Prescott AZ

Pride House	Jefferson TX
Prince George Inn	Annapolis MD
The Priory	Pittsburgh PA
Private Lodging	Cleveland OH
Prospect Hill	Gerrardstown WV
Prospect Hill	Trevilians VA
Providence Lodge	Lake Junaluska NC
Province Inn	Strafford NH
The Prytania Park Hotel	New Orleans LA
Pudding Creek Inn	Fort Bragg CA
Pueblo Bonito	Santa Fe NM
Quaker House	Nantucket MA
Queen Anne Inn	Denver CO
Queen Victoria	Cape May NJ
Quill & Quilt	Cannon Falls MN
Rabbit Hill Inn	Lower Waterford VT
Rainbow Hospitality	Niagara Falls NY
Rainbow Tarns	Crowley Lake CA
Raymond House Inn	Port Sanilac MI
Red Brook Inn	Mystic CT
Red Castle Inn	Nevada City CA
Red Fox Inn & Tavern	Middleburg VA
Red Hill Inn	Centre Harbor NH
The Red House Country Inn	Burdett NY
Red House Inn	Brevard NC
Red Lion B&B	Red Lion PA
Red Rose Inn	Santa Barbara CA
Redstone Inn	Dubuque IA
Reed House B&B	Asheville NC
Reluctant Panther Inn	Manchester VT
Remshart-Brooks House	Savannah GA
Renaissance Inn	Sister Bay WI
Rhett House Inn	Beaufort SC
Richardson House B&B	Jamesport MO
Richmond Hill Inn	Asheville NC
River Road Inn	Loudon TN
Riverfront House B&B	Mathews VA
Riverview Hotel	Saint Mary's GA
Riverwind	Deep River CT
Roberta's B&B	Seattle WA
The Rock House	Morgantown IN
Rockhouse Mountain Farm	Eaton Center NH
Rockwood Lodge	Homewood CA
Rocky Shores Inn	Rockport MA
Room with a View	El Paso TX
Rose Inn	Ithaca NY
Rose Victorian Inn	Arroyo Grande CA
Rosebriar Inn	Astoria OR
Rosenberry Inn	Wausau WI
Roserox Country Inn By-The-Sea	Pacific Grove CA
Rosewood Inn	Corning NY
Rosswood Plantation	Lorman MS
The Rough Riders	Medora ND
Round Barn Farm	Waitsfield VT
Royal Brewster B&B	Bar Mills ME
Royal Carter House	Ashland OR
RSVP Savannah B&B Reservation Service	Savannah GA
The Ruffner House	Luray VA
The Russell-Cooper House	Mount Vernon OH
Rutledge Museum Guest House	Charleston SC
The Ryan House B&B	Sonora CA
Saddle Rock Ranch	Sedona AZ
Sage Cottage	Trumansburg NY
Salem Inn	Salem MA
Salisbury House	Allentown PA
Salisbury House	Los Angeles CA
Salt Ash Inn	Plymouth VT
Samuel Watson House	Thompson CT
Sand Castle Guest House	Cape May NJ
Sandlake Country Inn	Cloverdale OR
Sandpiper Hotel	Spring Lake NJ
Santa Nella House	Guerneville CA
Sara's B&B Inn	Houston TX
Sardy House	Aspen CO
Sausalito Hotel	Sausalito CA
Scanlan House	Lanesboro MN
Scarlett's Country Inn	Calistoga CA
Schoolhouse Inn	Melvern KS
Seal Beach Inn & Gardens	Seal Beach CA
Seekonk Pines Inn	Great Barrington MA
Seven Wives Inn	St George UT
Seventh Sister Guesthouse	Cape May NJ
Shadowbrook B&B	Irvington-on-Hudson NY
Shady Oaks Country Inn	Saint Helena CA
Shaw House Inn	Ferndale CA
Shelburne Inn	Seaview WA
Shelter Harbor Inn	Westerly RI
Shenandoah Farm	Arlington VT
Sherman House Restaurant & Inn	Batesville IN
Sherman-Berry House	Lowell MA
Sherwood Inn	Skaneateles NY
Ships Inn	Nantucket MA
Ships Knees Inn	East Orleans MA
Shire Inn	Chelsea VT
The Shirley-Madison Inn	Baltimore MD
Shumway Mansion	Kirkland WA
Silas Griffith Inn	Danby VT
The Silver Fox Inn	West Rutland VT
The Silver Thatch Inn	Charlottesville VA
Silvermine Tavern	Norwalk CT
Simpson House Inn	Santa Barbara CA
Slavka's B&B	Columbus OH
Sleepy Hollow Farm	Gordonsville VA
The Smithton Inn	Ephrata PA
Snowvillage Inn	Snowville NH
Society Hill Government House	Baltimore MD
Society Hill Hotel	Baltimore MD
Society Hill Hopkins	Baltimore MD
Society Hill Hotel	Philadelphia PA
Somerset House	Provincetown MA
Sophie Kerr House	Denton MD
Southard House	Austin TX
Spencer House	San Francisco CA
Spray Cliff on the Ocean	Marblehead MA
Spreckels Mansion	San Francisco CA
Spring Bank Inn	Frederick MD
Spring Garden	Laurel DE
Spring House	Airville PA
The Spruces B&B	Salt Lake City UT
Squaw Peak Inn	Phoenix AZ
The Squire Tarbox Inn	Wiscasset ME
St. Charles Guest House	New Orleans LA
St. Francis Inn	St. Augustine FL
St. Francisville Inn	Saint Francisville LA
Stagecoach Inn B&B	Cedarburg WI
Standish House	Lanark IL
Starrett House Inn	Port Townsend WA
State House B&B	Salem OR
Staveleigh House	Sheffield MA
Stephen Daniels House	Salem MA
Stephen Potwine House	East Windsor CT
Stewart Manor	Indianapolis IN
Stillman's Country Inn	Galena IL
The Stone Hearth Inn	Chester VT
Stone Manor Hotel	New Orleans LA
Stone Post Inn	Spring Lake NJ
Stonebridge Inn	Poultney VT
Stonehurst Manor	North Conway NH
Storybook Inn	Sky Forest CA
Stout House	Dubuque IA
Stratford House Inn	Bar Harbor ME
Inn at Strawberry Banke	Portsmouth NH
Strawberry Castle B&B	Penfield NY
Strawberry Inn	New Market MD
Strawberry Lodge	Kyburz CA
Strong House Inn	Vergennes VT
Sugar Tree Inn	Vesuvius VA
The Summer House	Sandwich MA
Inn at Sunderland	Sunderland VT
Sundial Inn	Kennebunkport ME
Sunset Inn	Lake Junaluska NC
Surf Manor & Cottages	San Diego CA
Surry Inn	Surry ME
Swan-Levine House	Grass Valley CA
Swift House Inn	Middlebury VT
Sword Gate Inn	Charleston SC

Tamworth Inn .... Tamworth NH
The Taos Inn ....Taos NM
Tavern House .... Vienna MD
Telfair Inn ....Augusta GA
Ten Inverness Way .... Inverness CA
Terrace Manor .... Los Angeles CA
The Terrace Townhouse ....Boston MA
Inn at Thatcher Brook Falls .... Waterbury VT
Thayers Inn .... Littleton NH
Inn at the Green ....Poland OH
Thomas Huckins House .... Barnstable MA
Thomas Shepherd Inn .... Shepherdstown WV
Inn at Thorn Hill .... Jackson NH
Thorp House Inn & Cottages .... Fish Creek WI
Three Center Square Inn .... Maytown PA
Three Pheasant Inn .... Great Falls MT
Tide Watch Inn .... Waldoboro ME
Tolland Inn ....Tolland CT
Tollgate Hill Inn .... Litchfield CT
Tran Crossing .... Frederick MD
Troutbeck .... Amenia NY
Tuc'Me Inn ....Wolfeboro NH
Tudor Inn .... Port Angeles WA
Tulip Tree Inn .... Chittenden VT
Inn at Turkey Hill ....Bloomsburg PA
Turtleback Farm Inn ....Eastsound WA
Twin Gates .... Baltimore MD
Two Meeting Street Inn .... Charleston SC
Under Mountain Inn .... Salisbury CT
Under the Greenwood Tree .... Medford OR
Underledge Inn ....Lenox MA
Union Hotel ....Benicia CA
Union Street Inn ....San Francisco CA
University Club of St. Paul .... Saint Paul MN
Valley House Inn ....Orleans VT
Vendue Inn .... Charleston SC
The Veranda - (Hollberg Hotel) .... Senoia GA
The Vermont Inn .... Killington VT
Victorian B&B Inn .... Avoca IA
The Victorian Farmhouse .... Little River CA
Victorian Garden Inn .... Sonoma CA
Villa d' Italia ....Santa Barbara CA
Village Country Inn ....Manchester Village VT
Village Green Inn .... Falmouth MA
Village House .... Jackson NH
Village Inn ....Lenox MA
Village Victorian Inn ....Rhinebeck NY
Vincent-Doan Home .... Mobile AL
Vineyard House ....Coloma CA
Vintage Towers Inn ....Cloverdale CA
Voss Inn .... Bozeman MT
W.E. Mauger Estate ....Albuquerque NM
Wake Robin Inn .... Lakeville CT
Wakefield Inn .... Wakefield NH
Walker House ....Lenox MA
Wallowa Lake Lodge............................... Joseph OR
Walnut Street B&B .... Springfield MO
Warwickshire Inn ....Traverse City MI
The Washington House Inn .... Cedarburg WI
Washington School Inn .... Park City UT
Watercourse Way B&B .... South Strafford VT
Watson House ....Key West FL
The Waverly Inn .... Hendersonville NC
The Waybury Inn .... East Middlebury VT
Inn at Weathersfield .... Weathersfield VT
Weathervane Inn .... South Egremont MA
The Wedgwood Inn ....New Hope PA
Welbourne ....Middleburg VA
Welby Inn ....Kennebunkport ME
West Moor Inn .... Nantucket MA
The Westchester House ....Saratoga Springs NY
Westfield House ....Westfield NY
Weston House ....Eastport ME
Westways Resort .... Phoenix AZ
Whistling Swan Inn .... Stanhope NJ
The White Barn Inn ....Kennebunkport ME
White Lace Inn .... Sturgeon Bay WI
The White Oak Inn .... Danville OH

White Rocks Inn .... Wallingford VT
White Swan Inn .... San Francisco CA
White Swan Tavern ....Chestertown MD
Whitegate Inn ....Mendocino CA
The Widow Kip's Country Inn .... Mt Jackson VA
Wilburton Inn .... Manchester VT
The Wildwood Inn ....Ware MA
Wilkum Inn .... Idyllwild CA
Willcox Inn .... Aiken SC
William Penn Guest House .... New Castle DE
The William Seward Inn .... Westfield NY
Williams House Inn .... The Dalles OR
The Williams House .... Seattle WA
Willowtree Inn ....Tipp City OH
Wilson House Inn .... Mineral Point WI
Winchester Inn .... Allegan MI
Windham Hill Inn ....West Townsend VT
Wine Way Inn .... Calistoga CA
Wingscorton Farm Inn ....East Sandwich MA
Winters Creek Ranch .... Carson City NV
Winterwood at Petersham .... Petersham MA
Witmer's Tavern - Historic 1725 Inn ....Lancaster PA
The Woodbox ....Nantucket MA
Woodbury Guest House .... Cedar City UT
The Wooden Rabbit .... Cape May NJ
Woodruff House .... Barre VT
Woodstock Hall ....Charlottesville VA
Inn at Woodstock Hill .... Woodstock CT
Woolverton Inn .... Stockton NJ
Worthington Inn .... Worthington OH
Wyndemere House at Sippewissett ....Falmouth MA
Yankee Peddler Inn ....Newport RI
Yankee Pedler Inn ....Holyoke MA
Ye Olde Cherokee Inn .... Kill Devil Hills NC
Yesterdays Inn .... Niles MI
York Harbor Inn .... York Harbor ME
York House .... Mountain City GA
Zachariah Foss Guest House .... Washington MO
Zane Trace B&B .... Old Washington OH

Association of American Historic Inns

Discount Certificates

These are offered by innkeepers listed in this book to help promote historic inns. These are not paid advertisements.
Note: DO NOT REMOVE. These are only valid when presented with and attached to this book.
Advance reservations are required.

The Official Guide to American Historic Inns

20% discount weekday
10% discount weekends

Lafitte Guest House
1003 Bourbon St
New Orleans, LA 70116   Valid Thru 12/90
(504) 581-2678   Void if detached*

The Official Guide to American Historic Inns

15% discount midweek

Staveleigh House
PO 608, South Main St
Sheffield, MA 01257   Valid Thru 12/90
(413) 229-2129   Void if detached*

The Official Guide to American Historic Inns

20% discount on any room, any day except Saturday (December 1-May 25)

Harraseeket Inn
162 Main St
Freeport, ME 04032   Valid Thru 12/90
(207) 865-9377   Void if detached*

The Official Guide to American Historic Inns

$25 off 1 night stay from June 15 to August 15 or January 15 to March 15

200 South Street Inn
200 South St
Charlottesville, VA 22901   Valid Thru 12/90
(804) 979-0200   Void if detached*

The Official Guide to American Historic Inns

Peace and beauty at our White Mountain inn for 10% less during the week, except foilage and Christmas. Or chose a complimentary bottle of French house wine with your dinner during a stay at our inn, good anytime.

Inn At Thorn Hill
PO Box A, Thorn Hill Road
Jackson NH 03846   Valid Thru 12/90
(603) 383-4242, (603) 383-6448   Void if detached*

The Official Guide to American Historic Inns

10% discount good anytime

Starrett House Inn
744 Clay St
Port Townsend, WA 98368   Valid Thru 12/90
(206) 385-3205   Void if detached*

The Official Guide to American Historic Inns

20% discount midweek
(Sun.-Thurs. excludes holidays)

Rose Inn
813 Auburn Rd, Rt 34N, Box 6576
Ithaca, NY 14851-6576   Valid Thru 12/90
(607) 533-7905   Void if detached*

The Official Guide to American Historic Inns

Stay 2 nites and the 3rd nite is half price. Not valid holidays, special events or in July or August.

Westchester House
102 Lincoln Ave, PO Box 944
Saratoga Springs, NY 12866   Valid Thru 12/90
(518) 587-7613   Void if detached*

The Official Guide to American Historic Inns

10% discount anytime
(excludes foliage season and holidays)

Darby Field Inn   Not valid with
Bald Hill, PO Box D   any other offer
Conway, NH 03818   Valid Thru 12/90
(603) 447-2181   Void if detached*

The Official Guide to American Historic Inns

10% discount good anytime

Queen Anne Inn
2147 Tremont Place
Denver, CO 80205
(303) 296-6666
Valid Thru 12/90
Void if detached*

The Official Guide to American Historic Inns

*$10 off 2 night stay
(Monday-Thursday)*

Rhett House Inn
1009 Craven St
Beaufort, SC 29902
(803) 524-9030
Valid Thru 12/90
Void if detached*

The Official Guide to American Historic Inns

10% discount good anytime

High Meadows Inn
Rt 4 Box 6
Scottsville, VA 24590
(804) 286-2218
Valid Thru 12/90
Void if detached*

The Official Guide to American Historic Inns

*Complimentary bottle of champagne
good anytime*

Old Miners Lodge
615 Woodside Ave, PO 2639
Park City, UT 84060
(801) 645-8068
Valid Thru 12/90
Void if detached*

The Official Guide to American Historic Inns

*Double matted, hand painted lithograph
of Rose Victorian Inn*

Rose Victorian Inn
789 Valley Rd
Arroyo Grande, CA 93420
(805) 481-5566
Valid Thru 12/90
Void if detached*

The Official Guide to American Historic Inns

*10% discount good anytime on Melissa's
Room with the secret door*

Seven Wives Inn
217 N 100 W
St. George, UT 84770
(801) 628-3737
Valid Thru 12/90
Void if detached*

The Official Guide to American Historic Inns

*Special blend of coffee to take home
(Thanksgiving Coffee Company)*

Grey Whale Inn
615 N Main St
Fort Bragg, CA 95437
(707) 964-0640
Valid Thru 12/90
Void if detached*

The Official Guide to American Historic Inns

*A return to Grandma's Victorian
Bedroom and receive a 10% discount
(Monday-Thursday)*

John Palmer House Inn
4314 N Mississippi
Portland, OR 97217
(503) 284-5893
Valid Thru 12/90
Void if detached*

The Official Guide to American Historic Inns

*Extraordinary dessert for two $15 value,
good anytime*

Wilburton Inn
Box 468, River Rd
Manchester, VT 05254
(802) 362-2500
Valid Thru 12/90
Void if detached*

The Official Guide to American Historic Inns

*10% discount for breakfast by
candlelight and classical music (subject
to availability)*

Captain Mey's Inn
202 Ocean St
Cape May, NJ 08204
(609) 884-7793
Valid Thru 12/90
Void if detached*

The Official Guide to American Historic Inns

10% discount Monday through Thursday

White Oak Inn
29683 Walhonding Rd
Danville, OH 43014   Valid Thru 12/90
(614) 599-6107   Void if detached*

The Official Guide to American Historic Inns

*25% discount on any room,
Monday through Thursday.*

Prospect Hill
PO Box 55, RFD 1, Rte 613
Travellians, VA 23093   Valid Thru 12/90
(703) 967-0844   Void if detached*

The Official Guide to American Historic Inns

10% discount Monday through Thursday

The Russell-Cooper Home
115 E Gambier St
Mount Vernon, OH 43050   Valid Thru 12/90
(614) 397-8638   Void if detached*

The Official Guide to American Historic Inns

*10% discount on room/meals
(excludes bar area) Good anytime*

The Inn at Long Last
PO Box 589
Chester, VT 05143   Valid Thru 12/90
(802) 875-2444   Void if detached*

The Official Guide to American Historic Inns

*$10 off already discounted mid-week
rates (excludes foliage season, Christmas
& other holidays)*

Kedron Valley Inn
Rt 106 Box 145
South Woodstock, VT 05071   Valid Thru 12/90
(802) 457-1473   Void if detached*

The Official Guide to American Historic Inns

*10% discount good anytime
(if space available)*

Kalorama Guest House at Woodley Park   Advanced
2700 Cathedral Pl NW   Reservations Required
Washington, DC 20008   Valid Thru 12/90
(202) 328-0860   Void if detached*

The Official Guide to American Historic Inns

*20% discount good anytime
(if space available)*

The Shirley-Madison Inn   Advanced
205 W Madison   Reservations Required
Baltimore, MD 21201   Valid Thru 12/90
(301) 728-6550   Void if detached*

The Official Guide to American Historic Inns

*2nd nite half price
(November '89 - April '90)*

Captain Dexter House of Vineyard Haven   Advanced
100 Main St   Reservations Required
Vineyard Haven, MA 02568   Valid Thru 4/90
(508) 693-6564   Void if detached*

The Official Guide to American Historic Inns

*2nd nite half price
(November '89 - April '90)*

Captain Dexter House of Edgartown   Advanced
PO Box 2798   Reservations Required
Edgartown, MA 02539   Valid Thru 4/90
(508) 627-7289   Void if detached*

The Official Guide to American Historic Inns

*10% discount good anytime
(if space available)*

Kalorama Guest House at Kalorama Park   Advanced
1854 Mintwood Pl NW   Reservations Required
Washington, DC 20009   Valid Thru 12/90
(202) 667-6369   Void if detached*

Association of American Historic Inns
PO Box 336   Dana Point CA 92693   (714) 496-6953

Inn Evaluation Form

The Inn we visited: _____

	A	B	C	D	F
Location for our needs					
Cleanliness					
Bathroom facilities					
Beds					
Attitude & Friendliness of host					
Food & Presentation					
Worth the price					

A = Outstanding
B = Good
C = Average
D = Needs to be improved
F = Disaster

Any comments on the above: _____

_____

I especially appreciated: _____

_____

Suggestions for improvement: _____

_____

Name (optional): _____

Date of stay: _____

Please COPY and complete this form for each stay and mail to the address above. Since 1981 we have maintained files that include thousands of evaluations by inn goers. We value your comments which help us to keep abreast of the hundreds of new inns that open each year and to follow the changes in established inns.

Thank you.

American Historic Inns Publications

How to Start and Operate a Bed and Breakfast Inn

A set of six tapes from seminars given by Tim and Deborah Sakach.

Hundreds of prospective innkeepers have taken these classes and rated them highly. Do you have the right mix of entrepreneurial spirit, creativity, energy, and people skills to start and operate a quality bed and breakfast inn? This course will help you find out. Packed with valuable information and helpful tips.

Former students said:

"I certainly got my money's worth. I'm leaving with a renewed vitality."

"Excellent information on financing an inn and on cash flow management. I learned a great deal." Dave R., Innkeeper.

"Much preparation. Thoughtfully and sensitively shared."

Includes a wealth of information on topics such as:

- What location should you choose? (Location test provided.)
- Should you buy an existing inn, restore a historic property, or build your own?
- How much should you pay for an inn?
- How should it be financed?
- What are the regulations governing inns, and how can you meet them?
- How to estimate income and expenses.
- What is it like to be an innkeeper?
- How to manage an inn.
- How to obtain free advertising.
- How to develop a media kit.

$69.95

Innkeeping, How to Keep it Fun.

Cassette tape by Kathleen Salisbury, of Salisbury House in Los Angeles.

$9.95

How to Market Your Inn — The Key to Success.

Cassette tape by Lynn Montgomery, former innkeeper of Gold Mountain Manor and Emmy-winning screen writer.

$9.95

Professional Inn Management.

Cassette tape by Jerry Seigel, innkeeper, Casa Laguna, and former hotel consultant for 20 years.

$9.95

Save! Order all nine tapes for $89.95.

The Official Guide to American Historic Inns

By Tim and Deborah Sakach.

Includes more than 5,000 historic inns and B&Bs throughout the United States.

320 pages, more than 650 illus., $14.95

Become a member of the Association of American Historic Inns.

The Association of American Historic Inns was founded to promote historic preservation through inns and B&Bs. The combination of travel plus history provides the most effective use of old worthy properties and encourages a renewal of interest in our heritage and roots.

Annual Membership includes:

- Subscription to the association newsletter which provides travel information, new inn listings, and keeps you informed as to the latest happenings in historic inns.
- The next edition of the **The Official Guide to American Historic Inns** as soon as it comes off the press.
- Membership Discount Certificates.
- Discounts on American Historic Inns seminars and inn keeping classes.

$48.00